S0-BJR-600

COMPANION TO RUSSIAN HISTORY

COMPANION TO RUSSIAN HISTORY

by John Paxton

Published by Facts On File, Inc.
460 Park Avenue South, New York, N.Y. 10016

Library of Congress Cataloging in Publication Data

Paxton, John.
Companion to Russian history.

1. Soviet Union—Dictionaries and encyclopedias.
I. Title.
DK36.P39 947'.003'21 82-5192
ISBN 0-8160-1192-3 (pbk.) AACR2
Printed in the United States of America

10 9 8 7 6 5 4 3 2

COMPANION TO RUSSIAN HISTORY

by

John Paxton

Facts On File Publications
460 Park Avenue South
New York, N.Y. 10016

Edward
for a long friendship and
a memorable visit to
Russia

CONTENTS

PREFACE

The aim of the *Companion to Russian History* is to reach as wide a general readership as possible and to answer questions for those with an interest in Russian historical affairs. It is hoped that the book will stimulate its readers and inspire them to read more deeply and widely on the subject.

The period covered is a long one—from the Christianization of Kiev in the 10th century to the end of the Khrushchev era. There are a few entries beyond this date, but it is always difficult to evaluate current events with great accuracy.

Initially, the *Companion* was intended as an immediate reference tool for readers of Russian literature. In the course of this pursuit, the editor and compiler decided that a more comprehensive coverage was desirable. Who were the Decembrists? What was the background of Alexander Kerensky and Grigory Rasputin? What is hemophilia? Where is Krasnodar? St. Petersburg, Petrograd, Leningrad—when did the names change and why? What was a *duma* and how many were there? What was an *arshin, desyatin, pood* or *verst?* The *Companion* gives the answers, but it takes no political stand in favor of or against the current regime in the Soviet Union.

The book contains more than 2,500 entries with maps covering a period of a thousand years. It consists of a Who's Who, Gazetteer, Dictionary, Atlas, and Chronology, supplemented by a Select Bibliography. The entries cover people, including the great, the eccentric, the wicked, the good, and the talented; places, from Moscow to the village where Tolstoy lived and worked; movements from the religious to the revolutionary fervor of the 19th century and beyond; the ideas of notable figures, from Peter the Great to Lenin; books, including *Das Kapital,* which was written in German but translated first into Russian; and the arts, including icons, abbeys, the Hermitage, cathedrals, and the influence of foreigners on the art and culture of Russia. And a large proportion of the entries include bibliographic suggestions for further reading.

Most Russian literature before Peter the Great was in the classical language of the church, Old Church Slavonic, which has influenced Russian to the same extent, though not as visibly, as Latin has influenced English. In modern times, Russian has been receptive to the international terminology of science and politics: e.g., *telefon, Kommunizm*. There are also borrowings from German, Tatar, French, English (sports terms), and Dutch (naval terms). As writers and readers know, transliteration problems arise in any book on Russia. I used the Library of Congress transliteration system, but it was necessary to break the rules from time to time. Certain forms, such as "Alexei Sergeyevich" do not belong to the Library of Congress or to the British Standard schemes. Instead, they usually trace back to the idiosyncratic schemes of early translators who mixed equivalents (Alexis) with transliterations. Some idiosyncratic spellings, such as "Tchaikovsky," are hallowed by tradition and, of course, I have used English forms for such people as "Catherine the Great" and such places as "Moscow." (*See also* entry on **Alphabet**.)

Dates also present confusion because until 1918, the Julian rather than the Gregorian calendar was used in Russia. Consequently, dates determined by the Julian calendar are 12 days behind the Gregorian calendar in the 19th century and 13 days behind in the 20th century. When Russia adopted the Gregorian system, the Julian date January 31 became Gregorian date February 14. In this *Companion*, I have used the old style up to 1918 and the new style after that, except for external events, where I have used new style throughout. (*See also* entry on **Calendar**.)

Of the pathfinders in Russian studies, two books are sadly out of print or out of date—M. T. Florinsky's *Encyclopaedia of Russia and the Soviet Union* and S. V. Utechin's *Everyman's Concise Encyclopaedia of Russia*. The *Cambridge Encyclopaedia of Russia and the Soviet Union*, edited by A. Brown, J. Fennell, M. Kaser, and H. T. Willetts, was published in early 1982. The format, style, and level of the book make it a useful source for further reading and reference.

John Paxton

Bruton, Somerset,
England.
June 1983

ACKNOWLEDGMENTS

The compilation and writing of this *Companion* was undertaken over a period of six years, and naturally the work would not have seen the light of day without the help and constructive criticism of a large number of people. Among those I should like to thank are Eve Beadle, Dione Daffin, Comus Evans, Sheila Fairfield, Brian Hunter, Bohdan Nahaylo, Andrew Rothstein, Annemarie Swainson, Lynda White, and particularly Kathryn Pocock and Teresa Cherfas for much valuable research. Additionally, the help given to me by the staff of London Library was tremendous as was that of Anthony C. Hall, a bookseller specializing in Russian books, of Twickenham, Middlesex, England.

Penny White typed drafts of the *Companion* at least six times and was her usual tower of strength. If errors are found, as sometimes happens in first editions of reference books, they are my own and I shall be pleased (although sad at the time) to be alerted so that they can be corrected for future editions.

A

ABAKAN. Capital of Khakass Autonomous Region in Krasnoyarsk Territory, Russian Soviet Federated Socialist Republic (*q.q.v.*). It is situated 150 miles (242 km) SSW of Krasnoyarsk on the Yenisey River and is an industrial center with sawmills and metalworks. Bronze Age tumuli and Turkic inscriptions have been discovered in the city, which was founded as a fort in 1707. Population (1981) 123,000.

ABAZA. Language spoken by people, numbering about 25,000, in the W part of the N Caucasus. Abaza is a written language but has no grammatical cases.

ABAZA, ALEXANDER (*fl.* late 19th century). Minister of finance (1880–81) under Tsar Alexander II who resigned upon the succession of Alexander III (*q.v.*), following the latter's proclamation of his intention to suppress revolution and maintain an autocracy.

ABBEYS. Abbeys were first established in Russia during the 10th century and played an important role in the economy of feudal Russia in the 14th and 15th centuries, as well as encouraging the spread of literacy, culture, and Orthodox Christianity. In the 17th century they became centers of military strength, assisting in warding off attacks by Tatars. In the Soviet Union there are relatively few abbeys, and they are divested of all functions other than religious ones.

ABEL, RUDOLF IVANOVICH (*c.* 1902–71). Intelligence officer convicted and sentenced to 30 years' imprisonment by a U.S. court in 1957 for conspiring to hand over U.S. military secrets to the USSR. In 1962 he was exchanged for Gary Powers, U.S. air force officer whose U-2 reconnaissance plane had been forced down near Sverdlovsk in 1960.

ABKHAZIAN AUTONOMOUS SOVIET SOCIALIST REPUBLIC. Region situated in Georgia. It has an area of 3,320 square miles (8,600 sq km). Its capital is Sukhumi, situated 100 miles (160 km) NNW of Batumi. The region was annexed from Turkey in 1810 and became an autonomous soviet socialist republic in 1921. The Abkhazian coast, along the Black Sea, possesses a famous chain of health resorts—Gagra, Sukhumi, Akhali-Antoni, Gulripsha and Gudauta—sheltered by thickly forested mountains. The republic produces coal, electric power, and building materials and has light industries. In 1971 there were 116 collective farms and 34 state farms; the main crops are tobacco, tea, grapes, oranges, tangerines, and lemons. Population (1972) 492,000.

ABRAHAM OF SMOLENSK, SAINT. A saint of Kievan Russia (*q.v.*). Local and contemporary saints were extremely important to the clergy and the faithful of the era.

Obolensky, Dimitri, *The Byzantine Commonwealth: Eastern Europe 500–1453*, 1971.

Vernadsky, George V., *Kievan Russia*, 1948.

ABRAMTSEVO. A village and farmstead in the Moscow region, bought by the industrialist Mamantov in the 19th century. It became an important center of Russian folk culture and art, visited by Turgenev and Gogol. It also has several picturesque churches. After 1917, Abramtsevo became a museum and a small town for artists including Vasily Polenov, Ilya Ye. Repin, the Serovs, the Vasneknovs, the Mamontovs, and Michael Vrubel. Abramtsevo now belongs to the Academy of Sciences of the USSR.

ACADEMY OF ARTS OF THE USSR. Founded in St. Petersburg in 1757 as the Russian Academy of Arts. It comprises the departments of painting, sculpture, graphic art, and decorative art.

ACADEMY OF SCIENCES OF THE USSR. Founded in St. Petersburg in 1724 by Peter the Great as the Russian Academy of Sciences. It later became the St. Petersburg Academy of Sciences and then the Imperial Academy of Sciences. From the Revolution until 1925 it was known as the Academy of Sciences of Russia. It is the chief coordinating body for scientific research within the USSR, directing the work of over 260 scientific institutions.

Vucinich, Alexander S., *The Soviet Academy of Science*, 1956.

ACMEISTS. A group of poets based in St. Petersburg who founded the Poets' Guild in 1912. The most outstanding members were Anna Akhmatova and Osip Mandelstam. Other members included Nicholas Stepanovich Gumilev, Michael Kuzmin, and Sergey Gorodetsky. They published a journal, *Apollon* (1909–17), under the editorship of Sergey Makovsky. Their poetry is generally individualistic with a strong emphasis on aesthetics and form. The group disbanded in 1917.

Mandelstam, Nadezhda, *Hope Against Hope*, 1971.

Poggioli, Renato, *Poets of Russia 1880-1930*, 1960.

ADASHEV, ALEKSEY FEDOROVICH (?–1561). An influential favorite of Tsar Ivan IV who advocated domestic reform and died in prison.

ADMIRALTY. Built by Andreyan Dmitriyevich Zakharov in St. Petersburg. Its gilded spire is the nodal point of three main streets or prospects.

Gosling, Nigel, *Leningrad*, 1965.

ADRIAN, PATRIARCH (1627–1700). The 10th and last of the original line of patriarchs. The archimandrite of Chudov Monastery and metropolitan of Kazan, Adrian was chosen as the new patriarch in 1690. A devout and godly man, he held extremely conservative views and opposed Peter the Great's plans to reform the church. He strove to prevent the tsar from interfering with the life of the church. A number of his religious writings have been preserved. After Adrian's death, the patriarchate was abolished, and the church was brought under the jurisdiction of the state and the new holy governing synod.

French, R. M., *The Eastern Orthodox Church*, 1951.

ADRIANOPLE, TREATY OF. Pact signed on September 14, 1829 at the conclusion of hostilities between Russia and Turkey (1828–29). As a result Russia obtained the right to unlimited transit of commercial ships through the Dardanelles and free trade throughout the Ottoman Empire. Autonomy was granted for Serbia and was recognized for Greece. In addition, Moldavia and Walachia were to be occupied until Turkey paid an indemnity.

ADYGEI AUTONOMOUS REGION. Region situated in Krasnodar Territory (*q.v.*). It has an area of 2,934 square miles (7,599 sq km). It was established 1922 and its capital is Maikop, situated approximately 220 miles (352 km) S of Rostov. The chief industries are timber, carpentry, food processing, and engineering, and cattle are bred in the area. Population (1980) 405,300.

ADZHARIAN AUTONOMOUS SOVIET SOCIALIST REPUBLIC. Region situated in Georgia. It has an area of 1,160 square miles (3,004 sq km). Previously under Turkish rule, it was annexed to Russia after the Treaty of Berlin (1878), and constituted as an autonomous republic within Georgia in 1921. The capital is Batumi. Subtropical crops include tea, tangerines, lemons, grapes, bamboo, and eucalyptus. It has livestock breeding, important shipyards and oil refining, food processing, and canning industries. Manufactures include clothing, building materials, and pharmaceutical supplies. Population (1981) 362,000.

AEHRENTHAL, COUNT ALOIS LEXA VON (1854–1912). Diplomat and politician of the Austro-Hungarian Empire. He was ambassador to St. Petersburg (1898–1906) and foreign minister (1906–12). While he was foreign minister, Austria-Hungary, with German approval, annexed Bosnia and Herzegovina (1908); this action raised the threat that Russia would make war and was one of the incidents leading to the First World War.

AEROFLOT. The world's largest airline and sole organization for air services in the Soviet Union. In 1980 the airline transported 104 million passengers and 3 million tons of freight. It serves 67 countries and its extensive domestic routes cover 3,600 towns.

AFGHANISTAN. Situated in central Asia, Afghanistan is bounded on the N by the USSR, by the Republics of Turkmenia, Uzbekistan, and Tadzhikistan, on the W by Iran, and to the E and S by Pakistan. Since the time of Alexander the Great, Afghanistan has been at the crossroads between Europe and Asia. Different ethnic groups passing through or settling in Afghanistan have bequeathed a legacy of internal troubles. Influence in Afghanistan was contested by Great Britain and Russia in the 19th century and by the USSR, the People's Republic of China, and the United States after the Second World War. Afghanistan was reorganized as an independent state in 1921. In 1973 the monarchy was overthrown and King Zahir Shah abdicated. A republic was established under President Daoud, but he was killed in the coup of April 1978. A government was then set up under Nur Mohammad Taraki. The Khalqs became the dominant faction. There were a number of violent uprisings in 1978 as a result of the government's reform program that threatened to undermine Afghan traditions. Hafizullah Amin was made prime minister in 1979 and, following the collapse of the Afghan army, asked for Soviet help. In September 1979 armed confrontation took place between supporters of Taraki and Amin in which Taraki was killed. The Soviets began their invasion of Afghanistan on December 24, 1979, and Babrak Karmal returned from the Soviet Union to be appointed prime minister and president of the revolutionary council. Internal resistance to Karmal and the Soviets has continued for some time. Population (1981) 16,276,000.

AFINOGENOV, ALEXANDER NIKOLAYEVICH (1904–41). Playwright and one of the few important dramatists to emerge immediately after the Revolution. *The Strange Fellow* (1928) and *Fear* (1931) were his best-known plays and dealt with the difficulties of change in a new social order. Subsequent plays, *The Distant, Greetings Spain, Mashenka,* and *On the Eve* were more acceptable politically to the regime. He was killed in a German air raid.

AGITPROP. Word derived from initial syllables of the words *agit*ation and *prop*aganda, and it refers to a department of the central committee of the Communist Party of the Soviet Union. It is responsible for agitation and propaganda on behalf of communism. It is also applied to anyone engaged in agitprop.

Clews, J. C., *Communist Propaganda Techniques*, 1964.

Schapiro, Leonard B., *The Communist Party of the Soviet Union*, rev. ed. 1971.

AGRARIAN REFORMS. The first major agrarian reform was the abolition of serfdom, an institution that had developed in the period of Kievan Russia and was consolidated in Muscovite Russia as a means of providing a bonded labor force to support the gentry in their obligation to defend the country. Serfs of private landowners were freed in 1861, royal serfs in 1863, and state serfs in 1866. In all cases the serf's homestead became his own property, hereditary within his family; other land was vested in the village as a whole.

Serfs of private landowners were obliged to surrender part of their former allotments in return for freedom; royal serfs kept the maximum amount of allotment land permitted; state serfs kept all their land against cash rent; Cossacks (*q.v.*) kept two-thirds of their land against 20 years of army service. The land to be held in common. The system of holding land in common did not succeed; redemption cost was an excessive burden and the rules imposed by the villages were restrictive. Village allotment areas declined; the overall amount of land held by former serfs was still insufficient for their support.

Stolypin's government enacted a second major agrarian reform in 1906; this was revised and extended in 1911. Peasants in communities that did not redistribute land periodically were given their current holdings outright; those in communities which did redistribute were given the right to apply for permanent ownership at the time of redistribution. The community was required to consolidate land into united holdings where it had been held in scattered strips. In 1911 such partitions into private holdings were extended from arable to grazing land, with the exclusion of traditional common lands. There was provision for the abolition of the non-distributing commune by majority vote, of the distributing commune by a two-thirds majority vote. The land held by the peasant household was vested in the head of the household.

In 1918 the Soviet government abolished all private ownership and made farming the sole basis of landholding, but did not immediately proceed to collectivization. During the first Five-Year Plan (1928–32) all land, whether formerly owned by peasants or gentry, was collectivized. In 1930 the central government conceded that enforced collectivization had been too severe, and that peasants in collective farms were to be permitted small private holdings. Policy since then has been gradually to industrialize agriculture in order to eliminate traditional peasant values and replace them with those of an urbanized socialist proletariat. The *kolkhoz* (collective farm) (*q.v.*) is owned by its members, but its production policy is state controlled and its produce state allocated. The *sovkhoz* farm (*q.v.*) is state owned with hired peasant labor, and is usually highly mechanized and industrial in its approach.

Blum, Jerome, *Lord and Peasant in Russia from the Ninth to the Nineteenth Century*, 1961.

Emmons, Terence, *The Russian Landed Gentry and the Peasant Emancipation*, 1968.

Laird, Roy D., *Collective Farming in Russia*, 1958.

Lewin, Moshe, *Russian Peasants and Soviet Power*, 1968.

Pavlovsky, George A., *Agricultural Russia on the Eve of the Revolution,* 1930.

Robinson, Geroid T., *Rural Russia under the Old Régime,* (2nd ed.) 1967.

Shanin, T., *The Awkward Class,* 1970.

Volin, Lazar, *A Century of Russian Agriculture: From Alexander II to Krushchev,* 1970.

Vucinich, Alexander S. (ed.), *The Peasant in Nineteenth Century Russia,* 1968.

AGRICULTURE. Until 1928 the USSR was predominantly agricultural in character, but it has since become an industrial-agricultural country. Of the gross national product, industry and transport accounted for 42.1 percent in 1913 and 78.8 percent in 1977; agriculture for 57.9 percent in 1913 and 14.6 percent in 1977. Of the total state land fund of 2.2 billion hectares, agricultural land in use in 1977 amounted to 1.1 billion hectares, and state forests and state reserves to 1.1 billion hectares. Twenty-two percent of all those gainfully employed in 1977 were engaged in agriculture (in 1913, 75 percent).

The total area under cultivation (including single-owner peasant farms, state farms, and collective farms) was (in the same territory) 118.2 million hectares in 1913, and 226.4 million hectares in 1980.

Collective farms (*kolkhozy*) on November 1, 1980 controlled 248.3 million hectares, of which 102.8 million were under crops of various kinds; state farms and other state agricultural undertakings controlled 794.9 million hectares, of which 102.2 million were under crops; manual and clerical workers held 4 million hectares as allotments.

Produce marketed (after consumption by collective farmers) was, in units of 1 million tons, for the present area of the USSR in 1980: grain, 81.3; seed cotton (unginned), 10; sugar beets, 64.4; potatoes, 16.6; other vegetables, 20.6; meat (slaughtered weight) and fats, 11.8; milk and milk products, 59.4; wool, 453; and eggs (1 billion), 46.6.

Between 1953 and 1980 the number of collective farms was reduced, mainly by amalgamation and partly by transformation into state farms, from 93,300 to 26,000, their cultivated area falling from 132 million hectares to 95.5 million hectares.

Investments in agriculture in 1979 were 21.6 billion rubles by the state and 10.2 billion rubles by collective farms.

An All-Union Academy of Agricultural Sciences, founded in 1929, has regional branches in Siberia and Central Asia and 196 research institutes.

Hahn, W., *The Politics of Soviet Agriculture,* 1972.

Jasny, N., *The Socialized Agriculture of the USSR,* 1949.

Laird, Roy D., *Collective Farming in Russia,* 1958.

Laird, Roy D. (ed.), *Soviet Agricultural and Peasant Affairs,* 1963.

Lewin, Moshe, *Russian Peasants and Soviet Power,* 1968.

Robinson, Geroid T., *Rural Russia under the Old Régime,* (2nd ed.) 1967.

Smith, Robert E., *Peasant Farming in Muscovy,* 1977.

Strauss, Erich, *Soviet Agriculture in Perspective,* 1969.

Symons, Leslie, *Russian Agricul-*

ture: A Geographic Survey, 1972.

Volin, Lazar, A *Century of Russian Agriculture: From Alexander II to Krushchev*, 1970.

AGRIGORODY. Plans were devised at the beginning of 1951 for *agrigorody* (farm-cities) to be established; agricultural settlements were to be transformed into large centralized towns, surrounded by collective fields. Because the peasants were likely to object strongly to this idea, it did not win the support of all the party leaders and was dropped. Similar plans, however, have been implemented in the Ukraine since 1957.

AIGUN, TREATY OF. One of the "unequal treaties" signed by China (1858) in which it ceded to Russia 400,000 square miles (1,036,000 sq km) of territory on the left bank of the Amur River, including the city that became Vladivostok.

AIR FORCE. The Soviet air force was believed to consist, in 1981, of over 470,000 officers and men and some 9,000 first-line aircraft, excluding second-line and training types. To supplement long-range missiles (limited by the SALT I interim agreement to 1,618 ICBM and 600 MRBM/IRBM), the DA strategic bomber force is estimated still to have 113 Tupolev Tu-95 ("Bear") four-turboprop bombers, 80 Myasishchev M-4 four-jet bombers and flight refueling tankers ("Bison"), 420 Tupolev Tu-16 ("Badger") and 140 supersonic Tupolev Tu-22 ("Blinder") twin-jet bombers, and at least 100 Tupolev Tu-26 ("Backfire") swing-wing bombers.

The fast attack tactical air forces, under local army command in the field, have an estimated total of 4,800 ground-attack and reconnaissance aircraft.

Operating 1,200 fixed-wing aircraft and helicopters, the Soviet navy has the world's second largest naval air arm.

Kilmarx, Robert A., A *History of Soviet Air Power*, 1962.

AIX-LA-CHAPELLE, CONGRESS OF (1818). Meeting of the Quadruple Alliance (*q.v.*) (Great Britain, Austria, Prussia, and Russia) and France at Aix-la-Chapelle (now Aachen), attended by Tsar Alexander I (*q.v.*). The Alliance reaffirmed the political reorganization of Europe established by the Congress of Vienna (1814–15) and restored France's status as an independent power. It withdrew its occupying forces and admitted France into what thus became the Quintuple Alliance (*q.v.*).

AKADEMGORODOK. A "scientific city" near Novosibirsk, where some of the most famous Soviet research institutes work in cooperation with advanced industrial enterprises.

AKHMADULINA, BELLA (1937–). Her poetry is based on the tradition of the Acmeists (*q.v.*); sober, prosaic images, calm diction, and structural compactness are features of her work. Her active and lively imagination frequently leads her poetry beyond the bounds of accepted reality to express avant-garde themes. Themes of Akhmadulina's work include sickness and neurotic states of mind, the importance of intimate human concerns, nature, and technology. Akhmadulina has been published only sporadically, although a volume, *Struna,* appeared in 1962. Akhmadulina was at one time married to the poet Yevgeny Yevtushenko.

Brown, Edward J., *Russian Literature since the Revolution,* 1963.

Holthusen, J., *Twentieth Century Russian Literature,* 1972.

AKHMATOVA, ANNA (1889–1966). Pseudonym of Anna Andreyevna Gorenko. She was a poet of the school of Acmeists (*q.v.*). Her poems, inspired by the poetry of Pushkin, brought her great renown. Her most popular collections were *The Rosary* (1914) and *The Willow Tree* (1940). She married another Acmeist, Nicholas Stepanovich Gumilev, who was executed by the Bolsheviks in 1921, and she subsequently became an "un-person" until 1940. In 1946 she again incurred the displeasure of the authorities for "bourgeois decadence" and was expelled from the Union of Soviet Writers, but she was rehabilitated in 1959.

Driver, S. J., *Anna Akhmatova,* 1972.

Haight, Amanda Chase, *Anna Akhmatova: A Poetic Pilgrimage,* 1976.

Kunitz, Stanley and Hayward, Max (eds.), *Poems of Akhmatova,* 1973.

Mandelstam, Nadezhda, *Hope Against Hope,* 1971.

AKKERMAN, CONVENTION OF. An agreement signed on October 7, 1826 in Akkerman, Rumania, between the Ottoman Empire and Russia, by which Russia's demands concerning Serbia and the Danubian principalities of Moldavia and Walachia were accepted, under threat of war, by the Ottomans. The terms were that the earlier Treaty of Bucharest (1812) was confirmed; Serbia's autonomy was recognized; Russia was granted the right to protect the autonomy of Moldavia and Walachia, with the guarantee that the *hospodars* (princes) would thereafter hold office for seven-year terms and could only be dismissed with the consent of the Russian ambassador in Istanbul; Russian ships were given the freedom of the Black Sea and the Danube River; and the straits of the Bosporus and the Dardanelles were opened to any merchant vessels sailing to or from Russia. Subsequently the Ottomans renounced the convention and attempted to regain control of Serbia, Moldavia, and Walachia, compelling the Russians to declare war on the Ottoman Empire in 1828.

AKMOLINSK. Until 1961 a city and oblast. It was renamed Tselinograd (*q.v.*).

AKSAKOV, IVAN SERGEYEVICH (1823–86). Poet, essayist and critic. He was the son of Sergey Timofeyevich Aksakov. An ardent Slavophile journalist, he was frequently in trouble with the authorities. His greatest critical work was a biography of the poet Fedor Tyutchev (*q.v.*).

Lukashevich, S., *Ivan Aksakov, 1823–1886: A Study in Russian Thought and Politics,* 1965.

Riasanovsky, Nicholas V., *Russia and the West in the Teachings of the Slavophiles,* 1952.

AKSAKOV, KONSTANTIN SERGEYEVICH (1817–60). Critic and writer. He was the son of Sergey Timofeyevich Aksakov. He was an ardent Slavophile and a writer of historical and philological essays.

Chmielewski, E., *Tribune of the Slavophiles: Konstantin Aksakov*, 1961.

Riasanovsky, Nicholas V., *Russia and the West in the Teachings of the Slavophiles*, 1952.

AKSAKOV, SERGEY TIMOFEYEVICH (1791–1859). Novelist and one of the founders of Russian Realism. He was the father of Ivan and Konstantin. After retiring from the civil service he wrote a notable autobiographical trilogy of Russian family life: *Family Chronicle* (1856), *Years of Childhood* (1858), and *Reminiscences* (1856).

Fennell, J.L.I. (ed.), *Nineteenth-Century Russian Literature*, 1973.

AKSELROD, P. B. *See* **AXELROD, P. B.**

AKSYONOV, VASILY (1932–). Aksyonov spent the early part of his life in the Far East and then studied medicine. His first stories appeared in 1959 in the magazine *Yunost'*. In his novel *Zvezdny Bilet* (1961) he dispenses with the traditional narrative framework and uses the technique of reporting from shifting points of view. The novel, which concerns the protest of teenagers against the adult world, has been compared with Salinger's *The Catcher in the Rye* (1951). It is written in the language of teenagers; *Apelsiny iz Marokke* (1963) largely consists of teenage dialogue. Aksyonov's heroes like jazz, sports, and dance and experiment with love affairs; they are doctors, workmen, athletes, and engineers at the start of their careers, having to make important decisions for the first time. The stories are humorous, ironic, and critical of society. In 1980 Aksyonov left Moscow for the United States, and was stripped of his Soviet citizenship in 1981.

Holthusen, J., *Twentieth Century Russian Literature*, 1972.

AKTYUBINSK. Capital of Aktyubinsk Region, Kazakhstan *(q.v.)*. It is situated 90 miles (145 km) SW of Orsk. Manufactures include chemicals, metals, and electrical equipment. The city was founded in 1869. Population (1977) 184,000.

ALAI MOUNTAINS. Mountain range of SW Kirghizia and part of the W branch of the Tien Shan system. It extends 200 miles (320 km) W of the Chinese border and rises to 19,280 feet (5,880 m) in the W.

ÅLAND ISLANDS, PEACE CONGRESS (1718). Peace Congress held on the Åland Islands in the Gulf of Bothnia between Russia and Sweden. The Russian delegation was led by Bruce and Osterman, the Swedish delegation by Goertz and Count Gyllenborg. Sweden wished to regain some of its territories from Peter the Great. While Goertz eventually agreed with some of the Russian proposals, Charles XII of Sweden disapproved of them. After several months of abortive negotiations,

Goertz was told that Peter would terminate the conference if a treaty was not concluded in December. Goertz set off to consult with Charles but was arrested, and Charles himself was killed in battle.

Massie, R. K., *Peter the Great,* 1980.

ALASKA. The coasts of Alaska were explored in 1741 by Vitus Bering, a Danish explorer employed by Russia. Various Russian trading companies were established after 1784 when Grigory Shelekhov founded the first permanent settlement (on Kodiak Island). The Russian American Company was granted a monopoly in 1799 and prospered under the direction of Alexander Baranov, who founded Sitka as his capital in 1799. In 1812 he established a colony in northern California.

In 1821 Tsar Alexander I claimed the 51st parallel as the territory's S boundary but this was disputed by Great Britain and the United States, and in 1824 the boundary was fixed at 54° 40′ N. Subsequently Russian influence in Alaska declined, and the territory was sold to the United States for $7 million in 1867.

Brown, D., *Alaska,* 1974.

Cooper, B., *Alaska: The Last Frontier,* 1972.

Hulley, C. C., *Alaska: Past and Present,* 1970.

ALATAU MOUNTAINS. A group of four ranges (Dzungarian, Kungei, Talass, and Terskei) in the Tien Shan system. All except Talass rise to over 16,000 feet (4,880 m).

ALCOHOLISM. *See* **Drunkenness.**

ALDAN. Town built for gold miners situated 160 miles (416 km) SSW of Yakutsk on the route from Yakutsk to the Trans-Siberian Railway. Population (1973) 20,000.

ALDAN RIVER. River rising in the Aldan Mountains and flowing NE and then N and W for 1,700 miles (2,720 km) to join the Lena River. Gold is found in its basin and it is navigable for 1,000 miles (1,610 km) upstream.

ALDANOV (1886–1957). Pseudonym of Mark Aleksandrovich Landau. He was a novelist who left Russia for France in 1919 and wrote a series of books on the French revolutionary period. His essay on Lenin (1921) compared the Russian and French revolutions, and in *The Fifth Seal* (1939) he depicted the decline in revolutionary idealism that followed the Russian revolutions. Among his later works are *A Night at the Airport* (1949) and *The Escape* (1950). After 1941 he lived in the United States.

ALEICHEM, SHALOM (or **SHOLOM**) (1859–1916). Pseudonym of Shalom (or Sholom) Rabinovich. He was a celebrated writer in Yiddish who became known in the United States as the "Jewish Mark Twain." He was born in the Ukraine and his many plays have popularized the image of Jewish characters in a small Russian town during the tsarist era. He emigrated to America and died in New York.

Grafstein, M. (ed.), *Shalom Aleichem Panorama,* 1949.

Samuel, M., *The World of Shalom Aleichem,* 1943.

Waife-Goldberg, M., *Shalom Aleichem,* 1968.

ALEKHINE, ALEXANDRE ALEXANDROVITCH (1892–1946). A Russian who became a French citizen. He was world chess champion (1927–33), when he defeated Capablanca, and again from 1937 until his death.

Alekhine, A., *My Best Games of Chess, 1924–1937,* 1939.

ALEKSANDROV. City situated 65 miles (104 km) WNW of Vladimir. It came under the control of the Muscovite princes in 1302. Tsar Ivan resided in the city (1564–81), and it was here that he organized his political police (*oprichnina*). The first printing presses in Russia were established here and it is the site of the Uspensky convent. Population (1967) 46,000.

ALEKSANDROVSKOYE. Village situated 47 miles (75 km) NW of Irkutsk in S Siberia. Established as a hard-labor camp in 1873, it took political prisoners from 1904. It later became a special prison administered by the Committee of State Security (KGB) for political prisoners serving life sentences, generally in solitary confinement.

ALEKSANDROVSK-SAKHALINSKY. City situated on the W coast of N Sakhalin on the Tatar strait. It was founded as a penal settlement in 1881. There are coal deposits in the vicinity. Anton Chekhov visited the area in 1890 and subsequently published *The Island of Sakhalin* (1893–94). Population (1975) 25,000.

ALEKSEYEV, MICHAEL VASILYEVICH (1857–1918). General who was commander in chief on the W front (1915) and chief of staff to Tsar Nicholas II *(q.v.)* (1915–17) during the First World War. For a brief period after the overthrow of the tsar he was chief of staff to Kerensky. In 1918 he took the initiative to organize the White (anti-Bolshevik) forces in the Civil War. He died soon afterwards of pneumonia.

ALESHA (or ALYOSHA) POPOVICH. A favorite hero of the epic poems *(byliny) (q.v.).*

ALEUTIAN ISLANDS. A continuation of the Alaskan peninsula consisting of 150 mountainous islands, some rising to 8,000 feet (2,438 m), and many of them volcanic. They separate the Bering Sea from the Pacific Ocean. The Aleutian Islands were discovered in 1741 by Vitus Bering *(q.v.)*, a Danish explorer employed by Russia. The islands were included in the purchase of Alaska by the United States in 1867. Because of their proximity to the USSR the islands play an important part in U.S. defense strategy.

ALEXANDER I, GRAND PRINCE OF BULGARIA (1857–93). Son of Prince Henry of Hesse (Battenberg). He served with the Russian forces in the Russo-Turkish War (1877–78), the result of which was the autonomy of Bulgaria. Alexander was elected constitutional prince in 1879. In 1883 he restored the constitution to combat Russian influence. After the war with Serbia he was forced to abdicate in 1886.

ALEXANDER I (1775–1825). Tsar of Russia (from 1801). He came to the throne after the murder of his father, Paul I. Having received a progressive humanitarian education, Alexander's policies were at first liberal in outlook, but later the "enigmatic tsar" was strongly influenced by reactionary mysticism. In the first part of his reign censorship was relaxed, restrictions on travel abroad were lifted, and the council of state and ministries were established as were a state school system and several universities. The serfs were liberated without land in the Baltic, torture was abolished, and Poland was granted a constitution. Alexander planned to transform Russia with the help of the unofficial committee, but he became disillusioned and abandoned his plans to abolish serfdom and the autocracy, and the plans of Michael Speransky for a constitution were not implemented. Under the influence of General Arakcheyev and Prince Alexander Golitsyn, Alexander carried out a number of increasingly reactionary policies, particularly in the field of education. At the time of Alexander's death a group of revolutionary liberals later known as the Decembrists, infuriated by the tsar's policies, were planning an uprising. Abroad, Alexander alternated between alliances with England and France, formed the Holy Alliance with Austria and Prussia, gained part of the Caucasus, Finland, and Bessarabia and fought the patriotic war of 1812 against Napoleon and was a leading figure at the Congress of Vienna (1814–15). Toward the end of his life he withdrew into seclusion. He was succeeded by his brother, Nicholas I.

Jenkins, M., *Arakcheev: Grand Vizier of the Russian Empire*, 1969.

Paléologue, Maurice, *The Enigmatic Tsar: The Life of Alexander I of Russia*, 1938.

Palmer, Alan, *Alexander I, Tsar of War and Peace*, 1974.

Troyat, Henri, *Alexander of Russia: Napoleon's Conqueror*, 1984.

ALEXANDER II (1818–81). Known as the Liberator. He was tsar of Russia from 1855. Although conservative in outlook, Alexander implemented a series of great reforms in many spheres of life. After much discussion, 10 million serfs and their families were emancipated in 1861, 1863, and 1866. The *zemstvo* (*q.v.*) system of local government was reformed in 1864, and the various *zemstva* made a valuable contribution to public health and education, while the municipal government was reformed in 1870. Judicial reforms were also implemented in 1864, and the judiciary became a separate part of the government and lost its air of secrecy. In 1874 military service was reorganized and the length of service reduced. There were a number of peasant riots, however, and a series of mysterious fires in St. Petersburg and in towns by the Volga, while the radical populist group grew and increased its activity. Abroad, Alexander dealt with the Polish uprising of 1863, finally conquered the N Caucasus, liberated Bulgaria from Turkey in 1878, and presided over the Russian expansion in Central Asia. He was assassinated in 1881 by a terrorist bomb thrown at his coach. *See* **Grinevitsky, Ivan.**

Almedingen, Edith Martha, *The*

Emperor Alexander II, 1962.
Graham, Stephen, *Alexander II: Tsar of Russia,* 1935.
Moss, W. E., *Alexander II and the Modernization of Russia,* 1958.
Nolde, B. E., *L'Alliance franco-russe,* 1936.
Seton-Watson, Hugh, *The Russian Empire, 1801–1917,* 1967. *The Decline of Imperial Russia, 1855–1914,* 1952.

ALEXANDER III (1845–95). Tsar of Russia from 1881. Alexander III wished above all to curb changes introduced by Alexander II and to suppress revolts and strengthen the autocracy; his reactionary policies were influenced by Constantine Pobedonostsev, and to a lesser extent by Dmitry Tolstoy and Ivan Deliyanov. As a result of the "Temporary Regulations" of 1881, officials had the power to search, exile, and try by courts-martial any who were considered to be a threat to state security. Restrictions on the peasants were introduced; the post of *zemstvo* chief was created in 1880; the *zemstvo* chief, a member of the gentry, had direct bureaucratic and judicial power over his group of peasants. The State Gentry Bank, founded in 1885, further consolidated the position of the gentry. Counter reforms were also implemented in town government and in the *zemstvo* system, and the electorate decreased. University autonomy was abolished, as was higher education for women. National minorities such as Poles, Georgians, Armenians, and Finns were russified, while restrictions were placed on the Jews; from 1881 pogroms occurred, and pressure was applied to all who were not of the Orthodox faith. A protectionist economic policy encouraged the rapid growth of industrialization; he promoted Russian colonization in Central Asia and formed an alliance with France.

ALEXANDER NEVSKY (*c.* 1220–63). Prince of Novgorod (1236–63) and grand prince of Vladimir (1252–63). He was a Russian hero who gained his name of Nevsky defeating the Swedes on the Neva River in 1240. Two years later he overcame the Teutonic Knights on the frozen Lake Peipus (on the Estonian border). He was canonized after his death. A knightly order named after him was founded by Peter the Great and revived by Soviet Russia in 1942 for deeds of valor.

ALEXANDRA FEDOROVNA (1872–1918). Born a princess of Hesse-Darmstadt and a granddaughter of Queen Victoria, she married (1894) Nicholas II (*q.v.*) of Russia. Her belief in the powers of the monk Rasputin (*q.v.*) to cure the young tsarevich of hemophilia brought her under Rasputin's disastrous domination and encouraged her to exert a nefarious political influence, much resented by the tsar's ministers and the population at large. After the 1917 Revolution she was murdered along with her husband and children.

ALEXIS (1690–1718). The son and heir of Tsar Peter I (the Great). Alexis's unhappy relations with his father progressively worsened and he fled to Vienna (1716). Peter lured him back and condemned him to death for treason. He died before his execution.

ALEXIS MIKHAILOVICH (1629-76). Tsar who succeeded Michael Romanov, the first Romanov tsar, in 1645, known as the "quiet one." Viewed by some as the epitome of Muscovite culture and as a pioneer of interest in the West, Alexis relied heavily on advisers, in particular on Boris Morisov and Prince Elijah Miloslavsky. In an attempt to solve financial problems, Alexis debased the coinage in 1656, but this led to inflation and a number of revolts, including the copper coin riot of 1662. Other revolts during Alexis's reign include the Cossack and peasant rebellion in the Ukraine (1624–38) and the celebrated uprising led by Stenka Razin (*q.v.*) in 1670. Other important events in Alexis's reign are the granting of the new legal code (*Ulozheniye*) of 1649, which remained in force until the early 19th century and which favored the landowners and confirmed serfdom, and a permanent schism in the Orthodox Church. He fought Poland (1654–67) and Sweden (1656–61) and won the Ukraine for Russia.

ALEXIS (Sergey Vladimirovich Simanksy) (1873–1970). Patriarch of Moscow and All Russia (1945–70). He was ordained bishop in 1913 and was archbishop (1929), metropolitan of Novgorod (1932), and metropolitan of Leningrad (1933). From about 1925 he cooperated with the Soviet authorities and secured considerable expansion of church activity as a result.

Hackel, Sergei, *The Orthodox Church*, 1971.

ALGIRDAS (?–1377). Also known as Olgierd. He was grand duke of Lithuania from 1345 to 1377. A pagan ruler, Algirdas was nevertheless tolerant of the Orthodox Church. He fought Poles, Mongols, and Teutonic Knights, and extended Lithuania eastward to make it one of the largest European states of its time.

Gerutis, A., *Lithuania: 700 Years*, 1971.

ALIGER, MARGARITA IOSIFOVNA (1915–). Poet who was first published in 1933 but who gained fame during the Second World War with her patriotic poems, including *Zoya* (1942). Her poem *The Most Important Thing* (1948) caused her to be criticized by the authorities.

ALISHAN, LEON (1820–1901). Armenian poet and historian. He wrote historical, geographical, and botanical works on Armenia.

ALLAN, SIR WILLIAM (1782–1850). British painter of scenes of Russian life. His most famous Russian picture was *Peter the Great Teaching his Subjects Shipbuilding* (1844).

ALLILUYEVA, SVETLANA IOSIFOVNA (1927–). Daughter of Stalin by his second wife, Nadezhda Alliluyeva. She left the USSR in 1967 and published *Twenty Letters to a Friend* (1967).

"ALL POWER TO THE SOVIETS". A slogan adopted by Lenin. In the name of the Soviets, the Bolshevik Party was able to dominate the political organization of post-revolutionary Russia: the newly formed Soviet Union.

Daniels, Robert V., *Red October,* 1968.

Daniels, Robert V. (ed.), *The Russian Revolution Documents,* 1972.

Ulam, Adam, B., *Lenin and the Bolsheviks,* 1969.

ALL-RUSSIAN CONGRESS OF SOVIETS. The first congress met in Petrograd in June 1917 with representatives from more than 350 units from all over Russia. It appointed a central executive committee, which sat permanently in Petrograd. Some of the leaders of this committee were also leaders of the executive committee of the Petrograd Soviet, having attended the congress as delegates.

Katkov, George and Shukman, H., *Lenin's Path to Power,* 1971.

Pipes, Richard, *The Formation of the Soviet Union,* 1964.

ALL-RUSSIAN DIRECTORY. A counterrevolutionary organization consisting of five members. It was established in Omsk in September 1918.

ALL-RUSSIAN PERIOD. The reign of Peter the Great (1682–1725). Also known as the Imperial Age and the St. Petersburg Era.

Sumner, Benedict H., *Peter the Great and the Emergence of Russia,* 1950.

ALMA RIVER. Site of a Crimean War battle in which the British, French, and Turkish troops defeated the Russian forces on September 20, 1854. The allies did not, however, pursue their victory and so failed to gain Sebastopol without a struggle.

ALMA-ATA. Capital of Kazakhstan republic and region. It produces agricultural and horticultural products and manufactures machinery, textiles, food, and tobacco products. Population (1977) 871,000.

ALMETYEVSK. City in Tatar Autonomous Soviet Republic situated on the left bank of the Stepnoy Zoy River. Founded in 1950, it is the center of the republic's oil fields. Population (1973) 95,000.

ALPHABET AND TRANSLITERATION. Russian uses the Cyrillic alphabet, traditionally attributed to Saints Cyril and Methodius, ninth-century Greek Orthodox missionaries who reduced Old Slavonic to writing in order to spread the Gospel. It bears a marked resemblance to Greek. The modern Russian alphabet has 32 letters; 4 more were in use in the "old orthography" before 1917. National transliteration schemes reflect the pronunciation of the transliterating language—e.g., English: Khrushchev, French: Khrouchtchev, German: Chruschtjow. There is also an international "scholarly" scheme which uses diacritics to achieve a letter-for-letter transliteration (except щ = SC): Hruščēv. Some idiosyncratic transliterations have become sanctioned by use, e.g., Tchaikovsky (British Standard would be Chaikovskii). ъ ь (hard and soft signs) indicate only that a preceding consonant is nonpalatalized or palatalized respectively. Prerevolutionary letters: I (now И), Ѣ (E), Ѳ (Ф), V (I).

The American Library of Congress transliteration is to be adopted by the British Library and the *British Na-*

Russian	Transliteration: British Standard	Transliteration: International
А	A	A
Б	B	B
В	V	V
Г	G	G
Д	D	D
Е	E	E
Ж	ZH	Z
З	Z	Z
И	I	I
Й	I	J
К	K	K
Л	L	L
М	M	M
Н	N	N
О	O	O
П	P	P
Р	R	R
С	S	S
Т	T	T
У	U	U
Ф	F	F
Х	KH	H
Ц	TS	C
Ч	CH	Č
Ш	SH	Š
Щ	SHCH	ŠČ
Ъ		Ŭ
Ы	Y	Y
Ь		J
Э	E	E
Ю	YU	JU
Я	YA	JA

tional Bibliography. This differs from British Standard only by the addition of some diacritics and the use of IU and IA for Ю and Я.

Auty, R. and Obolensky, D. (eds.), "An Introduction to Russian Language and Literature," *Companion to Russian Studies*, Vol. 2, 1977.

ALTAIC LANGUAGES. Turkish is the best known of the languages in the Altaic group, the others being Mongolian and Manchu-Tungus. Altaic-speaking peoples, of which there are some 70 million, live mainly in W, Central, and NE Asia.

Poppe, N., *Introduction to Altaic Linguistics*, 1965.

ALTAY MOUNTAINS. The Altay Mountains proper and the Greater Altay stretch from the Gobi desert NW in two parallel ranges across the Siberian frontier. The upper streams of the Ob and Irtish rivers lie within the range. The highest peak in the USSR Altay is Belukha Mountain at 14,783 feet (4,506 m) above sea level. Lead, zinc, and silver are mined.

ALTAY TERRITORY. Territory situated within the Russian Soviet Federated Socialist Republic, SW of Siberia. Its capital is Barnaul. It has an area of 101,000 square miles (261,590 sq km). Although the Altay Mountains form part of the territory, there is considerable fertile agricultural land. Population (1970) 2,500,000.

ALTRANSTÄDT, FIRST TREATY OF. Agreement made by Charles XII of Sweden with Augustus II the Strong, king of Poland and elector of Saxony, during the Great Northern War (1700–21) (*q.v.*). Shortly after his succession, Augustus formed an alliance with Denmark and Russia against Sweden, a move that precipitated the war; Charles soon proved victorious and demanded the deposition of Augustus (Stanislaw Leszczynski was elected in his place). Following a Swedish invasion of Saxony, where he had taken refuge, Augustus was forced to accept the first Treaty of Altranstädt of September 24, 1706 by which he renounced his claim to the Polish throne, acknowledged Stanislaw, withdrew Saxony from the war against Sweden, and repudiated his alliance with Russia. In 1709, however, Peter the Great of Russia defeated Charles at the Battle of Poltava, enabling Augustus to declare his former agreement void and to return to Poland and recover his throne.

ALTYN. Monetary unit in medieval Russia. One *altyn* equaled six *dengas* or three *kopeks*.

ALVENSLEBEN-ERXLEBEN, GUSTAV, GRAF VON (1803–81). Prussian general. He was the chief personal adviser to King William I. In 1863 he negotiated a Prusso-Russian agreement, termed the Alvensleben Convention, providing for cooperation in the suppression of Polish rebels.

AMALRIK, ANDREY ALEKSEYEVICH (1938–80). Author. He was expelled from Moscow University in 1963 for political reasons and in 1965 was sentenced to two and one-half years' internal exile for "parasitism." His experiences in exile formed the subject of his book *Involuntary Journey to Siberia* (1970). He also wrote *Will the Soviet Union Survive until 1984?* (1970).

Karlinsky, Simon and Appell, A., Jr (eds.), *The Bitter Air of Exile: Russian Writers in the West, 1922–1972,* 1977.

AMASTRIS. Town situated on the S shore of the Black Sea. It was reportedly attacked and plundered by the Rus in 820–42 although some, including Vasilev, refused to recognize the validity of this story, claiming that it referred to Igor's campaign in 941.

AMBARTSUMINA, VIKTOR AMAZASPOVICH (1908–). Astronomer who has researched interstellar absorption of light, the luminance of interstellar substance, and the calculation of mass ejected by newly formed stars. His works include *Dispersion and Absorption of Light in the Atmosphere of Planets* (1941), *Evolution of Stars and Astrophysics* (1947), *Star System* (1949), and *Theoretical Astrophysics* (1958).

AMFITEATROV, ALEXANDER VALENTINOVICH (1862–1938). Journalist who was exiled for his satirical piece "The Obmanovs" (1902). In 1905 he went abroad and published *Krasni Flag,* a revolutionary magazine. On his return to Russia he became editor of the newspaper *Russkaya Svoboda* (Russian Freedom). He left Russia again after the Revolution and wrote articles against the Bolsheviks. His books include *Maria Luseva* (1904), *Those of the Eighties* (1907–08), and *Those of the Nineties* (1910).

AMU DARYA. River of Central Asia rising in the Pamirs and flowing W and N to the Aral Sea. It forms a large part of the Afghanistan-USSR frontier. Its total length is 1,500 miles (2,400 km) and it is navigable for over 800 miles (1,450 km). It is much used for irrigation and enters the Aral Sea as a large delta. It was known in ancient times as the Oxus.

AMUR RIVER. River formed by the junction of the Shilka and Argun rivers at the USSR-China border. It flows for 1,800 miles (2,880 km) SE and then NE, forms part of the border between the USSR and China, and enters the Sea of Okhotsk at Nikolayevsk opposite the N end of Sakhalin. The Amur River system has 8,400 miles (13,440 km) of navigable waterways, which are open from May to October each year, and drains nearly 800,000 square miles (2,072,000 sq km).

ANADYR RANGE. Mountain range in NE Siberia extending SE from the East Siberian Sea.

ANADYR RIVER. River rising in the Gidan range of NE Siberia and flowing for 500 miles (800 km) SW and then E, entering the Bering Sea at the Gulf of Anadyr.

ANARCHISM. Theory that equality and justice can only be sought through the abolition of the state. Central to all anarchist logic is the emphasis on individual freedom and the denial of any authority. Anarchism is of particular emotional appeal whenever an agrarian society is undergoing the upheavals caused by industrialization. In Russia anarchism was influential in the late 19th and early 20th centuries; its chief theorists were Bakunin and Kropotkin *(q.q.v)*, both of whom also influenced populism. Bakunin believed that the social instinct within man rather than laws enforced by state or church was sufficient to make man behave in a socially acceptable manner. He was active in the international workers' movement, traveled abroad, and met Karl Marx and P.-J. Proudhon. Kropotkin believed that animal and primitive communities were based on mutual aid, and asserted that war was not a basic instinct of savage man. His desire to transform mankind into a federation of mutual aid communities is set out in his book *Mutual Aid* (1902). Toward the end of the 19th century the anarchists divided into individualists, syndicalists, and communists, and in 1917 a federation of anarchists was established. They joined the Soviets and at first assisted the Bolsheviks in the Civil War, but later alternated between opposing and supporting the Bolsheviks. Anarchist groups were finally suppressed in 1921 following the Kronstadt uprising.

Avrich, Paul, *The Anarchists in the Russian Revolution,* 1973.

Carr, Edward Hallett, *Bakunin,* 1937.

Joll, J., *The Anarchists,* 1964.

Masaryk, Tomáš G., *The Spirit of Russia,* 2 vols., 1955.

Runkle, G., *Anarchist, Old and New,* 1972.

Walicci, Andrzej, *A History of Russian Thought, From the Enlightenment to Marxism,* 1973.

Woodcock, G., *Anarchism,* 1962.

ANARCHIST-COMMUNIST. An utterly militant party whose members held many views similar to those of the Bolsheviks on individual issues, such as ownership of land, but, unlike them, did not believe in any state structure. They drew their inspiration from Bakunin and Kropotkin *(q.q.v.)*.

ANASTASIA (Anastasiya Nikolayevna) (1901–18?). Youngest daughter of Tsar Nicholas II. It was assumed that she had been murdered with the rest of the Russian royal family at Yekaterinburg (1918) until a German citizen named Anna Anderson claimed to be Anastasia (1929). Anderson's claim continues to provoke controversy.

ANASTASIYA ZAKHARIN (?–1560). The first of the seven wives of Tsar Ivan IV. They were married a month after his coronation in 1547. It is from her family that the next dynasty, the Romanovs, came. She was said to have exerted a beneficial influence on the Tsar; of their six children only two survived childhood.

ANDIZHAN. Capital of the Andizhan region in Uzbekistan, 160 miles (256 km) ESE of Tashkent. It dates from the ninth century and became important in the 15th century because of its position on the caravan route to China. In 1898 it was the center of an abortive uprising against tsarist rule. Industries are cotton and food production. Population (1975) 224,000.

ANDREYEV, LEONID NIKOLAYEVICH (1871–1919). Short-story writer and dramatist. Originally a lawyer, he became a journalist. His early stories were influenced by Maxim Gorky, who befriended him, and Anton Chekhov. Later he was influenced by the works of Tolstoy and Dostoyevsky and his style changed. Most of his works reveal his obsession with death, madness, and sex, although he was capable of an almost surrealistic humor. His best-known works are *Anathema, The Red Laugh, Seven Who Were Hanged,* and *He Who Gets Slapped.* He fled to Finland after the Revolution (1917) and died in poverty, a violent anti-Bolshevik.

Newcombe J., *Leonid Andreyev,* 1972.

Woodward, J. B., *Leonid Andreyev: A Study,* 1969.

ANDREYEVSKY, SERGEY ARKADYEVICH (1847–1918). Poet, critic, and author. He was the first to translate Edgar Allan Poe's *The Raven* into Russian. His works include *Kniga smert'* (1925), and he wrote much criticism of Dostoyevsky, Lermontov, Nekrasov, and Turgenev.

ANDREW, SAINT (?–A.D. 62 or 70). Patron saint of Russia and also of Scotland. One of the 12 Apostles and brother of St. Peter, according to early church legend, he was active as a missionary in Asia Minor, Macedonia, and the Black Sea area. He was often called *protokletos* (first-called) in early Byzantine tradition. He was crucified at Patras in Greece on an X-shaped (St. Andrew's) cross. St. Andrew's day is November 30.

ANDREY, GRAND PRINCE (*fl.* mid 13th century). Younger brother of Alexander Nevsky. He was grand prince of Vladimir (1246–52) but was deposed by Alexander, who succeeded him as grand prince.

ANDREY, YURYEVICH BOGOLYUBSKY (*c.* 1111–74). Prince of Rostov-Suzdal (1157) and grand prince of Vladimir (1169). On his father's death (1157) he was elected prince of Rostov and Suzdal. He fortified and enlarged Vladimir, which became his capital, encouraged settlers, built many churches and opposed feudal separatism. In 1169 he sacked Kiev and became grand prince. Later he forced Novgorod to accept a prince of his choice. He was assassinated after attempting to reduce the power of his nobles.

ANDREYEV, ANDREY (1895–). A member of the Communist Party since 1914, Andreyev was one of the organizers of the union of metalworkers in Petrograd from 1915 to 1917. He took part in the October Revolution and in the second All-Russian Congress of Soviets. He was president of the central committee union of railway workers (1922–27) and was secretary of the central committee of the All-Union Communist Party (1924–25). Andreyev was a member of the Politburo (1932–52) and was again secretary of the central committee of the All-Union Communist Party (1935–46). He was a people's commissar of the workers' and peasants' red army and of agriculture, and has held several other important positions within the party. He has been a member of the Presidium since 1953.

ANDRONIKOV MONASTERY. Built between 1410 and 1427, the Andronikov Monastery is the oldest building still standing in Moscow. It is probable that Andrey Rublev assisted in designing it. Its design makes use of *kokoshniki,* the upper tier of which was arranged in an octogon around the base of a drum. The monastery is now known as the Rublev Museum, as it has on display many of Rublev's works and other fine icons.

ANDROPOV, YURY VLADIMIROVICH (1914–84). A member of the Communist Party of the Soviet Union since 1932, Andropov interrupted his university education to become a telegraph worker, an apprentice cinematographic mechanic, and a seaman, graduating from a technical school for waterway transport. Having been a *komsomol* organizer at a shipyard, Andropov then became the first secretary of the Yaroslav committee of the All Union Komsomol (1936–40). From then on, his distinguished political career included being the first secretary of numerous committees; from 1962 he had been a member of the foreign affairs committee. From 1953–57 he was ambassador to Hungary, and from 1957–67, Andropov was head of the central committee of the Communist Party of the Soviet Union's liaison department for communist and workers' parties of socialist countries. From 1961, he had been a member of the central committee of the Communist Party, and between 1967 and 1973, a full member of the Politburo central committee. He was chairman of the

KGB and resigned in May 1982 to take up a post as secretary of the CPSU. On the death of Leonid Brezhnev on November 10, 1982 Yury Andropov was appointed general secretary of the CPSU central committee and later that month a member of the Presidium. In 1983 he was appointed president of the Presidium.

Medvedev, Zhores, *Andropov*, 1983.

ANDRUSOVO, TREATY OF (1667). Treaty ending the Russo-Polish war for control of the Ukraine (1654–67). By the treaty the Ukraine was divided along the Dncpr River, Russia receiving the E part, Kiev, and the provinces of Smolensk and Seversk.

O'Brien, C. B., *Muscovy and the Ukraine: From the Pereiaslavl Agreement to the Truce of Andrusovo*, 1963.

ANGARA RIVER. River leaving Lake Baikal at the SW end and flowing for 1,300 miles (2,092 km) through SE Siberia; at first NNW through a deep valley to Irkutsk, and then E to become a tributary of the Yenisey River 35 miles (56 km) SSE of Yeniseysk. At Bratsk is a dam with one of the world's largest hydroelectric plants.

ANGARSK. Town situated 30 miles (48 km) NW of Irkutsk on the Angara River in the Russian Soviet Federated Socialist Republic. Manufactures include machinery, petrochemicals, and building materials. It has an oil refinery. Population (1972) 213,000.

ANGLO-RUSSIAN ENTENTE. An agreement signed in St. Petersburg on August 31, 1907 which laid down English and Russian spheres of interest in Persia, England taking the Persian Gulf and Russia the N of Persia. The aim was to keep a check on German expansion in the Near East. The entente formed a link in the Entente Cordiale between England, France, and Russia and was a basis for the allied coalition in the First World War.

ANHALT-ZERBST, SOPHIA. *See* **CATHERINE II.**

ANNA IVANOVNA (1693–1740). Empress of Russia (1730–40). The daughter of Ivan V and the niece of Peter I, Anna married (1710) Frederich William, duke of Courland (?–1710). She was elected by the Supreme Privy Council to become empress on the condition that she accept a number of provisions curtailing her powers. In practice, on ascending the throne, she became an autocrat and gave herself up entirely to pleasure. Her administration was run by her German advisers. Azov was recaptured in the Russo-Turkish War (1736–39), during her reign.

Longworth, Philip, *The Three Empresses, Catherine I, Anne and Elizabeth*, 1972.

ANNA LEOPOLDOVNA (KARLOVNA) (1718–46). Duchess of Brunswick-Wolfenbüttel and regent of Russia (1740–41). She was the granddaughter of Ivan V, and the daughter of Charles Leopold, duke of Mecklenburg-Schwerin, and of Catherine, sister of Tsarina Anna Ivanovna. She married the prince of Brunswick-

Wolfenbüttel and their son Tsar Ivan VI succeeded Anna.

ANNALS OF THE FATHERLAND. A literary and political journal of progressive socialist persuasion, first published in 1818 in St. Petersburg by the civil servant Svinin. From 1820, it was published monthly, and at this stage, was not yet of particular political significance. Publication ceased in 1830. Later, in 1839, Krayevsny started publishing the *Annals* in the "thick" journals.

Vissarion Belinksy participated in this, as did Alexandar Herzen, T. N. Granovsky, and Nicholas Ogarev. Also published were works by Ivan Turgenev, Nicholas Nekrasov, and Michael Lermontov. Because of the political views voiced in the constitutions, the *Annals* was attacked by the censorship but its influence, however, was wide. Publication ceased in April 1884.

ANNENKOV, PAUL VASILYEVICH (1812–87). Critic and first scientific Pushkinist. He was the author of literary memoirs republished 1928.

ANNENSKY, INNOKENTY FEDOROVICH (1855–1909). Modernist poet influenced by Baudelaire, Mallarme, Tyutchev *(q.v.)*, and Verlaine. He began writing poems in 1904 and also translated Euripides into Russian. His works include *Quiet Songs* (1904) and *The Cypress Chest* (1910).

AN-SKI, SHLOIME (SOLOMON SAMUEL RAPPAPORT) (1863–1920). Author writing in Yiddish. He was a Socialist Revolutionary and a member of the Polish "Bund." His works include *Di Yiddishe Folkshaftung* (1921) and *Gesamelte Shriften* (1925).

ANTAE (ANTES). Group of E Slavonic nomadic tribes living in S Russia between the Dnepr and Dnestr rivers; they thrived in the sixth century.

ANTI-COMINTERN PACT. A five-year agreement for mutual defense against communist subversive activities which was signed by Germany and Japan on November 24, 1936 and later joined by Italy (1937). The Western democracies held that the pact was designed to dominate Europe rather than to combat communism. From 1939 to 1941 other countries, including Bulgaria, Finland, Hungary, Rumania, Slovakia, and Spain, signed the pact.

ANTI-COMMUNIST BLOC. Following the Second World War the USSR's hold over countries in E Europe grew stronger. In April 1949 a Western military alliance, the North Atlantic Treaty Organization, was established. Fear of communism in the anticommunist countries intensified, especially during the McCarthy era and especially after the USSR had announced that it possessed the hydrogen bomb. In 1955 West Germany joined NATO, and plans were made for the rearming of West Germany. The Soviet Union, alarmed, retaliated by creating the Warsaw Treaty Organization, which bound the E European countries in a close military alliance. Thus the world was divided roughly into the communist bloc and the anticommunist bloc, headed by the United States, and the nonaligned countries.

Feis, H., *From Trust to Terror: The Onset of the Cold War, 1945–50,* 1970.

Levering, Ralph B., *The Cold War, 1945–1972,* 1982.

ANTI-PARTY GROUP CRISIS. The Anti-Party was the name given by Khrushchev to large and inefficient central ministries which, he felt, were usurping the party's role in industry. Members of the group included Malenkov, Molotov, and Kaganovich. In meetings of the central committee and the Supreme Soviet, seven members of the Presidium had remained silent, forming a majority against Khrushchev, and calling on him to resign as first secretary. Khrushchev refused, and rallied his supporters. On June 22, 1957 the vast majority of central committee members supported Khrushchev, the Anti-Party group was thus defeated, and a new Presidium elected.

Leonhard, Wolfgang, *The Kremlin Since Stalin,* 1962.

Tatu, M., *Power in the Kremlin: From Khrushchev's Decline to Collective Leadership,* 1969.

ANTI-SEMITISM. In 1791 Catherine the Great instituted the "Pale of Settlement," a vast territory in the W provinces to which Jews *(q.v.)* were confined. For many years before this, Jews had been treated with contempt by Muscovite rulers. Repression increased under Tsar Nicholas I with the conscription of Jewish boys for 25 years from the age of 12. Although Alexander II was more liberal, there were violent pogroms under Alexander III and these, in turn, led to the large-scale emigration of Jews to W Europe and the United States.

"The Protocols of the Elders of Zion," a forged document outlining a plan for world domination by the Jews, caused further repression, and because many leaders of the October Revolution were Jews they were accused of trying to gain world domination through "Jewish Bolshevism." Anti-Semitism is "banned" in the USSR, but after 1930 Jews tended to be excluded from official positions. Stalin's policy from 1948 was to destroy Jewish cultural institutions; there were many imprisonments and executions, culminating in the "Doctors' Plot" (1953). With the death of Stalin the situation improved but anti-Semitism has continued.

Baron, S.W., *The Russian Jew under Tsars and Soviets,* 1964.

Israel, G., *The Jews in Russia,* trans. from the French by S. L. Chernoff, 1975.

Schwarz, S., *The Jews in the Soviet Union,* 1951.

ANTOKOLSKY, MARK (1842–1902). Sculptor, who lived abroad for a large part of his life and attempted in his work to break away from the academic tradition. In 1871 Tsar Alexander II purchased his statue *Ivan the Terrible.* Many of his works are in the Hermitage in Leningrad.

Chamot, M., *Russian Paintings and Sculpture,* 1963.

ANTONOV-OVSEYENKO, VLADIMIR ALEKSANDROVICH (1884–1939?). Revolutionary with Menshevik leanings who joined the Social-Democratic Labor Party in 1903. He was an organizer of the October rising and conducted the capture of the Winter Palace. He commanded various army groups during the Civil War, but as a supporter of Trotsky he was dismissed from the army in 1925. He then held diplomatic posts abroad and disappeared in the Great Purge of 1936–38.

Kochan, Lionel, *Russia in Revolution*, 1966.

ANTONOV UPRISING. An uprising in the Tambov province (1919–21) led by A. S. Antonov, a socialist revolutionary. It was anticommunist and as many as 50,000 peasants and deserters from the Red Army took part. Troops defeated the movement on several occasions, but it only collapsed with the onset of the New Economic Policy.

Footman, David, *Civil War in Russia*, 1981.

ANZHERO-SUDZHENSK. Town in the Russian Soviet Federated Socialist Republic situated 50 miles (80 km) NNW of Kemerovo in the Kuznetsk basin. It is an important coal-mining center. Manufactures are mining equipment and by-products of coal. Population (1970) 106,000.

APPANAGE. The land held by an individual prince. During the period of Appanage Russia such holdings multiplied at a considerable rate, as princes divided their territory between their sons. The Muscovite rulers eventually gained the upper hand partly because, while they divided their principality among their sons, the eldest son received the largest share and the title grand prince, putting him in a stronger position in relation to his brothers than was the case with the rulers of other appanages.

APPANAGE RUSSIA. The Kievan state collapsed in 1240 and the period that followed was known as Appanage Russia. An appanage was the land held by an individual prince; after 1240 the number of appanages increased greatly and the continual subdivision of land resulted in the destruction of political unity. During the period of Appanage Russia the country was controlled by the Mongols (1240–1380), while the W and SW were taken first by Lithuania, then by Poland. In the N the Teutonic Knights, Swedes, and Norwegians posed a constant threat. These factors contributed to the loss of Russia's international standing and its relative isolation from the rest of Europe, and it became increasingly inward-looking. Economic and cultural revival came only with the Muscovite unification of Russia.

Presniakov, A. E., *The Formation of the Great Russian State: A Study of Russian History in the Thirteenth to Fifteenth Centuries*, trans. A. E. Moorhouse, 1970.

Vernadsky, George, *The Mongols and Russia*, 1953.

Vernadsky, George et al. (eds.), *A Source Book for Russian History from Early Times to 1917*, 1972.

APPARAT. Name given to divisions staffed by professional communist workers and which carry out the party's directives under the guidance of the secretariat. The *apparat* influences every sphere of life in the USSR; it appoints and controls key personnel at all levels of party, state, and economic administration, disseminates propaganda, sounds out public opinion, and reports the mood of the people to the central authorities and maintains close links with thousands of party secretaries in local units.

Hough, J. F. and Fainsod, Merle, *How the Soviet Union is Governed,* 1979.

Lane, D., *Politics and Society in the USSR,* (London, 1970; New York, 1971).

APPARATCHIKI. Colloquial term for an official of government, trade unions, or party. The term has rather contemptuous connotations.

Skilling, H. G., *Interest Groups in Soviet Politics,* 1971.

White, Stephen, *Political Culture and Soviet Politics,* 1979.

APRAKSIN, COUNT FEDOR MATVEYEVICH (1661–1728). General-admiral and creator of the Russian navy. He was a life-long friend of Peter the Great. In 1700 he was made governor of Azov and was also put in charge of shipbuilding and the construction of naval installations. In 1708 he defeated the Swedish attempt on St. Petersburg, and was created a count (1709) for his services. In 1713 he won Russia's first naval victory against Sweden at Hangö, and in 1721 he concluded the Treaty of Nystadt (*q.v.*) with Sweden. He was tried three times for embezzlement and each time was punished with heavy fines.

Mitchell, Mairin, *The Maritime History of Russia: 848–1948,* 1949.

APRAKSIN, COUNT STEPAN FEDOROVICH (1702–58). General and nephew of Count Fedor Matveyevich Apraksin. He was commander in chief of the Russian army during the Seven Years' War and defeated the Prussians at the battle of Gross Egersdorf (1757).

APRIL THESES. On his return to Petrograd, April 16, 1917, Lenin published the so-called April Theses, a policy statement that defined his own position and was intended to direct the Bolsheviks toward the seizure of power. The theses contributed to the October uprising because in effect they were asking the Bolsheviks to withdraw support from the provisional government. In the theses Lenin opposed continuation of the war; proposed that power be handed over to the Soviets, including control of banks, production, and distribution of goods; advocated abolition of the existing police force, army, and bureaucracy and the confiscation of all private land; and suggested that the Social-Democratic Party be called the Communist Party, and that the Socialist International be reconstructed.

The theses met with considerable opposition even from within the Bolshevik Party; and the Petrograd and Moscow Bolshevik committees voted against them, but within a few weeks they were adopted by the Bolsheviks.

Schapiro, Leonard B., *The Communist Party of the Soviet Union* (2nd ed.) 1970.

Ulam, Adam B., *Lenin and the Bolsheviks,* 1969.

APUKHTIN, ALEKSEY NIKOLAYEVICH (1841–93). Writer. His first volume of poems appeared in

1886, and his complete works were published in two volumes in 1907. He was unusual in that his poetry did not expose the social problems of the day but treated emotional themes such as lost youth, lost chances of pleasure, or death. Several of his lyrics were set to music by Tchaikovsky.

ARAKCHEYEV, COUNT ALEXEY ANDREYEVICH (1769–1834). Soldier and statesman. He was a stern and conservative adviser to Tsar Paul I and Tsar Alexander I and minister of war (1808–10). During Alexander's frequent absences abroad he virtually ruled Russia. This period was known as the *Arakcheyevshchina.*

ARAKISHVILI, DMITRY IGNATYEVICH (1873-1953). Prominent in the musical world as a conductor, teacher, and composer, he was one of the founders of the Georgian school of music. In 1914 Arakishvili wrote the first Georgian opera, *Skazaniye o Sota Rustavel.*

ARAL SEA. Known as the Sea of Islands. It is a large inland sea separated in the W from the Caspian Sea by the Ust Urt plateau. It has an area of 24,000 square miles (61,160 sq km). It has no outlet but is fed by the Syr Darya and Amu Darya rivers. Fish, particularly sturgeon, carp, and herring, are an important resource. The water is brackish and generally shallow.

ARBUZOV, ALEKSEY NIKOLAYEVICH (1908–). Arbuzov is one of the best known of contemporary Soviet dramatists, both at home and abroad. His plays were first published in 1930, *Tanya* is generally considered to be one of the foremost plays of the 1930s. In later years, music hall and vaudeville features have colored his work.

ARCHANGEL. Region in the N Russian Soviet Federated Socialist Republic adjacent to the Arctic Ocean. It has an area of 229,000 square miles (593,110 sq km) and is mainly forested, with lumbering and wood processing industries. It is also the capital of the region of same name situated on the North Dvina River 25 miles (40 km) from the White Sea. Archangel is the principal sawmilling and timber-exporting center of the USSR. Other industries include shipbuilding, fish canning, and rope manufacture. The port is kept open from May to November with the aid of icebreakers. Population (1981) 391,000.

ARCHIPENKO, ALEXANDER (1887–1965). Sculptor. His development paralleled that of the Cubist painters. A gradual simplification of human contours brought him to the point of expressing the nude figure entirely in geometrical shapes.

Archipenko, Alexander, *Archipenko: Fifty Creative years: 1908–1958,* 1960.

Karshan, D. H. (ed.), *Archipenko: International Visionary,* 1970.

ARCHITECTURE. Traditional Russian building is based on a wooden structure *(klet)* with walls made of horizontally stacked timbers and a steep roof. In pre-Kievan Russia the *klet* formed the nucleus of all buildings; larger buildings were made from a cluster of *klety* joined by short passages. More important buildings were carved with decorative designs from folk art.

After the conversion of Kievan Russia to Christianity, the influence of Byzantium predominated; the wooden structures were sometimes translated into stone, which was scarce, and always adapted to strict Byzantine rules, as nearly all important buildings were religious. The Byzantine convention of a cube (the earth) surmounted by a dome or cupola (heaven) was adapted to custom, climate, and resources. Russian churches had smaller, darker interior spaces, greater verticality, and decoration on the outside. The Byzantine cupola became elongated into an "onion" dome on a cylindrical drum.

In the 16th century Italian architects were brought to Moscow to build in stone for Ivan III. Their main work was the Cathedral of St. Basil the Blessed in the Kremlin (1555–60), in which they used their expertise with stone to produce a traditional Russian design consisting of nine separate units on one foundation, each octagonal in shape.

The decorative baroque European style was popular in Russia before the deliberate Westernization of Russian art under Peter the Great. From then on Russian architects, notably Andreyan Zakharov (Admiralty, St. Petersburg, from 1805), worked in successive fashionable Western styles. In the early years of the 20th century the school of Constructivism produced outstanding modern buildings, but its inspiration declined into a politically motivated, massive monumentalism in the 1930s.

Auty, R. and Obolensky D. (eds.), "An Introduction to Russian Art and Architecture," *Companion to Russian Studies,* Vol. 3, 1980.

Berton, Kathleen, *Moscow: An Architectural History,* 1977.

Buxton, David Roden, *Russian Medieval Architecture,* 1934.

Faensen, Hubert and Ivanov, Vladimir, *Early Russian Architecture, 1975.*

Hamilton, George H., *The Art and Architecture of Russia,* (2nd ed.) 1975.

Kennett, Victor and Audrey, *The Palaces of Leningrad,* 1973.

Voyce, Arthur, *Russian Architecture: Trends in Nationalism and Modernism,* 1948.

ARCHIVES. The establishment of the Moscow Archive of the Ministry of Justice in 1852 marks the beginning of systematic archive-keeping in Russia, despite abortive efforts at centralization by Peter and Catherine the Great. Earlier archives were kept sporadically and go back to the 11th-century birchbark documents of Novgorod, but were subject to the ravages of accident and political expediency.

The Bolsheviks had a particular organizational, political, and philosophical interest in the preservation of records and have established the most centralized and state-directed system in the world.

Archives are in the hands of the Chief Archives Board, a government department that was part of the MVD (1938–60). Prior to 1938 archives were administered by a Central Archives Board, established in 1918 with minor changes in 1922 and 1929.

Major archives include: the Central State Archive of the City of Moscow (acronym TsGAgM), established in its present form in 1963, absorbing a previous Moscow archive which had gone back to the tsarist Moscow *gubernüg* archive; the Central State Archive of Ancient Acts (TsGADA), which took its present name and form in 1941, and is an amalgamation of the major pre-1917 historical archives; the Central State Archive of the National Economy of the USSR (TsGANKh), founded in 1961; the Central State Archive of the October Revolution, Superior Organs of State Power and Organs of State Administration of the USSR (TsGAOR), began in 1920 as Section 4 of the State Archive of the RSFSR; and the Central State Historical Archive of the USSR (TsGIA), which assumed its present form in 1941.

Grimsted, Patricia Kennedy, *Archives and Manuscript Depositories in the USSR: Moscow and Leningrad,* 1972.

ARCTIC. The USSR within the Arctic Circle consists mainly of tundra; those areas S of an isotherm having a July temperature of 50°F (10°C) will produce trees (notably in the E Siberian forest E of the Yenisey River), but even they are affected by permafrost. Land forms range from the rocky Karelian shield, ice-eroded, and the N tip of the Ural Mountains, to the much higher Central Siberian plateau (up to 5,000 feet/1,524 meters) and the E Siberian mountains (up to 10,000 feet/3,048 meters) beyond the Lena River. The main rivers flowing into the Arctic Ocean along its extensive coastline are the Ob, Yenisey, Kotuy, Lena, Indigirka, and Kolyma.

The native population is supported by fishing, hunting, and reindeer farming, the people being mainly Komi, Yakut, Tungus, Yukaghir, Koryak, Chukchi, Samoyeds, and Lapps. The Kola peninsula is urbanized and industrialized to some degree, with nickel, phosphate, and iron extraction and a major deepwater fishing base at Murmansk. Mineral resources also include copper, coal, lignite, petroleum (on the N Pechora River), and natural gas (near the mouth of the Ob). E. Siberia has reserves of copper, nickel, gold, platinum, cobalt, diamonds, tin, and mercury. Russian inhabitants are mainly employed in extractive industries. The main towns are Murmansk, Kandalaksha, Amderma, Novy Port, Igarka, Nordvik, Tiksi, and Srednye Kolymsk.

Levin, M. G. and Potapov, L. P. (eds.), *The Peoples of Siberia,* 1964.

McDonald, R. St. J., *The Arctic Frontier,* 1966.

ARCTIC EXPLORATION. Sporadic exploration by individual hunters and trappers had begun before the 16th century, when the Muscovite state reached the Arctic coast and established a sub-Arctic trading center at Archangel. In 1773 Peter the Great sent an expedition to find a NE passage between Europe and Asia; for 10 years its members mapped the Arctic coast from the White Sea to the Chukchi Sea and discovered the Aleutians, the Kuril Islands, and parts of Arctic America. The Soviet government under Lenin stimulated scientific study of the Arctic Ocean; this program inaugurated the drifting polar research stations which have been maintained since.

The most important result has been the discovery and survey (1948–49) of the Lomonosov Ridge, the central transoceanic submarine mountain range extending from the New Siberian Islands to the continental shelf off Ellesmere Island (1,100 miles/ 1,760 km). Exploration of the Russian Arctic has intensified since the introduction of long-range missiles has increased its strategic importance.

Armstrong, Terence E., *The Northern Sea-Route*, 1952.

Maxwell, A. E. (ed.), *The Sea*, Vol. 4, 1971.

Neatby, L. H., *Discovery in Russian and Siberian Waters*, 1973.

ARENSKY, ANTON STEPANOVICH (1861–1906). Composer and pianist. He is now mainly remembered for his Trio in D Minor and Variations on a Theme of Tchaikovsky.

ARGUN RIVER. Tributary of the Amur River. It rises in the Great Khingan Mountains in NE China and flows W past Hilar to the USSR frontier. Its total length is 900 miles (1,400 km). The Argun River forms part of the frontier after linking with Lake Hulun Nor and joins the Shilka River to form the Amur River.

ARGUNOV, IVAN PETROVICH (1727–1802). Portrait painter. He was originally a serf who had much influence on realistic portraiture in Russia.

Holme, C. (ed.), *Peasant Art in Russia*, 1912.

ARMAVIR. Town situated 105 miles (168 km) E of Krasnodar on the Kuban River in Russian Soviet Federated Socialist Republic. Manufactures include agricultural machinery, food products, and vegetable oils. Population (1981) 165,000.

ARMED NEUTRALITY. Policy devised in 1780 by Catherine the Great and directed against Britain. She persuaded Denmark, Sweden, and Prussia to adopt a wide interpretation of the rights of neutrals against Britain's enforcement of what Great Britain believed to be its maritime rights.

ARMENIAN CHURCH. The Armenian Apostolic (Orthodox) Church was, according to tradition, founded at Caesarea by the apostles Bartholomew and Thaddaeus. It was at first dependent on Syrian traditions for its liturgy; after being adopted as the national Armenian church in 300 A.D., it gradually developed a national liturgy, stimulated by St. Mashtots, who established Armenian as a literary language fit for use by the church. In 506 the church broke from the other Orthodox churches in its Monophysitism (insistence that Christ had only one nature); in this respect it followed St. Cyril of Alexandria, as did the Coptic Church.

The primate is the Catholicos of all Armenians; he resides at Echmiadzin. The Catholicos of Sis owes him spiritual allegiance but enjoys administrative autonomy. The patriarchate of Jerusalem dates from 1307, that of Constantinople from 1461.

Attwater, Donald, *The Christian Churches of the East*, 1961.

Gulesserian, P. C., *The Armenian Church*, 1970.

ARMENIAN LANGUAGE AND LITERATURE. Armenian is an Indo-European language spoken by an estimated 5.5 million people. It was introduced into the Transcaucasus by N Balkan immigrants *c.* 1500–1000 B.C. The written form developed after the Armenians became Christians at the beginning of the fourth century; it was based on an alphabet of 38 letters. The written form, called Grabar, was the medium of religious writing and court poetry; the spoken form deviated from it and split into dialects. National feeling and nationalist propaganda of the 18th and 19th centuries brought about a revival of the spoken language as a literary medium, and ensured its survival in place of Grabar. E Armenian (based on the speech of Yerevan and Ararat) is the language of the Armenian Soviet Socialist Republic; W Armenian (based on the speech of Istanbul) is used in Turkish Armenia.

The great period of Grabar literature was from the 5th to the 12th century, ending with the political decline of Greater Armenia. Its masterpiece is the *Refutation of the Sects* by Eznik Koghbatzi. The 18th- and 19th-century revival used spoken Armenian. In Russian Armenia, nationalist writers used plays, novels, and verse to inspire national feeling. The best known are the novelist Khachatur Abovean (*Wounds of Armenia,* 1841), the playwright Gabriel Sundukiantz, the novelist Hakob Meliq-Hakobian, and the poet Hovhannes Thumanian.

Boyajian, Z. C., *Armenian Legends and Poems*, 1958.

ARMENIANS. A people of NE Turkey and SW Russia speaking an Indo-European language. Approximately 1.5 million Armenians live in Turkey, Europe, and the United States and 3.1 million in the Armenian Soviet Socialist Republic, with smaller numbers in Georgia and Azerbaijan. Their culture is ancient and highly developed, with a literature written in an alphabet derived from Greek and Syriac script. Their language is the only representative of a distinct branch of the Indo-European family. Herodotus claimed they were related to the ancient Phrygians. They call themselves Hay and their land Hayastan. They are mainly Monophysite Christians and belong to the Armenian Apostolic Church. During the 19th century they suffered massacres at the hands of the Turks, who feared the growing influence of nationalism among them.

Burney, C. and Lang, D. M., *The Peoples of the Hills, 1971.*

Hovannisian, R.G., *The Republic of Armenia,* Vol. 1: *The First Year, 1918–1919,* 1971.

Kurkjian, V. M., *A History of Armenia,* 1959.

Lang, D. M., *Armenia: Cradle of Civilization,* 1970.

ARMENIAN SOVIET SOCIALIST REPUBLIC. In 1920 Armenia was proclaimed a Soviet socialist republic. The Armenian Soviet government, with the Russian Soviet government, was a party to the Treaty of Kars (1921), which confirmed the Turkish possession of the former government of Kars and of the Surmali district of the government of Yerevan. From 1922 to 1936 it formed part of the Transcaucasian Soviet Federated Socialist Republic. In 1936

Armenia was proclaimed a constituent republic of the USSR, with its capital at Yerevan. It has an area of 11,490 square miles (29,800 sq km). The country is mainly mountainous but the valley of the Araks River yields cotton, orchards, and vineyards, as well as subtropical plants. Important mineral deposits include copper, zinc, aluminum, and marble. Population (1979) 3,000,000.

ARMFELT, GUSTAV MORITZ, COUNT OF (1757–1814). First governor-general of Finland under Tsar Alexander I.

ARMY. The Russian army largely was established by Peter the Great, aided by foreign experts. The army rarely suffered defeat during the 18th century and was steadily improved by Rumyantsev and Suvorov. Military organization then came under the influence of rigid Prussian military doctrine, although later Suvorov's ideas were reimplemented. Demoralized by the February Revolution of 1917, the Imperial Army disintegrated soon after the Bolshevik seizure of power.

In 1981 the Soviet army consisted of approximately 187 divisions, of which some 100 were of combat readiness, numbering about 1.8 million men.

The mechanized and tank divisions are equipped with the T54 medium tank, mounting an 85-mm gun, and with the Stalin III heavy tank, mounting a 122-mm gun. The T54 is being replaced by the T62 medium tank, mounting a 115-mm gun. Rocket units are stated to be the main force of the army.

In addition to the Soviet army, there are some 560,000 security and border troops.

Erickson, John (ed.), *Soviet Military Power and Performance*, 1979.

Hellie, R., *Enserfment and Military Change in Muscovy*, 1971.

Liddell Hart, Basil H., *The Soviet Army*, 1956.

O'Ballance, E., *The Red Army*, 1964.

Wildman, A. K., *The End of the Russian Imperial Army: The Old Army and the Soldiers' Revolt (March–April 1917)*, 1980.

ARSENY. Metropolitan of Rostov who opposed the empress, Catherine II, when she secularized church lands in 1763–64. He excommunicated all those involved with this policy, but lacked the support of other hierarchs, and was brought to trial, defrocked, and imprisoned for life.

ARSHIN. Measure of length equal to 28 inches or 71 centimeters, also known as *archin, parmak,* or *pharoagh.*

ART. The strongest folk-art traditions in the early Russian principalities were wood carving, metalwork, and embroidery. These traditions reflected a high standard of craftsmanship and a lively, creative imagination; with the stimulus of Byzantine Christianity from *c.* 1000 all three rose to the level of art. Byzantine conventions were adopted, but they were interpreted with native imagery and a liking for linear design and natural forms.

Of large-scale work in metal, the most notable surviving pieces are the damascened copper doors of the Cathedral of the Nativity (*c.* 1233) in

Suzdal; each door has 35 figurative panels. Small pieces, secular and ecclesiastical, included church vessels, jewelry, book covers, icon covers, lamps, and tableware; they were made in chased, embossed, engraved, or relief-decorated copper and silver, with some gold and (in Kiev) gold cloisonné enamel.

Wood-carvers made devotional objects in the strict Byzantine tradition, including carved icons which, by the 15th century, consciously imitated painted icons. The introduction of the elaborate iconostasis, or icon-screen, *c.* 1400 brought together this type of work and the ornate, architectural wood-carving tradition with its intricate curvilinear patterns and undercut lace effects. Wood carving is the characteristic Russian art form, surviving all reversals.

Painting emerged as a great art in the 14th century with the work of Theophanes the Greek and his successor Andrey Rublev (*q.q.v.*). The Muscovite state produced the culminating style, a wholly Russian interpretation of religious subjects. This, together with similarly original secular and religious work in other media, came to an abrupt end under Peter the Great (1689–1725), who rejected all native, Byzantine, and Oriental schools in favor of Western European models. Russian artists began to follow European trends, with no particular distinction, until the emergence of a realist school in the 19th century. The genre paintings of Alexey Venetsiyanov (1779–1847) and Pavel Feodotov (1815–52) were popular, the former with his lyrical treatment of peasant scenes and Russian landscape, the latter imbued with satire or sentiment drawn from everyday bourgeois life. The first vigorous painter of peasant life was Ilya Repin (*q.v.*), inspirer of the later Socialist Realism.

The first modern movements developed under the influence of the painter Michael Vrubel (1856–1910) (*q.v.*) and of the circle of designers surrounding Sergei Diaghilev, Alexander Benois, and Leon Bakst (*q.q.v.*). Three later schools were of international importance: Rayonism was a style of abstract painting which flourished from 1911, the mass of an object being projected into space by radiating lines of color; Constructivism was a type of abstract sculpture practiced by the brothers Naum Gabo and Antoine Pevsner (*q.q.v*) from 1917, using movement and transparency as well as mass; Suprematism was a school of abstract painting founded by Kasimir Malevich (*q.v.*) in 1913, using only the geometric shapes of rectangle, triangle, circle, and cross.

The Russian avant-garde, flourishing in the early period after the Revolution, was rejected after the death of Lenin and replaced by a revival of Socialist Realism.

Gray, Camilla, *The Russian Experiment in Art 1863–1922*, 1962.

Sarabianov, D. and Bowlt, John E., *Russian and Soviet Painting*, 1977.

Talbot Rice, Tamara, *A Concise History of Russian Art*, 1963.

Vaughan James, C., *Soviet Socialist Realism*, 1973.

ARTEL. Russian artisans' or farm cooperative.

ARTEMOVSK. Ukrainian town situated 40 miles (64 km) NNE of

Donetsk in the Donbas. It is the largest center of salt mining in the USSR and manufactures iron and glass.

ARTSYBASHEV, MICHAEL PETROVICH (1878–1927). Novelist, essayist, and playwright. His novel *Sanin* (1907) was one of the first in Russia to include a frank discussion of sex. Other works include *Breaking Point* (1915) and *War* (1918). He left the USSR following the Revolution.

ASBEST. Situated in the foothills of the Urals in the Russian Soviet Federated Socialist Republic 33 miles (53 km) ENE of Sverdlovsk, it is a railway terminus leading to the largest asbestos-mining plant in the USSR. Population (1969) 76,000.

ASEYEV, NICHOLAS NIKOLAYEVICH (1889–1963). Poet. His early works include *Night Flute* (1914), *Letorey* (1915), and *Queen of the Cinema* (early 1920s). In 1923 he joined the literary LEF (Left Front) but although later works such as *The Steel Nightingale* (1922), *Twenty-Six* (1923), *The Sverdlov Storm* (1924), and *Semyon Proskakov* (1926) contained a political element, they still expressed much romanticism.

ASHKHABAD. Capital of Turkmenistan Soviet Socialist Republic situated at the foot of the Kopet Dagh 25 miles (40 km) from the Iranian frontier. It was rebuilt following an earthquake in 1948. Industries include textiles, glass, food processing, and meat-packing. Population (1981) 325,000.

ASIA, SOVIET CENTRAL. Soviet Central Asia embraces the Kazakh Soviet Socialist Republic, the Uzbek Soviet Socialist Republic, the Turkmen Soviet Socialist Republic, the Tadzhik Soviet Socialist Republic, and the Kirghiz Soviet Socialist Republic.

Turkestan (by which name part of this territory was then known) was conquered by the Russians in the 1860s. In 1866 Tashkent was occupied and in 1868 Samarkand, and subsequently further territory, was conquered and united with Russian Turkestan. In the 1870s Bokhara was subjugated, the emir, by the agreement of 1873, recognizing the suzerainty of Russia. In the same year Khiva became a vassal state to Russia. Until 1917 Russian Central Asia was divided politically into the khanate of Khiva, the emirate of Bokhara, and the governor-generalship of Turkestan.

In the summer of 1919 the authority of the Soviet government became definitely established in these regions. The khan of Khiva was deposed in February 1920, and a People's Soviet Republic was set up, the medieval name of Khorezm being revived. In August 1920 the emir of Bokhara suffered the same fate, and a similar regime was set up in Bokhara. The former governor-generalship of Turkestan was constituted an autonomous Soviet socialist republic within the Russian Soviet Federated Socialist Republic on April 11, 1921.

In the autumn of 1924 the Soviets of the Turkestan, Bokhara, and Khiva republics decided to redistribute the territories of these republics on a nationality basis; at the same time

Bokhara and Khiva became socialist republics. The redistribution was completed in May 1925, when the new states of Uzbekistan, Turkmenistan, and Tadzhikistan and several autonomous regions were established. The remaining districts of Turkestan populated by Kazakhs were united with Kazakhstan. Kirghizia, until then part of the Russian Soviet Federal Socialist Republic, was established as a union republic in 1936.

Grousset, René, *The Empire of the Steppes: A History of Central Asia,* 1971.

Wheeler, Geoffrey E., *The Modern History of Soviet Central Asia,* 1964.

Wheeler, Geoffrey E., *The Peoples of Soviet Central Asia,* 1966.

ASKANIA-NOVA. Ukrainian town situated 50 miles (80 km) WNW of Genichesk. A protected zoological nature reserve was established here in 1910.

ASSEMBLY OF 1471. Called by Ivan III before his campaign against Novgorod and usually considered a forerunner of the *zemsky sobor (q.v.)* of the Muscovite tsars, the assembly first appeared in its fully developed form during the reign of Ivan the Terrible (1549).

Fennell, John L.I., *Ivan the Great of Moscow,* 1963.

Vernadsky, George et al. (eds.), *A Source Book for Russian History from Early Times to 1917,* 1972.

ASTAPOVO. The author Count Lev Nikolayevich Tolstoy died of pneumonia on November 10, 1910 after his flight from home at the railway station of Astapovo. It was situated near his estate at Yasnaya Polyana in central Russia.

ASTRAKHAN. Region on the Lower Volga River in the Russian Soviet Federated Socialist Republic adjacent to the Caspian Sea. It has an area of 17,200 square miles (44,558 sq km). It is mainly agricultural, producing cotton and fruits. Some cattle and sheep are reared, especially lambs for fur. Salt deposits are in Lake Baskunchak. It is also the capital of the region of same name 60 miles (97 km) from the Caspian Sea on the delta of the Volga River. The principal port for the Caspian Sea, it trades in timber, grain, cereals, cotton, fruit, and rice. Industries include shipbuilding, sawmilling, textiles, and fish processing, especially caviar. Population (1977) 466,000.

ATAMAN. Military leader, commander of infantry and Cossack combat units. Initially in the Ukraine the title denoted an elected official, but from 1723 it referred to the appointed head of the military and civil administration. Leaders of popular uprisings such as Stenka Razin were also called by this title. It is also spelled *hetman.*

ATLANTIC CHARTER. The joint declaration of eight peace aims issued August 14, 1941 by Churchill and Roosevelt, which formed the basis of the charter of the United Nations. The main aspects were freedom, self-determination, and equality of opportunity for all nations. The USSR accepted the charter. Churchill suggested that Soviet demands for the postwar settlement be met in spite of the terms of the charter, a proposal rejected by Roosevelt.

Luard, E., *A History of the United States,* Vol. 1, 1981.

ATOMIC ENERGY. The world's first atomic power station began operation in Obninsk with a capacity of 5,000 kw in June 1954. Since that time, the Soviet Union has carried out an extensive program of development and experimentation in the peaceful use of atomic energy.

Some of the most important power stations in the USSR are the Leningrad atomic power station, with a capacity of 2,000,000 kw; the Siberian atomic power station in Novosibirsk, opened in 1958, with a total capacity of 600,000 kw; the Kurchatov atomic power station, opened in 1964, with a 300,000-kw capacity; the Novovoronezh atomic power station, opened in 1964, with a 2,455,000-kw capacity; and the Kola atomic power station with 880,000 kw capacity. The first fast-breeder reactor opened at Ulyanovsk in 1969, followed by the Shevchenko reactor in 1973.

In 1978 the Soviet Union had 19 atomic power stations in operation with a total capacity of 7,616,000 kw. By 1990 the USSR intends to raise the aggregate capacity of Soviet atomic power to 100,000,000 kw.

ATTILA THE HUN (*c.* 400–53). Ruler of a Central Asian nomadic people A.D. 434–53. Attila inherited the throne together with Bleda his brother. The inherited kingdom extended from the Alps and the Baltic in the W to the Caspian Sea in the E. He began his attacks on the Roman Empire in 441 with an onslaught on the Danubian frontier and continued them until 443, attacking again in 447 and 452. In *c.* 445 he killed Bleda and ruled alone. He never succeeded in taking Constantinople, but his ravages of large areas of the empire and the tribute he exacted earned him the title "Scourge of God."

Gordon, C. D., *The Age of Attila,* 1960.

Manchen Helfen, O., *The World of the Huns,* 1973.

Thompson, E. A., *A History of Attila and the Hun,* 1948.

AUGUSTOW. Town in Poland 50 miles (80 km) N of Bialystok where the S wing of the Russian army surrendered to the Germans in 1915.

AUGUSTUS II THE STRONG (1670–1733). King of Poland and elector of Saxony (known as Frederick Augustus I of Saxony), he regained Poland's former provinces of Podolia and the Ukraine. He joined with Russia and Denmark against Sweden, and began the Great Northern War (1700–21). Russia defeated Sweden but Augustus was defeated, and deposed by the Polish Diet. In 1710 he was restored to the throne by Peter the Great. In 1716–17 Russia once again intervened between Augustus and the Polish nobles and in 1720 annexed Livonia. Augustus at last acknowledged Russia's influence in Poland. He was, however, unable to reestablish a strong monarchy, and the court was known as the most dissolute in Europe. At his death Poland was no longer a major European power and had become a protectorate of Russia.

AUSTERLITZ, BATTLE OF. The first engagement of the War of the Third Coalition, also known as the Battle of the Three Emperors. Napoleon won the battle on December 2, 1805 in what is considered his most brilliant victory, engaging his 68,000 troops against 90,000 Russians and Austrians. Francis I of Austria agreed to a truce and Alexander I of Russia withdrew with his troops to Russia.

AUTOCRAT AND AUTOCRACY. Total power exercised by Russian tsars. Ivan III modeled his court on that of the Byzantine emperors and used the titles tsar and autocrat. The latter as used in Moscow originally referred to the complete independence of the Muscovite sovereign from any overlord after the withdrawal of the Tatars. Originally the title implied independence from any other ruler, but it came to mean an absolute monarch particularly under Peter the Great. Even when the power of the tsar was limited by that of the state duma and state council following the 1905 Revolution, the title "autocrat" was retained in the constitution.

Pipes, Richard, *Russia Under the Old Regime,* 1974.

Vernadsky, George, *The Tsardom of Muscovy,* 1969.

AUTONOMOUS OBLAST. Administrative territorial unit, often forming part of a *kray*. Autonomous oblasts are supposed to represent territorial autonomy for peoples who are not sufficiently numerous for the creation of an autonomous republic. Each autonomous oblast is represented in the Soviet of Nationalities of the USSR Supreme Soviet by five deputies. Internal administration is similar to that of an ordinary oblast. There are now nine autonomous oblasts, six in the Russian Soviet Federated Socialist Republic (Adyge, Jewish, Karachay-Circassian, Khakas, Mountainous-Altay, and Tuva) and one each in Georgia (South Ossetian), Azerbaijan (Mountainous-Karabakh), and Tadzhikistan (Mountainous-Badakhshan).

Hough, J. F. and Fainsod, Merle, *How the Soviet Union is Governed,* 1979.

McAuley, Martin, *Politics and the Soviet Union,* 1977.

AUTONOMOUS REPUBLIC. Administrative territorial unit that is supposed to represent territorial autonomy for peoples which did not qualify for a union republic of their own. There are at present 19 autonomous republics; they have such external symbols of statehood as constitutions, Supreme Soviets and councils of ministers, but in fact their administration is on the oblast level. Each autonomous republic is represented by 11 deputies in the Soviet of Nationalities of the USSR Supreme Soviet.

Hough, J. F. and Fainsod, Merle, *How the Soviet Union is Governed,* 1979.

McAuley, Martin, *Politics and the Soviet Union,* 1977.

AVARS. Warlike people who were settled in the Caucasus and one of 15 minor nationalities collectively known as Avarian.

Wallace-Hadrill, J. M., *The Barbarian West 400–1000,* 1967.

AVERCHENKO, ARKADY TIMOFEYEVICH (1881–1925). Author, particularly of humorous sketches and stories. He was a contributor to the magazine *Satyricon* published in St. Petersburg (1906–17). He left Russia in 1922.

AVKSENTEV, NICHOLAS DMITRIYEVICH (1878–1943). Politician and leader of the right wing of the Socialist Revolutionaries (*q.v.*). He was minister of the interior in the provisional government and a member of the Ufa Directory with Admiral Kolchak (1918). Later he emigrated.

AVVAKUM, PETROVICH (*c.* 1621–82). Priest and a member of the Old Believers sect. He disagreed with the reforms of Patriarch Nikon (*q.v.*). He was burned at the stake (1682).

Avvakum, Petrovich, *The Life of the Archpriest Avvakum by Himself*, trans. V. Nabokov, 1960.

AXELROD, PAVEL BORISOVICH (1850–1928). Leader, with Yuly Martov and Fedor Dan, of the Mensheviks. His two-part essay in *Iskra* in 1903–04, which expounded the differences between the two factions within a Marxist party, incurred the anger of Lenin.

Ascher, Abraham, *The Mensheviks in the Russian Revolution*, 1976.

Ascher, Abraham, *Pavel Axelrod and the Development of Menshevism*, 1972.

AZERBAIJAN. The independence of Azerbaijan was declared in 1918, with the capital first at Ganja, and later at Baku. In 1920 Azerbaijan was proclaimed a Soviet socialist republic. With Georgia and Armenia it formed the Transcaucasian Soviet Federated Socialist Republic. In 1936 it became one of the republics of the USSR. It has an area of 33,430 square miles (86,600 sq km). Subtropical agriculture includes cotton growing, orchards, and vineyards with silk culture, as well as tea plantations. The area is rich in natural resources, the most important industry being oil. Population (1981) 6,262,000.

AZEV, YEVNO FISHELEVICH (1869–1918). One of the founders of the Socialist Revolutionaries. An infamous police agent who played a double game and was exposed (1908), he was sentenced to death by the party but escaped to Germany and lived under an assumed name.

AZOV (ancient Tanaïs). River port in the Rostov oblast in the SW Russian Soviet Federated Socialist Republic 20 miles (32 km) from the mouth of the Don River. Azov was founded as a Greek colony in the third century B.C., became a Genoese colony in the 13th century, was subject to Turkey from 1471, and became Russian in 1739, when it was conditionally annexed as a dismantled fortress. It was not definitely secured until 1774 under the Treaty of Kuchuk-Kainarji. Now a rail junction, it is an important fishing center with fish processing plants. Because the port silted up, its functions were largely taken over by Rostov-on-Don. Population (1976) 73,000.

AZOV, SEA OF. N arm of the Black Sea, connected to it by the narrow Kerch strait (known in antiquity as Bosporus Cimmerius). It has an area of 14,000 square miles (71,070 sq km). Its greatest length is 220 miles (352 km); its average breadth is 80 miles (128 km); and its maximum depth is 49 feet (15 m). The water is very fresh and the sea is frozen for three or four months almost every year. The Don and Kuban rivers flow into the sea; its chief ports are Zhdanov, Taganrog, and Kerch. The Sivash, or Putrid Sea, a series of salty lagoons and marshes, lies to the W of the Sea of Azov, separated from it only by the long, narrow, sandy Arabat peninsula. This is one of several characteristic sandspits, created by counterclockwise currents. The freshness of the water and the low air and water temperatures cause the annual freezing from November to December until February to March. The Sea of Azov is linked to the Caspian Sea by the Manych canal, which has increased its economic importance; its freshwater fisheries are among the largest in the Soviet Union.

B

BABA-YAGA. A hideous hag or ogress in Russian folklore who is also guardian of the fountains of the water of life. She flies through the air in a fiery mortar, propelled by a pestle, causing storms and havoc. She captures children and after cooking her victims, eats them.

BABAR (ZAHIR UN-DIN MUHAMMED) (1483–1530). The founder of the Mongol empire in India and a descendant of Tamcrlane and Genghis Khan. Although not a diplomat, he established relations with Basil III.

BABEL, ISAAC EMMANUELOVICH (1894–1941). Novelist, playwright, and short-story writer. He wrote mainly about violence and brutality from the viewpoint of an intellectual both fascinated and repelled by his material, yet striving to be objective. He gained fame with *Odessa Tales* (1923–24), which was published by Maxim Gorky. *Red Cavalry* (1924) was written as a result of his service as a soldier in the war against Poland. He also wrote two plays *Sun Set* (1928) and *Maria* (1935). He was arrested in 1937 or 1938 and died in a concentration camp, a victim of the Stalin purges.

Carden, Patricia, *The Art of Isaac Babel*, 1972.

Hallett, R. W., *Isaac Babel*, 1973.

BABI YAR. Ravine near the middle of Kiev. In the Second World War the Nazis occupied the area for nearly two years, and the ravine contains the bodies of over 150,000 men, women and children, mainly Jews, slaughtered by the occupiers. It is the subject of a famous poem by Yevgeny Yevtushenko (*q.v.*) that became the focal point of activism against anti-Semitism.

Kuznetsov, Anatoli, *Babi Yar: A Documentary Novel*, 1967.

BADAKHSHAN. Province of Afghanistan, on the NE border. In the

5th century Badakhshan had formed part of Turkhmenistan, but was later ruled by the Turks and Arabs and came under the Khwanzmshah and the Timurids. In 1699, it became part of the Uzbek empire, and remained so until 1822, when it was taken over by Murad Beg. Following the penetration of E Pamir by Russia in 1895, Great Britain and Russia allotted Badakhshan to Afghanistan, and W Pamir to Bokhara, under Russian protection. In 1918, Pamir became the Gorno-Badakhshan Autonomous Oblast of the USSR.

BAGRATIDS. Royal Armenian and Georgian dynasty. It ruled Armenia from 885 to 1045, keeping the country free from the influence of the Byzantine Empire, and ruled Georgia from 1045 until its annexation in 1800 by Russia.

BAGRATION, PRINCE PETER IVANOVICH (1765–1812). A general of Georgian and Armenian extraction, descended from the Bagratids. He served against the French revolutionary and Napoleonic armies in Italy, Switzerland, and Austria, and against Turkey in 1809. He commanded the second Russian army against Napoleon during the advance on Moscow in 1812 and was killed at the Battle of Borodino. Nicholas I erected a monument to his memory on the site of the battle.

BAIKAL, LAKE. Lake in SE Siberia on the boundary between the Buryat-Mongol Autonomous Soviet Socialist Republic and Irkutsk oblast. It has an area of 12,150 square miles (31,104 sq km), and is the world's deepest freshwater lake. It is fed by over 300 rivers, drained only by the Angara River. It freezes over from January to April.

BAIKAL-AMUR MAGISTRAL (BAM), The. The recently constructed Baikal-Amur Magistral Railway provides a more direct route to the Pacific ports of Nakhodka and Vladivostok than that offered by the Trans-Siberian Railway and much of its route lies several hundred kilometers N of the Trans-Siberian Railway, avoiding the latter's lengthy detour around Lake Baikal, and eases the very heavy pressure on the Trans-Siberian route, which is only partially electrified and is not double-track throughout. It gives access to valuable raw materials such as coal, iron ore, copper, nickel, and timber.

Construction of the Baikal-Amur Magistral was the most arduous railway-building project ever tackled by Soviet engineers working under severe climatic and geological conditions. There is permafrost throughout the area, and winter temperatures fall to −132 °F (−60 °C). Severe danger exists in the mountains in winter from avalanches, and in summer freak streams of mud fill riverbeds and valleys, hindering construction.

Work was carried out from seven major construction sites, each equipped with its own reinforced concrete plant, steel fabrication works, and extensive engineering plant, and these sites will remain to form the nuclei of new heavy-industry towns.

Over 3,200 bridges, tunnels, and culverts were built for the Baikal-Amur Magistral, including 140 major river crossings and a 3,960 foot (1,200

m) bridge 132 feet (40 m) high over the Zeya River reservoir.

A 108 mile (180 km) link from the Trans-Siberian Railway at Skovorodino to Tyndin, about midway between Ust-Kut and Komsomolsk, was opened in 1975, and a northward extension of this route, to Berkakit, was opened in 1978. This line reaches the rich Chulman coalfields. The 456 mile (700 km) eastern section of the line from Urgal to Komsomolsk-on-Amur was opened to service traffic in June 1979.

BAKHCHISARAY. Capital of the Crimean oblast, Bakhchisaray has many buildings of historical interest, including the famous palace built in 1519, and various mosques.

BAKLANOV, GRIGORY (1923–?). Author. Having studied at the Gorky Institute of Literature, Baklanov embarked on a literary career; his works include *In Snegiri* (1954) and *Nine Days* (1958). He became a member of the CPSU in 1942.

BAKST, LEON SAMOYLOVICH (1866–1924). Painter and stage designer. He designed settings for the Imperial Theater at St. Petersburg and later for many of Diaghilev's ballets, including *The Sleeping Beauty, Carnaval, Scheherazade* and *L'Après-Midi d'un Faune.*

Lister, R., *The Muscovite Peacock,* 1954.

Spencer, Charles, *Bakst,* 1937.

BAKU. Capital of Azerbaijan and port situated on the S coast of the Apsheron peninsula on the Caspian Sea. Oil and gas wells were discovered and worshiped as early as the sixth century. Baku was independent until 1509 when it came under Persian influence. For a brief period (1723–35) it was under Russian rule and was finally annexed by Russia in 1806. It became capital of Azerbaijan in 1921 following the collapse of the anti-Bolshevik Azerbaijan Republic (1918–20). Industries include shipbuilding, oil refining, and the manufacture of oilfield equipment, chemicals, textiles, and cement. A pipeline runs to Batumi on the Black Sea and oil is exported. Population (1981) 1,046,000.

BAKUNIN, MICHAEL ALEKSANDROVICH (1814–76). Anarchist. An aristocrat, who, for a short time, served in the army, he left Russia in 1840. After taking part in a rising at Dresden in 1848 he was handed over to the Russian authorities and imprisoned. Later he was exiled to Siberia, but he escaped and reached England in 1861 and worked with Alexander Herzen. His life was then spent in a struggle with Karl Marx to decide upon the form which socialist doctrine should take. The anarchists were defeated and Bakunin was expelled from the International in 1872. His book *God and the State* (1882) called for militant atheism and the destruction of the state.

Berlin, Isaiah, *Russian Thinkers,* 1978.

Carr, Edward Hallett, *Michael Bakunin,* 1937.

Masaryk, Tomáš G., *The Spirit of Russia: Studies in History, Literature and Philosophy,* 1955.

Venturi, Franco, *Roots of Revolution,* 1960.

BALAKIREV, MILY ALEXEYEVICH (1836–1910). Composer and pianist. He was a pupil of Glinka and became a successful pianist. Later he taught Mussorgsky and Cui. He became a leading member of "The Five" (Cui, Balakirev, Borodin, Mussorgsky, and Rimsky-Korsakov) (*q.q.v.*), a group that revived the nationalist tradition in Russian music. Balakirev, who was much influenced by Glinka (*q.v.*), wrote two symphonies, piano music, incidental music for *King Lear* (1859–61), many songs, and the symphonic poems *Tamara* (1882) and *Russia* (1884).

Garden, E., *Balakirev*, 1967.

Seroff, Victor I., *The Mighty Five: The Cradle of Russian National Music*, 1948.

Zetlin, Mikhail O., *The Five: The Evolution of the Russian School of Music*, 1959.

BALAKLAVA. Port situated 8 miles (13 km) S of Sevastopol in the Crimea and since 1957 an urban district of Sevastopol. In the Crimean War it was held by the British (1854–56) following the Battle of Balaklava (October 25, 1854).

BALALAIKA. Russian triangular three-stringed guitar of Tatar origin. There are six sizes from piccolo to double bass. It is important in Russian folk music, but there are now also large balalaika orchestras.

BALANCHINE, GEORGE MELITONOVICH (1904–83). Choreographer. One of the seminal figures in the history of ballet, he left Russia in 1924 and was ballet master for Diaghilev (1925–29). In 1939 he went to the United States, where he choreographed for Broadway (*On Your Toes*) as well as for ballet. He founded the School of American Ballet (1934) and the New York City Ballet (1948). Balanchine introduced the concept of plotless ballet. Among his most important works are *Serenade, Orpheus, The Prodigal Son, Apollo,* and *Ballet Imperial.*

Taber, B., *Balanchine*, 1975.

BALIEV, NIKITA (1877–1936). Actor and impresario. He left Russia in 1920 and his Chauve-souris (Bat) company played in London for several years. The program consisted of song, dance, and folklore, and he performed in an attractive broken English that captivated his audiences.

BALKARS. Turkic-speaking people living in the Kabarda-Balkar Autonomous Republic on the N slopes of the main Caucasian range, E of Elbrus; they number about 40,000. They were subject to Russia from the 1820s. In 1921 they were included in the Mountain People's Autonomous Republic, and in 1922 in the Kabarda-Balkar Autonomous Oblast. For alleged collaboration with the Germans the Balkars were deported to Asiatic Russia in 1943 and were officially ignored as a people until 1957, when they were rehabilitated and permitted to return home.

Conquest, Robert, *The Soviet Deportation of Nationalities*, 1960.

BALKHASH. Town situated on the N shore of Lake Balkhash in Kazakhstan. Founded as Bertys in

1929, it is an important center of the copper industry. Population (1976) 78,000.

BALKHASH, LAKE. Lake situated 100 miles (160 km) W of the Chinese frontier between the Kazakh Hills in the N and the Sary-Ishik-Otrau desert in Kasakhstan. It has an area of 6,680 square miles (17,301 sq km) and an average depth of 20 feet (6 m). Fed chiefly by the Ili River, it has no outlet. Fishing and salt extracting are important. Its main ports are Balkhash, Burlyu-Tobe, and Burlyu-Baytal.

BALLADS. Russian ballads were mostly composed between the 13th and the 18th century. They recount dramatic tales such as the wife who murdered her husband. They are composed in a freer tonic verse than are *byliny (q.v.)*.

BALLET. Russian ballet began under the empresses Anna Ivanovna (1693–1740) and Elizabeth (1709–62), who engaged German and Italian directors to train Russian dancers. By 1740 the Imperial School of Ballet was established at the Winter Palace. Many of the dancers were serfs attached to the royal household and already trained in folk traditions; this introduced a virility into Russian ballet that ensured its ultimate victory over increasingly effete French and English styles of dancing. Productions were spectacular owing to the patronage of the tsar.

The arrival in St. Petersburg in 1811 of Charles Didelot (1767–1837), the French teacher and choreographer and an outstanding representative of the classical tradition, laid the foundations for the St. Petersburg school and the company's greatness. Jules Perrot (1810–92), Didelot's successor as ballet master, in 1851, continued his work until he was replaced by Marius Petipa (1818–1910), another French dancer, in 1862. Petipa combined the romantic style in vogue in Western Europe with the spectacle and formal approach that the tsar demanded.

By this time the ballet in Russia was firmly established as a serious art; in 1825 the Moscow Ballet, now the Bolshoi Ballet Company, had been founded, and productions were of a high quality in spite of a growing tendency for the dancing to become no more than a mechanical display of technique and stagecraft.

It was Peter Ilyich Tchaikovsky's (1840–93) ballet *The Sleeping Beauty* (1890) that brought about a revival of direct emotional appeal to the audience while retaining the spectacle.

Another major turning point occurred in 1909, the first season of Serge Pavlovich Diaghilev's (1872–1929) Ballets Russes in Paris, using dancers trained at the Maryinsky Theater, and avant-garde Russian composers and designers; Michel Fokine (1880–1942) was chief choreographer and Igor Fedorovich Stravinsky (1882–1971) principal composer, while its most notable designers were Alexander Nikolayevich Benois (1870–1960) and Leon Bakst (1866–1924). The company's principal dancers were Tamara Karsavina (1885–1978) and Vaslav Nijinsky (1890–1950). Through the Ballets Russes the influence of Russian ballet reached England, with Alicia Markova (1910–), France, with Serge Lifar

(1905–) and the United States, with George Balanchine (1904–83).

With Diaghilev's departure, the Moscow Bolshoi company became dominant with its vigorous, athletic style and lavish productions, well suited to the new socialist state's requirements for an impressive "state art."

The Kirov Ballet (formerly the Maryinsky) in Leningrad adhered to a more restrained classical style and became known for the pure, artistic creativity of its choreographers and outstanding line and movement of its dancers. Foreign influence was opposed as companies had to comply with the state policy of artistic self-sufficiency.

In 1929 René Blum (1884–1944) succeeded Diaghilev; he was joined by Colonel W. de Basil (1888–1951) in 1932 and under this partnership the Ballets Russes continued to make the influence of Russian ballet felt throughout the world, making its first tour of the United States in 1933.

In the Soviet Union ballet is encouraged; tours are frequent and dancers such as Rudolf Nureyev have made great contributions to ballet outside the USSR. For a brief period immediately after the Revolution, avant-garde styles and political content were attempted, but under Stalin there was a return to traditional forms and to the 19th century classics and neoclassics such as *Cinderella* and *Romeo and Juliet.* Particularly successful was Yury Grigorovich's version of *Spartacus* (1968).

Beaumont, C. W., *A History of Ballet in Russia, 1616–1881,* 1930.

Benois, Alexander, *Reminiscences of the Russian Ballet,* 1947.

Karsavina, Tamara, *Theatre Street,* 1950.

Lieven, P., *The Birth of the Ballets Russes,* 1936.

Roslavleva, Natalia, *Era of the Russian Ballet, 1770–1965,* 1966.

Swift, M. G., *The Art of the Dance in the USSR,* 1968.

BALLISTIC MISSILES. Ballistic missiles form an important part of the Soviet deterrent. It is thought that the USSR has about 1,400 intercontinental ballistic missiles, and 600 medium- to intermediate-range ballistic missiles deployed in the western USSR. In the 1950s the USSR started building submarines designed to carry ballistic missiles.

BALMONT, KONSTANTIN DMITRIYEVICH (1867–1943). Writer. Having been expelled from school and from Moscow University on political grounds, Balmont finally graduated from the Yaroslav College of Law. He began publishing verse and was considered the most promising "decadent" poet; his best works include *Buildings on Fire* (1900) and *Let us be as the Sun* (1903). He used accumulations of words for musical effect. An anti-Bolshevik in 1917, he emigrated, and it is felt that his later work is not truly "Russian."

BALTIC GERMANS. The descendants of the Teutonic Knights and their followers who settled in the Baltic provinces. In the 18th century the provinces became part of Russia. After the 1917 Revolution, the Baltic peoples formed independent republics, but as a result of the German-Soviet pact of 1939, the Baltic Germans were deported to Germany.

BALTIC PROVINCES. Name given in prerevolutionary times to the provinces of Estland, Livland, and Kurland. Once belonging to the Teutonic Knights, they later belonged to Sweden and Poland and were annexed by Russia in the 18th century, after which russification measures were instigated.

BALTIC REPUBLICS. Estonia, Latvia, and Lithuania. They were created independent states in 1918–19 and in 1940 were incorporated into the Soviet Union.

BALTIC SEA. Sea surrounded by Sweden, Denmark, Germany, and Poland and the republics of Lithuania, Latvia, and Estonia. It is connected to the North Sea by a channel between Denmark and the S of Sweden. The Baltic has been the principal maritime trade route between Russia and Western Europe since the Middle Ages.

BAM. *See* **Baikal-Amur Magistral, The.**

BANDUNG CONFERENCE (1955). First conference of various nonaligned nations, held in Bandung, Indonesia. The conference was encouraged by the Soviet government, but opposed by the United States.

BANKING. The state bank, Gosbank, was founded in 1921. In 1932 a number of specialized banks for long-term investments were established, but these were abolished in the same year. The Stroybank deals with investments, and the Vneshtorgsbank with foreign trade.

BAPTISTS. The sect appeared in continental Europe in 1834 in Hamburg, where Johann Gerhardt Oncken set up a church. Through his influence the sect's beliefs spread to Russia, where a Baptist Union was organized in 1884 and a sympathetic Union of Evangelical Christians (English-influenced) in 1908. Persecution, at first severe, was relaxed in 1905 and was further relaxed in 1917. In 1927 the Baptist Union had an estimated 500,000 members and the Union of Evangelical Christians, 4 million. Persecution began again in 1929. The two groups combined in 1944 as the All-Union Council of Evangelical Christians and Baptists in the USSR. The estimated 540,000 members (1970) enjoy limited toleration.

Bourdeaux, M., *Opium of the People*, 1965.

BARABA STEPPE. Wooded steppe in SW Siberia between the Irtysh and Ob rivers colonized since the 18th century by Russians and Ukrainians, and from 1941 by Volga Germans. The Baraba Steppe is one of the main areas of dairy farming in Siberia.

BARABASHNOV, N. P. (1894–). Astrophysicist who put forward theories about the nature of the moon's surface. He was also director of the Kharkovsky observatory.

BARANOV, ALEXANDER. *See* **Alaska.**

BARANOVICHI. Town in the Brest oblast in Belorussia, and center of the Baranovichiskaya oblast.

Founded in 1870 as a railway station, it is now an important railway junction. Baranovichi suffered great damage during the German occupation in the First World War, and was largely destroyed during the Second World War. Population (1979) 126,000.

BARATYNSKY, YEVGENY ABRAMOVICH (1800–44). Poet of aristocratic birth, Baratynsky was expelled from the *corps de pages* and was forced to become a private soldier. In 1820, he was transferred to Finland, where he wrote some of his best-known works. He eventually settled in Moscow. Among his best-known poems are *Death* (1833) and *The Bull* (1828).

BARCLAY DE TOLLY, PRINCE MICHAEL ANDREYEVICH (1761–1818). Soldier of Scottish descent. He was commander in Finland (1808–09) and is famous for his march across the ice of the Gulf of Bothnia and his capture of Umeo. He was minister of war from 1810–13 and commanded the Russian forces against Napoleon in 1812, but his strategy of retreat and his defeat at Smolensk (August 17–18, 1812) caused dissatisfaction in the country, and he was replaced as commander by Kutuzov. After Kutuzov's death in 1813 he again took command and achieved distinction at Leipzig and at the capture of Paris. Some describe him as the real architect of Napoleon's defeat in the 1812 campaign.

Josselson, M. and D., *The Commander: A Life of Barclay de Tolly*, 1980.

BARKHIN, GRIGORY (1880–1969). Architect who designed the *Izvestiya* newspaper building (1925–27) in Moscow in the Constructivist style.

BARMY. Part of the regalia of grand princes of Moscow consisting of a silk scarf on which jewels were sewn. It covered the ruler's shoulders on grand occasions.

BARNAUL. Capital of Altay territory in the Russian Soviet Federated Socialist Republic situated on the Ob River and Turksib railway. Formerly known for silver smelting, it was founded as a town in 1771. Industries include engineering, steel works, sawmilling, food processing, and the manufacture of textiles and footwear. Population (1981) 549,000.

BARSHAY, RUDOLF BORISOVICH (1924–). Founder and director of the Moscow Chamber Orchestra. Barshay is also an accomplished viola player and conductor.

BARSHCHINA. Labor without payment demanded by a landlord from a serf before the emancipation of serfs in 1861.

Blum, J., *Lord and Peasant in Russia from the Ninth to the Nineteenth Century*, 1961.

BARYATINSKY, PRINCE ALEXANDER IVANOVICH (1814–79). Commander of Russian troops who distinguished himself in campaigns in the Caucasus beginning in 1857. He completed the Russian conquest of the N Caucasian mountain peoples by defeating and capturing Shamil (*q.v.*) at Gunib in 1859.

BARYSHNIKOV, MIKHAIL (1948–). Ballet dancer and director. He danced with the Leningrad Kirov Ballet from 1969–74, when he defected to the West. He danced exclusively with the American Ballet Theatre and the New York City Ballet. In 1979 he was appointed artistic director of the American Ballet Theatre.

BASHKIR. Autonomous republic situated in the W foothills of the Ural mountains in the Russian Soviet Federated Socialist Republic. It has an area of 55,430 square miles (143,564 sq km). Annexed to Russia in 1557, it was constituted as an autonomous Soviet republic in 1919. Its capital is Ufa. Chief industries are oil, chemicals, coal, steel, electrical engineering, timber, and paper. Cereals, potatoes, and sugar beets are grown. The longest pipeline in the USSR connects the oil field at Tuymazy with the Omsk refineries. Population (1981) 3,860,000.

BASHKIRS. Turkic-speaking people living in the Bashkir Autonomous Republic. Muslims since the 14th century, in 1557 they came under the overlordship of Muscovy. Colonization by Russia in the 17th and 18th centuries caused a number of revolts. Although a Bashkir nationalist government was formed in 1917, two years later it joined the Bolsheviks.

Donnelly, A. S., *The Russian Conquest of Bashkiria: A Case Study in Imperialism, 1552–1740,* 1968.

BASIL I, GRAND DUKE OF MOSCOW (1371–1425). The son of Dmitry Donskoy, Basil was made grand prince after his father's death. He ruled from 1389 to 1425. He was a cautious ruler, enlarging the principality of Muscovy, acquiring new appanages and towns, and fought a continuous war with Lithuania in the hope of gaining extra territory. In 1408 the Golden Horde mounted a surprise assault on Moscow in order to punish Basil for not having paid homage to his overlord. Basil's principality was devastated, but Moscow remained intact. The grand duke is considered by some to have been a weak ruler because he was constantly adopting different policies and making alliances with different rulers.

Strakhovsky, Leonard I., *A Handbook of Slavic Studies,* 1949.

BASIL II (1415–62). The son of Basil I, he succeeded his father at the age of 10 only after Basil the Squint-eyed and Dmitry Shemiaka's claim to the throne had been suppressed. He ruled from 1425 to 1462. Having defeated his rivals, Basil began to extend the principality. In 1445 he was seriously wounded in a battle with Mongol leaders and taken captive. He was set free, and in 1452 the princedom of Kasimov was founded and a Mongol prince accepted Russian suzerainty. Basil's chief contribution to history, however, is the fact that he abolished the political system as it existed, and witnessed the birth of a national Russian state ruled by Moscow. Having liquidated those who opposed him, he became the uncontested leader of Vladimir as well as of Moscow.

Vernadsky, George, *A History of Russia,* 1943–69.

BASIL III (1479–1533). He ruled from 1505 to 1533, and continued many of the policies initiated by his father and predecessor, Ivan III, annexing the appanage of Pskov in 1511, the remainder of Riazan in 1517, and the principalities of Starodub, Chernigov-Seversk, and the upper Oka area. In 1514 he finally captured Smolensk, after having waged three campaigns against Lithuania. Basil also gained territory from the khanate of Kazan, as well as entering into diplomatic relations with the Holy Roman Empire.

Florinsky, M., *Russia: A History and an Interpretation,* 1947.

BASKAK. Resident Mongol overseer in Russia when it had become part of the Mongol Empire. The *baskak* guided the Russian princes' policies.

BASOV, NICHOLAS GENNADYEVICH (1922–). Radiophysicist who researched the interactions of radiation and atoms, which led to work on lasers. Basov has worked as director of physical-mathematical sciences, and from 1957 he has been a member of the USSR Academy of Sciences. He has been awarded various prizes, including the Nobel Prize in 1964 for work on quantum electronics.

BATORY, STEPHEN (1533–86). King of Poland (1576–86). Tsar Ivan IV of Russia tried to gain access to the Baltic Sea for Muscovy as a result of which Stephen began the war against Ivan. He forced Ivan to cede Polotsk and Livonia under the truce of Jam Zapolski (1582). He aspired to unite Muscovy, Poland, and Transylvania in one great state.

BATU KHAN (?–1255). Mongol-Tatar khan and grandson of Genghis Khan. Chosen as commander in chief in 1235 for the invasion of Europe, by 1240 Batu had conquered most of Russia. In the lower Volga he established the Golden Horde.

BATUMI. City and major seaport on the E coast of Black Sea in the Georgian Soviet Socialist Republic. It is the capital of the Adzhar Autonomous Soviet Socialist Republic in SW Georgia. It was ceded to Russia by Turkey in 1878. The main industries are refining oil from Baku and Alyaty, marine and railway engineering, and fruit and vegetable canning; manufactures include cans and clothing. It exports petroleum and manganese. There is also a naval base. Population (1973) 108,000.

BATURIN. Ukrainian village and regional center of the Chernigovsky oblast. It was founded in 1575 and from 1669 to 1708 was the residence of the Ukrainian hetman. The palace of Hetman K. Razumovsky is of particular architectural interest. It is now a center for light and heavy industry.

BATYUSHKOV, KONSTANTIN NIKOLAYEVICH (1787–1855). Poet. Having served in the army, by the end of the wars against Napoleon he was an important member of the Arzamas. His collected works were published in 1817. Influenced by the classical Latin and French elegaic poets as well as by German and English Romanticism, he was opposed to the use of Church Slavonic archaisms. Always lyrical and elegaic, the lyrical epigrams written when he was in an advanced state of mental illness are considered his best poetry. Having succumbed to melancholy, he spent the final 30 years of his life as a mental invalid.

BAYER, GOTTLIEB SIEGFRIED (1694–1738). Historian and philologist. From 1725 he worked in the Academy of Science at St. Petersburg. He was particularly interested in ancient Russian history.

BAZAROV. Nihilist hero of Turgenev's novel *Fathers and Sons* (1862). Contrary to Turgenev's expectations, the portrait of Bazarov and his negation of materialism and religious and aesthetic values, attempted negation of human relationships, and his zealousness at dissecting frogs was denounced as a caricature by the radicals. Turgenev based his character on the nihilist Nechayev (*q.v.*).

Freeborn, Richard, *Turgenev: A Study*, 1960.

BAZHENOV, VASILY IVANOVICH (1737–99). Architect. Having studied at Moscow University and at the St. Petersburg Academy of Arts, Bazhenov completed his studies in Paris and Rome. Unfortunately his plans for the Kremlin and Tsaritsyno were not a success and he fell into Catherine II's disfavor. One of his finest works, however, is Pashkov House in Moscow.

Snegirev, V., *V. I. Bazhenov*, 1950.

BAZHOV, PAUL PETROVICH (1879–1950). Writer. His stories are frequently about the strength of the Russian workers; his patriotism is reflected in his literary activity. He has been awarded several prizes and was a deputy at the Supreme Soviet.

BEARD TAX. Tax on beards instigated by Peter the Great in 1698 (and reenacted in 1701). Wishing to modernize Russia, Peter ordered that beards be shaven and Western dress adopted. For Peter the beard represented all that was backward and uncivilized in Russia; for the majority of Orthodox believers, however, the beard was a special religious significance, and they considered it shameful to shave their beards. At first all Russians except the clergy were ordered to shave, but eventually those who wished to keep their beards could do so providing they paid an annual beard tax. The amount paid ranged from 2 kopeks for peasants to 900 rubles for wealthy merchants. The taxpayer then received a bronze medallion with a picture of a beard and the words "tax paid" inscribed on it, which was to be worn on a chain round the neck.

Massie, R. K., *Peter the Great*, 1981.

BEDNY, DEMYAN (1883–1945). Poet. In the 1920s he was considered to be the chief proletarian poet. Official approval was such that Lenin advised Gorky to examine Bedny's fables. His Civil War poems did much to spur on the fighters, but his poems of the NEP period are considered lewd and in bad taste. The obedient puppet of Stalin, Bedny's poetry glorifies Stalin's policies and attacks his enemies. Bedny also produced pornographic and antireligious poetry. The production of his play *Ancient Warriors,* in which the Orthodox Church is ridiculed, occurred just as the party proclaimed that the church had had a positive effect on the development of early Russia, and brought Bedny's career to a halt. He was later allowed to continue publishing.

BEDNYAK. Impoverished peasant, owning some land but usually not enough to support a family.

BEKOVICH-CHERKASSY, PRINCE ALEXANDER (?-1717). In 1711 he was sent by Peter I as a diplomat to Karbada. He later worked to bring together the peoples of the Caucasus with the Russian people and then forged links with Persia. In 1715, after exploring the Caspian Sea, he drew the first map of it. He was fatally wounded en route to Khin, where he intended to look for gold and subjugate the khan.

BEKSULATOVICH, SIMEON (*c.* 16th century). Formerly Sain Bulat of Kasimov, a Tatar, he was rechristened and appointed Tsar and Great Prince of All Rus as a joke by Ivan the Terrible. He ruled from 1575–76, signing documents under his own name and seal, while Ivan lived as a boyar. He was subsequently dethroned and sent into exile in Tver.

Klyuchevsky, Vasili O., *The Rise of the Romanovs,* 1970.

BELAYA RIVER. River rising in the S Urals and flowing 700 miles (1,120 km) SW past Beloretsk, then N and NW past Sterlitamak and Ufa to join the Kama River. It is used for transport and irrigation.

BELAYA TSERKOV. Ukrainian town 45 miles (72 km) SSW of Kiev, founded in the 11th century. Industries include food processing, flour milling, and the manufacture of leather goods and clothing. The Aleksandriya Park, established in the 18th century, is famed for its botanical species. Population (1981) 162,000.

BELGOROD. Town 45 miles (72 km) NNE of Kharkov in the Russian Soviet Federated Socialist Republic, situated on the N Donets River. Industries include chalk quarrying, meat packing, flour milling, and tanning. Population (1981) 255,000.

BELGOROD-DNESTROVSKY. Ukrainian port situated at the mouth of the Dnestr River on the Black Sea, 25 miles (40 km) SW of Odessa. Founded by the Greeks in the sixth century, over the centuries it passed to Rome, Genoa, Moldavia, and Turkey. It was ceded to Russia in the 19th century but held by Rumania from 1918 to 1940 and by Germany during the Second World War. It trades in fish, salt, and wine. Population (1974) 37,000.

BELINSKY, VISSARION GRIGORYEVICH (1811–48). Leading representative of the radical intelligentsia, literary critic, and an ardent Westernizer, Belinsky founded the sociological school of literary criticism and changed the course of Russian literary criticism.

Bowman, H. E., *Vissarion Belinski, 1811-1848,* 1954.

BELKSKY FAMILY. Princes and leaders of the various struggles for the supremacy of the Russian Orthodox Church in the Polish and Litovian states during the 14th and 15th centuries. They originated from the town of Belkso. Semyon Ivanovich Belksky served under Ivan III, bringing with him the people of his towns and inherited estates, as did Fedor Ivanovich Belksky in 1481. In 1538, after the death of Helen, the regency was disputed between the Shuiskys and Belkskys. The Shuiskys prevailed.

BELL, JOHN (1691-1780). Scottish traveler and doctor. In 1714 Bell set out for St. Petersburg, joining an embassy there before going to Persia. Returning to St. Petersburg four years later, he spent the following four years in an embassy to China, thus passing through Siberia and Mongolia. In 1722 he was summoned by Peter the Great to accompany him on his voyage to Derbent and the Caspian Gates. After visiting Constantinople on a mission, he settled there before returning to his estate in Antermony. Bell's *Travels* (1783) were highly popular in Great Britain, providing a vivid picture of life in Russia.

BELL, THE (KOLOKOL). Journal founded in 1857 by Alexander Herzen (*q.v.*) while he was in exile in London. It was smuggled into Russia in large quantities. Herzen advocated reform but opposed violence. It was thought that Alexander I was a subscriber. Reforms were slow in coming and the views of Herzen and *The Bell* gave way to more radical means of achieving change.

BELLINGSHAUSEN, FABIAN GOTTLIEB VON (1778-1852). Russian explorer. He was the first, with M. P. Lazarev, to circumnavigate Antarctica (1819-21), and the Bellingshausen Sea on the Pacific side of Antarctica is named after him.

BELOOZERO CHARTER (1488). Charter granted by Ivan III that made some provision for elected local inhabitants to take an active part in certain judicial and administrative matters.

BELORETSK. Town 115 miles (184 km) ESE of Ufa in the Russian Soviet Federated Socialist Republic. It is a center of the iron and steel industry, using local iron and manganese ores. Population 63,000.

BELORUSSIA (White Russia). Area in the W part of the Russian plain with an area of 80,134 square miles (207,600 sq km). It has valuable forest land and rich deposits of rock salt. In the 9th century the area was inhabited by East Slavic tribes under the authority of the Kievan state. After the decline of the Kievan state, the principalities of Turov-Pinsk, Smolensk, and Volhynia grew stronger, but from the 13th to the 14th century the area became part of the grand duchy of Lithuania. Belorussia was annexed to Russia during the Polish partitions of 1772-95, but from 1920-39, W Belorussia was Polish. In 1918 Belorussia was occupied by the Germans, and an independent Belorussian republic was created. In 1921 a Belorussian republic was established and this became a constituent republic of the USSR the following year, and its territory was extended. From 1941 to 1944, however, together with the Baltic states, Belorussia formed part of the Reich Commissariat Ostland. The capital of the republic of Belorussia is Minsk; other principal towns include Gomel, Vitebsk, and Mogilyov. Population (1978) 9,500,000.

BELORUSSIANS. An E Slavic people living in Belorussia and surrounding areas, for 79.4 percent of whom Belorussian is the mother tongue. They first developed a national identity when the Lithuanians were outnumbered by Russians during the 13th and 14th centuries; this continued to grow, and by the late 17th century a Belorussian literature and press had appeared. There are Belorussian communities in Lithuania, Latvia, and the Byalystok district of Poland.

BELOVO. Town in S Siberia 55 miles (88 km) NW of Novokuznetsk, in the Kuznetsk Basin in the Russian Soviet Federated Socialist Republic. Industries include coal mining, zinc smelting, and the manufacture of radio equipment and metal products. Population (1977) 112,000.

BELTSY. Town in SW Moldavia 70 miles (112 km) NW of Kishinev. Industries include meat packing, sugar refining, and flour milling. Population (1971) 105,000.

BELY, ANDREY (1880–1934). Pseudonym of Boris Nikolayevich Bugayev, poet and Symbolist novelist and critic. He was a disciple of the Austrian educator Rudolf Steiner and wrote *St. Petersburg* (1913–16).

BENCKENDORFF, COUNT ALEXANDER KHRISTOFOROVICH (1783–1844). General and statesman, chief of police, and suppressor of liberal thought. A member of the band of officers who murdered Emperor Paul in 1801, Benckendorff then directed his attention to a predominantly military career and was commandant of Moscow after Napoleon's retreat, distinguishing himself time and time again. In 1819 he was aide-de-camp to Tsar Alexander I, and in 1825 Benckendorff commanded the troops that put down the Decembrists. He then took measures against any Russian noble families that had been connected with the Decembrists. In 1826 he was chief of the gendarmerie and the Third Section.

Monas, Sidney L., *The Third Section: Police and Society in Russia under Nicholas I*, 1961.

Riasanovsky, Nicholas V., *Nicholas I and Official Nationality in Russia, 1825–1855*, 1959.

BENDERY. Town on the Dnestr River in the Moldavian Soviet Socialist Republic. Known as Tigan or Tungaty, it is mentioned in the early Russian chronicles. From 1538 to 1812 it belonged to the Turks, who built a fortress there. Between the two world wars it belonged to Rumania. Population (1975) 100,000.

BENEDIKTOV, VLADIMIR GRIGORYEVICH (1807–73). Poet and clerk in the ministry of finance. Superficial in content, his poetry is showy in its use of images, rhymes, and vocabulary, and is romantic in outlook. Love and nature were his favorite themes. For 10 years Benediktov enjoyed great popularity among other officials and civil servants.

BENITSKY, ALEXANDER PETROVICH (1780–1809). Writer and civil servant in the Commission for the Compilation of Laws. Benitsky published work of different genres in various journals but is best known for his philosophical tales of the Orient, following in the footsteps of Voltaire. His style is considered the best example of lucidity in Russian before Pushkin (*q.v.*).

BENOIS, ALEXANDER NIKOLAYEVICH (1870–1960). Painter, art historian, and theatrical designer. In 1898 Benois and Diaghilev founded the periodical *Mir Iskusstva (q.v.)*, and in 1907 the two collaborated in *Le Pavillon d'Armide*. Benois later wrote the book and created the sets and costumes for *Petrushka*. Benois helped acquaint the Russian public with Western art and the West with Russian ballet and fine arts.

BENUA, NICHOLAS (1813–98). Architect who was responsible for the Imperial stables in Peterhof, which he built in the English Tudor style.

BERCHTOLD, COUNT LEOPOLD (1863–1942). Austro-Hungarian foreign minister. Pursuing a career in the diplomatic service, in 1906 Berchtold was made ambassador at St. Petersburg and was appointed foreign minister in 1912. His ultimatum to Serbia led to the outbreak of World War I. He resigned in 1915.

BERDICHEV. Ukrainian town 96 miles (152 km) WSW of Kiev. Acquired by Russia in 1793, it was founded in the 14th century. Industries include engineering, sugar refining, tanning, and food processing. Population (1976) 80,000.

BERDYANSK. Port in the Zaporozhe oblast of the Ukrainian Soviet Socialist Republic, situated on the Berdyansk Gulf of the Sea of Azov. Founded in 1827, the town is predominantly an engineering center. From 1939 to 1958 it was called Osipenko. Population (1975) 120,000.

BERDYAYEV, NICHOLAS ALEKSANDROVICH (1874–1948). Religious philosopher and Christian existentialist. At first adhering to Marxism, Berdyayev later replaced it with a neo-Kantian realism. After imprisonment for a political crime and a visit to Germany, he became involved in the religious revival in Russia and eventually joined the Orthodox Church. For a time he worked as professor of philosophy at Moscow University, but in 1922 he was forced to leave the USSR and in 1924 he founded a religious philosophical academy in Paris.

Seaver, George, *Nicholas Berdyayev: An Introduction to His Thought*, 1950.

BEREZHANY. Town in the center of the Berezhansky region of the Ternopolskaya oblast of the Ukrainian Soviet Socialist Republic. From the 16th to the 18th century Berezhany was an important trading center. Population (1970) 14,500.

BEREZINA RIVER. River rising approximately 37 miles (59 km) W of Lepel in N Belorussia and flowing 350 miles (560 km) S to join the Dnepr River above Rechitsa. Linked by canal with the W Dvina River and the Baltic Sea, it forms a waterway from the Baltic to the Black Sea. The remnants of Napoleon's Grand Army retreated across the river, on November 26-29, 1812, near Borisov.

BEREZNIKI. Town in the Russian Soviet Federated Socialist Republic 95 miles (152 km) N of Perm. It has deposits of sodium, potassium, and magnesium salts and is an important center of the chemicals industry. Population (1981) 188,000.

BEREZOVO. Settlement in the Khanty-Mansy National Okrug of the Tyumen oblast in W Siberia. Founded as a fortified town and administrative center in 1593, from the 18th century Berezovo has been a place to which those finding disfavor with the government have been sent. It is also a center for fishing and fur trapping.

BERG, AKSEL IVANOVICH (1893–). Radio engineer and pioneer of cybernetics. Berg started his career as a submarine navigator and from 1918 to 1921 commanded a submarine in the Baltic fleet. He later taught advanced training courses for naval radio operators at Leningrad Naval Academy. His main work concerns theories and methods of design and calculation of tube generators. He has been awarded many orders and medals and from 1946 has been a member of the USSR Academy of Sciences.

BERG, LEV SEMYONOVICH (1876–1950). Zoologist, geographer, and ichthyologist. He propounded the anti-Darwinist theory of nomogenesis.

BERGGOLTS, OLGA FEDOROVNA (1910–75). Poet. Born in St. Petersburg, she used Leningrad as the subject matter of much of her poetry. Her first book of poetry was published in 1934, but she is chiefly remembered for her moving war poems dealing with the siege of Leningrad, such as the poems of her *February Diary* (1942). Arrested in 1932 on a charge of "association with enemies of the people" and imprisoned for a year and a half, Berggolts was permitted to join the Communist Party in 1940. Her concern for individual human emotion, as expressed in her article "A Conversation about Lyric Poetry," did not meet with official approval, although her poem "Pervorossiysk" was awarded a Stalin prize in 1950. Her book *The Knot* (1965) contains many of her finest lyrical poems. A prominent member of the Writers' Union, Berggolts was an outspoken advocate of the need to express freely one's ideas in literature.

BERIA, LAVRENTY PAVLOVICH (1899–1953). Georgian communist. Having joined the Bolshevik Party in 1917, Beria worked in the

Cheka and the GPU (*q.q.v.*) in Transcaucasia. From 1932 to 1938 he was virtual dictator of Transcaucasia. Commissar for internal affairs from 1938 to 1945, he was deputy prime minister for security from 1941 to 1953. In 1945 he was created a marshal of the Soviet Union. He was responsible for the deportation of thousands of people from E Poland and the Baltic states and was responsible for the security police in the satellite states. In 1953 he was shot as an "imperialist agent."

BERING ISLAND. Island to the SW of the Bering Sea off the coast of Kamchatka. One of the Kormandorsky (Commander) group of islands, it belongs to the USSR.

BERING, VITUS JONASSEN (1681–1741). Danish-Russian explorer. He joined the fleet of Peter the Great and in 1724 was appointed by the tsar to direct the first Kamchatka expedition, which was to investigate whether there was a land connection between America and Asia. After building the ship, he set sail and named the Diomede Islands in the middle of the strait. In 1773 he again set sail, with 600 others, and eventually landed in the Gulf of Alaska. Worn out and suffering from scurvy, he went ashore on Bering Island, where he died. *See* **Dezhnev, Semen.**

BERKOVETS. Weight, varying in amount at different times and places.

BERLIN CONGRESS (1878). Congress that met on June 13 as a result of the Russo-Turkish War and that was presided over by Bismarck. Austria-Hungary, France, Great Britain, Russia, and Turkey took part. *See* **Congress of Berlin.**

BERLIN, TREATY OF (1878). Treaty that made official the "small Bulgaria" solution already proposed by Great Britain and Russia and that replaced the unsatisfactory treaty of San Stefano. In addition Bosnia-Herzegovina was placed under Austro-Hungarian occupation; Montenegro gained extra territory; Rumania and Serbia were officially recognized as independent; and Turkey ceded Ardahan, Kars, and Batum to Russia. Turkey was to observe religious toleration, and navigation on the Danube was to be internationally supervised.

BERZIN, JAN (1881–1938). Latvian communist. After 1917 he worked as a Soviet diplomat in Switzerland, Finland, Austria and Britain. One of the main organizers of the forced labor camps in Russia, he was a victim of the Great Purge.

BESSARABIA. Region in SW bounded on the N and E by the Dnestr River, on the S by the Danube River and on the W by the Prut River. The N and S parts are in the Ukrainian Soviet Socialist Republic; the main central area is the Moldavian Soviet Socialist Republic. It has an area of 17,100 square miles (44,289 sq km). An agricultural area, it produces maize, wheat, sugar beets, grapes, sheep, cattle, and pigs.

BESTUZHEV, ALEXANDER ALEKSANDROVICH (1797–1837). Writer and Decembrist. He was coeditor with Ryleyev (*q.v.*) of the

Polar Star. In 1829 Bestuzhev was transferred to the Caucasus as a private soldier, where he was recommended for the St. George's Cross and where he wrote his best novels. He was charged with the murder of his mistress and, although the inquest could not prove Bestuzhev's guilt, he lost all interest in life. In 1837 at the storming of Adler on the Black Sea coast, he was savagely killed by the Circassians.

BESTUZHEV-RYUMIN, COUNT ALEKSEY PETROVICH (1693–1766). Grand chancellor of Russia. In 1721 Bestuzhev-Ryumin was sent to Copenhagen as Russian minister and it was not until 1740 that he was summoned back to Russia by E. J. Biron *(q.v.)*. Appointed vice-chancellor by the empress, Elizabeth, for the following 16 years, he was in charge of the foreign policy of Russia. Despite his successful handling of the war of the Austrian succession, he was arrested and condemned to death, accused of instigating a plot. The sentence was commuted to banishment, although Catherine II recalled him and appointed him a field marshal.

BESTUZHEV-RYUMIN, KONSTANTIN NIKOLAYEVICH (1829–97). Professor of Russian history at St. Petersburg University. The author of more than 300 articles, Bestuzhev-Ryumin was an ardent Slavophile and editor of a Slavophile journal

BEZHITSA. Town in the Russian Soviet Federated Socialist Republic 133 miles (213 km) SE of Smolensk situated on the Desna River. It has been part of Bryansk since 1956. Manufactures include railway rolling stock, locomotives, and agricultural machinery.

BEZOBRAZOV, ALEXANDER MIKHAILOVICH (1866–1933). Statesman under Nicholas II. In 1903 he was promoted to state secretary and a member of the Special Committee for the Affairs of the Far East. It has been suggested that Russia was forced into the Russo-Japanese war of 1904–05 by the Bezobrazov group of adventurers, who made the tsar ignore the advice of Witte; certainly his comments on Far Eastern affairs aggravated international relations.

BIBIKOV, DMITRY GAVRILOVICH (1792–1870). Bibikov was appointed military governor of Kiev in 1837 and was minister of internal affairs from 1952 to 1955. He pursued a policy designed to strengthen the autocracy, and wishing to russify the Ukraine, replaced local clerks with Russians and altered the laws regarding the Polish gentry.

BILIBIN, IVAN YAKOVLEVICH (1876–1942). Illustrator of Russian folktales. He studied in Munich and in St. Petersburg under Repin. Influenced by Vasnetsov, he developed a style similar to that of the late medieval book illuminators.

BIOSPHERE RESERVES. Reserves managed by the ministry of agriculture and the Academy of Science and set up as a result of the UNESCO program of Man and the Biosphere. There are reserves at Berezina, the Caucasus, the Central

Black Earth reserve, Prioksko-Terrasny, Repetek, and Sikhotealin. A new wildlife reserve at Lake Ladoga is to be established.

BIROBIDZHAN. Town 100 miles (160 km) WNW of Khabarovsk on the Trans-Siberian Railway. It is the capital of the Jewish Autonomous Region, to which the name is also given. Industries include sawmilling and woodworking; manufactures include clothing. Population (1973) 60,000.

BIRON (BUHREN), ERNST JOHANN (1690–1772). German favorite of Tsaritsa Anna Ivanovna (1730–40). Having been expelled from the Academy of Königsberg for misbehavior in 1714, Biron went to Russia, and his influence over Anna grew steadily. In 1727 he became her lover, and was made grand chamberlain and count. He was extremely unpopular owing to his vindictive and corrupt character. Regent for three weeks after Anna's death, he was deposed and banished to Siberia. Peter III, however, permitted him to return to Russia.

BIRTHRATE. The birthrate varies from republic to republic; in the S non-Slavic republics, the birthrate is considerably higher than in the Russian Soviet Federated Socialist Republic. One percent of urban families in the Russian Soviet Federated Socialist Republic have four or more children, in contrast to 25 percent of urban families in Turkmenistan. In general, however, the birthrate in the Soviet Union is very low; the average number of children in a family was 1.7 in 1980. The authorities, concerned by the falling birthrate, provide financial and other incentives for those families with children.

BIYSK. Town in S Siberia in the Russian Soviet Federated Socialist Republic situated 80 miles (128 km) SE of Barnaul near the confluence of the Biya and Katun rivers. It was founded as a fortress in 1709. Industries include meat packing, sugar refining, and the manufacture of textiles. Population (1981) 215,000.

BJÖRKÖ, TREATY OF (1905). "Private" treaty concluded between Nicholas II and William II of Germany on July 24, 1905. The kaiser wished to improve Russo-German relations. Nicholas, however, was advised by his ministers to withdraw from the alliance.

BLACK EARTH. *Chernozem,* or black soil, covers approximately 9 percent of the USSR and was first identified on the steppes. Extremely fertile, it is a grassland soil with a dark humus layer more than 10 inches thick. It is neutral chemically (neither alkaline nor acid) and has a calcareous layer under the humus. In this last respect it differs from similar soils in the United States.

BLACK HUNDREDS. Name given to reactionary populist groups in the early 20th century. While endorsing national representation and the need to improve the life of peasants and workers, they also supported absolutism and anti-Semitism. The least harmful activity was the staging of popular demonstrations at which the crowds would carry icons and portraits of the royal family, accompanied by patriotic and religious songs. More sinister was the hatred of the Jews, which was encouraged. They organized pogroms directed against Jews and general terror against university students and members of free professions; "Beat the Yids and the Intelligents; Save Russia" became their slogan. The authorities tended to ignore the pogroms, and Nicholas II thanked the Black Hundreds for their support.

Ulam, Adam B., *Lenin and the Bolsheviks,* 1965. *Russia's Failed Revolutionaries,* 1981.

BLACK SEA. Sea bounded by the USSR, Rumania, Bulgaria, and Turkey. It joins the Sea of Azov by Kerch strait, and the Mediterranean by the Bosporus. As Russia's only year-round ice-free passage to the open sea, the Black Sea has played a critical role in Russian maritime development since Peter the Great.

BLAGONRAVOV, ANATOLY ARKADYEVICH (1894–). Soviet scholar and lieutenant general. A Doctor of Technical Science, he wrote many articles on the use and construction of weapons. From 1943 Blagonravov was a member of the Academy of Science, and from 1946 he was the president of the Academy of Artillery Science. From 1947 he was a deputy at the Supreme Soviet.

BLAGOVESHCHENSK. Town in the Russian Soviet Federated Socialist Republic 35 miles (56 km) from the Manchurian border on the Zeya River near its confluence with the Amur. It is on a branch of the Trans-Siberian Railway. Settled in 1644 it became Chinese territory in 1689. It became a Russian army post in 1856. Industries include flour milling and sawmilling; manufactures include machinery, footwear, and furniture. Population (1981) 179,000.

BLOCH, JEAN RICHARD (1884–1947). French socialist and man of letters. One of the *clarté* group of socialist writers, Bloch spent most of World War II in Moscow.

BLOK, ALEXANDER ALEKSANDROVICH (1880–1921). Leader of the Symbolist movement and its most outstanding poet. He had been deeply influenced by the works of Vasily Andreyevich Zhukovsky (1783–1852) and Vladimir Solovev (1853–1900) (*q.q.v.*) and began his literary career in 1904 with *Verses of the Lady Beautiful.* By 1911, however, he had bitterly reacted against his earlier ideals, and the poems of *Nocturnal Hours* are concerned with the human misery found in the city streets and restaurants. He welcomed the 1917 Revolution, and, sympathetic to the Left Socialist Revolutionaries, cooperated with the Bolsheviks. He published an epic poem *The Twelve* (1918), concerning 12 Red Guardsmen representing the Apostles, which was an apologia of the Bolshevik Revolution. *The Scythians* (1920), about the revolutionary period, was a call to the West to abandon the fight against the Bolsheviks. Disillusionment with the regime followed shortly before he died.

Poggioli, Renato, *Poets of Russia, 1880–1930,* 1960.

Pyman, Avril, *The Life of Alexander Blok,* 2 vols. 1978 and 1979.

BLOODY SUNDAY (1905). On Sunday, January 9, 1905 many innocent, peaceful demonstrators were fired upon by troops in St. Petersburg. The employees of the Putilov factory who were members of Gapon's *(q.v.)* organization of workers felt that some of their members had been victimized and went on strike. The employers decided upon a lockout, whereupon the workers decided to present their grievances to the tsar; a certain number of political demands were also included by the intellectuals. The large demonstrations were fired on by troops; as a result over 100 people were killed and many more wounded. The result was a wave of strikes that swept the country.

BLUDOV, DMITRY NIKOLAYEVICH (1785–1864). Civil servant under Nicholas I and a minor writer. In 1832 Bludov was minister of foreign affairs, from 1837 to 1839 minister of justice, in 1855 president of the St. Petersburg Academy of Science, and in 1862 president of the state council and committee of ministers.

BLUE ROSE ARTS SOCIETY. Radical arts society founded in 1907. It consisted of a group of Symbolist Impressionists, many of whom tended toward a lyric mysticism in their art; blue and lavender frequently dominated their work.

BOBORYKIN, PETER DMITRIEVICH (1836–1921). Journalist, novelist, and contributor to the journal *Vestnik Evropy*. Much influenced by the French naturalists, Boborykin's novels are widely considered of low quality.

BOBRIKOV, N. I. (1839–1904). Governor-general of Finland. He brought in Russian officials to enforce Russian commands in Finland. This met with much hostility from the Finns. Bobrikov was assassinated by Eugen Schaumann, one of the Finnish party of active resistance, thus bringing Finland virtually to a state of war with Russia.

Kirby, D. G., *Finland and Russia, 1808–1920*, 1975.

BOBROV, SEMYON SERGEYEVICH (1767–1810). Poet. Bobrov was particularly interested in the history of the Russian fleet. His poetry is rich in imagination, diction, and imagery.

BOBRUYSK. Town in Belorussia 85 miles (136 km) SE of Minsk on the Berezina River. It is a commercial center trading in timber and grain. Founded in the 16th century, industries include engineering; manufactures include paper, cellulose, clothing, and footwear. Population (1981) 203,000.

BOBYL. Term for tenant farmer or landless peasant.

BODAYBO. Town in the Irkutsk oblast on the Vitim River. It is the center of the Lena gold-mining area. In 1912, the Bodaybo gold mines went on strike; the strike was savagely suppressed, and more than 500 people were killed or wounded.

BOGDANOV, ALEXANDER ALEKSANDROVICH 1873–1928). Pseudonym of Malinovsky, politician, economist, sociologist, and philosopher. Having been a Social Democrat from the 1890s, in 1903 he joined the Bolsheviks. With Lenin he led the "stone-hard" Bolsheviks and was leader of the *Vpered* group. Although Bogdanov left the Bolshevik Party in 1917, his theories of proletarian culture (*proletkult*) were highly influential, especially *A Short Course of Economic Science* (1896) and *A Course of Political Economy* (1910). In the latter part of his life, Bogdanov turned his attention to blood transfusion, founded the first blood transfusion institute in Russia, and died as the consequences of an unsuccessful experiment on himself.

BOGDANOVICH, IPPOLIT FEDOROVICH (1743–1803). Poet. He is particularly remembered for his verse tales such as *Dushenka* (1775), an adaptation of La Fontaine's *Amours de Psyché et Cupidon*. Having found favor with Catherine II, he became the official court poet.

BOGOLEPOV, NICHOLAS PAVLOVICH (1847–1901). Jurist and civil servant with reactionary views. He occupied several important posts in the university world, including rector of Moscow University (1891–95) and minister for the education of the people (1898–1901). Under his jurisdiction professors were dismissed for exhibiting "harmful tendencies," and 183 Kiev students were handed over to soldiers.

BOGOLYUBOV, VENIYAMIN YAKOVLEVICH (1895–). Sculptor. Inevitably he is remembered for his wood and marble sculptures of Lenin and Stalin. From 1929 Bogolyubov worked closely with V. I. Ingal (*q.v.*). After the Second World War he sculpted many monuments.

BOGOLYUBSKY, ANDREY YURYEVICH (1111–74). Grand prince of Vladimir and the most powerful Russian prince of the 12th century. As ruler of the Rostov-Suzdal, he transferred the capital to Vladimir, on the Kliazma River. He enlarged his summer residence, Bogolyubovo, and built many beautiful churches, the most famous of which is the Cathedral of Our Lady in Vladimir. Wishing to expand his principality, in 1169 he stormed Kiev and put one of his allies on the throne there. His attempt to take Novgorod was not at first successful, but eventually the Novgorodians were forced to accept one of Andrey's princes. Having incensed his courtiers over the execution of a boyar, he was killed by them.

BOGOSLOVSKY, MICHAEL MIKHAILOVICH (1867–1929). Historian who was influenced greatly by Kliuchevsky. His works include a dissertation on Peter the Great's regional reforms, and one on self-government in the N of Russia in the 17th century, and his well-known book *Peter I, Material for a Biography*.

BOGROV, D. G. (*fl.* early 20th century). Former police agent and socialist revolutionary. Bogrov assassinated thc prime minister Peter

Stolypin (*q.v.*) at a theater in Kiev in 1911; it is still unclear whether Bogrov was acting as a revolutionary or as a police agent when he killed him.

BOKHARA. City in the Uzbek Soviet Socialist Republic 270 miles (432 km) SW of Tashkent in an oasis on the Zeravshan River, on a spur of the Trans-Caspian Railway. It was founded *c.* the first century A.D. and captured by the Arabs in 709. Noted as a medieval center of Islamic culture, it was dominated in turn by Arabs, Persians, Turks, and Uzbeks. Industries include karakul processing, silk spinning, and carpet making. Population (1981) 192,000.

MacLean, Fitzroy, *Eastern Approaches,* 1949.

BOLOTNIKOV, IVAN ISAYEVICH (?–1608). A leader of the peasant uprising at the beginning of the 17th century. Having fled to the Caucasus in his youth, Bolotnikov was captured by the Tatars and sold in Turkey as a slave. He eventually escaped and returned to Russia. An energetic and talented leader, he tried to promulgate a general uprising of bondsmen against their masters. Bolotnikov's revolt is thus one of the first in a long line of peasant revolts. Finally defeated and driven back to Tula he was captured by the tsar's forces and executed. *See* **Time of Troubles.**

BOLOTOV, ANDREY TIMOFEYEVICH (1738–1833). Writer, scholar, and one of the founders of the science of agronomy in Russia. His memoirs constitute an indispensable historical document.

BOLSHEVIKS. Those of the radical faction of the Russian Social Democratic Workers' Party when it split in 1903. The Bolsheviks, meaning those in the majority (Mensheviks were the minority), were headed by Lenin, who believed that the revolution must be led by a single centralized party of professional revolutionaries. After the Russian Revolution (1917) the Bolsheviks succeeded in eliminating other political parties, and from 1918 until 1952 the Communist Party of the Soviet Union was termed Communist Party (Bolsheviks). *See* **Communist Party.**

Carr, E. H., *A History of Soviet Russia.* Vols. I–III: *The Bolshevik Revolution, 1917–1923,* 1951–52.

Dan, Theodore, *The Origins of Bolshevism,* 1964.

Haimson, Leopold H., *The Russian Marxists and the Origins of Bolshevism,* 1955.

Ulam, Adam B., *The Bolsheviks,* 1965.

BOLSHOI THEATER. The best known of the chief Russian theaters is the Bolshoi Theater in Moscow. It was founded in 1776, but a theater was not built on the present site until 1821–24. It was rebuilt and altered considerably in 1856 by Alberto Kavos after it had suffered extensive damage in a fire. Opera and ballet have been performed at the Bolshoi Theater since 1825.

BOLSHOI THEATER. (St. Petersburg). Theater in St. Petersburg, also known as the Kamenny (stone) theater. Performances were first held there in 1783.

BONAPARTE, NAPOLEON (1769–1821). Emperor of France who attempted to conquer most of Europe. He met with almost unmitigated success until, in 1812, he tried to take Moscow, but he was forced to withdraw during the disastrous premature onset of winter. The myth of Napoleon as the self-willed hero, above ordinary morality, was to figure largely in the Russian literature of the 19th century, including Tolstoy's *War and Peace,* Pushkin's *The Queen of Spades,* and Dostoyevsky's *Crime and Punishment.*

Olivier, Daria, *The Burning of Moscow, 1812,* 1966.

BONDARCHUK, SERGEY FEDOROVICH (1920–). Ukrainian film actor. In 1959 he directed and took the lead in *A Man's Destiny,* which won first prize at the Moscow Festival. In 1960 he acted in Roberto Rossellini's *It Was Night at Rome.*

BONDAREV, YURY VASILYEVICH (1924–). Novelist and state official. A member of the CPSU from 1944, Bondarev was first deputy chairman of the Russian Soviet Federated Socialist Republic Writers' Union. From 1941 to 1945 he served in the Soviet army, and from 1975 has been deputy to the Supreme Soviet. His novels include *Young Comrades* (1959) and *A Choice* (1980).

BOR. Tax paid by the citizens of Novgorod in the 14th and 15th centuries.

BORESKOV, GEORGY KONSTANTINOVICH (1907–). Chemist and director of research in modern experimental and theoretical reactor studies. Boreskov has also researched fertilizers, insecticides, and fungicides. From 1961 he has been a member of the USSR Academy of Science.

BORETSKY FAMILY. Boyar family in Novgorod that was prominent in the 15th century. The Boretskys opposed union with Moscow. Marfa Boretskaya's house became a center of anti-Moscow intrigue. In 1478, after the union of Novgorod and Moscow, Marfa was sent to a nunnery, and the Boretskys' wealth was confiscated by the Moscow princes.

BORIS AND GLEB. Sons of Vladimir, they were savagely murdered by their elder brother, Svyatopolk, in 1015. Boris and Gleb were canonized and their feast celebrated three times a year. An idealized portrait of their lives is given in Nestor's *The Lection on the Blessed Martyrs Boris and Gleb* (c. 1078). *The Tale of the Holy Martyrs Boris and Gleb* enjoyed greater popularity.

BORISLAV. Ukrainian town 50 miles (80 km) SW of Lvov in an area producing oil and natural gas. Industries include oil refining; manufactures include oil-drilling equipment. Population (1970) 35,300.

BORISOGLEBSK. Town in the Russian Soviet Federated Socialist Republic 130 miles (208 km) ESE of Voronezh on the Khoper River. Industries include meat packing, flour milling, and tanning. Population (1970) 69,000.

BORISOV. Belorussian town 45 miles (72 km) NE of Minsk on the Berezina River. Industries include manufacturing matches, enamelware, glass products, food products, and musical instruments. Population (1970) 106,000.

BORISOV-MUSATOV, VIKTOR (1870–1905). Symbolist painter who associated with the Moscow school of literary Symbolism *(q.v.)*. A most influential painter in his day and pupil of Chistyakov, in 1895 he worked with Gustave Moreau in Paris, and having made the acquaintance of Puvis de Chavannes, began working in a historical style. Among his most famous paintings are *The Reservoir* (1902) and *Sunset Reflection* (1904).

BORODIN, ALEXANDER PORFIRYEVICH (1833–87). Composer. He was also a chemist who made important studies in organic chemistry. He was a mainly self-taught musician and was influenced by a meeting with Balakirev *(q.v.)* in 1862. A follower of Glinka *(q.v.)*, Borodin was also influenced by Russian folk music, Schumann, and Liszt. He composed the opera *Prince Igor* (1869–87), three symphonies, much chamber music, and the tone poem *In the Steppes of Central Asia* (1880).

BORODIN, MICHAEL MARKOVICH (1884–1952). Pseudonym of Grusenberg, a Jewish communist born in Belorussia. An immigrant to the United States, Borodin became a member of the Socialist Party there. Following the Bolshevik Revolution, Borodin returned to the Soviet Union and then worked abroad as a communist agent. He was arrested and imprisoned in Glasgow before being expelled. He was invited to China and acted as high adviser to the central executive committee of the Kuomintang. After returning once more to the Soviet Union he was deputy head of Tass agency, and from 1932, editor of the *Moscow Daily News*. Borodin was arrested during the Great Purge and died in a Siberian labor camp.

BORODIN, SERGEY PETROVICH (1902–). Pseudonym of Amir Sargrdzhain, writer. Borodin's patriotic *Dmitry Donskoy* (1941) won him great fame and a Stalin Prize. He also wrote the trilogy *Stars over Samarkand* (1953–62) and *The Wings of a Slave* (1932).

BORODINO. Village 70 miles (110 km) W of Moscow. It was the site of an inconclusive battle fought on September 7, 1812 between Napoleon's army and Russian forces.

BOROVIKOVSKY, VLADIMIR LUKICH (1757–1825). Portrait and icon painter. Having studied with Levitsky at the Academy of Arts, Borovikovsky painted portraits of prominent members of Russian society. His portraits are considered lacking in psychological detail. His icons are influenced by the Ukrainian school; one of his best-known icons is *The Annunciation* in the Cathedral of the Virgin of Kazan in Leningrad.

BORZHOMI. Town and health resort in Georgia on the Kura River.

BORZOI. Russian hound, bred to pursue wolves. The *borzoi* is descended from the Arabian greyhound and a collielike Russian sheepdog.

BOSPORUS. Strait uniting the Black Sea with the Sea of Marmara, dividing Europe from Asia. Securing open passage for Russian naval and commercial shipping through the warm waters of the Bosporus has been a touchstone of Russian diplomacy from the mid-17th century to the present. After 1841 no warships could pass through the strait without permission from Turkey, but from 1918 to 1923 it was necessary to obtain permission from an international commission of the straits. In 1923, following the Treaty of Lausanne, Turkey was given more power. The commission was abolished in 1936, and Turkey was allowed to reoccupy the straits.

BOTCHKA. A *botchka* was a measure of capacity of a cask or barrel and equivalent to 4.92 hectoliters or 108.28 gallons. There were 40 *vedró* to a *botchka* and 10 *krushka* to a *vedró*.

BOYAR. A member of the medieval Russian aristocracy in the 16th century, as distinguished from the service noble (*pomeshchik*). Boyars received their titles from the tsars, headed important offices, and participated in the deliberations of the *boyarskaya duma*. This was an advisory council to the Russian grand princes and tsars, consisting of important boyars, nobles, and high church dignitaries.

BRATSK. Town in the Russian Soviet Federated Socialist Republic 285 miles (456 km) NNW of Irkutsk on Angara River. Industries are based on an important hydroelectric power station, begun in 1954 and completed in 1964. They include sawmilling and the manufacture of wood pulp, cellulose, and furniture. Population (1981) 222,000.

BRATSTVO. Orthodox organizations in Belorussian and Ukrainian towns from the 16th to the 18th century at a time when these lands belonged to the Polish-Lithuanian state. Connected to a church, they had religious, educational, and charitable functions. They also fanned resistance to Catholicism and other aspects of Polish culture.

BRAUNSTEYN, ALEXANDER YESEYEVICH (1902–). Biochemist. Braunsteyn made an important advance in biochemistry with his discovery of transanimation. From 1928–56 he was the people's commissar of health. He has held a number of important posts, including head of the laboratory at the Institute of Molecular Biology from 1960.

BRENNA, VINCENZO (1740–1819). Italian artist and architect, who from 1780 to 1801 worked in Russia, mainly in Pavlovsk and also in St. Petersburg.

BRESHKO-BRESHKOVSKAYA, EKATERINA KONSTANTINOVNA (1844–1934). Revolutionary. As a result of her work as a member of the Socialist Revolutionary Party, Breshko-Breshkovskaya spent years in prison and in exile. Often called the "Grandmother of the Russian Revolution," she emigrated to Prague after the Bolshevik Revolution.

BREST. City in Belorussia on the Bug River where it forms the frontier with Poland. It was formerly known as Brest-Litovsk. Founded in 1017, it was invaded by the Mongols in 1241 and by Lithuania in 1319. It became Polish in 1569, Russian in 1795, and again Polish in 1919–39. It is a railway center and river port trading in timber, grain, and cattle. Industries include sawmilling, cotton spinning, food processing, and engineering. Population (1981) 194,000. *See also* **Brest-Litovsk, Treaties of.**

BREST, COUNCIL OF (1596). Council at which the Uniate Church was created. *See* **Uniates.**

BREST-LITOVSK, TREATIES OF (1918). The peace treaties between the Central Powers and, respectively, the Ukraine and Soviet Russia toward the end of the First World War. An independent Ukraine was recognized by the first treaty. By the second, Russia acknowledged Ukrainian independence and also lost its Polish and Baltic possessions. The treaties were repealed following the ultimate defeat of the Central Powers.

Freund, G., *The Unholy Alliance*, 1957.

Schapiro, Leonard., *The Communist Party of the Soviet Union*, 1960.

Wheeler-Bennett, J. W., *The Forgotten Peace: Brest-Litovsk, March 1918*, 1938.

BREZHNEV, LEONID ILYICH (1906–1982). Politician. Born in Dneprodzerzhinsk in the Ukraine, Brezhnev was educated at the Dneprodzerzhinsk Metallurgical Institute and later became deputy chief of the Urals regional land department. In 1935–36 he served in the Soviet army. From 1937–39 he was chief of a department in the Dnepropetrovsk regional party committee. A political officer in the army from 1941 to 1946, in 1944 he was made major general. The first secretary of the central committee of the Communist Party in Moldavia in 1950–52, Brezhnev was made a member of the central committee of the CPSU in 1952. His political career continued to climb, and in 1956 he was made a member of the Politburo, and from 1956 to 1960 he served as secretary of the central committee of the CPSU. Chairman of the Presidium of the Supreme Soviet of the USSR from 1960 to 1964, and also from 1977, in 1963 he was appointed as secretary of the central committee of the CPSU and general secretary from 1966. In 1976 he was made marshal of the Soviet Union and in 1977 became president of the Presidium of the Supreme Soviet. He died on November 10, 1982. Yury Andropov *(q.v.)* succeeded him.

BREZHNEV DOCTRINE. On September 28, 1968 *Pravda* published an article outlining how the USSR considered the sovereignty of the satellite states to be limited. It was dubbed "Brezhnev Doctrine" by Western commentators. The "Brezhnev Doctrine" was used to justify the invasion of Czechoslovakia in 1968.

BRODSKY, JOSEPH ALEKSANDROVICH (1940–). Russian-Jewish poet. His work has been largely neglected by the Soviet authorities.

He was sentenced to five years hard labor for "social parasitism," but this was commuted. In 1969 he went into voluntary exile in the United States. His publications include *Song without Music* (1969) and *A Stop in the Desert; Verse and Poems* (1970).

BRONSTEIN, LEV DAVIDOVICH. *See* **Trotsky, Lev.**

BRONZE HORSEMAN. *See* **Falconet, E. M.** and **Pushkin, A. S.**

BRUNNOV, FILIPP IVANOVICH (1797–1875). Russian diplomat and staunch supporter of the tsar. From 1818 he served in the ministry of foreign affairs and took part in congresses of the Quadruple Alliance and the Quintuple Alliance *(q.q.v.)*.

BRUSILOV, ALEKSEY ALEKSEYEVICH (1853–1925). General. A successful commander of the First World War, Brusilov became a prominent figure in national Bolshevism. Although supreme commander in chief of the Russian forces in the summer of 1917 under the provisional government, he joined the Red Army after the Bolshevik takeover.

BRYANSK. City in the Russian Soviet Federated Socialist Republic 210 miles (336 km) SW of Moscow on the Desna River and oblast capital. It is a railway center and industrial center. Industries include iron and steel, sawmilling, rope making, brick making, and the manufacture of road-making machinery and cement. There is a lumbering and forestry school. Bryansk forms the center of the Bryansk-Bezhitsa industrial area. Population (1981) 407,000.

BRYULOV, KARL PAVLOVICH (1799–1852). Painter. He was one of the first Russian artists to enjoy international repute. Born in Italy, Bryulov came to Russia as a child. He returned to Rome to paint and distinguished himself with his painting *The Last Day of Pompeii* (1828–30), of which Sir Walter Scott is said to have remarked that it was not a painting but an epic. He returned to Russia, hailed as the greatest painter of his time, but his subsequent work was disappointing, with the exception of his portraits.

Talbot Rice, Tamara, *A Concise History of Russian Art*, 1963.

BRYUSOV, VALERY YAKOVLEVICH (1873–1924). Poet. Bryusov's early work was largely misunderstood and ridiculed. *Russian Symbolists* (1894), written by Bryusov and A. L. Miropolsky, caused a scandal. By 1906, however, Symbolism was recognized, and Bryusov was hailed as the foremost Russian poet. His *Stephanos* (1906) was warmly received, although subsequently his poetic talents were on the wane. Bryusov also wrote stories and plays, translated poetry, reviewed books, and became an expert on Armenian poetry. After the events of 1917, he became a communist and worked as the head of censorship, but he was not felt to be sufficiently reliable and was replaced.

West, James D., *Russian Symbolism*, 1970.

BUBNOV, ANDREY SERGEYEVICH (1883–1940). Bolshevik. Having joined the party in 1903 Bubnov participated in the 1905 Revolution, after which he worked in the local party committees. Following the October Revolution of 1917, he was elected to the first Politburo, and during the Civil War he was a prominent commissar. A Left Communist in 1918, a Democratic Centralist and a Trotskyite in 1923, he supported Stalin after Lenin's death. In 1929 he was appointed commissar of education in the Russian Soviet Federated Socialist Republic. He disappeared in the Great Purge, but his name was subsequently rehabilitated.

BUDANTSEYEV, SERGEY FEDOROVICH (1896–*c.* 1938). Writer. Budantsev's early work, such as *The Revolt* (1922) was conventional in content, but his *Tale of the Sufferings of the Mind* was denounced as reactionary and extremely anti-Soviet, despite its apparently politically neutral theme. He died in a concentration camp in the late 1930s.

BUDDHISM. It is thought that there are still several hundred thousand Buddhists living in the USSR, the majority of whom live in areas bordering Mongolia. Bandido Hambo Lama is the head of the Buddhist Religious Central Board. It has been Soviet policy to reduce the number of lamas and to close many religious houses.

BUDYONNY, SEMYON MIKHAILOVICH (1883–). Russian military leader and marshal of the Soviet Union. Having served in the 48th Cossack regiment in the Far East, he was involved in revolutionary activity early in 1917. In 1918 he organized a cavalry unit to combat White forces. A member of the Communist Party from 1919, he took an active role in the Civil War. He pursued a highly successful military and political career; in 1939 he was deputy commissar for defense and in 1940 was first deputy. Despite a setback in his career in the Second World War, in 1953 he was made inspector of cavalry. From 1939 to 1961 he was a full member of the central committee.

BUG RIVER. The South Bug rises in the S Ukraine 37 miles (59 km) NE of Ternopol and flows 530 miles (848 km) SE past Vinnitsa and Nikolayev to enter the Dnepr estuary on the Black Sea. It is navigable for approximately 60 miles (96 km). The West Bug rises in the W Ukraine 35 miles (56 km) ENE of Lvov and flows 480 miles (768 km) NW forming the Poland/Ukraine frontier from NW of Sokal to NW of Brest and turning W to join the Vistula River below Warsaw. It is navigable below Brest. It is linked by the Mukhanets River to the Dnepr-Bug canal.

BUGAYEV, BORIS (1923–). Soviet government official and, from 1946, a member of the CPSU. A graduate of the higher flying school for civil aviation, he pursued a career in aviation, rising to the position of commander of a pilot's department of civil aviation (1947–66). He has been minister of the USSR civil aviation since 1970 and a member of the central committee since 1971.

BUGAYEV, BORIS NIKILAEVICH. *See* **Bely, Andrey.**

BUGULMA. Town founded in 1741, now in the Tatar Autonomous

Republic. Bugulma is one of the chief centers of the Tatar-Bashkir oil fields. Population (1977) 82,000.

BUGURUSLAN. Town in the center of the Buguruslan region of the Chkalovskaya oblast of the Russian Soviet Federated Socialist Republic. It was founded in 1748. Population (1977) 53,000.

BUKHARA. *See* **Bokhara.**

BUKHARIN, NICHOLAS IVANOVICH (1888–1938). Communist leader and Marxist theoretician. In 1908 he was made a member of the Moscow Bolshevik committee. He was imprisoned and deported. After the 1917 Revolution he returned to Russia, edited *Pravda* (1917–29), and in 1919 was elected to the executive committee of the Comintern. For a time he was editor of *Izvestia.* The following year he published *The Economy of the Transitional Period.* A member of the Politburo from 1924, Bukharin supported Stalin, despite distrusting him. In 1928 he disagreed with Stalin over the latter's industrialization policy and was expelled from the Politburo in 1929. He was shot in 1938.

Schapiro, Leonard, *The Communist Party of the Soviet Union,* 1960.

BUKOVINA (Beech-tree Land). Area situated in the Carpathian foothills and the upper stretches of the Dnestr, Prut, and Seret rivers. It was occupied by the Romans, Huns, East Slavs, and then by Rumanians. Part of the Moldavian principality in the 14th century, Bukovina fell under Turkish suzerainty in 1512, was ceded to Austria in 1775, granted autonomy in 1861, and was occupied by the Rumanians in 1918. Ceded to Rumania and then to the USSR at varying times, in 1947 it was finally ceded to the USSR.

BUKOVSKY, VLADIMIR (1942–). Writer and scientist. While working at the Moscow Center of Cybernetics, Bukovsky was arrested in 1963 for possessing banned literature and was confined to the Leningrad psychiatric prison hospital for 15 months; he spent another 8 months in similar institutions for having demonstrated on behalf of Soviet writers. Arrested in 1967 for civil rights work and sentenced to three years corrective labor, in 1972 Bukovsky was again arrested for having passed information on the abuse of psychiatry to the West. As a result of world outcry he was released and has now taken up residence in the United States. His writings include *To Build a Castle: My Life as a Dissenter* (1978).

BULAVIN, KONDRATY AFANASYEVICH (1660–1708). Leader of the Cossack revolt of 1707–08.

BULGAKOV, MICHAEL AFANASYEVICH (1891–1940). Author. Having graduated as a doctor in 1916, in 1920 Bulgakov directed his attentions to literature. In 1924 he wrote *The Day of the Turbine,* known in English as *The White Guard.* Although he wrote historical plays, Bulgakov achieved fame with his novel *The Master and Margarita* (1938, but not published until 1966). He earned his living as assistant producer and literary adviser at the Moscow

Art Theater. He wrote *Black Snow,* in which are thinly disguised portraits of his colleagues at the Moscow Art Theater, viewed in a generally unfavorable light. Persecuted from 1929, he appealed to Stalin for permission to emigrate, but permission was not granted. Bulgakov went blind in 1939 and died the following year.

BULGAKOV, SERGEY NIKOLAYEVICH (1871–1944). Philosopher, theologian, and economist. Once a legal Marxist, he became an Idealist, an Orthodox priest and then a Christian Socialist. A Constitutional-Democratic member of the Second Duma *(q.v.),* Bulgakov participated in the *Vekhi* Symposium. After being exiled from the Soviet Union in 1922 he became a professor at the Russian Theological Institute in Paris. He wrote a number of books, among which are those dealing with the doctrine of "Sophia, the Wisdom of God."

Kindersley, Richard K., *The First Russian Revisionists,* 1962.

Kolakowski, L., *Main Currents of Marxism,* 1980.

BULGANIN, NICHOLAS ALEKSANDROVICH (1895–1975). Communist. Having played a prominent role in the *Cheka* (1918–22), he rose steadily up the party machinery to the positions of defense minister (1953–55) and deputy prime minister (1947–55). In 1934 Bulganin was appointed a member of the central committee and in 1948 of its Presidium. Toward the end of the war he was made a marshal. In 1955 he was appointed prime minister, but in 1957 he joined the ill-fated antiparty group. In 1958 he was expelled from the Presidium, and retired.

BULGARIN, FADDEY VENEDIKTOVICH (1789–1859). Journalist. A Polish deserter from Napoleon's army, he found favor with the secret police by giving evidence against his Decembrist friends and then used his considerable influence at court to suppress talented young writers. He founded the daily newspaper *Northern Bee.*

BULGARS. An E European people. It is thought that they originated as a Turkic tribe of Central Asia and that they arrived in A.D. 370 in the steppe W of the Volga with the Huns. They formed a powerful khanate known as Greater Bulgaria under Kurt in the seventh century, but this split up after his death. One horde settled around the confluence of the Volga and Kama rivers, and although they enjoyed a considerable period of prosperity, they became subject to the Mongol Golden Horde in 1237, and the Volga Bulgars in time became integrated with the Russians. Following the disintegration of Greater Bulgaria, a second group finally settled in the SE Balkans, where they established the first Bulgarian empire. This was destroyed by the Byzantines. A second Bulgarian empire was established in the twelfth century, but this fell to the Ottoman Turks.

BUND. The General Union of Jewish Workers in Russia and Poland, it was a socialist political movement founded in Vilna in 1897. Its aims were an end to anti-Jewish discrimination and a reorganized, federal, Russian empire. It was recognized as the most powerful socialist body by 1900. In conflict with Lenin over its emphasis on Jewish interests, it seceded from the Russian Social Democrat Party in 1903–06, and after 1906 supported the Mensheviks. In 1920 it was divided; the majority of members joined the Communist Party, the minority continued as a separate group under Rafael Abramovich until it was suppressed by the government.

BUNGE, NICHOLAS KHRISTYANOVICH (1823–95). Statesman and economist. His official posts included professor and rector of Kiev University, manager of the Kiev branch of the state bank, minister of finance (1881–86), and chairman of the committee of ministers (1875–95). Bunge carried out extensive reforms of the budgetary system, abolished the poll tax, founded the Peasant Land Bank and the Nobility Land Bank, carried out industrialization measures, and introduced factory inspectors into Russia.

BUNIN, IVAN ALEKSEYEVICH (1870–1954). Author of the neo-Realist school. His works include *The Village* (1910), which gave a gloomy picture of Russian peasant life, and a collection of short stories, *The Gentleman from San Francisco* (1916, trans. 1923). Leaving Russia in 1919 he emigrated to Paris, and in 1933 was the first Russian to be awarded the Nobel Prize in literature.

BURYAT-AGINSKY. National area, situated in S Siberia in the Chita region of the Russian Soviet Federated Socialist Republic. It has an area of 9,000 square miles (23,310 sq km). The capital is Aginskoye. The main occupations are stock rearing and lumbering. Population (1970) 812,000.

BURYAT AUTONOMOUS SOVIET SOCIALIST REPUBLIC. Autonomous republic bounded on the S by Mongolia and on the W by Lake Baikal. It has an area of 135,650 square miles (351,334 sq km). The capital is Ulan-Ude. The region consists mainly of a plateau rising to the forested Barguzin mountains. The main occupation is rearing cattle and sheep. Population (1981) 929,000.

BURYATI. Mongolian-speaking people living in SE Siberia in the Buryat Autonomous Republic and in the Irkutsk and Chita oblasts. Self-governed by the Steppe Dumas in the 19th century, some of the Buryati formed a theocratic state opposed to the Bolsheviks.

BUSLAYEV, FEDOR IVANOVICH (1818–97). Philologist and historian of art. His academic appointments included professorship at Moscow University and membership of the Academy of Sciences. His subject was the interdependence of the Russian language, art, and folklore.

BUSLAYEV, VASILY. The hero of two Novgorod *byliny*, or heroic poems, of the 14th to the 15th century.

BUTASHEVICH-PETRASHEVSKY, MICHAEL (1821–66). Socialist. An employee of the foreign ministry, Butashevich-Petrashevsky was coauthor of a *Pocket Dictionary of Foreign Words,* in which socialist and radical ideas were explained. An admirer of Fourier, he held weekly meetings in which literary, political, and social topics were discussed. The government, in its alarm, sentenced 15 members of the Petrashevsky group to death and at the last minute informed them that their sentences had been commuted to forced labor in Siberia. One of the 15 was Fedor M. Dostoyevsky.

BUTURLIN, VASILY VASILYEVICH (?–1656). Diplomat who also pursued a military career. In 1655 he commanded the Russian troops sent to help Bohdan Khmelnitsky *(q.v.)* in the struggle against the Poles.

BYALIK, CHAIM NACHMAN (1873–1934). Russian-born Hebrew poet, essayist, and story writer. His poem *In the City of Slaughter* (1905) was written in reaction to the Kishinev pogrom; it is a moving account of human suffering and an admonition to the Jews for their passivity under oppression. In 1924 Byalik settled in Palestine where he was the leader of a cultural revival. He translated Shakespeare's *Julius Caesar* and Cervantes's *Don Quixote* into Hebrew and is regarded as the greatest modern Hebrew poet.

BYELORUSSIA. *See* **Belorussia.**

BYKOV, VASILY VLADIMIROVICH (1924–). Belorussian writer. Many of his novels deal with the Second World War. From 1966 he has been a presidium member of the Belorussian Union of Writers. Among his works are *A Crane's Cry* (1960) and *The Soldier's Fate* (1966).

BYKOVA, YELIZAVETA IVANOVNA (1913–). Chess player and economic planner. The women's world chess champion (1953–56 and 1958–62), Bykova has been an international chess master since 1953 and an honorary master of sport of the USSR. The author of *Soviet Women Chess Players* (1951 and 1957) and *Women's World Chess Championships* (1955), Bykova has won several awards.

BYLINY. Epic or heroic oral songs of Russia. The majority of *byliny* were composed before the 16th century; a few date back to the days before the coming of Christianity to Russia. Many recount heroic events in the Kievan age. They were superseded by historical songs and ballads. Richard James, an Englishman, was the first collector of *byliny,* in the 17th century.

Magnus, L. A., *The Heroic Ballads of Russia,* 1926.

BYZANTIUM (Constantinople and Istanbul). An ancient Greek city, Byzantium was the capital of the Byzantine empire and the center of Orthodox Christianity. After Kievan Russia had accepted Christianity, it was particularly influenced by Byzantine culture, art, and theology.

C

CABOT, SEBASTIAN (*c.* 1476–1557). Italian navigator, son of John Cabot. Employed as a cartographer and explorer by Henry VIII and then by Edward VI, in the later years of his life he organized an expedition to find a NE passage to the Far East. Although this met with little success, it helped develop trade with Russia.

CADETS. *See* **Constitutional Democratic Party, Kadet Party.**

CALENDAR. The Julian calendar was introduced under Julius Caesar. It was devised by Sosigenes of Alexandria, stipulating a length of 365.25 days to one year. To facilitate ordinary use, this was managed as a 365-day year, with one extra day every four years. The year was divided according to the activities of the sun, and not of the moon as had been done previously. The system was introduced in 45 B.C., but did not come into correct operation until A.D. 4. By that time the names of months and their length were the ones in current use.

This calendar was replaced in W countries by the Gregorian calendar, which was more accurate in its calculation of the length of the year (365.242199 days); the Julian error had produced a difference of seven days in 1,000 years. The improved calendar was devised under Pope Gregory XIII, who issued a papal bull concerning it in 1582. The Catholic European countries adopted it almost at once; the Protestant states later; Great Britain did so in 1752. Under this system, accuracy was maintained by limiting the number of leap years; centennial years are not leap years unless divisible by 400.

Russia had its own national calendar which reckoned the years, not from the birth of Christ but from an estimated beginning of the world. The year ran from September 1. In 1700 Peter the Great adopted the Julian calendar, which had been or was about to be abandoned by W Europe. It remained in force until 1918 when the Soviet government adopted the Gregorian system.

In 1929 a revolutionary calendar was devised, but it was never generally used. This replaced weeks with periods of five numbered days, and reckoned the era from 1917.

CAMERON, CHARLES (1740–1812). Scottish architect who brought the Palladian style to Russia. Cameron built the palace at Pavlovsk, the Agate pavilion and gallery in St. Petersburg, and redecorated rooms in the palace at Tsarskoye Selo.

Loukomski, George K., *Charles Cameron, 1740–1812*, 1943.

CANALS. Peter the Great instigated a program of large-scale canal building in the late 17th and early 18th century. These connected the main river systems and were of considerable importance before the days of rail transport. In later years, Stalin used forced labor to extend the Soviet Union's waterway network. The main canals include the Volga-Don, the White Sea-Baltic, the Volga-Baltic, and the Moscow-Volga. In 1977 the length of navigable canals and rivers was 85,860 miles (143,100 km).

CANTEMIR, DEMETRIUS (1673–1723). Linguist. Ruler of Moldavia from 1710, Cantemir concluded an alliance with Peter the Great at Lutsk in 1711. He fled to Russia following the Russian defeat at the Battle of Stanilesti, and was appointed imperial chancellor. Proficient in 11 languages, his best-known work is his *History of the Growth and Decay of the Othman Empire* (1734–35). Other works include the first critical history of Moldavia-Walachia, a geographical, economic, and ethnographical account of Moldavia, a history of the ruling houses of Brancovan and Cantacuzino, and the *Divan*, which deals with the conflicting demands of body and soul. Cantemir was elected to the Berlin Academy in 1714.

CAPITAL PUNISHMENT. *See* **Death Penalty.**

CAPO D'ISTRIA, GIOVANNI ANTONIO. *See* **Kapodistrias, Ioannis Antonios.**

CARAN D'ACHE (1858–1909). Pseudonym of Emmanuel Poiré, and pun on the Russian word *karandash* (pencil). French caricaturist and illustrator. Born and educated in Moscow, Caran d'Ache settled in Paris where he earned considerable popularity.

CARDIS, TREATY OF. Treaty concluded in 1661 as a result of Russia's war with Sweden. In 1656 Tsar Alexis marched into Livonia but was unable to capture Riga and the small towns on the Gulf of Finland. By 1659 Russia, exhausted, concluded a 20-years' peace at Valiesar. This was confirmed without setting a time limit in 1661 at Cardis. Russia agreed to relinquish all it had gained from Sweden.

Pares, Bernard, *A History of Russia*, 1926.

CARPATHIAN MOUNTAINS. Mountain system extending 900 miles (1,440 km) NW to SE across S Czechoslovakia, the Ukraine, and Rumania. The main ranges are the Little Carpathians, the White Mountains, the W and E Beskids, the High and Low Tatra, and the Transylvanian Alps. The highest point is Gerlachovka, at 8,737 feet (2,665 m) in the High Tatra. There are rich mineral deposits.

CASIMIR IV (1427–92). King of Poland from 1445 and grand prince of Lithuania. He strove to form a union between Poland and Lithuania and to recover the lost W and N lands of Poland; as a result of this policy, Poland became a great power in the 15th century. Ivan III, rehearsing for war, carried out a number of frontier skirmishes and raids on Lithuania in 1489; after Casimir's death these escalated into full-scale war (1500–03).

CASPIAN SEA. Sea between Asia and extreme SE Europe. It is bounded on the N, W, and E by USSR and on the S by Iran. Eighty percent of the shoreline is in the USSR. It extends 750 miles (1,200 km) N to S and is approximately 220 miles (352 km) wide. It is tideless with no outlet and is the largest inland sea in the world. Of lower salinity than the Black Sea, it receives fresh water from the Volga and Ural rivers. It is frozen in the N for 2–3 months a year.

CASTLEREAGH, VISCOUNT (Londonderry, Robert Stewart) (1769–1822). British statesman and diplomat, secretary of war (1805–09), and foreign secretary (1812–22). He was anxious to safeguard Europe against the military threat posed by Russia, and thus strongly resisted Russia's huge territorial demands following the Napoleonic wars.

CATHERINE I (Yekaterina Alexeyevna) (1684–1727). Empress of Russia and consort and successor to Peter the Great. After the death of her mother, a Lithuanian peasant, Marta Skowronska, as she was then called, worked as a servant for Pastor Gluck, before marrying a Swedish dragoon. Captured as a Russian prisoner of war, Marta was sold to Prince A. D. Menshikov at whose house she became the lover of Peter the Great. In 1703, she was received into the Orthodox Church, and rechristened Yekaterina Alexeyevna. Catherine and Peter officially married in 1712, and Catherine was crowned empress-consort in the Uspensky cathedral in 1724. After Peter's death, she was declared empress regent in 1725, and she established the supreme privy council the following year. She died in 1727.

CATHERINE II (1729-96). Known as the Great, she was empress of Russia from 1762 to 1796. Originally named Sophie Augusta Frederika and the daughter of Prince Christian of Anhalt-Zerbst (in Prussia), she was born in Stettin, entered the Orthodox Church (1744), and married (1745) the future tsar, Peter III. Catherine hated her degenerate and feeble-minded husband but realized that her marriage to him could be a path to power. Their only child was the future Paul I (born 1754). Peter became tsar in 1762, but six months later a military coup led by Grigory Orlov and Prince Grigory Potemkin *(q.q.v.)*, deposed him, and he was murdered some days later. Catherine supplanted her own son when she took the throne. Though in her zeal for self-education she read and corresponded with

Voltaire and others and practiced and patronized art and literature, she ruled as an enlightened despot, but a despot nonetheless. She never forgot her political dependence on the nobility and gentry who had set her on the throne. Although she abolished capital punishment, except for political crimes, and prepared comprehensive schemes of educational, legal, and administrative reform, little was actually accomplished during her reign. The number of serfs increased and the military and economic burdens on the peasantry grew worse. Following the revolt (1773–75) led by Yemelyan Pugachev *(q.v.)*, a pretender who claimed to be her dead husband Peter III, her domestic policy became increasingly repressive. She pursued an imperialist foreign policy and in two wars with Turkey (1768–72 and 1787–92) expanded her territories near the Black Sea and annexed the Crimea. The Ukraine was fully absorbed, and when Poland was obliterated by the three partitions of 1772, 1793, and 1795, Russia took the largest share.

Cronin, Vincent, *Catherine: Empress of all the Russians*, 1978.

de Madariaga, I., *Russia in the Age of Catherine the Great*, 1981.

Gooch, George P., *Catherine the Great and Other Studies*, 1954.

Grey, Ian, *Catherine the Great*, 1961.

Olivier, D., *Catherine la Grande*, 1965.

CATHERINE IVANOVNA (1684–1727). Duchess of Mecklenburg. The daughter of Tsar Ivan V, she was considered ineligible to ascend the throne because she had married an alien.

CATHERINE PAVLOVNA (1788–1819). Grand duchess, sister of Alexander I, and wife of the Duke of Oldenburg, governor-general of three central provinces.

CATHOLIKOS. Ecumenical heads of the Armenian, Georgian, and Albanian churches are given this title.

CAUCASUS. Region between the Black Sea and Caspian Sea. The N Caucasus consists mainly of plains, including the Stavropol Plateau and the Kuban Steppe. It is drained in the N by the Don River into the Sea of Azov and in the S by the Kuban River into the same sea, and by the Terek River into the Caspian Sea. Chief crops are cereals and cotton; industry is concentrated on Armavir, Astrakhan, Krasnodar, Rostov, and Stavropol. The Great Caucasus is mountainous with ranges extending 750 miles (1,200 km) WNW to ESE from Taman peninsula in the W to Apsheron peninsula in the E, and rising to Mount Elbruz. Rainfall is up to 100 inches (254 cm) annually on the S slopes and 10 inches (25 cm) in the E. There are important deposits of petroleum and manganese. Transcaucasia is mountainous with the Surami range extending N to S between the Great Caucasus and Little Caucasus. Pushkin, Lermontov, and many Russian writers from the end of the 18th century were influenced by the exotic and romantic appeal of the Caucasus.

Baddeley, J. F., *The Russian Conquest of the Caucasus*, 1908.

Baddeley, J. F., *The Rugged Flanks of the Caucasus,* 1940.
Maclean, Fitzroy, *To Caucasus, End of All the Earth,* 1976.

CAUCASUS MOUNTAINS. Name given to the mountain range, and also to the whole region, incorporating the Kuban, Kuma, and Manych basins, and Transcaucasia, including the Krasnodar and Stavropol Krays. The Chechen-Ingush, Daghestan, Kabarda-Balkar, and N Ossetian autonomous republics of the Russian Soviet Federated Socialist Republic, and the union republics of Armenia, Azerbaijan, and Georgia. At the beginning of the 20th century the Caucasus was the world's leading oil producer; it is also an area of horticulture, viticulture, and engineering. Parts of the area have been conquered by the Scythians, Persians, Macedonians, Romans, Parthians, Arabs, Byzantium, Khazars, Cumans, Mongols, and Turks. In the 18th century, Turkey, Persia, and Russia gradually increased their power in the Caucasus Mountains. The Caucasus was the scene of much fighting during the Russian Civil War and the Second World War.

CAVIAR. Hors d'oeuvre prepared from fish roe. The best caviar is from the sturgeon; it is black and in the USSR is a luxury commodity. On the other hand, the coarser variety, *payusnaya,* is freely available in the USSR and E Europe. Most caviar comes from the Caucasian coast of the Caspian Sea and the mouth of the Kura River and from the Volga-Caspian area.

CECCHETTI, ENRICO (1850–1928). Italian teacher and ballet master. He spent most of his life as a dancer and then as a teacher at the Imperial Theater, St. Petersburg. Cecchetti not only taught Nijinsky, Karsavina, Pavlova, and Karkova, but also profoundly influenced the Diaghilev company and modern ballet.

CENSORSHIP. First officially introduced by Peter the Great for theological articles, general censorship was instigated in 1803, although the first comprehensive laws on censorship were not drawn up until 1826. Although preventive censorship was abolished for newspapers and certain books in 1865, the revolutionary movement prompted stricter measures to be taken. In 1905–06, however, publication was greatly liberalized, with virtually only foreign books subject to censorship. Censorship of the press disappeared after the February Revolution of 1917, but was soon reinstated following the Bolshevik seizure of power. During Stalin's rule, censorship was extremely strict, although it was slightly relaxed under Khrushchev. Glaring anomalies have been known to occur; Solzhenitsyn's *One Day in the Life of Ivan Denisovich* was published, whereas Pasternak's *Dr. Zhivago* was not. All printed matter and written material, sometimes including telegrams and private correspondence, is censored. Authors themselves exercise "internal censorship," whereby they prudently write what they consider will pass the censor. *See* **Decree on the Press.**

Dewhirst, Martin and Farrell,

Robert (eds.), *The Soviet Censorship,* 1973.

Walker, Gregory P. M., *Soviet Book Publishing Policy,* 1978.

CENSUS. A census was ordered by Peter the Great in 1710 in the hope that it would show an increase of households from which tax could be exacted; in fact it revealed a 20 percent decline. A further census in 1719 indicated an increase in the number of male peasants, and thus poll tax on the individual male was introduced. This had the dual result of increasing revenue and extending the cultivated area.

CENTRAL ASIA. *See* **Asia, Soviet Central.**

CENTRAL COMMITTEE OF THE COMMUNIST PARTY, THE. The highest organ of the party between congresses. Its function is to direct all party activities between congresses. Members are elected at party congresses, and the committee's Presidium and Secretariat and the committee of party control are formed. From 1917 to 1934, it acted as a quasi-parliament, with room for discussions and factions. In order to free himself from dependency on majority support in the central committee, Stalin liquidated 70 percent of the central committee between the 17th and 18th party congresses (1934–39). Thus, until Stalin's death, its role was greatly diminished. During the period of "collective leadership," after Stalin's death, leaders again had to win the support of the various factions of the central committee. Wider in scope than the Supreme Soviet and the council of ministers, the central committee is the main tool of the government.

Hough, Richard Alexander and Fainsod, Merle, *How the Soviet Union is Governed,* 1979.

McAuley, M., *Politics and the Soviet Union,* 1977.

Schapiro, Leonard, *The Communist Party of the Soviet Union,* (2nd ed.) 1970.

CENTRAL EXECUTIVE COMMITTEE. From 1917–36 the executive organ of the congresses of Soviets of workers' and soldiers' deputies. It was elected at the first congress of Soviets in July 1917. In 1922, following the formation of the USSR, there were all-union and also republic central executive committees. The chairmen of the committee acted as the heads of state. As a result of the Stalin constitution of 1936, the role of the central executive committee was bestowed on the Supreme Soviet and its Presidium.

CHAADAYEV, PETER YAKOVLEVICH (1793–1856). Russian thinker. After university studies Chaadayev served as an army officer in the Napoleonic campaign. Having traveled in Europe (1823–26), he settled in Moscow, and composed his *Lettres Philosophiques* in French (1827–31). The first letter, published in Russian in the review *Teleskop* in 1836, caused great controversy; his unmitigated support of Western European values and his equally wholehearted condemnation of Russian culture resulted in his proclamation that the future of Russia could only lie in a reunion with the Roman

Catholic Church. This precipitated the great division between the Westernizers and Slavophiles. In answer to the authorities' declaration that he was insane, Chaadayev wrote his *Apologie d'un fou.*

CHAGALL, MARC (1887–). Artist. He was born in the Jewish community of Vitebsk in tsarist Belorussia, and studied painting in St. Petersburg (1907–10). In 1910, on a visit to Paris, Chagall was strongly influenced by Cubism and by the bright colors of the Fauves, Van Gogh, and Gauguin. After the 1917 Revolution, Chagall was commissar for fine arts at Vitebsk and commissioned to paint a mural for the State Jewish Theater in Moscow. After his work was judged officially to be incompatible with Socialist Realism, in 1922 Chagall went to Berlin and took up lithography and etching. He then lived in Paris, New York, and Venice. Religious themes and landscapes form much of the subject matter of his work. His paintings frequently depict a world that defies observable reality; it was as a result of seeing Chagall's work that Guillaume Apollinaire coined the word *Surréaliste*; although Chagall himself did not participate in this movement.

CHALIAPIN, FEDOR. *See* **Shalyapin, Fedor.**

CHANCELLOR, RICHARD (?–1556). British seaman who visited Russia in 1553–54 as pilot-general of Sir Hugh Willoughby's expedition to find a NE passage from England to China. His was the only one of three ships to get through to Vardø, Norway, and on into the White Sea. He traveled overland to Moscow where he was received favorably by Ivan IV. The tsar granted English merchants favorable trading conditions in a letter to Mary I; this led, on Chancellor's return, to the foundation of the Muscovy Company, with a monopoly of English-Russian trade and a base at Archangel. Chancellor visited Moscow again in 1555–56, but on his return drowned off the Scottish coast.

CHAPAYEV, VASILY IVANOVICH (1887–1919). A former laborer, he was hailed as a hero of the Red Army during the Civil War, when he commanded a division in the Urals. He has remained popular as a result of Dmitry Andreyevich Furmanov's book about him (1923) and the film *Chapaev* (1934), about his Civil War exploits.

CHAPYGIN, ALEXEY PAVLOVICH (1870–1937). Soviet writer. Having worked first as a shepherd and then as a decorator in St. Petersburg, Chapygin's first work was published in 1903. His novel *The White Monastery* (1913) depicts country life on the eve of the 1905 Revolution. He also wrote a number of short stories and sketches, including the autobiographic tale *My Life* (1929). His historical novel *Stepan Razin* was warmly received in Soviet Russia, particularly by Gorky.

CHARDZHOU. Capital of Chardzhou region in Turkmenistan situated 300 miles (480 km) ENE of Ashkhabad. Founded in 1886 when the Trans-Caspian Railway reached the Amu Darya River, it is a railway junction and river port. Industries include textiles, especially cotton. Population (1970) 102,000.

CHARLES XII (1682–1718). King of Sweden (1697–1718). In the Great/Second Northern War *(q.v.)* Charles defeated the Russians at Narva in 1700. In 1707 his troops left Saxony to invade Russia. Although Sweden won the Battle of Holowczyn the following year, Charles was forced to march on the Ukraine, instead of Moscow, as had been planned. By 1709 Charles had the choice of fighting the Russians or withdrawing to Poland. The Swedes attacked the Russian fortified camp at Poltava, and were forced to surrender. Charles spent the following five years in exile in Turkey. He was killed besieging a fortress in Norway in 1718.

Hatton, R. M., *Charles XII of Sweden*, 1968.

Stomberg, Andrew A., *A History of Sweden*, 1932.

CHARNOLUSKY, VLADIMIR IVANOVICH (1865–1941). Educationalist and author. Having finished studying at Kiev University, Charnolusky published works on education with G. Falbork *(q.v.)* before the 1917 Revolution. From 1921 he worked for the people's commissariat for education in the Russian Soviet Federated Socialist Republic. He was head of the State Library for Education of the People and taught at the Second Moscow State University.

Grant, Nigel, *Soviet Education*, (4th ed.) 1979.

CHARTER OF THE TOWNS. Charter issued by Catherine the Great in 1785. It deals with the rights of the individual and the collective, with craft guilds (*tsekhi*), and with urban self-government. According to the terms of the charter, however, the burghers were still subject to soul tax and were still unable to own peasants or estates.

de Madariaga, I., *Russia in the Age of Catherine the Great*, 1981.

CHARTER TO THE NOBILITY OF 1785. Charter issued under Catherine II, which recognized the privileged position of the nobility as the ruling class and which implicitly recognized the peasants' status as chattel slaves. It also provided for the creation of autonomous corporations of the nobility, with legal powers.

Dukes, Paul, *Catherine the Great and the Russian Nobility: A Study Based on the Materials of the Legislative Commission of 1767*, 1967.

CHEBOKSARY. Capital of Chuvash Autonomous Republic of the Russian Soviet Federated Socialist Republic. It is situated on the S bank of Volga River. Industries include textiles and electrical engineering and the city manufactures matches. Population (1977) 292,000.

CHEBYSHEV, PAFNUTY LVOVICH (1821–94). Russian mathematician. Born at Borovsk, he studied at Moscow University in 1859 and was professor of mathematics at St. Petersburg University until 1880. Chebyshev wrote on such topics as prime numbers, the problem of obtaining rectilinear motion by linkage, probability, quadratic forms, and the theory of integrals and gearings.

CHECHEN-INGUSH AUTONOMOUS SOVIET SOCIALIST REPUBLIC. Autonomous republic of the Russian Soviet Federated Socialist Republic on the N slopes of the Great Caucasus and bounded on the E by Dagestan and on the S by Georgia. It has an area of 7,350 square miles (19,037 sq km). Its capital is Grozny. Industries are based on the Grozny oil field and include engineering, chemicals, and food canning; manufactures include building materials, timber products, and furniture. Population (1981) 1.2 million.

CHECHENS. Caucasian-speaking people in the Chechen-Ingush Autonomous Republic. Until the 19th century they lived in local tribal groups and strongly resisted Russia's attempt to conquer them in the 19th century; after the Chechens' defeat, one-fifth of their number left for Turkey. They fought both the Cossacks and Bolsheviks during the Civil War and continued to oppose the Communists by means of guerilla warfare in the mountains. In 1943, as a result of their anti-Communist uprising they were all deported to Kazakhstan and W Siberia, but they were rehabilitated in 1957. They are Sunni Muslims.

CHEKA (CHREZVYCHAYNAYA KOMMISSIYA). All-Russia extraordinary commission for fighting counterrevolution and sabotage established on December 7, 1917. It was in operation until 1922, when it became the GPU *(q.v.)*. It was headed by Felix Dzerzhinsky. Although its sphere of work was wider than mere political repression (it also dealt with speculation and abuse of authority, for example), it did not hesitate to use terror as a means of eliminating inefficiency and opposition. It established concentration camps and internal security camps, as well as censoring the press. Although the original *Cheka* is now replaced by the KGB, its members are still often referred to as *chekisty*.

Leggatt, G., *The Cheka: Lenin's Political Police*, 1981.

CHEKHOV, ANTON PAVLOVICH (1860–1904). Dramatist and writer of short stories. Born at Taganrog on the Sea of Azov, he was educated at the gymnasium there and then went to Moscow, where he took his degree at the Faculty of Medicine in 1884. Chekhov began writing for comic newspapers while a student, in order to supplement his family's meager income. His collected stories, published in 1886, were warmly received by the public, and also by Aleksey Suvorin *(q.v.)*, editor of the daily paper *Novoy Vremya,* who invited him to contribute stories to it. In 1890 Chekhov visited the penal colony of Sakhalin Island, and his report on it, *Sakhalin Island* (1891), is alleged to have influenced reforms in prisons, which were introduced in 1892. Having settled with his family at Melikhovo in 1891, he spent time and money on local improvements, including working as head of a sanitary district during the cholera epidemic of

1892–93. He wrote many of his finest stories there. Consumption forced him to spend the rest of his life on the S coast of the Crimea and at foreign health resorts. Owing to his left-wing political views, he broke with Suvorin and met Gorky and at Yalta was a friend of Leo Tolstoy. His short stories are rich in suggestion, evoking moods in an economical way, and often contain a poignant blend of humor with the sadder aspects of life; examples include *Lady and the Lapdog, The House with an Attic,* and *A Dreary Story.* His plays, especially *The Seagull* (1896), *Uncle Vanya* (1897), *The Three Sisters* (1901), and *The Cherry Orchard* (1903) have won him lasting renown.

Hingley, Ronald, *A New Life of Anton Chekhov,* 1976.

Valency, M., *The Breaking String: The Drama of A. Chekhov,* 1966.

CHELOBYTNYE. Name (literally, "beating one's forehead") given to requests or complaints made to local or central organs of power from the 15th to the beginning of the 18th century. Collective bodies, such as the entire population of a village, or individuals could apply with their *chelobytnye.*

CHELYABINSK. Capital of Chelyabinsk region of the Russian Soviet Federated Socialist Republic situated in the S Ural mountains and on the Trans-Siberian Railway. Founded in 1736, its industries include iron and steel, zinc, chemicals, agricultural engineering, and flour milling. It trades in grain and coal. Population (1981) 1,055,000.

CHELYUSKIN, CAPE. The northernmost point of the continental USSR, extending into Boris Vilkitsky Strait in the Arctic Ocean at the N tip of Taymyr peninsula.

CHERDYN. Town in the center of the Cherdyn region of the Molotov oblast of the Russian Soviet Federated Socialist Republic. According to archaeological finds, Cherdyn is probably one of the most ancient towns of the Urals. In the 9th and 10th centuries, it was a center for trade. Population (1970) 39,000.

CHEREMKHOVO. Town in the S center of the Russian Soviet Federated Socialist Republic situated 80 miles (128 km) NW of Irkutsk on the Trans-Siberian Railway. Industries include coal mining, engineering, and chemicals. Population (1970) 110,000.

CHERENKOV, PAUL ALEXEYICH (1904–). Soviet physicist and one of a team who won a Nobel Prize in 1958 for their work on the nature of light emitted in liquids and solids exposed to radiation.

CHEREPNIN, NICHOLAS NIKOLAYEVICH (1873–1945). Composer and conductor. Having studied at St. Petersburg University, and then at the Conservatory under N. A. Rimsky-Korsakov *(q.v.),* Cherepnin taught for three years before being appointed professor at the Conservatory. From 1909–14 he was conductor at the annual ballet performances of the Diaghilev ballet company in Paris, where he was influenced by French Impressionist music and by the music of Strauss. He wrote a wide range of works for different instruments, orchestras, and voices, including the opera *The Marriage Broker,* the ballet *Le Pavillon d'Armide,* and the religious cantata *Pilgrimage and Passions of the Virgin Mary.*

CHEREPOVETS. Town 130 miles (208 km) NW of Yaroslavl in the Russian Soviet Federated Socialist Republic on the N side of the Rybinsk reservoir. A settlement around a monastery was established in the 14th century. Industries include shipbuilding, sawmilling, iron and steel, and agricultural engineering; manufactures include footwear and matches. Population (1981) 279,000.

CHERKASSOV, NICHOLAS KONSTANTINOVICH (1903–). Soviet actor. Having started with mime, comedy, and vaudeville in Leningrad, since 1926 Cherkassov has worked in film. He is internationally renowned for his interpretation of the title roles in Eisenstein's *Aleksandr Nevsky* (1938) and *Ivan the Terrible* (1944–45).

CHERKASSY. Ukrainian town situated 100 miles (160 km) SE of Kiev on the S bank of the Dnepr River. Founded in the late 13th century, it became part of Russian territory in 1793. Industries include sawmilling, engineering, metalworking, and food processing. Population (1981) 242,000.

CHERKASSY, PRINCE VLADIMIR ALEKSANDROVICH (1824–78). Slavophile of moderately liberal outlook. In 1857 Cherkassy presented the government with his article "On the Best Means for the Gradual Ending of Serfdom." From 1861 to 1863 he took an active part in preparations for the emancipation of the serfs in Poland, where he worked as chief director of the governmental commission for domestic and spiritual affairs.

CHERNENKO, KONSTANTIN (1911–). A member of the Communist Party of the Soviet Union since 1931, he was elected a full member of the central committee in 1978. In February 1984, he became general secretary of the central committee and chairman of the defense council, and on April 11, 1984 president of the Presidium.

CHERNIGOV. Ukrainian town 80 miles (128 km) NNE of Kiev situated on the Desna River. One of the oldest of the Kievan Russian cities, it declined after the Mongol invasion of 1239. Industries include textiles; manufactures include knitwear, footwear, and chemicals. It is a river port handling grain, flax, and potatoes. Population (1981) 252,000.

CHERNOV, VIKTOR MIKHAILOVICH (1876–1952). Leader of the Russian Social Revolutionary Party. Having helped found the party in 1902, he was a member of its central committee and editor of its journal *Revolutionary Russia.* Opposed to the left wing of his party, he was minister of agriculture in Kerensky's provisional government, and elected chairman of the constituent assembly in Petrograd in 1918, although the assembly only lasted a day. Having fought for the Reds on the Volga during the Civil War, he emigrated in 1920, living in Paris and the United States, where he wrote *The Great Russian Revolution* (1936) and also contributed to anti-Communist magazines.

CHERNOVTSY. Ukrainian city situated 140 miles (224 km) SE of Lvov on the Prut River. It is the capital of Chernovtsy region. One of the oldest cities in Russia, it was the center of the Ukrainian National Movement in the 19th and 20th centuries. Industries include sawmilling, engineering, food processing, textiles, and rubber products. Population (1981) 224,000.

CHERNOZEM. *See* **Black Earth.**

CHERNYAKHOVSK. Town in the Kaliningrad oblast of the Russian Soviet Federated Socialist Republic. It was founded by the Teutonic Knights in 1337 as a castle but was granted the status of a town in 1583. The town, until 1946 called Insterburg, was renamed at the Potsdam Conference (1945) after the Soviet general who captured it. It is an important railway junction. Population (1975) 35,000.

CHERNYAKHOVSKY, IVAN DANILOVICH (1906–45). General of the army and hero of the Soviet Union. Chernyakhovsky joined the Soviet army in 1924 and was a member of the Communist Party from 1928. In 1944 he was appointed commander of the troops at the third Belorussian front, and in 1945 he successfully drove out the German forces from Königsberg and was mortally wounded during the fighting.

CHERNYAYEV, MICHAEL GRIGOREVICH (1828–98). General who captured Ali-Atka in 1863, and together with Verevkin stormed Chimkent and took Tashkent *(q.q.v.)*. In 1871 he published the reactionary journal *The Russian World,* which opposed military reforms. At the invitation of the Serbian government in 1876, Chernyayev was chief commander of the Serbian army in the Serbian war with Turkey.

CHERNYSHEVSKY, NICHOLAS GAVRILOVICH (1828–89). Journalist, author, and leader of the radical intelligentsia in the 1850s and 1860s. Born in Saratov, he started his literary career working for the review *The Contemporary.* Following V. G. Belinsky *(q.v.)* and the English Utilitarians, he believed in egoism as the best motivator of human behavior, although he did draw attention to social injustices. He was arrested, imprisoned, and spent 19 years in exile in Siberia. His writings include the highly didactic novel *Chto Delat (What Is to Be Done)* (1863) and *Aesthetic Relations of Art and Reality.* His writings are highly praised by Soviet Marxists for the extent to which they paved the way for future Bolshevik thought.

Chernyshevsky, Nikolai Gavrilovich, A *Vital Question,* 1886.

Lampert, Evgeny, *Sons Against Fathers,* 1965.

Masaryk, Tomáš G., *The Spirit of Russia: Studies in History, Literature and Philosophy,* 2 vols. 1955.

Randall, Francis B., *N. G. Chernyshevsky,* 1967.

Ulam, Adam B., *Lenin and the Bolsheviks,* 1966.

CHERSKI RANGE. Mountain system in the Russian Soviet Federated Socialist Republic extending 600 miles (960 km) NW to SE in NE Siberia. It rises to Pobeda Peak, 24,406 feet (7,438 m) above sea level.

CHERTKOV, VLADIMIR GRIGORIYEVICH (1854–1936). Former officer of the Horse Guards, he was a fanatic and despotic man who greatly influenced Leo Tolstoy.

CHESME, BATTLE OF. Naval battle waged between the Russian and Turkish fleets in the Bay of Chesme in 1770, and won by the Russians. It is alleged that 10,000 Turks fell in the battle, while Russia lost 11 men. This victory led to a series of anti-Turkish uprisings in Egypt and Syria.

CHETARDIE, MARQUIS DE LA. French envoy at St. Petersburg in the 1740s.

CHETVERT. Dry measure equal to 5.95 bushels, or 2.099 hectoliters, also a land measure, one half of a *desyatin (q.v.).*

CHEVACHINSKY, SAVVA IVANOVICH (1713–70). Architect. From 1745–60 he directed work at Tsarskoye Selo and built the naval church and a baroque-style belfry for the church of St. Nicholas in St. Petersburg, as well as assisting in the design and construction of the Hermitage.

CHIATURA. Georgian town situated 100 miles (160 km) NW of Tbilisi on the Kvirila River. The main industry is manganese mining. It is one of the world's largest producers of manganese. Population (1975) 30,000.

CHICHERIN, BORIS NIKOLAYEVICH (1828–1904). Liberal politician, jurist, historian, and philosopher. He was a professor at Moscow University and mayor of Moscow (1882–83). A follower of Hegel, his *Philosophy of Law* (1900) asserts that law comes from freedom, man's true spiritual essence. He was viewed as the leader of the etatist school in Russian historiography. In politics he was anti-Socialist, supporting private property and freedom of contracts, although this did not rule out the possibility of the state taking measures to improve society.

CHICHERIN, GEORGY VASILYEVICH (1872–1936). Diplomat. He became a leading member of the Menshevik faction of the Social Democratic Labor Party in Berlin. After working for the labor movements in England, Germany, and France, Chicherin became a Bolshevik after the Revolution of 1917. He was imprisoned in Brixton jail, released, and expelled from Great Britain. He returned to Russia and worked as commissar for foreign affairs.

Mendel, Arthur P. et al., *Dilemmas of Progress in Tsarist Russia,* 1961.

Rubinstein, A. Z., *The Foreign Policy of the Soviet Union,* 1960.

Treadgold, Donald W., *Lenin and his Rivals: The Struggle for Russia's Future, 1898–1906,* 1955.

CHIMKENT. Town in Kazakhstan 90 miles (144 km) N of Tashkent on the Turksib Railway. Founded in the 12th century, it became part of

Russia in 1864. Industries include lead and zinc refining and chemicals and textiles. The town manufactures cement. Population (1981) 334,000.

CHINESE EASTERN RAILWAY. Railway line connecting Vladivostok with the Trans-Siberian Railway. It was built by the Russians in 1896–1903. It was controlled by the Whites and the Allies during the Russian Civil War.

CHIRCHIK. Town in Uzbekistan 20 miles (32 km) NE of Tashkent situated on the Chirchik River. Chirchik came into existence because of the exploitation of hydroelectric power on the river. Industries include agricultural engineering; manufactures are fertilizers and footwear. Population (1970) 108,000.

CHIRIKOV, YEVGENY NIKOLAYEVICH (1864–1932). Author and moderate representative of Gorky's *znanye* school of fiction.

CHITA. Town in the Russian Soviet Federated Socialist Republic in S Siberia, situated on the Chita River near its confluence with the Ingoda River and on the Trans-Siberian Railway. The Decembrists were exiled to this town. Founded in 1653, its industries include railway engineering, tanning, and flour milling. Population (1981) 315,000.

CHKHEIDZE, NICHOLAS SEMYONOVICH (1864–1926). Georgian Social Democratic leader. In the early 1890s Chkheidze assisted in spreading Marxist ideas in Georgia. In 1907 he was elected to the Russian State Duma, where he led the Social Democratic group. During the March Revolution of 1917 he was chairman of the Petrograd Soviet of workers' and soldiers' deputies. Following the November 1917 Revolution, he returned to Transcaucasia, and was president of the constituent assembly of the Independent Republic of Georgia. He emigrated to France following the Bolshevik occupation of Georgia.

CHMIELNICKI, BOGDAN (1595–1657). Hetman of Zaporozhian Cossacks. He was educated in Poland. After quarreling with the Polish governor of Czehryn, Chmielnicki fled to the Cossacks' Zaporozhian stronghold, where he allied with the Crimean khan. Cossacks and Tatars together rose against the Poles in 1648. Armed conflict continued until eventually the Poles defeated the Cossacks at Beresteckzo. He sought help from Moscow, but he was on the point of betraying Moscow when he died.

CHOSEN COUNCIL. A group of advisers who assisted Ivan IV (1533–84).

CHRISTIAN SECTS. Aside from the Orthodox Christian Church, Christian sects in the Soviet Union include the Baptist-Evangelical Christians, Pentacostalists, Catholics, the Lutheran Church, and the Old Believers. The Baptist-Evangelical Christians, recognized by the state, enjoyed official approval until 1929. In 1944, Baptists and Evangelicals were united in an All-Union Council of Evangelical Christians-Baptists. By the 1960s a large minority were increasingly frustrated by the way in which legislation prevented them from preaching the Gospel of Christ, and an "Action Group" broke away and established their own Council of the Evangelical Christian-Baptist Churches in 1965. This has not had official recognition, and many of its members have been persecuted. The Catholic Church had been dwindling, until the incorporation of the Baltic republics in 1940–44. Western-rite Catholics are officially recognized; the Eastern-Catholic Church, officially dissolved in 1949, is not. The incorporation of the Baltic states also resulted in an increase in the Lutheran Church in the USSR.

Bourdeaux, Michael, *The Opium of the People: The Christian Religion in the USSR*, 1965.

Marshall, R. H., *Aspects of Religion in the Soviet Union*, 1971.

CHRISTIANITY, CONVERSION TO. The origins of Christianity in Russia date back to the ninth century. In 944 Russian Christians signed a Byzantine-Russian treaty and *c.* 955 Princess Olga, regent of Kiev, was baptized. However, subsequent rulers, Svyatoslav (942–72) and Vladimir (died 1015), preferred paganism. Vladimir, however, realized that since Kiev was surrounded by powerful countries, each of which had accepted either Islam, Judaism, or Christianity, it was necessary for the security of Kiev to accept one of these faiths. He chose Byzantine Christianity, was baptized in 988, and married the emperor of Constantinople's sister in 989. Personal "conversion" was judged necessary only for the upper echelons of society, who enforced Christianity on the masses.

Obolensky, Dimitri, *The Byzantine Commonwealth: Eastern Europe 500–1453*, 1971.

CHRISTIANS OF THE UNIVERSAL BROTHERHOOD. *See* ***Dukhobory.***

CHRONICLES. Largest and one of the most valuable pieces of Kievan literature. The chronicles, or annals, started at the same time as Russian literature, and the tradition continued until the 17th century. They were written partly by monks, partly by laymen, and in Muscovite times, by official scribes. The *Primitive Chronicle* covers the period up to 1110; the *Kievan Chronicle* continues the history as far as 1200.

Mirsky, D. S., *A History of Russian Literature*, 1949.

Pipes, Richard (ed.), *Karamzin's Memoir on Ancient and Modern Russia*, 1959.

CHU RIVER. River rising in the SE Kazakh desert and flowing 600 miles (960 km) E to enter Lake Issyk Kul in the Kirghiz Soviet Socialist Republic. It is used for power and irrigation, especially for cotton crops.

CHUDSKOYE, LAKE, BATTLE OF. A battle took place on the ice in 1224 on Lake Chudskoye, situated in NW Russia, in which the Novgorodians under Alexander Nevsky defeated the Teutonic Knights. *See* **Peipus, Lake.**

CHUKCHI. People of the Chukchi peninsula in extreme NE Siberia. One branch lives as nomadic reindeer herders; the others are maritime fishing people who also hunt whale, walrus, and seal and live in fixed villages. Their language is of the Paleo-Siberian family.

CHULKOV, GEORGY IVANOVICH (1879–1939). Poet. He was hailed as prophet of the new revolutionary philosophy, or mystical anarchism, which revolted against all external conditions.

CHULKOV, MICHAEL DMITRIYEVICH (*c.* 1743–92). Novelist and translator of Marivaux and Fielding. He is remembered for his novel *The Fair Cook or the Adventures of a Debauched Woman* (1770).

CHURCH AND STATE. Church and state were separated by the Bolshevik government's decree of January 23, 1918. Church schooling ceased; the church was stripped of her legal rights and her property confiscated. The Bolsheviks strove to undermine the church's influence on the spiritual life of the people, and an intensive antireligious propaganda campaign was instigated in 1922.

Curtiss, John S., *The Russian Church and the Soviet State 1917–1950,* 1953.

CHUVASH. Autonomous republic in the Russian Soviet Federated Socialist Republic located in Volga valley bounded on the N by the Volga River and on the S by the Sura River. It has an area of 7,064 square miles (18,296 sq km). Its capital is Cheboksary, situated 360 miles (576 km) E of Moscow. The main occupations are farming and lumbering, with related industries as well as engineering, chemicals, and textiles. Population (1981) 1,311,000.

CINEMA, SOVIET. In 1919 the cinema was nationalized and put under the people's commissariat for education; in 1922 the first centralized state cinema, Goskino, was organized; in 1924 this was reorganized into Sovkino. The first films were mostly newsreels and documentaries about the Civil War, and propaganda. The doctrine of Socialist Realism was to limit the scope of cinema, although extremist groups, and masters of the cinema, such as Dovzhenko, Vsevolod Pudovkin and Sergey Mikhailovich Eisenstein, reacted against this. The most famous Soviet silent films, such as Eisenstein's *Battleship Potemkin* (1926) and *October* (1927) and Pudovkin's *Mother* (1926) and *The End of Petersburg* (1927) were made in the 1930s during the Soviet cinema's "golden era." The most popular films were the melodramas, produced with the assistance of Lunacharsky. After the death of Stalin, Soviet cinema entered a new period, although the principles of Socialist Realism still apply.

Leyda, Jay, *Kino: A History of the Russian and Soviet Film,* 1960.

Taylor, R., *The Politics of the Soviet Cinema, 1917–1929,* 1979.

CIRCASSIA. Obsolete name for an area in the N Caucasus in which the Circassians of the early 19th century lived.

CIVIL WAR (1917–22). War following the October Revolution and the enforced dissolution of the constituent assembly, fought between the

Reds, organized by Trotsky *(q.v.)*, and the White generals who supported the provisional government or one of the former parties. In the winter of 1917–18 the Bolsheviks overthrew General Kaledin's *(q.v.)* regime of Don Cossacks and fought anti-Bolshevik supporters in Orenburg and on the Manchurian frontier. The E and S fronts were constituted in the summer of 1918. In March 1919 the Whites under Admiral Kolchak *(q.v.)* were nearing the Volga but were forced back until the capture of Kolchak in 1920. The N front was liquidated in 1920 following the departure of Allied troops in 1919. The Baltic states and the German troops led by General von der Goltz complicated the position as did the intervention of Japan, Finland, Poland, Turkey, and Rumania. The ultimate Red victory was due to the failure of the Whites to organize the peasants and unify their aspirations.

Footman, David, *Civil War in Russia*, 1961.

CMEA. *See* **Council for Mutual Economic Assistance (Comecon).**

COLD WAR. Term used by Bernard Baruch, a United States presidential adviser, in 1947 to describe the state of rivalry between the United States and its allies on the one hand and the USSR and its allies on the other. The "war," which stopped short of actual armed conflict, was fought with political, economic, and propaganda weapons, and gave rise to a great increase in the use of espionage; it arose from the Soviet dominance of E Europe after the Second World War, and the Allies' fear of Soviet military strength as seen against the weakness of W European states. There was also fierce ideological competition as both the capitalist and communist groups sought to extend their spheres of influence.

The struggle was seen most clearly in postwar Germany, particularly in the Soviet attempt to isolate Berlin in 1948–49. This and other Soviet initiatives prompted the formation of the North Atlantic Treaty Organization for mutual defense, set up by the Western powers in 1949. The Cold War has continued since, but fear of nuclear weapons has prevented any outbreak of actual warfare.

Feis, H., *From Trust to Terror: The Onset of the Cold War, 1945–50*, 1970.

La Feber, W., *America, Russia and the Cold War, 1945–1975*, (3rd ed.) 1976.

Seton-Watson, H., *Neither War nor Peace*, 1961.

Yergin, D., *Shattered Peace: The Origins of the Cold War and the National Security State*, 1978.

COLLECTIVE FARMING. *See* **Kolkhoz.**

COLLECTIVISM. Political theory stressing the priority of the collective as opposed to the individual. First formulated in the 18th century, collectivism was to influence future socialist and communist theories.

COLLECTIVIZATION OF AGRICULTURE. Attempt by Stalin to amalgamate individual peasant holdings into collective farms (*kolkhozy*), instigated by the Communist Party in 1929. This met with much resistance, but it was overcome by harsh measures, and by 1937, 93.5 percent of all peasant holdings had been collectivized. However, millions died of starvation, or were sent to forced labor camps, and the agricultural output did not recover its former level until 1938.

Carr, Edward Hallett, *A History of Soviet Russia*, 14 vols., 1952–78.

Davies, R. W., *The Socialist Offensive: the Collectivisation of Soviet Agriculture, 1929–30,* 1976.

Lewin, Moshe, *Russian Peasants and Soviet Power,* 1968.

Nove, Alec, *An Economic History of the USSR,* 1969.

COLLINS, SAMUEL. Physician to Tsar Alexis in Moscow in the early 1660s.

COMECON. *See* **Council for Mutual Economic Assistance.**

COMINFORM (Communist Information Bureau). Established in 1947 by Zhdanov and Malenkov in Belgrade. It aimed to coordinate the activities of world Communist parties but membership was limited to Bulgaria, Czechoslovakia, France, Hungary, Italy, Poland, Rumania, the USSR, and Yugoslavia. In 1948 Yugoslavia was expelled and the headquarters transferred to Bucharest. It was dissolved in 1956.

COMINTERN. The Communist International (Comintern), founded on the initiative of the Russian Communist Party in 1919, was dissolved on May 15, 1943. Its aim was to claim the leadership of communism in the world socialist movement.

Carr, Edward Hallett, *A History of Soviet Russia,* 14 vols., 1952–78.

Degras, Jane (ed.), *The Communist International 1919–1943: Documents,* Vols. 1–3, 1956–65.

Schapiro, Leonard, *The Communist Party of the Soviet Union,* (2nd ed.) 1970.

COMMANDER ISLANDS. *See* **Komandorsky Islands.**

COMMISSAR. Title of various high-ranking officials. Commissars were first appointed by the provisional government after the February 1917 Revolution as the new regime's representatives at the headquarters of army groups on the front and in the provinces where they replaced the former governors. The Bolsheviks extended the use of the title after the October Revolution. The most important of these were the people's commissars, who took the place of the former ministers, and military commissars, who were party functionaries attached in a supervisory capacity to military commanders. People's commissars were renamed ministers in 1946.

COMMITTEE OF MINISTERS. Collective name given to ministers from 1804 to 1906, although in actual fact the committee had few duties and no corporate responsibilities.

COMMUNE (*mir*). The basic unit of Slavic organization was the commune or village. Basically an extended family unit, the commune may have consisted of one dwelling or of many households. Revolutionaries such as Herzen extolled the virtues of the commune. The Socialist-Revolutionary Party strove to strengthen the commune. The Bolsheviks proposed that properties should be administered by the state or commune. Individual communes took it upon themselves to confiscate land from landlords. The commune later referred to a type of *kolkhoz* in which members lived and worked communally and in which private ownership was virtually abolished.

Blum, Jerome, *Lord and Peasant in Russia from the Ninth to the Nineteenth Century,* 1971.

Malia, Martin E., *Alexander Herzen and the Birth of Russian Socialism,* 1961.

Venturi, Franco, *Roots of Revolution,* 1960.

COMMUNISM. State of society that the Communist Party is striving to achieve. The basic aims of communism were first expounded in the *Communist Manifesto* of Marx and Engels. Its main characteristics are the absence of social classes, private property, and the state. Socialism, viewed as a preliminary stage in achieving a communist society, was declared to have been built in the Soviet Union in 1936.

Carew Hunt, Robert N., *The Theory and Practice of Communism: An Introduction,* 1957.

COMMUNIST PARTY. Following the Russian Revolution (1917) the Bolsheviks *(q.v.)* under Lenin emerged as the single, dominant party and adopted the name Communist Party (Bolsheviks). Under Stalin the party grew from a relatively small, elite group to a ruling bureaucracy with a much larger membership. In 1952 "Bolsheviks" was dropped from the party's official name. According to the rules adopted by the 22nd congress of the party on October 31, 1961, the Communist Party of the Soviet Union "unites, on a voluntary basis, the more advanced, politically more conscious section of the working class, collective-farm peasantry and intelligentsia of the USSR," whose principal objects are to build a communist society by means of gradual transition from socialism to communism, to raise the material and cultural level of the people, to organize the defense of the country, and to strengthen ties with the workers of other countries.

The party is built on the territorial-industrial principle. The supreme organ is the party congress. Ordinary congresses are convened not less than once in four years. The congress elects a central committee, which meets at least every six months, carries on the work of the party between congresses, and guides the work of central Soviet and public organizations through party groups within them.

The central committee forms a political bureau to direct the work of the central committee between plenary meetings, a secretariat to direct current work, and a commission of party control to consider appeals against decisions about expulsion. Similar rules hold for the regional and territorial party organizations.

Over 398,340 primary party organizations exist in mills, factories, state machine and tractor stations, and other economic establishments, in collective farms, units of the Soviet army and navy, in villages, offices, educational establishments, and so forth, where there are at least three party members. On January 1, 1978 nearly 42 percent of the members were industrial workers; 13 percent were collective farmers; and 44 percent were office and professional workers. Women accounted for 25.1 percent of all members.

In 1981 the Communist Party had 17,500,000 members. Membership of the Young Communist League was 37,800,000 in 1978.

McAuley, Martin, *Politics and the Soviet Union,* 1977.

Schapiro, Leonard, *The Communist Party of the Soviet Union,* (2nd ed.) 1970.

CONGRESS OF BERLIN (1878). Congress following Alexander II's war with Turkey. Russia had wished to liberate the Balkan Slavs. The San Stefano treaty (1878), which concluded the war, met with much international opposition, as Russia had created a large Bulgaria dependent on Russia. At the Congress of Berlin, Bulgaria was divided and reduced in size, although Russia did obtain S Bessarabia.

CONGRESS OF VIENNA (1814–15). European congress following the downfall of Napoleon. Russia gained most of the Duchy of Warsaw, which became a constitutional kingdom of Poland in union with Russia.

CONSCRIPTION. *See* **Military Service.**

CONSTITUENT ASSEMBLY. Democratically elected assembly that met in Petrograd on January 18, 1918 and which was dissolved by the Bolsheviks after one session. The Bolsheviks lost the election, receiving only 9.8 million votes out of 41.7 million votes; the Socialist Revolutionaries won, and 707 deputies were elected. Some leading Socialist Revolutionaries and Constitutional Democratic deputies were arrested on arriving at Petrograd. At the assembly, the Bolsheviks' request that the Soviet government should be recognized was rejected. They walked out, followed by the Left Socialist Revolutionaries, and the assembly was dispersed by guards following orders from the Bolsheviks.

Carr, E. H., *The Bolshevik Revolution 1917–1923,* 3 vols., 1966.

Schapiro, Leonard, *The Origin of the Communist Autocracy 1917–1922,* 1955.

CONSTITUTION. The first Russian Soviet Federated Socialist Republic constitution adopted in 1918 was replaced in 1924 by the federal constitution, and in 1936 by the Stalin constitution. In 1977 a new constitution was adopted, although, as it states, its intent is to preserve "continuity of ideas and principles." The first part of the constitution deals with the social and political principles of the system, the second with the state and the individual, and the third with the federal nature of the union.

Rigby, T. H., *Rules of the Communist Party of the Soviet Union,* 1977.

Topornin, B., *The New Constitution of the USSR* (trans. M. Saifulin and K. Kostrov), 1980.

CONSTITUTIONAL DEMOCRATIC PARTY (Kadets). Party formed in 1905 of left-wing liberals who wished to establish the English governmental system of a ministry responsible to an elected legislature, elected by universal suffrage. In 1918 they showed little interest in reestablishing the Constituent Assembly and were eventually outlawed by the Bolsheviks.

Hosking, Geoffrey A., *The Constitutional Experiment: Government and Duma, 1907–1914,* 1973.

Mendel, Arthur P., *Dilemmas of Progress in Tsarist Russia: Legal Marxism and Legal Populism,* 1961.

CONSTRUCTIVISM. Movement in art in the 1920s. The Constructivists wished to remove bourgeois elements from art, and to adopt a scientific approach, using industrial materials. The constructions of Rodchenko, such as his *Suspended Construction* of 1921, are examples of this. Tatlin *(q.v.)* designed a fantastic monument to the Third International, commissioned by the government, but it was never built. Constructivism considerably influenced architecture and interior design.

Bowlt, John E. (ed.), *Russian Art of the Avant-Garde: Theory and Criticism 1902–1934,* 1976.

Gray, Camilla, *The Great Experiment: Russian Art, 1863–1922,* 1962, (new ed. 1971).

CONTEMPORARY, THE *(Sovremennik).* Literary quarterly, founded by Pushkin in 1836. After his death it was edited by P. A. Pletnev and was the most influential literary monthly for 20 years. It published most of Turgenev's *Sportsmen's Sketches* and his first two novels. Suppressed by the authorities in 1866, it was replaced by *Otechestvenniye zapiski,* edited by Yevgrafovich Saltykov-Shchedrin and Nicholas Alekseyvich Nekrasov.

COPYRIGHT. Since 1928 copyright in literary and artistic works covers the period of the life of an author and for a subsequent 10–15 years. The author has no copyright in a translation of his work, and in some cases the copyright can be appropriated by the state in the public interest. In this case royalties are payable. Foreign works are not protected unless there is a special treaty with the state concerned.

CORRECTIVE LABOR CAMPS. There are four different kinds of corrective labor colonies, varying by different degrees of severity. A series of laws has been passed from 1961 onward in order to make the conditions harsher. The majority of convicted prisoners serve their sentences in these camps. *See also* **GULag.**

Solzhenitsyn, Alexander, *The Gulag Archipelago,* 3 vols. 1974–78.

COSSACKS. People of S and SW Russia descended from independent Tatar groups and escaped serfs from Poland, Lithuania, and Muscovy. They established a number of independent self-governing communities, which were given special privileges by Russian or Polish rulers in return for military services. Known for their horsemanship, each Cossack community provided a separate army. The Cossacks slowly lost their autonomy as Russia expanded in the 17th and 18th centuries and there were occasional rebellions. Many fled Russia after the Revolution (1918–21), and collectivization subsumed remaining Cossack communities.

COUNCIL FOR MUTUAL ECONOMIC ASSISTANCE (Comecon). The council was founded in 1949 to assist the economic development of its member states through joint utilization and coordination of efforts, particularly industrial development. Development of trade between members has not progressed at the rate expected because of artificial exchange rates between member countries.

Founding members were the USSR, Bulgaria, Czechoslovakia, Hungary, Poland, and Rumania. Later admissions were Albania (1949; ceased participation 1961), Cuba (1972), East Germany (1950), and Mongolia (1962). Since 1964 Yugoslavia has enjoyed associate status with limited participation. Observers are China, North Korea, and North Vietnam.

The supreme authority is the session of the council, usually held annually in members' capitals in rotation under the chairmanship of the head of the delegation of the host country; all members must be present and decisions must be unanimous.

The executive committee is made up of one representative of deputy premier rank from each member state. It meets at least once every three months and has a Bureau of Common Questions of Economic Planning in which each member country is represented by a deputy chairman of its national planning body. The secretariat is based in Moscow.

There is a committee for cooperation in the field of planning and a committee for scientific and technical cooperation set up in 1971 and a committee for material and technical supply set up in 1974. There are permanent commissions on statistics, foreign trade, currency and finance, electricity, peaceful uses of atomic energy, geology, the coal industry, the oil and gas industry, the chemical industry, the iron and steel industry, the nonferrous metals industry, the engineering industry, the radio engineering and electronics industries, light industry, the food industry, agriculture, construction, transport, posts and telecommunications, standardization, civil aviation, and public health.

There are seven standing conferences: for legal problems; of ministers of internal trade; of chiefs of water resources authorities; of chiefs of patent authorities; of chiefs of pricing authorities; of chiefs of labor authorities; and of representatives of freight and shipping organizations.

There are three semiautonomous bodies within the CMEA: the institute of standardization; the bureau for the coordination of ship freight, and the international institute of economic problems of the world socialist system.

In 1980 there were 20 technical and economic agencies associated with the CMEA.

CMEA is the official abbreviation. Other unofficial abbreviations are Comecon and Cema. Comecon is also current in French and German along with vernacular formulations. The working language of the organization is Russian. The Russian form of the name is Soviet Ekonomicheskoy Vzaymopomoshchi (SEV).

The flag is red with a white central emblem consisting of a star and five curved arrows pointing to the center.

Kaser, Michael, *Comecon,* (2nd ed.) 1967.

Kaser, Michael, *Soviet Economics,* 1970.

COUNCIL OF NATIONALITIES. One of two chambers of the All-Union Congress of Soviets. The council chooses its own presidium, which in turn constitutes the presidium of the congress. Under the Stalin constitution of 1936, the Supreme Council also consisted of two chambers, one of which was the Council of Nationalities.

COUNCIL OF PEOPLE'S COMMISSARS. Council formed at the all-Russian Congress of Soviets held in 1917, headed by Lenin. Although legislative authority was theoretically the responsibility of the central executive committee, legislative power was frequently exercised by the Council of People's Commissars. In 1946, it was renamed the Council of Ministers.

COUNCIL OF STATE. Council formed in 1810 by Tsar Alexander I, in the charge of the Council of Ministers. Its members were appointed by the emperor. It was an advisory rather than legislative body, and the emperor was not obliged to follow their advice. In 1906, Count Witte redefined its role; only half of its members were to be appointed; the rest were to be elected.

COURLAND, DUCHY OF. Duchy, at times under Polish and Russian rule. *See* **Kurland.**

COURLAND, LATVIA. Region between the Gulf of Riga and the Lithuanian border. It is mainly agricultural. The main products are cereals, flax, and potatoes. *See* **Kurland.**

COZENS, ALEXANDER (1717–86). Russian-born English draftsman and landscape artist.

CPSU. Communist Party of the Soviet Union.

CRIMEA. Ukrainian peninsula extending 120 miles (192 km) into the Black Sea and approximately 210 miles (336 km) from W to E. It is joined to the mainland by the Perekop isthmus. It has an area of 9,880 square miles (25,590 sq km). The capital is Simferopol. Its terrain consists of dry but fertile steppes with mountains parallel to the S coast. The climate on the steppes is arid, and Mediterranean on the coast. The main occupations are farming and fishing. Metallurgical industries are based on the iron fields of Kerch, and tourism is important on the coast.

CRIMEAN WAR (1854–56). War fought by Turkey, Great Britain, and France against Russia. France and Turkey disputed over rival claims to control the Holy Places in Palestine; Tsar Nicholas I demanded that the

Turkish government recognize the Orthodox Church and population in Turkey. Despite Nicholas's desire for a peaceful settlement, Turkey declared war on Russia in 1853 and was shortly followed by Great Britain and France. Russia was defeated and at the Treaty of Paris (1856) ceded Bessarabia to Moldavia and agreed to the neutralization of the Black Sea area. Its influence in Europe was by then considerably diminished.

Anderson, M. S., *The Eastern Question 1774–1923: A Study in International Relations,* 1966.

French Blake, R. L. V., *The Crimean War,* 1971.

CUBAN CRISIS (October 1962). Crisis which brought the world to the brink of nuclear war. Khrushchev shipped intercontinental missiles to Cuba, which if installed, would have resulted in most of the United States being within reach of land-based Soviet rockets armed with nuclear warheads. President Kennedy, however, forced Khrushchev to remove the missiles from Cuba.

Talbott, Strobe, *Khrushchev Remembers,* 2 vols. 1971 and 1974.

CUI, CÉSAR ANTONOVICH (1835–1918). Russian composer of songs, operas, and piano music. He was also a music critic. The son of a French prisoner of 1812, he entered the St. Petersburg Academy of Military Engineering in 1857 and later lectured there. He began to compose and was music critic of the *St. Petersburg.* The sources of his operas are both Russian and French. His short piano compositions are considered his best work.

Zetlin, Mikhail O., *The Five: The Evolution of the Russian School of Music,* 1959.

CUMANS. *See* **Polovtsians.**

CURZON LINE. Polish-Soviet armistice line proposed by Lord Curzon, British foreign minister, in 1920. Although not intended to be the Polish E frontier, it was publicized as such during the Second World War.

CYRIL AND METHODIUS, SAINTS. Cyril (827–?); Methodius, (825–?). Two Greek brothers who influenced the religious development of the Slavs. They translated the Holy Scriptures into what is now known as Old Church Slavonic, inventing a Slavic alphabet based on Greek characters, which later evolved into the Cyrillic alphabet.

Obolensky, Dimitri, *The Byzantine Commonwealth: Eastern Europe 500–1453,* 1971.

CYRIL OF TUROV, SAINT. Bishop of Turov in the 12th century. Some of his sermons, carefully composed and full of subtle rhetorical devices, have been preserved.

CYRILLIC ALPHABET. Saint Cyril (827–?) composed an alphabet based on Greek characters, used originally for writing Old Church Slavonic. This evolved into the present-day Cyrillic script. *See* **Alphabet**.

CZAR. *See* **Tsar.**

D

DACHA. A small Russian country house or villa.

DAGESTAN. Autonomous republic in the Russian Soviet Federated Socialist Republic. It lies between the E ranges of the Great Caucasus mountains and the Caspian Sea. Annexed from Persia in 1723, it was formally ceded to Russia by the Treaty of Gulistan in 1813 and was constituted an autonomous republic in 1921. It has an area of 19,416 square miles (50,287 sq km) and is mountainous with a narrow coastal plain. The capital is Makhachkala. The chief occupation is farming, especially cattle and sheep, wheat, grapes, and cotton. Some deposits of oil and natural gas are in the region, and industries include engineering, oil, chemicals, textiles, woodworking, and food processing. Population (1979) 1,600,000.

DAGMAR, PRINCESS MARY (MARIA FEDOROVNA) (1847–1928). Daughter of King Christian IX of Denmark and sister of Queen Alexandra of Great Britain, she was betrothed to Nicholas, heir of Tsar Alexander II. Nicholas died at the age of 22, before succeeding to the throne, and the future tsar, Alexander III, married her in his stead in 1866. Later, as dowager empress, she retained considerable influence over her son, Tsar Nicholas II.

DAHL, VLADIMIR IVANOVICH (1801–72). Writer who also used the pseudonym Kazak Luganski. Pioneer of the realistic ethnographic school. He compiled the *Comprehensive Dictionary of the Living Great-Russian Language,* in four volumes (1861–68), and *Proverbs of Russian Folk* (1862), which contains over 30,000 proverbs. His complete works, including songs, novels, and essays, were published in 10 volumes (1897–98). He was an honorary member of the St. Petersburg Academy of Sciences from 1863.

DALSTROY (Far Eastern Construction Trust). A state corporation in the Magadan oblast and NE Yakutia established in 1930 to exploit mineral resources. Until 1953 it was supervised by the chief of administration of corrective labor camps. The trust was abolished in 1957.

Petrov, V., *It Happens in Russia*, 1951.

DAN, FEDOR ILYICH (1871-1947). Socialist writer and leader. He initially collaborated with Lenin, but later joined the Mensheviks. In 1894 he joined the Social Democratic movement and actively supported the St. Petersburg "Union of Struggle for the Liberation of the Working Class." In 1902 the Marxist paper *Iskra* began to publish his articles. Although frequently imprisoned or exiled, he remained active and in 1906 became a permanent member of the Menshevik central committee. Following the February Revolution, Dan was one of the most influential leaders in the executive council of the Soviets and aroused the opposition of the Bolsheviks, who arrested him in 1921. In 1922 he emigrated, first to Berlin, and later to Paris. He became an editor of the *Sotsialisticheskiy Vestnik* (Socialist Courier) and was the Menshevik representative to the Second International. In 1940, he settled in the United States and wrote *The Origin of Bolshevism* (1946).

Ascher, Abraham (ed.), *The Mensheviks in the Russian Revolution*, 1976.

DANIEL, YU (or Yuliy) (1925-). Verse translator and writer. Before his trial in 1966, Daniel published four stories—*This is Moscow Speaking*, *Hands*, *The Man from M.I.N.A.P.*, and *The Atonement*—under the pseudonym of Nikolai. His writing is frequently bitterly satirical and critical of the Soviet regime. In 1965, Daniel was arrested in Moscow at the time of a new wave of arrests of dissidents and intellectuals, and was tried in February 1966, with A. Sinyavsky (also known as Abram Terts). For the first time in the history of the Soviet Union, authors were thus put on trial for what they had written. The trial was also unusual in that Daniel and Sinyavsky surprised the prosecution by pleading not guilty. Despite substantial internal support and much international concern, Daniel was sentenced to five years hard labor and Sinyavsky to seven years. Daniel was released in 1979.

Labedz, Leopold and Hayward, Max (eds.), *On Trial: The Case of Sinyavsky and Daniel*, 1967.

DANIELSON, NICHOLAS FRANTSEVICH (1844-1918). Liberal populist. He translated the first volume of Marx's *Capital* into Russian, but although he agreed with much of the Marxian theory of capitalism he could not agree that the theory was applicable to Russia.

DANIIL (?-1547). Metropolitan of Moscow from 1521, he continued the teachings of St. Joseph of Volokolamsk (1439-1515) in supporting those known as the possessors, who maintained that the church needed luxurious surroundings for the performance of its functions.

Fennell, John L. I., "The Attitude of the Josephians and the trans-Volga Elders to the Heresy of the Judaizers," in *Slavonic and East European Review*, 1951.

DANIIL ALEKSANDROVICH (1261–1303). Youngest son of Alexander Nevsky and grand prince of Moscow. In 1276 the appanage principality of Moscow was created for Daniil by his father. Daniil extended the principality downstream along the Moscow River, eventually gaining control of the river mouth and lower course from a Riazan prince. He was succeeded by his son Yury, who ruled from 1303 to 1325.

DANIIL, PRINCE OF VOLYNIA (1202–64). Also known as Daniil of Galicia and Danilo Romanovich. Son of Prince Roman, he ruled from 1221 to 1264. He encouraged migrants and trade, and was also a great patron of learning and the arts. He founded many cities, including Lvov, which rivaled Kiev as a center for trade. Much of his enlightened rule was negated by the Mongol invasion of 1240–41. He submitted to the khan's suzerainty but gradually developed his power and forged links with the West with a view to defeating the khan. He drove the Mongols out of Volynia *c.* 1257 and fought off another invasion in 1260. As part of his development of links with his western neighbors, he married off his sons to princesses of Austria, Hungary and Lithuania, and acknowledged Pope Innocent IV as head of the church in his domain. For this last action he received a king's crown from the pope, the only Russian ruler ever to do so.

DANILEVSKY, GRIGORIY PETROVICH (1829–90). Historical novelist. His works include *Mirovich* (1879), *Moscow in Flames* (1886, English translation 1917), *The Black Year* (1888–89), and *The Princess Tarakanova* (trans. 1891).

DANILEVSKY, NICHOLAS YAKOVLEVICH (1822–85). Naturalist and Slavophile. He was the first to propound a biological foundation for the Slavophile philosophy and doctrine, which envisaged the final triumph of the Slavs over the West.

McMaster, R. E., *Danilevsky: A Russian Totalitarian Philosopher*, 1961.

Petrovich, Michael B., *The Emergence of Russian Pan-Slavism, 1856–70*, 1956.

Simmons, Ernest J. (ed.), *Continuity and Change in Russian and Soviet Thought*, 1955.

DANILOVA, ALEXSANDRA (1906–). Ballerina. After training at the Russian Imperial and Soviet State ballet schools in Leningrad, she worked at the Maryinsky Theater. She left the Soviet Union in 1924, joined Diaghilev and the Ballet Russe, and worked with them from 1925 to 1929. Her most important roles included *Le Pas d'Acier, Apollon Musagètes,* and *The Gods go a'Begging.* From 1933 to 1937 she was a member of Colonel de Basil's company, and from 1938–58 she was prima ballerina of Massine's Ballet Russe de Monte Carlo. For many years she taught and lectured on ballet. In 1975 she choreographed

Coppélia with George Balanchine for the New York City Ballet and she made her screen debut in *The Turning Point* in 1977.

DANNENBERG, P. A. (1792–1872.) Senior general at the battle of Inkerman, a major engagement of the Crimean War fought in thick fog on November 5, 1854. He had previously been unsuccessful in the Danube campaign and on this occasion, in spite of considerable reserves that would have won the day for Russia had he utilized them, he ordered a retreat and allowed the allies to regain lost territory.

DANUBE, MOUTH OF THE. By the Treaty of Adrianople (1829), the settlement ending the Russo-Turkish War of 1828, Russia was granted control over the mouth of the Danube in addition to territory in the Caucasus, the right to establish a protectorate over the Danubian principalities, and other gains. However, in 1856 the Russians ceded the mouth of the Danube to Turkey by the Treaty of Paris. Russian influence in the area was diminished when Danubian principalities were placed under the guarantee of the signatory powers, and an international commission was established to ensure the safe navigation of the Danube.

DANUBIAN PRINCIPALITIES. In 1812 Napoleon objected to Russian control of the Danubian principalities of Moldavia and Walachia *(q.q.v.)*, as they were a threat to the growth of French influence in the Near East. By the Treaty of Adrianople (1829) Turkey recognized a Russian protectorate over the principalities, which were, however, to enjoy an autonomous existence. In 1848 Russia intervened to suppress a revolution by the Rumanian national movement. Russian occupation of the Danubian principalities in 1853, in an attempt to force the Turks to come to terms in the so-called Holy Land controversy, precipitated the Crimean War *(q.v.)*, which began in the same year. Moldavia and Walachia were occupied by Austria to separate the Russians from the Turks in the Balkans; eventually peace was established in 1856. Under the Treaty of Paris (1856) the Danubian principalities were placed under the joint guarantee of the signatory powers.

DARDANELLES. Straits separating European and Asiatic Turkey, and connecting the Aegean Sea with the Sea of Marmara. They are about 45 miles (72 km) long and between 1 and 5 miles (1.6 to 8 km) wide. The straits were part of Turkey from 1453. From the days of Catherine the Great, Russia wanted to secure free passage for its warships through the straits, while preventing non-Black Sea powers from doing so. Great Britain, on the other hand, wished to prevent Russia from reaching the Aegean Sea. However, the Treaty of Kuchuk Kainarji *(q.v.)* in 1774, between Russia and Turkey, opened the straits to Russian commercial navigation, and by the Treaty of Unkiar Skelessi *(q.v.)* in 1833, Turkey promised to close the straits to all non-Black Sea powers. The Treaty of Paris in 1856, the Treaty of London in 1871, and the Treaty in Berlin *(q.q.v.)* in 1878 prohibited the warships of all nations from using the straits. After the First World War, at the Treaty of London in 1915, the straits became part of Russia, although the October revolutionaries later canceled imperial secret treaties. The role of the straits in peacetime and in wartime was further discussed in Lausanne in 1923, and at Montreux in 1936. Turkey modified the Montreux agreement in 1945 to allow unrestricted transportation of Allied supplies to the USSR.

DARGINS. Caucasian-speaking Muslim people inhabiting the central part of E Dagestan and numbering about 160,000.

DARGOMYZHSKIY, ALEXANDER SERGEEVICH (1813–69). Composer. Largely self-taught, he became a talented amateur musician when young. He received encouragement from Glinka and decided to compose. His first opera, *Esmeralda* (1847), performed eight years after its composition, was not a success. *The Russalka* (1856) and *The Triumph of Bacchus* (1867) were received more warmly. He wrote some songs and orchestral fantasias. From 1866 he started work on setting *The Stone Guest*, a play by Pushkin, to music. The work was completed by César Antonovich Cui (1835–1918) and orchestrated by Rimsky-Korsakov (1844–1908) *(q.q.v.)*. It was performed in Leningrad in 1872.

Abraham, Gerald, E. H., *On Russian Music*, 1935 and *Studies in Russian Music*, 1939.

DARUGA. Head of a special department handling Russian affairs established when Batu Khan, grandson of Genghis Khan, made his headquarters at Old Savay in 1240 following the subjugation of most of Russia by the Golden Horde.

DARWINISM. The evolutionary theories of Charles Darwin (1809–82) influenced the Pan-Slavism *(q.v.)* movement, which recognized the struggle for survival and aimed to unite all Slavic-speaking peoples.

DARYAL (DARIEL). Pass through the Caucasus mountains situated 70 miles (112 km) N of Tbilisi and overlooked by Mount Kazbek (16,558 feet/5,050 meters). The Georgian Military Highway crosses the pass. Mentioned in *The Demon* by Lermontov, it was fortified from early times, and was known in the classical period as the Gates of Alan and the Caucasus or Iberian Gates.

DAS KAPITAL. *See* ***KAPITAL, DAS.***

DASHAVA. Rich natural gas field in the Ukraine that has been worked since 1924. The town of Dashava is at the head of a 325-mile (523-km) gas pipeline to Kiev, Lvov, Minsk, and Moscow.

DASHKOVA, PRINCESS CATHERINE ROMANOVNA VORONTSOVA (1743/4–1810). Patron of literary arts in Russia during the 18th century. She belonged to an influential family. Her uncle was chancellor under Tsaritsa Elizabeth and her sister was mistress to Peter III, the husband of Catherine. In 1759, she married Prince Michael Ivanovich Dashkov. Princess Dashkova was associated with the plans, after Tsaritsa Elizabeth's death (1761), to overthrow Peter III and to make Catherine regent for her son Paul. She also took part in the plans to place Catherine on the throne in 1762.

Princess Dashkova traveled and lived much in Europe, but in 1782 she was appointed by Catherine II to direct the St. Petersburg Academy of Arts and Sciences. In September 1783 she became first president of the Russian Academy, which, under her supervision and influence, compiled a Russian dictionary. Her other literary activities included editing a journal and writing plays.

Following the death of Catherine and the accession of Paul, Princess Dashkova was forced to retire and was banished to a village near Novgorod. When Alexander I became tsar she was allowed to live just outside Moscow.

Memoirs of the Princess Dashkova Written by Herself (in English), 1840.

Troyat, Henri, *Catherine the Great* (English edition), 1979.

DASHNAKTSUTYUN. The "Confederacy" party, commonly called Dashnaks, was a national revolutionary grouping founded in Turkish Armenia in 1890. The party started to recruit Russian Armenians, with the aim of establishing an independent state of Great Armenia. When Tsar Nicholas II closed many Armenian schools, libraries, and newspaper offices in 1903, and took over the property of the Armenian Church, the Dashnaks carried out a policy of civil disobedience in Russia in 1903–05. They supported the provisional government but were opposed to the Bolshevik Revolution Party in the independent Armenian republic of 1918–20, which became the chief party. Even today the party is in existence and aims at achieving an independent Armenia.

DATOV, SARYM (*fl.* late 18th century). Leader of an anti-Russian uprising of the Kazakhs in 1783–97.

DAUGAVPILS. Town on the W Dvina River in Latvia, founded by the Livonian Knights in 1278. A trading center for grain, flax, and timber, it also manufactures textiles and food products. Industries include railway engineering. Population (1976) 112,000.

DAVLET-GERAY, KHAN. Leader of the Crimean Tatars. He led his army against Moscow in 1571, having failed to take Astrakhan in 1569. He failed to storm the Kremlin but much of the city and surrounding area was destroyed. The troops departed with 100,000 prisoners and considerable loot. He was defeated by the Russians in 1572.

DAVIDOV, DENIS VASILEVICH (1784–1839). Cossack general, poet, and military writer. He led a partisan force during Napoleon's retreat from Moscow. His theories on partisan warfare included combining the discipline of the European command system with primitive Asian methods. He wrote *Essay on the Theory of Partisan Action* and several collections of patriotic verse, including *The Hussar Feast* and *Contemporary Songs*. Tolstoy is said to have used him as a model for Denisov in *War and Peace*.

DEATH PENALTY. Capital punishment was abolished on May 26, 1947, but was restored on January 12, 1950, for treason, espionage, and sabotage; on May 7, 1954, for certain categories of murder; in December 1958, for terrorism and banditry; on May 7, 1961, for embezzlement of public property, counterfeiting and attack on prison warders, and, in particular circumstances, for attacks on the police and public order volunteers; on February 15, 1962 for rape; and on February 20, 1962 for accepting bribes.

DEBORIN (IOFFE), ABRAM MOYSEEVICH (1881–). Historian and philosopher. He became a Bolshevik in 1903, went over to the Mensheviks in 1907, but eventually joined the Communist Party in 1928. He was editor of the chief Marxist philosophical journal, *Under the Banner of Marxism,* and secretary of the department for history and philosophy in the Academy of Sciences (1935–45). His writings argued against mechanical materialism, but he was condemned as a "Menshevik idealist." His works included *Introduction to the Philosophy of Dialectical Materialism,* 1916; *Dictatorship of the Proletariat and the Theory of Marxism,* 1927; *Dialectical Materialism,* 1929; and *Lenin and the Crisis of Modern Physics,* 1930.

Hecker, J., *Moscow Dialogues,* 1933.

Wetter, Gustav A., *Dialectical Materialism,* 1958.

DECEMBRISTS (DEKABRISTY). Members of an anti-tsarist revolt in December 1825, following the death of Alexander I. They were members of various clandestine organizations organized following the Napoleonic Wars by former military officers, who, after being exposed to Western liberalism, had become discontented on their return to Russia with the country's reactionary government. The revolt failed largely because of poor organization, and five leaders were executed and their followers imprisoned or exiled to Siberia.

Mazour, Anatole Grigorevich, *The First Russian Revolution, 1825,* 1966.

Raeff, Marc, *The Decembrist Movement,* 1966.

Zetlin, Mikhail O., *The Decembrists* (trans. George Panin), 1958.

DECREE ON THE PRESS. A set of rules issued by the provisional government in April 1917 to control printing and publishing. A number of copies of the book or journal had to be submitted to various officials for their perusal. Authors and editors were also obliged to print an official denial or correction as directed by the provisional government in the place of passages disapproved of by the government, without altering the text of the alteration provided by the government. *See* **Censorship.**

DE LA MOTHE, VALLIN (1729–80). Architect. De la Mothe, who was of French extraction, worked as an architect in St. Petersburg, Moscow and the provinces from 1759 to 1775. In St. Petersburg he built the Catholic church of St. Catherine on the Nevsky Prospekt, and the Small Hermitage (1764). De la Mothe's work contains the characteristics of the Russian early classical style.

DE LONG ISLANDS. A group of islands in the Yakut Autonomous Soviet Socialist Republic, NE of the New Siberian Islands in the E Siberian Sea, which include Bennett, Henrietta, and Jeannette Islands. They were named after George Washington De Long, the American navigator and explorer, who discovered them in 1879.

DELVIG, BARON ANTON ANTONOVICH (1798–1831). Poet. He became a leading member of Pushkin's "Pleiade" circle, and chief organizer of its literary activities. His few poems are in the classical manner while his songs were modeled on folk poetry. He was editor of *Severniye tsvety* from 1825 and in 1830 began publication of *Literaturnaya Gazeta* (Literary Gazette).

DELYANOV, IVAN (1818–97). Alexander III appointed him head of the Ministry of Education in 1882. He supported autocracy and was opposed to revolutionaries, but he continued Dmitry Tolstoy's *(q.v.)* education policies, keeping a tight control on education and exercising discipline. A circular he issued in 1887 appealed to his subordinates to keep socially undesirable elements or "children of coachmen, servants, cooks, washerwomen, small shopkeepers, and persons of similar type" out of the classical gymnasiums, which were the only places of secondary education that one could advance to a university from.

DEMIDOV, PAUL GRIGOREVICH (1738–1821). Member of a wealthy family and patron of the arts. He founded the Demidov law school at Yaroslavl in 1805.

DEMOCRATIC CENTRALISM. The guiding principle of the Communist Party organization. Elections of party members or delegates are held by all leading party bodies. Inspection of and reporting on the efficiency of the lower to higher bodies takes place regularly. There is strict party discipline and the subordination of the minority to the majority. All decisions of the higher authority are binding on the lower.

Hough, J. F. and Fainsod, Merle, *How the Soviet Union is Governed,* 1979.

Schapiro, Leonard, *The Communist Party of the Soviet Union,* 1977.

DEMOCRATIC MOVEMENT. During the 19th century at the time of growing dissatisfaction with autocracy, democracy was not emphasized in the programs of the various political movements struggling for reform. The Decembrists had a democratic wing, but the radicals were more interested in spreading socialist ideas. There was, however, a democratic trend among liberal reformers of the 1860s and 1870s, which also manifested itself in the People's Right Party (1894–95), in the Liberation movement of the early 1900s and subsequently in the Constitutional Democratic Party. For 20 years following the revolution, the word "democracy" had bourgeois connotations, and was therefore a pejorative term until the introduction of the Stalin constitution in 1936, which was described as "the most democratic constitution in the world." Measures taken following the death of Stalin were described officially as "further democratization of the regime." In contrast, various dissidents in the Soviet Union are struggling for a very different form of democracy.

***DENGA* (pl. *DENGI*).** A medieval Russian monetary unit, borrowed from the Tatars,w hich ceased to circulate after the 17th century. One silver *denga* equaled half a kopck. In modern Russian *dengi* means "money."

DENIKIN, ANTON IVANOVICH (1872–1947). Distinguished Russian general of the First World War who rose from the ranks. After the Russian Revolution he was imprisoned for supporting Kornilov's attempted revolt against Kerensky's socialist government but escaped to raise an army in the S. Meanwhile (November 1917) the Bolsheviks under Lenin had seized power and Denikin's "White" army, with Allied support, occupied the Ukraine and N Caucasus. As Bolshevik power grew, the "Red" army gradually forced the "Whites" back to the Crimea and in 1920 Denikin abandoned the struggle; he died in exile in France.

Footman, David, *Civil War in Russia,* 1961.

Lehovich, D. V., *Denikin,* 1974.

DENISOV, ANDREI AND SIMEON. Brothers and leaders of the reorganized Old Believers faith in the 18th century. They came from a princely family in N Russia.

DEPRESSION OF 1900. Economic depression following the great industrial expansion of the previous decade. During this period there was considerable political agitation, culminating in the 1905 Revolution five years later.

DERBENT. Port town in Dagestan, Russian Soviet Federated Socialist Republic, situated on the Caspian Sea. Although held by Peter the Great for a short period in 1722, it was not annexed to Russia until 1806. Industries include fishing and fish processing, textiles and wine making, with glassworks nearby. Population (1976) 66,000.

DERZHAVIN, GABRIEL ROMANOVICH (1743–1816). Poet and civil servant. Following a period in the army he worked as a civil servant for over 20 years, becoming in turn provisional governor and minister of justice (1802–05). He dedicated his ode *Felisa* (1783) to Catherine the Great and served briefly as her private secretary. His most influential work was his ode *God* (1784). His poetry is marked by vigor of thought and expression and gives a rich portrait of his time.

Clardy, J. V., *Derzhavin,* 1967.

Cross, Anthony G. (ed.), *Russian Literature in the Age of Catherine the Great,* 1976.

DESNA RIVER. River of the Russian Soviet Federated Socialist Republic, rising approximately 50 miles (80 km) ESE of Smolensk and flowing 700 miles (1,120 km) SSW past Bryansk to join the Dnepr River above Kiev. Navigable below Bryansk, it is used for carrying timber, grain, and other agricultural produce.

DE-STALINIZATION. Name given to official policy that undermined Stalin's hitherto uncontested infallibility. In February 1956, at the Twentieth Congress of the Communist Party of the Soviet Union, Khrushchev attacked the cult of Stalin's personality, and drew attention to the injustices of Stalin's regime. After the Twenty-Second Party Congress, the central committee of the Party published a decree condemning the "cult of the individual" and stressing the need for collective leadership. In 1961, Stalin's body was removed from beside Lenin's in the mausoleum on Red Square, and the numerous busts and pictures of Stalin were destroyed. Places named after Stalin had their names changed, a number of prisoners were released, a freer intellectual atmosphere ensued, and the excesses of forced assimilation were condemned. De-Stalinization also stimulated a process of change in eastern European countries.

Medvedev, Roy V., *Let History Judge,* 1972.

Payre, Roy, *The Rise and Fall of Stalin,* 1966.

Randall, Francis B., *Stalin's Russia,* 1966.

DESYATIN. Land measure equal to 2.7 acres, or 1.092 hectares. *See* **Chetvert.**

DESYATOVSKIY'S REPORT (1841). A. P. Zablotskiy-Desyatovskiy, a government official under Alexander II, produced a report in 1841 on the condition of the serfs, mainly in central European Russia, which gave a horrifying account of the lives of peasant serfs and of the callousness of the average landlord. The report is printed in full in A. P. Zablotskiy-Desyatovskiy, *Graf Kiselev i ego Vremya,* Vol. IV, 1882.

DÉTENTE. Attempts at relaxing or easing tension, particularly between the countries of E and W Europe. Intense hostility between the United States and the USSR ended in 1953 after Stalin's death. After 1963, and the Cuban missile crisis, both superpowers became aware of the need to prevent nuclear warfare. Accordingly, in 1967, the Outer Space Treaty, and in 1968 the Treaty on the Non-Proliferation of Nuclear Weapons, worked toward this goal, as did the normalization of relations between East and West Germany, the Treaty of Non-Agression between the USSR and West Germany in 1970, the Four Power Agreement on Berlin in 1971, and the Seabed Arms Control Treaty, also of 1971. In 1971–72 the United States' decision to end its military intervention in Vietnam enabled the Kremlin to feel more able to seek détente, although the Sino-American rapprochement made the Soviet leaders apprehensive that the United States would curry favor with Mao, thus providing Beijing (Peking) with technological aid. In 1972, after his visit to Moscow, President Nixon proclaimed the end of the Cold War, and the beginning of Soviet-American détente. Such events as the invasion of Afghanistan and the nuclear arms debate have not, however, enhanced détente.

DETY BOYARSKIYE. Lesser gentry who were minor servitors of the princes.

DEULINO, TRUCE OF (1618–19). Truce that lasted 14½ years and that terminated Russian-Polish hostilities begun in the Time of Troubles (1606–13). In 1609 the Polish King Sigismund III declared war on Russia and besieged Smolensk. In 1610 the leading Muscovite boyars accepted Sigismund's son Wladyslaw as their ruler, but Sigismund decided to take the throne himself and resumed the war. His troops burned large parts of Moscow and occupied the Kremlin, and in 1611 they took Smolensk. A Russian army succeeded in recapturing Moscow and Michael Romanov was elected tsar by a *zemsky sobor.* The Wladyslaw campaign of 1617–18, in which Michael reached but did not take Moscow, ended with the Truce of Deulino, by which the Poles kept Smolensk and other conquered W Russian lands. The Poles had to release Russian envoys taken prisoner in 1610. Hostilities were resumed in 1632 when the truce expired, but the Russians were unable to retake Smolensk and had to accept the Treaty of Polyanov (1634), by which they were obliged to pay 20,000 rubles to the Poles. In return Wladyslaw renounced his claim to the Russian throne and recognized Michael as the rightful tsar.

DEUTSCH, LEV GRIGOREVICH (1855–1943). Revolutionary. He joined the populists in Kiev (1876), participated in the Chigirin conspiracy (1877), and was a joint founder of the populist "Black Repartition" and later of the "Liberation of Labor," the first Russian Marxist group abroad. In 1884 Deutsch was arrested in Germany and handed back to Russia, where the government sentenced him to 16 years' hard labor; as a result he wrote *Sixteen Years in Siberia.* In 1903 he joined the Mensheviks and, having participated in the 1905 Revolution, he was again arrested in 1906. He lived for some years in W Europe and the United States, where he became editor of the socialist paper *Noviy Mir* (New World).

DEVELOPED SOCIALISM. A once obscure term used by Lenin, currently predominant in Soviet theory, used to describe the stage between primitive socialism, in which the foundations of socialism were laid down, and full communism, which had not yet been achieved. In 1969, Brezhnev referred to a "developed socialist society" and after the Twenty-Fourth Party Congress in 1971, the term became widespread in theoretical journals.

Kelly, D. R. (ed.), *Soviet Politics in the Brezhnev Era,* 1980.

DEYNEKA, ALEXANDER ALEKSANDROVICH (1899–). Painter and sculptor. When Socialist Realism was imposed by the Soviet authorities he managed to preserve some of his earlier style in his works, which included sports, industrial, and military scenes. Many of his murals can be seen in Moscow underground stations.

James, C. Vaughan, *Soviet Socialist Realism,* 1973.

DEZHNEV, SEMEN (1605–72/3). Explorer and Cossack adventurer. He was the first known person to navigate the Bering Strait (1648), thus establishing that Asia and North

America were separate land masses. With Fedor Popov he was the first to sail round the NE corner of Asia. His reports of various expeditions were not discovered until 1736, and in the meantime (1728) Vitus Bering *(q.v.)* had sailed through the strait that bears his name.

DIAGHILEV, SERGE PAVLOVICH (1872–1929). Ballet impresario, born in Novgorod. In pursuit of his goal of introducing Russian art to W Europe, he presented (1908) Shalyapin *(q.v.)* in a season of Russian opera in Paris. He followed this up with his famous Ballets Russes, presented in Paris (1909) and London (1911), in the conviction that in ballet he could form a union of all the arts. To this end he secured the services of dancers of outstanding skill—Pavlova, Nijinsky, Karsavina, and Lopokova—and choreographers such as Fokine and Massine; he commissioned Benois, Bakst, Matisse, Picasso, Braque, and others to design the decor, and Debussy, Ravel, Stravinsky, and Prokofiev to compose ballet scores. The Revolution broke his links with Russia, but with Paris as its headquarters his company continued to enjoy the highest reputation.

Grigoriev, Sergey L., *The Diaghilev Ballet,* 1953.

Spencer, Charles, *The World of Serge Diaghilev,* 1974.

DIALECTICAL MATERIALISM. The philosophy of the world communist movement, propounded by Marx and Engels, and later adopted by Lenin. Materialism stresses the priority of matter and the secondary importance of the mind, thus denying the possibility of a transcendental reality. Marx and Engels argued that materialism ceases to be mechanistic, and becomes dialectical; chemical processes give rise to living processes, and living organisms develop consciousness. Thus everything is in a continual state of becoming; nothing is permanent, and all things contain contradictory aspects, the tension of which will transform them. The materialist conception of history states that environment conditions human development; man must therefore cooperate to change the institutions of society, thus becoming in charge of his own condition. Hitherto, the state has been the instrument of the ruling class; the exploited must destroy it and create a workers' socialist state.

Wetter, Gustav A., *Dialectical Materialism*, 1958.

DICKSON ISLAND. Island situated at the mouth of Yenisei gulf in the Kara Sea, Arctic Ocean, off Krasnoyarsk Territory in the Russian Soviet Federated Socialist Republic. It has an area of 12 square miles (31 sq km). The chief settlement is Dickson Harbor, a government polar and coaling station.

DICTATORSHIP OF THE PROLETARIAT. In Marxist theory, the temporary continuation of state power after the Revolution. Eventually there will be no need of government, because government is based on class, and so therefore it follows that the state will "wither away."

Lenin, Vladimir Ilyich, *The State and Revolution*, 1927.

Walker, A., *Marx: His Theory and Its Context*, 1978.

DIDELOT, CHARLES (-LOUIS) (1767–1837). Swedish-born French dancer, choreographer, and teacher who anticipated the Romantic ballet in his work. In 1801 he left Paris to become ballet master and choreographer of the St. Petersburg Imperial School of Ballet (now the Soviet State School of Ballet, Leningrad), where he stayed until 1811. After a time in London and Paris he returned (1816) to St. Petersburg, where he remained for the rest of his life, producing over 50 ballets there. These illustrated the principles of his own teacher, Jean-Georges Noverre, and had a marked Romantic element. As a teacher he was himself considered revolutionary. His ballets included *Flore et Zéphere*, produced in 1796 in London and considered his finest work. His wife, Rose (Colinette) Didelot, was also a dancer.

Rozlavleva, N., *Era of the Russian Ballet, 1770–1965*, 1966.

DIDEROT, DENIS (1713–84). French man of letters and philosopher, chief editor of the French *Encyclopédie*. The first three volumes of this monumental work were translated into Russian very quickly after publication and the work was supervised by the director of Moscow University. The completion in 1772 left Diderot without any source of income; on learning of this Catherine the Great bought his library and appointed him librarian on an annual salary for the duration of his life, asking him to keep the books until she needed them. In 1773 Diderot went to St. Petersburg to thank her, staying five months and being received with honor and warmth. He wrote *Plan d'une université pour le gouvernement de Russie* (published 1813–14) for Catherine. However, he soon became disillusioned with Russia's enlightened despotism, as can be gleaned from his *Observations sur les instructions de Sa Majesté Impériale aux députés* (1774).

Crocker, L. G., *Diderot, the Embattled Philosopher*, revised edition, 1966.

DIEBITSCH, COUNT HANS FRIEDRICH ANTON (IVAN IVANOVICH DIBICH-ZABALKANSKIY) (1785–1831). Field marshal chiefly responsible for the Russian victory in the Russo-Turkish War (1828–29), owing to his Balkan campaigns. German-born and educated in Berlin, he joined the Russian army in 1801 and fought in the Napoleonic Wars, acquiring the rank of major general. In 1815 he was present at the Congress of Vienna and subsequently became adjutant general to Alexander I. In 1824 he was appointed chief of the Russian general staff, helping to suppress the Decembrist uprising (1825), and from 1826 to 1832 he served on a secret committee formed by Nicholas I to examine programs for administrative and social reform.

In 1829 he was made commander of the Russian forces in Europe and inflicted three serious defeats on the Turks (at Silistria, at the Kamchyk River near Varna, and at Burgas). A fourth battle at Sliven ensued and Adrianople was forced to capitulate, precipitating the conclusion of the peace treaty of Adrianople. For his successful campaigning Diebitsch was made a field marshal and given the name Zabalkanskiy to commemorate his march across the Balkans. He died of cholera while leading the Russian army against the Polish insurgents of 1830.

DIKIY, ALEKSEI DENISOVICH (1889–1955). Stage and film actor and, from 1922, producer. He is probably best remembered for his portrayal of Stalin in *The Third Blow* (1948).

DIKOE POLE. Steppe frontier.

DINAMO. One of 36 sports societies founded in 1923, having branches throughout the Soviet Union. The Dinamo football teams are particularly well known.

DISRAELI, BENJAMIN (1804–81). British statesman. The Russo-Turkish War was fought during his second period of administration (1874–80) and became a major issue in his foreign policy, because Russian victories posed a threat to the route to India. Disraeli calculated that Russia was exhausted by the war and would react to a threat of British intervention. The result was the Treaty of San Stefano (1878). This was later modified by the Congress of Berlin (1878), which Disraeli attended.

DISSIDENTS. The right to dissent remained politically unacceptable under tsarist and Soviet regimes. After the death of Stalin many dissenting intellectuals made their appearance; these included Amalrik, Sakharov, and Solzhenitsyn.

Conybeare, F. C., *Russian Dissenters*, 1921.
Reddaway, Peter, *Uncensored Russia: The Human Rights Movement in the Soviet Union*, 1972.
Rothberg, Abraham, *The Heirs of Stalin: Dissidence and the Soviet Regime, 1953–1970*, 1972.
Shatz, M. S., *Soviet Dissent in Historical Perspective*, 1980.
Tokés, R. L. (ed.), *Dissent in the USSR*, 1975.

DISTRICT DUMA. Pre-Revolutionary local municipal council, elected by limited franchise.

DIVORCE. Legal changes in the 1960s caused divorce to become easier and thus more widespread: in 1950, there were .4 cases of divorce per thousand; in 1979, there were 3.6 per thousand. The divorce rate is higher in cities such as Moscow and Leningrad than it is in rural areas. Divorce costs between 50 and 200 rubles, depending on the couple's income, and the authorities decide in each case who is to pay.

DJILAS, MILOVAN. (1911–). One-time Yugoslav party and government official, chief propagandist, and closest friend of Tito. Djilas was born of peasant origins in 1911 in Montenegro. After studying at Belgrade University he joined the illegal CPY in 1932, in 1938 was made a member of the central committee by Tito, and in 1940 was made a member of the Politburo. During the Second World War Djilas was a member of Tito's supreme headquarters, and for a while led partisan forces in Montenegro. After Tito had fallen from Moscow's favor in 1948, Djilas was blamed by Moscow for being responsible for "revisionist heresies." Denouncing Stalinism, Djilas assisted Tito in creating Yugoslavia's "self-management socialism." After publishing a series of articles in which he stressed the need for greater freedom, Djilas was brought to trial. He continued to write articles criticizing the regime, and although he was released from prison in 1966, he is forbidden to publish in Yugoslavia. His publications include *The New Class* (1957), *Conversations with Stalin* (1962), and *Memoirs of a Revolutionary* (1973).

DMITRIY (born and died 1553). In 1553 Ivan IV persuaded the Muscovite boyars to swear an oath of allegiance to his newborn son, Dmitriy. The tsar was ill and believed he was dying, and feared that his family would be in danger. The action was resented by the boyars and added to the tension between the monarch and his nobles. Dmitriy died later that year.

DMITRIY DONSKOY (1350–89). Grand prince of Moscow (from 1363), one of the heroes of Russian history. He asserted his dominance over rival princes, but his real importance lies in the fact that, by his two victories over the Golden Horde at the Vozha River and more decisively at Kulikovo, near a crossing of the Don River (hence his additional name), he destroyed the legend of Tatar invincibility. Moreover, even though subsequently defeated, his prestige was so great that the princes of Moscow were thenceforth regarded as national rulers. He was also responsible for the introduction of firearms into the Russian army.

Vernadsky, George, *The Mongols and Russia,* 1953.

Zenkovsky, Serge A., *Medieval Russian Epics, Chronicles and Tales,* 1963.

DMITRIYEV, IVAN IVANOVICH (1760–1837). Author and poet. He wrote much sentimental poetry, principally court and monarchistic odes. He was also the author of proverbs and satires, some lyric poetry and folk-style songs, and 68 didactic fables. He stopped writing in 1803.

Drage, C., *Russian Literature in the Eighteenth Century: The Solemn Ode, the Epic, Other Poetic Genres, the Story, the Novel, Drama,* 1978.

DMITRIYEV, RADKO (1859–1919). Soldier. Bulgarian who served as a general in the Russian army during the First World War. He was murdered at Pyatigorsk by communists in 1919.

DMITRIY, FALSE. Name of three pretenders to the Muscovite throne during the Time of Troubles. All three claimed to be Dmitriy, son of Ivan IV (ruled 1533–84), who had died under mysterious circumstances in 1591 while still a boy.

Fedor I (ruled 1584–98) was the last of the Rurik dynasty and was succeeded by his brother-in-law, Boris Godunov, during whose rule the first False Dmitriy appeared and claimed the throne. Thought by many historians to have been Yuriy Otrepev, one of the Russian gentry who had been a friend of the Romanovs before becoming a monk, the first False Dmitriy seems to have believed that he was who he claimed to be. He pursued his claim in Moscow (1601–02) but fled to Lithuania when threatened with exile. In 1603 he sought armed assistance from Lithuanian and Polish nobles and from the Jesuits, and in 1604 he marched on Russia. Although he was defeated, when Boris died (1605) the government decided to support the pretender and he was proclaimed tsar. Dmitriy enjoyed considerable support until he began to favor Polish friends, disregarding the traditions and customs of the Muscovite court. When he planned a Christian alliance to drive the Turks from Europe, Vasiliy Shuiskiy, one of the boyars, led a coup against him in 1606, murdered him, and became tsar himself.

In August 1607 a second pretender appeared claiming to be the recently murdered tsar; although quite unlike the first Dmitriy in appearance, he attracted a large body of supporters and gained control of S Russia. In spring 1608, he established a base, including a full court and government administration, at Tushino (hence his nickname, Thief of Tushino). His troops ravaged N Russia, and his authority soon rivaled that of Shuiskiy, who, in 1610, forced the pretender to flee to Kaluga. While there the second Dmitriy continued to press his claims until fatally wounded (October 1610) by one of his own followers.

In March 1611 a third False Dmitriy, identified as a deacon named Sidorka, laid claims to the throne; he gained the support of the Cossacks (1612), who were laying waste to the environs of Moscow, and of the people of Pskov (from which he is called Thief of Pskov), but was betrayed and executed.

Platonov, Serge F., *The Time of Troubles: A Historical Study of the Internal Crisis and Social Struggle in Sixteenth- and Seventeenth-Century Muscovy* (trans. J. Alexander), 1970.

Vernadsky, George, *The Tsardom of Moscow, 1547–1682*, 1959.

DMITRIY, PRINCE OF SUZDAL (*c.* 14th century). The death of Ivan the Meek (1359) resulted in a struggle for the title of grand prince between Prince Dmitriy of Suzdal and Ivan's 9-year-old son Dmitriy. Both were descended from Vsevolod III, but Dmitriy of Suzdal was a generation older and therefore claimed seniority. The Mongol suzerain was finally won over by the arguments of Dmitriy of Moscow, who had direct succession in his favor, and Dmitriy of Suzdal abandoned his headquarters in Vladimir without a fight.

DMITRIY, PRINCE OF UGLICH (1581–91). Son of Ivan IV who was mysteriously murdered in 1591 during the rule of his brother Fedor. The regent, Boris Godunov, who ascended the throne on Fedor's death (1598), was suspected of the murder, which, with Fedor's death, brought to an end the Rurik line of imperial succession and necessitated an election. In June 1606, he was canonized and his remains brought to Moscow in a further attempt to convince people that he was dead.

Vernadsky, George, *The Death of the Tsarevich Dmitriy*, (Oxford Slavonic Papers, V), 1954.

DMITRIY ROSTOVSKIY (1651–1709). Ecclesiastical writer and preacher. He entered a monastery in 1668. His most famous works include *Chet'u-Minei* (biographies of saints), a polemic against the Old Believers, and a manuscript of the Bible.

DNEPRODZERZHINSK. Ukrainian town situated 20 miles (32 km) WNW of Dnepropetrovsk on the Dnepr River with important metallurgical industries, especially iron and steel. It also manufactures fertilizers and cement. Population (1974) 242,000.

DNEPROPETROVSK. Ukrainian city situated on the Dnepr River. It is the capital of region of same name and a railway center. It was founded by Potemkin in 1786 as Ekaterinoslav, after Catherine the Great. Industries are based on nearby coal, iron, and manganese, and power from the Dneproges reservoir; they include iron and steel, agricultural engineering, and chemicals. The city manufactures machine tools. Population (1977) 995,000.

DNEPR RIVER. River rising S of Valday hills approximately 170 miles (272 km) W of Moscow in the Smolensk region and flowing 1,400 miles (2,240 km) S and then W through Smolensk, then S through Belorussia to form part of the border with the Ukraine. It passes Kiev and turns SE, widening to a lake approximately 77 miles (123 km) long. It then passes Kremenchug and forms a further lake and then passes Dnepropetrovsk and turns S with a further lake before entering the Black Sea by an estuary below Kherson. It is navigable in the upper course for eight months of the year and in the lower for nine. It forms the Dneproges reservoir for hydroelectric power. The chief tributaries are the Berezina, Pripet, Sozh, and Desna rivers.

DNESTR RIVER. River rising in the Carpathian mountains in W Ukraine and flowing 870 miles (1,392 km) on a meandering course, SE into the Moldavian Soviet Socialist Republic and through it to enter the Black Sea by an estuary W of Odessa. It is ice-free for 10 months.

DOBROLYUBOV, NICHOLAS ALEKSANDROVICH (1836–61). Literary critic from 1856 of the *Contemporary* and essayist. He was a protégé of Nicholas G. Chernyshevsky (*q.v.*), and like him rejected religion. A revolutionary socialist in politics, he was, together with his friend Chernyshevsky, a believer that a critic should explore the deeper meaning of works of art and this school of critical realism had great influence until the end of the century.

Dobrolyubov, Nikolai A., *Selected Philosophical Essays*, 1956.

Masaryk, Tomas G., *The Spirit of Russia: Studies in History, Literature and Philosophy*, 2 vols., revised edition 1955.

DOBRYNYA NIKITICH. A mythological hero set in the Kievan age who was associated with the uncle of St. Vladimir.

DOCTOR ZHIVAGO. Novel by Boris Pasternak, the last part of which consists of poetry written by the main character, Yuriy Zhivago. Pasternak was refused permission to publish it in the Soviet Union, and the manuscript was smuggled out and published in Italy in 1958. It attracted international acclaim. Because of the constant attacks on him within the Soviet Union he refused the Nobel Prize in Literature. The novel encompasses life in Russia between 1903 and 1929, although the epilogue takes place after the Second World War.

"DOCTORS' PLOT." Alleged plot by some Moscow doctors to kill well-known government officials. The "conspiracy" was fully reported in the press in January 1953. The doctors, many of whom were Jewish, were said to have murdered Andrei Zhdanov (1896–1948), head of the Leningrad Party Organization. This was probably the pretext for starting another great purge and was part of Stalin's anti-Semitic policy, but the death of Stalin in March 1953 saved the country from this. All but two of the doctors survived their ordeals and were released, and later Khrushchev stated that there had been no plot whatsoever and that it all had been engineered by Stalin.

Hingley, Ronald, *Joseph Stalin: Man and Legend*, 1974.

Rush, M., *The Rise of Khrushchev*, 1958.

Whitney, J., *Khrushchev Speaks*, 1963.

DOGGER BANK INCIDENT. International incident occurring on October 21, 1904, in the Russo-Japanese War when a Russian fleet under Admiral Zinoviy Rozhdestvenskiy had, while on its way to the Far East, fired by mistake at some English fishing boats on the Dogger Bank, an extensive sandbank in the North Sea, and inflicted casualties. Russia claimed by way of excuse that there were Japanese torpedo boats with the fishing boats.

DOKLADCHIK. Novgorodian 13th century high court jury consisting of 10 men, including a boyar and a commoner from each of the five *kontsy*, presided over by a *posadnik*.

DOLGORUKAYA, PRINCESS (*c.* 18th century). Princess Dolgorukaya was engaged to Peter III in 1729, but the marriage did not take place as he died of smallpox in 1730. She was a member of the Dolgorukiy family, who managed to replace the Menshikovs as court favorites and leading government ministers.

DOLGORUKAYA, PRINCESS CATHERINE (1847–1922). Mistress of Tsar Alexander II (1855–81). The tsar morganatically married her in 1880 on the death of the empress, Maria Aleksandrovna, and conferred on her the title Princess Yurevskaya.

DOLGORUKIY, PRINCE IVAN (1708–39). Adviser to Peter II *(q.v.)* following the downfall of Menshikov.

DOLGORUKIY, PRINCE VASILIY LUKICH (1670–1739). Diplomat. He was ambassador to Denmark (1707–20) and later minister in Paris (1720–22). He was also a member of the Supreme Privy Council and on the death of Peter II (*q.v.*) he was in favor of the "conditions" that would have transferred much of the monarch's power to the nobles. He was beheaded, together with others of his family, for forging Peter II's will.

DOLGORUKIY, PRINCE VASILIY VLADIMIROVICH (1667–1746). Field marshal. He was responsible for the suppression of the mutiny of Bulavin and for this he gained the confidence of Peter I, although later Dolgorukiy opposed many of the tsar's reforms. He was deprived of his rank and title by Peter because of intrigue but was subsequently reinstated. He supported the accession of Anna Ivanovna and helped to compile the "conditions" for her to gain the throne. He was again deprived of his rank and title. In 1741 Empress Elizabeth restored these and he was made president of the War College.

DOMOSTROY. Literary work of Muscovite Russia dating from *c.* 1550, consisting of 63 chapters of instructions to a Muscovite family on "house managership." The work reflects the patriarchal society of the period.

Fennell, J. and Stokes, A., *Early Russian Literature*, 1974.

DON RIVER. River, rising near Tula approximately 130 miles (208 km) SSE of Moscow in the Russian Soviet Federated Socialist Republic, and flowing 1,200 miles (1,920 km) S to Voronezh. It then flows SE to a canal link with the Volga River near Volgograd, then SW by an extensive lake to Tsimlyanskiy, and on to Rostov. It enters the Sea of Azov by a delta. It is navigable to Voronezh, but closed by ice for 3–4 months annually. The river is used for transporting coal, grain, and timber, and for fisheries. Its chief tributaries are the Voronezh, Donets, and Medveditsa rivers.

DONETS BASIN. Coal-mining and industrial region. It has an area of 10,000 square miles (25,000 sq km) and lies N of the Sea of Azov and W of the Donets River. Development of the region began in the 1870s. The name is sometimes abbreviated to Donbas(s).

DONETS RIVER. River, rising in SW of the Russian Soviet Federated Socialist Republic 80 miles (128 km) NNE of Kharkov, and flowing S and SE through the Ukraine, which it enters at Volchansk and leaves again in the SE near Kadiyevka to join the Don River below Konstantinovskiy. It flows through an extensive coalfield and industrial area.

DONETSK. Capital of region in the Ukraine situated N of the Sea of Azov, in a large industrial region in the Donets basin coalfield, with an important metallurgical industry. Manufactures include iron and steel machinery, chemicals and cement. Formerly called Yuzovka, after the Welshman John Hughes (*q.v.*), its name was changed to Stalino after 1917 and in 1961 to Donetsk. Population (1977) 984,000.

DONKEY'S TAIL EXHIBITION. Exhibition of painters held in Moscow (1912) organized by Vladimir Tatlin (*q.v.*), Michael Larionov, Natalya Goncharova (*q.v.*), Kazimir Malevich (*q.v.*), and others. Bright color combinations derived from Russian folk art were a feature of the exhibition.

DOROSHENKO, HETMAN PETER (*fl.* 17th century). Seventeenth-century Ukrainian leader. During this period Muscovy was defending new possessions in the Ukraine against Turkey.

DORPAT. *See* **Tartu.**

DOSTOYEVSKY, FEDOR MIKHAILOVICH (1821–81). Russian novelist. His father, a Moscow doctor, was murdered (1839) by his serfs at his country home, an event which haunted Dostoyevsky all his life. He studied at the Military Engineering College at St. Petersburg but resigned (1844) to take up a literary career. His first novel, *Poor Folk* (1846), achieved considerable success. Disaster overtook him when he was arrested (1849) on a charge of sedition (on the flimsiest of grounds) and condemned to be shot; he was already facing a firing squad when a reprieve arrived. He had to endure four years as a convict and two years of exile in Siberia, an experience that undermined his health, and that he described in his *Memoirs from the House of the Dead* (1861). On his return from exile he engaged in journalistic enterprises that failed and left him deeply in debt, a state aggravated by his passion for gambling. The unhappy marriage that he had contracted while in Siberia ended in 1863 on the death of his wife. In 1865 he traveled to Germany with a young woman, Polina Suslova, to retrieve his fortune by an "infallible" method of winning at roulette. This, of course, failed. On his return he set about writing a potboiler to satisfy his creditors (*The Gambler*). He hired a stenographer, Anna Snitken, and shortly afterwards married her. They again had to go abroad to avoid creditors, a humiliating time for Dostoevsky. His wife gradually restored order to his finances and they returned to Russia. In his later years he evolved a peculiar Slavophilism compounded of hatred for aristocrats and socialists alike, and of religious obsessions. A naturalistic writer, acclaimed by Vissarion Belinsky *(q.v.)*, he was particularly interested in the psychology of the abnormal, because he believed that through a study of abnormality he would come to understand the true nature of man. Passionately interested in religion, he shows in his work a preoccupation with good and evil, and the search for God. His attitude toward his characters is one of great compassion. Even in his lifetime he won recognition both inside and outside Russia as a great novelist.

Carr, Edward Hallett, *Dostoevsky*, 1931.

de Jonge, Alex, *Dostoevsky and the Age of Intensity*, 1975.

Goldstein, D. I., *Dostoevsky and the Jews*, 1981.

Grossman, Leonid, *Dostoevsky*, 1974.

Peace, R., *Dostoevsky: An Examination of the Major Novels*, 1971.

DOSTOYEVSKY, MICHAEL MIKHAILOVICH (1820–64). Brother of Fedor Dostoyevsky, with whom he founded the magazine *Vremya* (The Time) in 1860 in St. Petersburg. The publication was banned by the government in 1863 because of a misunderstanding, but the brothers began a new magazine, *Epokha* (Epoch), in which Fedor's *Notes from the Underground* appeared (1864).

DOVZHENKO, ALEXANDER PETROVICH (1894–1956). Film director, of a Cossack family. He was appointed People's Artist of the Russian Soviet Federated Socialist Republic in 1950. He started in films in 1926, having previously been a teacher and a painter. His *Arsenal* (1929) and *Earth* (1930), in which he used a variety of techniques, all infused with poetic lyricism, brought him fame, but were denounced by official critics as counterrevolutionary. *Shchors*, made in 1939, is the story of a Ukrainian Red Army hero. Among his other films were *Battle of the Ukraine* (1943), an important war documentary made by giving personal instruction to 24 different cameramen distributed along a battle front, the color film *Michurin* (1949), and *Poem of the Sea*, completed in 1958 after his death.

Taylor, R., *Film Propaganda: Soviet Russia and Nazi Germany*, 1979.

DRAGOMANOV, MICHAEL PETROVICH (1851–95). Ukrainian historian and publicist. He was the leader of a moderate Ukrainian national democratic movement of "federalists." He was dismissed from his post at Kiev University because of his nationalism. He published *Songs of the Ukrainian People.*

DREGOVICHIY. An ancient Slavic tribe of primitive forest people, whose center was in Turov. According to ancient manuscripts, the *dregovichiy* had their own princes who ruled them, until the ninth century, when they came under the leadership of Kiev.

DREIKAISERBUND. *See* **Three Emperors' League.**

DREVLANS. An E Slavic tribe who, in the 10th century, opposed the expansion of Kievan influence and were responsible for the death of Prince Igor in 945.

DROGOBYCH. Town 42 miles (67 km) SW of Lvov in the Ukraine. It was part of Kievan Russia until the 14th century, when it passed to Poland. Acquired by Austria in 1772, it was returned to Poland in 1919 and taken by the USSR in 1939. Center of production for petroleum and natural gas. Industries include oil refining, metalworking and chemicals. Population 43,000.

DROZHZHIN, SPIRIDON DMITREVICH (1848–1930). Poet. His first verse was published in 1873 and his poetry was greatly influenced by Aleksey Koltsov, Ivan Nikitin, and Nicholas Nekrasov *(q.q.v.)*. The main themes of his poetry are the life of the Russian peasant, village poverty, and the countryside of Russia, and his works include *In a Peasant Cottage* (1882), *Autumn Holiday* (1886), *Give Me Wings* (1905), and *Centuries of Wicked Slavery are Past* (1918).

DRUNKENNESS. Drunkenness is generally considered a national failing in Russia. St. Vladimir is reputed to have said, "It is Russia's joy to drink: we cannot do without it." Many working days are lost in the Soviet Union through the effects of alcohol. The Soviet authorities have increased the price of vodka from time to time to curb excessive drinking, but with no noticeable results. Drunkenness was for long associated with the unhappiness of life in Russia.

Connor, W. D., *Deviance in Soviet Society: Crime, Delinquency and Alcoholism*, 1972.

DRUZHINA. Military retinue of Kievan princes and great lords.

DRUZHININ, ALEXANDER VASILEVICH (1824–64). Writer and critic. He started his literary career by publishing the story *Polinka Saks* in 1847, which dealt with the question of women's rights. Druzhinin's humanistic and democratic tendencies did not, however, continue to find expression during the period of strict censorship following 1848, and he subscribed to the theory of pure art for art's sake.

DUAL POWER. Situation whereby the authority of the provisional government established March 2, 1917 was constantly undermined by the rival influence of the Soviet of the Workers' and Soldiers' Deputies, thus enabling the Bolshevik takeover at the October Revolution.

Daniels, Robert V., *Red October*, 1968.

Shukman, H., *Lenin and the Russian Revolution*, 1966.

Ulam, Adam B., *Lenin and the Bolsheviks*, 1969.

DUBASOV, F. V. (1845–1912). Soldier. General responsible for the suppression of the Moscow uprising of 1905. Initially unsuccessful because the loyalty of his troops was uncertain, he was given reinforcements in the form of the Semenovsky Guards, who ruthlessly quelled the revolt in a few days.

Harcave, S., *First Blood: The Revolution of 1905*, 1964.

DUBBELT, GENERAL LEONTIY VASILYEVICH (1792–1862). Soldier and police chief under Nicholas I. He was in charge of the Third Section and created the renowned Gendarmerie. He fought at the Battle of Borodino and survived being under suspicion during the investigations following the Decembrist conspiracy. On retiring from the army he was appointed to the new Corps of Gendarmes, the executive arm of the Third Section.

Monas, Sidney L., *The Third Section*, 1961.

DUBČEK, ALEXANDER (1921–). Former Czechoslovak party official, born in Uhrovice, Slovakia. A machine fitter, he joined early and rose steadily until he became the first secretary of the central committee of the Communist Party of Czechoslovakia. Moscow considered Dubček's liberal reforms to be unacceptable and invaded Czechoslovakia on August 21, 1968. In April 1969, Dubček was replaced by the less liberal Husak. Subsequently, Dubček was appointed Czech ambassador to Turkey (1969–70) and, after 1975, worked in a forestry enterprise in Bratislava.

DUBNOW, SIMON (1860–1941). Jewish historian born in Belorussia.

He was a founder of the Jewish Historico-Ethnological Society and contributed to the Russian-Jewish *Voskhod* (Rising). He left Russia for Riga, Latvia, in 1922 and was murdered by the Nazis in 1941. He believed that Jews would retain their identity in the Diaspora. His works included *World History of Jewish People* in 10 volumes, 1925–29, and *History of the Jewish People in Russia and Poland* in 3 volumes, 1916–20.

Selzer, R. M., *Dubnow*, 1970.
Steinberg, A., *Simon Dubnow*, 1963.

DUDINSKAYA, NATALYA MIKHAILOVNA (1912–). Soviet ballerina. She joined the Leningrad Academic Theater Opera and ballet troupe, and within a year was dancing the main roles. Dudinskaya participated in the creation of new Soviet ballets such as *The Flame of Paris*, *Laurensya*, and *The Bronze Horseman*.

DUDINTSEV, VLADIMIR DMITRIYEVICH (1918–). Author. Trained as a lawyer, he served as defense counsel with a Siberian military tribunal from 1942 to 1945. He began writing seriously in 1946 as a contributor to *Komsomolskaya Pravda*. His works include a collection of short stories (1952), *Not By Bread Alone* (1957), and *A New Year's Tale* (1960). *Not By Bread Alone*, a frank description of the Soviet social and political system, was his most successful work and was censored by the authorities.

Stonum, M., *Soviet Russian Literature*, 1967.

***DUKHOBORY* (SPIRIT WRESTLERS).** Religious sect founded in the 18th century. They called themselves Christians of the Universal Brotherhood until 1939 and then Union of Spiritual Communities of Christ. The sect preached equality and opposed all authority which conflicted with their conscience. They were opposed to the priesthood and the sacraments and their approach to religious matters resembled that of the Quakers. They were persecuted under Catherine II. Alexander I persuaded them to settle near the Sea of Azov, where they farmed and flourished. They were forcibly moved from their farms and shifted eastward in 1840 when they refused to accept military conscription. In 1887 they again resisted conscription and their leader, Peter Veregin, was exiled to Siberia. Leo Tolstoy persuaded the tsar to let the sect emigrate and English Quakers provided funds for them to settle in Canada. They flourished in Canada until the 1930s when the communal settlements were abandoned. The Sons of Freedom, an extreme group of Dukhobors, still resist some of the Canadian laws on education, land, and tax, but many have been assimilated into Canadian society. There are probably 20,000 Dukhobors in Canada.

Hawthorn, H. B. (ed.), *Doukhobors of British Columbia*, 1955.
Woodcock, G. and Avakumoniv, I., *The Doukhobors*, 1968.

DUKHONIN, GENERAL NICHOLAS NIKOLAYEVICH (1876–1917). Soldier. He was commander-in-chief of all Russian forces when the October Revolution started. Having helped several senior officers to escape, then refusing to obey an order to open truce negotiations with the Germans, he was, in November 1917, shot by the mutinous troops.

DUKHOVNAYA GRAMOTA. A will or testament.

DUMA. Duma was the name of a Kievan political institution consisting of a council of boyars; but is better known as the elected legislative assemblies which, with the State Council, comprised the Russian legislature from 1906 to 1917, and which were established in response to the 1905 Revolution. The tsar could rule absolutely when the duma was not in session and he could dissolve it at will. The first state duma, elected by universal male suffrage but with limited power over financial and other matters, met for 73 days in 1906 and the second met in 1907 for 102 days. The first and second dumas were unsuccessful in that, although it was expected that the representatives would be conservative, they were mainly liberal and socialist, and their demands for reform were totally unacceptable to the government. The franchise was then restricted, and the third duma ran its full five-year term (1907–12) and gave support to the government's agrarian reforms and military reorganization. The fourth duma sat from 1912 to 1917, but it gradually became opposed to the government's war policy and increasingly critical of the imperial regime. On the abdication of Tsar Nicholas II the provisional committee established by the duma asked Prince Lvov to form a provisional government.

Gurko, V. I., *Features and Figures of the Past: Government and Opinion in the Reign of Nicholas II,* 1939.

Harper, Samuel N., *The New Electoral Law for the Russian Duma,* 1908.

Hosking, Geoffrey A., *The Russian Constitutional Experiment,* 1973.

Levin, Alfred, *The Second Duma: A Study of the Social-Democratic Party and the Russian Constitutional Experiment,* 1940.

Maklakov, V. A., *Memoirs of* V. A. *Maklakov: The First State Duma: Contemporary Reminiscences,* Arthur P. Mendel, ed., 1967.

Pares, Bernard, *Russia and Reform,* 1907.

Sack, A. J., *The Birth of the Russian Democracy,* 1918. *Memoirs of Count Witte* (trans. A. Yarmolinsky), 1921.

DUMBARTON OAKS CONVERSATIONS. From August 21 to October 7, 1944, representatives of China, the USSR, the United States, and Great Britain met at Dumbarton Oaks, a mansion in Georgetown, Washington, D.C., to formulate proposals for an organization that eventually became the United Nations. Paragraph 4 of the Moscow Declaration of 1943 had stressed the need for such a postwar organization to succeed the League of Nations. The Dumbarton Oaks proposals for the establishment of a general international organization did not establish the voting procedures or qualifications for membership; these were settled at the Yalta Conference in February 1945, at which a trusteeship system was agreed upon to replace the league mandates. The final proposals formed the basis of negotiations at the San Francisco Conference in 1945, from which the Charter of the United Nations was published.

Luard, E., *A History of the United Nations*, Vol. 1, 1981.

DUMNIY DYAK. Chief secretary or clerk who had the right to attend meetings of the *boyarskaya duma.*

DUMY. Ukrainian lyric-epic songs. A mixture of folk and literary influences, they extol Cossack exploits against the Turks, Poles and Tatars.

DUNAYEVSKIY, ISAAK (1900–). Soviet composer. Dunayevskiy worked as conductor and composer in Moscow, Kharkov, and Leningrad. In 1932 Dunayevskiy began to compose for film. Dunayevskiy was one of the creators of the operettas *The Golden Valley* (1937), *The Road to Happiness* (1941), and *The Son of the Clown* (1950). He was one of the first composers in the USSR to use jazz forms (1933).

DURNOVO, PETER NIKOLAYEVICH (1844–1915). Politician. Minister of the interior under Nicholas II, he replaced General Dmitriy Trepov (*q.v.*) and was largely responsible for the downfall of Sergei Witte (*q.v.*), to whom he owed his post. His measures to quash the 1905 Revolution were ruthless and harsh. His successor as minister of the interior was Peter Stolypin (*q.v.*).

DUSHANBE. Capital of the Tadzhik Soviet Socialist Republic situated N of the border with Afghanistan. Its industries include textiles and meat packing, and it manufactures cement and leather. It is connected with the Trans-Caspian Railway. It was formerly known as Stalinabad. Population (1977) 460,000.

DUXOBORY. *See* ***DUKHOBORY.***

DVINA RIVER. The N Dvina is formed by the confluence of the Sukhona and Yug rivers and flows 470 miles (752 km) NW through N Russian Soviet Federated Socialist Republic to enter the White Sea above Arkhangelsk. Its chief tributaries are the Vychegda, Pinega, and Vaga rivers. Navigable from May to November, it is linked with the Mariynsk canal system. The W Dvina rises in the Valdai hills in NW Russian Soviet Federated Socialist Republic and flows 640 miles (1,024 km) SW into Belorussia, past Vitebsk, then NW to Riga and the Gulf of Riga. It is partly navigable from May to November.

DVOR. Peasant homestead, also the court of the prince.

Blum, J. T., *Lord and Peasant in Russia from the Ninth to the Nineteenth Century*, 1971.

DVOROVIYE LYUDI. Household serfs.

DVORYANIN. A courtier or member of the Russian nobility.

DVORYANSTVO. A member of the Russian nobility. In the 17th century, military service for the *dvoryanstvo* was hereditary. In 1642 and 1649 it was established that only the *dvoryanstvo* could own land worked by serfs. Peter the Great extensively reformed the rights and position of the *dvoryanstvo*; although from then on the *dvoryanstvo* were virtually forced to serve either in the army, navy, or bureaucracy. In 1785, a charter reaffirmed and consolidated their status, and the *dvoryanstvo* enjoyed such privileges as exemption from poll tax and the fact that they could not be stripped of estates, title, or status without trial by their peers. Their rights over the serfs were also reaffirmed, and so by this time, the *dvoryanstvo* was a full-fledged class of nobles.

Dukes, Paul, *Catherine the Great and the Russian Nobility*, 1968.

Jones, R.E., *The Emancipation of the Russian Nobility 1762–1785*, 1973.

Kochan, Lionel, *The Making of Modern Russia*, 1962.

Pipes, Richard, *Russia Under the Old Regime*, 1974.

DVOYEVERIYE. Duality of belief between official Christianity and popular paganism put forward as a hypothesis because it was felt that Christianity had only a superficial hold on its Russian converts initially, because of the speed at which the country was converted.

DYAK. Clerk in an office of the central government in Moscow or in the provinces.

DYBENKO, PAUL EFIMOVICH (1889–1938). Sailor. He organized revolutionary sailors of the Baltic fleet in 1917 and was later appointed people's commissar of the navy. He narrowly escaped execution by the Germans in the Ukraine during the Civil War. He lost his post during the purge of the armed forces in 1937.

Mawdsley, E., *The Russian Revolution and the Baltic Fleet*, 1978.

DYKH-TAU. Mountain peak. It is the third highest mountain of the central Greater Caucasian range, rising to 17,190 feet (5,240 m).

DZERZHINSK. Town, situated 20 miles (32 km) W of Gorky on the Oka River, in the Russian Soviet Federated Socialist Republic. Industries include sawmilling and engineering; manufactures include chemicals, especially fertilizers. Population (1977) 248,000.

DZERZHINSKIY, FELIKS EDMUNDOVICH (1877–1926). Communist politician, of Polish noble descent. He was imprisoned for revolutionary activities several times and was the first head (1917–24) of the postrevolutionary secret police (Cheka) and of its successors, the OGPU and the GPU.

Leggett, G., *The Cheka: Lenin's Political Police*, 1981.

DZERZHINSKIY, IVAN IVANOVICH (1909–). Composer. He studied at the Leningrad Conservatory. His works comprise several operas, including *Quiet Flows the Don*, composed 1923–24, but first performed in 1935. This was based on the novel by Michael Sholokhov *(q.v.)*, as was another opera, *Virgin Soil Upturned*. He also composed orchestral and vocal works and music for plays and films.

DZHAMBUL. Town, situated 285 miles (456 km) W of Alma-Ata on the Turkish railway. It is the capital of Dzhambul region of Kazakhstan.

Founded in the seventh century, it passed to Russia in 1864. Industries include fruit canning and sugar refining; manufactures include superphosphates and prefabricated buildings. Population (1970) 188,000.

DZHUGASHVILI, IOSIF VISSARIONOVICH. *See* **Stalin, Joseph.**

DZUNGARIAN GATE. Mountain pass between the Dzungarian Alatau and the Pa-erh-lu-k'o and Ma-li ranges. It links the Balkhash-Alakol depression, Kazakh Soviet Socialist Republic, with the Lower Ai-pi Hu basin in the W People's Republic of China. Its width is 6–25 miles (10–40 km). It was used from olden times by nomadic tribes from Inner Asia en route to the Kazakhstan steppes, and by warriors, including Genghis Khan, from Central Asia. The Aktogay-China railway was to have used the pass but only the Soviet half was completed and this reached Druzhba on the frontier.

E

EASTERN ORTHODOX CHURCH. Traditionally the main faith in Russia. For the origins of Orthodoxy in Russia, *see* **Christianity, Conversion to.** The influence the Orthodox Church (*q.v.*) has had on the Russian character and culture cannot be overestimated. The Orthodox Church was particularly important in times of national difficulty, such as under the Tatar yoke. There are two autocephalous Orthodox churches in the country; the Russian and the Georgian; the Russian Orthodox Church is led by the patriarch (*q.v.*) of Moscow and All Russia. The bishops of Moscow, Leningrad, Kiev, Minsk, and Novosibirsk are known as metropolitans. There are still some functioning theological academies and monasteries, although many monasteries have been turned into museums.

Bourdeux, Michael, *Opium of the People: The Christian Religion in the USSR*, 1965.

Kolarz, Walker, *Religion in the Soviet Union*, 1962.

Ware, Timothy, *The Orthodox Church*, 1963.

EASTERN QUESTION. Term describing the problem created by the instability of the Ottoman empire in the 19th century. The whole area was a source of conflict between the great powers. At first only Austria, France, Great Britain, and Russia were involved, but from 1879 the German empire became more concerned with Balkan affairs, as did Italy toward the end of the century. Russia was particularly anxious to gain access from the Black Sea to the Mediterranean Sea.

ECHMYADZIN. Monastery and town in the Armenian Soviet Socialist Republic of the USSR. It is the seat of the supreme Catholicos, or primate of the Armenian Church. A church was first built there in 309, following

St. Gregory the Illuminator's vision. The present cathedral dates from the seventh century. The town of Vagharshapat was renamed Echmyadzin in 1945 and dates from the sixth century BC, and in the second and early part of the third century AD it was the capital of Armenia.

EDUCATION. Education is free and compulsory from ages 7 to 16/17. Coeducation was reintroduced in all schools on September 1, 1954. There are two types of general schools, with an 8-year or a 10-year curriculum. The minimum school-leaving age is now 17. Pupils who leave an 8-year school continue their education at either a 10-year school or a vocational training school. A 10-year school pupil may also transfer to vocational school after the 8th year. Vocational school pupils must reach the same standard of general education as those at 10-year general schools, and so stay on at school longer. Instruction is given in more than 100 languages.

In 1980–81 there were 145,000 primary and secondary schools. Pupils in general educational schools numbered 44.3 million, 9.9 million of them in the 9th and 10th forms, and the teachers 2.6 million. Those at vocational and specialized technical secondary schools number 8.5 million.

At the end of 1940 labor reserve schools, both vocational and industrial, were organized, admitting applicants from 14 to 17 years of age. From 1959 onward these and other technical schools were reorganized as town and rural vocational and technical schools, at which pupils stay for a year longer than at general schools, combining completion of general secondary education with vocational training. From 1940 to 1977, inclusive, they trained 35 million skilled workers. In 1978, 2.3 million graduated from such schools, including 628,000 for agriculture; 600,000 agricultural mechanics were trained on state and collective farms. Over 4,300 vocational training schools existed in 1981, training 2.17 million boys and girls, all of whom receive a full secondary education. In 1979, 13.9 million children of from 3 to 7 years of age attended kindergartens. Children in boarding schools numbered over 800,000 in 1972–73.

In 1980–81 there were 4,383 technical colleges, with 4.6 million students, and 883 universities, institutes, and other places of higher education, with 5.2 million students, including 1.6 million taking correspondence or evening courses.

Among the 65 university towns are: Moscow, Leningrad, Khar'kov, Odessa, Tartu, Kazan, Saratov, Tomsk, Kiev, Sverdlovsk, Tbilisi, Alma-Ata, Tashkent, Minsk, Gorky, and Vladivostok. On January 1, 1981 there were 1.37 million scientific workers in places of higher education, research institutes, and Academies of Sciences. There are 33,000 foreign students from 130 countries.

The Academy of Sciences of the USSR had 732 members and corresponding members. The total number of learned institutions under the USSR Academy of Sciences is 244, with a scientific staff of 46,000. Fourteen of the union republics have their own Academies of Sciences, with scientific staff numbering 49,079. There are also Siberian, Far Eastern, and other branches of the USSR Academy. On January 1, 1981 there were 96,820 postgraduate students. The Academy of Pedagogical Sciences had 14 research institutes with a staff of 1,712.

In 1980–81 about 100.2 million people were studying at schools, colleges, and training or correspondence courses. Of the employed population 181 per 1,000 had a higher education (in 1939, 13; in 1959, 33).

Grant, Nigel, *Soviet Education,* 1972.

EHRENBURG, ILYA GRIGOROVICH (1891–1967). Writer, of Jewish origin, who spent much of his life in Paris. A Symbolist poet at the start of his career, Ehrenburg was a skillful master of all the genres. His works include *A Street in Moscow* (1932), *Out of Chaos* (1934), and *European Crossroad* (1934). A one-time member of the Supreme Soviet, he was a pioneer of the de-Stalinization of literature, and wrote the influential novel *The Thaw* (1954–56). While permitted to strive for the rehabilitation of victims of the Terror, such as Osip Mandelstam (*q.v.*), at the same time he had to make considerable concessions to the authorities.

Muchnik, H., *From Gorky to Pasternak,* 1963.

EISENSTEIN, SERGEI MIKHAILOVICH (1898–1948) Film director. He directed the film *Battleship Potemkin* (1925), intended as one episode in a full coverage of the 1905 Revolution. He edited it to produce an emotional reaction in his audience by a startling juxtaposition of real and symbolic images. Such carefully manipulated successions of shots were important in Soviet didactic films. Other notable films included *Alexander Nevsky* (1938), his first talking film, and *Ivan the Terrible* (1944–45). Although he was awarded many honors he also had many disagreements with the authorities, who criticized his works as "formalistic," "unrealistic," and "exaggerating the destructive aspects of the Revolution." The first part of *Ivan the Terrible* (1944) was praised by Stalin but the second part (1945) was denounced.

Barna, Yon, *Eisenstein,* 1973.

ELBRUZ, MOUNT. Kabardino-Balkar/Georgia. The highest peak in the Caucasus mountains, comprising two extinct volcanoes, the W 18,482 feet (5,633 m) above sea level and the E 18,356 feet (5,595 m) above sea level.

ELECTORAL SYSTEM. All Soviet citizens over the age of 18 have the right to vote. Although theoretically more than one candidate may run, voters are never given a choice of candidates; this is justified officially by the democratic nature of the selection procedure and by the basic consensus of opinion. Nominations, in theory freely discussed, are tightly controlled by the Communist Party. The district party and local election committee organize the three-week campaign. Polling takes place on a Sunday and is not compulsory. Screened polling booths are provided, but very few voters use them. Electors wishing to vote for the candidate put an unmarked ballot paper in the box; those in disagreement cross out the name. All-Union and Supreme Soviet elections take place every five years, and those for local Soviets occur every two and a half years.

Churchward, L. G., *Contemporary Soviet Government,* 1975.

Fainsod, Merle, *How Russia is Ruled,* 1953.

Hazard, John N., *The Soviet System of Government,* 1960.

ELECTRICITY. In 1982 there were 57 fuel-burning power stations of over one million kw capacity, and these account for nearly 80 percent of the country's electricity. Hydroelectric stations have been constructed on major rivers. Among them are the Bratsk (4.5 million kw), completed in 1967 and until recently the world's largest; Ust'-Ilimsk, Central Siberia (3.6 million kw); Krasnoyarsk (6 million kw); and a 1.26 million kw station on the Pechora River (Far North). The Sayano-Shushenskaya hydropower station, part of the Yenisei chain, and already partly in operation, will have a 6.4 million kw capacity when completed in 1983. A high dam has to be constructed before completion, in a gorge in the Sayan Range. Another large hydroelectric station is under construction on the Kureika River, Siberia, to provide energy for the mining and metallurgical center at Norilsk in the Arctic.

Total installed capacity of power stations in 1938 was 8.7 million kw and 266.7 million kw in 1980. Industry consumes about 70 percent of the total output of electricity. Over 35,000 small rural power stations have been closed in recent years owing to supply from state stations becoming available, but there are still many operating in the countryside. In 1980 10 percent of total electricity supply came from nuclear-powered plants. Some 800 towns and urban settlements were heated by central thermal plants. The total output of electricity in 1980 was 1,295,000 kwh.

ELEKTROSTAL. Town, 32 miles (51 km) E of Moscow, in the Russian Soviet Federated Socialist Republic. Industries include heavy engineering, steel works, and the manufacture of stainless steel. Population (1977) 135,000.

ELENA, GRAND DUCHESS OF LITHUANIA (*fl.* late 15th century). Daughter of Ivan III, married to Grand Duke Aleksandr of Lithuania. Marriage was meant to secure better relations between Moscow and Lithuania.

ELISTA. Town, 180 miles (288 km) W of Astrakhan, it is the capital of the Kalmyk Autonomous Soviet Socialist Republic. Called previously Stepnoy, (1943–57), it is a communications and trading center. Industries include processing of farming products, especially sheepskins, wool, meat, and grain. Elista manufactures bricks and tanning extract. Population (1973) 56,000.

ELIZABETH PETROVNA (1709–62). Daughter of Peter the Great and of his second wife, Catherine I, who acceded to the throne as empress in 1741, having overthrown the infant emperor Ivan VI with the assistance of the Preobrazhenskiy Guards. She took the duties of government seriously and attempted to carry on the policies of her father. She abolished the death penalty, was one of the founders of Moscow University, built the Winter Palace in St. Petersburg, and introduced French culture to the court.

Talbot Rice, Tamara, *Elizabeth, Empress of Russia,* 1970.

ELTON, LAKE. Lake with salt content of approximately 25 percent and an area 62 square miles (161 sq km). It is situated in steppe country 90 miles (145 km) E of Volgograd near the Kazakh Soviet Socialist Republic border.

EMANCIPATION, EDICT OF. Edict of 1861, by which some serfs, hitherto regarded as chattels of the landowner, were liberated. Although a landmark in the history of Russia—the serf could marry, take legal action, own property in his name, and engage in business or trade—he was in fact economically dependent on the landlord. The serf had to buy the land from his previous owner; the amount and type of land often depended on the individual landowner's whim. The land could be redeemed by 30–40 days' labor annually, or by *obrok,* a 6 percent tax paid to the landowner. In many cases the serfs were worse off following the 1861 edict. *See* **Agrarian Reforms.**

Kochan, Lionel, *The Making of Modern Russia,* 1962.

EMBA RIVER. River rising in S Mugodzhar hills, Kazakh Soviet Socialist Republic, and flowing 384 miles (614 km) SW past Zharkamys to enter the Caspian Sea near Zhilaya Kosa. Its lower course flows through the Emba oil field. Its main tributary is the Temir River.

EMIN, FEDOR ALEKSANDROVICH (1735–70). Author, thought to have been born in what is now Yugoslavia. He arrived in Russia in 1761 and wrote some of the first Russian novels. Previously, mainly translations were available. His best-known work is *The Letters of Ernest and Doravia* (1766).

ENGELS, FRIEDRICH (1820–95). German social philosopher, businessman, and friend of Karl Marx (*q.v.*). Having retired from directing a textile firm, he devoted himself to political agitation and writing and attempted to prove that Marxist dialectical materialism is implicit in the theory and practice of modern science. Thus he believed that all events are interrelated, and no one phenomenon can be understood outside the context of social evolution. Engels predicted the obsolescence of war, as increased industrialization would bring international unity.

Coates, Zelda K., *The Life and Teaching of F. Engels,* 1945.

ENGELS. Town situated on Volga River opposite Saratov, in the Russian Soviet Federated Socialist Republic. Industries include railway engineering, meat packing, flour milling, and the manufacture of textiles and leather goods. Population (1981) 168,000.

ÉON, CHARLES de BEAUMONT, CHEVALIER d' (1728–1810) French secret agent whose first mission was to the Tsaritsa Elizabeth in 1755, disguised as a woman. The term "eonism," meaning a tendency to adopt the clothing and mannerisms of the opposite sex, is derived from his name.

ERFURT CONFERENCE. Conference held at Erfurt, Germany, in March 1808 between Napoleon I and Tsar Alexander I, in the presence of German princes. The meeting was intended to consolidate agreements reached at Tilsit (1807), but mutual resentment and suspicion prevented a lasting alliance. Relations deteriorated after the conference and Napoleon attacked Russia in 1812.

ERIVAN. *See* **Yerevan.**

ESENIN, SERGEI ALEKSANDROVICH (1895–1925). Poet. Founder of the Imagist (*q.v.*) school of Russian poets. He presented himself as a "peasant poet" and recited in Moscow salons wearing a peasant smock. He welcomed the Revolution, without really understanding it. He married Isadora Duncan, the American dancer, in 1922, but they separated after a year and he returned to Russia with an international reputation as a drunken exhibitionist. He never succeeded in adapting either to the new urban Soviet society or to the changed peasant world; he hanged himself in Leningrad in 1925. His *Confession of a Hooligan* was published in 1918.

Davies, J. (ed.), *Esenin: A Biography in Memoirs, Letters and Documents*, 1982.

McVay, G., *Esenin: A Life*, 1976.

McVay, G., *Isadora and Esenin*, 1980.

ESTONIAN SOVIET SOCIALIST REPUBLIC. Constituent republic of the USSR, bounded on the N by the Gulf of Finland, on the S by Latvia, on the W by the Baltic Sea, and on the E by the Russian Soviet Federated Socialist Republic. Area 17,400 square miles (45,100 sq km). Estonia was a tribal territory supporting a peasant and seafaring community until conquered by German knights under Albert of Buxhoevden in 1217–27. This German (Catholic) domination was ended when the Estonians adopted Protestant beliefs and placed themselves under the protection of Sweden in 1561. The country was taken from Charles XII of Sweden by Peter the Great in 1721 and became a province of Russia. After a brief period of independence following the 1917 Revolution, the secret protocol of the Soviet-German agreement in 1939 assigned Estonia to the Soviet sphere of interest. An ultimatum in 1940 led to the formation of a government acceptable to the USSR, which applied for Estonia's admission to the Soviet Union; this was effected by decree of the Supreme Soviet later that year. The incorporation has been accorded de facto recognition by the British government, but not by the United States government, which continues to recognize an Estonian consul-general in New York. The chief towns are Tallinn (capital) and Paldiski. The terrain consists of mainly lowland rising to glacial moraine ridges in the S, with poor, sandy soil. About 20 percent of the land is forest. Agriculture is based on intensive dairy farming and grain production. Industries include distilling gas, petrol and asphalt from local oil shale, of which deposits are considerable; textiles; and shipbuilding. Manufactures include matches, paper, and furniture. Industries and manufactures all center on Tallinn. The chief exports are dairy and oil-shale products. Population (1981) 1,500,000.

Parming, Tönu, *A Case Study of a Soviet Republic: The Estonian SSR*, 1978.

ETTINGER, SALOMAN (*c.* 1803–56). Dramatist. A Russian Jew who wrote in Yiddish. In 1825 he wrote, among others, the play *Serkele* for the Jewish festival of Purim to replace the traditional, popular festival plays that had become vulgar.

EUDOXIA (EVDOKHIYA FEDOROVNA LOPUKHINA) 1669–1731). First wife of Peter the Great. She was married at 17, and soon found that she had little in common with Peter, and in 1698 he forced her to take the veil. Later she reversed her decision, and entered into a liaison with Stepan Glebov, but did not assist her son Alexis with his flight to Austria. She was tried, sent to the Uspensky convent, and officially rehabilitated on the accession of Peter II.

EVENKI NATIONAL AREA. Situated in Krasnoyarsk Territory, in the Russian Soviet Federated Socialist Republic. It consists mainly of tundra and coniferous forest. Area 285,900 square miles (740,481 sq km). The chief rivers are Lower Tunguska and Stony Tunguska. The principal occupations are reindeer breeding and fishing. The capital is Tura. Population (1970) 13,000.

EVREYNOV, NICHOLAS NIKOLAYEVICH (1879–1953). Dramatist and Symbolist. Among his plays was *The Chief Thing* (1921), which was written to show the drama of the inner self. He also wrote extensively on the origin of the drama.

EXECUTIVE COMMITTEE OF THE ALL-RUSSIAN CONGRESS OF SOVIETS. Committee consisting of about 300 members, theoretically in charge of the all-Russian Congress of Soviets, which stands at the pinnacle of thousands of Soviets in the union. In actual fact, power tends to be with the 10 members of the Council of People's Commissars.

Kochan, Lionel, *The Making of Modern Russia*, 1962.

EYLAU, BATTLE OF (1807). Battle fought in appalling conditions in E Prussia (now Bagrationovsk) between Russia and France. Augereau's corps were decimated by the Russian battery, but Napoleon was saved by his artillery of the guard. There was no clear outcome of the battle, but the French occupied the battlefield.

Pares, Bernard, *A History of Russia*, 1926.

F

FABERGÉ, PETER CARL (1846–1920). Russian-born jeweler. He achieved fame through the ingenuity and extravagance of the jeweled objects he devised for the tsar and the Russian nobility in an age of ostentatious extravagance that ended at the outbreak of the First World War.

FADEYEV, ALEXANDER ALEXANDROVICH (1901–56). Novelist. He was influenced by Tolstoy's psychological realism and led campaigns against unorthodox trends in literature. He fought in the Revolution and became a member of the Communist Party in 1918. During the 1930s and 1940s he was implicated in the purge of writers. His work includes *The Rout* (1927) and *The Young Guard* (1945), which is probably his best book and which he revised in 1951 following criticism that he had failed to show the Party's leading role. He committed suicide after the official denunciation of Stalin.

Slonim, Marc, *Soviet Russian Literature*, 1967.
Zelinsky, K., A. A. *Fadeyev*, 1948.

FADEYEV, GENERAL ROSTISLAV (1824–83). He published a memorandum, *Opinion on the Eastern Question*, issued in serial form in the late 1860s and as a book in 1870. This work influenced the acceptance of Pan-Slavism as the official ideology of a new imperialism in Russia.

FAINZILBERG, ILYA ARNOLDOVITCH. *See* **Ilf and Petrov.**

FALBORK, HEINRICH ADOLFOVICH (1864–?). Writer and supporter of popular education. Falbork and V. I. Charnolusky organized the first statistical investigation of the education of the Russian people, and as a result of his work the League of Learning and the Pedagogic Academy were formed. In 1891 he visited the famine-stricken regions of Russia and submitted an account of the famine to the Free Economic Society. In 1904 he was banished from St. Petersburg as a result of his membership in the Social Democratic group.

Gurko, V. I., *Features and Figures of the Past*, 1939.

FALCONET, ÉTIENNE MAURICE (1716–91). French sculptor. He worked under the patronage of Madame Pompadour at Bellevue and was employed by Catherine II in St. Petersburg (1766–78), where he executed the bronze equestrian statue of Peter the Great situated in Decembrists' Square. Nicknamed "The Bronze Horseman," it was the subject of a poem by Pushkin in 1832 and shows Peter reining in his horse on the brink of a rock. The plaster cast was completed in 1779 and the finished statue weighed 16 tons. The 1,600-ton block of granite on which the statue stands came from Lasht, a village 7 miles from St. Petersburg, and was maneuvered by 500 men taking five weeks. The statue was unveiled in August 1782. The pedestal bears the inscription PETRO PRIMO—CATHARINA SECUNDA MDCCLXXXII on one side and the same in Russian on the opposite side.

Falconet, E. M., *Correspondence avec Catherine II*, 1921.

Levitine, G., *The Sculpture of Falconet*, 1972.

FALK, ROBERT (1886–1956) Artist. After studying at the Moscow College, Falk exhibited work at the first "Knave of Diamonds" (*q.v.*) exhibition and was one of the most influential members of the group. He subsequently worked as an art teacher.

Gray, Camilla, *The Russian Experiment in Art*, 1962.

FALSE DMITRIY I. *See* **Dmitriy, False.**

FALSE DMITRIY II. *See* **Dmitriy, False.**

FAR EASTERN REPUBLIC. It existed from 1920 to 1922. The Far Eastern Republic served as a buffer state between Soviet Russia and Japan. One of the first "people's democracies," it was annexed to Russia following the Japanese leaving Vladivostok.

FEBRUARY REVOLUTION (1917). Revolution during which the monarchy fell and the provisional government and the Soviets of workers' and soldiers' deputies were established. Over 14 million peasants were engaged in military service, which in turn led to acute food shortages; this proved to be one of the factors that triggered the Revolution. Having taken command of the army in 1915, Tsar Nicholas II was at the front and the tsarina, with the help of Rasputin, was responsible for much of the decision making on domestic matters. In February 1917 there were widespread bread riots, strikes, and demonstrations in Petrograd, and the troops, summoned to restore order, mutinied. This led to the abdication of the tsar and a provisional government, led by Kerensky, assumed power. The provisional government and the Soviets vied with one another for power, and the government proved to be incapable of dealing with the rising power of the Bolsheviks.

Florinsky, M. T., *End of the Russian Empire*, 1961.

Katkov, George, *Russia 1917: The February Revolution*, 1967.

Rothstein, Andrew, *A History of the USSR*, 1950.

FEDIN, KONSTANTIN ALEKSANDROVICH (1892–1977). Novelist, fellow-traveler and one of the Serapion Brothers (*q.v.*). His *Cities and Years* (1924) is an attempt to analyze the revolution. His work is frequently about revolution, civil war, and the intellectual's task of redefining his role in a much-changed world. Head of the Moscow Writers' organization, in 1959 he was appointed secretary-general of the Writers' Union.

Slonim, Morc, *Soviet Russian Literature*, 1964.

FEDOR I (1557–98). Tsar of Russia from 1584, and third son of Ivan IV. Somewhat feeble-minded, he was tsar in name only; Russia was at this time governed by Boris Godunov (*q.v.*). Fedor was the last member of the house of Rurik to be tsar.

Florinsky, Michael T., *Russia: A History and an Interpretation*, 2 vols., 1953.

FEDOR II (1589–1605). Tsar of Russia in 1605. The son of Boris Godunov, Fedor was proclaimed tsar on his father's death. His mother, however, attempted to take charge of matters, and aroused the fury of the boyars, who murdered both Fedor and his mother.

Florinsky, Michael T., *Russia: A History and an Interpretation*, 2 vols., 1953.

FEDOR III (1661–82). Educated by Simeon of Potolsk, and tsar of Russia from 1676. I. M. Yazykov and Alexis Likhachev virtually ruled on his behalf, and from 1681 Vasily Vasilyevich Golitsyn was highly influential. *Mestnichestvo* (*q.v.*) was finally abolished during Fedor's reign.

Florinsky, Michael T., *Russia: A History and an Interpretation*, 2 vols., 1953.

FEDOR KUSMICH. *See* **Kusmich, Fedor.**

FEDOROV, IVAN FEDOROVICH (?–1583). First printer in Russia. Ivan IV asked Christian III of Denmark for help with printing in 1552, and Hans Missenheim, a Copenhagen printer, was sent to Russia, where he taught Fedorov his craft. He produced the first printed book in Moscow in 1563. He fled from Muscovy and continued his work in Lithuania and Poland.

FEDOROV, NICHOLAS FEDOROVICH (1828–1903). Philosopher. According to his philosophy, the ideal classless society would be realized when the forces of nature were brought under man's control, following which it would be of vital importance to resurrect the dead. His ideas on space travel, solar energy, and the labor armies in 1920 have been particularly influential.

FEFER, ITSIK (ISAAK SOLOMONOVICH) (1900–52). Yiddish poet. Having joined the Communist

Party in 1919, Fefer volunteered for the Red Army and took part in the Civil War of 1917–20 and in the war of 1941–45. His first work was published in 1919. In 1943 he toured the United States and Great Britain in the capacity of the first official representative of Soviet Jews. He held a number of important government offices, but was arrested in 1948 during the purge of Jewish writers. He was executed in 1952. The author of lyrical poems, Fefer drew upon his experiences in the Civil War for subject matter for much of his writing. He also wrote several plays.

FELDSCHER. In tsarist times, a supervised medical auxiliary at rural hospitals. Under the present regime, a *feldscher* is a highly trained nurse who acts as doctor at a polyclinic. The Soviet Union is trying to replace *feldschera* with trained doctors.

FELLOW-TRAVELER. Term coined by Trotsky in 1925 for those intellectuals, especially writers, who were not communists but had sympathy with communism or a modified Soviet regime.

Caute, David, *Fellow Travellers*, 1973

FEODOSIYA. Port and health resort, situated on Black Sea in SE Crimea and 96 miles (154 km) ENE of Sevastopol, in the Russian Soviet Federated Socialist Republic. Founded in the sixth century by the Greeks, it was destroyed several times and only grew to any size in the 13th century with the arrival of the Genoese. It was conquered in 1473 and remained under Tatar/Turkish rule until 1783. Industries include fishing, fish canning, flour milling, engineering, and brewing. Population (1976) 75,000.

FEODOTOV, PAUL ANDREYEVICH (1815–52). Realist painter who depicted Russian customs with gentle satire in order to focus attention on social injustice. Although his work paved the way for the radical *Peredvizhniki*, the *Peredvizhniki* believed Feodotov's paintings were not sufficiently critical of society. His most famous painting is generally considered to be "The Major's Courtship" (1848).

Hamilton, George H., *The Art and Architecture of Russia*, 1954.

FEOFAN THE GREEK (*c.* 1307–*c.* 1405). Painter of Greek origin. Feofan painted a series of frescoes at the Church of the Transfiguration in Novgorod, which were discovered during restoration work in 1918. There is evidence that he modified the Byzantine renaissance style to suit simpler Russian tastes. He was also important as a book illustrator.

FEOKTISTOV, KONSTANTIN PETROVICH (1926–). Cosmonaut and spacecraft designer, candidate of technical science since 1955, and space pilot of the USSR since 1964. Having served as a Soviet Army scout in World War II, Feoktistov was shot by the Germans, but managed to escape from a burial trench. After working in an engineering factory, in 1953 he graduated from N. E. Bauman Higher Technical College in Moscow and from 1955 has worked in the Soviet space program. Feoktistov was closely involved in the launching of the first artificial satellite and with the first successful manned flight by Yury Gagarin (1961) (*q.v.*). He also carried out important experiments during the flight of *Voskhod I* (1964) and has completed 16 orbits in *Vostok*.

FERGANA. Town in the region of the same name 145 miles (232 km) ESE of Tashkent, Uzbekistan. Manufactures include textiles and food products. Minerals are found in the area, including coal, oil, and uranium. Population (1981) 180,000.

FET, AFANSY AFANASEVICH (also known as Foeth and Shenshin) (1820–92). Leading lyrical poet of the 19th century. His four-volume *Evening Lights* was published in 1883–91. He also translated Shakespeare, Horace, Goethe, and Schopenhauer.

Fedina, V., A. A. *Fet*, 1915.
Gustafson, R. F., *The Imagination of Spring: The Poetry of* A. *Fet*, 1966.
Pokrovsky, V., A. A. *Fet*, 1911.

FIELD, JOHN (1782–1837). Pianist and composer. The son of an Irish violinist and grandson of an organist, his piano nocturnes were used as models by Chopin. He was apprenticed at the age of 11 years to Clementi, who took him to France, Germany, and Russia. He achieved great popularity as a pianist and composer, and settled in St. Petersburg in 1803. After a long illness in Naples, he died in Moscow.

Piggott, P., *The Life and Times of John Field, Creator of the Nocturne*, 1973.

FIERAVANTI, ARISTOTLE. *See* **Fioravanti.**

FIGNER, VERA NIKOLAYEVNA (1852–1942). Revolutionary and leading supporter of populism (*q.v.*). Educated at boarding school until 1869, in 1870 she married the lawyer A. V. Filippov and then studied medicine at Zurich University. Captivated by progressive politics, she abandoned her marriage in order to devote herself to revolutionary activities. Back in Russia she worked as a district nurse and eventually condoned and actively supported the terrorist organization Narodnaya Volya (*q.v.*), which was responsible for the assassination of Tsar Alexander II in 1881. Sentenced to death in 1884, the sentence was commuted and she spent 20 years in solitary confinement. Finally permitted to go abroad in 1906, she took part in the work of the Russian Socialist Revolutionary Party. Her *Memoirs of a Revolutionist* were published in 1927.

Footman, D., *Red Prelude*, 1968.
Venturi, F., *Roots of Revolution*, 1961.

FINDELSON, NICHOLAS FEDOROVICH (1868–1928). Musical historian and journalist. He founded *Russkaya Muzikalnaya Gazeta* in 1894, which was, for many years, the only musical periodical in Russia.

FINLAND. Finland was a dependency of Sweden from the 13th century, but the country was always under threat from Russia. By the Peace of Nystad the province of Vyborg was ceded to Russia in 1721, and in 1743 the Russian frontier was extended to the Kymmene by the Peace of Turku. A further extension occurred in 1809 when Sweden ceded the remainder of Finland with the Åland Islands at the Peace of Hamina. Finland, however, retained its autonomy and the tsars became grand dukes of Finland. The government was headed by a governor-general who was the personal representative of the tsar. In 1899 Russia declared its right to legislate on Finnish affairs and in 1900 undertook the first stage of incorporating the Finnish army into the Russian army. The governor-general was assassinated and his successor made some concessions. In 1910 the Imperial Legislation Law deprived the Finnish parliament of the right to legislate on taxes, maintain law and order, and control prices.

In 1917, following the collapse of the Russian empire, Finland declared itself independent and, following a period of civil war, peace was concluded with Russia in 1920. In 1930 the Communist Party was proscribed.

Russia attacked Finland in 1939 and the Finns sued for peace in 1940 following heroic resistance. Finland ceded the Rybach peninsula, the Karelian isthmus, and other territory in SE Finland and granted a 30-year lease for the port of Hanko. Finland retained its independence but ceded 16,170 square miles (41,880 sq km) of territory. Finnish troops reoccupied most of the ceded areas when Germany invaded the USSR. In 1944 the Russians overcame the Finns' resistance and under the armistice ceded the Petsamo area, its only Arctic outlet, leased the Porkkala headland for a 50-year period, and paid reparations.

Since 1945 Finland has been an uncommitted neutral country and has aimed at peaceful relations with the USSR.

Chew, A. F., *The White Death: The Epic of the Soviet-Finnish Winter War*, 1971.

Kirchner, W., *The Rise of the Baltic Question*, 1970.

FINNIC. A group of languages of the Finno-Ugric branch of the Uralic family, which includes Finnish and Estonian among a number of other languages, most of which are dwindling in significance. The Finnic peoples, ancestors of the modern Finns and Estonians, migrated in prehistoric times from central Russia to the area of the E Baltic, Finland, and Karelia, bringing grain cultivation with them. Estonia became an important trading area and established a sense of national identity while the Finns inhabited more remote regions and remained fragmented until recent times. The Lapps in the far N of the region retain their separate identity and language but other groups have mainly lost theirs. All these peoples were Christianized during the 11th and 12th centuries.

Hakulinen, L., *The Structure and Development of the Finnish Language*, 1967

FINNO-UGRIC LANGUAGES. Family of languages and branch of the Uralic language group.

FINNS. Group of peoples belonging to the Nordic, Baltic, and Uralic subraces of the European old race; they consist of the Finns of Finland, the Karelians, Estonians, Lapps, Volga Finns, and Permian Finns, some of which have now been assimilated by the Russians.

FIORAVANTI (FIERAVANTI), RODOLF (nicknamed ARISTOTLE) (*c.* 1418–80). Bolognese architect, engineer, and mathematician summoned to Moscow by Ivan III to rebuild the Cathedral of the Ascension. He lived in Moscow from 1475 to 1479.

FIRES OF 1862. A series of outbreaks, the cause of which was unknown but suspected to be arson, in St. Petersburg and in towns on the Volga River. They formed part of a general unrest that was otherwise marked by peasant riots, student actions, and revolutionary propaganda.

FIRST WORLD WAR. *See* **World War I.**

FISHING INDUSTRY. The most important fishing areas include the Barents and White seas, the Far East, the Baltic Sea, and the Caspian Sea. Whaling is carried out in the Antarctic. The most important fish processing plants are in Murmansk and Astrakhan. The fishing catch including whales totaled (in 1,000 tons): in 1913, 1,051; in 1940, 1,422; in 1960, 3,541; and in 1980, 9,526.

FIVE, THE. *See* ***Moguchaya Kuchka.***

FIVE-YEAR PLAN. Plan during which the economic growth of the country is structured for the following five years, the first of which lasted from 1928 to 1932. In 1958 the Seven-Year Plan replaced it.

Bergson, A., *The Economics of Soviet Planning,* 1964.

Carr, Edward Hallett and Davies, R. W., *Foundations of a Planned Economy,* Vol. 1, 1969.

Kaser, Michael, *Soviet Economics,* 1970.

Nove, Alec, *An Economic History of the USSR,* 1969.

FLAG (STATE). Red, with a hammer and sickle in gold in the upper left corner and above them a five-pointed star bordered in gold.

FLETCHER, GILES, THE ELDER (1548–1611). English poet, author, and diplomat. Having studied at Eton College, where he began to compose Latin verse, Fletcher was admitted as a scholar to King's College, and in 1572 was appointed a lecturer at King's. After serving as deputy senior orator and senior fellow, in 1580 Fletcher was made dean of arts. Elected to Parliament in 1583, two years later he was made remembrancer of the city of London. Dispatched on an important mission to Hamburg as second agent of the queen, in 1588 he was sent as ambassador to Russia. He concluded an alliance between England and Russia at the court of Tsar Fedor I; trade with Russia was restored, and better conditions obtained for the English Muscovy Company. In 1591 he published *Of the Russe Commonwealth,* a comprehensive account of Russian government, law, manners, geography, and military strategy.

Berry, L., *The English Works of Giles Fletcher the Elder,* 1964.

FLORENCE, COUNCIL AND UNION OF (1439). Act of union signed between the Western Church and the Orthodox Church in 1439. The reunion of Rome and Constantinople was short-lived. Metropolitan Isidor of Moscow, who had agreed to the decisions taken by the council, was imprisoned on his return to Moscow, and a new metropolitan, Metropolitan Yiona, was made head of an independent Orthodox Church in 1448.

FLORENSKIY, PAUL ALEKSANDROVICH (1882–?). Orthodox priest, philosopher, and physicist. One of the founders of the Union of Christian Struggle as a student, he then lectured at the Moscow Theological Academy. Banished to Central Asia before the 1917 Bolshevik seizure of power, he returned and studied advanced physics at the Academy of Sciences. Deported to a concentration camp in the 1920s, nothing more is known about him. His *The Pillar and Foundation of Truth* (1914) has influenced philosophical and theological thought in the Soviet Union.

FLOROVSKIY, GEORGIY VASILEVICH (1893–). Orthodox priest, theologian, and philosopher. A professor at the Russian Theological Institute in Paris, and then at the St. Vladimir Theological Seminary in New York, his *The Ways of Russian Theology* (1937) was particularly influential.

FOKINE, MICHAEL (1880–1942). Russian dancer and choreographer. He was one of the founders of modern ballet. Isadora Duncan inspired him to free himself from the rigid classical discipline of the Imperial Ballet to create ballets in which dancing, music, and scenery are combined in a related whole. *Le Cygne* (*The Dying Swan,* 1905) created as a solo for Anna Pavlova (*q.v.*), and *Chopiniana* (later known as *Les Sylphides,* 1906) were early works. His great period was with Diaghilev in Paris (from 1909), when he created *Petrushka, Scheherazade, The Firebird,* and *Le Spectre de la Rose.* He left Russia for France at the outbreak of the Revolution and moved to the United States during the Second World War.

Beaumont, C. W., *M. Fokine and His Ballets,* 1945.

FONVIZIN, DENIS IVANOVICH (1744–92). First Russian playwright. Fonvizin entered the civil service, and in 1777–78 traveled to Montpellier. He is particularly noted for his two comedies, *The Brigadier-General* (1766) and *The Minor* (1782), both considered masterpieces that combine native Russian comedy with 18th-century French comedy.

Brown, W. E., *A History of Eighteenth-Century Russian Literature,* 1978.

Cross, Anthony G. (ed.), *Russian Literature in the Age of Catherine the Great,* 1976.

Welsh, D. A., *Russian Comedy, 1765–1825,* 1966.

FORCED LABOR CAMPS. *See* **GULag.**

FORESTRY. Of the 791.6 million hectares of forest land of the USSR, a large portion is administered and worked by the state, and the other, about 38 million hectares in extent, is granted for use to the peasantry free of charge. The largest forest areas are 515 million hectares in the Asiatic part of the USSR; 51.4 million along the N seaboard; 25.4 million in the Urals; and 17.95 million in the NW.

On October 24, 1948, a plan was published for planting crop-protecting forest belts, introducing crop rotation with grasses and the building of ponds and water reservoirs in the steppe and forest-steppe areas of the European part of the USSR. By the middle of 1952, some 2.6 million hectares had been planted with shelter-belt trees and 13,500 ponds and reservoirs had been built. The planting of the shelter belts in the Kamyshin-Volgograd and Belgorod-Don areas has in the main been completed. A Volga forest belt has been planted along 1,200 km of railway. Reforestation was carried out on 2.5 million hectares of land in 1980.

FORMALISTS. Name given to the group of literary critics belonging to the Opoyaz group (Society for the Study of Poetic Language). Leading Formalist critics include V. Shklovskiy, B. Eykhenbaum, and R. Jakobson. The Formalists issued their manifesto, a collection of essays entitled *Poetika*, in 1919. For the Formalists, art is mainly a collection of devices and techniques; attention is paid to style rather than to ideas expressed or the "message" conveyed; a typical work of Formalist criticism is Shklovskiy's essay "The Plot as a Phenomenon of Style." The extremists amongst the Formalists identified the study of literature with that of linguistics and were interested primarily in the phonetic qualities of poetry; Osip Brik, for instance, produced a study of the phonetic structure of Pushkin's verse. The more moderated Formalists, the "Petersburg Group," shared a keen interest in the way in which historical processes have affected literature. The school as a whole was suppressed in 1930.

Mirsky, D. S., *Contemporary Russian Literature, 1881–1925*, 1972.

FOURIER, FRANÇOIS MARIE CHARLES (1772–1837). French social philosopher who advocated the peaceful transformation of society into small self-supporting communes. In Russia, Fourierism had a considerable influence on the thought of the *Petrashevtsy* (*q.v.*), an informal group of radicals arrested in 1849.

FRANK, ILYA MIKHAILOVICH (1908–). Physicist, and joint Nobel Prize winner with Pavel A. Cherenkov and I. Ye. Tamm for discovering and interpreting the "Kereskov effect." Of great importance in the field of nuclear physics. Frank has also conducted research into electron radiation and gamma ray quanta.

FRANK, SEMEN LYUDVIGOVICH (1877–1950). Philosopher. A Marxist and Social Democrat, Frank was interested in idealism before becoming involved with the Orthodox Church. A university teacher from 1912 to 1922, in 1922 he was exiled and then lived in Berlin, Paris, and London. His philosophic ideas on All-Unity are discussed in his works, such as *Philosophy and Life* (1910) and *God with Us* (1946).

Kalakowski, L., *The Main Currents of Marxism,* Vol. 3, 1980.

FRANZ JOSEF LAND. Archipelago of approximately 187 islands in the Arctic Ocean off Novaya Zemlya and N of the Barents Sea, in the Russian Soviet Federated Socialist Republic. It has an area of 8,000 square miles (20,720 sq km). It was discovered by Austrians in 1873 and claimed by the USSR in 1926. Three main sections are separated by the British Channel on the W and the Austrian Sound on the E. The main islands are Aleksandra, George, Wilczek, Graham Bell, Hooker, and Rudolf Islands. Formed of basalt and almost covered by glacier ice and lichen, the land rises to 2,410 feet (735 m) above sea level on Wilczek Land. There are government observation stations with permanent settlements.

FREE TRADE UNION ASSOCIATION. Union established by 43 workers in 1977 and 1978, and quashed by police action in 1978.

FREEMASONRY. Undenominational "religion" for men, based on philanthropy and mysticism. In Russia freemasonry flourished from 1770 to 1810, but it later degenerated into an incredible and bigoted mysticism. The former freemasons' lodge in Moscow now houses the Writers' Union.

FRENCH INFLUENCE ON RUSSIA. Under Elizabeth and Catherine II, French was the language spoken by the aristocracy. Adulation of Voltaire was excessive, and French culture was widely imitated; French classicism left its mark on architecture and the arts, and the Russian language assimilated some French words. Michael Speransky (*q.v.*) reorganized local government on the Napoleonic model. During the Slavophile/Westernizer controversy, however, there was much heated debate as to whether Russia should continue to look to the West, or whether it should preserve its own heritage; Fedor M. Dostoyevsky was among those highly critical of France.

Billington, James, *The Icon and the Axe; A Cultural History of Russia,* 1966.

FRIEDLAND, BATTLE OF (November 14, 1807). A battle during the Napoleonic Wars fought near Friedland, East Prussia (now Pravdinsk, Russian Soviet Federated Socialist Republic). The French under Napoleon defeated the Russians, under General Levin Bennigsen (1745–1826). The victory enabled the French to occupy Königsberg and led to the Treaty of Tilsit between Napoleon and Alexander I of Russia.

FRUG, SIMON SAMUEL (1860–1916). Russian-Yiddish poet. After the publication of his first poem in Russian in 1880, Frug became a prominent figure in Russian literary circles in St. Petersburg. In 1888 he began to write in Yiddish. Although his Russian poetry is considered to be more successful, Frug helped modernize Yiddish poetic techniques. Most of his writing deals with the suffering encountered by Jewish people in Russia.

FRUNZE. Capital of Kirghizia situated 120 miles (192 km) WSW of Alma Ata in the Chu River valley.

Founded as a fortress in 1878. Industries include meat packing, floor milling, tanning, and the manufacture of agricultural machinery and textiles. Population (1981) 552,000.

FRUNZE, MICHAEL VASILEVICH (1885–1925). Bolshevik military leader. Having taken part in the 1905 Revolution, Frunze defeated Admiral Kolchak in 1919 and General Wrangel (*q.q.v.*) in 1920 during the Civil War. During the intra-party struggle Frunze sided with Stalin, and was appointed people's commissar for military and naval affairs in 1925.

FRYAZIN, IVAN (GIOVANNI BATTISTA VOLPE) (*c.* 15th century). Italian master of the mint in Moscow under Ivan III.

FUNT. A pound (measure of weight).

FURMANOV, DMITRIY ANDREYEVICH (1891–1926). Writer. Originally a journalist, he wrote several "Sketches from the Front" after joining the army in 1914. They were published in *Russkoye Slovo* in 1916. He joined the Communist Party in 1918 and served as a political commissar with Chapayev's guerrilla forces. In 1923 he wrote the novel *Chapayev* about his experiences, which was later successfully made into a film. Other works are *Red Sortie* (1922), *Riot* (1923–25), and an unfinished novel, *Writers.*

FUTURISM. Movement in literature and art that occurred between 1910 and 1930. Influenced by artistic developments in France and Italy, Russian Futurists strove to create a new art that belonged to the 20th century. There were several groups of Futurists, the most famous of which was the Cubist-Futurist group led by Velemir Khlebnikov (*q.v.*). Khlebnikov developed a "trans-sense" language, designed to free the word from its meaning. The poet Vladimir Mayakovsky (*q.v.*) also belonged to this group. The Futurists, at first cooperating with the government, organized the Left Front in the arts, but owing to disenchantment with the regime, split up in 1930.

Markov, Vladimir, *Russian Futurism: A History,* 1969.

FYODOR I, II, III. *See* **Fedor I, II, III.**

G

GABO, NAUM (1890–1977). Gabo and his brother Anton Pevsner *(q.v.)* returned to the USSR in 1917 from Munich and became the founders of the Constructivist school of art. Gabo was the most noted sculptor of this school, specializing in constructions of colored transparent materials, metals, glass, and plastic, which illustrated new theories of sculptural space. In 1920, with his brother, he published the *Realistic Manifesto*, challenging the right of governments to interfere with an artist's right to explore new ways of expression. In that year he made a sculpture with a single moving part; this became known as kinetic sculpture. In 1922 he left Russia for Germany and later lived in England before going to the United States in 1946. He wrote *Gabo* (1957) and *Of Divers Arts* (1962).

Bowlt, John E. (ed.), *Russian Art of the Avant-Garde: Theory and Criticism 1902–1934*, 1976.

Gray, Camilla. *The Russian Experiment in Art, 1863–1922*, 1971.

Olson, R. and Chanin, A., *Naum Gabo, Antoine Pevsner*, 1948.

Read, H. and Leslie, M., *Naum Gabo*, 1957.

GAGARIN, PRINCE PAUL PAVLOVICH (1789–1872). From 1864 he was president of the state council and committee of ministers, and from 1857 to 1861 a member of the secret council for peasant affairs. He was a staunch supporter of the autocracy.

GAGARIN, YURY ALEKSEYEVICH (1934–68). Astronaut. In April 1961 he became the first man to orbit the earth in a space capsule and return safely. He wrote *Till We Reach the Stars* (1962), and (with V. Lebedev) *Psychology and Space* (1971). He died in an air crash in 1968.

Gagarin, V., *My Brother Yuri: Pages from the Life of the First Cosmonaut*, 1974.

GAGAUZ. Turkic-speaking people living in Dobniya, S Bessarabia in the

Zaporozhye oblast of the Ukraine, totaling about 150,000. Their forefathers were Orthodox Christians, who migrated there as a result of the Russo-Turkish wars and the savage Turkish persecution of Christians.

GAGRA. Town situated 45 miles (72 km) NW of Sukhumi on the Black Sea, in the Abkhazian Autonomous Soviet Socialist Republic. Health resort and port. Industries include distilling, sawmilling, and metalworking. Coast guard station.

GALICIA. Region extending N from the Carpathian mountains across SE Poland and NW Ukraine. It is rich in minerals, especially oil and natural gas.

GAPON, FATHER GEORGI APOLLONOVICH (1870–1906). Priest. He believed in police socialism and founded the Assembly of Russian Factory and Mill Workers in St. Petersburg in 1903, which was financed by police funds. A strike at the Putilov works in St. Petersburg began because of alleged victimization of assembly members and soon spread. Gapon decided to make an appeal to the tsar. He promoted a petition which was revolutionary in its demands, and organized an illegal march of 200,000 to the Winter Palace. The police fired on the demonstrators, killing 130 people, and January 9, 1905 became known as "Bloody Sunday" and saw the start of a year of revolutionary unrest. Gapon was not, however, trusted by his fellow revolutionaries and was murdered.

Harcave, Sidney, *First Blood: The Revolution of 1905*, 1964.

Sablinsky, W., *The Road to Bloody Sunday: The Role of Father Gapon and the Assembly in the Petersburg Massacre of 1905*, 1976.

GARIN (real name **Mikhailovsky, Nicholas Georgyevich**) (1852–1906). Writer, although for most of his life, Garin worked as a railway engineer. His main work as an author is a trilogy describing the early life of Tema Kartashov; *Tema's Childhood* (1892), *Schoolboys* (1893), and *Students* (1895). This well-written work of literature is also considered an important historical document.

GARSHIN, VSEVOLOD MIKHAILOVICH (1855–88). Novelist. He fought in the war with Turkey (1877) and then wrote the short story *Four Days*, which established his reputation as a writer. Mental instability and the fear of madness drove Garshin to suicide. His literary output consists of 20 stories, the best known of which is *The Red Flower*. His writing shows great sensitivity and human understanding.

Mirsky, D. S., *A History of Russian Literature*, 1949.

GASTEV, ALEKSEI KAPITONOVICH (1882–1939). Poet and labor theorist. Gastev's poetry deals with industrialization, the necessity of building an "iron state," for which sacrifices are called. In his prose writings, Gastev expounded his theory of "mechanized collectivism," in which the workers synchronize their movements with the movements of machines, thus making individual thinking and a "normalized psychology" impossible. His reputation as a poet rests on his *Shockwork Poetry* (1918) and *A Stack of Orders* (1921). Gastev directed the central institute of labor, but disappeared during the Great Purge.

Zavalishnin, Vyacheslav, *Early Soviet Writers,*1958.

GATCHINA. Town in the Leningrad oblast, 28 miles (45 km) SW of Leningrad. The village of Khotchino was founded there in the 15th century, but a town developed there after a summer palace was built (1766–1772) for Catherine II. It was later transformed into a palace, barracks and fortress, but was held by the Germans in the Second World War and was extensively damaged in the siege of Leningrad. Gatchina was a favorite residence of the tsars in the 19th century. Its main industries are paper production and tractor repairing. Population (1970) 63,000.

GAZLI. Largest natural gas field in the USSR, discovered in the 1950s. Situated 63 miles (100 km) NW of Bukhara in the Bukhara oblast of Uzbekistan.

GE, NIKOLAI NIKOLAIYEVICH (1831–94). Artist of French origin who joined the Academy in 1850. He settled in Florence and concentrated mainly on landscapes and religious paintings, before returning to Russia. Turning his back on a career as a professor, Ge spent 10 years in the Ukraine studying Tolstoy's religious writings. His religious paintings, particularly *Golgotha* (1892) and *The Crucifixion* (1891), are particularly expressive and stand out from the comforting familiarity of other religious paintings of this era.

Hamilton, George H., *The Art and Architecture of Russia,* 1954.

GENGHIS KHAN (1162–1227). Mongol emperor who succeeded his father at the age of 13. He was responsible for uniting the Mongols under his leadership and established his capital at Karakorum in 1206. A great warrior, he conquered the whole of North China (1211), the area from Lake Balkash to Tibet (1217), and the empire of Kharezm (1218), and became the ruler of Central Asia; in addition he was a most skillful administrator and promulgated a code of laws for his people. The result was that his organization of states lasted for longer than was usual in Asia at that time.

Desmond Martin, H., *The Rise of Chingis Khan and His Conquest of Northern China,* 1950.

Fox, R., *Ghenghis Khan,* 1937.

GEORGIAN SOVIET SOCIALIST REPUBLIC. Constituent republic in SW USSR, bounded in the W by the Black Sea and in the SW by Turkey. It has an area of 26,900 square miles (69,670 sq km). The chief towns are Tbilisi (the capital), Kutaisi, Batumi, Sukhumi, Poti, Rustavi, and Gori. Georgia includes the Abkhazian Autonomous Soviet Socialist Republic, the Adzhar Autonomous Soviet Socialist Republic, and the South Ossetian Autonomous Republic. It is mountainous in the N and S, sloping to central valleys, and drained by the Kura and Rion rivers. The main products are manganese, coal, oil, baryta, tobacco, tea, fruit, and wines. Population (1981) 5,100,000.

GEORGIANS. Caucasian-speaking people living in most of Georgia. They are not an ethnically homogenous people; tribes from Asia Minor settled here and mingled with Greek, Scythian, Iranian, and Armenian elements. Although Georgians are predominantly Orthodox Christians, there are some groups of Sunni Muslims. They are intensely proud of their national heritage.

Antadze, K. D., *Soviet Georgia,* 1972.

GERMAN-SOVIET NON-AGGRESSION PACT. *See* **Russo-German Non-aggression Pact.**

GERSHENZON, MICHAEL OSIPOVICH (1869–1925). Historian, editor, and critic. After the Revolution he lectured at the Literary Art Institute of Moscow. He was associated with the Symbolists (*See* **Symbolism**) and the Neo-Idealist philosophers. His works include *P. Ya. Chaadaev* (1908), *History of Young Russia* (1908), *Historical Sketches* (1910), *Images of the Past* (1911), and are mostly concerned with the history of ideas in 19th-century Russia.

Berman, Y. A., *M. O. Gershenzon,* 1928.

GIERS, NICHOLAS KARLOVICH (1820–95). Statesman and foreign minister. He started work in the Asiatic department of the foreign ministry. In 1875 Giers was appointed director of the Asiatic department and deputy minister of foreign affairs. In 1882 he was foreign minister under Alexander III.

GILYAKS. Paleo-Asiatic people, numbering about 4,400, who live near the mouth of the Amur River and on Sakhalin Island in E Siberia. Until the 20th century they retained a form of group marriage. They are mostly fishermen and hunters. Since collectivization they have undertaken some crop production and cattle rearing.

GINZBURG, ALEXANDER (1936–). Writer and dissident. An employee of the State Literary Museum. Ginzburg edited the journal *Syntaxis* which expressed discontent with the Soviet way of life. In 1960 Ginzburg was prosecuted by the KGB in connection with this, was convicted, and given a sentence of two years in corrective labor camps. In 1964 the KGB charged Ginzburg with possessing "anti-Soviet" literature, but the case was dismissed. In 1967 Ginzburg and Yuri Galanskov were arrested on the grounds of anti-Soviet agitation and propaganda and tried in 1968. Despite massive support at home and abroad, Ginzburg was sentenced to five years and Galanskov seven years hard labor.

Reddaway, Peter (ed.), *Uncensored Russia,* 1972.

GIPPIUS (HIPPIUS), ZINAIDA NIKOLAYEVNA (1867–1945). Symbolist poet. She was a member of the Religious and Philosophical Society and wrote in a metaphysical vein. Leaving Russia in 1919, she continued writing poetry, plays, novels and short stories, many of which displayed bitter opposition to Bolshevism. Her most important novel is *The Devil's Puppet* (1911).

West, James D., *Russian Symbolism,* 1970.

GLADKOV, FEDOR VASILYEVICH (1883–1958). Author. His *Story of My Childhood* (1949) was widely acclaimed. His other works include *Cement* (1926), published after the Revolution, which was the first novel to portray Soviet economic and industrial activity.

Alexandrova, Vera, *A History of Soviet Literature,* 1963.

Struve, Gleb., *Russian Literature under Lenin and Stalin,* 1972.

GLAGOLITHIC ALPHABET. According to legends, the alphabet invented by St. Cyril of Thessalonica in the ninth century for Slavonic translations of religious works during his mission to Moravia. Some of the earliest Old Church Slavonic manuscripts are written in the Glagolithic alphabet. It was soon replaced by the Cyrillic alphabet, also invented by St. Cyril.

GLAVLIT. Abbreviation for the Chief Literary Administration, or Soviet censorship office. Nothing in the USSR can be published unless it has been submitted to *Glavlit. Glavlit*'s representative reads the work, indicating what alterations are necessary. After changes are made, the revised version is resubmitted. It is then stamped and signed.

GLAZUNOV, ALEXANDER KONSTANTINOVICH (1865–1936). Composer and conductor. He studied under Rimsky-Korsakov. In 1899 he was appointed professor of music at the St. Petersburg Conservatory, and in 1909 he was appointed director. Glazunov's musical output includes the ballets *Raymonda, Les Ruses d'Amour,*and *The Seasons,* eight symphonies, choral music, orchestral works, piano and violin concertos, and chamber, vocal and instrumental music. Toward the end of the his career, Glazunov became more and more interested in form and abstract music. He left Russia in 1928 and finally settled in Paris where he died.

Fedorova, G., *A. K. Glazunov,* 1947.

GLEB. *See* **Boris and Gleb.**

GLIÈRE, REINHOLD MORITZOVICH (1875–1956). Composer. He studied in Kiev and Moscow and became professor of composition (1913) and director (1914) at the Kiev Conservatory, and professor of composition at the Moscow Conservatory (1920). He taught Prokofiev, Khachaturian, Knipper, and Myaskovsky (*q.q.v.*). A prolific composer, his works include several symphonies, of which the best known is No. 3, *Ilya Mouromets* (1909–11), the ballet *The Red Poppy* (1926–27), and a cello concerto. In his later works he used folk music from the E USSR.

GLINKA, FEDOR NIKOLAYEVICH (1786–1880). Mystical and religious poet. He wrote mystical, religious verse, but also some secular poems, one of which, *Troika,* is known throughout Russia as a song. He fought in the 1812 campaign and also wrote on military affairs.

GLINKA, MICHAEL IVANOVICH (1804–57). Composer. He studied in St. Petersburg and Berlin. His work laid the foundation of the Russian school of music, as he rejected the influence of Western European composers and used folk music. His *A Life for the Tsar*, now called *Ivan Susanin* (1836), is the first important Russian opera and one of the first examples of nationalism in music. He also composed the opera *Ruslan and Ludmilla* (1842), after a poem by Pushkin. He also wrote *Memoirs* (trans. R. B. Mudge), in 1963. *See* **Moguchaya Kuchka.**

Brown, David, *Mikhail Glinka*, 1974.

Calvocoressi, Michael D., *A Survey of Russian Music*, 1944.

GLINSKAYA, ELENA (?–1538). Mother of Ivan IV. Following the death of her husband, Basil III, in 1533, she governed for her son Ivan IV, who was then a minor. She came from the Glinsky family, but ignored the boyars and turned to her uncle, Prince Michael Glinksy, for help in governing. Later she relied on Prince Telepnev-Obolensky for assistance. She was extremely unpopular and died suddenly in 1538; poisoning was suspected.

GNEDICH, NICHOLAS IVANOVICH (1784–1833). Poet. He successfully translated Homer's *Iliad* (1829) from the Greek, and his poems include some excellent paraphrases of Greek folk songs.

GNESSIN, MICHAEL FEBIANOVICH (1883–1957). Composer. He studied at St. Petersburg Conservatory and helped to found the Don Conservatory, becoming director in 1920. Later he was a professor at the Moscow and Leningrad conservatories. His compositions include an opera-poem *The Youth of Abraham* (1921–23), works for chorus and orchestra, including *Symphonic Monument, 1905–17* (1925), incidental music, and folk song arrangements. After the Revolution he set a poem by Sergei Esenin *(q.v.)* to music for chorus and orchestra to commemorate the revolutions of 1905 and 1917.

GODUNOV, BORIS FEDOROVICH (*c.* 1551–1605). Tsar of Russia (from 1598). He rose to importance under Ivan the Terrible; his sister, Irene, married Ivan's heir, the feeble-minded Fedor. During Fedor's reign (1584–98) Boris acted as regent, and after his death the *Zemsky sobor* elected him tsar. His reign inaugurated the "Time of Troubles," but he was an able if tyrannical ruler. He was suspected of the murder of the rightful heir, Fedor's younger brother, Dmitry, who had died mysteriously (1591). Boris was killed in suppressing a revolt during the advance on Moscow of a false claimant to the throne. His life is the theme of Mussorgsky's well-known opera *Boris Godunov*.

Grey, Ian, *Boris Godunov: The Tragic Czar*, 1973.

GODUNOV, FEDOR (?–1605). Son and heir of Boris Godunov, deposed and murdered, together with his mother, in Moscow by supporters of the False Dmitry after a reign lasting just a few weeks.

GOGOL, NICHOLAS VASILYEVICH (1809–52). Author and dramatist of Cossack origin. While some critics claim Gogol as one of the first Realist writers, his work has elements of Surrealism, depicting the reality of a nightmare world. His short story *The Overcoat* (1842) was to have a considerable influence on subsequent writers, while *The Nose,* in which a character loses his nose, clearly discredits the theory that Gogol was purely a Realist. The comedy *Government Inspector* (1842) has brought Gogol lasting fame, but his best-known work, *Dead Souls* (1842), is one of the masterpieces of Russian literature. This *poema* is a satirical account not only of the deficiencies of life in Russia, but of the human condition. Convinced of his divine mission as an instrument in bringing about the moral regeneration of Russia, Gogol fell increasingly under the influence of Father Matthew Konstantinovsky, a fierce ascetic, who strengthened Gogol's fear of hell. As an act of self-mortification, Gogol burned the second part of the manuscript of *Dead Souls*. He fell into a state of melancholy and died.

Magarshack, D., *Gogol: A Life,* 1957.

Nabokov, Vladimir, *Nikolai Gogol,* 1961.

Troyat, Henri, *Gogol: The Biography of a Divided Soul* (trans. 1973).

GOLDEN HORDE. The Empire of the Golden Horde (also known as Western Kipchaks) was formed in the 13th century by Batu, a grandson of Genghis Khan. It comprised European Russia and W Siberia. Its capital was Sarai on the Aktuba River, an arm of the lower Volga, but in the 14th century the capital was moved to a point 45 miles E of modern Volgograd but still named Sarai. The rise of the Golden Horde ended the growth of Kievan Russia, and Kiev itself was sacked by the Horde in 1240. During the period 1237–40 nearly all Russian principalities came under the Horde's control and paid tribute to the khans. The Golden Horde were eventually defeated at the battles of Kulikovo (1380) and Timur (1395).

Curtis, J., *The Mongols in Russia,* 1908.

Presnyakov, A. E., *The Formation of the Great Russian State,* 1970.

Vernadsky, George V., *The Mongols and Russia,* 1953.

GOLDEN HORN BAY. Inlet of Peter the Great Gulf on the Sea of Japan, on which stands the port of Vladivostok.

GOLDFADEN, ABRAHAM (1840–1908). Hebrew and Yiddish poet and playwright born in Russia. After graduating from the Zhitomir rabbinical seminary in 1866, Goldfaden taught in Russia before emigrating to Poland and Rumania, where he founded the first Yiddish theater. In 1878 he returned to Russia, but later moved to Poland and the United States. Among Goldfaden's best works are *Shulamit* (1880) and *Bar Kochba* (1882).

GOLDMAN, EMMA (1869–1940). Anarchist. She left Russia for the United States in 1885 and was politically active from about 1890 to 1917. She was imprisoned in 1893 for inciting a riot. After meeting Alexander Berkman in 1906, she became an active anarchist and was imprisoned in 1916 and in 1917, and after two years in prison she was deported to Russia. She later lived in England and Canada and was involved in the Spanish Civil War. Her writings include *Anarchism and Other Essays* (1911), *My Disillusionment in Russia* (1923), and an autobiography *Living My Life*, (1931).

Shulman, A., *Emma Goldman*, 1971.

GOLENISHCHEV-KUTUZOV, COUNT ARSENY ARKADYEVICH, (1843–1913). Poet and contributor to the journals *Delo* and *Vestnik Evropi*. In his poetry Golenishchev-Kutuzov attempted to revive a classical style, but it is generally considered that the result is wooden and lifeless, although poems dealing with destruction and death are not entirely devoid of merit. Mussorgsky set some of his poetry to music, for which it is remembered.

GOLIKOV, IVAN IVANOVICH (1735–1801). Merchant and historian. Golikov collected and published a compendium of source material for a biography of Peter the Great, *The Acts of the Great Peter*.

GOLITSYN, ALEXANDER NIKOLAYEVICH (1773–1844). Prince, minister of education under Alexander I, and from 1813, president of the Russian Bible Association. His considerable influence at court continued into the days of Tsar Nicholas I.

Palmer, Alan, *Alexander I: Tsar of War and Peace*, 1974.

GOLITSYN, BORIS ALEKSEYEVICH (1654–1713). Russian statesman and tutor of Peter the Great. In 1683 the regent, Sophia Alekseyevna appointed Golitsyn head of the government department for the administration of the lower Volga region. In 1689 he directed the Naryshkin faction, which brought Peter to power, and then helped with many of Peter's undertakings, although in 1697–98 he remained at home during Peter's trip abroad, and acted as one of the triumvirate in charge. After taking harsh measures against the *streltsy* (*see* ***Strelets***), Golitsyn directed his attention to the lower Volga, ruling it despotically. He took monastic vows shortly before dying.

GOLITSYN, (PRINCE) DMITRY MIKHAILOVICH, (1665–1737). Russian statesman. In 1704 Golitsyn commanded the auxiliary troops in Poland against Charles XII. From 1715 to 1719 he was governor-general of Kiev, in 1719 was made senator, and from 1719 to 1722 was president of the Kamer-Kollegra, which was a finance ministry created by Peter I in 1718 to manage the state's income and estimate its expense. His career was marred by involvement in the disgrace of vice-chancellor P. P. Shafirov. He developed the concept of limiting the autocracy, and drew up a constitution which Empress Anna Ivanovna was forced to sign. Golitsyn was arrested in 1736 and sentenced to death, ostensibly for his part in a conspiracy, but actually for his antimonarchical views. The sentence was commuted to lifelong imprisonment.

GOLITSYN, PRINCE MICHAEL MIKHAILOVICH (1675–1730) Soldier. An accomplished strategist, he was made a field marshal under Peter I. He fought in many battles against Sweden including the battle of Poltava. Later he was president of the War College (ministry), a senator, and member of the Supreme Privy Council.

GOLITSYN, PRINCE VASILY VASILYEVICH, (1643–1714). Russian statesman in charge of foreign affairs prior to 1689. In 1682, under the rule of Tsar Fedor Alekseyevich, Golitsyn assisted in the reorganization of military service and the abolition of *mestnichestvo*. Under Sophia Alekseyevna, Golitsyn was principal minister and head of the foreign office. He achieved a successful outcome of his negotiations with Poland, but his expeditions against the Crimean Tatars met with failure, as a result of which Peter the Great stripped him of his rank and wealth and banished him.

GOLOMYANKA. *Comephorus baikalensis.* Species of fish unique to Lake Baikal. It has no scales and gives birth to live young.

GOLOVIN, ALEXANDER YAKOVLEVICH (1863–1930). Soviet theater director and painter. Having studied art, Golovin started his career in the theater in the early 1900s. Influenced by Mikhail Vrubel he developed an ornamental decorative Impressionist-style. He was particularly famed for his scenery for operas such as *Carmen*. He also painted portraits of prominent actors of the day.

GOLOVKIN, GAVRIL IVANOVICH (1660–1734). The first state chancellor of the Russian Empire. Golovkin accompanied Peter the Great on his first tour of W Europe. In charge of foreign affairs from 1706, he was made state chancellor at Poltava in 1709, and a count of the Russian Empire a year later. Under Catherine I, Golovkin was a member of the Supreme Privy Council, and under Anna a member of the first Russian cabinet, which opposed suggestions for the limitation of the rights of the autocracy.

GOLOVNIN, ALEXANDER VASILYEVICH (1821–86). Minister for education (1862–66), of a relatively liberal outlook. He was responsible for the University Statute of 1863, which gave universities greater autonomy than before, and he also introduced a statute for secondary education, which was officially accepted in 1864.

GOLOVNIN, VASILY MIKHAILOVICH (1776–1831). Navigator who explored the coasts of Kamchatka and Russian America (Alaska). He served in the British navy (1801–06), was captured by the Japanese (1811–13), and circumnavigated the world (1817–19). As vice-admiral, he was responsible for the construction of ships, including the first 10 Russian steamships. His writings included *Journey Round the World* (1822) and *Narrative of My Captivity in Japan* (1816, trans. 1824).

GOLUBINSKY, YEVGENY YEVSTIGNEYEVICH (1834–1912). Church historian and professor of the

Moscow Ecclesiastical Academy. He wrote the two-volume *History of the Russian Church, 1900–17.*

GOMEL. Capital of Gomel region situated on the Sozh River, in Belorussia. It became part of Lithuania in 1537, was ceded to Poland under the Treaty of Andrusovo in 1667, and became a Russian possession in 1772. Industries include railway engineering; manufactures include electrical goods, agricultural implements, footwear, textiles, and furniture. Population (1977) 360,000.

GONCHAROV, IVAN ALEKSANDROVICH (1812–91). Novelist and censor. His psychological study, *Oblomov* (1847), which made him famous, portrays a hero who symbolizes Russian agreeable laziness. Oblomov's disease, *oblomovshchina,* is shown as common to man. In *The Frigate Pallas* (1858) Goncharov describes his sea journey to Japan.

GONCHAROVA, NATALYA SERGEYEVNA (1881–1962). Painter. Unlike other artists of the Cubist-Futurist movement, Goncharova came of a family of noble origin. In 1898 she began studying sculpture at the Moscow College, where she met Michael Larionov (*q.v.*), a fellow student, and life-long friend. In 1906 Goncharova sent work to the "World of Art" exhibition. Diaghilev invited Goncharova and Larionov to contribute to the Russian exhibition in Paris. Two streams can be discerned in her work: a vigorous revival of national traditions, influenced by icon painting, and the current European styles, particularly Impressionism. By 1910, however, under the influence of the French *fauves,* the two styles became reconciled.

Gray, Camilla, *The Russian Experiment in Art,* 1962.

GORBATOV, BORIS LEONTYEVICH (1908–54). Writer and journalist, a member of the Communist Party from 1930. A member of the writer's organization RAPP, Gorbatov wrote about it in his novel *Our Town* (1930). The Great Fatherland war provided inspiration for a number of novels and stories, including *Letter to a Comrade* (1942). *The Unvanquished* won him the Stalin prize, and deals with life in a town occupied by the Germans.

GORCHAKOV, ALEXANDER MIKHAILOVICH (1798–1883). Statesman. Gorchakov's diplomatic career started in 1817. After serving in embassies in various European capitals, in 1854 he was made an ambassador. Gorchakov succeeded Count Nesselrode as foreign minister in 1856, and as a result of his great success in this post, he was made chancellor in 1866. In the 1870s, however, in the face of Bismarckian Germany, his popularity lessened, although in 1873 he played an important part in forming the Three Emperors' League (*q.v.*). His influence in Russia's policy in the Balkan crisis (1875–78) was less considerable, yet he remains one of the most noteworthy diplomats of 19th century Europe.

GORCHAKOV, PRINCE MICHAEL (1795–1861). Soldier. He served with distinction in the Napoleonic campaigns of 1812–14, and in

1853 became chief of staff of the army. He gained fame by his gallant and skillful defense of Sevastopol (1854–55) and was viceroy of Warsaw (1856–61).

GORDON, PATRICK (1635–99). Scottish soldier. Following service in the Swedish-Polish wars (1655–60), in which he fought for each side in turn, he joined the Russian army in 1661. A friend of Peter the Great, he rose to the rank of general, having helped the tsar to overthrow the regent, Sophia, in 1689 and to suppress the *streltsy* revolt of 1698. *Passages from the Diary of General Patrick Gordon of Auchleuchries* was published in 1859.

GOREMYKIN, IVAN LONGINOVICH (1839–1917). Minister of the interior under Nicholas II from 1895–99 and chairman of the council of ministers in 1906 and from 1914–16. He was considered to have taken little action against Rasputin (*q.v.*) and was forced to resign.

GORI. Town 40 miles (64 km) WNW of Tbilisi, in Georgia. Mentioned in the seventh century as Tontio, it became a Russian town in 1801. It is situated in a horticultural area. Industries include fruit and vegetable canning and sawmilling. It is the birthplace of Joseph Stalin (1879). Population (1976) 54,000.

GORKY. Formerly Nizhny Novgorod, Russian Soviet Federated Socialist Republic city and capital of the oblast of the same name situated at the confluence of the Volga and Oka rivers. Founded by Prince Vladimir in 1221. Industries include shipbuilding, sawmilling, oil refining, chemicals, and textiles; manufactures include locomotives, aircraft, cars, machine tools, and electrical goods. It is famous for its annual trade fairs established in 1817. Gorky is the birthplace of Maxim Gorky, the author, in 1868, and of Mily Alekseyevich Balakirev, the composer, in 1836. Population (1981) 1,367,000.

GORKY, MAXIM (real name **Aleksei Maksimovich Peshkov**) (1868–1936). Literary theorist, novelist, playwright, and critic. His pen name is Russian for "bitter." Orphaned as a child, Gorky wandered about Russia, had no formal education, and held various jobs. He describes this period of his life in *Childhood* (1913), *My Apprenticeship* (1918), and *My Universities* (1923). Gorky first achieved fame in 1898 with his collected tales. While his early writings tended toward romanticism, later stories were often Chekhovian and finally his work is a denunciation of capitalist society. *Mother* (1907) and *Klim Samgin* (1927–36) are examples of this. A supporter of the Bolsheviks, he lived the life of an émigré on Capri (1906–13), and established the *Vperëd* faction with Alexander Alexandrovich Bogdanov. Following the February Revolution of 1917, Gorky set up the New Life group, a non-Bolshevik Left Social Democratic group. Opposed to the Bolshevik seizure of power, he nevertheless cooperated with them from 1919, although he lived in Italy from 1921 to 1928. After his return to the USSR, he headed the Writers' Union from 1932, and was proclaimed founder of Socialist Realism. He was a close friend of Stalin. It is uncertain whether Gorky died from natural causes, or whether his death was engineered by the anti-Soviet Bloc of Rightists and Trotskyists.

Kaun, Alexander, *Maxim Gorky and His Russia,* 1932.

Levin, Dan, *Stormy Petrel,* 1965.

Muchnik, Helen, *From Gorky to Pasternak,* 1963.

GORLOVKA. Town 20 miles (32 km) NNE of Donetsk situated in the Donbas coalfield, in the Ukraine. Industries include mining; manufactures include mining machinery, chemicals, and fertilizers. Population (1981) 338,000.

GORNO-ALTAY AUTONOMOUS REGION. Region in the Altay Mountains on the Mongolian frontier, in the Russian Soviet Federated Socialist Republic. It has an area of 35,740 square miles (92,567 sq km), and is forested. Its capital is Gorno-Altaysk. Main occupations are lumbering, cattle rearing and goldmining; some 133,000 hectares are under crops. The main industries are mining (gold, mercury, and brown coal) and chemicals. Population (1973) 166,000.

GORNO-ALTAYSK. Capital of Gorno-Altay Autonomous Region, 140 miles (224 km) SE of Barnaul. Industries include meat packing and textiles; manufactures include furniture. Population (1970) 98,000.

GORNO-BADAKHSHAN AUTONOMOUS REGION. Autonomous region in the Pamirs between the borders of China and Afghanistan, in Tadzhikistan. It has an area of 24,590 square miles (63,688 sq km). Its capital is Khorog, which is situated 165 miles (264 km) SE of Dushanbe. The region is mountainous. The chief occupations are farming, especially cattle and sheep, cereals and fodder crops; and mining, especially gold, coal, salt, mica, and rock crystal. Population (1972) 163,000.

GORODETSKY, SERGEI MITROFANOVICH (1884–). Poet. His first book, *Yar* (1907), demonstrated his considerable promise as a Symbolist poet. His later work was disappointing. In 1912 Gorodetsky repudiated Symbolism, and together with Nicholas Gumilev (*q.v.*) founded the Acmeist school. After Gorodetsky had joined the Communist Party, he denounced any connection with the Acmeists largely as a result of Gumilev's execution. His later collections of verse, *The Sickle* (1921) and *Mirolom* (1923), idealize the life of the Soviet workers.

GORODOVYE PRIKAZCHIKY. Locally elected town administrators in the first half of the 16th century. In towns in which the population guaranteed to pay taxes to the treasury, election of local administrative officials was allowed. Elsewhere, local officials were appointed by the central government.

GOSBANK. The Soviet state bank.

GOSIZDAT. The state publishing house in the USSR.

GOSKINO. The state cinema.

GOSPLAN. Abbreviation for State Planning Commission government departments which plan and coordinate economic activities founded 1921. The Gosplan consists of three types of departments, according to regional differences and branches of the economy. The party leadership disapproved of Gosplan's first five year plan, which provoked a wave of terror against some of those in charge. Since then, Gosplan has been directed by people from the party leadership. In 1960 responsibility for long-term economic planning was transferred to the *Gosekonomsoviet* or state scientific economic council.

Miller, M., *Rise of the Russian Consumer*, 1965.

GOST. Member of the highest ranking merchants in Moscow in medieval times, appointed by the tsar to handle his domestic and foreign trade in monopolized goods. *Gosti* could buy land and were exempt from certain taxes.

GOSTINNAYA SOTNIYA. Merchants' association (guild) of lower-ranking merchants in Moscow in the 16th and 17th century. The membership of the association varied from 100 to 350 members, who, though influential, did not enjoy the same rights and privileges as those of the *gosti*.

GOSTINNY DVOR. Marketplace in Moscow and St. Petersburg where foreign, or "outside," merchants could display their goods.

GOSUDAR. "Great Sovereign" or "Sovereign of All Russia." The former title was bestowed on Patriarch Philaret (*q.v.*) in 1619 by his son, Tsar Mikhail. Tsar Alexis bestowed the same title on Patriarch Nikon. The title established the recipient, in effect, as the tsar's colleague. The title "Sovereign of All Russia" was assumed by Ivan III in 1493, to emphasize his claim to the entire inheritance of Kievan state.

GPU (GOSUDARSTVENNOYE POLITICHESKOE UPRAVLENIYE). Abbreviation for State Political Administration Soviet Security Service, which was founded in 1922, replacing the *Cheka* (*q.v.*). Its work was directed against the church, private entrepreneurs, kulaks, the old intellectuals, and former members of opposition parties. The GPU was also concerned with the conflict within the party. In 1924 its name was changed to OGPU and in 1934 to NKVD. *See* **Secret Police.**

Deacon, R., *A History of the Russian Secret Service*, 1972.

Levytsky, B., *The Uses of Terror: The Soviet Secret Police, 1917–1970*, 1972.

Wolin, Simon and Slusser, Robert M., (eds.), *The Soviet Secret Police*, 1957.

GRABAR, IGOR EMMANUILOVICH (1871–1960). Art historian whose works include the six-volume *Istoriya russkogo iskusstva*.

GRAHAM, STEPHEN (1884–1975). Writer. An Englishman who lived in Russia and there studied the lives of peasants and students. His works include *A Vagabond in the Caucasus* (1911), *Undiscovered Russia* (1912), and *Summing-up on Russia* (1951).

GRAMOTA. Russian word denoting a written document.

GRAND EMBASSY. An embassy of 250 organized by Peter the Great. It consisted of three ambassadors headed by François Lefort (*q.v.*). It left Moscow on March 9, 1697 and over a period of 18 months traveled through Sweden, Holland, and England, and in the Hapsburg Empire. One of the main aims was to obtain greater knowledge of shipbuilding. Peter traveled with the embassy incognito as "Pëtr Mikhailov" and spent many months working as a craftsman in the docks of Amsterdam and London. Because of the revolt of the *streltsy* he was forced to return to Russia and curtail his travels and so did not visit France and Italy as planned. During the 18 months he recruited over 750 foreigners to work in Russia.

Anderson, M. S., *Peter the Great,* 1978.

GRANOVSKY, ALEXANDER (1890–1937). Theater director. In 1919 he founded the Jewish Theater studio in Leningrad; its repertoire was based on the work of Sholom Aleichem (*q.v.*). Later it transferred to Moscow as the Moscow State Jewish Theater.

GRANOVSKY, TIMOFEI NIKOLAYEVICH (1813–55). Historian and writer. He was professor of European history at Moscow University. His scholarly output was not great but he had, through his writings, teaching and personality, a great influence on his students. He was considered to be a typical "Westerner" of that period.

Masaryk, Tomás G., *The Spirit of Russia,* rev. ed. 1955.
Stankevich, A. V., *T. N. Granovsky,* 1914.

GREAT/SECOND NORTHERN WAR (1700–21). Fought by Russia, Denmark/Norway, and Saxony/Poland against Sweden. Charles XII (*q.v.*) of Sweden defeated Russia at Narva (1700), resulting in the withdrawal of Norway from the anti-Swedish alliance. In 1706, after six years' fighting, he defeated Poland and it too was forced to leave the alliance. Peter the Great meanwhile increased his military strength in the Baltic and finally beat the Swedish forces at Poltava in 1709. Turkey attempted to intervene 1710 but from then on the Swedes lost ground and initiated peace negotiations, 1717–18, during the course of which Charles XII was killed. The Treaties of Stockholm (1719–20) and the Treaty of Nystad (1721) established the peace and also made Russia a powerful state in the Baltic.

GREAT PURGE (1934–38). A repressive wave of terror by which Stalin aimed at eliminating the opposition. It was followed by a number of show trials that resulted in the arrest, exile, or death of about 8–10 million people. In 1934, following the death of Sergey Kirov (*q.v.*), which was used as the pretext for the purge, at first only former political opponents were arrested, but the number and range increased and the arrests became almost indiscriminate. Guilt was established by extracting confessions through torture. The charges made against "the enemies of the people" ranged from treason to sabotage and espionage. NKVD tribunals sentenced the prisoners to death or to long terms of imprisonment in corrective labor camps. Stalin justified the purge by stating that as progress toward full socialism is realized the class struggle must be intensified. The result of the purge was to give Stalin supreme power.

Conquest, Robert, *The Great Terror,* 1973.

Mandelstam, Nadezhda, *Hope Against Hope,* 1971.

Tucker, Robert C. and Cohen, Stephen F. (eds.), *The Great Purge Trial,* 1965.

GREAT REFORMS. Radical changes instituted by Alexander II, including the emancipation of the serfs (1861) (*see* **Agrarian Reforms**), the reform of the serfs, *mir* (*q.v.*) or system of self-government, provincial and municipal government reform, the autonomy of the universities, universal military service, and some judicial reform. These liberal reforms met with fierce opposition from both the Conservatives and the Revolutionaries. Assassinated in 1881, Alexander was not able to implement reforms for the police or civil service.

Mosse, W. E., *Alexander II and the Modernisation of Russia,* 1970.

GREAT RUSSIANS. People forming the largest proportion of the Russian population, totaling about 100 million. They are the descendants of the inhabitants of medieval Kievan Rus. Together with the Belorussians and Ukrainians, they constitute the Russian section of the Slavic family. They represent a very large proportion of the population of the Russian Soviet Federated Socialist Republic and important minorities in other republics.

GREBENSHCHIKOV, GRIGORY DMITRIYEVICH (1882–?). Author. He was most widely known for his *V prostorakh Sibiri* (1914–15); his writings comprise stories and novels about Siberian peasants.

Buyanovich, M., *A Turbulent Giant,* 1940.

Yakushev, I., *G.D.G.,* 1926.

GRECHANINOV, ALEXANDER TIKHONOVICH (1864–1956). Composer. He studied at the St. Petersburg Conservatory under Rimsky-Korsakov and at the Moscow Conservatory with Vassily Ilich Safonov. In 1922 he made his first European tour. He lived in Paris from 1925 and finally settled in the United States. His works comprise operas, including *Dobrynya Nikitich* (1902) and *Sister Beatrice* (1912), five symphonies, chamber music, Catholic church music, piano pieces, songs, and folk songs. He intended his *Missa Oecumenica,* which was performed in Boston in 1944, to unite all creeds, both Eastern and Western.

GREGORIAN CALENDAR. *See* **Calendar.**

GREGORY, SAINT (THE ILLUMINATOR) (240–332). Apostle of Armenia. The reputed founder of the Armenian Church and its first metropolitan. He succeeded in persuading King Tividates of Armenia to abandon paganism. The king then imposed Christianity on his subjects.

The office of metropolitan remained in his family until the fifth century.

GREGORY XIII (1502–85). Pope. He published the Gregorian calendar in 1582, which was the corrected version of the Julian calendar established by Julius Caesar in 46 B.C. The Gregorian calendar was adopted by the Soviet Union in 1918.

GREKOV, BORIS DMITRIYEVICH (1882–1953). Historian and pupil of Vasily Klyuchevsky (*q.v.*). He was professor of history at Moscow University where his main field of research was medieval Russian history. His works include *Kievan Russia* (1939), *Peasants in Russia from the Earliest Times to the Seventeenth Century* (1946), and *The Golden Horde and Its Fall* (1950).

GRIBOYEDOV, ALEXANDER SERGEYEVICH (1795–1829). Dramatist and diplomat. He is famous for his comedy *Woe from Wit* (1823), the first Russian comedy of manners. It was not published until 1833 because of censorship. He was murdered by an anti-Russian mob while serving as a diplomat in Persia.

Welsh, D. A., *Russian Comedy, 1765–1823*, 1966.

GRIGORIEV, APOLLON ALEKSANDROVICH (1822–64). Poet and literary critic. His writings emphasized the early roots and simple nature of Russian popular life. One of his modern admirers was Alexander Blok (*q.v.*).

GRIGORIEV, SERGEI (1883–). Ballet master. He studied at the Imperial Ballet School, St. Petersburg, and was employed by Diaghilev as *régisseur* for the first Paris season of the Ballets Russes in 1909, remaining with the company until 1919. After 1932 he worked with Colonel de Basil in the Ballets Russes de Monte Carlo. Later he was attached to the Royal Ballet.

Grigoriev, S., *The Diaghilev Ballet, 1909–29*, 1953.

GRIGOROVICH, DMITRY VASILYEVICH (1822–99). Author. One of the first of the Realists to depict scenes of peasant life; his stories *The Village* (1846) and *Anton Goremyka* (1847) produced a strong effect on those who advocated greater realism in literature, but the stories themselves are not considered as intrinsically important. In 1845 Grigorovich introduced Fedor Dostoyevsky to Nicholas Nekrasov and Vissarion Belinsky, and later helped to promote Anton Chekhov (*q.q.v.*).

GRIN, ALEXANDER (real name **Alexander Stepanovich Grinevsky**) (1880–1932). Writer. As a schoolboy Grin read avidly, although he was at times suspended from school for laziness. After a short time in the merchant marine he led a tramp's existence, and finally started a career as a writer. After fighting with the Red Army, ill and penniless he was rescued by Maxim Gorky. A chronic alcoholic, he spent the last few years of his life as a failed writer and geography teacher, turned to carving for a living, and died in poverty. His stories, frequently romantic and exotic in flavor, are underestimated by Soviet critics, but they convey the turmoil the Soviet

Union was undergoing. His best-known works include *The Ratcatcher* (1924), *Fantastic Tales,* and *The Road to Nowhere* (1930).

GRINEVITSKY, IVAN (1857–81). He assassinated Alexander II on March 13, 1881 near the Winter Palace in St. Petersburg. A group of Nihilists agreed to make an attempt on the tsar's life but the first of their bombs were not successful. Grinevitsky's bomb achieved its aim but he himself was also killed.

GRIVNA. Monetary unit in medieval Russia consisting of 10 *kopeks,* or 20 *dengas,* or 20 *nogatas,* or 25 *kunas,* or 50 *rezanas.* Originally *grivna* meant a circular ingot of silver.

GRODNO. Town 96 miles (154 km) SW of Vilnius near the Polish border, situated on the Neman River, in Belorussia. Founded in the 10th century, it became part of Lithuania in 1398. It was acquired by Poland in 1569, passed to Russia in 1795, and back to Poland in 1920. In 1939 it was incorporated in Byelorussia. Industries include sugar refining and textiles; manufactures include fertilizers, leather goods, and electrical equipment. Population (1976) 176,000.

GROMYKO, ANDREI ANDREYEVICH (1909–). Diplomat. He became a member of the Communist Party in 1931 and was elected to the central committee in 1956. He was ambassador to the United States (1943–46) and served as Soviet representative to the United Nations Security Council from 1946–1948. Later he was ambassador to Britain from 1952 to 1953. He became foreign minister in 1957, having been deputy foreign minister in 1947–52 and 1953–57 and in 1983 was appointed first deputy premier. He is respected for his ability as a negotiator and for his grasp of international affairs.

GROSS GÖRSCHEN. Village situated 13 miles (21 km) SW of Leipzig now in the German Democratic Republic. It was the scene of a battle (May 1813) in which Napoleon defeated the Prusso-Russian forces.

GROSSMAN, VASILY SEMYONOVICH (1905–). Writer. Grossman worked as an engineer in Donbas and Moscow. In 1934 his novel *Glyukauf* attracted the attention of Maxim Gorky, who published it. From 1941 to 1945 Grossman wrote stories and sketches for *The Red Star,* mostly about the war. After the war he turned his attention to writing a novel concerning the defense of Stalingrad, and his play *If We Were to Believe the Pythagorians* (1946) was banned by the authorities.

GROZNY. Capital of Chechen-Ingush Autonomous Soviet Socialist Republic situated W of the Caspian Sea, in the Russian Soviet Federated Socialist Republic. The center of one of the richest oilfields in the USSR, it is connected by pipeline with the oil fields and oil ports at Makhachkala on the Caspian Sea, and of Tuapse on the Black Sea. Oil production began in 1893. Manufactures include oil-drilling machinery and chemicals. Population (1977) 387,000.

GROZNY. Epithet applied to Ivan IV, the Terrible.

GUBERNIYA. An administrative unit in Russia introduced by Peter I and abolished by the Soviet government in 1923.

GUBNYE. Locally elected officials in Muscovite Russia in the first half of the 16th century. They were engaged in combating crime.

GUCHKOV, ALEXANDER IVANOVICH (1862–1936). Leader of the moderate liberals in Russia (1905–17). Founder and chairman of the Octobrists' *(q.v.)* party and president of the third state duma. In the First World War he was chairman of the duma committee on military and naval affairs, and subsequently chairman of the nongovernmental central war industries committee. He became the minister for war and navy in the provisional government. He was a critic of the imperial regime and in March 1917 went to Pskov and secured the abdication of the tsar. He left for Paris after the October Revolution.

GUDZY, NICHOLAS KALINIKOVICH (1887-). Literary historian. From 1922 he was professor at the Moscow State University. Gudzy was particularly interested in ancient Russian literature, and in the literature of the 19th century. He wrote several volumes on Tolstoy.

GULAG. An acronym for the chief administration of corrective labor camps, which were publicly acknowledged 1934–60, but which, according to Alexander Solzhenitsyn, have existed since 1918. Apart from the administration of these penal colonies, the GULag was also responsible for much economic production using forced labor.

Solzhenitsyn, A., *The Gulag Archipelago,* 3 vols. 1973–76.

GULISTAN, TREATY OF (1813). Treaty concluded following Russia's dispute with Turkey and Persia. Russia gained the N part of Azerbaijan, with the cities of Baku, Derbent, and Gundja.

GUM. Acronym for *Gosudarstvenny Universalny Magazin* (Universal State Store). Major department store situated in Red Square, Moscow.

GUMILEV, NIKOLAI STEPANOVICH (1886–1921). Poet and husband of Anna Akhmatova (*q.v.*). His early writings show the influence of the Symbolist school, but he later rejected its tenets and formed his own Acmeist group (*q.v.*), using the journal *Apollon* as a vehicle for the group's ideas. His verses are of a patriotic and monarchist nature, and are concerned with adventure, struggle, and heroism. He was shot for anti-Soviet activity in 1921.

Hingley, Ronald, *Nightingale Fever,* 1981.

Poggioli, Renato, *Poets of Russia, 1880–1930, 1960.*

GUREV. Town situated on the Ural River near its mouth on the Caspian Sea, in Kazakhstan. Founded in 1645, it has only grown since the development of the oil industry. Industries include fishing and fish canning, and oil refining. It is a terminus of the oil pipeline from the Emba field. Population (1970) 113,000.

GURKO, IOSIF VLADIMIROVICH (1829–1901). Army officer who took a major part in the Russo-Turkish war of 1877–78. Having fought in the Crimean War, and the suppression of the Polish uprising in 1863, he defeated the Turkish armies and occupied Sofia, Plovdiv, and Erdine, thus bringing the war to an end in 1878. From 1882–1883 he was governor-general and military commander in Odessa before serving in similar posts in Warsaw (1883–94), where he repressed Polish nationalistic tendencies and implemented a policy of russification in Poland. In 1884 Gurko was made a member of the imperial council.

GURO, ELENA (real name **Eleonora Genrikhovna von Norenberg**) (1877–1910). Russian Futurist poet. She was a professional painter who had graduated from the school of the Society for the Encouragement of the Arts, and was interested in French, German, and Scandinavian literature. Guro is one of the most neglected of the early Russian Futurists. Her literary career started with *Early Spring* (1905), followed by *The Hurdy-Gurdy* (1909), *The Autumnal Dream* (1912), *The Baby Camels of the Sky* (1914), and other works. Her work remains unjustly overlooked.

Mirsky, D. S., A *History of Russian Literature,* 1949.

GYPSIES. Gypsies number about 130,000 in the USSR, leading a nomadic existence. They reached central and N Russia by the 18th century. The majority speak Romany as their mother tongue but they are generally bilingual. There have been many attempts, before and after the Revolution, to resettle the gypsies but none has been entirely successful.

H

HAGUE CONVENTIONS. International conferences convened by Nicholas II which met May 18, to July 19, 1899 and June 15, to October 18, 1907, with the aim of "a possible reduction of the excessive armaments which weigh upon all nations" by "putting a limit on the progressive development of the present armaments." The first convention's achievements were limited but did include agreement on the use of gas, expanding bullets, the banning of explosives launched from balloons, and the creation of a court of arbitration. The second convention reached agreement on a number of naval matters and on the employment of force to recover debts. A further convention was planned for 1915 but because of the First World War did not meet. The two conventions did influence the form of the League of Nations.

HAJI-GERAY. Khan of the Crimea. In 1428 Haji-Geray was rescued from persecution by neighboring khans of the grand duke, Vitovt of Lithuania, and then granted the former possessions of the khan of the Golden Horde in W Russia to Lithuania. In 1449, however, he seized the Crimea, and there founded the Geray dynasty, which ruled until the end of the 18th century.

HANGÖ, BATTLE OF (1714). Site of the battle during which the Russian fleet defeated the Swedes, which led to the peace treaty of Nystad (1721) (*q.v.*), as a result of which Russia gained Ingria, Estonia, and Swedish Livonia. *See* **Great Northern War.**

HANNIBAL, ABRAHAM (*fl.* early 18th century). Engineer general, known as "Peter the Great's Negro." Hannibal was Pushkin's great-grandfather, and his life history is the subject of the poet's unfinished historical novel *The Negro of Peter the Great* (1828).

HANSEATIC LEAGUE. Trading

association of N German towns and German merchants abroad. From the late 13th century to the end of the 15th century, the League played a leading role in N European trade, thus exercising considerable economic and political power. In 1478, Ivan III, grand prince of Moscow, captured Novgorod (*q.v.*) and expelled the Hanseatic merchants who lived there, and in 1494 Novgorod ceased to be a Hanseatic trading post.

HARBIN. City in NE China on the S bank of the Sungari River. The headquarters of the Chungchang Railway started by the Russian government was at Harbin. The city was also a center of tsarist activity in Manchuria following the October Revolution. Harbin has earned the name the "Moscow of the Orient."

HARRIMAN, WILLIAM AVERELL (1891–). American businessman and diplomat. In 1941 he coordinated lend-lease aid with Great Britain and the Soviet Union, and from 1943 to 1946 served as ambassador to the Soviet Union. Thereafter he advised several U.S. presidents on relations with the Soviets. He wrote *Peace with Russia?* (1960), *America and Russia in a Changing World* (1971), and, with Elie Abel, *Special Envoy to Churchill and Stalin, 1941–1946.*

HEHN, VICTOR (1813–90). German historian. Having taught in Dorpat, in 1855 Hehn was appointed as a librarian in St. Petersburg, but returned to Berlin in 1873. His main works are about his travels in France and Italy, but he is also remembered for his *Diary from Russia* (1892).

HEMOPHILIA. Grand Duke Alexis Nicolayevich (the tsarevich), the fourth child and first son of Tsar Nicholas II and Tsaritsa Alexandra Fyodorovna, suffered from hemophilia, a hereditary condition characterized by excessive bleeding. The Tsaritsa was a granddaughter of Queen Victoria, several of whose descendants suffered from it. His apparently successful treatment of Alexis gave Rasputin (*q.v.*) ascendancy over Alexandra.

HERBERSTEIN, BARON SIGISMUND VON, (*fl.* early 16th century). Diplomat. He was sent to Russia in 1517 and 1526. He was a competent linguist and had an understanding of the Russians; he wrote *Commentaries on Muscovite Affairs* (new edition 1956).

HERMANN, DAVID (1876–1930). Founder of the Vilna Troupe in 1916 for the production of Jewish folk drama. Later the troupe split up, some members remaining with Hermann, the rest going to New York.

HERMITAGE MUSEUM. Museum situated in the buildings of the Old Hermitage (1775–84), the New Hermitage (1839–50), and the Hermitage Theater (1787). The Hermitage was originally constructed in order to house the art collection of Catherine I, and under Catherine the Great it was a center of musical and theatrical activity. It now houses one of the world's great art collections.

Descargues, Pierre, *The Hermitage,* 1961.

HERZEN, ALEXANDER IVANOVICH (1812–70). Radical journalist and political thinker, and probably the greatest European publicist of his day. He disliked the social order of Russia and as a result of his association with a radical discussion group he was exiled (1834–42). His father, who died in 1846, left him a fortune and Herzen left Russia, never to return, the following year. He lived mainly in London, where he set up the Free Russian Press and published *The Bell* (Kolokol) (*q.v.*), the first Russian *émigré* journal, which had considerable influence inside Russia. His works include *Childhood, Youth and Exile.*

Malia, Martin E., *Alexander Herzen and the Birth of Russian Socialism, 1812–1855,* 1961.

HETMAN. Commander in chief of the army in Poland, Lithuania, and among the Zaporozhye, or Dnepr Cossacks. The word is derived from the German *Hauptmann. See* **Ataman.**

HINDENBURG, PAUL VON (1847–1934). German field marshal and hero of the First World War, and the second president of the Weimar Republic. Following the Russian Revolution of March 1917, Hindenburg and Ludendorff imposed the treaty of Brest-Litovsk on Russia. Lenin and the Bolsheviks accepted its terms in the belief that peace was necessary to secure their authority in the new Soviet state.

HIRSCHBEIN, PERETZ (1881–1949). Founder of the first Yiddish Art Theater in Odessa after the ban on Yiddish plays was lifted in 1908.

HOFMAN, MODEST LYUDVIGOVICH (1887–). Literary historian. He was a prominent scholar of Pushkin's work and edited the work of many of the poets belonging to the Pushkin circle. He left Russia in 1923.

HOLY ALLIANCE. *See* **Quadruple** and **Quintuple Alliances.**

HOLY SYNOD. The administrative organ of the Russian Orthodox Church, founded by Peter the Great (1720) on the Lutheran model.

Cracraft, James, *The Church Reform of Peter the Great,* 1971.

HORDE. *See* **Golden Horde.**

HUGHES, JOHN (*fl.* late 19th century). Welshman. In 1869 he succeeded in obtaining a concession for a company to be called the New Russia Company. It produced coal, iron, and rails. The mining settlement of Yuzovka, which was to become one of the great metallurgical cities in the world, is named after him.

HUMBOLDT, FREIHERR VON (FRIEDRICH HEINRICH) ALEXANDER (1769–1859). German naturalist and traveler, known primarily for his work on the current off the W coast of S America now named after him. In 1829 the tsar of Russia invited him to journey to Central Asia, during which meteorological data and other information were tabulated and diamonds discovered in the gold mines of the Urals. As a result of Humboldt's efforts, the Russian government allowed a line of magnetic and meteorological stations to be established across N Asia. He is considered a great representative of German scientific culture.

HUNS. A nomadic people who invaded SE Europe *c.* 370, and who then built up a large empire which extended into central Europe. Having appeared from beyond the Volga River in the fourth century, they occupied the plains between the Volga and the Don, and then the lands between the Don and Dnestr. After this, the Huns defeated the Visigoths in what is now Rumania, thus bringing their empire to the Danubian frontier of the Roman Empire. Although the warring Huns were greatly feared, from 455 they no longer played an important part in European affairs.

HYPERBOREAN MOUNTAINS. Early name for the Ural mountains.

I

ICON. Image of Christ or the Virgin, or of a saint or saints, painted to signify the presence of the subject, and used as an object of veneration and a channel for prayer. The use of icons was established in the Byzantine church during the sixth century and was partly inspired by the former custom of venerating images of the Roman emperors. By *c.* 700 a reactionary Iconoclastic movement arose, asserting that the images had become the subjects of idolatry. Icons were restored in places of worship and formed part of the Byzantine Christian devotion adopted by Russia. The most outstanding medieval icon painter was Andrei Rublev; his *Trinity* (*c.* 1410) became the most popular of all Russian icons and was widely copied. (The earlier *Our Lady of Vladimir* (*c.* 1100) is thought to have been painted in Constantinople and brought to Kiev). Dionissy (*c.* 1450–*c.* 1507) was the greatest of his time, painting in patterns of line and flat color as a personal exploration of holy mysteries.

A strong group of 17th-century icons was painted for use in the homes of the faithful, as simple aids to Christian living; they included homely scenes and near-portraits. With the accession of Michael Romanov (1613) icon painting came to reflect a new determination to establish the Muscovite church and state as the true heirs of Byzantium. Simon Ushakov (*fl.* 1650–1700) is considered the last great icon painter. The tradition became debased under the Westernizing influence of Peter the Great.

Onasch, K., *Russian Icons*, 1977.
Stuart, J., *Ikons*, 1975.
Talbot Rice, Tamara, *Russian Icons*, 1963.
Unesco, *Early Russian Icons*, 1958.
Uspensky, L. A. and Lossky, V. N., *The Meaning of Icons*, 1952.

IGARKA. Port situated 425 miles (680 km) from the mouth of the

Yenisey River in the Krasnoyarsk territory, in the Russian Soviet Federated Socialist Republic. The main industries are timber and graphite. It is the site of a permafrost research station. Population (1970) 16,000

IGNATIEV, COUNT NICHOLAS PAVLOVICH (1832–1908). Diplomat and Conservative politician. As envoy to China from 1859 he secured the Ussuri region for Russia by the Treaty of Peking (1860). In 1864 he became ambassador of Turkey, where his encouragement of nationalistic and Pan-Slavic feeling against the Turkish empire was partly responsible for the Bulgarian rebellion.

Having urged Russia to declare war on Turkey in 1877, he negotiated the concluding Treaty of San Stefano (1878); this would so greatly have strengthened Russian influence in the Balkans that it was immediately challenged by Great Britain and Austria-Hungary, and its terms were not implemented. As minister of the interior (1881–82), he was active in promoting ultraconservative and Slavic nationalist policies.

IGNATOVICH, INNA IVANOVNA (1879–1967). Soviet historian whose works include *Borba Krestyan za Osvobozhdenye* (The Peasants' Struggle for Emancipation) and *Pomeshchik; Krestyane nakanune osvobozhdeniya* (Landowner and Peasants on the Eve of Emancipation).

IGOR, GRAND PRINCE (*c.* 877–945). Succeeded as ruler of Kiev in 912. Much of his reign was devoted to expeditions against neighboring powers, not all successful. He led a disastrous expedition into Transcaucasia in 913–14; in 941 and 944 he made unsuccessful raids on Byzantium, but saved his position sufficiently to conclude a treaty. His conquest of nomadic tribes to the SE was followed by an attempt to extract an extra tribute from them; in the course of this attempt he was murdered. He was the husband of St. Olga (*q.v.*), who acted as regent for their son Svyatoslav after Igor's death.

Vernadsky, George V., *Kievan Russia,* 1948.

IGOR, LAY OF THE HOST OF. *See* **Lay of the Host of Igor.**

IGOR SVYATOSLAVICH (1151–1202). Prince of Novgorod-Seversk from 1178 and of Chernigov from 1198. The one notable event of his rule was his defeat by the Polovtsy in 1185, and his capture, subsequent escape, and return to Novgorod-Seversk. This is the subject of *The Lay of the Host of Igor,* thought to be the first important Russian epic. Borodin's opera *Prince Igor* is based on it.

IGUMEN. An abbot, head of a monastery, or father superior.

ILARION (*fl.* 11th century). Metropolitan of Kiev; he was regarded as one of the great Kievan writers. In 1049 he wrote his sermon *On Law and Grace,* which was widely disseminated.

ILF AND PETROV. Pseudonym of a literary partnership between Ilya Arnoldovich Fainzilberg (1897–1937) and Yevgeny Petrovich Katayev (1903–42) (*q.v.*). In 1928 they published *The Twelve Chairs* and in 1931 *The Golden Calf*, both novels satirizing aspects of Soviet society. They also visited the United States and wrote *Little Golden America* (1936). They were frowned upon under Stalin, but their work later recovered its popularity.

Slonim, Marc, *Soviet Russian Literature*, 1967.

Struve, Gleb, *Russian Literature under Lenin and Stalin*, 1972.

ILI RIVER. River rising in the Tien Shan as the Tekes and Kunges rivers, flowing E into China and back to the Soviet frontier through Kuldja, whence it is navigable for small vessels. It flows into Lake Balkhash. It is 890 miles (1,439 km) long from the source of the Tekes.

ILIODOR, S. T. Monk. He was a supporter of Rasputin (*q.v.*) who became abnormally influential in Saratov province, largely through Rasputin's own influence with the tsaritsa, Alexandra. A government attempt to have him removed failed because of the murder of the minister of the interior, Peter Stolypin (*q.v.*). It was Iliodor who published Alexandra's letters to Rasputin.

de Jonge, Alex, *The Life and Times of Grigorii Rasputin*, 1981.

ILMEN, LAKE. A lake situated 100 miles (160 km) SSE of Leningrad, in the Russian Soviet Federated Socialist Republic. It has an area of 350 square miles (906 sq km) and is drained by the Volkhov River into Lake Ladoga.

ILYA OF MUROM. Hero of a Kievan epic poem that depicts him as a semifantastic warrior defending Kiev from its enemies in the age of St. Vladimir. A peasant and an invalid, Ilya was cured of his illness by a miracle and, at the age of 33, became a champion of Christian Kiev against the surrounding nomads.

ILYUSHIN, SERGEI VLADIMIROVICH (1894–1977). Aircraft designer. He first became known for his Il-2 Stormovik, a dive bomber widely used by the Soviet Union during the Second World War. He later worked on commercial aircraft, designing the jet airliner Il-62 (1962).

IMAGISTS. A postrevolutionary literary movement. Russian Imagism evolved more or less separately from Anglo-American Imagism. The Imagists founded the movement in 1919 as a successor to Futurism. Characteristics of Imagism are the primacy of the image, coarse language, and pessimism; these features can be seen in Sergei Esenin's (*q.v.*) *Confession of a Hooligan* (1920). In the first manifesto or declaration of Imagism, signed by Esenin, Ivnev (*q.v.*), Mariengov, and Shershenevich (1893–1942), the image was defined as "the naphthalene preserving a work of art from thc moths of time." The movement, although in agreement with the ethic of the October Revolution, found itself unable to maintain an apolitical stance during the Civil War, and by 1927 it had disintegrated.

Markov, Vladimir, *Russian Futurism*, 1969.

Poggioli, Renato, *Poets of Russia*, 1960.

IMANDRA, LAKE. A lake situated approximately 64 miles (102 km) S of Murmansk, in the Russian Soviet Federated Socialist Republic. It is 50 miles (80 km) long and 15 miles (24 km) wide, with an area of 330 square miles (855 sq km). Its outlet flows S into the Kandalaksha gulf of the White Sea.

IMERITIA. Region of Georgia in the upper Rion River basin. It is agricultural, producing vines and mulberry trees, and has some coal and manganese mines. The region was first mentioned in 1442 when Alexander I of Georgia gave it to one of his sons. It was raided by Turks during the 16th century and forced to pay tribute, but regained total independence, which it retained until the early 19th century. Russia claimed overlordship in 1804, and, after bitter opposition, annexed Imeritia in 1810. The chief cities are Kutaisi (the historic capital) and Chiatura.

IMPERIYA VSEROSSYSKAYA. Designation of the Russian state from Peter the Great's act of October 1721 until the abdication of Nicholas II in March 1917.

IMPRESSIONISM. A term denoting one of the most important movements of modern art, which reacted against Romanticism and Realism, and emphasized color and light. Impressionism began in France, and French Impressionism can be divided into two phases: the first lasting from 1862–71, led by Manet (1832–83), and the second starting in 1870, known as the Argenteuil phase, named for the town where Monet (1840–1926) and other Impressionists gathered. Impressionism reached Russia later. In 1885, Ilya Repin (*q.v.*) was painting in an Impressionist style learned in Paris. Michael Larionov (1881–1964), strongly influenced by his sojourn in Paris, was dubbed "the finest Russian Impressionist" as a result of his work of 1902–06. The influence of Impressionism on Russian art cannot be underestimated since it affected the subsequent assumptions about the nature of art and technique in general. *See* **Alexander Golovin, Konstant Korovin,** and **Natalya Goncharova.**

Gray, Camilla, *The Russian Experiment in Art*, 1962.

Hamilton, George H., *The Art and Architecture of Russia*, 1954.

INBER, VERA MIKHAILOVNA (1890–?). Poet. She published her first collection of verse (*Sad Wine*) in 1912 and was briefly associated with the Constructivist (*q.v.*) group. Other works are *Bitter Delight, Fragile Words, Goal and Way*, and *The Pulkovo Meridian*. She was best known in later years for *Nearly Three Years*, a diary of the siege of Leningrad. She received the Stalin prize in 1946.

INDGIRKA RIVER. River rising SE of Oimyakon on the Oimyakon plateau and flowing 1,113 miles (1,780 km) N through the Cherski range into the tundra, past Khonu, Druzhina, and Chokurdakh to the E Siberian Sea, entering it by a delta. Ice-free from June to September, it is navigable up to Khonu. Its main tributaries are the Selennyakh and Moma rivers.

INDUSTRIAL PARTY. An allegedly subversive group of the technical intelligentsia, which was said to be wrecking the first Soviet Five-Year Plan at capitalist instigation. The members were tried and condemned in 1930, together with a number of those considered sympathetic to them.

INFORMERS. The Soviet regime to a large extent relies on informers in order to expose transgressions of the law. The threat of constant surveillance also prevents dissent, making coordination between dissenters difficult. There are two kinds of informers: professional informers who are employed by the secret police, and private citizens who denounce infringements of the law. Official informers may be placed as house porters, domestics, students, teachers, factory employees, or prisoners in labor camps, and may employ the technique of *agents provocateurs*. Informers embark on this role in order to enhance their career prospects, or as a result of police threats, and they may win much public acclaim; such was the case of the informer in the "Doctors' Plot" of 1953, who was proclaimed a national heroine. Citizens are encouraged to denounce criminals; failure to denounce embezzlers or people preparing to flee the Soviet Union is a crime, and in extreme cases, wives have denounced husbands, and children parents. Denunciation is, of course, largely motivated by fear for one's own life.

Mandelstam, Nadezhda, *Hope Against Hope*, 1971.

Smith, Hedrick, *The Russians*, 1973.

INGAL, VLADIMIR IOSIFOVICH (1901–). Sculptor. Educated at the All-Russian Academy of Art in Leningrad, Ingal has worked in collaboration with the sculptor V. Y. Bogolyubov. Together they have carved a number of statues of Lenin and Stalin, and the famous statue of G. K. Ordzhonikidze, for which they were awarded the Stalin prize in 1941.

INGRIANS (LENINGRAD FINNS). Finns living in or near Leningrad who are the direct descendants of the original inhabitants of the area. They number about 90,000.

INGUSH. Caucasian-speaking people (and their language) of the Nakho-Dagestanian group. They are closely related to the Chechens. They live in the Chechen-Ingush Autonomous Republic (N Caucasus) and number about 100,000. They are Sunni Muslims. They were deported to Kazakhstan in 1944, charged with collaboration with the Nazis, but were rehabilitated in 1957 and permitted to return.

INHERITANCE. Although the Bolsheviks abolished inheritance in 1918, it was reintroduced during the New Economic Policy (1921–29). Inheritance is not taxed although a small registration fee is charged. The testator is free to leave his property to whomever he chooses, and also to state agencies or public organizations, with the exception of religious bodies, although dependents may not be disinherited.

INKERMAN, BATTLE OF (November 5, 1854). A decisive battle of the Crimean War, in which the French and British defeated the Russians at Inkerman, near Sevastopol. In spite of poor direction, the Anglo-French force withstood the Russian attack. The Russians lost about 12,000 men, the British, about 2,500, and the French, about 1,000.

Pemberton, W. B., *Battles of the Crimean War*. 1962.

INTELLIGENTSIA. Prior to 1917, the intelligentsia was a term referring to the sector of society holding radical left-wing views, who were highly critical of the tsarist regime. Marxists, however, traditionally regarded the intelligentsia with mistrust, while the Makhayevists (*see* **Makhayevism**) viewed the intelligentsia as a class of exploiters. Following the Bolshevik seizure of power, "intelligentsia" became a derogatory word, and in the 1920s and early 1930s, the intelligentsia was discriminated against. Since Stalin's cultural revolution, however, the status of the intelligentsia has grown considerably. The intelligentsia is now viewed officially as a stratum rather than a class of society.

Pipes, Richard (ed.), *The Russian Intelligentsia*, 1961.

Raeff, Marc, *Origins of the Russian Intelligentsia: The Eighteenth-Century Nobility*. 1961.

Schapiro, Leonard, *Rationalism and Nationalism in Russian Nineteenth-Century Political Thought*, 1967.

INTERNATIONAL, THE. The First International was formed in London by Karl Marx in 1864; its aim was to coordinate working-class movements in different countries and thereby to establish international socialism. There were disputes between the Marxist and anarchist members, culminating in the final separation between Marx and Bakunin (1872) (*q.q.v.*). The movement was dissolved in 1876.

The Second International was formed in Paris in 1889, comprising the radical parties of Austria, Belgium, Denmark, Germany, Spain, Sweden and Switzerland. A nonrevolutionary movement, it collapsed with the outbreak of the First World War.

The Third International (Comintern) was formed in Moscow by Lenin and the Bolsheviks in 1917 and comprised the communist elements excluded from the Second International. Its aim is world revolution.

A Fourth International was formed by Trotsky in Mexico in the 1930s, and there was also a Fifth—the Situationist International—formed in 1954.

There have been two revivals of the Second, nonrevolutionary socialist, International. The first (1923) ceased to operate in 1940. The second (1951) is the currently operative Socialist International. Its congress meets at least once every two years and its council, in which the Socialist Union of Central-Eastern Europe is represented, at least twice a year.

Braunthal, J., *History of the International*, 1967.

Drachkovitch, M. M. (ed.), *The Revolutionary Internationals, 1864–1943*, 1966.

Joll, Y., *The Second International, 1889–1914* (2nd ed.), 1975.

Marx, Karl and Engels, Friedrich, *The Communist Manifesto*, 1848.

Rose, S., *The Socialist International*, 1955.

Stekloff, C. M., *History of the First International* (repr.), 1968.

INTERREGNUM (1610–13). Period following the deposition of Vasili Shuisky in July 1610 and the accession of Michael Romanov in February 1613 (*q.q.v.*). Muscovite Russia was administered by a council of seven boyars under the leadership of Prince Fedor Mstislavsky, but they lacked the authority to deal with Polish attacks and domestic risings inspired by pretenders to the throne. Stabilizing influence came from the strength of the church and from the army, which ultimately defeated the Poles and set up the *zemsky sobor*, which elected Michael Romanov.

INTOURIST. *See* **Tourism.**

IOFFE, ADOLF ABRAMOVICH (1883–1927). Supporter of Trotsky, revolutionary, and Soviet diplomat. A member of the Menshevik party, he joined Trotsky in Vienna in 1908. They both joined the Bolsheviks in 1917. After the Revolution he was one of the negotiators of the Russian-German treaty at Brest-Litovsk (*q.v.*), and he was made ambassador to Germany in 1918. He headed diplomatic missions to Geneva (1922) and China (1923). He remained a strong supporter of Trotsky in the power struggle after Lenin's death (1924). When Trotsky was defeated by Stalin he committed suicide.

IPATYEFF, VLADIMIR NIKOLAYEVICH (1867–1952). Chemist. He pioneered work on high-pressure catalytic reactions in hydrocarbons. He was made chairman of the government's chemical committee in 1914 and continued to work for the Soviet government after the Revolution. He was, however, anti-Communist and in 1927 he left the USSR to settle later in the United States. He is best known for his work during the Second World War when his process for manufacturing high-octane gasoline from low-octane fuels was used to produce aviation fuel.

IPPOLITOV-IVANOV, MICHAEL MIKHAILOVICH (1859–1935). Composer and conductor. He studied under Rimsky-Korsakov at St. Petersburg and was an associate of Borodin and Balakirev (*q.q.v.*). He became professor at the Moscow Conservatory in 1893, after working in Tbilisi, Georgia, where he returned in 1924 to reorganize the Georgian State Conservatory. He was director of the Moscow Conservatory (1906–22). His work, including seven operas, showed strong folk influence.

IRBIT. Town in the Sverdlovsk oblast in W central Russian Soviet Federated Socialist Republic, situated 125 miles (200 km) NE of Sverdlovsk. Founded in 1631, Irbit became internationally renowned for its annual fair, which was a center for Russian trade with China, Central Asia, and Siberia. Population (1970) 49,000.

IRKUTSK. Capital of region of same name situated at the confluence of the Angara and Irkut rivers, in the Russian Soviet Federated Socialist Republic. Founded in 1652 as a wintering station, it became the capital of E Siberia in 1822. It is an important center with industries including engineering, mica processing, automobile plants, meat packing, and sawmilling. Population (1977) 532,000.

IRON CURTAIN. Term coined by Winston Churchill on March 5, 1946, referring to the border between the Communist bloc and Western European countries. It is closely guarded by the Soviet countries, and access from E to W is strictly regulated.

IRTYSH RIVER. River rising in Sinkiang in the Mongolian Altay range and flowing 1,844 miles (2,950 km) W, as the Black Irtysh, into Lake Zaysan in the Kazakh Soviet Socialist Republic. It leaves as the Irtysh River and flows N and NW through mountains and the Kulunda Steppe into the Russian Soviet Federated Socialist Republic, past Omsk and Tobolsk, to enter the Ob River at Khanty-Mansy. It is navigable to Semipalatinsk from April to November and to Tobolsk from May to November. Its middle course drains the agricultural areas of W Siberia.

ISAKOVSKY, MICHAEL VASILYEVICH (1900–73). Poet of peasant background. He published his first book of poems in 1927. His writing, mainly in the folk-song idiom and on rural themes, has been widely popular. He won Stalin prizes in 1943 and 1949, and has been a deputy to the Russian Soviet Federated Socialist Republic Supreme Soviet since 1947. His poems include *Wire in the Straw* (1927), *Masters of the Land,* (1931) and *Song of the Motherland* (1948).

ISINGLASS. An almost pure collagen produced mainly in the USSR, Canada, Brazil, and the West Indies. It is derived from the swim bladders of fish and is used as a gelatinous stiffening and to clarify wine and beer. Russian isinglass is mainly derived from sturgeon.

ISKANDER, FAZIL (1929–). Writer. Although born in Abkhazia, Iskander's stories and poetry are written in the Russian language. The plots of his stories are simple, and the style is conversational and witty, although this does not weaken the strong satire. Iskander's best-known novel is *The Goatibex Constellation* (1966), in which bureaucrats aspire to crossbreed an ordinary goat with a mountain wild ox, thus resolving the problem of food production in the Soviet Union and affirming Michurinist genetics.

Brown, Dana, *Soviet Russian Literature since Stalin*, 1978.

ISKRA GROUP, THE. An unofficial body within the Social Democratic Workers' Party ("iskra" means "the spark"). It was organized by Lenin, Yuly Martov, and Alexander Potresov (*q.q.v.*) in 1900. They aimed to unite the active Marxist members, and were successful in gaining control of local branches of the party. During the second party congress, which they organized, the group split; the more revolutionary faction formed the Bolshevik group. The Iskra provided Lenin with his first position of influence, and he also founded the newspaper of the same name, which after 1900 was published abroad.

Haimson, Leopold H., *The Russian Marxists and the Origins of Bolshevism*, 1955.

Wolfe, Bertram, D., *Three Who Made a Revolution*, 1966.

ISOLATORS. Type of special prison established in the 1920s for particularly important political prisoners who are kept incommunicado, usually for life. The best-known isolators were those of Vladimir, Verkhneuralsk, and Aleksandrovskoye near Irkutsk. It is also an expression used for that section of the labor camps containing punishment cells.

ISPRAVNIK. Local government official.

ISSYK-KUL. A lake situated between two mountain ranges at 5,200 feet (1,584 m) above sea level, in Kirgizia. It has an area of 2,390 square miles (6,190 sq km). Many streams run into its salty waters, which contain quantities of fish.

ISTOMINA, AVDOTYA ILINICHNA (1799–1848). Dancer of the classical school. She was mentioned by Pushkin in the first chapter of *Eugene Onegin.*

ITIL. Town near the mouth of the Volga and capital of the Khazars in the 10th century. In 965 it was taken and sacked by Svyatoslav of Kiev, permanently reducing Khazar power.

IURII. *See* **YURY.**

IVAN (?–1581). Son and heir of the tsar, Ivan IV, the Terrible, who killed him in a violent fit of anger by striking him with a staff. He was commemorated in folklore as a lost hero who might one day return to save Russia.

IVAN I (*c.* 1304–41). Succeeded his brother Yury Danilovich as Prince of Moscow in 1325, and obtained the title of grand prince when the Mongol army of the Golden Horde devastated the principality of Tver and put Grand Prince Alexander to flight (after 1327). Nicknamed "kalita" or "moneybag," he consolidated his position not by warfare but by buying land and cultivating the good opinion of the khan of the Golden Horde, whose tributes he collected. He also persuaded the head of the Russian church (Metropolitan Theognost, whose predecessor had died in Moscow and become a focus of veneration) to establish himself in the city.

Fennell, John L. I., *The Emergence of Moscow, 1304–1359*, 1968.

IVAN II (1326–59). Grand prince of Moscow (1353–59). He succeeded his brother Simeon the Proud and was called, by comparison, "the Meek." His reign was characterized by the growing threat of Lithuania under Olgerd, and by the able statesmanship of his primary counsellor, Metropolitan Alexis. A decline in the power of the Mongol Golden Horde began during his reign and was successfully exploited by his son, Grand Prince Dmitry Donskoy.

Vernadsky, George V., *The Mongols and Russia*, 1953.

IVAN III, THE GREAT. (1440–1505). Grand prince of Moscow from 1462. He was regarded as the unifier of appanage Russia. Ivan's first wife was Princess Maria, sister of the grand prince of Tver, who died in 1467. There was one son by this marriage, Ivan Molodoy (the Young). In 1472, Ivan III married Zoë (or Sophia) Palaeologa (died 1503), niece of the last Byzantine emperor, transferring to himself much of the imperial prestige. He adopted the emperor's emblem of the two-headed eagle. Between 1470 and 1480 he greatly enlarged Moscow by annexation, taking Novgorod and Tver among the other principalities. In 1480 he ceased paying tribute to the khan, and ended Russian subordination to him. His principality became not only independent but the dominant Russian power. In 1493 he took the title of Sovereign of All Russia, claiming inheritance of Kievan Russia, and challenged the right of Poland and Lithuania to former Kievan land. His use of the title 'tsar' was inspired by his Byzantine marriage. He greatly increased the standing of the sovereign above that of the nobility, and fostered all the legends and traditions glorifying the Muscovite state.

Fennell, John L.I., *Ivan the Great of Moscow*, 1961.

Grey, Ian, *Ivan III and the Unification of Russia*, 1964.

Norrctrandcrs, B., *The Shaping of Tsardom under Ivan Grozny*, 1964.

IVAN IV, VASILYEVICH (the Terrible) (1530–84). Tsar of Muscovy from 1533, he was crowned at the age of 17. His youth was dominated by the threats and conspiracies of the boyars. The early years of his reign, influenced by the good advice of the church and loyal boyars, and of his first wife Anastasia Romanova, were constructive and progressive. He called the first *zemsky sobor* in 1549, and this body approved reforms in the law and in local administration. In 1551 a church council took place that regulated and improved the church's position in the state. In 1550 and 1556 reforms were made in the army and in the military service owed by the gentry.

With improved forces Ivan succeeded in conquering the most important of Muscovy's traditional enemies, Kazan, Astrakhan, and the Livonian Order (*q.q.v.*). He had by 1560 established the authority of the tsar, greatly strengthened the state, and established commercial relations with England.

The second half of his reign was characterized by extreme behaviour—uncontrollable rages, suspicion of the whole boyar class, and a harsh personal despotism. His deterioration was exacerbated by the death of Anastasia, (1560) and his belief that she had been murdered. His withdrawal from the boyars and the church, and his insistence on personal control, found its most extreme form in the creation of the *oprichnina* (*q.v.*)—parts of the state that were separately governed by officials directly under his control, *oprichniki*, who acted as his personal police and whose function it was to kill those whom he considered his enemies. The internal disintegration of the state coincided with pressure from its enemies in the Crimea and in the NW, where the Livonian war was revived, with Poland and Sweden joining forces against Muscovy.

In 1581 the tsar killed his son and heir in a fit of rage; the event appeared finally to destroy his mental balance. He was succeeded in 1584 by his son Fedor.

Carr, F., *Ivan the Terrible*, 1981.
Grey, Ian, *Ivan the Terrible*, 1964.
Payne, Robert and Romanoff, N., *Ivan the Terrible*, 1975.
Skrynnikov, R.G., *Ivan the Terrible*, 1981.
Vernadsky, George V., *The Tsardom of Muscovy*, 1969.

IVAN V, ALEKSEYEVICH (1666–96). Tsar of Russia (1682–96). He was the son of Tsar Alexis, and succeeded his brother Fedor III. He was an invalid and mentally retarded. Because of his condition it was agreed that he and his half-brother Peter I (the Great) should rule together under the regency of Ivan's sister Sophia. The regency was overthrown in 1689 and Peter became the effective ruler; Ivan retained his title but never participated in government.

O'Brien, C. B., *Russia under Two Tsars*, 1952.

IVAN VI, ANTONOVICH (1740–64). Tsar and great-grandson of Ivan V. Ivan was the son of Anna Leopoldovna and Prince Anthony of Brunswick-Bevern-Lüneburg. He succeeded his great-aunt, Tsaritsa Anna, when still an infant, under the regency first of the duke of Courland and second of his mother; she was an unpopular regent and was overthrown in favor of Peter the Great's daughter Elizabeth, who was tsaritsa from 1741. Ivan's youth was spent in confinement and his psychological development remained that of a child. In 1764 an army officer, Vasily Mirovich, tried to liberate him. This, a threat to the new empress, Catherine II, led to Ivan's murder by his guards.

IVANO-FRANKOVSK. Town 12 miles (19 km) SSE of Lvov, in the Ukraine. Industries include railway engineering, oil refining, woodworking, textiles, and food processing. Population (1970) 105,000.

IVANOV, ALEXANDER ANDREYEVICH (1806–58). Artist. He is best known for his painting *The Appearance of the Messiah to the People*, to which he devoted 30 years preparation. The finished work was not considered successful, but many of the individual studies (over 200) of its figures were brilliant. He was unusual in his time in his feeling for Byzantine art.

Talbot Rice, Tamara, *A Concise History of Russian Art*, 1963.

IVANOV, VSEVOLOD VYACHESLAVOVICH (1895–1963). Writer. He is best known for his short stories and novels, notably *The Partisan* (1921) and *Armoured Train 14-69* (1922), which described Soviet expansion into Siberia. A protégé of Gorky, he used his wide experience as partisan fighter, sailor, actor, and circus performer in his writing. His plays include *The Compromise of Niab Khan* and *Twelve Young Lads from a Snuffbox*. He published his memoirs, *Meeting with Gorky*, in 1947. His early work, with its vivid, naturalistic description that attracted Gorky's attention, is considered to be his best.

Slonim, Marc, *Soviet Russian Literature*, 1964.

IVANOV, VYACHESLAV IVANOVICH (1866–1949). Poet of the

Symbolism (*q.v.*) school. In 1903 he published a volume of lyric poetry, *kormchiye zvezdy*, which established him as leader of the St. Petersburg Symbolist movement. *Cor Ardens* (1911) is considered his most important poetical work. He was also a philosopher and classical scholar. He was made professor of Greek at Baku University in 1921 and in 1924 emigrated to Italy where he became a Catholic.

West, James, *Russian Symbolism*, 1970.

IVANOV-RAZUMNIK (1878-1946). Pseudonym of Razumnik Vasilyevich Ivanov. He was a writer and critic and leader of "The Scythians," an intellectual group who believed in Russia's destiny as a part-Asian nation. Before the Revolution he wrote populist and revolutionary works; after 1917 his even stronger inclination toward the Left brought about his arrest in the 1930s, as a "populist ideologist." He left the Soviet Union for Germany during the war and died in Munich. He wrote an account of his life, including his imprisonments and exile.

IVANOVO. Capital of region of same name 155 miles (248 km) NE of Moscow situated on the Uvod River, in the Russian Soviet Federated Socialist Republic. Created in 1871 and known as the "Russian Manchester," it took a prominent part in both the 1905 and 1917 revolutions. It manufactures cotton, textile machinery, and chemicals. Population (1977) 461,000.

IVNEV, RYURIK (1893-). Pseudonym of Michael Alexandrovich Kovalev. He was a Soviet writer who was a member of the "fellow-traveler" movement. His novels include *Neschastny angel* (1917) and *Geroy romana* (1928). In 1919 he was, with Esenin (*q.v.*), a founder of Imagist poetry. His later work depicted bohemian characters in Soviet society.

IZBA. Peasant hut made of wood. It is known that *izby* were in existence as early as the fourth century A.D., and widespread use of *izby* continued until the 18th century. The first *izby* were built with a stone or clay fireplace but without a chimney; chimneys were not incorporated into the design of the *izby* until the 12th century. To the N and center of Russia, the roofs were steep, and the *izby* had cellars; to the S roofs were less steep. *Izby* traditionally are constructed with birch, or occasionally lime logs, and are 7-9 meters long.

IZGOY. A feudal serf, bound to the owner and to the soil.

IZHEVSK. Capital of the Udmurt Autonomous Soviet Socialist Republic situated 350 miles (560 km) ENE of Gorky on the Izh River, in the Russian Soviet Federated Socialist Republic. Founded in 1760, it became an important metallurgical center with manufacture of firearms and armaments, motorcycles, lathes, and machinery. Population (1977) 534,000.

IZMAIL. Capital and port of the Izmail region 120 miles (190 km) SW of Odessa on Dnestr River, in the

Ukraine. Founded in the 16th century, it was part of Rumania from 1918 to 1939. Industries include flour milling and tanning. Izmail trades in cereals and hides. Population (1970) 48,000.

IZMAILOV, ALEXANDER EFIMOVICH (1779–1831). Novelist and writer of fables. He is best known for *Evgeny* (1799–1801), a didactic novel of manners.

IZMAILOVO GLASS FACTORY. The Izmailovo glass factory, the first recorded in Russia, was founded in 1668, employing Venetian glassblowers.

***IZVESTIYA* (NEWS).** Daily newspaper published by the Supreme Soviet Presidium, which was founded after the February 1917 Revolution as the organ of the Petrograd Soviet. It was published jointly by the central executive committee of Soviets and the Petrograd Soviet from August 1917, but became very similar to *Pravda* from October 1917. In 1918 publication was transferred to Moscow and in 1957 the circulation stood at 1,550,000. However, under the editorship of Alexey Adzhubey (editor, 1959–64) the style of the newspaper changed and it became an evening publication in 1960. It became and remains popular, and in the late 1970s the circulation was 8,600,000. A weekly supplement *Nedeliya* (The Week), as of 1980 sold separately, is also published.

IZVOLSKY, COUNT ALEXANDER PETROVICH, (1856–1919). Diplomat and minister. As foreign minister he concluded a treaty with Britain resolving Anglo-Russian disagreements in the Middle East, but he was dismissed in 1910 following an unsuccessful agreement with Austria. In 1910, he was transferred to Paris where he served as the Russian ambassador from 1910 to 1917. He had sought Austrian help in 1908 in asserting Russia's right to use the Dardanelles. The resulting agreement strengthened Austria in the Balkans at Russia's expense, and no aid was given in the Dardanelles question.

IZYASLAV, GRAND PRINCE (1027–78). One of the three sons of Yaroslav the Wise (*q.v.*) of Kiev. He received the princedom of Kiev and Novgorod on his father's death, but his reign was marked by constant and inconclusive wars with his brothers.

Vernadsky, George V., *Kievan Russia*, 1948.

J

JACOBINS. Minor revolutionary organization in Russia in the early 19th century. The Jacobins were led by Jacobin Frédéric-César La Harpe, the former chief tutor of Alexander I. Influenced by the French radicals, they advocated republicanism, although La Harpe himself extolled the merits of both radical ideas with enlightened absolutism to Alexander I.

Clarkson, Jesse Dunsmore, *A History of Russia,* 1961.

Palmer, Alan, *Alexander I,* 1974.

JADWIGA, QUEEN OF POLAND (*c.* 1373–1399). At 10 or 11 years of age (1384), Jadwiga, younger daughter of Louis I of Hungary, was invited by the Poles to be their queen. Her father had ruled Poland (1370–82), being the nephew of the Polish King Casimir III (died 1370). In 1386 she was married to Jagiello (*q.v.*), grand duke of Lithuania, with whom she ruled until her death in 1399. The marriage produced a powerful united empire dominant in E Europe until 1569.

JAGIELLO, KING OF POLAND (*c.* 1350–1434). As grand duke of Lithuania he was invited by the Poles to marry their queen, Jadwiga, and to rule with her, on the condition that he and his people become Christian. He ruled Poland as Wladyslaw II Jagiello (1386–1434). The union of the crowns produced a dominant state that defended E Europe from the Teutonic Knights of Germany and from the Mongols. He recognized Lithuania (under his cousin Vytautas) as an autonomous dukedom on the condition that in foreign policy the two states be united.

JAPAN, SEA OF. Marginal sea of the Pacific Ocean, bounded on the E by Japan and Sakhalin Island (USSR) and on the W by the USSR and Korea. It has an area of 405,000 square miles (1,048,950 sq km) and an average depth of 4,429 feet (1,350 m) with a maximum depth of 12,278 feet (3,742 m). There is a continental shelf about 19 miles (30 km) wide along the Siberian coast, where the sea freezes in winter. Fish include shellfish, salmon, and squid, with some herring, sardines, and tuna. There are oil and gas reserves off Sakhalin Island.

JASSY, TREATY OF. Treaty signed at Jassy, Moldavia, in 1792, ending the Russo-Turkish war of 1787–92. It confirmed the 1774 Treaty of Kuchuk Kainarji (Küçük Kaynarca) narca) (*q.v.*). Turkey was to hold Bessarabia, Moldavia, and Walachia, and the Russian frontier advanced to the Dnestr River. Russia gained the fortress of Ochakov. *See* **Russo-Turkish Wars**

JAWLENSKY, ALEXEI VON (1864–1941). A Russian-born painter of the Expressionist school. He trained under Ilya Repin and moved to Munich in 1896 where he came under the influence of Wassily Kandinsky. In 1905 he worked in France and was influenced in his use of color by Matisse. As a member of the German Blue Rider group he painted Expressionist portraits with vivid Fauvist colors. He remained best known for his portraits; later in his life these became mystical in quality and almost abstract.

JELGAVA. Latvian town 30 miles (48 km) SW of Riga on the Lielupe River. Formerly known as Mitau, it was founded in the 13th century and passed to Russia in 1795. The main industries are textiles, sugar refining, sawmilling, and processing agricultural produce; manufactures are linen goods, oilcloth, rope, woolen goods, bricks, tiles, and leather goods. Population (1972) 58,000.

JENA, BATTLE OF. Battle fought on October 14, 1806 between the armies of France and Prussia. Napoleon's decisive action against Prussia followed a secret pact between Prussia and Russia, signed in July 1806. The French defeated Prince Friedrich of Hohenlohe-Ingelfingen at Jena, fielding 54,000 men against a Prussian force of 51,000. The news of the victory helped a second French force of 25,000 to withstand and ultimately to defeat the main Prussian army (numbering 63,000) at Auerstadt. Prussia was thus conquered before the Russian promise of aid could be implemented.

JEWISH AUTONOMOUS REGION. It is located in Khabarovsk Territory and bordered on the S by the Amur River. A Jewish National District was established in 1928 and was enlarged as an autonomous region in 1934. The capital is Birobidzhan. It has an area 13,895 square miles (35,988 sq km). The chief industries are nonferrous metallurgy, building materials, timber, engineering, textiles, paper, and food processing. There are 50 factories and 140,000 hectares under crops. Population (1980) 193,400; Jews, 15,000.

JEWISH SOCIAL DEMOCRATIC PARTY. The Jewish movement split from the Russian Social Democrats in 1903 and had a separate identity until rejoining in 1906. *See* **Bund.**

JEWS. The Soviet Union has one of the largest Jewish populations in the world (2.2 million at the 1970 census, but about 1.8 million by some Western estimates). There are large communities in Moscow and Kiev and the major synagogues maintain bakeries for producing unleavened bread. There were relatively few Jews in Russia until the partitions of Poland in the 19th century. Thousands of Jews, seeking to escape political persecution and harassment, emigrated to the West in the 1970s. A recent tightening of emigration rules by the Soviet authorities had cut the flow from a high of about 51,000 in 1979 to less than 3,000 in 1982. The Jewish Autonomous Region has only 15,000 Jews out of a population of 190,000 (1979 figures). *See also* **Anti-Semitism.**

Brym, Robert J., *The Jewish Intelligentsia and Russian Marxism*, 1978.

JINGOISM. Term said to have originated with those who supported sending a British fleet into Turkish waters in 1878 to resist the advance of Russia; it became associated with an attitude of belligerent nationalism. The phrase appears in a popular song of the time, "We don't want to fight, yet by jingo, if we do . . ."

JOB, PATRIARCH. In 1589 the patriarch of Constantinople raised the head of the Russian Orthodox Church to the rank of patriarch. Thus, Metropolitan Job, adviser to Boris Godunov, became the first Russian patriarch. The church under him was reorganized with a stronger hierarchy and gained greatly in prestige and influence. He was removed by the pretender False Dmitry after Godunov's death in 1605.

Medlin, William K., *Moscow and East Rome*, 1952.

JOHANSSEN, PER CHRISTIAN (1817–1903). Swedish ballet dancer. He taught at the Imperial Ballet School, St. Petersburg from 1860 and helped to establish the Russian style of ballet. He taught Mathilda Kshesinskaya, Olga Preobrajenski, and Paul Gerdt.

JOHN, KING OF DENMARK (*c.* 1460–1513). Reigned as king of Denmark and Norway (1483–1513). He succeeded his father, Christian I. Recognized as sovereign of Sweden by the state council, he forced the Swedish regent to resign in 1497, and was crowned king. In 1493 he had formed an alliance with Ivan III, the Great, of Moscow. Strengthened by this alliance and by his own strong navy, he attempted the control of the Baltic for Danish trade and the suppression of the German Hanseatic League.

JOHN OF KRONSTADT, FATHER (IVAN ILIYCH SERGEYEV) (1829–1909). Russian Orthodox priest. After his ordination he went to Kronstadt where his sermons attracted large congregations from all classes of society. He opposed the teachings of Tolstoy, concentrating his work on the unskilled poor and establishing a center for training in industrial skills. He rejected all radical political reform.

JOHN SOBIESKI, KING OF POLAND (1674–96). Sobieski was a member of the nobility and was appointed field commander of the Polish army in 1666. He came to prominence through his victories against the Cossacks and Tatars and was confirmed in popularity after a victory over the Turks in 1673. He was elected king in 1674. In 1686 he concluded a treaty (The Eternal Peace) with Russia, the traditional enemy of Poland, in order to secure Russian aid against Turkey.

JOSEPH II, HOLY ROMAN EMPEROR (1765–90). Ally of Catherine the Great, whom he visited twice and with whom he made two important agreements. The first was the tripartite partition of Poland in 1772 among Austria, Russia, and Prussia. The second was an alliance sharing power in E and SE Europe between Austria and Russia. Catherine declared war on Turkey in 1787, and Joseph raised an army in support. His policy, however, was unpopular at home, and Austria withdrew from the war. *See* **Russo-Turkish Wars.**

JOSEPH OF VOLOKOLAMSK (1439–1515). Theologian. From 1477 he was abbot of the prosperous Monastery of Abbot Pafnutius at Borovsk SW of Moscow, but after disagreements with Prince Ivan III, Joseph founded his own monastery at Volokolamsk 80 miles (129 km) W of Moscow. He then engaged in ecclesiastical controversies, including the suppression of the Judaizing Christian sects and the important dispute on possessions. In 1503 Abbot Nil Sorsky accused the monasteries of following a course of perdition because of their emphasis on possessions, but Joseph believed in a binding relationship between the natural protector of the church, the autocrat, and in a wealthy and powerful church, and won the day. His most important work was *The Enlightener.*

JUDAIZERS. Religious sect that opposed several Christian doctrines, such as the Trinity and the divinity of Christ, as well as the existing structure of the Orthodox Church, particularly with regard to church property, monks, and the hierarchy. It flourished at the end of the 15th century in Novgorod and was suppressed early in the 16th century. *See* **Joseph of Volokolamsk.**

JUDICIARY REFORMS OF 1864. Dmitry Zamyatnin, minister of justice, brought in legislation which separated the judiciary from the executive government and reformed court procedures. Formerly a branch of general administration, with all cases relying on secrecy and written evidence, the judiciary acquired independent judges, and public hearings in court, with cases debated by lawyers. Procedure was simplified by introducing two ways of conducting a case, the general and the abbreviated procedure. Minor cases came before justices of the peace; serious criminal cases were tried by jury. The system did not apply to military courts. The central government attempted to sidestep the new legislation (when dealing with suspected revolutionary activity) by reserving certain categories of offense for special courts-martial. The reform is considered the most important and most successful of the "Great Reforms" (*q.v.*) of the 1860s.

Kucherov, Samuel, *Courts, Lawyers and Trials under the Last Three Tsars,* 1953.

JULIAN CALENDAR. *See* **Calendar.**

JULY DAYS. Period from July 16 to 18, 1917, when servicemen and civilians, in sympathy with the Bolsheviks, tried to seize power from Kerensky's provisional government in Petrograd. Lenin considered their uprising inopportune; they received no significant support and the attempt failed. Bolshevik involvement was ascribed to pro-German sympathies and Bolsheviks in general were accused of treason. Lenin fled to Finland.

Carr, Edward Hallett, *The Russian Revolution: from Lenin to Stalin,* 1979.

Katkov, George and Shukman, H., *Lenin's Path to Power,* 1971.

Shukman, H., *Lenin and the Russian Revolution,* 1977.

JUSTICE. The basis of the judicial system is the same throughout the Soviet Union, but the constituent republics have the right to introduce modifications and to make their own rules for the application of the code of laws. The Supreme Court of the USSR is the chief court and supervising organ for all constituent republics and is elected by the Supreme Soviet of the USSR for five years. Supreme Courts of the union and autonomous republics are elected by the Supreme Soviets of these republics, and territorial, regional, and area courts by the respective Soviets, each for a term of five years.

Court proceedings are conducted in the local language with full interpreting facilities as required. All cases are heard in public, unless otherwise provided for by law, and the accused is guaranteed the right of defense.

Laws establishing common principles of legislation, criminal responsibility for state and military crimes, judicial and criminal procedure, and military tribunals were adopted by the Supreme Soviet on December 25, 1958 for the courts of both the USSR and the constituent republics.

The law courts are divided into people's courts and higher courts. The people's courts consist of the people's judge and two assessors, and their function is to examine, at the first instance, most of the civil and criminal cases. Some of the more important cases are tried at the regional courts, and those of the highest importance at the Supreme Court. The regional courts supervise the activities of the people's courts and also act as courts of appeal from the decisions of the people's court. Special chambers of the higher courts deal with offenses committed in the military and the public transport services.

People's judges and assessors, who serve on a rotating basis, are elected directly by the citizens of each constituency: judges for five years, assessors for two and one-half years. Should a judge be found not to perform his duties conscientiously and in accordance with the mandate of the people, he may be recalled by his electors.

The people's assessors are called on for duty for two weeks a year. The people's assessors for the regional court must have had at least two years' experience in public or trade-union work. The list of assessors for the Supreme Court is drawn up by the Supreme Soviet of the republic.

The labor session of the people's court supervises the regulations relating to the working conditions and the protection of labor and gives decisions on conflicts arising between management and employees, or the violation of regulations.

Disputes between state institutions must be referred to an arbitration commission. Disputes between Soviet state institutions and foreign business firms may be referred by agreement to a foreign trade arbitration commission of the All-Union Chamber of Commerce.

The procurator-general of the USSR is appointed for five years by the Supreme Soviet. All procurators of the republics, autonomous republics, and autonomous regions are appointed by the procurator-general of the USSR for a term of five years. The procurators supervise the correct application of the law by all state organs, and have special responsibility for the observance of the law in places of detention. The procurators of the union republics are subordinate to the procurator-general of the USSR, whose duty it is to see that acts of all institutions of the USSR are legal, that the law is correctly interpreted and uniformly applied. He also has to participate in important cases in the capacity of state prosecutor.

Capital punishment was abolished on May 26, 1947 but was restored on January 12, 1950 for treason, espionage, and sabotage; on May 7, 1954 for certain categories of murder; in December, 1958 for terrorism and banditry, on May 7, 1961 for embezzlement of public property, counterfeiting, and attack on prison warders and, in particular circumstances, for attacks on the police and public order volunteers; on February 15, 1962 for rape; on February 20, 1962 for accepting bribes.

Berman, Harold J., *Justice in the USSR*, 1963.

——*Soviet Criminal Law and Procedure*, 1972.

K

KABALA. Form of servitude in medieval Russia under which an individual accepted an obligation to work for a definite and agreed period of time.

KABALEVSKY, DMITRI BORISOVICH (1904–). Composer, conductor and musicologist. He studied composition under Nicholas Myaskovsky and piano under Scriabin at the Moscow Conservatory. He taught at the conservatory from 1932, becoming a professor there in 1939. His works include the operas *Colas Breugnon* (1938), *Semya Tarasa* (1950), and *Nikita Vershinin* (1955). He has composed four symphonies, including his No. 1 in commemoration of the 15th anniversary of the Revolution, three piano concertos, a violin concerto, and a cello concerto, as well as many choral works, songs, and piano works.

Abraham, Gerald E.H., *Eight Soviet Composers,* 1943.

Calvocoressi, Michel D., *A Survey of Russian Music,* 1944.

Tcherepnin, A., *Anthology of Russian Music,* 1966.

KABARDINO-BALKAR AUTONOMOUS SOVIET SOCIALIST REPUBLIC. Region annexed to Russia in 1557 and constituted an autonomous republic in 1936, (as part of the Russian Soviet Federated Socialist Republic). It has an area of 4,825 square miles (12,500 sq km). The capital is Nalchik, situated 320 miles (512 km) SE of Rostov. The chief industries are ore mining, engineering, coal, food processing, timber and light industries. The region also manufactures building materials and has a varied agriculture. Population (1981) 688,000.

KACHALOV, VASILY IVANOVICH (1875–1948). Soviet actor. Kachalov's services to acting and to the Soviet Union were twice rewarded by the Order of Lenin.

KADET PARTY. The name was formed by the initials of the Constitutional-Democratic Party (*q.v.*), which represented members of the bourgeoisie and petty bourgeoisie, civil servants, army officers, shopkeepers, and the like. It was founded in October 1905 and was headed by Pavel Miliukov, who advocated government on a constitutional basis to be attained by legal methods. He looked to Great Britain for a model of his ideas. Nearly all the ministers in the provisional government were Kadets. The party was suppressed in 1917.

Hosking, Geoffrey A., *The Constitutional Experiment*, 1973.

McNeal, Robert H. (ed.), *Russia in Transition: 1905–1914: Evolution or Revolution?* 1976.

KADIYEVKA. Coal-mining town situated approximately 104 miles (168 km) NNW of Rostov, in the Ukraine, with important metallurgical and chemical industries. Population (1977), 141,000.

KAGANOVICH, LAZAR MOYSEYEVICH (1893–). Communist and disciple of Lenin. In 1911 Kaganovich joined the Bolshevik Party and played a prominent role in the leather workers' union. He assisted in organizing party affairs and rapidly advanced from post to post, including membership in the central committee from 1924, head of party organization in the Ukraine 1925–28, and from 1930, membership in the Politburo. He was in charge of the collectivization of agriculture from 1929 to 1934 and the party purge in 1933–34. He became one of Stalin's chief lieutenants, but in 1957, as a member of the "anti-party group," Kaganovich was expelled from the central committee and the Presidium.

Carr, Edward Hallett, *A History of Soviet Russia,* 14 vols., 1952–78.

KAGUL. Town situated 30 miles (48 km) NNW of Galati in the Moldavian Soviet Socialist Republic, on the Prut River where it forms the frontier with Rumania. Industries include wine making and flour milling.

KAKHETIA. Region of E Georgia in the Georgian Soviet Socialist Republic. It is drained by the upper Alazan River. The chief towns are Telavi, Signakhi, and Gurdzhaani. It is an important wine-producing area.

KAKHOVSKY, PETER GRIGOREVICH (1797–1826). Decembrist (*see* **Decembrists**). He was active in all the preparations for the unsuccessful uprising of December 1825 and was responsible for killing General-Governor Michael Andreyavich Miloradovich. Kakhovsky was sentenced to death and hanged in July 1826.

Mazour, Anatole Grigorevich, *The First Russian Revolution, 1825,* 1937.

Raeff, Marc, *The Decembrist Movement,* 1966.

Zetlin, Mikhail O., *The Decembrists,* 1958.

KALEDIN, ALEKSEY MAKSIMOVICH (1861–1918). Cossack leader and soldier. He served from 1914 in command of a cavalry division but opposed the military reforms of the provisional government and in 1917 was forced to resign. Returning to the Don region, he was elected hetman of the Cossacks and organized an anti-Bolshevik campaign, but he suffered many defeats and shot himself in February 1918.

KALININ (Formerly Tver). Capital of Kalinin region situated 105 miles (168 km) NW of Moscow at the confluence of the Volga and Tversta rivers. Established in the 12th century, it became, from *c.* 1240, the capital of the powerful grand principality of Tver rivaling Moscow. An important icon school flourished there; one of the most famous of the Tver icons is the 15th century *Blue Dormition.* There are large textile and engineering industries. Population (1981) 422,000.

KALININ, MICHAEL IVANOVICH (1875–1946). Communist statesman, born at Tver (now Kalinin). An active revolutionary arrested many times after 1898, he became one of the first supporters of Lenin. He supported Stalin in the party struggle following Lenin's death. In 1919 he became chairman of the all-Russian executive committee of the Soviets and a member of the central committee. He was a member of the Politburo from 1926 and chairman of the Supreme Soviet of the USSR from 1938 to 1946.

Schapiro, Leonard B., *The Communist Party of the Soviet Union,* 1977.

KALININGRAD (Formerly Königsberg). Capital of Kaliningrad region. An important ice-free Baltic port, it is situated at the mouth of the Pregel River on the Bay of Vistula. Founded as a fortress for the Teutonic Knights in 1255, it joined the Hanseatic League in 1340. Seat of the dukes of Prussia from 1525 to 1618, it became the coronation city of the kings of Prussia in 1701. It became Russian territory in 1945 as a result of the Potsdam Conference. Exports include grain, flax, and timber. Industries include shipbuilding, engineering, chemicals, food products, and paper and flour milling. Population (1981) 366,000.

KALISZ, TREATY OF. Treaty concluded between Russia and Prussia on February 28, 1813, in Kalisz, in central Poland, which stipulated the restoration of Prussia to its 1806 frontiers, the independence of the German states, and an agreement by both Russia and Prussia not to sign a separate peace with Napoleon I.

KALKA, BATTLE OF. Battle that took place on the Kalka River in 1223 between Russian and Polovtsy forces and the Mongols. Having won the battle, the Mongols disappeared and did not reappear until 1237–40.

KALMYK AUTONOMOUS SOVIET SOCIALIST REPUBLIC. It is part of the Russian Soviet Federated Socialist Republic. Its area is 29,300 square miles (75,887 sq km). First constituted an autonomous republic in 1935, it was dissolved in 1943 and reconstituted in 1958. The capital is Elista, situated 180 miles (288 km) W of Astrakhan. Chief industries are fishing, canning, and the manufacture of building materials. There is also cattle breeding and irrigated farming. Population (1981) 301,000.

KALMYKS (KALMUCKS). Mongol people of the Tibetan Buddhist faith living in the Kalmyk Autonomous Soviet Socialist Republic. They migrated from W China to Russia (Nogay Steppe) in the early 17th century. In 1920 a Kalmyk autonomous oblast was established and in 1933 it became an autonomous republic. It was occupied in part by the Germans in 1942, and it was thought that the Kalmyks had collaborated with the enemy and as a result were exiled to Soviet Central Asia. Rehabilitation of the Kalmyks was announced in 1957 and they returned to their homes. In 1979 Kalmyks numbered about 150,000.

Conquest, Robert, *The Soviet Deportation of Nationalities,* 1960.

KALUGA. Capital of the Kaluga region situated 100 miles (160 km) SSW of Moscow on the Oka River. Industries include saw-milling, engineering, and the production of iron and steel goods, bricks, glass, matches, and food products. Population (1981) 276,000.

KAMA RIVER. River rising N of the Udmurt and flowing N, E, and finally SW for 1,200 miles (1,920 km) to join the Volga River below Kazan.

KAMCHATKA. Mountainous, volcanic region in the Khabarovsk territory in the NE USSR, including the Kamchatka peninsula, the Chukot and Koryak national areas, and the Komandorsky Islands. It has an area of 490,425 square miles (1,270,200 sq km). Industries include fishing, fish processing, fur trapping, and woodworking. Population (1975) 317,000.

KAMENEV, LEV BORISOVICH (1883–1936). Politician. A prominent leader of the Bolshevik movement before the Revolution. Although he opposed Lenin's seizure of power in 1917 he remained prominent in the party. Initially he supported Stalin against Trotsky and later he supported Trotsky and Zinoviev. He was expelled from the party several times. Finally, in 1935, he was sentenced to five years' imprisonment; at a retrial in 1936 he was again sentenced and was executed.

Carr, Edward Hallett, *The Russian Revolution: From Lenin to Stalin,* 1979.

Schapiro, Leonard B., *The Communist Party of the Soviet Union,* 1977.

KAMENSK-URALSKY. Town situated 80 miles (128 km) ESE of Sverdlovsk. Manufactures include machine tools and pipes. The town also has aluminum refining and bauxite mining. Population (1981) 191,000.

KANDINSKY, WASSILY. (1866–1944). Artist. He was trained as a lawyer and economist before taking up art at the age of 30. He studied in Munich where he formed the *Blaue Reiter* group in 1911 with Franz Marc, and became the first Russian pure abstract artist. He returned to Russia in 1914 and helped to reestablish the arts after the Revolution. He left Russia in 1921 to join the Bauhaus, a school of design and architecture in Weimar, Germany. From 1933 he lived in Paris. His written works include *Concerning the Spiritual in Art* (1912) and *Point and Line to Plane* (1926).

Grohmann, W., *Wassily Kandinsky: Life and Work,* 1959.

Kandinsky, W., trans. H. Rebay, *On the Spiritual in Art,* 1947.

KANKRIN, COUNT YEGOR FRANTSEVICH (1774–1845). Russian government official of German birth. He was minister of finance (1823–44) and played a dominant role in the economic strategy of that period, which included an attempt to stabilize the currency.

KANSK. Industrial town situated 110 miles (176 km) E of Krasnoyarsk in the Krasnoyarsk Kray of the Russian Soviet Federated Socialist Republic on the Kan River. Important mining includes coal, lignite, and mica. Industries include textile production, wood processing, and sawmilling. Population (1970) 75,000.

KANTEMIR, PRINCE ANTIOCH DMITRIYEVICH (1708–44). Poet. He wrote exclusively in conversational Russian and used Polish syllabic verse form. During the reign of Peter the Great Church Slavonic was restricted to the church, but a practical language was required for textbooks and manuals and spoken Russian as a literary language began to develop.

Drage, C., *Russian Literature in the Eighteenth Century: The Solemn Ode, the Epic, Other Poetic Genres, the Story, the Novel, Drama,* 1978.

Segal, H. B., *The Literature of Eighteenth-Century Russia,* 2 vols., 1967.

KAPITAL, DAS. The most famous work of Karl Marx, in which he develops his theories about the capitalist system, emphasizing its self-destructive nature. The first volume of *Das Kapital* appeared in 1867; the second and third volumes were published posthumously in 1885 and 1894 and were edited by Engels. *Das Kapital* was first published in Russian in 1872 and was the first translation into a foreign language.

KAPITSA, PETER LEONIDOVICH (1894–). Physicist. Educated at Leningrad and at Cambridge (under Lord Rutherford), he was assistant director of research in magnetism at the Cavendish Laboratory (1924–32) and Messel Research Professor at the Royal Society's Mond Laboratory (1932–35). He did important work on the magnetic and electrical properties of substances at low temperatures and also designed an improved plant for the liquefaction of hydrogen and helium. Kapitsa was detained in the USSR in 1935, but later became director of the Institute for Physical Problems at the Academy of Sciences in Moscow. He was awarded the Stalin Prize for Physics (1941 and 1943), and holds the Order of Lenin. He was elected a Fellow of the Royal Society of Great Britain in 1929, the first foreigner in 200 years to gain membership.

KAPODISTRIAS, COUNT IOANNIS ANTONIOS (1778–1831). Greek statesman. After serving as secretary of state in the "septinsular republic" of the Ionian Isles, then under Russian protection, in 1809 Kapodistrias embarked on a career in the Russian foreign service. He was later chosen by Tsar Alexander I for a mission to Switzerland in 1814, between 1815 and 1821 he greatly influenced the tsar, and from 1816 he was second secretary of state. Finding the tsar's attitude toward the war of Greek independence intolerable, however, he withdrew from Russian service and spent five years actively supporting the Greeks. In 1827 he was elected governor of Greece. He was assassinated in 1831.

KARA BOGAZ GOL. Gulf on E side of Caspian Sea, in Turkmenistan, with large deposits of chemical salts caused by rapid evaporation. It has an area of approximately 8,000 square miles (20,720 sq km).

KARACHAY. Turkic-speaking people who live in the Karachayevo-Cherkess Autonomous Oblast.

KARACHAYEVO-CHERKESS AUTONOMOUS REGION. The present autonomous region, part of Stavropol oblast, was reestablished in 1957, having been originally established in 1926 and dissolved in 1943. It has an area of 5,442 square miles (14,048 sq km). The capital is Cherkessk, situated approximately 225 miles (360 km) NNW of Tbilisi. Chief industries are ore mining, engineering, chemicals, and woodworking. Livestock breeding and grain growing are also important, and 501,613 acres (203,000 hectares) under crops. Population (1980) 370,000.

KARAGANDA. Capital of the region of the same name situated NNW of Lake Balkhash. Founded in 1857 as a copper-mining village, its economic importance is related to its being the center of the Karaganda coal basin. Manufactures include iron, steel, and cement. Population (1981) 583,000.

KARA-KALPAK AUTONOMOUS SOVIET SOCIALIST REPUBLIC. Constituted as an autonomous region within the Kazakh Autonomous Republic in 1925, the region then became an autonomous republic within the Russian Federation in 1932, and then part of the Uzbek Soviet Socialist Republic in 1936. It has an area of 63,920 square miles (165,553 sq km). The capital is Nukus, situated 500 miles (800 km) WNW of Tashkent. Chief industries are the manufacture of bricks, leather goods, and furniture, and canning and wine making. Agriculture includes cotton growing and the rearing of cattle, sheep, and goats. Population (1974) 779,700.

KARA KALPAKS (BLACK CAPS). Turkic-speaking people numbering about 250,000 who live in the Kara-Kalpak Autonomous Soviet Republic in Uzbekistan.

KARAKOZOV, DMITRY VLADIMIROVICH (1840–66). Student and member of the Ishutin group. He was executed following an unsuccessful attempt to assassinate Alexander II in 1866.

KARA-KUL, LAKE. The "Black Lake" situated on the plateau between the Pamir and the Alai mountains, in Tadzhikistan, near the China-USSR border. It is nearly 13,000 feet (3,962 m) above sea level. Its area is 140 square miles (363 sq km).

KARA-KUM. The "Black Sands," a desert between the Caspian Sea and the Amu Darya River, in Turkmenistan, S and SE of the Ust Urt plateau. It has an area of 110,000 square miles (284,900 sq km). The 500-mile (800-km) Kara-Kum canal runs from the Amu Darya River through two oases to Ashkhabad.

KARAMZIN, NICHOLAS MIKHAILOVICH (1766–1826). Historian and author. He wrote *Letters of a Russian Traveller* (1790–1801), which was modeled on Laurence Sterne's *Sentimental Journey* and based his prose on the colloquial speech of the Russian gentry, excluding all Church Slavonic influences. Interest in his work created a reading public. His *Memoir on Ancient and Modern Russia* (1811) was given to Alexander I, who appointed him court historian. His finest work was *History of the Russian State* (1818–24) in 11 volumes. He also wrote literary works, including the most famous *Poor Liza* (1792).

KARA SEA. Part of the Arctic Ocean situated N of the USSR between Severnaya Zemlya and Novaya Zemlya. The Ob, Yenisey, Pyasina and Taymyra rivers flow into the sea. It is extremely shallow (650 feet/198 meters) and fishing is important at river mouths. It is ice-free only in August and September.

KARELIAN AUTONOMOUS SOVIET SOCIALIST REPUBLIC. Formed as a republic 1923, and formerly a labor commune, it is part of the Russian Soviet Federated Socialist Republic. Its area is 66,564 square miles (172,400 sq km). The capital is Petrozavodsk, situated 185 miles (296 km) NE of Leningrad. Chief industries include timber, papercellulose, mica, chemicals, electrical goods, and furniture. There is also varied farming. Population (1981) 746,000.

KARELIAN ISTHMUS. A strategically important piece of land between the Gulf of Finland and Lake Ladoga. The chief city is Leningrad.

KARL MARX PEAK. Highest peak in the Shakhdara mountains situated in the SW Pamirs in the Tadzhik Soviet Socialist Republic. Rising to 22,067 feet (6,726 m) above sea level, it was first climbed in 1946 by Soviet mountaineers.

KARPOV, ANATOLY (1951–). Soviet chess player. Karpov won the world individual championship for junior chess players in 1969 and became an International Grandmaster, and in 1975 became world champion.

Richards, David J., *Soviet Chess: Chess and Communism in the USSR*, 1965.

Wade, R. G., *Soviet Chess*, 1968.

KARPOVICH, MICHAEL MIKHAILOVICH (1888–1959). Historian and editor. He was influential in the advancement of Russian studies in the United States and was editor of *Novy Zhurnal* (New Review), the New York Russian-language periodical. His works include *Imperial Russia 1801–1917* (1932).

KARS. Capital of Kars province, Turkey, situated 115 miles (184 km) SW of Tbilisi, USSR. It was attacked by Russia in 1807, 1828, and 1855. The city and surrounding area was ceded to Russia in 1878 at the Congress of Berlin. It was returned to Turkey in 1921. Population (1975) 54,787.

KARSAVIN, LEV PLATONOVICH (1882–1952). Historian and philosopher, brother of Tamara Platonovna Karsavina *(q.v.)*. In 1922 he was expelled from Russia and went to live in Germany. Later he was appointed professor of history at Kaunas University in Lithuania. He was arrested in 1948 and died in a concentration camp. His works include *Philosophy of History* (1923).

KARSAVINA, TAMARA PLATONOVNA (1885–1979). Prima ballerina and sister of Lev Platonovich. She made her debut in 1902 and was prima ballerina of the Maryinsky Theater in St. Petersburg. In 1909 she was one of the founders of Diaghilev's Ballets Russes and scored a particular triumph with Nijinksy in *Le Spectre de la Rose*. She settled in London in 1918 and helped to found the Royal Academy of Dancing. Her writings included *Classical Ballet: The Flow of Movement* (1962) and an autobiography *Theatre Street* (1930).

KASIMOV, PRINCEDOM OF. In 1452 Basil II created a Mongol princedom under Prince Kasim. The prince was subject to the grand prince of Moscow and this marked a turning point in the decline of power of the Golden Horde.

KATAYEV, VALENTIN PETROVICH (1897–). Novelist and playwright. He was the older brother of Yevgeny who used the surname Petrov. Writing on social affairs with a light touch, he achieved his first success with *The Embezzlers* (1926). *Time Forward* (1933) describes the trials and tribulations and the successes of workers through the period of the first Five-Year Plan. His comedies were popular, especially *Squaring the Circle* (1929). His more recent work includes a volume of memoirs, *Grass of Oblivion* (1967).

KATKOV, MICHAEL NIKIFOROVICH (1818–87). Editor. He was an assistant professor of philosophy at Moscow University (1845–50) until the subject was eliminated from the disciplines studied. In the following year he was appointed editor of the daily newspaper *Moscow Record* and in 1856 he also became editor of the monthly *Russian Herald.* He edited these publications until his death and had considerable influence on government officials. Although initially a liberal and in favor of change, after the Polish uprising (1863) he became an opponent of the liberal reforms of Alexander II.

KATORGA. Hard labor.

KATYN. The German government announced in 1943 that a mass grave of 4,250 Polish officers had been found in the forest near Katyn, a village 12 miles (19 km) W of Smolensk. An additional 10,000 officers had been killed elsewhere. The International Red Cross was denied access to investigate and in 1944 a Soviet commission stated that the officers were killed by Germans. However, in 1951–52 a U.S. investigatory commission accused the Soviets of the crime.

Anders, General Wladyslaw, *The Crime of Katyn*, 1965.

Mackiewicz, J., *The Katyn Wood Murders*, 1951.

Zawodny, J. K., *Murder in the Forest*, 1972.

KATYREV-ROSTOVSKY, PRINCE IVAN MIKHAILOVICH (?–1640). A member of one of the most important boyar families and a sort of Russian "Vicar of Bray" in that he changed allegiance several times. Katyrev-Rostovsky served under Boris Godunov. He was exiled to Siberia by Vasily Shuisky, but returned to Moscow to assist in the election of Michael Romanov. Katyrev-Rostovsky is chiefly remembered as the possible author of the *Tale of his Book of Former Years*.

KAUFMAN, GENERAL KONSTANTIN PETROVICH (1818–82). Army officer. His early career was spent in the Caucasus. In 1867 he became the first governor-general of Turkestan. After taking Samarkand in 1873, he was in charge of the successful campaign against the khanate of Khiva and in 1876 he won the khanate of Kokand for Russia. Protests from the British government, which felt that there was a threat to British interests in Afghanistan, thwarted his expansionist plans, after Alexander II decided that he was unwilling to give his support to Kaufman for further expeditions.

KAUNAS (Russian: Kovno, German: Kauen). City in the Lithuanian Soviet Socialist Republic, situated on the Neman River. Kaunas was first established as a fortress in 1030 and was granted a municipal charter in 1403. Owing to its position on the main route E the Teutonic Knights frequently attacked and destroyed it. As a result of the third partition of Poland in 1795 Kaunas was given to Russia. In 1915–18 and 1941–44 the town was occupied by the Germans, and from 1918 to 1940, was the de facto capital of independent Lithuania. Following the Second World War Kaunas was made part of the USSR. The town is an important river port and railway junction and has numerous industries, including the manufacture of agricultural machinery, textiles, metal goods, chemicals, and food products. Population (1981) 383,000.

KAVERIN, VENYAMIN ALEKSANDROVICH (ZILBER) (1902–). Author. Some of his successful publications, *Nine Tenths of Fate* (1926), *The Larger View* (1934–35), and *Two Captains* (1940–45), exploit a dramatic psychological plot, but his best novel, *Artist Unknown* (1931), has a political content. He was a founding member of a Russian literary group, the Serapion Brothers (*q.v.*), named after E.T.A. Hoffman's hero. The group was founded in Petrograd in 1921.

Slonim, Marc, *Soviet Russian Literature*, 1967.

KAZACHOK. The *kazachok* is a Cossack dance and a feature of most Russian dances in the *vprisyadku* style, which involves a peculiar method of bending the knees.

Tkachenko, T., *Folk Dances of the USSR*, 1954.

KAZAKHSTAN. In 1920 Uralsk, Turgay, Akmolinsk, and Semipalatinsk provinces formed the Kazakh Soviet Socialist Republic within the Russian Soviet Federated Socialist Republic. Kazakhstan was made a constituent republic of the USSR in 1936. To this republic were added parts of the former governorship of Turkestan inhabited by a majority of Kazakhs. It has an area of 1,049,155 square miles (2,717,300 sq km). The capital is Alma-Ata. Agriculture of all kinds, especially the growing of grain and cotton, is important, and the sheep of Kazakhstan produce particularly high-quality wool. The country is rich in mineral resources, including coal, tungsten, oil, copper, lead, zinc, and manganese, and it has important heavy-engineering industries. Population (1981) 15,000,000.

KAZAKOV, MATVEY FEDOROVICH (1738–1813). Architect. His work, in the classical style, is found mainly in Moscow. Working with Vasily Bazhenov (*q.v.*), he built the Senate Building (1776–88), now the meeting place of the council of ministers, and constructed many buildings including the present House of Unions.

Berton, Kathleen, *Moscow: An Architectural History*, 1977.

Hamilton, George H., *The Art and Architecture of Russia*, 1954.

KAZAN. Capital of the Tatar Republic, situated at the confluence of the Kazanka and Volga rivers. Founded in 1401, it became the capital of an independent Tatar khanate subjugated by Ivan IV (the Terrible) in 1552. An important trading center in the Middle Ages, Kazan revived in the 18th century when Siberia was developed. Industries expanded after the city was rebuilt under Catherine II (the Great) in 1762–96. It is an important transport and industrial center with large engineering works and oil refineries. Other manufactures are chemicals, soap, textiles, typewriters, and musical instruments. Its fur industry handles half the Russian output. Population (1981) 1,011,000.

KAZBEK, MOUNT. Mountain peak in the Caucasus, situated 65 miles (104 km) N of Tbilisi. It rises 16,546 feet (5,043 m) above sea level.

KAZENNAYA. Treasury office.

KAZIN, VASILY VASILEVICH (1898–). Poet. For a time he was a member of the Smithy (*Kuznitsa*) group of poets. His work shows nostalgia for the countryside rather than the city. His work includes *The Fox-Fur Coat and Love* (1925–26) and *Confessions* (1928).

Poggioli, Renato, *Poets of Russia, 1880–1930*, 1960.

KEISTUT (KESTUTIS) (*c.* 14th century). Brother of Grand Prince Algirdas of Lithuania who helped to defend the western part of the Lithuanian state against the Teutonic Order while Algirdas pressed eastward.

KEMEROVO. Capital of the region of the same name situated on the Tom River, in Siberia. Important industries are chemicals, engineering, and coal mining. Population (1981) 486,000.

KENNEDY, JOHN FITZGERALD (1917–63). President of the United States of America (1961–63). Kennedy suffered two serious setbacks during the first year of his presidency: an unsuccessful attempt to overthrow the Castro regime in Cuba in April 1961 and the building of the Berlin Wall by the USSR in August. His major triumph occurred in October 1962, when he ordered a full alert and a naval blockade of Cuba (*see* **Cuban Crisis**).

KERCH. Ukrainian port and chief industrial center of the Crimea situated 79 miles (126 km) NW of Novorossiysk at E end of the Kerch peninsula. Industries include iron and steel, shipbuilding, and fisheries. Kerch was founded by the Greeks in the sixth century B.C. and has many ancient monuments. Population (1981) 159,000.

KERCH PENINSULA. Ukrainian peninsula situated between the Sea of Azov in the N and the Black Sea in the S. It is 60 miles (96 km) long and a maximum of 30 miles (48 km) wide and is separated from the Crimean mainland by the Kerch Strait.

KERENSKY, ALEXANDER FEDOROVICH (1881–1970). Statesman and lawyer. A moderate socialist, he was elected to the Fourth Duma in 1912 and there led the Labor group of socialist peasant members; he was a brave opponent of the tsarist government. Later he joined the Socialist Revolutionary Party. During 1917 he held many government posts: minister of justice (February), minister of war and navy (May), and in July prime minister. As prime minister he aimed to continue the war against Germany but this undermined his popularity and in November he was ousted by the Bolsheviks. He then lived in exile, first in France and then in Australia, and finally, from 1946, in the United States.

Kerensky, Alexander Fedorovich, *The Kerensky Memoirs: Russia and History's Turning Point*, 1965.

KEYNES, LADY LYDIA. *See* **Lopokova, Lydia.**

KGB. Abbreviation of *Komitet Gosudarstvennoy Bezopasnosti*, the Committee of State Security, which has been the Soviet security service since 1953. Earlier similar organizations have been the Cheka, OGPU, NKVD, and MGB (*see* **Secret Police**).

Hingley, Ronald, *The Russian Secret Police*, 1970.

Levytsky, B., *The Uses of Terror: The Soviet Secret Service 1917–1970*, 1971.

Wohn, Simon and Slusser, Robert M., *The Soviet Secret Police*, 1957.

KHABAROVSK. Capital of the territory of the same name. It is located on the Amur River and the Trans-Siberian Railway. It is the chief industrial center of E Siberia, in which is carried out oil refining, engineering, brewing, tanning and flour milling. Population (1981) 545,000.

KHACHATURIAN, ARAM ILYICH (1903–78). Composer. Born in Georgia, he studied at the Moscow

Conservatory (1923–34). His compositions were influenced by Armenian, Georgian, and other folk tunes that he collected. His first symphony (1934) drew attention to his talent and this was followed by a piano concerto (1936) and a violin concerto (1940). His best-known works are two ballets, *Gayanch,* which includes the saber dance (1942), and *Spartak* (1954), revised 1958. He also composed music for films and plays. For a short period he was under censure during the worst of the Zhdanov "formalist" (*q.v.*) pressures. He received many awards, including the Order of Lenin (1939).

Abraham, Gerald E.H., *Eight Soviet Composers,* 1943.

Shneerson, Grigory, A. *Khachaturian,* 1959.

KHAKASS. Turkic-speaking Siberian people living in the Khakass Autonomous Region and numbering about 60,000. They were formerly nomadic herdsmen and are now collectivized.

Kolarz, Walter, *The Peoples of the Soviet Far East,* 1954.

KHAKASS AUTONOMOUS REGION. Region established in 1930. It has an area of 23,855 square miles (61,784 sq km). The capital is Abakan, situated 150 miles (240 km) SSW of Krasnoyarsk, in Krasnoyarsk territory. Chief industries are coal and ore mining, and timber and woodworking. There is also livestock breeding, dairy and vegetable farming, with 1.5 million acres (621,000 hectares) under crops. Population (1979) 500,000.

KHALTURIN, STEPAN NIKOLAYEVICH (1856–82). Political agitator. He led the short-lived Northern Union of Russian Workers (*q.v.*), one of the early labor movements in St. Petersburg. He later joined a group engaged in terrorist activity. Having worked on the imperial yacht as a carpenter, he obtained employment at the Winter Palace and managed to smuggle in dynamite in his tool bag. He hid beneath the dining room and in February 1880, 11 people were killed in an explosion that he engineered, but Alexander II, the real target, was unhurt. Khalturin was later executed for his part in another assassination.

KHAN TENGRI. Mountain peak in the Tien Shan ranges, situated on the border of the Kazakh Soviet Socialist Republic with China. It rises to 22,949 feet (6,995 m) above sea level.

KHANKA, LAKE. Lake situated 100 miles (160 km) N of Vladivostok on the China-USSR frontier. It has an area of 1,700 square miles (4,400 sq km). Fed by the Mo and Lefu rivers, it is drained by the Sungacha River into the Ussuri River.

KHANTY-MANSIY NATIONAL AREA. A national area in W Siberia crossed by the Ob River. It has important deposits of oil and natural gas. Its area is 215,000 square miles (556,850 sq km). The capital is Khanty-Mansiysk, situated at confluence of the Ob and Irtysh rivers and 300 miles (480 km) NNE of Tyumen. Population (1970) 272,000.

KHARKOV. Capital of the region of the same name in the Ukraine. Founded in 1656 as a Russian frontier fortress, the city became an important trading center. It was made a provincial capital in 1732. Rapid expansion followed the opening of the nearby Donets basin coalfield, for which it was the main communication and supply center from 1869. It is an important industrial and transportation center. Manufactures are agricultural machinery, including tractors, equipment for coal mining, oil drilling, and electrical products, locomotives, machine tools, and many other goods. Important buildings include the 17th-century Pokrovsky Cathedral and A. M. Gorky University, formerly Kharkov University, (1805). Population (1981) 1,485,000.

KHATANGA RIVER. River rising in central Siberia, in Krasnoyarsk, and flowing NE for 412 miles (659 km) to enter the Laptev Sea at Khatanga Bay. It abounds with fish.

KHAZARS. Turkic-speaking people mentioned in documents dated up to the 12th century, but unknown since. They lived on the banks of the lower Volga and their capital was at Itil at the river's mouth. The Khazar state covered an area from the Urals to beyond the Dnepr River, and from the Caucasus to the Oka and Kama rivers. The Khazars were defeated in 966 by Prince Svyatoslav when he destroyed their fortresses at Samandar and Sarkil, and their power declined. The Jewish religion predominated among them, but other religions were also tolerated.

Koestler, Arthur, *The Thirteenth Tribe,* 1978.

Vernadsky, George, *Ancient Russia,* 1959.

KHEMNITSER (CHEMNITZER), IVAN IVANOVICH (1745–84). Writer. He was of German origin but dealt with the idiom of the time with great skill. His fables were distinguished by their realism and simplicity and dealt with human failings.

KHERASKOV, MICHAEL MATVEYEVICH (1733–1807). Poet and author. His long poems *Rossiada* (1771–79), a description of Ivan the Terrible's capture of Kazan, and *Vladimir vozrozhdenny* (1785), the story of Vladimir's Christianization of Russia, were attempts to give Russia a national epic.

Drage, C., *Russian Literature in the Eighteenth Century: The Solemn Ode, the Epic, Other Poetic Genres, the Story, the Novel, Drama,* 1978.

KHERSON. Capital of the region of the same name in the Ukraine, situated 18 miles (29 km) from the mouth of the Dnepr River. It was founded in 1778 as a naval base by Prince Potemkin (*q.v.*), whose tomb is in the cathedral. It is a river port exporting grain and timber, and its manufactures are textiles and food products. There are also engineering, flour milling, shipbuilding, and brewing industries. Population (1981) 329,000.

KHETAGUROV, KOSTA (KONSTANTIN) LEVANOVICH (1859–1906). Ossetic poet and revolutionary democrat. Khetagurov is regarded by many as the founder of Ossetic literature. Of peasant stock, he studied in St. Petersburg from 1881 to 1885 but was unable to complete the course because of financial difficulties. Much of his prose reflects his grievances with the tsarist regime in the Caucasus, while Khetagurov's poetry deals with the historical fate of the Ossetes.

KHIBINY MOUNTAINS. Mountains on the Kola peninsula near Murmansk. They rise to over 3,000 feet (915 m) above sea level and are noted for the range of minerals found there, including titanium, vanadium, and molybdenum.

KHIVA. Town situated 18 miles (29 km) SW of Urgench on the Khiva oasis, in the Uzbek Soviet Socialist Republic. Industries include cotton milling, metalworking, and carpet making. Formerly it was the capital of the Khiva Khanate. Population (1974) 26,000. (*See* **Kaufman, General R.P.**)

KHLEBNIKOV, VELEMIR VLADIMIROVICH (1885–1922). Poet and Slavophile. He was the founder of Russian Futurism (*q.v.*), which aimed at shocking the reader and made an attempt at breaking with past conceptions of the use of words by creating a "trans-sense" language. Futurism was both a literary and artistic movement at the beginning of the 20th century.

Brown, Edward J. (ed), *Major Soviet Writers: Essays in Criticism*, 1973.

KHMELNITSKY. Capital of the region of the same name situated 170 miles (272 km) WSW of Kiev on the S Bug River, in the Ukraine. It became part of Russia in 1795. Industries include engineering, food processing, and furniture. Population (1970) 113,000.

KHMELNITSKY, BOGDAN (*c.* 1595–1657). He was the Ukrainian leader (hetman) from 1648 to 1657 and led the rebellion of the Cossacks against Polish rule in the Ukraine (1648). Although peace was made with the Poles in 1649, it proved less than satisfactory to his followers and the war was renewed in 1651. Bogdan was defeated at the battle of Boresteczko and the subsequent treaty was less advantageous. He then approached Moscow and, with the signing of the Pereyaslav agreement (1654), the autonomy of the Ukraine began to wane.

Vernadsky, George, *Bohdan, Hetman of Ukraine*, 1941.

KHODASEVICH (CHODASIEWICZ), VLADISLAV FELITSYANOVICH (1886–1939). Poet. A Symbolist whose most accomplished poems *Tyazholaya lira*, were published in 1922, when he was already in exile.

West, James D., *Russian Symbolism*, 1970.

KHODYNKA FIELD DISASTER. Celebrations for the coronation of Nicholas II on May 18, 1896, ended in disaster when a too large crowd, numbering 500,000, gathered at Khodynskoye Field. There was inadequate organization, and panic led to a stampede that caused the deaths of over 2,000 people with many more injured.

KHOLOP. A captive and a personal slave of a prince, a boyar, or a monastery. The *kholop* was a dependent individual, and next to the peasants, the most numerous class in Russia. There were various categories of *kholopy* in medieval Russia.

KHOLOPSTVO. Surrender of freedom because of economic necessity; captivity or slavery.

KHOMYAKOV, ALEKSEY STEPANOVICH (1804–60). Philosopher and poet. Basically his philosophy was summed up in the concept of *sobornost (q.v.)*: love, freedom and truth of believing. He was the greatest thinker in the 19th century Slavophile movement and preached, as a lay theologian, universal Christianity and the coming together of all Christian denominations, so long as the Orthodox Church was supreme. He was opposed to Western ways of life and felt that Holy Russia had a special mission in the world.

Hare, Richard, *Pioneers of Russian Social Thought,* 1951.

Masaryk, Tomás G., *The Spirit of Russia: Studies in History, Literature and Philosophy,* 2 vols., rev. ed., 1955.

Petrovich, Michael B., *The Emergence of Russian Panslavism, 1856–70,* 1956.

Riasanovsky, N. V., *Russia and the West in the Teachings of the Slavophiles,* 1952.

Zernov, Nicholas M., *Three Russian Prophets,* 1944.

KHOPER RIVER. River in the Russian Soviet Federated Socialist Republic rising 26 miles (42 km) WSW of Penza and flowing SSW for 600 miles (960 km) to join the Don River.

KHOREZM (KHWARIZM, CHORASMIA). Oasis of Khiva situated along the left bank of the Amu Darya River in Uzbekistan. In the 16th century it became the center of the khanate of Khiva. The khanate repelled Russian advances in 1717 and 1839, but in 1873 it became a Russian protectorate. After the Revolution the khanate was abolished and a Khorezm People's Soviet Republic was established in 1920, but it was abolished again in 1924.

KHOROMY. Old Russian word referring to a type of wooden house with two or more stories.

KHOTIN. Town in the Chernovtsy oblast in N Bessarabia in the Ukraine. Khotin was conquered by the Moldavians, Poles, and also by the Turks. In 1812, Khotin became part of Russia, but it was part of Rumania from 1918 to 1940 and from 1941 to 1944.

KHRENNIKOV, TIKHON NIKOLAYEVICH (1913–). Composer. He was a pupil of Shebalin at the Moscow Conservatory from 1932. His works include an opera, *The Brothers,* two symphonies, a piano concerto, piano works, music for plays and films, including incidental music for *Much Ado About Nothing,* and many songs, including some to words by Robert Burns. In 1948, acting in his capacity as secretary of the Union of Soviet Composers, he condemned many of his colleagues, including Prokofiev, for "formalism."

KHROMOV, PAUL ALEKSEYEVICH (1907–). Soviet economist and specialist in the theory and history of economics, and from 1929, a member of the CPSU. From 1935 Khromov was director of the Institute of Economy at the USSR Academy of Sciences; from 1942 to 1948, professor at Lomonosov University; and from 1946, a member of the staff academy of social sciences of the central committee. Khromov's numerous publications include *The Economic Development of Russia in the Eighteenth and Nineteenth Centuries* and *The Economic Development of Russia* (1967).

KHRUSHCHEV, NIKITA SERGEYEVICH (1894–1971). Soviet politician. He was from 1953 to 1964 the first secretary of the central committee of the party. He joined the party in 1918 while working as a locksmith in the Donets Basin. Khrushchev became second secretary of the Moscow Party Organization in 1934, its first secretary in 1935, and first secretary of the Ukrainian Party Organization in 1938. Khrushchev took a prominent part in the Great Purge. In 1939 he became a member of the Politburo and during the Second World War was an important political officer in the army. Toward the end of Stalin's rule Khrushchev was the party's chief agricultural expert, but his policy of "rural cities" was a disaster. After Stalin's death Khrushchev was first secretary of the central committee, proving to be the most powerful member of the "collective leadership." After denouncing Stalin in a four-hour secret speech at the congress of the CPSU in 1956, he pursued a policy of destalinization with a degree of inconsistency. His plans for greater industrialized state farming eventually resulted in lower agricultural production. While Khrushchev's reforms improved the standard and quality of life in the USSR, they did not win him much popularity. In his dealings with the West, Khrushchev alternated peaceful gestures with threats, and his decisions led to the Cuban missile crisis with the United States in 1962. Khrushchev was forced out of office in 1964.

Crankshaw, Edward, *Khrushchev*, 1966.

Khrushev, Nikita, *Khrushchev Remembers*, 2 vols., 1971 and 1974.

Leonhard, Wolfgang, *The Kremlin Since Stalin*, 1962.

KHUTOR. Individual farmstead.

KHVOROSTININ, PRINCE IVAN (1623–?). Prince, writer, and political figure. He is remembered for his polemics against Catholicism and for his writings recording the peasant war and the Polish-Swedish intervention.

KIBALCHICH, NICHOLAS IVANOVICH (1854–81). Populist and scientist. From 1871 to 1875 Kibalchich studied medicine in St. Petersburg, but he was arrested in 1875 for possessing subversive literature and was imprisoned for three years. He joined the populist organizations *Zemlya i Volya* and *Narodnaya Volya*. His scientific studies of outer space were curtailed by his arrest for his part in the assassination of Alexander II. Kibalchich was executed in 1881.

KIEV. Capital of the region of the Ukraine, situated on the right bank of the Dnepr River. It is the third largest city in the USSR. The city is first recorded as occupied by Prince Oleg in 882. His successor Igor (913–45) established and expanded Kiev's authority over the surrounding Slavic tribes, a policy carried further by Svyatoslav (962–72) *(q.v.)*. Under Vladimir (*c.* 980–1015) *(q.v.)* Kiev was recognized as the center of Russia; his conversion to Christianity brought strong Byzantine influences into the city's culture, law, and government. River-borne trade with Byzantium had flourished since the ninth century, with the city as the main gathering point. Under Prince Yaroslav (The Wise) (1019–54) *(q.v.)* Kiev was the capital of a state extending from the Baltic to the Black Sea, a great cultural, religious, and trading center, but threatened by nomadic warrior hordes and internal conflict in the ruling house. Temporarily halted by the strong rule of Vladimir Monomakh (1113–25), barbarian attacks were resumed after his death and civil wars reduced the city's power until its destruction by the Mongols in 1240. The Upper Town, or capital, remained a ruin; Lithuanian and then Polish rulers garrisoned the town, of which only the artisan community of the Lower Town remained active. The Upper Town revived with the end of Polish rule in 1654, and became a symbol of Ukrainian national feeling. Russian annexation stimulated a revival of the city's economic and cultural importance. The government of the Ukrainian Soviet Republic was moved to Kiev in 1934. It is a commercial, industrial, transportation, and cultural center. Industries are extremely diverse, including light and heavy engineering products, chemicals, textiles, and food products. There are many fine ancient buildings, including the Byzantine Cathedral of St. Sophia and the Pechersky Monastery. Prince Yaroslav's Golden Gate survives as a ruin. Population (1981) 2,248,000.

KIEV UNIVERSITY. One of the most important universities of the Soviet Union, founded in 1834. The university includes 11 faculties, and its library houses more than 500,000 volumes.

KIEVAN RUS. A 9th to 13th century state, ruled over by princes of the House of Ryurik *(q.v.)*. It incorporated the land of the E Slavic tribes; the Dnepr Basin, and the land to the N of it; Finnish tribes in the upper Volga and the Gulf of Finland; the land of the W Slavs, the ancestors of the present Lithuanians and Latvians; and two Turkish-speaking peoples to the E. Its most noteworthy rulers included Princess Olga *(q.v.)*, who became a Christian and was canonized, Svyatoslav, who rid Kievan Rus of the Khazars, St. Vladimir *(q.v.)*, who in 998 brought Christianity to Russia, Yaroslav the Wise (1019–54) *(q.v.)*, who introduced the first legal code, and Vladimir Monomakh (1113–25) *(q.v.)*. Feuds between Yaroslav's sons after Vladimir's death, growing regionalism, and the shifting pattern of world trade as a result of the Crusades led to the gradual decline of Kievan Rus. Kievan Rus was finally destroyed by the Mongol conquest of 1237–40.

Vernadsky George V., *Kievan Russia,* 1948.

KINESHAMA. Industrial town situated 50 miles (80 km) ENE of Ivanovo on the Volga River, in the Russian Soviet Federated Socialist Republic. It is a center for textiles, sawmilling, and paper manufacture. Population (1976) 100,000.

KIREVSKY, IVAN VASILEVICH (1806–56). Editor. He became a Slavophile and founded the review *Evropeyets* (The European), which was suppressed by the censor. In 1845 he took over the editorship of another journal, which was again suppressed. His most influential article was "About the Character of European Education and its Bearing on Education in Russia," which was published in another journal, *Moskovsky sbornik,* which he founded in 1852.

Riasanovsky, Nicholas V., *Russia and the West in the Teaching of the Slavophiles,* 1952.

KIRGHIZ. Turkic-speaking people living in the Kirghiz Republic, although 70,000 Kirghiz live in the Sinkiang-Uoigur autonomous region of China. It is thought that the present-day Kirghiz are descended from the Kirghiz who inhabited the area around the Yenisey River between the sixth and the ninth century, and from invading Mongol and Turkic tribes. The Kirghiz are predominantly Muslim and are a pastoral people.

Wheeler, Geoffrey E., *The Peoples of Soviet Central Asia,* 1966.

KIRGHIZIA. After the Revolution, Kirghizia became part of Soviet Turkestan, which itself became an autonomous Soviet socialist republic within the Russian Soviet Federated Socialist Republic in 1921. In 1926 the government of the Russian Soviet Federated Socialist Republic transformed Kirghizia into an autonomous Soviet socialist republic within the Russian Soviet Federated Socialist Republic. Finally in 1936 Kirghizia was proclaimed one of the constituent Soviet socialist republics of the USSR. It has an area of 76,460 square miles (198,500 sq km). Its capital is Frunze. Generally mountainous, it rises to 24,406 feet (7,439 m) above sea level in Pobeda. It has fertile valleys growing wheat, sugar beets, and cotton. It is famous for its livestock breeding, and has general engineering industries. Population (1978) 3,500,000.

KIRILLIN, VLADIMIR ALEKSEYEVICH (1913–). Soviet government official. A graduate of the power engineering institute, Kirillin gained membership in the CPSU in 1937 and served in the Soviet army from 1941 to 1943. Kirillin's numerous posts include the head of the department of science, high schools, and schools (1954–55) and the head of the ideologies department of the central committee (1955–63). From 1961 to 1966 Kirillin was a member of the central committee, and from 1963 to 1966 the chairman of the all-union society for the dissemination of political and scientific knowledge. Since 1965 he has been the chairman of the Comecon committee for scientific-technological cooperation. Kirillin has been decorated with various orders, medals, and prizes.

KIRILOV, IVAN K (?–1737). The editor of the first national atlas of Russia.

KIROV. Capital of the region of the same name in the Russian Soviet Federated Socialist Republic, NE of Gorky on the Vyatka River. Founded in 1174, it became part of Russia in 1489. During the nineteenth century it was used as a place of political exile. Industries include railway and agricultural engineering. Manufactures are textiles, footwear, and matches. Population (1981) 396,000.

KIROV, SERGEY MIRONOVICH (KOSTRINOV) (1886–1934). Politician. He became a Bolshevik in 1905. His first task after the Revolution was to establish Soviet power in the Caucasus. From 1926 he was party secretary in the Leningrad area, and became a Politburo member in 1930. Kirov gave support to Stalin but opposed Stalin's personal rule after the 17th party congress in 1934. His assassination in December 1934 began the witch-hunt that developed into the Great Purge *(q.v.)*, which resulted in the judicial execution of over 100 suspected opponents of Stalin's regime.

Conquest, Robert, *The Great Terror*, 1971.

Wolfe, Bertram D., *Khrushchev and Stalin's Ghost*, 1957.

KIROVABAD. Town situated 110 miles (176 km) SE of Tbilisi, in Azerbaijan. Founded in the sixth century just to the E of the present city, it was destroyed in an earthquake in 1139. It was conquered by Russia in 1804. It is the second largest town of the Azerbaijan republic and the industrial and cultural center of the region. Manufactures are textiles and wine. Population (1981) 243,000.

KIROVOGRAD. Capital of the region of the same name in the Ukraine, situated 160 miles (256 km) SE of Kiev. It was founded in 1734 as a fortress. Manufactures include agricultural machinery, clothing, soap, and food products. Population (1981) 246,000.

KISELEV, PAUL DMITRIYEVICH (1788–1872). Political force in 19th century Russia. In 1816 Kiselev presented Alexander I *(q.v.)* with some articles dealing with the possible gradual emancipation of the serfs *(q.v.)*. From 1835, he was a member of secret committees on the serf question, and drew up some measures that met with little success. In 1856 he was sent to Paris as a diplomat and supported a policy of creating closer links between Russia and France.

KISELEVSK. Town situated 156 miles (250 km) SE of Novosibirsk in the Novosibirsk region of the Russian Soviet Federated Socialist Republic. It is an important coal-mining and mining equipment center in the Kuznetsk basin. Population (1977) 124,000.

KISHINEV. City situated WNW of Odessa, in the Moldavian Soviet Socialist Republic. Founded in the 15th century around a monastery, it was conquered by Turkey in the 16th century and by Russia in 1812. It was Rumanian from 1918 to 1940. It is the capital and the commercial and cultural center of a rich agricultural area with an extensive food industry. Manufactures include leather goods, wine, and hosiery. Population (1981) 539,000.

KISLOVODSK. Health resort situated 110 miles (176 km) NW of Ordzhonikidze in N Ossetian Autonomous Soviet Socialist Republic, in the Russian Soviet Federated Socialist Republic. It is famous for its mineral waters. Population (1974) 125,000.

KITAY GOROD. An ancient trading center near Moscow to the E of the Kremlin. In the 11th century artisans settled in this area. In the 14th and 15th centuries, as the population of Moscow grew, Kitay Gorod became an important trading center, especially for leather goods, ironware, and jewelry. By the 16th century, Kitay Gorod was beginning to lose its independence as a trading center and became more of a suburb. The large old bankers' and merchants' buildings have now been mostly replaced by modern buildings.

KIZEL. Town situated 305 miles (488 km) S of Krasnoyarsk on the Yenisey River. It is the capital of the Tuva Autonomous Soviet Socialist Republic and the center of a mining, farming, and lumbering area. Industries include tanning; manufactures include sheepskin and timber products. Population (1976) 57,000.

KLAIPÉDA. Lithuanian port situated at the entrance to Kursky Zaliv, a large lagoon on the Baltic Sea. It has been an important center since the sixth century for trade in timber, grain, and fish. Manufactures include textiles and products associated with timber. Population (1981) 181,000.

KLENZE, LEO VON (1794–1864). German architect and painter. The majority of his work was undertaken in Germany, but in 1839 he began work on additions to the Hermitage in St. Petersburg in the Greek Revival style.

KLET. Also known as *scrub*. A rectangular building similar to a shed, made of stacked beams, approximately 7 meters (23 feet) long, and 2 to 3 (6½ to 10 ft.) meters high. The roof was steep and two-sloped, while moss and hemp were used to fill in holes. In ancient Russia, *klety* were constructed to house livestock and animals. Usually the *klet* inhabited by the family was linked by a passageway to the *klet* containing supplies and animals.

KLIN. Town situated 50 miles (80 km) NW of Moscow that was totally destroyed by the *oprichniki* c. 1570.

KLYUCHEVSKAYA SOPKA. Active volcano in Kamchatka peninsula situated 220 miles (352 km) NNE of Petropavlovsk-Kamchatsky at 15,666 feet (4,775 m) above sea level.

KLYUCHEVSKY, VASILY OSIPOVICH (1841–1911). Historian. Born in Voskresenskoye in Penza oblast, Klyuchevsky started studying at the ecclesiastical seminary, but, inspired by the reforms of the 1860s, switched to the faculty of history and philology at the University of Moscow. After graduating, Klyuchevsky continued his studies and lectured. In 1879 he was appointed to the chair of history at Moscow University. His *Kurs russkoy istorii* (English translation, *A History of Russia*) brought him worldwide fame and is considered an important landmark in world historiography.

KLYUN, IVAN (1870–1942). Artist. He was a minor Suprematist (*q.v.*), a member of the "Union of Youth," and a close friend of Kazimir Malevich (*q.v.*). His work is considered to show how the concern for ornamentation and beauty deteriorated into standard formulas after the Revolution.

Gray, Camilla, *The Great Experiment: Russian Art 1863–1922*, 1962.

KLYUSHNIKOV, VIKTOR PETROVICH (1841–92). Writer of somewhat reactionary tendencies. His novel *Marevo* (1864) attacked the emancipation of the serfs. Klyushnikov also wrote children's stories, translated English authors, and from 1887 to 1892 edited the magazine *Niva*.

KNAVE OF DIAMONDS. Society of painters, founded in Moscow in 1909 for exhibition purposes, by Michael Larionov (*q.v.*) and others. For two years the Knave of Diamonds was the leading movement of the Soviet avant-garde.

Gray, Camilla, *The Russian Experiment in Art 1863–1922*, 1962.

Markov, Vladimir, *Russian Futurism*, 1968.

KNIPPER, LEV KONSTANTINOVICH (1898–). Composer. After studying in Berlin, Freiburg, and Moscow he attempted to follow modern European musical developments, but eventually he accepted the Soviet conception of music, and composed much music for the Red Army and Navy. He also composed 3 operas, including *Candide* (1926–27), several ballets, and 14 symphonies, which include *Poem about Komsomols* in praise of communist youth. The song *Polyushko* from the Fourth Symphony has an international reputation.

KNIPPER-CHEKHOVA, OLGA LEONARDOVNA (1870–?). One of the most outstanding actresses of the first generation of the Moscow Art Theater. In 1901 she married Anton Pavlovich Chekhov (*q.v.*). Knipper-Chekhova is especially remembered for her interpretation of the leading female roles of the plays of Chekhov, Gorky, and Turgenev, as well as for her performance in plays by Molière, Gogol, and Griboyedov. She was awarded the Order of Lenin and twice received the Order of the Red Banner of Labor.

KNYAZ. The Russian word for prince.

KNYAZHATA. Collective name for the serving princes of Muscovite Russia.

KNYAZHNIN, YAKOV BORISOVICH (1742–91). Dramatist. He was a writer of classical tragedies and comedies. To an extent, his work can be seen as an imitation of Voltaire's; his tragedy *Vadim* is almost revolutionary in its political freethinking. Knyazhnin's comedies are mostly in verse. *An Accident with a Carriage* (1779) is considered to be one of his best works.

Drage, C., *Russian Literature in the Eighteenth Century: The Solemn Ode, the Epic, Other Poetic Genres, the Story, the Novel, Drama*, 1978.

Segel, H. B. (ed.), *The Literature of Eighteenth-Century Russia*, 2 vols., 1967.

KOCHUBEY, VIKTOR PAVLOVICH (1768–1834). Diplomat and state official. Kochubey's diplomatic career included service in Sweden, London, and Turkey. He occupied various important posts at home and abroad both under Alexander I and Nicholas I (*q.q.v.*).

KOGAN, LEONID BORISOVICH (1924–). Violinist. He graduated from the Moscow Conservatory in 1948. He is the winner of many awards, including first prize at the Queen Elizabeth International Contest of Violinists in Brussels (1951). In 1952 he began teaching at the Tchaikovsky Conservatory in Moscow. He has toured in the United States and W Europe.

KOGAN, PETER SEMYONOVICH (1872–1932). Soviet literary historian and critic. His most famous works include *Essays on the History of the Western European Literature* (1943) and *Essays on the History of Ancient Literatures* (1923).

KOKAND. Town situated 350 miles (560 km) ENE of Bokhara in the Fergana valley, in Uzbekistan. An important town since the 10th century and capital of the Uzbek Khanate in the 18th century, it was taken by General Konstantin P. Kaufman for Russia in 1876. In 1917–18 it was the capital of the anti-Bolshevik government of Turkestan. Manufactures are textiles, including silk, and fertilizers. Population (1977) 155,000. *See* **Kaufman, Gen. K. P.**

KOKCHETAV. Town in the center of the Kokchetav oblast of the Kazakh Soviet Socialist Republic, founded in 1824. Population (1977) 98,000.

KOKOVTSOV, COUNT VLADIMIR NIKOLAYEVICH (1853–1942). Politician. He served as state secretary (1902) and minister of finance (1906). In 1911 he became prime minister following the death of Stolypin but was dismissed in 1914 for taking a stand against corruption, especially as personified by Rasputin, and died in exile in Paris.

KOLA PENINSULA. Peninsula lying between the Barents Sea to the N and the White Sea to the S. It has an area of 50,000 square miles (129,500 sq km). Its low granite plateau yields important minerals, especially apatite and nepheline, which are exported from Kandalaksha. There is an important naval base on the Murmansk fjord.

KOLCHAK, ADMIRAL ALEXANDER VASILYEVICH (1873?–1920). Naval commander and explorer. He served with distinction in the Russo-Japanese War and later with the Black Sea fleet during the First World War. He was leader of the anti-Bolshevik troops in Siberia (1918–20). He overthrew the Ufa Directory and was recognized by anti-Bolshevik organizations as representing the provisional government. His early successes were followed by withdrawals and after the fall of Omsk in 1919 he retreated to Irkutsk and was taken prisoner, tried, and executed.

Fleming, Peter, *The Fate of Admiral Kolchak,* 1963.

KOLKHOZ. Widespread form of agricultural organization in the Soviet Union; *kolkhoz* is the Russian abbreviation for "collective economy." In theory a *kolkhoz* is a cooperative of a number of peasants who pool land and equipment and who are paid according to the amount of work done. In fact *kolkhozy* are managed by the Party which appoints the chairman. Owing to the system of compulsory selling of produce to the state at prices fixed by the state, it is difficult for many *kolkhozy* to receive an adequate income. Also, the *kolkhoz* system offers few incentives for the workers to take an interest in the work. Membership of a *kolkhoz* is automatic for those born in it; it is difficult to leave. *See* **Agrarian Reforms.**

Davies, R. W., *The Socialist Offensive: the Collectivisation of Soviet Agriculture, 1929–1930,* 1976.

KOLLONTAY, ALEXANDRA MIKHAILOVNA (1872–1952). Politician and propagator of "free love." A Bolshevik in the 1890s, Kollontay subsequently became a Menshevik "liquidationist." After 1908, she lived in exile and joined the International Bureau of Women Socialists. From 1915 Kollontay assisted Lenin, and after her return to Russia in February 1917 she became a member of the Bolshevik central committee. Her interest in women's affairs found its outlet in 1920–21 when she was head of the women's department of the central committee. In 1921–22 she was secretary of the International Women's Secretariat of the Comintern. She continued her political career as a diplomat in Norway (1923–26 and 1927–30), Mexico (1926–27), and Sweden (1930–45). She developed the Bogdanovist approach to the question of relations between the sexes, and advanced the "winged eros theory," in which individuals in a socialist society should be free to associate with different persons of the opposite sex. Although Lenin disapproved, this theory was popular with others, since by making the family appear an outmoded institution, family ties were weakened. Her works include *The Workers' Opposition in Russia* (1923) and *Free Love* (1932).

KOLMOGOROV, ANDREY NIKOLAYEVICH (1903–). Mathematician. From 1931 he has been a professor at Moscow University and, from 1939, a member of the Academy of Sciences. Kolmogorov is a leading international authority on the theory of probability, having put forward the widely accepted axiomatic theory, and is an authority on mathematical logic. He is also interested in cybernetics.

KOLOKOL. *See* **Bell, The.**

KOLOMENSKOYE. Village in the Lenin region of the Moscow oblast. From the 15th to 17th century, Kolomenskoye was part of the tsar's country estate; there are many buildings of architectural note dating from this period. In 1923 the former estate was made into a museum.

KOLOMNA. City situated 64 miles (104 km) SE of Moscow on the Moskva River near its confluence with the Oka River, in the Russian Soviet Federated Socialist Republic. It became an outpost of Moscow in 1301 and has been an industrial city since the mid-19th century. It is a railway engineering center manufacturing locomotives, diesel engines, wagons, and textile machinery. Population (1977) 145,000.

KOLOMYYA. Town situated 110 miles (176 km) SE of Lvov on the Prut River, in the Ukraine. It was formerly Polish but was ceded to the USSR in 1945. It manufactures chemicals and textiles. Population (1974) 141,000.

KOLTSOV, ALEKSEY VASILYEVICH (1809–42). Poet. His early life was hard and he had no formal education. His poetry describes nature and peasant life, and he has been called the "Russian Burns." Much of his work shows the influence of Pushkin, and when he was first published in 1835 he was noticed by the critic Belinsky *(q.v.)*. *See* **Drozhzhin, Spiridon.**

KOLYMA RANGE. Mountain range in Khabarovsk, extending NE for 500 miles (800 km) between the Kolyma River and the Sea of Okhotsk, in the Russian Soviet Federated Socialist Republic.

KOLYMA RIVER. River rising on the Pacific divide N of the Sea of Okhotsk and flowing for 1,600 miles (2,560 km) through the Cherskogo Mountains to the tundra of the Kolyma depression. The principal tributaries are the Omolon River, 700 miles (1,120 km) long, and the Anyui River.

KOMANDORSKY ISLANDS. A group of treeless islands between the Kamchatka peninsula and the Aleutian Islands in Khabarovsk territory. The two largest islands of the group are Bering and Medny and the main village is Nikolskoye.

KOMI. A people living in the NE European part of the Soviet Union. Finnish speaking, they are the most civilized of the "Northern Peoples." There are two groups of the Komi people: the Komi, who live in the Komi Autonomous Republic, and the Komi-Permyaki, who live in the Komi-Permyak National Area.

KOMI AUTONOMOUS SOVIET SOCIALIST REPUBLIC. It has an area of 160,540 square miles (415,000 sq km). Constituted as an autonomous republic 1936, it is the North-Western part of the Russian Soviet Federated Socialist Republic. The capital is Syktyvkar, situated 140 miles (224 km) ENE of Kotlas. It is mainly tundra in the N. Chief industries are coal, oil, timber, gas, asphalt, and building materials; livestock breeding and dairy farming are also important. Population (1981) 1,147,000.

KOMI-PERMYAK NATIONAL AREA. A national area in the Perm region of the Russian Soviet Federated Socialist Republic. It has an area of 160,540 square miles (415,900 sq km). The capital is Kudymkar, situated 90 miles (144 km) NE of Perm.

The region is mainly forested and has industries associated with timber. Population (1974) 1,012,000.

KOMISSARZHEVSKAYA, VERA (1864–1910). Actress and manager of the St. Petersburg theater.

KOMMUNA. The most completely collective farm in which there is no private property, all land is worked collectively, and its produce is shared. Sometimes this includes collective eating and living.

KOMMUNARSK. Town situated 90 miles (144 km) NW of Abakan in the Kuznetsk Ala-Tau, Krasnoyarsk territory, in the Russian Soviet Federated Socialist Republic. It is a gold-mining center. Population (1977) 129,000.

KOMMUNIST. Main theoretical journal of the Communist Party of the Soviet Union, published by Pravda publishing house for the central committee (18 issues a year). It was founded in 1924 and was called *Bol'shevik* until 1952.

KOMMUNIZMA PEAK. Highest mountain in the USSR. It is situated in the Akademiya Nauk range of the Pamirs, in Tadzhikistan at 24,590 feet (7,495 m) above sea level.

KOMSOMOL (ALL-UNION LENINIST COMMUNIST UNION OF YOUTH). A youth organization attached to and founded by the Communist Party in 1918, it now caters to the 14–28 age range. The Komsomol has worked closely with the party; Komsomol members participated in the Civil War, collectivization, and industrialization, and recently more than 70 percent of party recruits have come from the Komsomol. Komsomol members are encouraged to play a full part in sociopolitical life; membership and service also enhances employment and further education prospects.

Kassof, A., *The Soviet Youth Program: Regimentation and Rebellion*, 1965.

KOMSOMOLSK. Town situated 165 miles (264 km) NE of Khabarovsk on the Amur River. It was founded in 1932 by the Komsomol (the communist youth movement) (*q.v.*). It has developed into a center for shipbuilding and sawmilling. Manufactures include steel, chemicals, wood pulp, and paper. Population (1981) 274,000.

KONCHALOVSKY, PETER (1876–1956). Painter. Expelled from Moscow College in 1909 for leftism, Konchalovsky exhibited paintings in the first Knave of Diamonds exhibition (*q.v.*). His *Portrait of Georgy Yakulov* is reminiscent of Matisse's style, although later Konchalovsky was to be more influenced by Cézanne, in that his former predilection for color was replaced by a monochromatic palette.

Gray, Camilla, *The Russian Experiment in Art 1863–1922*, 1962.

KONDAKOV, NIKODIM PAVLOVICH (1844–1925). Russian scholar who specialized in Byzantine and ancient Russian art.

KONDRATENKO, ROMAN ISIDOROVICH (1857–1904). General in the Russian army who heroically fought in the defense of Port Arthur in 1904. Prior to Port Arthur, Kondratenko commanded the Seventh East-Siberian Infantry. Once in Port Arthur, he greatly increased its fortifications. *See* **Russo-Japanese War.**

KONDRATEV, VIKTOR NIKOLAYEVICH (1901–). Soviet physical chemist. From 1948 he has been a member of the CPSU. Kondratev's main work has been in the fields of chemical kinetics, molecular spectroscopy, photochemistry, the structure of matter, and the fundamental processes of chemical transformation.

KÖNIGSBERG *See* **Kaliningrad.**

KONSTANTIN PAVLOVICH (1779–1831). Russian grand duke, second son of Emperor Paul I, and brother of Alexander I and Nicholas I. He embarked on a military career in 1799 in Italy. In 1805 he was in command of the guards and was partially responsible for the Russian defeat at Austerlitz. In 1815 he was made commander in chief of the Polish armed forces. Preferring Poland to Russia, Konstantin renounced any claim to the throne; the Decembrists, on the other hand, unsuccessfully demanded that Konstantin should rule. He was, however, most unpopular in Poland, incompetent, and taken by surprise at the 1830 insurrection in Warsaw.

KONSTANTINOVKA. Ukrainian town situated 36 miles (58 km) N of Donetsk in the Donbas. Manufactures include iron and steel, glass, and chemicals. Population (1976) 111,000.

KOPEK (COPEK). Russian coin equaling 1/100 of a ruble. In medieval Russia 1 *kopek* equaled 1/10 of a *grivna (q.v.).*

KOPELEV, LEV ZINOVYEVICH (1912–). Soviet author, critic, translator, and literary historian. Graduating from the Moscow Foreign Language Institute in 1938, Kopelev pursued his studies before serving in the Second World War. He was expelled from the party in 1945 and sentenced to 10 years' imprisonment and five years' exile, but was released prematurely and rehabilitated. However, Kopelev was criticized for his role in the Human Rights Movement and expelled from the Writer's Union in 1965. His publications include *The Heart is Always on the Left* (1960), *Myths and Truths of the American South* (1958), and *To be Preserved Forever* (1976).

KOPEYSK. Town situated 11 miles (18 km) SE of Chelyabinsk, in the Russian Soviet Federated Socialist Republic. It is a center for lignite mining. Population (1977) 157,000.

KORCHNOI, VICTOR (1931–). Soviet chess player. He was Soviet champion in 1960, 1962, and 1964 and is an International Grandmaster. He left the USSR in 1976.

Wade, R. G., *Soviet Chess*, 1968.

KOREAN WAR (1950–53). An indecisive war in which the Soviet government risked losing its North Korean outpost and which was sparked by the crossing of the 38th parallel by the North Korean army. Resistance was organized by the United Nations, with the United States bearing the brunt of the fighting, and the Chinese intervened on the side of the North Koreans when the United Nations forces approached the Yalu River dividing Korea from China. An armistice was signed in July 1953.

KORF, NICHOLAS ALEKSANDROVICH (1834–83). Pedagogue and investigator of teaching methods. Wishing to improve education for the masses, Korf devised a special system of village schools; each school was to consist of one class divided into three sections and presided over by one teacher. Anxious to develop a network of primary education, Korf insisted that primary education should be compulsory and given in the mother tongue. He also stressed the need to improve the training of teachers. His work did not meet with the approval of the tsarist authorities, and in 1872 Korf felt it prudent to settle in Geneva. He returned to Russia in 1883.

KORMLENIYE. A system of local administration prevalent from the 14th through the 16th century, under which local administrators, who were appointed from Moscow, received payments in kind from the local population.

Blum, Jerome, *Lord and Peasant in Russia from the Ninth to the Nineteenth Century*, 1971.

KORMLENSHCHIK. Recipient of the *kormleniye*; a local administrator and tax collector, and as a rule a member of the nobility.

KORNILOV, GENERAL LAVR GEORGEVICH (1870–1918). Soldier. He served in the Russo-Japanese War (1904–05) and in the First World War. He was captured by the Germans but made a spectacular escape. He was Petrograd military district commander in 1917 and was responsible for the arrest of Nicholas II (*q.v.*) and his family. As commander in chief of all Russian forces in August 1917, he believed that the provisional government was incapable of dealing with any threat from the Bolsheviks, and mistakenly believing that Alexander Kerensky (*q.v.*) was in agreement, he organized his troops to march on Petrograd but was arrested on Kerensky's orders. This action strengthened the Bolsheviks, and after the fall of Kerensky Kornilov escaped to join the anti Bolshevik forces of Anton Denikin (*q.v.*) on the Don, where he was killed in action.

Kerensky, Alexander Federovich, *Prelude of Bolshevism, the Kornilov Rising*, 1919.

KORNILOV, VLADIMIR ALEKSEYEVICH (1806–54). Russian sailor. After the Russo-Turkish war of 1828–29 Kornilov was promoted to the rank of lieutenant, and rose to the rank of vice-admiral. He was in charge of defense at Sevastopol during the Crimean War, where he was wounded and died.

KOROBYA (pl. *Korobei*). Medieval dry measure equal to about 12 bushels.

KOROLENKO, VLADIMIR GALAKTIONOVICH (1853–1921). Short-story writer and novelist. Educated at the St. Petersburg Technological College and the Moscow College of Agriculture and Forestry, Korolenko was expelled in 1876 for his part in revolutionary activities. Arrested in 1879, he spent five years in exile in Siberia. Korolenko is particularly famed for his story *Makar's Dream* published in 1885. His other stories include *The Blind Musician* (1898).

Mirsky, D. S., *A History of Russian Literature* , 1949.

KOROLEV, SERGEY PAVLOVICH (1906–66). Aeronautical engineer. He designed missiles, rockets, and spacecraft. In 1933 he headed development of the Soviet Union's first liquid-propellant rocket. From 1945 he worked on a series of ballistic missiles that led to the Soviet Union's first intercontinental ballistic missile. Later he supervised the Vostok and Soyuz manned spaceflight program.

KOROVIN, KONSTANT (1861–1939). Painter. Korovin is considered by many to be the first Russian artist to be influenced strongly by the Impressionists (*q.v.*), whose work he saw in Paris in 1885. Korovin's transposition of French Impressionist ideas brought about a complete change in theatrical design. Appointed professor of the Moscow College in 1901, he supervised the work of almost all the avant-garde of the first decade of the 20th century.

Gray, Camilla, *The Russian Experiment in Art 1863–1922,* 1962.

KORYAK NATIONAL AREA. Region located in NE Siberia, including part of the Kamchatka peninsula, Russian Soviet Federated Socialist Republic. It has an area of 152,000 square miles (393,680 sq km). The capital is Palana. Main occupations include reindeer breeding, fishing, and hunting. Population (1970) 31,000.

KORYAKI. A Paleo-Asiatic people living in the Koryak National Okrug of the Kamchatka oblast. Traditionally the main occupations of the Koryaki are fishing and reindeer breeding.

KOSCIUZKO, TADEUSZ ANDRZEY BONAVENTURA (1746–1812). Polish army officer and statesman. Having entered the corps of cadets in Warsaw, Kosciuzko was sent abroad to complete his education at the expense of the state; in France Kosciuzko studied fortification and painting. In 1776, he enlisted in the American Continental army as a volunteer, and pursued a brilliant military career during the American Revolution, as a result of which he was awarded U.S. citizenship, the rank of brigadier general, lands, and an annual pension. In 1784 Kosciuzko returned to Poland and took a leading part in the war following the proclamation of the constitution of 1791. In 1794 he was invited by Polish insurgents to lead the Polish armies against the Russians, and was finally defeated at Szczekociny, and later at Maciejowice, where he was seriously wounded. Imprisoned in St. Petersburg, Kosciuzko was released in 1796.

KOSTROMA. Capital of the region of the same name situated 45 miles (72 km) ENE of Yaroslavl at the confluence of the Volga and Kostroma rivers, in the Russian Soviet Federated Socialist Republic. It was founded in 1152 and annexed to Moscow in 1364. Noted for linen products since the 16th century, it now manufactures footwear, paper, and clothing. Population (1981) 259,000.

KOSTROMA RIVER. A 250-mile (400 km) tributary of the Volga River.

KOSTROV, ERMIL IVANOVICH (*c.* 1750–96). Poet and translator. Kostrov studied at Moscow University and his translation of Homer's *Iliad* into Alexandrine was the first instance of the use of this verse form in Russia. Kostrov spent the latter part of his life in poverty.

KOSYGIN, ALEKSEY NIKOLAYEVICH (1904–80). Soviet government official and a member of the CPSU from 1927. Kosygin studied at a textile institute and was a textile engineer in a Leningrad factory, where he attracted Zhdanov's attention. During the Great Purge, Kosygin was chairman of the Leningrad City Soviet (1938) and in 1939 was chairman of the USSR commissariat for the textile industry. From 1940 to 1953 he was deputy chairman of the USSR council of people's commissars, USSR minister of finance (1948), and minister of light industry (1948–53). A member of the central committee in 1939, Kosygin became a full member of the Politburo in 1948. Kosygin's political career waned temporarily after Zhdanov's death, but from 1958 he was chairman of Gosplan, and in 1960 he was a first deputy of the central committee's presidium. In 1964 he took Khrushchev's place as chairman of the council of ministers.

Brown, Archie and Kaser, Michael (eds.), *The Soviet Union Since the Fall of Khrushchev,* 1975.

KOTLAS. Town in the Arkhangelsk region of the Russian Soviet Federated Socialist Republic, situated near the confluence of the N Dvina and Vychegda rivers. It is an important transportation center and river port. Industries include shipbuilding and repairing, wood processing, and cellulose paper works. Population (1970) 40,000.

KOTOSHIKHIN, GRIGORY KARPOVICH (?–1667). Foreign office official. He left Russia for Sweden in 1664 and wrote a political pamphlet bitterly critical of Russian rulers. He was executed in 1667 for murdering his landlord.

KOTZEBUE, OTTO VON (1787–1846). Navigator who commanded two voyages of circumnavigation. Having accompanied Adam Ivan Krusenstern (*q.v.*) on his voyage of 1803–06, Kotzebue led an expedition (1815–18) on the ship *Rurik,* during which he entered the Pacific Ocean at Cape Horn and visited Easter Island, and the Tuamotu Archipelago, where he discovered some islands. He went on to chart part of the Alaskan coast before making his way back to

Russia, visiting the Marshall Islands on the way. During his second voyage, commissioned by Alexander I, Kotzebue carried out important oceanographic investigations. He also brought back previously unknown plants.

KOUSSEVITZKY, SERGEY ALEXANDROVICH (1874–1951). Conductor. His early career was as a double-bass virtuoso. He made his debut as a conductor in Berlin in 1908 and in 1910 he founded a symphony orchestra with which he toured Russia. In 1918 he was appointed conductor of the State Symphony Orchestra in Petrograd but he left Russia in 1920. After visiting most of the countries of Europe, he settled in the United States as conductor of the Boston Symphony Orchestra (1924–49). He encouraged many composers, including Aaron Copland and Samuel Barber.

Leichtentritt, H., *Serge Koussevitsky*, 1946.

KOVALECHENKO, IVAN DMITRIYEVICH (1923–). Soviet historian and member of the CPSU from 1944. Having graduated from Moscow University (1967), Kovalechenko became a professor there. From 1969 he has worked as chief editor of the periodical *Istoriya SSSR*, (History of the USSR), and had been chairman of the committee for applied mathematics and electronic data processing in historical research at the USSR Academy of Sciences in the department of history.

KOVALEVSKAYA, SOFIYA VASILYEVNA (1850–91). Mathematician and writer. Having studied at Heidelberg, Berlin, and Moscow, Kovalevskaya was appointed lecturer at the University of Stockholm and became professor there. Her work dealing with the rotation of a solid body about a fixed axis won her the Prix Bordin at the Academy of Paris (1888). She also wrote several plays and novels.

KOVALEVSKY, VLADIMIR ONUFRIYEVICH (1842–83). An early theorist of evolution and expounder of Darwin's theories, geologist, and paleontologist. Kovalevsky married the mathematician Sofiya Vasilevna Kovalevskaya. He was director of an unsuccessful oil firm, and as a result of its failure Kovalevsky committed suicide.

KOVROV. Town situated 44 miles (70 km) SSE of Ivanovo, on the Klyazma River, in the Russian Soviet Federated Socialist Republic. It is an important railway center. Industries include railway engineering, textiles, and excavator production. Population (1977) 140,000.

KOZELSK. Town in the center of the Kozelsk region of the Kaluzhskaya oblast, on the Smolensk-Tula railway line. Kozelsk is an ancient Russian town, first mentioned in manuscripts *c.* 1146. Kozelsk is particularly remembered for its tragic and heroic defense when it was attacked in 1238 by Batu Khan.

KOZINTSEV, GRIGORY MIKHAILOVICH (1905–). Soviet film director and script writer. Kozintsev began his career in film in 1920 in Kiev. In 1924, he was the director of the Lenfilm Studio in Leningrad. One of his best-known works is the *Maksim Trilogy*, which he produced at Trauberg. From 1947 Kozintsev worked in the theater and produced *King Lear* (1941) and *Othello* (1943).

Leyda, Jay, *Kino: A History of the Russian and Soviet Film*, 1960.

KOZLOV, IVAN IVANOVICH (1779–1840). Poet and translator. Kozlov began writing poetry in 1820, after he had gone blind. His poetry is considered sentimental, appealing to easily aroused emotions; technique and content are comparatively inadequate. He achieved fame among his contemporaries as a result of *The Monk* (1825), written in imitation of Byron and Pushkin. Kozlov's translations of poetry are, however, more highly valued; his translation of Charles Wolfe's *Burial of Sir John Moore at Corunna* is particularly well done.

KRAMATORSK. Ukrainian town situated 110 miles (176 km) SSE of Kharkov. It is a center of heavy engineering and a railway junction. Population (1981) 183,000.

KRAMSKOY, IVAN NIKOLAYEVICH (1837–87). Painter. He studied at the Academy of Arts, and became the leader of the first professional society of independent painters, the Association of Traveling Art Exhibitions, also known as the Wanderers. His paintings include *Christ in the Wilderness*.

Talbot Rice, Tamara, *A Concise History of Russian Art*, 1963.

KRASIN, LEONID BORISOVICH (1870–1926). Communist. Having become a member in 1890 of one of the earliest social democratic organizations in Russia, from 1900 to 1903 Krasin was a leading member of *Iskra* (*q.v.*). From 1904 to 1905, Krasin opposed Lenin's methods in the party and had him expelled from the central committee. In 1905, however, with Lenin reinstated in favor, Lenin, Krasin, and Bogdanov led the Bolshevik faction of the Revolution. In 1909 he broke with Lenin. Krasin's important political positions include membership in the presidium of the supreme council of national economy, commissar for foreign trade, and ambassador to Britain twice and to France once. His technical skills and business acumen helped him to play a leading part in reorganizing the Soviet economy.

KRASNODAR. Capital of the territory of the same name on the lower Kuban River, in the Russian Soviet Federated Socialist Republic. It was founded by Catherine II in 1794. The principal industries are food processing, oil refining, and railway engineering. Population (1981) 581,000.

KRASNOVODSK. Port situated on the SE coast of the Caspian Sea, in Turkmenistan. Founded in 1869, it is an important railway and oil pipeline terminus. Population (1976) 54,000.

KRASNOYARSK. Capital of the territory of the same name, situated on the Yenisey River and the Trans-Siberian Railway, in the Russian Soviet Federated Socialist Republic.

Founded in 1628, it is an industrial center of a gold-producing area and the site of one of the world's largest hydroelectric plants. Manufactures include heavy-engineering products, textiles, paper, and cement. Population (1981) 820,000.

KRAVCHINSKY, SERGEY MIKHAILOVICH (1851–95). A member of the clandestine populist movement, *Zemlya i Volya*, his pseudonym was Stepnyak. After assassinating the chief of the gendarmes, Mezentsev, in 1878, Kravchinsky fled to Switzerland and England. Kravchinsky's literary accomplishments include *Underground Russia*, published in Russian in London (1873), *The Little House on the Volga* (1906), and the novel *Andrey Kozhukhov* (1889).

Venturi, Franco, *Roots of Revolution*, 1961.

KRAY. Administrative territorial unit. All *krays* are located within the Russian Soviet Federated Socialist Republic. It is similar to an oblast but generally has an autonomous oblast within its borders.

KREMENCHUG. Ukrainian town situated 165 miles (264 km) ESE of Kiev on the Dnepr River. Founded in 1571, it is an industrial center with a large hydroelectric plant. Industries include engineering, textiles, food processing, and sawmilling. Population (1981) 215,000.

KREMLIN. The main fortress in a medieval Russian city, usually built on the high bank of a river or rivers, in the case of a confluence, and separated from the rest of the city by a wall with ramparts, a moat, and towers and battlements. The *kremlin* itself contained the palaces for the bishop and prince, their offices, a cathedral, and stores and weapons in case of siege. The best-known *kremlin* is the Moscow Kremlin, built according to a triangular design at the confluence of the Moskva and Neglinnaya rivers. The rampart and red-brick towers were built by Italian architects in the days of Ivan III. The ornate spires were added in the 17th century. The Kremlin contains the Cathedral of the Dormition, the Cathedral of the Archangel Michael, and the Cathedral of the Annunciation, as well as the Palace of the Pacets and Terem Palace. The present Great Kremlin Palace was built in 1839–40 by Konstantin Thon, in the Russo-Byzantine style. The Supreme Soviet now holds its sessions in it.

Berton, Kathleen, *Moscow: An Architectural History*, 1977.

Buxton, David Roden, *Russian Medieval Architecture*, 1975.

KREMLINOLOGY. Name derived from the Moscow Kremlin, where the Supreme Soviet of the USSR holds its sessions. Kremlinology is the study of the policies of the Soviet government. It also implies gleaning information or clues about the conduct of Soviet politics which give an indication of what goes on behind the facade of "monolithic unity" among the leadership.

Conquest, R., *Power and Policy in the USSR*, 1961.

Hough, J. and Fainsod, M., *How the Soviet Union is Governed*, 1979.

Nove, A., "The Uses and Abuses of

Kremlinology," in *Was Stalin Really Necessary?*, 1964.

Tatu, M., *Power in the Kremlin*, 1969.

KRESTNOYE TSELOVANIYE. An oath affirmed by the kissing of the cross.

KRESTYANIN. A peasant. In medieval Russia there were different varieties of peasants according to whether they belonged to the tsar, boyars, the church, or monasteries.

Blum, Jerome, *Lord and Peasant in Russia from the Ninth to the Nineteenth Century*, 1971.

KRIVICHY. A savage people who had settled in the Dnepr region, and in the land to the E of Lake Peipus from the 6th to the 10th century. Their chief towns were Smolensk, Polotsk, and Pskov. They abandoned this area in favor of more northern latitudes and settled along the Volga and W Dvina rivers.

KRIVOY ROG. Ukrainian town situated 81 miles (130 km) SW of Dnepropetrovsk on the Ungulets River. Center of a very rich iron-ore area. There is archaeological evidence from the burial grounds that Scythians inhabited the area and worked the iron deposits. The present town was founded in the 17th century, and industrial expansion took place after a syndicate of French, Belgian, and other nationals was established in 1881. Manufactures include chemicals, iron and steel, and machine tools. Population (1981) 663,000.

KRIŽANÍC, JURAJ (1618-83). Pan-Slavist who invented a language, *Krizanica*, which he hoped would unify the Slavonic people

KROKODIL. Satirical weekly magazine published by the Pravda publishing house. It is outspoken on most subjects dealing with many topical issues in political and social spheres and is nearer to the old *Simplicissimus* in Germany than to *The New Yorker* in the United States or *Punch* in Great Britain.

KRONSTADT. City situated 14 miles (22 km) W of Leningrad on SE Kotlin Island in the E Gulf of Finland, in the Russian Soviet Federated Socialist Republic. Founded by Peter the Great in 1703, it is a naval base with an arsenal, docks, and shipyards, and naval forts and batteries commanding the approach to Leningrad. Industries include sawmilling; manufactures include clothing and shoes. Naval mutinies occurred in 1825 and 1882 and the garrison played an important part in the 1905 and 1917 revolutions. Population (1970) 50,000.

KRONSTADT REBELLION. An uprising among Soviet sailors in Kronstadt (Kronshatdt) in the Gulf of Finland March 7-18, 1921. The sailors, who had supported the Bolsheviks in the October Revolution, demanded economic reforms and an end to Bolshevik political domination. The Red Army, led by Leon Trotsky and Michael Tukhachevsky (*q.q.v.*), crushed the rebels, and Lenin's New Economic Policy (1921) was introduced to relieve the privations that had given rise to the revolt.

Avrich, Paul, *Kronstadt, 1921.*

KROPOTKIN, PRINCE PETER ALEKSEYEVICH (1842–1921). Geographer, explorer, and anarchist. He explored parts of Manchuria, Siberia, and Scandinavia and was secretary of the Russian Geographical Society. From 1872 he was associated with the most revolutionary wing of the International. He was arrested in 1874 and spent two years in prison but escaped to England in 1876, and later went to Switzerland. He was deported from Switzerland and went to France, where he was imprisoned (1883–86). He lived in England from 1886 until 1917, visiting the United States twice during these years. Although opposed to communism, he returned to Russia after the Revolution and was held in great esteem. His literary output was great and included *The Great French Revolution 1789–93* (1909). The basis of his views on anarchism was given in *Ethics: Origin and Development* (1924), which expounded the theory of the abolition of states and private property and the establishment of voluntary self-help associations.

Joll, J., *The Anarchists*, 1964.
Miller, M. A., *Kropotkin*, 1976.

KROPOTKIN. Town situated 80 miles (128 km) ENE of Krasnodar on the Kuban River, in the Russian Soviet Federated Socialist Republic. The main industry is railway engineering. The town trades in agricultural products. Population (1970) 55,000.

KRUCHENYKH, ALEKSEY YELISEYEVICH (1886–1970). Futurist poet who began his career as a painter. Together with Velemir Khlebnikov *(q.v.)*, Kruchenykh was the originator of "trans-sense" (or *zaumney)* verse. Although somewhat an outsider among postrevolutionary Futurists *(q.v.)*, he developed the Cubo-Futurist theory. His artistic output includes a "non-sense" play *Gli-Gli*, in which the senses of audience were bombarded from all sides, and the opera *Victory over the Sun* (1913), which, with its songs in Kruchenykh's language of the future, Kazimir Malevich's costumes and scenery representing partial objects and individual letters, and Matushin's quarter-tone music, constituted a landmark in theater.

Barooshian, V. D., *Russian Cubo-Futurism, 1910–1930*, 1975.
Markov, Vladimir, *Russian Futurism*, 1968.

KRUDENER, BARBARA JULIANE (Baroness von) (1764–1824). Russian romantic-pietistic visionary. Having separated from her husband, Baron von Krudener, Krudener pursued happiness in love affairs and literature, and in 1802 wrote *Valérie*, a largely autobiographical novel. In 1804, however, Krudener was converted, which radically changed the course of her life. Influenced by apocalyptic visionaries, including J. H. Jung-Stilling, she occupied her days in Germany and Switzerland with Bible classes and confessions. Krudener's most important convert was Alexander I, who for several months attended her classes. In 1821, however, he expelled her from St. Petersburg. Krudener claimed the Quadruple Alliance (*q.v.*) as her personal achievement, although it is probable that this claim is exaggerated.

KRUGOVAYA PORUKA. Joint liability for taxes and dues.

KRUPSKAYA, NADEZHDA KONSTANTINOVNA (1869–1939). Educator and wife of Lenin. Educated at the Women's College in St. Petersburg, she aided Lenin in his revolutionary work and married him in 1898, accompanying him in his exile. After their return to Russia, Krupskaya was a member of the commissariat of education and developed and expounded the party's plans for education. She was later to become vice-commissar of education and a member of the central committee of the Communist Party and the Presidium of the USSR. She died in the Kremlin on February 27, 1939.

McNeal, Robert Hatch, *Bride of the Revolution: Krupskaya and Lenin*, 1972.

KRUSENSTERN, ADAM IVANOVICH (1770–1846). Russian navigator and admiral. After serving in the British fleet (1793–99), Krusenstern was commander of the first Russian expedition which explored the South Pole, circumnavigating the world. His *Voyage Round the World* was published in 1809–13.

KRUSHKA. *See* ***BOTCHKA.***

KRYASHIN. Christian Tatars who were baptized by force in the 16th and 18th centuries. Those baptized in the 18th century readopted Islam a century later.

KRYLOV, IVAN ANDREYEVICH (1768–1844). Journalist, critic and playwright. He began by translating the works of La Fontaine but later wrote his own collection of fables, *Basny* (1809), satirizing the bureaucracy in particular. He used colloquial language and idioms.

KSHESINSKAYA, MATHILDA (1872–1971). Ballerina and pupil of Per Christian Johanssen (*q.v.*).

KUBAN RIVER. River rising on Mount Elbruz in the Caucasus and flowing for 570 miles (920 km). It flows N in a wide arc and enters the Sea of Azov and the Black Sea through two tributaries.

KUBENA, LAKE. Lake situated in the Vologda region of the Russian Soviet Federated Socialist Republic. It has an area of 140 square miles (363 sq km). Drained by the Sukhona River to the N Dvina River, it is linked by canal with the Sheksna River.

KÜCHELBECKER, WILHELM KARLOVICH (1797–1846). Russian poet of German origin. He was at the school at Tsarskoe Selo with Pushkin and became a close friend. He took part in the abortive Decembrist uprising in 1825 and was imprisoned and later exiled to Siberia. His first poems were published in *Mnemozina* (1824–25).

Raeff, Marc, *The Decembrist Movement*, 1966.

KUCHKA. *See* **Mognchaya Kuchka.**

KUCHUK-KAINARJI, TREATY OF (1774). Peace treaty following Turkey's war with Russia (1770). According to this treaty, Russia was to restore to Turkey the captured Aegean Islands and Moldavia and Walachia and conceded to the Austrian annexation of Bukovina. Russia, for its part, gained the N shoreline of the Black Sea, with the exception of the Crimea. This arrangement was not a satisfactory solution to the Turkish problem. *See* **Russo-Turkish Wars.**

KUCHUM (*fl.* 16th century). Last khan of the Siberian khanate. Defeated by Ermak (Yermak) in 1581, Kuchum relinquished his struggle with Russian warriors in 1598, and fled to Asia, where he died.

KUDYMKAR. Capital of the Komi-Permyak National Okrug in the Perm oblast. Founded in the 16th century, Kudymkar was made capital of the national okrug in 1929.

KULAKS. Wealthy peasants in later imperial and early Soviet Russia. Before the Russian Revolution (1917) they were prominent in village affairs. After the Revolution, they were favored by the New Economic Policy (1921) until 1927, when Stalin raised their taxes and then transformed their lands into collective farms. The dekulakization program led to the execution and exile of many kulaks.

Lewin, Moshe, *Russian Peasants and Soviet Power,* 1968.

KULESHEV, LEV VLADIMIROVICH (1899–1970). Film director and theorist. He directed his first film, *The Project of Engineer Prite,* in 1917 and in the same year published a series of articles on film theory. In 1922 he made his first experiments with montage, "the Kuleshev effect," to show that cutting could completely alter the perception of an audience. He formed the Kuleshev Workshop in 1920 to train actors and film directors. His published work includes *Fundamentals of Film Direction* (1941).

Taylor, R., *The Politics of the Soviet Cinema, 1917–1929,* 1929.

KULIKOV, VIKTOR GEORGYEVICH (1921–). Soviet military official, and, from 1942, a member of the CPSU. Having served at the front during the Second World War, Kulikov rose through various positions and responsibilities, and was made a member of the central committee in 1971. In 1977 he was appointed commander in chief of Warsaw Pact forces and marshal of the Soviet Union.

KULUNDA. Steppe land in SW Siberia divided between the Altay Kray and the Kazakh Republic. Its wheat cultivation and cattle and sheep breeding make Kulunda one of the main agricultural areas of W Siberia.

KUNA. Former monetary unit in Kiev and Novgorod. *See* **Grivna.**

KUNAYEV, DINMUKHAMED AKHMEDOVICH (1900–). Soviet official. Kunayev joined the party in 1939 after graduating from the Institute of Non-Ferrous and Fine Metallurgy in Moscow in 1936. He pursued his career in science, rising to the position of chief engineer at *Altaypolymetall* combine, and was director of Leninogorsk Ore Board from 1936 to 1942. In 1949, Kunayev was made a member of the central committee of the Kazakh Communist Party. He was then elected to various governmental posts and in 1971 was made a member of the Politburo central committee.

KUNGAR. Town situated 48 miles (77 km) SSE of Perm, in the Russian Soviet Federated Socialist Republic. It is noted for leather goods. Population (1970) 65,000.

KUPRIN, ALEXANDER IVANOVICH (1870–1939). Writer. Having served in the army for four years, he engaged in various professions before deciding to devote his life to literary pursuits. His first story, *Moloch,* was published in 1896, but *The Duel* (1916) was to bring him fame. Kuprin's novels include *Yama* (The Pit) (1927) and *Yunkera* (1933), although he is chiefly remembered for his collections of short stories, such as *The River of Life* (1916) and *Sasha* (1920). He was associated with Gorky's publishing enterprise, *Znanye,* and the Realist writers. Following the 1917 Revolution Kuprin lived in Paris, but he returned to the USSR in 1938.

KURBSKY, PRINCE ANDREY MIKHAILOVICH (1528–83). Military commander. Advisor to Ivan IV. From 1563, however, he lost favor and eventually left Russia. He wrote a *History of the Grand Duke of Muscovy* (1560–70) while living in exile in Lithuania. It is in marked contrast to official histories of the period, which glorified Russia and her rulers at the expense of the truth. Kurbsky is also famous for his angry letters to Ivan IV in defense of the nobility.

Vernadsky, George, V., *The Tsardom of Muscovy,* 1969.

KURGAN. Capital of the Kurgan region of the Russian Soviet Federated Socialist Republic, situated 160 miles (256 km) E of Chelyabinsk on the Tobol River. Founded in the 17th century, it is the center of an agricultural area with associated industries. Population (1981) 322,000.

KURIL ISLANDS. Island chain extending 650 miles (1,040 km) between Cape Lopatka on the Kamchatka peninsula to Hokkaido, Japan, and separating the Sea of Okhotsk from the Pacific Ocean. Japan ceded Sakhalin to Russia in 1875 in return for the Kuril Islands and Japan held them until 1945. By the terms set out at the Yalta Conference the islands were awarded to the USSR. They have remained a source of friction between the Japanese and the Soviets. The total area is 5,700 square miles (14,763 sq km), consisting of 50 islands and numerous rocks. The main chain is volcanic and includes Shumshu, Paramushir, Onekotan, Simushir, Urup, Hurup, and Kunashir; there is a parallel nonvolcanic chain extending approximately 65 miles (104 km) ENE of Hokkaido, including Shikotan, Shibotsu, and Shuishio. The chief towns are Servo-Kurilsk, Kurilsk, and Yuzhno-Kurulsk. The Kuril Islands have a humid climate, with hot springs, active volcanoes, and sulphur deposits. Other minerals include iron, copper, and gold. The main occupations on the islands are fishing, mining (mainly sulphur), lumbering, fur trapping, and market gardening.

KURLAND (COURLAND). A Baltic area originally inhabited by the Cours, who were related to the Finns. It was ruled by the Livonian Knights in the 13th century. In 1561 it was governed by Poland as a duchy and passed to Russia in 1795. In 1920 it became part of Latvia.

KUROPATKIN, GENERAL ALEKSEY NIKOLAYEVICH (1848–1925). Soldier. He served in the Russo-Turkish war of 1877, and following service in the Caucasus, he became minister of war in 1898. His campaigns in the early stages of the Russo-Japanese War were disastrous and brought about his resignation. He served in the first years of the First World War, but in 1916 was appointed governer of Turkestan. He wrote *The Russian Army and the Japanese War* (1909).

KURSK. Capital of Kursk region of the Russian Soviet Federated Socialist Republic, on the Seym River. Founded in the ninth century, it was destroyed by the Mongols in 1240 and was rebuilt as a fortress in 1586. It is the industrial center of a rich agricultural district. Manufactures include chemicals, electrical equipment, food products, and alcohol. Population (1977) 373,000.

KURSKY ZALIV. A large coastal lagoon in Lithuania separated from the Baltic Sea by a narrow sandbar, the Kurskaya Kosa. It is 56 miles (90 km) long.

KUSKOVA, EKATERINA DMITRYEVNA (1869–1959). Journalist. She was the author of *Credo,* which advocated the raising of living standards of the working people rather than following the main aim of orthodox Marxists, which was to overthrow the autocracy. In 1921 she was active in Gorky's famine relief committee, whose appeals to the world public resulted in the Nansen and Hoover relief missions. She was expelled from Russia in 1922, together with many leading intellectuals; she lived first in Prague and later in Geneva.

KUSMICH, FEDOR (?–1864). Siberian holy man, or *starets* (*q.v.*). There are no facts about his age or background but he spent his life in prayer and meditation. He settled in a village near Tomsk. A belief developed that Alexander I had not died in 1825 at Tagenrog, but had gone into voluntary exile in Siberia under the name Kusmich. Certainly Kusmich's knowledge of court life was quite great and it is possible that he had connections with the imperial family.

Palmer, Alan, *Alexander I: Tsar of War and Peace,* 1974.

KUSTANAY. Capital of Kustanay region in Kazakhstan, situated 150 miles (240 km) SE of Chelyabinsk on the Tobol River. Founded in 1871, it is a center of an agricultural district with associated industries. Population (1977) 154,000.

KUSTAR. A peasant engaged in a cottage industry.

KUTAISI. Town situated 120 miles (192 km) WNW of Tbilisi in Georgia, on the Rion River. It was originally founded as the capital of Colchis in the 8th century B.C. and was the capital of Imeritia (West Georgia) in the 13th, 15th, and 16th centuries. It was taken by Russia in 1810. Industries are engineering, including vehicle assembly, chemicals, and silk and food production. Population (1981) 200,000.

KUTRIGURS. Bulgarian tribes who settled near the Sea of Azov in the sixth century.

KUTUZOV, PRINCE MICHAEL ILARIONOVICH (1745–1813). Soldier. He served with distinction against the Turks (1768–74, 1787–92), and was commander of the Russian troops at Austerlitz (1805), a battle which was fought against his advice. In 1812 he replaced Barclay de Tolly (*q.v.*) as commander in chief against Napoleon. At first he continued de Tolly's strategy of avoiding a pitched battle, but he revised tactics at Borodino where, after great losses on both sides, the Russians withdrew. Kutuzov then reverted to de Tolly's tactics and Napoleon occupied Moscow. The advent of winter and the Russian military forces caused Napoleon to begin his disastrous retreat. Kutuzov won a victory at Smolensk and harassed the Grand Army continuously on its homeward route.

KUYBYSHEV. Capital of the Kuybyshev region of the Russian Soviet Federated Socialist Republic, situated at the confluence of the Volga River with the Samara River. Important industrial, commercial, and transportation center. Manufactures include aircraft, locomotives, tractors, chemicals, and textiles. Population (1981) 1,238,000.

KUZBAS. *See* **KUZNETSK BASIN.**

KUZMIN, MICHAEL ALEKSEYEVICH (1875–1936). Poet. A member of the Symbolist group, although his work is not considered part of the Symbolist school, in that his poetry is less solemn. Kuzmin's poems are often a blend of religious themes with a refined sensuality and are very carefully crafted. *Songs of Alexandria* (1906) is usually considered his best collection of verse. This was followed by *The Seasons of Love* (1907). Kuzmin also wrote scenarios for plays, ballets, and operettas. In 1910 Kuzmin wrote *Concerning Beautiful Clarity*, a manifesto on poetry that marked the transition from Symbolism (*q.v.*), to Acmeism.

West, James D., *Russian Symbolism*, 1970.

KUZNETSK. *See* **NOVOKUZNETSK.**

KUZNETSK BASIN. Important coal-mining area (10,000 square miles, 25,900 sq km) in the Kemerovo region of the Russian Soviet Federated Socialist Republic. An iron-smelting works was founded in 1697 and coal was first mined in 1851, although it was discovered in 1721. The chief city is Novokuznetsk.

KVAS. Fermented beverage.

KVITKA-OSNOVYANENKO (1778–1843). Pseudonym of Hryhory Kvitva. He was the first modern Ukrainian writer and the author of humorous stories and novels, the most famous of which is the village romance *Marusya* (1834).

KYAKHTA. Town in the Buryat Autonomous Republic, situated 144 miles (232 km) S of Ulan-Ude in SE Siberia near the Mongolian border. Founded in 1728, it was a trading center between Russia and China until the mid-19th century. Industry includes footwear manufacture. Population (1970) 15,000.

KYAKHTA, TREATY OF. A treaty negotiated after the death of Peter the Great by an agent whom he had sent to China to forge commercial contacts. Ratified in 1728, the treaty also enabled the maintenance of a Russian ecclesiastical mission and some diplomatic functions at Peking.

KYZYL-KUM (Red Sands). Desert situated SE of the Aral Sea between the Amu Darya and Syr Darya (*q.q.v.*) rivers in Kazakhstan and Uzbekistan. It has an area of approximately 115,000 square miles (297,850 sq km). Important gold deposits have been found in the central area, and natural gas has been found in the SE.

KYZYL-ORDA. Administrative region of S Kazakhstan on the Aral Sea. It has an area of 88,150 square miles (220,500 sq km). The capital is Kyzyl-Orda. In the irrigated areas rice is the most important crop and cotton and melons are grown. Fishing and fish processing are the chief occupations. Population (1981) 163,000.

L

LABOR CAMPS. In 1956–58 corrective labor camps were renamed corrective labor colonies, with four levels of punishment depending on the nature of the crime committed. It is estimated that labor camps, organized by the GULag, or main administration for corrective labor institutions, now hold 99 percent of all convicted prisoners. The system of camps developed rapidly under Stalin; in 1953 approximately 10 million people were in labor camps and colonies, and it is thought that between 1930 and 1953, 15–16 million people perished in them.

Dallin, David J. and Nicolaevsky, Boris I., *Forced Labour in the Soviet Union,* 1948.

Solzhenitsyn, Alexander I., *The Gulag Archipelago,* 1–3, 1974–78.

LABOR UNIONS. Outlawed until 1906, the work of labor unions in imperial Russia was considerably hampered by the government, which was deeply suspicious of them. The only unions permitted were at the local rather than national level. Under the Soviet regime almost all workers belong to unions, but to a large extent the unions have become tools of the state whose foremost interest is in gaining the workers' support for the state's policies. An important function is the administration of the state social insurance funds. The activities of the different unions are coordinated by the Trade Union councils.

LACY, COUNT PETER (1678-1751). Irish soldier and Russian field marshal. He joined the Russian army in 1697 and in 1725 was appointed commander in chief for St. Petersburg, Ingria, and Novgorod. He fought in the 1733–35 war to put Augustus of Saxony on the Polish throne, and in 1736 was made a field marshal. He is also noted for having captured Azov from the Turks and the Swedish port of Wilmanstränd. Lacy was also responsible for many reforms within the Russian army.

LADOGA, LAKE. Lake emptying into the Neva River in the Gulf of Finland. It has an area of 7,100 square miles, (18,389 sq km). A railway, built for the winters of 1941–43, across the S part, helped to sustain Leningrad during the siege.

LA HARPE, FRÉDÉRIC-CÉSAR DE (*c.* 1754–1838). Swiss political leader and tutor to the future tsar Alexander I from 1784. Having left Switzerland because of his opposition to the Bernese government, La Harpe plotted a Vaudois rebellion from St. Petersburg. In 1794 he obtained French assistance in freeing Vaud from Bern, and in 1798 La Harpe and Ochs formed a unitary government for Switzerland. Having deposed Ochs in 1799, he was deposed in a coup the following year. In 1815 he represented his canton and Switzerland at the Congress of Vienna. La Harpe is important in Russian history because of his attempt to instill democratic and liberal ideas in Alexander. It is sometimes felt that his teaching had little in common with Russian reality, and that this was partly responsible for the contrast between the theory and the practice of Alexander I's reign.

LAIBACH, CONGRESS OF. Meeting of the Holy Alliance (*see* **Quadruple Alliance**) powers from January 26, to May 12, 1821, attended by the rulers and chief ministers of Russia, Austria, and Prussia, by the kings of the Two Sicilies and Sardinia-Piedmont and the dukes of Modena and Tuscany. Great Britain and France sent observers. The congress decided on the terms for the Austrian occupation of the Two Sicilies. It opposed revolutionary regimes and accordingly decided to put an end to the Neapolitan constitution; Austria was to restore the absolutist monarchy there.

LAND AND LIBERTY ORGANIZATION (*Zemlya i Volya*). Populist organization founded in 1876. It consisted of a highly organized group of 200 intellectuals who believed that the land should be given to the serfs, and that the state as it existed should be destroyed. In seeking to promote expressions of popular discontent they staged a mass demonstration in front of Kazan Cathedral in St. Petersburg, at which Georgy Plekhanov (*q.v.*) delivered a speech on populism. Acts of terrorism occurred more and more frequently; Vera Zasulich (*q.v.*) fatally shot the governor of St. Petersburg, General Trepov; Sergey Stepnyak shot General Nicholas Vladimirovich Mezentsov, chief of the Third Section; and attempts were made on the tsar's life. In 1879, owing to differences of opinion on the use of violence, Land and Liberty was dissolved and was replaced by the People's Freedom group.

Kochan, Lionel, *The Making of Modern Russia*, 1962.

Tompkins, Stuart Ramsay, *The Russian Intelligentsia*, 1957.

LAND CAPTAIN (*zemsky nachalnik*). The office of chief of the *zemstvo*, established in 1889, was one of the fruits of Alexander III's "counter-reforms." Appointed by the minister of the interior, the land captain was under the authority of the minister, and as such he represented the immediate bureaucratic supervision of the peasants. He exercised complete control over the peasant officials and could fine or imprison them. He was responsible for confirming the decisions made at peasant meetings. The land captain therefore replaced independent elected justices of the peace. Since they had to be appointed from members of the local gentry with a certain property qualification, the position of land captain emphasized the role of the gentry in the countryside. Their powers were diminished by the reforms of Peter Stolypin *(q.v.)* of the early 1900s.

LANDAU, LEV DAVIDOVICH (1908–68). Physicist. Educated at the universities of Baku and Leningrad, he was made head of the general physics department at Kharkov A. M. Gorlay State University. A leading figure in Soviet space technology, he also helped make the first Soviet atomic bomb. He was awarded the Nobel Prize in 1962 for his theory of the behavior of liquid helium. He won international renown for his work in the fields of atomic and nuclear physics, plasma physics, stellar energy, and low-temperature physics.

LANDAU, MARK ALEKSANDROVICH. *See* **Aldanov.**

LAPPS. Lapps in Russia live in the Kola peninsula and number about 2,000, making up only a small percentage of the total Lapp population. The Pechenga monastery was founded for the conversion of Lapps in the 16th century.

LARIONOV, MICHAEL FYODOROVICH (1881–1964). Painter. Born in Teraspol, Larionov was educated at the Moscow College of Painting, Sculpture, and Architecture. His first mature works earned him the title of "the finest Russian Impressionist," although his later work was primitivist in style. He broke away from the Knave of Diamonds *(q.v.)* group in 1912 and joined the Donkey's Tail group (*see* **Donkey's Tail Exhibition**). He developed a Rayonist theory of painting with Natalya Goncharova, and produced a number of Futurist works.

Gray, Camilla, *The Russian Experiment in Art, 1863–1922,* 1962.

LATVIA. Bounded on the E and S by the Gulf of Riga, on the N by Estonia, on the E by the USSR, on the S by Lithuania, and on the W by the Baltic Sea, Latvia was a tribal territory supporting a peasant and seafaring population until it was conquered by German knights under Albert of Buxhoevden, who founded Riga in 1201. German (Catholic) domination ended when Latvia adopted Protestant beliefs and placed itself under the protection of Sweden in 1561. In 1721 Peter the Great took it from Charles XII of Sweden, following the Great Northern War for control of the Baltic, and it became a Russian province. After the Revolution of 1917 it was declared an independent state. The secret protocol of the Soviet-German agreement of 1939 assigned Latvia to the Soviet sphere of interest. An ultimatum in 1940 led to the formation of a government acceptable to the USSR, which applied for Latvia's admission to the Soviet Union, which was later effected. The incorporation has been accorded de facto recognition by the British government but not by the United States. It has an area of 25,590 square miles (63,700 sq km). The capital is Riga. Agriculture is not now as important as industrial production, which includes the manufacture of railway equipment. Population (1981) 2,500,000.

Bilmanis, Alfred, *A History of Latvia,* 1951.

Grant Wilson, Herbert A., *The Latvian Republic: The Struggle for Freedom,* 1965.

LATVIANS. Baltic-speaking people, most of whom live in Latvia, although some have colonized Siberia. Throughout history they have been dominated either by the Russians, Scandinavians, or Swedes. There were many peasant uprisings in Latvia during the 1905 Revolution.

LAVRENYOV, BORIS ANDREYEVICH (1894–1952). Soviet author. Lavrenyov joined the army in 1915 and served as a cavalry officer in the First World War. In 1921 he began to write seriously. In the early stages of his literary career Lavrenyov was attracted to Futurism *(q.v.),* but he later came under the influence of Acmeism *(q.v.).* He was a member of the Leningrad literary group *Sodruzhestvo.* Lavrenyov's stories are romantic and his plots dynamic. Among his stories are the collections *Crazy Tales* (1925) and *The Forty-First* (1924). He also wrote the plays *Smoke* and *The Debacle* (1928). Much of his work recounts incidents from the Civil War and the days of War Communism *(q.v.).*

Fromberg, D. L., *Stout Heart and Other Stories,* 1943.

Struve, N., *Russian Literature under Lenin and Stalin, 1917–53,* 1971.

LAVROV, PETER LAVROVICH (1823–1900). Russian socialist thinker, mathematician, and populist leader. Lavrov advocated that the intelligentsia should strive to educate the peasants in the hope that ultimately this would produce a socialist society. He emigrated in 1868 and settled in Paris, where he was a leader of the Russian revolutionary movement abroad. Influenced by Comte and Feuerbach, he described his philosophy of history in his *Historical Letters* (1868–69), which stressed the significance of the individual in history. This had a considerable impact on followers of populist thought who made use of the ideas expressed in the *Historical Letters* to justify political violence. He was editor of the revolutionary journal *Forward* until 1872 when he joined the First International.

Krizhnik, I. S., *Peter Lavrovich Lavrov,* 1930.

LAY OF THE HOST OF IGOR. Poetic account of the Russian wars of Igor Svyatoslavich against the Polovtsy in 1185. It is written by an anonymous poet in a vivid style. Some scholars maintain that the *Lay* is a modern forgery.

LEAGUE OF ARMED NEUTRALITY. League based on Doctrine of Armed Neutrality at Sea, advanced by Russia in 1780 in order to protect the trade of neutral states against the British. A number of European countries accepted Catherine the Great's proposals, which became part of international maritime law. Neutral ships were not to be interfered with, even when trading with combatants; combatants' goods in neutral ships were not to be seized, and blockades were not to be legal until they were enforced.

LEAGUE OF NATIONS. League formed at the end of the First World War. The Soviet Union was a member from September 1934 to December 1939, although the government tended to view it as a league of imperialists conspiring against the "first workers' state."

LEBEDEV, PETER NIKOLAYEVICH (1866–1912). Physicist. He studied at the Moscow Higher Technical School and at the universities of Strasbourg and Berlin and was appointed professor at Moscow University. He founded and built up the first large school of physics in Russia. Lebedev conducted research in Maxwell's electromagnetic theory and succeeded in proving the pressure of light on solids and gases. His *Experimental Research on Light Pressure* was published in 1901.

LE BLOND, ALEXANDRE-JEAN-BAPTISTE (1679–1719). French landscape designer. His designs of parterres gained widespread popularity following their publication in 1709. As a result, he was summoned to Russia by Peter the Great in order to design the Peterhof garden. It was the first great garden in Russia and, as part of Peter's plans for the Westernization of Russia, it was built in the style of Versailles.

LEF (Left Front of Art). Literary organization named after the journal founded by Vladimir Mayakovsky (*q.v.*) in 1922. Descended from the Moscow Cubist-Futurists, the group's membership of 25 included Mayakovsky, V. V. Kamensky, and Aleksey Kruchenykh (*q.v.*). In 1926 LEF abandoned revolutionary Futurism for a more "socially constructive" program. In 1929 the group became known as REF (Revolutionary Front of Art), and the following year it joined RAPP (All Russian Association of Proletarian Writers).

Muchnic, Helen, *From Gorky to Pasternak*, 1963.

LEFORT, FRANÇOIS JACOB (1653–99). Swiss soldier who fought for the Russian army. A close friend of Peter the Great, he had a considerable influence over Peter. It is thought that he suggested to Peter that he undertake foreign travels. He assisted in the reorganization of the army and the navy and was appointed a general and an admiral. In 1697 he headed the Grand Embassy (*q.v.*).

LEFT OPPOSITION or **LEFT DEVIATION.** General term for the radical trend within the Communist Party opposing the policy of the majority of members. The left opposition was led by Nicholas Bukharin in 1918, and by Leon Trotsky (*q.q.v.*) in 1923. Trotsky felt that Russian socialism could succeed only if there was a world revolution. The left opposition accordingly supported revolutionary movements abroad, while pursuing a militant socialist policy at home. It therefore opposed the New Economic

Policy, disagreeing with Stalin who believed that socialism could be achieved in the Soviet Union without a world revolution. In 1925, Grigory Zinoviev and Lev Kamenev *(q.q.v.)* took over the leadership of the left opposition.

Daniels, Robert V., *The Conscience of the Revolution: Communist Opposition in Soviet Russia,* 1960.

Schapiro, Leonard B., *The Origin of the Communist Autocracy,* 1977.

LEFT SOCIALIST REVOLUTIONARIES. The heirs of the *narodnik* (*See* **Narodnaya Volya**) tradition, the Left Socialist Revolutionaries enjoyed the support of many of the peasants. The one-time allies of the Bolsheviks, the alliance foundered when the Bolsheviks strengthened the power of the army and police. The Left Socialist Revolutionaries, however, lacked clearly devised policies, since, although angered by the reintroduction of the death penalty, they kept their men in the *Cheka (q.v.).* They opposed Lenin over the Treaty of Brest-Litovsk, in 1918; Muravev attempted to declare war on Germany and the Bolsheviks; and several groups of the Left Socialist Revolutionaries attempted to overthrow the Bolshevik leadership of the local Soviets in provincial towns. After the assassination of the German ambassador, Count Mirbach, Maria Spiridonova and other leading members were shot, and the Left Socialist Revolutionaries lost credibility and ceased to threaten the position of the Bolsheviks.

Ulam, Adam, *The Bolsheviks,* 1965.

LEGAL MARXISTS. Group of economists and sociologists that included P. B. Struve, Tugan-Baranovsky, Sergey Bulgakov, and Nicholas Berdyayev *(q.q.v.).* They understood that Marxism, having originated in the highly industrialized countries of the West, posed special problems in its application to Russia, and they advocated "moderate" Marxism. They believed that the improvement of social and economic conditions should be a first priority because capitalism was in its infancy in Russia. These views were published as a declaration by Ekaterina Kuskova *(q.v.)* in *Credo* in 1889 but it was sharply attacked by Paul Axelrod, Vladimir Lenin, and Sergey Nikolayevich Prokopovich in 1902–03.

Kindersley, Richard K., *The First Russian Revisionists,* 1962.

LEGISLATIVE COMMISSION (1767–68). Commission set up by Catherine II in order to introduce fundamental changes of policy based on the ideas of the Enlightenment. Catherine prepared *The Instruction (Nakaz)* for the commission, which was to undertake the codification of laws and work towards the modernization of Russian law and life. At its first session in 1767, the commission consisted of 564 deputies; 28 had been appointed and 536 elected. Thus state institutions and many different sections of society, with the inevitable exception of the serfs, were represented. Despite its 203 sessions, the commission bore little fruit and divided into different factions. It did, however, provide Catherine with a large source of information about Russia, which influenced her later reforms. She disbanded the commission in 1768.

LENA GOLDFIELD MASSACRE. In April 1912 workers in the Lena goldfield went on strike in order to obtain better living and working conditions and higher wages. About 5,000 protesters were confronted by troops, who fired on them, killing approximately 200 and wounding many others. As a result, the Russian work force became incensed, and during that year some 725,000 workers went on strike. The duma, also angered, called for an investigation of the massacre, which resulted in heavy criticism of the way in which the goldfield was managed.

LENA RIVER. The largest river in the USSR and fifth largest in the world. It rises in the Baikal mountains W of Lake Baikal in Siberia, and flows for 1,200 miles (1,920 km) to reach the Arctic Ocean through a large delta. It drains approximately 1,000,000 square miles (approximately 2,600,000 sq km). Its chief tributaries are the Aldan, Olekma, Vitim, and Vilyui rivers.

LEND-LEASE. Aid given during the Second World War by the U.S. Lend-Lease program and the British and Canadian Mutual Aid programs to the Soviet Union. The Soviet Union received considerable amounts of military equipment, food, textiles, metals, and vehicles on generous credit terms. Although the United States has requested a token repayment, this has been refused, apart from the return of some ships.

Dawson, R. H., *The Decision to Aid Russia,* 1941.

LENIN (VLADIMIR ILYICH ULYANOV) (1870–1924). Russian revolutionary, leader of the Bolsheviks, and chief theoretician of Russian Marxism. He was born at Simbirsk into a middle-class family. His brother Alexander (*see* **Ulyanov, Alexander**) was hanged in 1887 for planning an attempt on Tsar Alexander III's life, greatly influencing Lenin's early life. Lenin studied law at Kazan University, but was expelled for subversive activity. Having studied Marx extensively, he went to St. Petersburg and organized the League for the Liberation of the Working Class. As a result he was arrested in 1897 and exiled for three years to Siberia, where he married Nadezhda Krupskaya *(q.v.)*. He continued his revolutionary activities abroad. In 1903, in London, Lenin became the leader of the Bolshevik faction of the Russian Social Democratic Labor Party. He returned to Russia for the 1905 Revolution. In 1907 he fled to Switzerland, and by means of underground organizations, continued to mastermind the Russian revolutionary movement. He was living in Switzerland during the First World War and in March 1917 the Germans clandestinely arranged for Lenin to return home in a sealed train. Once in Petrograd, he turned his attention to the overthrowing of Alexander Kerensky's *(q.v.)* provisional government, and was appointed chairman of the council of people's commissars. The April Theses *(q.v.)* were published, and during that summer he took refuge in Finland before returning to organize, with Trotsky, the October Revolution. He secured peace with Germany by the Treaty of Brest-Litovsk and in 1919 set up the Comintern to work towards world revolution. Lenin and the Red Army fought until 1921 before defeating the Whites. His position as chairman was strengthened, and Lenin became a virtual dictator. To restore the economy, he instituted the New Economic Policy *(q.v.)* in 1921. Lenin's health, which had been failing since an assassination attempt in 1918, grew worse. Although he warned that Stalin should not be allowed to continue as secretary general of the Communist Party, Lenin's warning went unheeded. He died in 1922, and his body, now embalmed, lies in a mausoleum in Red Square, where it is visited by thousands every year.

Fischer, Louis, *The Life of Lenin,* 1965.

Gorky, Maxim, *Days with Lenin,* 1932.

Krupskaya, Nadezhda K., *Memories of Lenin,* 1930.

Payne, Robert, *The Life and Death of Lenin,* 1964.

Shub, David, *Lenin: A Biography,* 1948.

Weber, Gerda and Hermann, *Lenin: Life and Works* [Chronology], 1980.

LENIN PRIZES. Lenin Prizes, established in 1925, are awarded yearly for outstanding work in science, technology, literature, or the arts. There is also an International Lenin Peace Prize awarded for services to the "peace campaign." The award of a Lenin Prize carries a substantial sum of money and the title of "Laureate of the Lenin Prize." Lenin Prizes were originally established after Lenin's death, but renamed Stalin Prizes in 1935; they reverted to Lenin Prizes in 1956. The awards are announced on Lenin's birthday and generally total 50, with an award of 75,000 rubles.

LENINABAD. Town situated 125 miles (200 km) NNE of Dushanbe on the Syr Darya River, in Tadzhikistan. The town is located on an ancient caravan route between China and the Mediterranean and was named Alexandria Eskhat after Alexander the Great. Successively plundered and ruled by Arabs and Mongols, it was annexed to Russia in 1866. Manufactures include textiles (including silk) and footwear. Population (1976) 121,000.

LENINAKAN. Town situated 55 miles (88 km) NW of Yerevan in Armenia. Founded in 1837 on the site of a Turkish fortress. Manufactures include textiles, carpets, bicycles, and food products. Population (1981) 213,000.

LENINGRAD. Originally St. Petersburg (until 1914) and later Petrograd (1914–24), it is the former capital of Russia and the second city of the USSR. It was founded by Peter the Great in 1703 and situated at the mouth of the Neva River where the Neva enters the Gulf of Finland. The strategic Neva delta had been contested by German and Swedish forces since the 13th century. Peter the Great finally drove out the Swedes during the Great Northern War of 1700–21 *(q.v.)*, and secured a Russian outlet to the Baltic, which he proceeded to fortify. The city's first defensive function changed rapidly. Government buildings, shipbuilding yards, and trading companies were established. Members of the governing, trading, and skilled classes were obliged to live there. The city was proclaimed the capital of Russia in 1712. Continuous expansion was achieved by bridging the many channels of the Neva River and building on the islands. Moscow became the capital of the new Soviet socialist republic in 1918, but the established industries of Leningrad were still dominant. The city's destruction was considered essential to a successful German invasion of Russia in 1941, and German forces besieged it from September 1941 until January 1944.

Leningrad has magnificent palaces and important educational institutions, particularly the Leningrad State University, the Summer and Winter Palaces, and the Hermitage Museum. Industries include heavy engineering, metalworking, instrument making, sugar refining, brewing, distilling, shipbuilding, papermaking, and printing. Manufactures include chemicals, tobacco, soap, crystal and glass, cotton and cloth, leather, cordage, pottery, porcelain, and machinery. The city is connected by river, lake, and canal with the Volga and Dnepr rivers and the Caspian and Black seas. It is also an important railway center and one of the largest seaports of the USSR. Population (1981) 4,676,000.

Gosling, N., *Leningrad,* 1965.

Kelly, Lawrence (ed.), *St. Petersburg: A Traveller's Companion,* 1981.

LENINGRAD, SIEGE OF (1941–44). Siege during the Second World War. On June 22, 1941 the Germans had 500,000 troops over the Russian frontier, and by November 1941 the army was outside Leningrad. The Soviet forces, weakened by the Great Purge, were unprepared. Leningrad was besieged and 750,000 people perished. On January 15, 1944 the Russians began to break out of the town, and on January 20 succeeded in cutting the German corridor to the Gulf of Finland. On January 27 the two-and-a-half-year siege ended.

Fadeyev, Alexander A., *Leningrad in the Days of the Blockade, 1941–43,* 1945.

Salisbury, Harrison, *Nine Hundred Days,* 1969.

LENINOGORSK. Town 50 miles (80 km) NE of Ust-Kamenogorsk in the NW Altay mountains of the Kazakh Soviet Socialist Republic. It is an important lead and zinc mining center (first exploited in the 18th century), with smelting industries. Population (1975) 70,000.

LENINSK-KUZNETSKY. Town situated 18 miles (29 km) S of Kemerovo in the Kuznetsk basin of the Russian Soviet Federated Socialist Republic. Founded in 1864, its main growth was in the 1930s. Industries include coal mining, iron mining, railway engineering, and brick making. Population (1977) 131,000.

LENKORAN. Town 120 miles (192 km) SSW of Baku on the Caspian Sea, 20 miles (32 km) from the Iranian frontier, in the Azerbaijan Soviet Socialist Republic. Industries include sawmilling, food canning, and fishing. Population (1974) 38,000.

LEONOV, LEONID MAKSIMOVICH (1899–). Novelist. Having served in the Red Army, Leonov settled in Moscow and had his first work published in 1922. At the outset of his career he was a member of the Serapion Brotherhood (*see* **Serapion Brothers**). At the same time, he was profoundly influenced by the writings of Dostoyevsky. Much of Leonov's work reflects his concern for universal ethical and moral problems and the fate of Russia. His novels include *The Badgers* (1924) and *The Thief* (1927). He was later obliged to conform to the demands of Socialist Realism, demands which he found easier to fulfill in plays rather than in novels. His psychological plays include *The Invasion* (1924) and *The Golden Carriage* (1954).

Muchnic, H., *From Gorky to Pasternak,* 1963.

LEONTYEV, KONSTANTIN NIKOLAYEVICH (1831–91). Philosopher, publicist, and essayist. Having served as a surgeon in the Crimean War, he pursued a career in the Consular Service and was posted to Crete and Salonika. He was assistant editor of the *Warsaw Diary* in 1879 and in 1880 he was appointed censor in Moscow. Although he secretly took monastic vows in 1887, Leontyev did not live a life of strict asceticism. An extreme antiliberal, opposed to democracy, he seriously questioned whether Russia would benefit from following the contemporary egalitarian and industrial trends of W Europe. He also rejected the ideas of the Slavophiles. Leontyev's best-known work includes *The East, Russia and Slavdom* (1885–86).

LEPESHINSKAYA, OLGA VASILYEVNA (1916–). Ballerina. She graduated from the Bolshoi Theater School. One of the greatest Soviet dancers of her day, her style is characterized by her virtuosity and strength. A member of the Communist Party since 1943, Lepeshinskaya has served on numerous boards and committees.

LERMONTOV, MICHAEL YURYEVICH (1814–41). Romantic poet and author. He became a cavalry officer in 1832 but was exiled to the Caucasus for a year for having published a revolutionary poem, *The Death of a Poet.* On the death of Alexander Pushkin *(q.v.)* in 1840, Lermontov was again banished for taking part in a duel. Most of his poems are romantic lyrics, many of which were inspired by the natural beauty of the Caucasian topography. His Byronic narrative poem *Demon* (1856) is a portrait of supernatural demoniac love; his best-known work, the celebrated and highly influential short novel *A Hero of Our Time* (1840), is the first of a long line of Russian psychological novels. Lermontov was killed in a duel in 1841.

Freeborn, Richard, *Rise of the Russian Novel,* 1973.

Kelly, Lawrence, *Lermontov: Tragedy in the Caucasus,* 1977.

Lavrin, Janko, *Lermontov,* 1959.

LESKOV, NICHOLAS SEMYONOVICH (1831–95). Russian writer. Having worked as a copying clerk in provincial government offices, Leskov obtained the job of chief steward of the estates of a wealthy nobleman and worked under a Nonconformist Englishman. In 1860 he began work as a journalist. He was expelled from the progressive papers for demanding an investigation into the great fires in St. Petersburg (1862), and he turned his hand to fiction. His novel *Cathedral Folk* (1872) and his stories in the *The Enchanted Wanderer* (1873) and *The Sealed Angel* (1873) are all concerned with the church and with popular beliefs. An antiradical, Leskov failed to win the support of the conservatives. A somewhat neglected author in the West, Leskov's writings contain a vast wealth of information about Russia and the Russian people.

Mirsky, D. S., *A History of Russian Literature*, 1948.

LESNAYA, BATTLE OF (October 9, 1708). The Russians, under the leadership of Peter the Great, scored a decisive victory over the Swedes in the Great Northern War *(q.v.)*. Russia also managed to capture a large supply train on its way to Charles XII of Sweden.

LEVITAN, ISAAK ILYICH (1861–1900). Landscape painter. He is considered by some to be the greatest of all Russian landscape painters of the late 19th century. Having studied at the Moscow Art School (1873–85), Levitan joined the Peredvizhniki. His ability to express the poignant lyrical beauty of the countryside of Central Russia has never been equaled. Levitan's best-known paintings include *The Golden Autumn* and *Evening on the Volga*. Most of his work is characterized by a feeling of melancholy.

LEVITSKY, DMITRY GRIGOREVICH (1735–1822). Painter of portraits and icons. He studied in Kiev and St. Petersburg under Antropov, and from 1771 Levitsky supervised the portrait-painting classes at the Academy of Arts. Technically brilliant, he is highly esteemed and is considered one of the great Russian masters of the psychological portrait. Many of his portraits of young girls from the Smolny Institute were highly successful, and Catherine II commissioned a series of portraits of herself. To a certain extent Levitsky created the style and character of society in St. Petersburg. By the mid-1780s, however, his style had changed; French influences were replaced by a simpler English style. He retired from the Academy of Arts in 1788. During the reign of Paul I his work was not appreciated. He went blind and died in 1822.

Hamilton, George H., *The Art and Architecture of Russia*, 1954.

LIAPUNOV BROTHERS, PROTOPY PETROVICH PROCOPIUS (?–1611) and **ZACHARY PETROVICH.** They were leaders of the gentry armies of Riazan during the Time of Troubles *(q.v.)*. In 1606 their force and that of other rebels were impeded by Prince Michael Skopin-Shuisky *(q.v.)*. At this stage the brothers decided to desert the rebel Bolotnikov *(q.v.)* and join forces with Tsar Vasily Shuisky *(q.v.)*. Faced with a Polish invasion in 1610, Procopius formed an army of gentry and peasants from Riazan and in 1611 marched on Polish-occupied Moscow. Joined by others as he marched, Procopius found himself leading the first national army and a form of government. Procopius was killed in 1611 by Cossacks, against whom measures were later taken, and without its leader, the army disbanded.

LIBEDINSKY, YURY NIKOLAYEVICH (1898–). Author and one of the founders of the proletarian "October Group" in 1922. His short novel *A Week* (1922) won Libedinsky the party's favor, in spite of his nonproletarian origins. His next novel, *Tomorrow* (1923), implied that the Soviet Union should be rescued from the New Economic Policy and was thus obviously less successful. Something of a political speculator, in his play *Heights* Libedinsky emphasized Lenin's warning that the party should not depend on officials trained by the tsarist regime. He was expelled from the party in 1933 as a result of his novel *Birth of a Hero* (1930), but he was later reinstated.

LIBERALS. Under many tsars, such as Nicholas I, liberals were suppressed, and the only means for expressing liberal ideas, such as sympathy with the lot of the peasant, or the land question, was through the medium of literature. Tsar Alexander **II** *(q.v.)*, however, implemented liberal reforms, and emancipated the serfs (*q.v.*) in 1861. His reforms were not considered radical enough and he was assassinated in 1881. By the early 20th century liberalism began to develop as a political force, based on the *zemstvo* (*q.v.*) movement. In 1904 the Union of Liberation (*q.v.*) demanded the abolition of the autocracy, equality before the law, universal suffrage, freedom of the press, and freedom of assembly.

Fischer, George, *Russian Liberalism, from Gentry to Intelligentsia,* 1958.

LIBERATION, THE. Russian socialist journal, established in 1902 by Paul Milyukov and published abroad by the economist Peren Struve. *See* **Union of Liberation.**

LIBERATION OF LABOR GROUP. Early Russian Marxist organization founded by the former populists Georgy Plekhanov and Pavel Axelrod *(q.q.v.)* in 1883, who were living in exile in W Europe. They translated the works of Marx and Engels and smuggled them into Russia. In 1888 the "Liberation of Labor Group" organized a Russian Social Democratic Union abroad, but they left it in 1900. Having worked with Lenin on *Iskra* (*q.v.*) in 1903, they joined the Russian Social Democratic Workers' Party at the Brussels-London Congress, and with this action the group dissolved.

LIBRARIES. The first libraries in Russia were the collections of manuscripts held by Orthodox monasteries. In 1714 the Academy of Sciences received Peter the Great's books, and in 1755, the Moscow University Library was founded. In 1814 the Imperial Public Library opened in St. Petersburg. Following the October Revolution libraries were nationalized, and a large number of private collections were requisitioned. Libraries now are closely controlled by the government and are the responsibility of the Ministry of Culture. In 1978 there were 350,000 libraries of all types with 4,200 million books.

Other important libraries are: Moscow's Lenin State Public Library, founded 1862, taking its present name in 1925; Leningrad's Saltykov-Shchedrin State Public Library, founded in 1795; Moscow's All-Union State Library of Foreign Literature, founded 1922; and Moscow's State Public Library of Science and Technology, founded 1958.

Horecky, Paul L., *Libraries and Bibliographic Centers in the Soviet Union*, 1959.

LIEGNITZ, BATTLE OF (1241). Important battle during the Mongol invasion of Russia and surrounding countries in the early 1240s. The Mongols scored a decisive victory over an army of Poles and Germans.

LIEPÀJA. Ice-free Latvian port on the Baltic Sea. Industries include steelworks, engineering, woodworking, food processing and fish canning. Founded in 1263 by the Teutonic Knights, it first became a Russian possession in 1795. Timber and grain are exported. Population (1973) 95,000.

LIFAR, SERGE (1905–). Dancer and choreographer. In 1923 he studied at the State Central Studio but later joined Serge Diaghilev and the Ballets Russes. Having created the leading roles in Prokofiev's *Fils prodigue* and Stravinsky's *Apollo*, in 1932 Lifar became ballet master and first dancer of the Paris Opera. In 1947, he was appointed director of the Institut Chorégraphique in Paris. He is celebrated for having been instrumental in the revival of French ballet, and he won much acclaim for his ballets *Lucifer* (1948), *Phèdre* (1950), and *Daphnis and Chloë* (1958). A. Haskell translated his *A History of the Russian Ballet from its Origins to the Present Day* (1954).

LIPETSK. Town situated 70 miles (112 km) NNE of Voronezh on the Voronezh River, in the Russian Soviet Federated Socialist Republic. It was rebuilt by Peter the Great in 1707, having been built in the early 13th century and destroyed by the Tatars toward the end of that century. Industries include iron and steel works and the manufacture of tractors and chemicals. It is noted as a health spa with chalybeate springs. Population (1981) 415,000.

LIPRANDI, GENERAL P. P. (1796–1864). Commander of the artillery during the Crimean War. Having captured positions held by Turkish troops, Liprandi advanced to Balaclava and destroyed the legendary Light Brigade.

LITERACY. The majority of the people of Russia were illiterate until the second half of the 19th century. By 1917 about 40 percent of the population over 10 years of age was literate and this rose to over 80 percent by 1939. In 1980 it was claimed that 99.9 percent of the population between 9 and 49 years of age was literate and that 60 percent had received secondary or higher education.

LITERATURNAYA GAZETA (LITERARY GAZETTE). A weekly publication founded in 1929, and after 1932 the organ of the USSR Union of Writers. Since Stalin's death it has moved from a hard party line to occasional critical and liberal observations. The circulation in 1979 was over 2,000,000.

LITHUANIA. Republic situated on the Baltic Sea and bounded on the N by Latvia, on the E and S by Poland, and on the W by the Baltic Sea. Lithuania was a tribal territory supporting a peasant and seafaring community, led by a warrior caste, until it was unified by Mindaugas, who was crowned king in 1253. A Christian, he negotiated peaceful relations with the German order of knights who controlled Latvia and Estonia *(q.q.v.)*. Under his successors the country expanded to the S and E. Grand Duke Gedimin conquered the principality of Kiev in 1320. Grand Duke Jagiello *(q.v.)* joined the Lithuanian empire to Poland in a personal union with the Polish royal house. In 1569 the Union of Lublin effected a full political union, with Lithuania subject to Poland, and Lithuania passed to Russia at the third partition of Poland in 1795. After the Revolution of 1917 Lithuania became an independent state. The secret protocol of the Soviet-German frontier treaty of 1939 assigned the greater part of Lithuania to the Soviet sphere of influence. In that year the province and city of Vilnius were ceded to Germany by the USSR. An ultimatum in 1940 led to the formation of a government acceptable to the USSR. This incorporation has been accorded de facto recognition by the British government, but not by the United States. Lithuania has an area of 25,170 square miles (65,200 sq km). Its capital is Vilnius. Before 1940 Lithuania was a mainly agricultural country but has since been considerably industrialized. The urban population was 23 percent of the total in 1937 and 53 percent in 1972. The resources of the country consist of timber and agricultural produce. Of the total area, 49.1 percent is arable land, 22.2 percent meadow and pastureland, 16.3 percent forests, and 12.4 percent unproductive lands. Heavy engineering, shipbuilding, and building-material industries are developing. Population (1980) 3,400,000.

Jurgela, Constantine Rudyard, *History of the Lithuanian Nation*, 1948.

Vardys, V. Stanley, *Lithuania under the Soviets: Portrait of a Nation*, 1965.

LITHUANIANS. Baltic-speaking people dwelling in Lithuania. The aristocracy was prominent in the affairs of the Polish commonwealth following the fusion of Poland and Lithuania. Traditionally the Roman Catholic Church has been strong in Lithuania.

Balys, Jonas, *Lithuania and Lithuanians: A Select Bibliography*, 1961.

LITTLE RUSSIA. Name for the Ukraine, now obsolete.

LITVINOV, MAXIM MAXIMOVICH (1876–1951). Pseudonym of Meir Wallach. He was a Soviet diplomat and politician. Of Jewish background, Litvinov joined the Social Democratic Labor Party in 1898 and its Leninist faction in 1901. Having taken part in the 1905 Revolution, in 1907 he moved to London where he worked as a clerk. Named representative of the Soviet government in Great Britain after the 1917 Revolution, he was arrested and later exchanged for the British ambassador.

Deputy foreign commissar in 1921–30 and 1939–46, Litvinov was foreign commissar from 1930 to 1939. He made a considerable impression at the League of Nations by advocating disarmament. Removed from the post in 1939, shortly before the pact with Hitler, he was reappointed as deputy foreign minister (1941–46) and was ambassador to Washington (1941–43).

LIVONIA. Latinized form of Livland, land on the E coast of the Baltic N of Lithuania. In the 13th century, Livonia incorporated most of Latvia and Estonia. Following the Livonian wars (1558–83), Livonia was divided between Poland and Sweden, and a war between Poland and Sweden ensued in 1621. In 1656, Livonia was the scene of the Russo-Polish, Polish-Swedish and Russo-Swedish wars. At the Treaty of Kardis (1661), Russia relinquished its claim on Livonia. In the Great Northern War *(q.v.)*, however, Peter the Great obtained Swedish Livonia. Following the 1917 Revolution, Estonia and Latvia announced their independence.

LIVONIAN ORDER (or **Knights of the Sword** or **Order of the Brothers of the Sword).** Crusading knights who between 1202 and 1237 conquered and Christianized most of what is now modern Latvia and Estonia. The order was founded in 1202 by the third bishop of Livonia, Albert von Buxhoevden, and it was intended to be a permanent military force protecting the church in Livonia. It was consecrated by the pope in 1204, but was forced to disband. It was reorganized by the pope in 1237 as a branch of the Teutonic Knights. However, the Livonian Knights again ruled the region from 1525 until Livonia was divided and the order dissolved in 1561.

LIVONIAN WAR (1558–83). A confrontation over Russian expansion toward the Baltic Sea. In 1558, Ivan the Terrible invaded Livonia and defeated its rulers, the Livonian Knights, who had placed Livonia under Lithuanian protection. Russia was eventually defeated by the Polish-Lithuanian commonwealth (*see* **Lublin, Union of**) and Sweden and lost its Livonian conquests and some border towns on the Gulf of Finland.

LOBACHEVSKY, NICHOLAS IVANOVICH (1793–1856). Mathematician and founder (with Janos Bolyar) of non-Euclidean geometry. He was a professor at Kazan University in 1816 and its rector from 1827 to 1846. He made a number of valuable contributions to geometry. He was later dismissed from his posts by the government. Lobachevsky's most important works include *Principles of Geometry* (1829–30) and *Imaginary Geometry* (1835).

LODYGIN, ALEXANDER NIKOLAYEVICH (1847–1923). Electrical engineer. He invented in 1872, and patented in 1874, the first incandescent lamp, which, though it did not find practical use, apparently influenced Edison's work. (Edison invented his carbon thread vacuum incandescent lamp in 1879.) From the early 1880s Lodygin lived mostly abroad. He died in the United States.

LOMBARD. St. Petersburg's pawnshop in the mid-19th century.

LOMONOSOV, MICHAEL VASILYEVICH (1711–65). Poet and scientist, sometimes called the father of modern Russian literature. The son of an Archangel fisherman, Lomonosov ran away to Moscow, where he was educated at the Slavo-Graeco-Latin Academy. He then studied at the universities of Marburg and Freiburg, where he wrote the poem *Ode on the Taking of Khotin* (1739). As an assistant professor at the Academy of Science in St. Petersburg, Lomonosov did research in the principles of matter and partially anticipated the atomic theory of the structure of matter. He established the first chemical laboratory in Russia and wrote the first Russian grammar (1755). He also wrote a history of Russia (1766) and altered the character of Russian prosody by adopting tonic versification in his poetry. He has long been venerated in Russia as a symbol of Russian creative genius.

Menshutkin, Boris N., *Russia's Chemist, Courtier, Physicist, Poet,* 1952.

LONDON, CONFERENCE IN (1871). As a result of the denunciation by Russia of the Black Sea Clauses of the Treaty of Paris (*q.v.*), during the Franco-Prussian War, a conference was held in London. This was attended by representatives of Austria-Hungary, Great Britain, Italy, North Germany, Russia, and Turkey. The neutralization of the Black Sea was ended, but the representatives asserted the inviolability of treaties.

LONDON, CONVENTION OF (1841). Convention at which it was decided that no power had the right to send warships through the Dardanelles and the Bosporus when Turkey was at peace. This still left Russia in a vulnerable position should Turkey and a Turkish ally decide to go to war against it.

LONDON, TREATIES OF. A number of international conferences have been held in London. In 1827–32 Russia, Great Britain, and France demanded self-government for Greece and negotiated boundaries for the new kingdom of Greece. In 1830–31 Russia, together with France, Great Britain, Prussia, and Austria recognized Belgium's independence from the Netherlands. In 1852 Russia, Austria, France, Prussia, Sweden, Denmark, and Great Britain recognized Danish rule over Schleswig and Holstein as autonomous duchies. In 1871 Russia, Great Britain, Italy, Austria-Hungary, North Germany, and Turkey agreed that the Black Sea should be no longer neutral. In 1914 Russia, Great Britain, and France decided against any one of the powers making a separate peace in World War I.

LOPOKOVA, LYDIA (1892–1981). Dancer and actress. Her first stage appearance was at the Maryinsky Theater, St. Petersburg, in 1901. She graduated from the Imperial Ballet School in St. Petersburg in 1909, joining the Diaghilev Ballet in 1910. She danced with the company intermittently until 1926, the year after her marriage to Maynard Keynes. She also danced as guest artist with the Vic-Wells Ballet in 1931 and 1933, which she helped found with her husband. She created the role of Mariuccia in *Les Femmes de Bonne Humeur* and the female cancan dancer in *La Boutique Fantasque.*

LOPUKHINA, YEVDOKIYA FYODOROVNA (1669–1731). Tsaritsa and first wife of Peter the Great (*q.v.*). Peter's mother hoped that the marriage would make the 17-year-old tsar abandon his wild and libertine behavior. The marriage was not a success; the tsaritsa was unintelligent and was sent by Peter to a monastery for having sympathized with the *streltsy* rebellion in 1698. Although she took vows, she left soon afterward. In 1718 her son, the tsarevich Alexis, was tried for treason, and Yevdokiya was imprisoned in a fortress on Lake Ladoga. In 1727, however, her grandson, Peter II, freed her and installed her in a convent. Following his death in 1730, she made an unsuccessful and halfhearted attempt for the throne.

LORIS-MELIKOV, GENERAL COUNT MICHAEL TARYELOVICH (1826–88). Russian general and statesman. He joined the army in 1843, and from 1863 to 1875 was governor of the Terek region. He distinguished himself during the Russo-Turkish War, as a result of which he was made a count. After a period as governor-general of the lower Volga region, he was transferred to Central Russia. He advocated a number of modest reforms of the economy, administration, and educational system and was appointed chairman of a commission whose task was the suppression of the revolutionary movement. As minister of the interior he devised a plan for a representative assembly and a cabinet government. This was rejected by Alexander III (*q.v.*), as a result of which Loris-Melikov resigned his post.

LOSEV, A. F. (1892–?). Philosopher. His books include *Antique Cosmos and Modern Science, The Philosophy of Name, Dialectics of Artistic Form,* and *Music as a Subject of Logic,* all published in Russia in 1927. *Outlines of the Antique Symbolism and Mythology,* Vol. I, was published in 1930. Little is known about his life.

LOVERS OF WISDOM, THE. Influential philosophic circle, active toward the end of the reign of Alexander I. Formed in 1823, the circle was, to some extent, a continuation of the Masonic Astrea Lodge. The circle consisted of a dozen members who met in secret, many of whom later were to become leading intellectuals. The most prominent Lovers of Wisdom included Dmitry Venevitinov and Vladimir Odoyevsky (*q.q.v.*). The circle, influenced by Schelling and by Romanticism, tended to disregard politics and published the journal *Mnemosyne.* The group disbanded after the Decembrist rebellion.

Billington, James H., *The Icon and the Axe,* 1966.

LUBLIN, UNION OF (1569). The act that created a Polish-Lithuanian commonwealth. Poland and Lithuania (*q.v.*) were to share a common monarch and diet (parliament) but each was to maintain its own laws, administration, treasury, and army.

LUGANSK. *See* **Voroshilovgrad.**

LUGANSKY, KAZAK. *See* **Dahl, Vladimir Ivanovich.**

LUKACS, GJÖRGY (1885–1971). Hungarian writer, Marxist philosopher, and literary critic. In 1918 Lukács joined the Hungarian Communist Party. In 1930 he moved to Moscow and from 1933 to 1944 worked at the Institute of Philosophy of the Soviet Academy of Science. He exerted considerable influence on European communist thought and is noted for having formulated a Marxist system of aesthetics that opposes political control of artists and that defends humanism. Having returned to Hungary in 1945, Lukács twice served as minister of culture. His publications include *Studies on Lenin* (1970) and *Solzhenitsyn* (1970, trans. 1971).

LUNACHARSKY, ANATOLY VASILYEVICH (1875–1933). Russian author, literary critic, and politician. Deported in 1898 for revolutionary activities, Lunacharsky joined the Bolsheviks and worked on the party's journal *Vperyod.* Imprisoned during the 1905 Revolution, in 1909 he started a school for an elite of Russian factory workers on Capri; he was assisted by Maxim Gorky and Alexander Bogdanov *(q.q.v.).* The three of them broke from Lenin, forming their own left-wing subfaction. In 1917 he joined Lenin and Trotsky in Russia and was appointed people's commissar for education. A supporter of Bogdanovism during the 1920s, he introduced many innovations into the educational system. In 1933 he was appointed ambassador to Spain but died shortly after the appointment. The author of some 14 plays, Lunacharsky also produced many works of literary criticism.

Fitzpatrick, Sheila, *The Commissariat of Enlightenment: Soviet Organization of Education and the Arts under Lunacharsky, October 1917–1921,* 1970.

LUNTS, LEV NATANOVICH (1901–24). Soviet essayist and playwright. A member of the Serapion Brothers (*q.v.*), Lunts wrote the plays *The Apes are Coming* and *The City of Truth,* a courageous anti-Bolshevik play. He emigrated and died abroad.

LUTSK. Ukrainian town situated 85 miles (136 km) NE of Lvov on the Styr River. Lutsk was part of Kievan Russia until 1154 when it became an independent principality. It was then, in turn, the possession of Lithuania and Poland until taken by Russia in 1791. It passed to Poland in 1919–39 and was ceded to the Ukraine in 1939. Industries include flour milling, tanning, and the manufacture of agricultural machinery. Population (1976) 128,000.

LVOV, ALEKSEY FEDOROVICH (1798–1870). Violinist and composer. He was director of the Imperial Court Chapel (1836) and leader of a string quartet. His works comprise three operas, including *Bianco e Gualtiero* and *Undine,* and some church music. Lvov is best known as the composer of the Imperial Russian National Anthem *God Save the Tsar.*

Montagu-Nathan, M., *A History of Russian Music,* 1914.

LVOV, PRINCE GEORGY YEVGENEVICH (1861–1925). Social reformer and statesman. He was active in the *zemstvo* movement (*q.v.*) and chairman of the All-Russian Union of Zemstvos. He formed a provisional government at the request of the provisional committee of the state duma February 1917 following Nicholas II's abdication and was prime minister until Kerensky replaced him in July of that year. He lived in exile in France after the Bolshevik seizure of power.

LVOV. Capital of Lvov region of the Ukraine. It was founded *c.* 1256 and became the capital of Galicia in 1772. It was taken by Poland in 1919 and ceded to the USSR in 1945. Lvov is an important industrial and railway center with industries including railway engineering, automobile assembling, and oil refining. Manufactures include chemicals, textiles, agricultural machinery, and glass. Population (1981) 689,000.

LYADOV, ANATOLY KONSTANTINOVICH (1855–1914). Composer and teacher. Lyadov studied composition under Rimsky-Korsakov at the St. Petersburg Conservatory. He was expelled for idleness in 1876, but was readmitted two years later and became a professor. From 1897 he was involved with the arrangement of folk songs collected by the Imperial Geographical Society. The skilled composer of beautifully polished piano pieces, he is also noted for his children's songs and for the symphonic poems *Baba-Yaga* (*q.v.*) and *The Enchanted Lake.*

LYASHKO, NICHOLAS (1884–1953). Pseudonym of Nicholas Lyashchenko. Soviet novelist and revolutionary. Lyashko began writing in 1905. Most of his work describes the life of the worker, drawn from his own experience, and tends to idealize the proletariat. A prolific writer, Lyashko's work includes *The Blast Furnace, Sweet Penal Servitude,* and *Russian Nights.*

LYATSKY, YEVGENY ALEKSANDROVICH (1868–?). Russian literary historian. He was editor of the correspondence of Vissarion Belinsky and Nicholas Chernyshevsky (*q.q.v.*), but he is most noted for his studies of Ivan Goncharov (*q.v.*).

LYSENKO, TROFIM DENISOVICH (1898–1976). Ukrainian biologist, agronomist, and member of the USSR Academy of Sciences. The president of the All-Union Lenin Academy of Agricultural Science from 1940 to 1965, Lysenko's main fields of research were heredity and its variability, individual development of organisms, crop nutrition, and laws of the formation of species. He was most influential during Stalin's rule. Afterward Lysenko's popularity lessened, owing to adverse results in agriculture when his theories were applied. Although he regained a degree of authority under Khrushchev, in 1964 the press announced the failure of Lysenko's agrobiological practices.

LYUBECH MEETING (1097). Meeting of the sons of Yaroslav the Wise (*q.v.*), at which the five princes decided to adhere to the practice of succession from father to son. This agreement was short-lived and in practice the principle of rotation from brother to brother prevailed. This resulted in constant civil war between uncles and nephews.

LYUBERTSY. Town situated 12 miles (19 km) SE of Moscow. Manufactures include electrical equipment, machinery, and plastics. Population (1981) 163,000.

LYUDI (literally people). Term used to denote the Kievan middle class.

M

MACARIUS, METROPOLITAN OF MOSCOW (1482–1563). Metropolitan who strongly influenced the young Ivan the Terrible, stressing the concept of Moscow as the Third Rome.

MacMAHON, MARIE EDMÉ PATRICE MAURIE (1808–93). Marshal of France and second president of the Third Republic. During the Crimean War MacMahon commanded the division that stormed Malakhov, which resulted in the fall of Sebastopol. He was elected president of the republic in 1873, but the majority of his policies met with little success.

MAGADAN. Port situated on the Sea of Okhotsk, Khabarovsk territory, in. the Russian Soviet Federated Socialist Republic. Industries include ship repairing, fishing, and the manufacture of mining equipment. Population (1976) 112,000.

MAGDEBURG LAW. German law, and a form of urban self-government, in use in towns governed by Lithuania and Poland. By the middle of the 15th century it had been introduced into the towns of W Russia. According to the law, the *mestnichestvo* were exempt from paying certain taxes, gained trading privileges, and were no longer subject to the legal jurisdiction of the *voyevodi*. Each town under this system was administered by two councils, the *lava* and the *rada*. In return for a comparative autonomy, the burghers supplied the prince with workers and an army.

MAGNITNAYA, MOUNT. Mountain situated in the S Ural mountains 2,000 feet (610 m) above sea level.

MAGNITOGORSK. Town 130 miles (208 km) SW of Chelyabinsk situated on the Ural River in the Russian Soviet Federated Socialist Republic. It was built 1929–31 under the first

Five-Year Plan and is an important metallurgical center using magnetite iron ore from nearby Mount Magnitnaya. Other manufactures include machinery, cement, chemicals, and clothing. Population (1981) 413,000.

MAGNITSKY, MICHAEL LEONTYEVICH (1778–1885). Politician. In 1810–11 Magnitsky helped Michael Speransky *(q.v.)* compile his state reforms. He was later governor of Simbirsk and from 1819 worked for the ministry of education. He wished to shut down Kazan University but instead dismissed 11 professors. In retirement he worked as editor of the reactionary journal *Raduga.*

MAHMUD II (1785–1839). Sultan of Turkey. During his reign the Russo-Turkish war of 1828–29 occurred, during which the Turkish army was defeated, and peace was concluded at Adrianople *(q.v.)*. However, when Mohammed Ali Pasha's army was advancing to the Bosporus, Russia came to Turkey's help, which led to the Treaty of Unkiar Skelessi *(q.v.)*.

MAIKOP. *See* **MAYKOP.**

MAKAROV, ALEKSEY VASILYEVICH (1675–1750). Private secretary to Peter the Great. Although he had no official post, he considerably influenced Peter's domestic policies.

MAKAROV, ADMIRAL STEPAN OSIPOVICH (1848–1904). Admiral in charge of defense during the Russo-Japanese War. Makarov went down with his flagship, the *Petropavlovsk,* outside Port Arthur.

MAKEYEVKA. Ukrainian town 8 miles (13 km) E of Donetsk in the Donets basin. Founded in 1899, it is an important iron and steel center and has coal-mining and coking plants. Population (1981) 442,000.

MAKHACHKALA. Capital of the Dagestan Autonomous Soviet Socialist Republic and port situated on the W shore of the Caspian Sea. Industries include oil refining served by the pipeline from the Grozny oil field, shipbuilding, railway engineering, fish canning, and food processing. Manufactures include textiles and footwear. Population (1981) 269,000.

MAKHAYEVISM. Russian social and political trend which was adhered to by the Bolshevik Party until the early 1930s. According to Makhaysky (J. W. Machajski), a Polish Social Democrat, in his book *The Brain Worker* (1905), knowledge is a means of production. The intelligentsia, it follows, is a class of exploiters. Accordingly, the working class must assist the intelligentsia to socialize knowledge. This theory resulted in the confiscation of private libraries and in the opening of educational institutions to all, regardless of their social origins.

MAKHNO, NESTOR IVANOVICH (1889–1935). Ukrainian anarchist. Imprisoned for terrorism in 1907, he was released 10 years later. The organizer of a peasant gang opposed to both Reds and Whites during the Civil War, from 1919–20 he worked with the Red Army and then emigrated.

MAKLAKOV, VASILY ALEKSANDROVICH (1870–1957). Liberal and lawyer. A member of the second, third and fourth dumas, he acted as counsel for the defense for political cases during the 1905 Revolution. A member of the Constitutional Democratic Party, he was appointed ambassador to France by the provisional government in 1917. He subsequently acted as leader of the Russian émigrés in Paris.

MAKSIMOV, NICHOLAS ALEKSANDROVICH (1880–1952). Specialist in plant physiology. Having studied at St. Petersburg University, from 1917 he was professor at Tiflis University, and then at Petrograd Saratov. From 1946–52 Maksimov was director of the K. A. Timiryazev Institute of Plant Physiology. He researched the effect of frost on plants.

MALENKOV, GEORGY MAKSIMILYANOVICH (1902–). Statesman and Communist Party official. Having joined the party in 1920, Malenkov worked for the apparatus of the party's central committee and in the party's Moscow committee. He was deeply involved in the Great Purge. From 1941 to 1945 he was a member of the state defense committee in charge of military equipment. He was secretary of the central committee and a deputy prime minister, and in 1946 was a member of the Politburo. Malenkov was prime minister, and the unofficial head of the collective leadership following the death of Stalin. In 1955 he confessed to having chosen the wrong policies, and in 1957 as a member of the anti-party group, he was expelled from the central committee.

Ebon, Martin, *Malenkov: Stalin's Successor,* 1953.

MALEVICH, KAZIMIR (1878–1935). One of the first abstract painters. Influenced by Impressionism, Fauvism, and Cubism, in 1913 Malevich evolved his own abstract geometrical style known as Suprematism *(q.v.)*, in which only geometrical elements were used in construction. After teaching painting from 1919 to 1921 in Moscow and Leningrad, he traveled to Weimar, where he met Wassily Kandinsky, and published his *The Non-Objective World.* His best-known paintings include the famous *White Square on a White Background.* Unfortunately his work met with official disapproval, and Malevich died in poverty in 1935.

Gray, Camilla, *The Russian Experiment in Art, 1863–1922,* 1971.

MALIK, YAKOB ALEKSANDROVICH (1906–). Diplomat. After joining the party in 1938, Malik worked in the Ukraine before studying at the institute of diplomats and consuls. From 1937 to 1939 he served on the people's commissariat of foreign affairs before being appointed to Japan and later to Britain.

MALINOVSKY, RODION YAKOVLEVICH (1898–1967). Soviet marshal. Having served with the French army in the First World War, and having fought in the Civil War, Malinovsky joined the party in 1926. In 1930 he graduated from the M. V. Frunze Military Academy. During the

Second World War, he proved to be a distinguished commander during the Stalingrad offensive (1942). He then led the SW army group (1943) and the second Ukrainian army group (1944), which occupied Rumania and Hungary. In 1945 he liberated Czechoslovakia and commanded the Transbaikalian army group in the war against Japan, and in 1945–46 he commanded the Soviet forces in Manchuria. A candidate member of the party's central committee from 1952, in 1957 he was appointed minister of defense.

MALYSHKIN, ALEXANDER GEORGYEVICH (1892–1938). Soviet writer. After studying at St. Petersburg University, Malyshkin took part in the 1917 Revolution, joined the Red Army in 1918 and in 1920 was involved in the liberation of the Crimea. His first stories expose the injustices of the autocratic regime, but his *The Fall of Daiv* describes the Red Army. His best-known work is the novel *People from the Back of Beyond* (1937–38).

MAMAY (?–1380). Tatar vizier and khan. In 1373 Mamay laid waste Ryazan; the following year his envoys and 1,500 Tatars were slaughtered in Nizhny-Novgorod. He was eventually overthrown by the rival khan, Toktamysh *(q.v.)*.

MANCHURIA. Frontier area of NE China. Tsarist Russia viewed Manchuria as an E outpost; Japan, too, wished to control the region. The ensuing Russo-Japanese war *(q.v.)* was sparked by Japan's demanding the Liaotung peninsula. Russia, France, and Germany forced Japan to renounce this demand. After the Second World War the USSR was granted the use of the naval base at Port Arthur, but this was returned to China on May 24, 1955.

MANDELSTAM, LEONID ISAAKOVICH (1879–1944). Physicist. Of Jewish background, Mandelstam was educated at the universities of Odessa and Strasbourg. He was appointed professor at the Odessa Polytechnical Institute in 1918, and at Moscow University in 1925. He did extensive research in optics, radio, and the theory of vibration. In 1928, Mandelstam and G. S. Landsberg discovered the combinational dispersion of light. Mandelstam's collected works were published in 1947–50.

MANDELSTAM, OSIP (1892–1938). Poet. His output was small, particularly after the Revolution, but his influence great, and he refused to participate in politics. He was arrested in 1934 and exiled. Arrested again in 1938, he was thought to have died on the way to a camp. His first volume of poems, *Stone,* was published in 1913, and this was followed by *Tristia* (1922) and *Poems* (1928).

Brown, Clarence, *Mandelstam,* 1973.

Mandelstam, Nadezhda, *Hope Against Hope,* 1971. *Hope Abandoned,* 1974.

MANNERHEIM, BARON CARL GUSTAF EMIL (1867–1951). Russian, and subsequently Finnish, army officer. He served in the Russo-Japanese War and in the First World War. In 1917 Mannerheim was made lieutenant general of the Russian army. In 1918, he led the White forces, and became regent of Finland in that year. In 1939–40, he was commander in chief during the "winter war" against the Soviet Union. He was president of Finland from 1944 to 1946.

MANYCH. System of lakes and rivers in the Russian Soviet Federated Socialist Republic NW of the Caucasus mountains. Navigation is possible as far as Proletarskaya. A large barrage and reservoir has been constructed at Vesely.

MANYCH DEPRESSION. Broad valley in the S Russian Soviet Federal Socialist Republic extending approximately 350 miles (560 km) SE from the lower Don River to the Caspian Sea and drained by the W and E Manych rivers.

MARI AUTONOMOUS SOVIET SOCIALIST REPUBLIC. Constituted an autonomous republic of the Russian Soviet Federated Socialist Republic in 1936, it has an area of 8,955 square miles (23,193 sq km). The capital is Yoshkar Ola, 400 miles (640 km) E of Moscow. Chief industries are metalworking, timber, paper, woodworking, and food processing. Grain is the main crop occupying 70 percent of the cultivated land. Minerals, including coal, are located at Pechora. Population (1981) 711,000.

MARIA, PRINCESS OF TVER (*c.* 14th century). Daughter of Vassily of Yaroslavl, Maria ruled after his death. She married Fedor of Mohilev and thus founded a new line of princes.

MARIA FEDOROVNA, EMPRESS. *See* **Dagmar, Princess Mary.**

MARSHAK, SAMUIL YAKOVLEVICH (1887–1964). Poet and writer of stories for children. His first work appeared in 1902, and he was assisted in his literary career by Gorky. He is considered one of the creators of Soviet literature for children and an able political satirist. Marshak also translated some of the works of Shakespeare, Burns, Byron, and Heine. He was awarded the Order of Lenin and other medals.

MARSHALS OF THE NOBILITY. Elected representatives of the nobility, a system initiated under Catherine II in 1766. Organized locally, there were both provincial and district marshals, elected by assemblies of deputies every three years.

Pares, Bernard, *A History of Russia*, rev. ed. 1965.

MARTOV, YULY OSIPOVICH (1873–1923). Leader of the Mensheviks (*q.v.*). Martov joined the Social Democrats in 1892. After working with Lenin on the union for the struggle of the working class, he parted company with him in 1903. He was appointed official leader of the Menshevik Party after 1917. In 1920 he settled in Berlin and edited the *Socialist Courier*.

Getzler, Israel, *Martov: A Political Biography of a Russian Social Democrat*, 1967.

MARTYNOV, ALEXANDER YEVSTAFEVICH (1816–60). Actor. Born in St. Petersburg, Martynov studied there at the Theater School (1827–35) and started acting publicly in 1832. One of the first actors of the Realist school, he influenced the future development of theatrical art. He died of tuberculosis.

MARX, KARL HEINRICH (1818–83). German political philosopher and social thinker. His main thesis was that humankind developed politically through three stages, leading to the dictatorship of the proletariat, the withering away of the state and the emergence of a classless society. Born in Trier, in what is now the Federal Republic of Germany, of Jewish parents, Marx studied at the universities of Bonn, Berlin, and Jena. In 1842 he was editor of the *Rheinische Zeitung,* but this was suppressed by the Prussian government in 1843. In the same year he married Jenny von Westphalen (1814–81). He met Friedrich Engels in Paris and in Brussels in 1847 produced his *Misère de la Philosophie* and the *Manifest der Kommunistischen Partei* (1848). Exiled in London, and although helped financially by Friedrich Engels *(q.v.),* Marx lived a life of poverty. He worked in the British Museum (now the British Library) and wrote his best-known work *Das Kapital,* Vol. 1 (1867). He died in 1883 and was buried at Highgate cemetery, London. His works are often quoted, although generally inaccurately, and the influence of these writings has been immense.

Berlin, Isaiah, *Karl Marx: His Life and Environment,* 1978.

MARXISM-LENINISM, INSTITUTE OF. Moscow's chief institution of study and research into the history and theory of communism. In 1931 the Marx-Engels Institute and the Lenin Institute merged to form the Marx-Engels-Lenin Institute and served as a tool of Stalin during his lifetime. From 1953 to 1957 many of the main ideological policies of the party leadership allegedly were based on the findings of the institute.

MARYINSK CANAL. Canal extending 5 miles (8 km) between Vytegra (NW) and Kovzha (SE) rivers as part of the Maryinsk system joining the Volga River and Rybinsk reservoir with the Neva River.

MASSINE, LÉONIDE (1894–). Dancer and choreographer. He studied at the Imperial School. In 1913 Massine met Diaghilev *(q.v.),* and the following year he danced in Fokine's *Légende de Joseph.* From 1924 to 1928 he worked with Diaghilev, from 1933 to 1936 with Colonel de Basil's company, and then with René Blum. Massine's work as a choreographer includes *Contes Russe, Le Tricorne,* and *Pulcinella,* but the ballet *La Symphonie Fantastique,* which he choreographed in 1936, contained some of his most successful work, in which he combined Expressionist effects with classical economy.

MATERIALISM. Metaphysical theory according to which the world consists of hard material objects, and according to which all immaterial concepts such as the mind or the soul are reducible to material things. In the Soviet Union, materialism is the official base of the sociological and ontological positions of Marxism, and Marxist philosophy is often known as dialectical and historical materialism. Before the Bolshevik seizure of power materialism was propagated by Michael Bakunin, Nicholas Chernyshevsky, Dmitry Pisarev, and Ivan Sechenev *(q.q.v.)*.

MATVEYEV, ARTAMON SERGEYEVICH (1625–82). Diplomat and statesman. Chief of the *streltsy* in 1654, in 1671 Matveyev was head of the foreign department, and in the following year he played a leading role in concluding an agreement with Poland concerning Turkey. His influence on Tsar Alexis was considerable. In 1674 he was appointed privy councillor. Exiled by Tsar Fedor Alekseyevich, he was pardoned in 1682. Recalled to Moscow by Peter I, Matveyev was killed by the *streltsy*.

MATYUSHIN, MICHAEL VASILYEVICH (1861–1934). Having studied at the Moscow Conservatory of Music, Matyushin worked as a violinist at the Court Orchestra in St. Petersburg until 1913; he also studied at the school for the encouragement of arts, studied under Yan Tsionglinsky, and studied at the Zvantseva School of Art. He joined Nicholas Kulbin's Impressionist group in 1909, but he left it to help found the Union of Youth. He collaborated for a while with Kazimir Malevich, Alexey Kruchenykh, and Velimir Khlebnikov. Matyushin conducted a studio in spatial realism for the Zorved group from 1918 to 1922 and later produced a book on the study of color, *The Rules of the Variability of Colour Combinations: A Colour Manual* (1932). He is also remembered for his music written for the Futurist opera *Victory Over the Sun* (1913).

MAXIMALISTS. Small terrorist group of populists that split off from the Socialist Revolutionaries in 1904. Having taken an active part in the Revolution of 1905, they continued to organize violence, and in 1906, blew up Peter Stolypin's *(q.v.)* summer residence. As a result, many Maximalists were executed, and others escaped abroad. They worked with the Bolsheviks after the latter's seizure of power in 1917, and were represented in the central executive committee. In 1920 the group disintegrated, and most of its members joined the Bolshevik Party.

MAYAKOVSKY, VLADIMIR VLADIMIROVICH (1894–1930). Poet. In 1908 Mayakovsky joined the Communist Party, and in 1911 he met some of the early Futurists *(q.v.)*. His first collection of poems, *As Simple as Mooing* (1916), met with success. He wrote many poems about the Revolution, including *150,000,000* (1920), in which President Wilson personifies capitalism. He also wrote satirical plays, including *The Red Bug* (1921). He was the leading representative of the Futurist school, and Mayakovsky had considerable influence on subsequent poets. Disenchanted with the party, he committed suicide in 1930, although later he was eulogized by Stalin.

Brown, Edward J., *Mayakovsky: A Poet of the Revolution*, 1973.

Shklovsky, Viktor Borisovich, *Mayakovsky and His Circle*, 1974.

Woroszylski, Wiktor, *The Life of Mayakovsky*, 1972.

MAYKOP (or **Maikop**). Capital of the Adygei Autonomous Region of the Russian Soviet Federated Socialist Republic, situated 60 miles (96 km) SE of Krasnodar on the Belaya River. Founded as a fortress in 1857, it manufactures furniture, leather, and food and tobacco products. Nearby are the Maikop oil fields, which were discovered in 1900. Population (1976) 127,000.

MAZEPA, IVAN STEPANOVICH (*c.* 1645–1709). Ukrainian hetman from 1687. He conspired with the Polish king, Stanislaw Leszczynsky, and Charles XII (*q.v.*) of Sweden with the aim of overthrowing Peter the Great. Mazepa and the Zaporozhe Cossacks supported Charles XII's invasion of the Ukraine. They were defeated in 1709 at the battle of Poltava.

MAZOVIA. Historic territory in Poland, consisting of part of the Mazovia-Podlasia lowland. Incorporated with the Duchy of Warsaw (1807–14), Mazovia was part of Russian Poland until 1918. It is now part of the Warsaw and Bialystok provinces in Poland.

MECKLENBURG, GRAND DUKE OF, KARL LEOPOLD (*fl.* early 18th century). In 1716 Mecklenburg married Catherine, niece of Peter the Great. Under the terms of the marriage treaty Mecklenburg was to support a Russian armed force, to put his troops at the disposal of the Russian army, and to annex Wismar and Warnemünde.

MELITOPOL. Ukrainian town 70 miles (112 km) S of Zaporozhe on Molochnaya River. Industries include meat packing and flour milling; manufactures include agricultural machinery, diesel engines, and clothing. Population (1981) 165,000.

MENGLI-GIREY, KHAN OF THE CRIMEA (*fl.* late 14th century). Mengli defeated Shah-Ahmed and, with the help of Ivan III, put an end to the Golden Horde.

MENSHEVIKS. Political party established in August 1917 at a congress of several Social Democratic groups. The Mensheviks proposed a proletarian party working with the liberals in order to replace the autocracy with a democratic constitution. Before 1917 "Menshevik" referred to the non-Leninist faction of the Russian Social Democratic Labor Party. Although the Mensheviks worked with the Bolsheviks during the 1905 Revolution, and reunited with them the following year, relations were strained. The Mensheviks themselves were divided into the "liquidationalists," the "party-minded Mensheviks" of the center, the followers of Pavel Axelrod (*q.v.*), and the followers of Trotsky. In 1922 the Mensheviks were suppressed, and in 1931 a show trial took place in Moscow. In 1920 a group of Mensheviks left Russia and settled in the United States.

Ascher, Abraham (ed.), *The Mensheviks in the Russian Revolution*, 1976.

Dan, Theodore, *The Origins of Bolshevism*, 1964.

Haimson, Leopold H., *The Russian*

Marxists and the Origins of Bolshevism, 1955.

MENSHIKOV, PRINCE ALEXANDER DANILOVICH, (1673–1729). Statesman and field marshal. A friend of Peter the Great, whose reforms he influenced and helped, Menshikov ruled Russia during the reign of Catherine I and the minority of Peter II. Eventually because of intrigue at court, he was banished to Siberia.

MENSHIKOV, ALEXANDER SERGEYEVICH (1787–1869). General. Menshikov unsuccessfully led the Russian army at the time of the Crimean War (*q.v.*) at Alma, Inkerman, and Sevastopol.

MEREZHKOVSKY, DMITRY SERGEYEVICH (1865–1941). Writer and leader of the older Symbolists, who influenced the religious revival among intellectuals at the beginning of the century. His essay "On the Causes of Decline of Contemporary Russian Literature" was important in the development of Symbolism. His works also include *Christ and Anti Christ* (1893–1902) and *The Coming Hamite* (1906). After 1917 he lived in France.

West, James D., *Russian Symbolism*, 1970.

MERV. One of the main oases of Central Asia near the Murgals River in the Mari (*q.v.*) oblast of Turkmenia. It has been ruled by the Arabs, Persia, Khorezm, the Zeravshan valley states, nomadic Turkmens, and Genghis Khan's Mongols. In 1884 it was annexed by Russia.

MESHCHERSKY, PRINCE VLADIMIR PETROVICH, (1839–1914). Editor of the reactionary weekly *Grazhdanin* (The Citizen). Influential with members of the court and the government, Meshchersky aimed at returning Russia to the conditions existing prior to the Great Reforms.

MESSERER, ASAF MIKHAILOVICH (1903–). Dancer, choreographer, and teacher. He studied at the Leningrad School until 1921. Messerer was the choreographer of many ballets and was appointed ballet master at the Bolshoi Theater in Moscow. He was one of the greatest male dancers and teachers of dance in the Soviet Union.

MESTNICHESTVO. System by which appointment of court officials, ambassadors, and army officials depended upon inherited rank and status. Records of genealogical tables were burned in 1682, thus abolishing *mestnichestvo.*

METROPOLITAN. Title bestowed upon the Orthodox bishops of Moscow, Leningrad, Kiev, Minsk, and Novosibirsk.

MEYERHOLD, VSEVOLOD YEMILYEVICH (1874–1942). Actor and director. Meyerhold worked with V. I. Nemirovich-Danchenko and Konstantin Stanislavsky (*q.v.*) at the Moscow Art Theater (1898–1902). In 1902 he founded the Society of New Drama in Russia. His method of production known as "biomechanics," involved reducing the actor to the status of a puppet under the control of the producer. He used a bare stage and stylized gestures. In 1920 he became head of theater in the people's commissariat for education. He founded his own theater in Moscow. Innovative and modernistic, he worked closely with Vladimir Mayakovsky (*q.v.*). In 1915 he made two films, now lost, *The Strong Man* and *Dorian Grey*, which are known to have influenced contemporary filmmakers. From 1920 Meyerhold had a working studio with student directors, including Sergei Eisenstein (*q.v.*). Accused of Formalism, he was arrested in 1939 and "disappeared."

Braun, E. (ed.), *Meyerhold on Theatre*, 1969.

Hoover, Margorie L., *Meyerhold: The Art of Conscious Theater*, 1974.

MEZENTSOV, GENERAL NICHOLAS VLADIMIROVICH (1827–78). Chief of the political police, assassinated in 1878. *See* **Land and Liberty Organization.**

MGB. Russian abbreviation for Ministry of State Security. Name of the Soviet security service (1946–53), and responsible for internal security; the MGB replaced the NKVD and NKGB. Under Beria's leadership and Stalin's orders the MGB became exceedingly powerful. Jewish intellectuals were harassed in 1949, and an operation was led against the former supporters of Zhdanov. The wave of terror and the powerful position of the MGB reached its zenith with the discovery of the "Doctors' Plot" of 1952. Following the death of Stalin the ministry was once again subordinated to party control and was reorganized as the KGB (Committee of State Security). *See* **Secret Police.**

MICHAEL ALEKSANDROVICH, GRAND DUKE (1878–1918). Brother of Nicholas II. Following Nicholas II's abdication Michael was offered the crown, but he refused it, consenting to accept it only if he were offered it by a democratically elected constituent assembly. Although Paul Milyukov and Alexander Guchkov (*q.v.*) of the provisional government implored Michael to accept the throne, he declined, thus bringing to an end the Romanov dynasty.

MICHAEL ALEKSANDROVICH, OF TVER, PRINCE (1333–99). Ruler of Tver from 1368. Much of his reign was dominated by conflict with Dmitriy Donskoy (*q.v.*) of Moscow. In the first year of his reign, Dmitriy besieged Tver and Michael fled to Lithuania. In 1371 Michael was given the throne of Vladimir by Mamay (*q.v.*) but the people of Vladimir refused to accept him. He was invited to Moscow, where he was showered with presents before being sent back to Mamay, who agreed to cancel Michael's patent. Dmitriy was given the title of duke of Vladimir. In 1372, after an alliance with Olgerd, Michael attacked the lesser Tverian princes; Dmitriy defended them. After the conflict between Tver and Moscow, which lasted for three years, Michael eventually had to make peace, and in 1375 he declared himself the "younger brother," that is, vassal of Dmitriy.

MICHAEL BORISOVICH OF TVER, PRINCE (1453–1505). The last of the Great Princes of Tver, Michael ruled Tver from 1461. In 1471 and 1477 Tver troops took part in the Novgorod mission against Khan Akmat. In the mid-1480s Michael officially recognized the overlordship of Ivan III, but he clandestinely engineered a rapprochement with King Kasimir III of Poland. Ivan III accordingly lay siege to Tver, and Michael fled to Lithuania. Tver's days as an independent principality were over; it became part of Rus, and Michael spent the rest of his days in Lithuania.

MICHAEL ROMANOV (1596–1645). Elected tsar of Muscovy and Russia in 1613 by the *Zemsky Sobor (q.v.)*, he was a weak ruler. Faced with internal problems and attacks from Poland and Sweden, he relied upon his father, the Patriarch Philaret *(q.v.)* of Moscow, and the *Zemsky Sobor.*

MICHAEL VSEVOLODOVICH OF CHERNIGOV, PRINCE (1179–1246). Ruler of Chernigov. Having fought in the campaign against the Tatars on the Kalka River, in 1223 Michael ascended the throne. In 1235 he succeeded in taking Galicia and Kiev. In 1238, turning over the rule of Galicia to his son, Michael became prince of Kiev. He then killed the Tatar envoy to Kiev and fled to Hungary. His Russian domain was then divided among several princes. He returned home in 1241, and was killed by the Tatars for refusing to perform a pagan ritual.

MICHAEL YAROSLAVICH OF TVER, GRAND PRINCE (1271–1318). Prince of Tver from 1285. In 1305 Michael became the first Russian prince to assume the title of Grand Prince of All Rus. Michael contended for years with Yury Danilovich (*q.v.*) for the title of Grand Prince of Vladimir, the leadership of the NE of Rus. Supported by the Orthodox Church, Michael was given the tsar's *yarlyk* (*q.v.*). He blundered in connection with the election of a new metropolitan and lost the blessing of the church; unfortunately, he also lost the support of the Novgorodians as a result of his harsh treatment of them. Yury was then granted the title of grand prince by Khan Uzbeq, and aided by Mongol forces, he challenged Michael's supremacy. Eventually accused of murdering Uzbeq's sister, Michael was executed in 1318.

Dmytryshyn, Basil, *A History of Russia*, 1977.

MIGHTY BUNCH. *See* **Moguchaya Kuchka.**

MIGHTY HANDFUL. *See* **Moguchaya Kuchka.**

MIKESHIN, MICHAEL OSIPOVICH (1836–96). Artist. He studied at the St. Petersburg Academy of Artists under B. Villebald, specializing in sculpting statues and monuments, such as his *Victory of the Russian Fleet.* He is also noted for his illustrations of Gogol's *Viy* and of the works of Taras Shevchenko, Alexander Pushkin, and Nicholas Nekrasov (*q.q.v.*).

MIKHAILOV, A. D. (1855–84). Decembrist and member of the Northern Society (*q.q.v.*) who became the party's expert on conspiracy and security.

MIKOYAN, ANASTAS IVANOVICH (1896–1978). Communist. After studying at a theological seminary, Mikoyan joined the Bolshevik Party in 1915, and rose to become a member of the Politburo in 1926 and deputy prime minister in 1937. A supporter of Khrushchev, he was an extremely influential member of the party.

MILITARY SERVICE. Prior to the Great Reforms of Alexander II, there was no standardized recruiting system for the army. Those to whom the lot of military service fell had to serve for 25 years, although this was reduced to 16 years in 1861. In 1874, however, Count Dmitry Milyutin inaugurated universal military service for all men of 20 years of age. The length of service depended on the education of the conscript, but service could last for as long as 6 years. Although the Bolsheviks abolished conscription in 1918, it was soon reintroduced and according to the constitution of 1936, it is a fundamental duty of Soviet citizens. Those leaving school at the age of 17 or 18 are automatically called up on finishing their education; others begin their service at the age of 19. Service may last for 2 to 5 years. Afterward, former soldiers are in the reserves until the age of 50, or in some cases, until age 65. Reservists may be called upon to undergo short periods of training. Psychological and technical preparation for military service begins at an early age. Young children are trained how to survive a nuclear attack and undergo basic training one afternoon a week, as well as for several weeks during the summer. In addition, military activities are arranged by pioneer and Komsomol (*q.v.*) groups. The young Soviet citizen is brought up to regard the USSR as a camp, besieged by hostile forces. This, and the memory of the appalling losses sustained in the two world wars help explain the significance accorded to military service.

MILITARY SETTLEMENTS. Military legislation, enacted under Nicholas I, by which crown peasants were turned into hereditary soldiers, often bringing great hardship.

MILITARY TRIBUNALS. Separate federal tribunals within the Soviet legal system subject to the military chamber of the supreme court of the USSR. The army, navy, and organs of state security have their own military tribunals, which have jurisdiction over crimes committed by military and security personnel and jurisdiction over crimes committed by civilians in case of espionage or complicity in military crimes. Prior to the 1958 statute on military tribunals, they had jurisdiction over all state crimes committed by civilians, and as such, the military tribunals were an important part of the terror apparatus.

MILITIA. Name used since the February Revolution of 1917 for the police. It is organized by the Ministry of Internal Affairs (MVD) (*q.v.*). According to the 1973 *ukaz* of the USSR Supreme Soviet, the militia is subject to the local Soviet. The militia chief has to confer with the local Soviet when enrolling recruits. The militia's main spheres of work are crime investigation and prevention, maintaining public order, exposure of "social parasites," enforcing the internal passport system, traffic control, and the licensing of the possession of firearms, photocopiers, and printing equipment.

MILOSLAVSKY. Family of boyars, powerful in the 17th century after Maria Miloslavsky had married Tsar Alexis (*q.v.*).

MILYUTIN, COUNT DMITRY ALEKSEYEVICH (1816–1912). Minister of war. He is remembered for having introduced universal military service (*q.v.*) in 1874 and for having reorganized the administration of the army.

MILYUTIN, NICHOLAS ALEKSEYEVICH (1818–72). Deputy minister of the interior. Milyutin played a prominent part in the Great Reforms, notably in preparations for the emancipation of the serfs. He was then made state secretary in Poland.

MININ, KUZMA (?–1616). A butcher from Nizhny Novgorod, he organized Prince Pozhaysk's army, which removed the Poles from Muscovy during the Time of Troubles (*q.v.*).

MINISTRIES. First established in 1804 as a replacement of Peter the Great's "Colleges," they constitute governmental departments in the USSR and in the union and autonomous republics. The first category of ministry exists on the all-union level, the second on the republic level, and the third on both. The second and third categories have been accorded greater importance since Stalin's death.

MINKUS, ALOISIUS LUDWIG (1827–90). Violinist and composer. In 1861–72 he was a soloist at the Moscow Conservatory, and in 1866–72, a professor there. He also composed ballet music, including music for *The Golden Fish* (1867) and *Don Quixote* (1869).

MINSK. Capital of the Belorussian Republic and of the Minsk oblast. Originally part of the Polotsk principality, it became capital of the Minsk principality in 1101. It became Lithuanian in 1326, and Russian in 1793. Occupied by the Germans in 1918 and 1941–44, and by the Poles in 1920, it suffered extensive damages during the Second World War. It is now an important center of food production, engineering, and transportation. Population (1981) 1.3 million.

MIR. Name of village communities before 1917. The *mir* was a form of peasant self-government, in charge of collecting taxes and distributing the land. The Slavophiles and populists wished to perpetuate the tradition, but it impeded agricultural progress and was abandoned.

Blum, Jerome, *Lord and Peasant in Russia from the Ninth to the Nineteenth Centuries*, 1961.

MIR ISKUSSTVA (World of Art). Movement in Russian art at the turn of this century. It took its name from the periodical founded by Diaghilev, which appeared from 1898 to 1904 and which published articles on modern W European painting. At the same time, it also evaluated traditional Russian art. Diametrically opposed to the utilitarian idea that art should serve a socially useful function, the society advocated art for art's sake. It also organized several exhibitions to which the leading Russian artists of the day sent their work. Following the events of 1917, many of the *Mir Iskusstva* group emigrated. Among their number were Leon Bakst, Alexander Benois, Mstislav Dobuzhinsky, Michael Larionov, and Nicholas Roerich (*q.q.v.*). Some of them helped with Diaghilev's ballet company.

MIRNY, PANAS (1849–1920). Pseudonym of Afanasy Yakovlevich Rudchenko. Ukrainian writer and considered to be the father of Ukrainian Realism in literature. Born in Mirgorod, he wrote mostly about life in the Ukraine between the Great Reforms of the 1860s and the 1905 Revolution. He had considerable influence on later Ukrainian writers.

MIRONOV, ALEKSEY FEDOROVICH (1745–1808). Architect. Having studied under Fedor Argunov and E. S. Nazarova from 1770 to 1792, he worked in Kuskov, where he built the open theater, and in 1792–98 he assisted with the building of the palace of Ostankin and then with the building of Strannoprinimy house in Moscow.

MIROVICH, VASILY YAKOVLEVICH (1740–64). A member of the guards, Mirovich plotted, with Ushakov, to rescue Ivan VI, seize the fortress of St. Peter and St. Paul, and imprison Catherine the Great (*q.v.*) and Paul. In 1764 Mirovich entered the fortress of Schlüsselburg, but the jailers killed Ivan, who was then secretly buried. Mirovich was executed.

MNISZEK, MARINA. She was engaged to False Dmitry (*q.v.*) in 1604, but her marriage was to be deferred until Dmitry had ascended the throne. After his death, she left Moscow but met the new pretender and eventually married him.

MOCHALOV, PAUL STEPANOVICH (1800–48). Actor at the Maly Theater in Moscow. After studying acting with his father, also an actor, in 1817 Mochalov was accepted by the Imperial Theater (in 1824 renamed the Maly Theater). His most celebrated roles include Chatsky in Griboyedov's *Woe from Wit,* Don Carlos, Ferdinand, and Karl Moor from Schiller, and Coriolanus, Hamlet, King Lear, Othello, Richard III, and Romeo from Shakespeare. His acting was greatly admired by Vissarion Belinsky, Nicholas Gogol, Michael Lermontov, and Ivan Turgenev (*q.q.v.*) . Konstantin Stanislavsky (*q.v.*) was later to consider Mochalov one of the geniuses of world theater.

MOGILA, PETER (*c.* 1596–1647). An Orthodox priest, he was metropolitan of Kiev from 1632. The Synod of Jerusalem in 1672 accepted his *Catechisms* and *Confession of Faith.*

MOGILEV. Town in Belorussia in central W USSR situated on the

Dnepr River. The town was established at the end of the 13th century and was part of Lithuania. It passed to Poland, Sweden, and then to Russia in 1772. Industries include the manufacture of machinery, rayon, clothing, and leather. Population (1981) 308,000.

MOGUCHAYA KUCHKA. Russian for The Mighty Handful, also known as The Five. It was the name given to a group of composers comprising Mili Balakirev, Borodin, Cesar Cui, Modest Mussorgsky, and Rimsky-Korsakov (*q.q.v.*), who created the national Russian school of music. By drawing on a rich source of Russian folk songs, melodies, and legends they created a romanticized view of Russia's past and to a large extent freed Russian music from the German academic tradition. Mussorgsky produced his famous opera *Boris Godunov*; Borodin wrote *Prince Igor*; and Rimsky-Korsakov wrote *Sadko* and *The Tale of the Town of Kitezh*. The Mighty Handful incurred the hostility of the brothers Anton and Nicholas Rubinstein (*q.q.v.*) who were staunch admirers of Western art and music. Tchaikovsky may be considered to occupy an intermediary position between the Five and the Westerners. The music of this group has become part of the basic musical repertoire of the world. *See* **Glinka, Michael.**

Seroff, Victor I., *The Mighty Five*, 1948.

MOISEYEV, IGOR ALEKSANDROVICH (1906–). Choreographer and founder of the State Folk Dance Ensemble. After graduating from the Choreographic School of the USSR Bolshoi in 1924, from 1924 to 1939 Moiseyev worked as a dancer and choreographer at the Bolshoi Theater. Fascinated by the folk dances of the Soviet republics and wishing to create a national folk ballet, he founded the State Folk Dance Ensemble. The ensemble has toured extensively both abroad and in the Soviet Union, and has won much popularity. Moiseyev's dances include *Three Fat Men* (1935) and *The Snow Storm* (1959).

MOLDAVIA. Principality founded by a group of Vlachs in the first half of the 14th century on the Lower Danube River. In *c.* 1349 Moldavia gained its independence under Prince Bogdan. It resisted Hungary and Poland and expanded to include Bessarabia. The principality was bounded on the W by Transylvania, on the N and NE by the Dnestr River, and on the S by the Black Sea and the regions of Dobruja and Walachia. By the mid-16th century, however, Moldavia had become a tribute-paying vassal-state of the Ottoman Empire. The Turks heavily fortified Moldavia, but in the 18th century Russian influence in Moldavia grew stronger. In 1774 Moldavia was placed under Russia's protection, although it still acknowledged Turkish suzerainty. In 1859 Moldavia united with Cuza to form the state of Rumania, and in 1924 the Soviet Union created the Moldavian Autonomous Soviet Socialist Republic.

MOLDAVIAN SOVIET SOCIALIST REPUBLIC. Constituent republic bounded on the NE and the S by the Ukraine and on the W by Rumania, across the Prut River. It has an area of 13,000 square miles (33,670 sq km). The chief towns are Kishinev (the capital), Tivaspol, and Beltsy. The region is mainly lowland with a fertile black soil and is drained by the Dnestr River. The main occupation is viticulture, with sturgeon fishing in the S, and agriculture. Population (1981) 4 million.

MOLDAVIANS. A Rumanian people living in the N of Rumania and in the Moldavian Republic of the USSR.

MOLOTOV, VYACHESLAV MIKHAILOVICH (1890–). Party and government official whose real name was Skyrabin. After joining the Bolsheviks in 1906, from 1909 to 1911 Molotov was banished for revolutionary activities to Vologda Guberniya. A contributor to the illegal paper *Zvezda* he became the editorial secretary of *Pravda.* A member of the Russian bureau of the party's central committee, after the Bolshevik seizure of power he held a number of important positions, including head of party organization in the Ukraine (1920–25); second secretary (after Stalin) of the central committee (1921–30); member of the Politburo and the presidium of the executive council; chairman of the council of people's commissars (1930–40); deputy chairman of the state defense committee (1939–49 and 1953–56); and commissar for foreign affairs. Second only to Stalin, Molotov's influence waned after Stalin's death. In 1957, owing to his membership in the "anti-party group," he was expelled from the central committee and its presidium and relegated to the position of ambassador to the Mongolian People's Republic (1957–60). In 1960 he served as the USSR's delegate to the International Atomic Energy Agency.

MOLOTOV-RIBBENTROP PACT. *See* **RUSSO-GERMAN NON-AGGRESSION PACT.**

MONASTERIES. Kiev's Monastery of the Caves and the St. Sergius Trinity Monastery (Troitse-Sergieva Laura) are two of the best-known functioning monasteries.

MONGOL CONQUEST. Having conquered China, Central Asia, Iran, and Transcaucasia in the early 13th century, by 1240 the Mongols had invaded the Slavic principalities. In 1242 they established their headquarters at Sarai on the Lower Volga, and the Golden Horde, Batu Khan's state, set up its suzerainty over the Russian princes. Mongol overlordship resulted in taxes, conscription, and the Mongols demanding the right to confirm in office every ruler of the principalities. Slavic uprisings were suppressed harshly. During this period Rus was almost completely cut off from the West and suffered a time of cultural degeneration. By the 14th century the grip of the Horde over its vassal territories grew less secure, and many of the W and S Russian principalities came under the new power of the Grand Duchy of Lithuania. At the same time, the principality of Moscow consolidated its strength until it was able to challenge the Horde. In 1380, a group of Russian princes under the command of Dimitriy Donskoy *(q.v.)* defeated the Tatars, but Moscow continued to pay tribute to the Tatars for another hundred years. The Mongols left their mark on the Russian language, contributed to the cultural backwardness which was to characterize Russia for centuries, and paved the way for the future Muscovite style of autocracy.

Kochan, Lionel, *The Making of Modern Russia*, 1962.

MONGOLIA. Plateau region in E central Asia and home of the Mongol people. At present, Mongolia is divided into Inner Mongolia (an autonomous region of the People's Republic of China) and Outer Mongolia, now the Mongolian People's Republic. A Mongolian feudal state became extremely powerful in the 13th century and, under Genghis Khan and his successors, the Mongols captured much of Eurasia.

MONOMAKH, VLADIMIR. Great prince of Kiev from 1113 to 1125, and author of the *Testament* recounting his life, including his wars against nomads and rebellious princes, voyages, and conferences.

Vernadsky, George, V., *Kievan Russia*, 1948.

MONS, ANNA IVANOVA. One-time lover of Peter the Great. According to Prince Kurakin, Peter and his friends spent three days in Anna's house, indulging in debauchery and alcohol, as a result of which many died.

MONTFERRAND, AUGUST AUGUSTOVICH (1786–1858). Russian architect and draftsman. Born in France, Montferrand studied in Paris. After 1816, however, he worked in St. Petersburg. Representative of the late classical period, Montferrand's works include the Lobanov-Rostovsky house, the Round Room in the Winter Palace, and the famous Cathedral of St. Isaac, a neoclassical building, the dome of which is framed in iron.

MORDOVIAN AUTONOMOUS SOVIET SOCIALIST REPUBLIC. Autonomous republic within the Russian Soviet Federated Socialist Republic in the bend of the Volga River ESE of Moscow. It has an area of 10,110 square miles (26,185 sq km). The capital is Saransk, 320 miles (512 km) ESE of Moscow. Mainly agricultural, the chief products of the region are grain, sugar beets and sheep and dairy products. Industries include the manufacture of electrical goods, textiles, furniture, and building materials. Population (1981) 984,000.

MORDVINOV, NICHOLAS SEMYONOVICH (1754–1845). Statesman and economist. Mordvinov aspired to change Russia's backward economy. He wrote several works on manufacturing, tariffs, and banking.

MOROZOV, BORIS I. Tutor of Tsar Alexis (1645–76). His corrupt practices made him extremely unpopular and were the cause of violent riots in Moscow in 1648.

MOROZOV, SAVVA. Serf who founded a ribbon factory in 1797, as a result of which he was able to buy freedom for himself and his family. The Morozov family eventually became the leading industrialists of Russia in the late 19th century.

MOROZOV FAMILY. Family of Old Believers, of serf origin, who became industrial entrepreneurs. Even before the emancipation of 1861, they had amassed considerable wealth from their textile business at Orekhovo-Zuevo and from their potash business. One of the most prominent members of the family, Savva Morozov, was a patron of the arts. He founded the Moscow Art Theater, befriended artists and writers such as Gorky, and collected post-Impressionist works. He also helped finance the Russian Social Democratic Party. The strike at the Morozov textile mill in 1885, organized by the populists, attracted attention to the plight of the working class. Another notable member of the family was Boris Ivanovich Morozov (1590–1662), one-time tutor and favorite of Tsar Alexis, who exercised considerable influence over the tsar's policies.

MOSCOW. Name of oblast of the Russian Soviet Federated Socialist Republic and capital of the USSR, situated on the Moskva River. First mentioned in 1147 in the *Chronicles,* Moscow was capital of a separate principality in the 13th century, of the grand principality of Vladimir in the 14th century, and then of Muscovy. In 1712 Peter the Great transferred the capital to St. Petersburg, but in 1918 Moscow was again made the capital. A commercial center since the Middle Ages, large manufacturing enterprises were established in Moscow in the mid-17th century, and textiles and metalworking from the 1830s. Moscow became the center of the Slavophile and *zemstvo* movements, and a center of the labor movement. The most famous buildings include the Kremlin, the Cathedral of the New Convent of the Virgin, the Intercession Cathedral, the Old Printing House, and the Bolshoi Theater. The center of the railway network, Moscow has three river ports and three passenger airports. Population (1981) 8,200,000 (without suburbs, 8,015,000).

Berton, Kathleen, *Moscow: An Architectural History,* 1977.

MOSCOW ART THEATER. Founded in 1898 by Konstantin Stanislavsky and Vladimir Nemirovich-Danchenko, the Moscow Art Theater achieved worldwide acclaim for its theatrical naturalism. Stanislavsky, who was in charge of stage direction, strove to strip the theater of commercialism and stereotyped mannerisms by concentrating on inner moods and emotions; in this he was influenced by the German Meiningen Company. The original ensemble was composed of amateur actors from the Society of Art and Literature. The theater performed plays by Gorky, Andreyev, Maeterlinck, and Hauptmann, and in particular the works of Chekhov. The theater continued to flourish after the Revolution. It has undertaken several international tours and has influenced theaters all over the world.

MOSCOW UPRISING (June 1648). Rebellion of the common people against the boyars and clergy who had seized common grazing lands, occupied them, and ploughed up the roads leading from the city to the country, thus leaving the people with nowhere to graze animals or cut firewood. The tsar was greatly alarmed, and the uprising sparked off minor rebellions in other cities.

MOSCOW-VOLGA CANAL. Man-made waterway connecting the Upper Volga and the Moscow River. It was built between 1932 and 1937 by forced labor.

MOSKVA (MOSCOW) RIVER. River rising on the W boundary of Moscow region and flowing 310 miles (496 km) E past Moscow and Kolomna to join the Oka River, in the Russian Soviet Federated Socialist Republic. It is linked with the Volga River by the Moscow canal.

MSTISLAV OF TMUTARAKAN (?–1036). Having fought with Yaroslav the Wise *(q.v.)* between 1024 and 1026 for the Russian territories, Mstislav achieved a division of the land, thus gaining Chernigov and Pereyaslavl in addition to Tmutarakan.

MSTISLAV VLADIMIROVICH (?–1540). Son of Vladimir Monomakh and ruler of Kiev from 1125 to 1152.

MTS. A network of Machine Tractor Stations under central direction, set up in 1929 during the "second agrarian revolution."

MUKDEN, BATTLE OF (March 1905). Battle between Russia and Japan. Each side lost over 70,000 men, and the Russian General Aleksey Kuropatkin *(q.v.)* resigned the command, after having been able to retreat only with great difficulty.

MURATOV, PAUL PAVLOVICH. (1871–1947). Essayist. He was prominent in the revival of artistic culture in Russia in the 1890s.

MURAVEV, NIKITA (1796–1843). Guards officer and key figure in the Northern Society *(q.v.)* in Moscow. After studying at Moscow University, in 1813 he embarked on a military career. He was one of the initiators of the Decembrist *(q.v.)* organization Union of Salvation *(q.v.)* in 1816, and he later was one of the leaders of the Northern Society. Muravev wished to replace the existing regime with one that was less autocratic and relied less on serfdom. Although he did not participate in the uprising of December 14, 1925, he was arrested and banished to Siberia.

Mazour, Anatole Grigorevich, *The First Russian Revolution, 1825*, 1937.

MURAVEV-AMURSKY, NICHOLAS NIKOLAYEVICH (1809–81). In 1847–61 Muravev-Amursky was general governor of the E Siberian province, and in 1858 he signed the Aygun agreement with China defining the Russo-Chinese border.

MURAVEV-APOSTOL, SERGEY IVANOVICH (1796–1826). Decembrist *(q.v.)* who unsuccessfully led a military uprising from January 11-15, 1826. He started his military service in 1810 and was a member of one of the first Decembrist groups, the Union of Salvation *(q.v.)*, in 1816 and was one of the three directors of the Southern Society in 1825. He led the Chernigov regimental uprising on December 29, 1825 but was not supported in this by other regiments. He was fatally wounded.

MURMANSK. City on E shore of the Kola Bay in the Russian Soviet Federated Socialist Republic, in extreme NW of the USSR. Port and railway to Leningrad were built in 1915–16. Main industries are shipbuilding, fishing, fish canning, and sawmilling. It is a sheltered port, on an inlet of the Barents Sea and ice-free, exporting timber and apatite. Allied military forces occupied the area in 1918–20. Population (1981) 394,000.

MUROM. Town 180 miles (288 km) E of Moscow, in the Russian Soviet Federated Socialist Republic, situated on the Oka River. First mentioned *c.* 862, it was razed by the Mongols in the 13th century and became part of the grand duchy of Moscow in 1393. Industries include railway engineering, flax spinning, and tanning. Population (1970) 99,000.

MUSCOVY. State from the 14th to the 18th century. The grand princes of Vladimir were the first princes to rule Muscovy. As Moscow became more powerful it took over as capital of the grand principality. Ivan the Great gained extra territory, including the Republic of Novgorod in 1478. By the time of Ivan the Terrible Muscovy had extended its rule over Vyatka, Pskov, Tver, and Ryazan, as well as over the Tatar khanates of Kazan, Astrakhan, and part of Siberia. Under the house of Romanov the rest of Siberia and the Ukraine were incorporated as well. The last tsar of Muscovy was Peter the Great, the first emperor of Russia.

Vernadsky, George V., *The Tsardom of Muscovy,* 1969.

Wilson, Francesca, *Muscovy: Russia Through Foreign Eyes, 1553-1900,* 1970.

MUSCOVY COMPANY. The first important English joint-stock company. Founded in 1553 to discover a NE passage to the Orient, it was chartered in 1555 and granted a Russian trade monopoly, which it lost in 1698. It was dissolved in 1917.

MUSSAVAT. Muslim democratic party in Baku, established in 1911. Mussavat was the main Muslim party in Transcaucasia and in the Azerbaijan Republic. It maintained an uneasy alliance with the Bolsheviks, but this disintegrated in January 1918 and the Mussavat joined the rebellion against Soviet power.

MUSSORGSKY, MODEST PETROVICH. (1839–81). Composer. An officer in the Preobrazhensky guards regiment, he resigned as a result of his alcohol problem, and worked as a government clerk. He joined Balakirev's *(q.v.)* circle in 1857. In 1874 he composed *Pictures at an Exhibition,* the first great work for solo piano in Russia. The same year, his opera *Boris Godunov* (1870), which is probably his best-known work, was given its first performance. *See* **Moguchaya Kuchka.**

Calvocoressi, Michal D., *Mussorgsky,* 1946.

Leyda, Jay and Bertensson, S., *The Mussorgsky Leader,* 1947.

MUZHI (literally "men"). Kievan upper classes.

MVD (Ministry of Internal Affairs). Ministry that controls the ordinary police (militia). From 1853 to 1854, the MVD was also in charge of security at home and intelligence work abroad. *See* **Secret Police.**

MYASKOVSKY, NICHOLAS YAKOVLEVICH (1881–1950). Polish-born Russian composer and teacher. Myaskovsky studied under Glière, Lyadov, and Rimsky-Korsakov (*q.v.*) before serving in the front as a military engineer (1914–18). In 1921 he was appointed professor at Moscow Conservatory. A prolific symphony writer, he was considered to be the foremost teacher of composition in Russia. Myaskovsky's works include 27 symphonies, 2 cantatas, 13 string quartets, songs, orchestral works, and piano pieces.

MYTISHCHI. Town 14 miles (22 km) NNE of Moscow. Industries include textiles and the town manufactures railway rolling stock. Population (1977) 136,000.

N

NABEREZHNYE-CHELNY. Town situated 10 miles (16 km) ESE of Yelabuga on the Kama River in the Tatar Autonomous Soviet Socialist Republic of the Russian Soviet Federated Socialist Republic. It is a grain trading and distribution center. Industries include flour milling, sawmilling, metalworking, the manufacture of bricks, railway cars and railroad ties, and the production of wine. Population (1981) 346,000.

NABOKOV, VLADIMIR VLADIMIROVICH (1899–1977). Novelist. Born in St. Petersburg, he went into exile in Europe in 1919. He resided in the United States after 1940 but later moved to Switzerland. He was professor of Russian literature at Cornell University from 1948 to 1958. He translated *Alice in Wonderland* into Russian (1923) and had already made a name for himself with a brilliant series of novels in Russian, *Mashenka, King, Queen, Knave, Invitation to a Beheading,* and others, before publishing his first English novels, *The Real Life of Sebastian Knight* (1938) and *Bend Sinister* (1947). *Lolita* (1955), his most famous work, is a story of the infatuation of a middle-aged intellectual for a 12-year-old girl. He also translated Pushkin's *Eugene Onegin* (1964) with commentary, in 14 volumes. Subsequent novels included *Pale Fire* (1962) and *Ada* (1969). He also published many scientific papers on entomology.

Dembo, L. S., *Nabokov: The Man and his Work,* 1968.

Field, Andrew, *Nabokov: His Life in Art,* 1967.

Nabokov, V., *Speak, Memory,* 1967.

NACHMAN OF BRATSLAV (1772–1811). Jewish writer and teller of Hassidic tales. In 1798 he visited Palestine and then went to live at Bratslav. His disciples published his stories, parables, and aphorisms, which have a fine poetic quality. His own writings, of a more esoteric nature, are unpublished.

Buber, M., *Geschichten des Rabbi Nachman,* 1908.

Horodezky, S. A. (ed.), *Torath R. Nachman mi-Bratzlav,* 1923.

NADEZHDIN, NICHOLAS IVANOVICH (1804–56). Editor and critic. He directed his scathing critical attacks against Russian Romanticism. In 1831 he founded *Telescope,* a monthly periodical. It was suppressed five years later for printing the famous philosophic letter of Peter Chaadayev *(q.v.).* Nadezhdin was exiled, and he redirected his energies into archaeological activities.

NADSON, SEMYON YAKOVLEVICH (1862–87). Poet. One of the populists (*see* **Populism**), following the tradition of Nicholas Nekrasov *(q.v.),* but he later became a pessimist. His technique, never of a very high quality, detracts from the poignancy and sincerity of his work.

NAGORNO-KARABAKH AUTONOMOUS REGION. From the 18th century it formed a separate khanate, but was established as an autonomous region in 1923 and is part of the Azerbaijan Soviet Socialist Republic. It has an area of 1,700 square miles (4,403 sq km). The capital is Stepanakert, situated 165 miles (264 km) WSW of Baku. Chief industries are silk, wine, dairying, and building materials. Agriculture includes cotton, grapes, and winter wheat, with 118,608 acres (48,000 hectares) under crops. Population (1981) 164,000.

NAKHICHEVAN. Capital of the Nakhichevan Autonomous Soviet Socialist Republic, situated 80 miles (128 km) SE of Yerevan near the Aras River. Industries include cotton ginning, wine making, and food processing; manufactures include metal goods, furniture, clothing, and building materials. The ancient city was ruled in turn by Persians, Arabs, Mongols, Turks, and Armenians. Population (1973) 35,000.

NAKHICHEVAN AUTONOMOUS SOVIET SOCIALIST REPUBLIC. Part of the Azerbaijan Soviet Socialist Republic situated on the borders of Turkey and Iran near the SW slopes of the Zangezur mountains. It has an area of 2,120 square miles (5,490 sq km). It was annexed by Russia (1828) and constituted as an autonomous republic in 1924. The capital is Nakhichevan, situated approximatley 80 miles (128 km) SE of Yerevan. Chief industries are agriculture (mainly cotton and tobacco), silk, clothing, cotton, canning, and meat packing. Fruit and grape growing are also important, and mulberry trees are grown for sericulture. Population (1981) 247,000.

NAKHIMOV, ADMIRAL PAUL STEPANOVICH (1802–55). Naval commander. In 1822–24 he circumnavigated the world. He commanded the Russian navy in the Black Sea during the Crimean War *(q.v.),* and in 1853 he destroyed the Turkish squadron at Sinop, capturing its commander. He was killed during the siege of Sevastopol, which he led after the death of Admiral Vladimir Kornilov *(q.v.).* The Nakhimov Order and Medal were instituted in 1944, and several naval cadet schools are named after him.

NAKHODKA. Port situated 55 miles (88 km) ESE of Vladivostok on the Pacific coast, in the Russian Soviet Federated Socialist Republic. Industries include ship repairing, food processing, fishing, sawmilling, and the manufacture of plywood and matches. Population (1976) 127,000.

NALCHIK. Capital of the Kabardino-Balkar Autonomous Soviet Socialist Republic, situated 105 miles (168 km) W of Grozny, in the Russian Soviet Federated Socialist Republic. It was founded in 1818 as a fort and has developed since the October Revolution as a vacation and health resort. Industries include meat packing, flour milling, and the manufacture of oil-field equipment, textiles, footwear, and furniture. Population (1977) 199,000.

NAMANGAN. Town situated 120 miles (192 km) E of Tashkent in the Fergana valley of Uzbekistan. It was captured by the Russians in 1875. Manufactures include cotton and food products. Namangan trades in livestock and fruit. Population (1981) 241,000.

NAMES. Before the October Revolution first names were limited to saints' names. Name days of the saints were celebrated more commonly than birthdays. Other limitations on names were imposed, some relating to social status and occupation. Nowadays no restrictions exist, but during the 1920s it became fashionable to use names of political achievements, ideals, and rulers.

Each person has at least three names: a first name, a patronymic (*q.v.*), and a surname. The patronymic is formed by adding the endings -ovich, -evich, and -orich to the father's first name in the case of a man, or by adding -ovna, -evna, and -inichna or -ichna to the father's name in the case of a woman. In addition, a wide number of diminutive forms of the first name are also used.

According to B. O. Unbegaun, in *Russian Surnames* (1972), the 12 most popular surnames in St. Petersburg in 1910 were: Ivanov, Vasilyev, Petrov, Smirnov, Mikhailov, Fedorov, Sokolov, Yakovlev, Popov, Andreyev, Alekseyev, and Aleksandrov.

NAMESTNICHESTVO. Large administrative unit in medieval Russia.

NAMESTNIK. Administrator of a *namestnichestvo,* usually a high-born nobleman appointed by the tsar.

NAPHTHA. Name originally applied to the more volatile types of petroleum that came from the ground in the Baku district of the USSR and Iran.

NAPIER, ADMIRAL SIR CHARLES (1786–1860). British admiral. After a career in many parts of the world, he was made commander in chief of the Baltic fleet. He refused to attack Kronstadt because of insufficient firepower and was recalled. He was not offered another command.

NAREZHNY, VASILY TROFIMOVICH (1780–1825). Novelist. Many of his narratives are indictments of serfdom, provincial gentry, and the Russian administration in the Caucasus, and he is an important predecessor of Gogol (*q.v.*). *The Russian Gil Blas* (1814) is his best-known publication. Other works include *Bursak* (1824) and *Dva Ivana* (1825).

NARODNAYA VOLYA (People's Freedom or **Will).** Revolutionary organization which came into being after the split of the Zemlya i Volya organization in 1879. It believed in the seizure of power, and in practice concentrated on the killing of high government officials. It was responsible for the assassination of Alexander II (1881). Led by Alexander Ulyanov, Lenin's older brother, the St. Petersburg group attempted the assassination of Alexander III. Although some members later joined the Social Democrats and became Bolsheviks, by 1902 a large proportion had become members of the Socialist Revolutionary Party.

Footman, David, *Red Prelude: A. I. Zhelyabov,* 1968.

Venturi, Franco, *Roots of Revolution,* 1960.

NARVA. Estonian city and port situated on the Narva River 8 miles (13 km) from the Gulf of Finland. It was founded by the Danes in 1223. Possession was contested between Sweden and Russia and in 1704 Peter the Great captured it. It remained Russian until 1919 when it was incorporated into independent Estonia. In 1945 it again became Russian territory. It has an important textile industry, the power for which is produced from the falls of the Narva River. Population (1976) 71,000.

NARYN RIVER. River rising in the Tien Shan mountains with the main stream flowing from the Petrov glacier. It flows 449 miles (718 km) W through fertile wheatlands past Naryn, then N and W through the Ketmen-Tyube valley to Toktogul, then SW into the Fergana valley, and enters the Uzbek Soviet Socialist Republic to join the Kara Darya River near Balykchi. Together, the Naryn and Kara Darya rivers form the Syr-Darya River. It is used for irrigation. The main tributaries are the Lesser Naryn, Son-Kul, and Kokomeren rivers.

NARYSHKIN. Baroque style which became very popular in the last part of the 17th century in Muscovy. The name Naryshkin came from Peter the Great's maternal relations who, together with Prince Galitsyn, were interested in Western styles.

NARYSHKIN, LEV (*fl.* late 17th century). Brother of Natalya Naryshkin, the second wife of Tsar Alexis and mother of Peter the Great.

NARYSHKIN, NATALYA KIRILLOVNA (1651–94). Second wife of Tsar Alexis and mother of Peter the Great.

NATANSON, MARK ANDREYEVICH (1850–1919). Revolutionary who also used the pseudonym Bobrov. He was a leader, together with his sister, Olga, and Sophia Perovskaya, of the Narodnaya Volya (*q.v.*) movement, which advocated terrorism as a means of achieving social change.

NATIONAL ANTHEM. "Soyuz nerushimy respublik svobodnykh" (Indestructible Union of Free Republics). The words are by Sergey Mikhalkov and G. El-Registan, and the music is by Alexander Vassilyevich Alexandrov. It first came into general use in 1944 and was revised in 1977.

NATIONAL BOLSHEVIKS. A political movement of the years following 1917. Although National Bolshevik supporters were not communists, they nevertheless regarded the Bolsheviks as the party best qualified to govern Russia. During the 1920s they founded the "Change of Landmarks Movement," which flourished during the Second World War. Prominent among the National Bolsheviks were A. N. Tolstoy, General Aleksey Alekseyevich Brusilov, and B. D. Grekov.

NATIONAL DEMOCRATIC PARTIES. Parties in Georgia and Belorussia. In the 1920s, in spite of being suppressed as an organized party, the Belorussian National Democrats were influential and assisted the Bolsheviks to implement "Belorussianization." The majority of the two parties' members were purged in 1933.

NATIONALITIES. The most numerous nationalities in the USSR at the 1979 census were: Russians (137 million), Ukrainians (42 million), Uzbeks (12.5 million), Belorussians (9.4 million), Kazakhs (6.5 million), Tatars (6.3 million), Azerbaijanins (5.4 million), Armenians (4.1 million), Georgians (3.6 million), Moldavians (3 million), Tadzhiks (2.9 million), Lithuanians (2.8 million), Turkmenians (2 million), Germans (1.9 million), Kirgiz (1.9 million), Jews (1.8 million), Chuvash (1.8 million), Latvians (1.4 million), Bashkirs (1.4 million), Mordovians (1.2 million), Poles (1.2 million), and Estonians (1 million). The great majority (in each case 84–99 percent) indicated the language of their nationality as their native tongue; exceptions were the Bashkirs (66 percent), Poles (33 percent), and Jews (17.7 percent).

Hooson, David J. M., *The Soviet Union: People and Regions*, 1966.

Katz, Zev, *Handbook of Major Soviet Nationalities*, 1975.

NAVAL ACADEMY. Established in St. Petersburg in 1715 for 300 pupils, it was one of several similar establishments founded by Peter the Great in an attempt to educate his people. The first All-Russian Congress of Soviets of Workers' and Soldiers' Deputies met at the academy from June 16 to July 7, 1917.

NAYDENOV (1869–1922). Pseudonym of Alexeyev, Sergey Aleksandrovich. Playwright, regarded as Alexander Ostrovsky's (*q.v.*) successor. Naydenov's play *Deti Vanyushina* (1901) reflects his interest in the conflict between generations.

NEBIT-DAG. Town situated 80 miles (128 km) ESE of Krasnovodsk in the Turkmen Soviet Socialist Republic, on the Trans-Caspian railway. It is an oil-refining center serving the Vyshka oil field. Population (1976) 65,000.

NECHAYEV, SERGEY GERRADIYEVICH (1847–82). Revolutionary. After the failure of the Narodniki (*see* **Narodnaya Volya**) to incite the peasants to rebel, Nechayev became a ruthless advocator of terrorism in order to obtain the reforms he felt necessary for Russia. He established a secret "Society of the Axe" in the late 1860s and wished to create a professional revolutionary cadre linked with a conspiratorial organization that would cover all Europe. Having won the approval of Michael Bakunin and Nicholas Ogarev *(q.q.v.)*, he set up groups of "revolutionary fives," all unknown to each other. In order to obtain absolute obedience, Nechayev deliberately involved his fellow revolutionaries in a common crime. His theories on revolution are outlined in his *Revolutionary Catechism*. He was imprisoned and spent 10 years in a dungeon. A legendary figure, he had considerable influence on his contemporaries and was Dostoyevksy's model for Peter Verkhovensky in *The Possessed*.

NEIZVESTNY, ERNST (1925–). Artist and sculptor. After studying at the V. I. Surikov State Institute of Arts, Neizvestny served in the Soviet army in 1942–45 and then worked as a sculptor at the studios of the USSR Agricultural Exhibition. He became an influential figure among unorthodox Soviet artists. A member of the Artists' Union of the USSR from 1953 to 1954 and from 1955 to 1957, in 1976 he was granted an exit visa to emigrate to Israel. His main works include *Mother* and *Great Mistakes*.

NEKRASOV, NICHOLAS ALEKSEYEVICH (1821–77). Poet. Much of his work was satire, and he wrote mainly of the misery of poor people. He owned and edited the radical journal *Sovremennik* (The Contemporary), in which Turgenev and Tolstoy were published. This became a mouthpiece for the radical intelligentsia and was suppressed in 1866. In 1868 Nekrasov took over editorship of the journal *Annals of the Fatherland*. He identified with the people, and many of his nonsatirical poems show how completely he had absorbed the spirit of folk songs. His poems include *Who Lives Well in Russia?*, *The Railway*, and *Peasant Children*, and *Russian Women*. Interest in his work has revived in Soviet Russia. *See* **Drozhzhin, Spiridon.**

NEKRASOV, VIKTOR PLATONOVICH (1911–). Writer. From 1944 he was a member of the CPSS. After studying architecture and drama, Nekrasov served in the war of 1941–45. He was awarded a Stalin Prize for his short story *In the Trenches of Stalingrad* (1940) in 1947.

NELEDINSKY-MELETSKY, YURY ALEKSANDROVICH (1752–1828). Poet. He wrote sentimental light verse, and cleverly stylized imitations of folk songs, some of which were very popular.

NELIDOVA, BARBARA. Mistress of Tsar Nicholas I with whom he had several children.

NEMAN RIVER. River rising 30 miles (48 km) SSW of Minsk in the Belorussian Soviet Socialist Republic and flowing 597 miles (955 km) W to Grodno, then N into the Lithuanian Soviet Socialist Republic past Neman and Sovetsk to enter the Courland

Lagoon. Main tributaries are the Viliya, Nevezys, Dubysa, Shchara, and Sheshupe rivers. It is used for logging. In 1807 Alexander I met Napoleon on a raft in the middle of the river. The meeting resulted in the Treaty of Tilsit *(q.v.)*.

NEMETS (literally "a German"). A foreigner and in the narrow sense it means any W European.

NEMETSKAYA SLOBODA. NE district of Moscow, established in the period following the Time of Troubles, and known as the "German suburb." At this time there was a considerable increase in the number of foreigners in Russia, and Tsar Alexis made over the area for their use. The word "German" denoted all Europeans.

NEMIROVICH-DANCHENKO, VASILY IVANOVICH (1848–1936). Author and journalist. He wrote prolifically, producing a vast number of narratives and novels directed at the general reader. Although superficial, his works are versatile and entertaining. They include *Personal Reminiscences of General Skobeleff* (1884), *The Princes of the Stock Exchange* (1914), and *Peasant Tales of Russia* (1917).

NEMIROVICH-DANCHENKO, VLADIMIR IVANOVICH (1858–1943). Cofounder, with Stanislavsky *(q.v.)*, of the Moscow Art Theater (1898) and a famous producer. Together with Stanislavsky, Nemirovich-Danchenko played a decisive role in the development of prerevolutionary and Soviet theater. He also instigated the Moscow Art Theater *(q.v.)* school, later named after him. He wrote *My Life in the Russian Theatre* (1937).

NENETS. *See* **Samoyeds.**

NENETS NATIONAL AREA. Area of the Russian Soviet Federated Socialist Republic situated in the N of the Arkhangelsk region. The principal occupations are reindeer breeding and fishing. The capital is Naryan-Mar, situated 400 miles (640 km) NE of Arkhangelsk. Population (1970) 39,000.

NEOPOPULISM. A development of liberal populism promoted in the 1920s by N. D. Kondratev and A. N. Chelinsev. Since neopopulism maintained that Marxist theory was not relevant to the peasant economy, and that individual peasant farming should be encouraged, it met with official disfavor, and its leaders were imprisoned.

NEP. *See* **New Economic Policy.**

NERCHINSK, TREATY OF (1689). A political and commercial agreement between Russia and China that also established boundaries between the two countries. The agreement gave Russia Transbaikalia (E of Lake Baikal) and gave China the Amur valley, and it permitted Russian trade caravans to enter Peking. The agreement was enlarged in 1727 and remained the basis of Russo-Chinese relations until the mid-19th century.

NERONOV, IVAN (1591–1670). The first of the archpriests of 17th-century Russia. He was one of the leaders of the religious and moral revival in the Orthodox Church, championing its traditions of piety, poverty, and prophecy. In 1653 he started to oppose Patriarch Nikon's *(q.v.)* reforms and, although reprimanded, he attracted support from other priests including Avvakum *(q.v.)*. He was exiled in 1654 and rejected the authority of the church council and Nikon, thus paving the way for the Old Believers *(q.v.)*.

NESSELRODE, COUNT KARL ROBERT (1780–1862). Statesman and foreign minister. He was a Protestant and was educated in Germany. For a period he was naval aide-de-camp to Paul I but soon chose to enter the diplomatic service instead. His friendship with Metternich resulted in Nesselrode's favoring Russo-Austrian cooperation and Metternich's anti-revolutionary policies. As diplomatic secretary to the Russian generals during the 1806–07 war against France, he subsequently served as an intermediary between Talleyrand and Alexander in Paris. He unsuccessfully implored Alexander to negotiate with Napoleon rather than fight, but went with the Russian army to Paris and signed the treaty of Chaumont in 1814. Appointed director of the college of foreign affairs in 1816, he frequently disagreed with Count Ioannis Kapodistrias *(q.v.)*. It was Nesselrode, however, who accompanied Alexander to the congresses of Aix-la-Chapelle, Troppau, Laibach, and Vienna.

NESTOR (1056–1113). Russian chronicler and hagiographer. In *c.* 1074 he was received as a monk into the Monastery of the Caves of Kiev. His works include the lives of Saints Boris and Gleb, the life of St. Theodosius, and of the sons of St. Vladimir, while *The Tale of Bygone years (The Russian Primary Chronicle)* (trans. 1930) has been ascribed to him since the 13th century. It is now thought that this is a composite work, with only a basic version being ascribed to Nestor.

NESTOR CHRONICLE. History of Slavic and Russian events from 1040 to 1110, credited to a Kiev monk, Nestor, the biographer of Theodosius.

Vernadsky, George V. (ed.), *A Source Book for Russian History from Earliest Times to 1917*, 1972.

NESTOROV, MICHAEL VASILYEVICH (1862–1942). Painter. He studied at the Moscow School of Art and at the Academy of Arts. Nestorov's style of painting tended toward sentimental realism and he was one of the *Peredvizhniki* (*see* **The Wanderers**). A religious painter, his favorite subjects are figures of monks, holy old men, and young saints, conveying the unworldly nature of Russian medieval Christianity. He was a recipient of the Stalin Prize.

NEVA RIVER. River issuing from Lake Ladoga and flowing 46 miles (74 km) W to enter the Gulf of Finland by a delta at Leningrad. In 1240 Alexander Nevsky conquered the Swedes on the banks of the Neva. Main tributaries are the Mga, Tosna, and Izhora rivers. It is connected by canals with the Volga River and the White Sea.

NEVEROV, ALEXANDER (1886–1923). Author and teacher. His most famous book was *Tashkent gorod khlebny* (1921). *Tashkent Gusilebedi,* his most ambitious novel, was incomplete at his death. His works deal with the impact of the Revolution on his own village.

Fatov, N. N., *Alexander Sergeyevich Neverov,* 1926.

NEVSKY, ALEXANDER. *See* **Alexander Nevsky.**

NEVSKY, DANIEL ALEKSANDROVICH (?–1303). Ruler of Moscow in the latter half of the 13th century.

Vernadsky, George V., *Russia at the Dawn of the Modern Age,* 1959.

NEW ECONOMIC POLICY. Economic policy practiced by the government in 1921–28, replacing the policies of War Communism (1918–21) (*q.v.*). It aimed at revitalizing the economy by allowing greater freedom in agriculture, industry, and trade. In this, the government was successful and raised the national income above that of 1913. The NEP was followed by the first Five-Year Plan (*q.v.*).

Carr, Edward Hallett, *Foundations of a Planned Economy,* 1971.

Dobb, Maurice H., *Soviet Economic Development Since 1917,* 6th ed., 1966.

Nove, Alec, *An Economic History of the USSR,* 1969.

Zaleksi, Eugene, *Planning for Economic Growth in the Soviet Union, 1918–1932,* trans. 1971.

NEW RUSSIA. An expression, now obsolete, for the steppe area N of the Black Sea and the Sea of Azov. This area was mostly taken from the Turks in the 18th and early 19th centuries.

NEW SERBIA. An area of Russia W of the Dnepr River settled by Serbian colonists in the 18th century.

NEW SIBERIAN ISLANDS. An archipelago in the Arctic Ocean situated between the Laptev Sea and the E Siberian Sea. They were discovered in 1773 by Ivan Lyakhov, a Russian merchant. The total area is 11,000 square miles (28,500 sq km). The islands are uninhabited, the three largest being Kotelny, Fadeyev, and New Siberia.

NEWSPAPERS. In 1980, 8,088 newspapers with a total circulation of 176 million copies, were published in 57 languages in the USSR.

NEYELOV, VASILY IVANOVICH (1722–82). Architect of the early classical period. One of the first to create landscaped gardens in 1744, Neyelov began work at Tsarskoe Selo. He also assisted in planning the Yekaterinsky park.

NEZHIN. Ukrainian town and center of Nezhinsky region of the Chernigovsky oblast. Nezhin is situated on the Ostyov River. From 1649 to 1782 the largest Cossack regiment was stationed here. In the 18th century, Nezhin was an important trading center for S Russia. Industries include machinery, chemicals, building materials, and whaling equipment. Population (1973) 68,000.

NICHOLAS I (1796–1855). Tsar of Russia from 1825. The commander of a brigade of the guard and inspector general of the engineering branch, Nicholas came to the throne in 1825 following the assassination of his brother Alexander I (*q.v.*). Nicholas began his reign by suppressing the Decembrist movement (*see* **Decembrists**). Aware of his country's need for reform, he appointed a committee to investigate the state of the country, and the codification of existing laws was undertaken. Alarmed by the revolutionary movement sweeping W Europe in 1830, Nicholas became increasingly dictatorial; his motto was "autocracy, orthodoxy, and nationality." Accordingly, discipline in the army, civil service, and universities was tightened, travel abroad restricted, and the dreaded Third Section (secret police) was established. He did, however, improve the lot of the serf and encourage the development of industry. The "iron tsar" suppressed the Polish rising of 1830–31 with great cruelty and in 1849 assisted the emperor of Austria to quell the Hungarian revolt. Eager to support Turkey's Christian subjects against the sultan, Nicholas's policies led to the Crimean War, during which he died.

Grunwald, Constantine, *Tsar Nicholas I,* 1954.

Lincoln, W. B., *Nicholas I,* 1978.

NICHOLAS II (1868–1918). Last tsar of Russia and the eldest son of Alexander III. He ascended the throne in 1894 and declared in his accession speech to the Tver Zemstvo that he intended to preserve the autocracy. In 1905, however, he granted a constitution providing for the establishment of a legislative assembly *(duma)* (*q.v.*), following the humiliating defeat of Russia in the war with Japan (1904–05). After the outbreak of the First World War, Nicholas acted as commander in chief of the armed forces. His wife Tsaritsa Alexandra (*q.v.*) had come under the influence of Rasputin (*q.v.*) and she in turn influenced the tsar. This lost Nicholas the support of the aristocracy, his rational allies. He abdicated at the beginning of the February Revolution. He was later banished to Siberia and was shot by the Cheka on Lenin's orders, together with his family.

Alexandrov, Victor, *The End of the Romanovs,* 1966.

Bing, E. J. (ed.), *The Secret Letters of the Last Tsar,* 1938.

Charques, Richard D., *Twilight of Imperial Russia: The Reign of Tsar Nicholas II,* 1965.

Frankland, Noble, *Imperial Tragedy,* 1961.

Massie, R. K., *Nicholas and Alexandra,* 1969.

Vulliamy, C. E. (ed.), *The Letters of the Tsar to the Tsaritsa,* 1929.

NICHOLAS, GRAND DUKE (1831–91). Son of Tsar Nicholas I. He was a statesman and commander in chief in the field toward the end of the Russo-Turkish war of 1872. In 1846 he began his military career serving as an officer in the cavalry. He was general inspector for engineering from 1852; from 1864 he was general inspector of the cavalry, and from 1855 a member of the state Soviet. Nicholas served in the Crimean War. In 1876, in spite of his manifest unsuitability for the post, Nicholas was appointed commander in chief of the Russian army in the Balkans. It is felt that Russia's victory in the Russo-Turkish war of 1877–78 was achieved in spite of rather than as a result of Nicholas's leadership. In 1880, he was appointed director of the military district of St. Petersburg.

NICHOLAS, GRAND DUKE (1843-65). Son and heir of Alexander II and brother of Alexander III. It was hoped that Nicholas would prove to be an enlightened and wise monarch. However, he contracted meningitis at his betrothal to the Danish Princess Dagmar (Maria Fedorovna) *(q.v.)* and died.

NICHOLAS, GRAND DUKE (1856–1929). Son of Grand Duke Nicholas and grandson of Tsar Nicholas I. He was a grand duke and army officer. Commissioned in 1872, he introduced major military reforms while serving in the Russo-Turkish war of 1877–78 and as inspector general of the cavalry (1895–1905). In 1905 he was appointed commander of the military district of St. Petersburg and first president of the imperial committee for national defense. He was commander in chief at the beginning of the First World War and then was sent to the Caucasus as viceroy of Nicholas II. He remained there until 1917. He was then reappointed commander in chief by the tsar, but Prince Georgy Lvov (*q.v.*), head of the provisional government, cancelled the appointment. Nicholas then settled in France.

NICHOLAS, SAINT (?– *c.* 350). Bishop of Myra in Lycia and patron saint of Russia, Greece, Sicily, children, scholars, merchants, and travelers. His feast day is December 6. He is also associated with Christmas as Santa Claus (Klaus). Little is known of his life, but tradition holds that he was imprisoned under Diocletian and later released. In 1087 his bones were brought from Myra (modern Dembre in Turkey), and they now rest in the crypt of the Basilica of S. Nicola, Bari. They reputedly exude a pure water as a testimony to his sanctity and power with God.

NIEMAN. *See* **Neman River.**

NIHILISM. Radical intellectual movement of the 1860s. Nihilism grew up largely as a result of the rejection of the historical and aesthetic idealism of the 1830s and 1840s. Nihilism represented a revolt against the established social order and it negated the authority of the state, family, and church. Social sciences and classical philosophical systems were rejected. In place of these structures and values were scientific materialism and positivism. The existence of the soul and the spiritual world was denied utterly. Nihilist thinkers had been influenced by Feuerbach, Darwin, Buckle, and Henry Spenser. The concept of nihilism was popularized by Ivan Turgenev (*q.v.*) in his famous novel *Fathers and Children* (1862), with its depiction of Bazarov, the nihilist. The liberal Chernyshevsky in his novel *Chto Delat* (What Is To Be Done?) concentrated on the positive aspects of nihilism, while the anarchist Kropotkin viewed it as the revolt of an adolescent generation struggling against tyranny.

Hingley, Ronald, *Nihilists: Russian*

Radicals and Revolutionaries in the Reign of Alexander II, 1855–81, 1967.

NIJINSKA, BRONISLAVA (1891–1972). Dancer, choreographer, and teacher and sister of Vaslav Nijinsky. She studied at the Imperial Theater School, in St. Petersburg, and appeared with Nijinsky in the first season of the Ballets Russes. She enjoyed the distinction of being the first woman choreographer and was called "La Nijinska" by Diaghilev. The most important ballets in her varied and brilliant career were *Les Noces* (1923), *Les Comediens Jaloux* (1932), and *Pictures from an Exhibition* (1944). Her work as a teacher has been of the greatest significance.

NIJINSKY, VASLAV (1890–1950). Ballet dancer and choreographer. He trained at the Imperial Ballet School, in St. Petersburg, from 1900. His performance in *Le Pavilion d'Armide* by Fokine in 1907 attracted attention and from 1909 he was the leading dancer in Diaghilev's Ballets Russes in Paris, where he enjoyed enormous popularity, especially in *Le Spectre de la Rose* and *Petrushka.* Relationships with Diaghilev *(q.v.)* were not easy, mainly due to Nijinsky's mental instability. Finally, he refused to dance and was dismissed, and this point marked a deterioration in his mental state. Only 10 years after his debut he gave his last performance, and he spent the rest of his life in a mental home. His unique powers of dancing earned him the title of *le dieu de la danse,* and he is remembered as one of the greatest male dancers.

Beaumont, C. W., *Vaslav Nijinsky,* 2nd ed., 1943.

Buckle, Richard, *Nijinsky,* 1971.

Reiss, F., *Nijinsky,* 1960.

NIKANOV, ARCHBISHOP (1826–90). Lay name: Alexander Ivanovich Brokovich. Philosopher and archbishop of Kherson. He opposed L. N. Tolstoy's *(q.v.)* views on the role of church and state and played an important part in leading the polemics against him. Nikanov's three-volume *Positive Philosophy and Supersensual Being* can be seen to anticipate Husserl's phenomenological constructions.

NIKITENKO, A.V. (1804–77). Professor of Russian literature. Born a serf, he rose to become secretary of a district branch of the Bible Society. In 1824, Vasily Zhukovsky *(q.v.)* helped him to buy his freedom. As censor he was lenient and was of liberal views.

Seton-Watson, Hugh, *The Russian Empire 1801–1917,* 1967.

NIKITIN, AFANASY (?–1472). Merchant of the 15th century. He journeyed to India via Derbent, Baku, and Persia in 1466–72 and described his experiences in clear and simple language in his book *Khozhdenie za tri morya* (Journey Beyond the Three Seas). It contained one of the earliest descriptions of India and its people in any European literature.

Nikitin, A., *The Travels of Athanasius Nikitin,* trans. 1857.

NIKITIN, IVAN SAVVICH (1824–61). Poet. His works are full of pessimism and his best-known work is the narrative poem ***Kulak.*** ***See* Drozhzhin, Spiridon.**

NIKITIN, NICHOLAS (1897–1963). Writer who was one of the Serapion Brothers (*q.v.*). After studying at the university, in 1918 Nikitin enlisted in the Red Army, and much of his earlier work such as *Fort Vomit* (1922) and *Stones* (1923), deals with the Civil War. It is felt that his literary talents waned as he tried to conform to the limiting demands of Socialist Realism, as in his novel *Kirik Rudenko's Crime* (1927), and his play *Baku* (1937).

NIKOLAYEV. Ukrainian port situated 16 miles (26 km) N of the Black Sea on the estuary of the Bug and Ingu rivers. It was founded in 1784 and is an important shipbuilding center and naval base. Flour milling is also important and some of the largest grain elevators in Europe are located here. Manufactures include machinery and footwear. Grain, timber, ores, and sugar are exported. Population (1981) 458,000.

NIKON (1605–81). Patriarch of Moscow (1652–66). His reforms created a schism in the Orthodox Church and alienated a section of the clergy and of laymen (the Old Believers) (*q.v.*). These reforms included the standardization of the ritual and the introduction of a new prayer book (1654). He aroused powerful opposition and was condemned by a church council in 1666–67 and deposed and confined to a monastery. His reforms, however, were continued after his fall.

Fedotov, Georgii P., *The Russian Religious Mind,* 2 vols., 1946–66.

Hackel, Sergei A., *The Orthodox Church,* 1971.

NIKOPOL. Ukrainian town situated 65 miles (104 km) SSW of Dnepropetrovsk on the Dnepr River. Located in a rich manganese-mining area, it is a major center of metallurgy and engineering, as well as a source of supply for the Donbas and Dnepropetrovsk steel plants. Population (1976) 143,000.

NIL SORSKY (NILUS OF SORA), ST. (1433–1508). Nil Sorsky, a monk from St. Cyril's monastery on the White Lake, was the leader and spokesman of the non-possessors (*q.v.*), or "elders from beyond the Volga," in their controversy within the Russian Orthodox Church in the late 15th and early 16th centuries. The non-possessors objected to the church's wealth and particularly its landholding. However, in 1503 a church council ruled in favor of the possessors, and some of Nil's followers were declared heretics. Nil Sorsky himself was canonized. *See* **Joseph of Volokolamsk.**

Billington, James H., *The Icon and the Axe,* 1966.

Fedotov, Georgii P., *The Russian Religious Mind,* 2 vols., 1946–66.

NIVKHI. *See* **Gilyaks.**

NIZHNY-NOVGOROD. *See* **Gorky.**

NIZHNY TAGIL. Town situated 80 miles (128 km) NNW of Sverdlovsk near the Tagil River, in the Russian Soviet Federated Socialist Republic. It is an important metallurgical and engineering center, manufacturing railway rolling stock, aircraft, agricultural machinery, machine tools, and chemicals. Population (1981) 404,000.

NKGB. Abbreviation for *Norodny Komitet Gosudarstvennoy Bezopasnosti* (people's commissariat for state security), which was the Soviet security force from 1943 to 1946. It was mainly concerned with "unreliable elements," many of whom were deported or sent to corrective labor camps. In 1946 the NKGB was renamed the MGB and, after the death of Stalin, the KGB. *See* **Secret Police.**

NKVD. Abbreviation for *Norodny Komitet Vnutrennykh Del* (people's commissariat of internal affairs), which was, from 1934 to 1943, the Soviet security service in charge of police and civil registry offices and of the corrective labor camps. It was one of Stalin's main tools during the Great Purge. In 1943 it was divided into two commissariats, the NKVD and the NKGB. *See* **Secret Police.**

Hingley, Ronald, *The Russian Secret Police,* 1970.

Levytsky, B., *The Uses of Terror: The Soviet Secret Service 1917–1970,* 1971.

NOBEL PRIZES. The Nobel Prizes have been awarded since 1901 by three Swedish and one Norwegian fund established under the will of Alfred Nobel. Since the prizes were instituted there have been 115 awards for physics, and Russian and Soviet awards have totaled 7; chemistry, 95 awards (1); physiology and medicine, 126 awards (2); literature, 77 awards (4); peace, 75 (1). Prizewinners include I. P. Pavlov (1904) and E. Metchnikoff (1908). In 1958 the physicists P. A. Cerenkov, I. M. Frank and I. E. Tamm shared the award, in 1962 it was awarded to L. D. Landau, in 1964 to N. G. Basov and A. M. Prokhorov and in 1975 A. D. Sakharov, the physicist, received the award for peace. In the field of the arts, the Nobel Prize was given to the novelist Ivan Bunin in 1933, to M. Sholokhov in 1965 and to Alexander Solzhenitsyn in 1970. In 1958, Boris Pasternak was awarded the Nobel Prize for literature, but did not accept it.

NOBILITY. In Muscovite Russia, the government promoted the interests of the gentry by passing laws that limited the peasants' movements. From 1475 boyar families in state service were entered in a state genealogical book; many squabbles ensued as the boyars fought to maintain their rank. In 1722 Peter the Great *(q.v.)* introduced compulsory state service, and with his Table of Ranks *(q.v.),* advancement was open to all. Titles of nobility were conferred on those who deserved it, regardless of social standing. In 1785, during what is considered the Golden Age of the Nobles, Catherine the Great issued a Charter to the Nobility *(q.v.);* this recognized the gentry of each district and province as a legal body, headed by an elected district or regional marshal of nobility. Members of the gentry were also exempt from tax obligations and personal service. The position of the nobility began to decline considerably under Alexander I and Nicholas I; according to the 1877 census, the nobility owned 73.1 million *desyatin* of land, but by 1911, it owned only 43.2 million *desyatin.*

Dukes, Paul, *Catherine the Great*

and the Russian Nobility: A Study Based on the Materials of the Legislative Commission of 1767, 1967.

NOGATA. A monetary unit in Novgorod and Kiev. One *nogata* equaled 1/20th of a *grivna (q.v.)*.

NOGINSK. Town situated 32 miles (51 km) E of Moscow on the Klyazma River. Manufactures include textiles, chemicals, and metal goods. Population (1976) 111,000.

NOLDE, BARON BORIS E. (1876–1948). Russian-French historian and legal scholar. His works include *L'alliance Franco-russe: Les Origines du système diplomatique d'avant guerre* (1936), *L'ancien régime et la révolution russe* (1929), *La formation de l'empire russe* and (in English) *Russia in the Economic War* (1928).

NON-POSSESSORS. A group in dispute within the Russian Orthodox Church in the late 15th and early 16th centuries. The "possessors," under the leadership of Joseph of Volokolamsk *(q.v.)*, believed that the tsar, being the church's protector, should in turn receive ecclesiastical obedience including the tsar's right to a say in the administration of the church.

The non-possessors, under the leadership of Nil Sorsky *(q.v.)*, came from the monasteries of the NE and, as such, are sometimes called the "elders from beyond the Volga." They objected to the church's wealth, particularly to monastic landholding. They also agreed that the state should not interfere in ecclesiastical affairs.

In 1503 a church council ruled that the church needed its wealth to carry out its work, particularly charitable work.

Fedotov, Georgii P., *The Russian Religious Mind*, 2 vols., 1946–66.

NORILSK. Town situated 50 miles (80 km) ESE of the port of Dudinka, in the Russian Soviet Federated Socialist Republic. It was founded in 1935 and is an important mining center for nickel, copper, platinum, and gold. Population (1981) 184,000.

NOROV, A. S. (1795–1869). Norov succeeded Prince Shirinsky-Shikhmatov *(q.v.)* as minister of education in 1853. He was influenced by Nikitenko *(q.v.)*, the ex-serf, and he made some steps in the move toward educational reform.

NORTHEAST PASSAGE. *See* **Northern Sea Route.**

NORTHERN SEA ROUTE. Shipping route running along the N coast of Europe and Asia. The route was first traversed by a Swedish explorer, and since the late 1960s Soviet icebreakers have kept the shipping lanes open with the aid of aerial observations.

NORTHERN SOCIETY. Group formed in 1822 from the Union of Salvation *(q.v.)* and the later group the Union of Welfare. The theorist of the Northern Society, Nikita Muravev *(q.v.)*, advocated a constitutional monarchy along the lines of the 13 original states of N America, civil liberties, and the emancipation of the serfs, although in general, the Northern Society was less radical than

Pestel's (*q.v.*) Southern Society. The group unsuccessfully plotted a coup during the interregnum between Alexander I and Nicholas I; an uprising was planned to occur when the soldiers would be swearing allegiance to Nicholas I. Morale failed, some defected, and others failed to give the order to rise. Nicholas I dispersed the mutineers by firing at them, many arrests followed, and five, including the poet Kondraty Ryleyev (*q.v.*), were executed.

Mazour, Anatole G., *The First Russian Revolution,* 1825, 1937.

Raeff, Marc, *The Decembrist Movement,* 1966.

NORTHERN UNION OF RUSSIAN WORKERS. Union organized in December 1878 by Stephan N. Khalturin (*q.v.*) in St. Petersburg. It cooperated with the populist movement *Zemlya i Volya (See* **Land and Liberty Organization**), and wished to destroy the existing regime in order to establish a socialist society. The union was suppressed in 1879.

Thaden, E. C., *Russia since 1801: The Making of a New Society,* 1971.

NORTH OSSETIAN AUTONOMOUS SOVIET SOCIALIST REPUBLIC. It has an area of 3,088 square miles (7,980 sq km). Constituted as an autonomous region (1924) and as an autonomous republic (1936), it is part of the Russian Soviet Federated Socialist Republic. The capital is Ordzhonikidze, situated 350 miles (560 km) SE of Rostov. Chief industries include nonferrous metals (mining and metallurgy), maize processing, timber and woodworking, textiles, building materials, distilleries, and food processing. The region also has varied agriculture. Population (1981) 601,000.

NOVAYA ZEMLYA. An Arctic land mass situated between the Barents Sea and the Kara Sea, consisting of two main islands separated by the narrow strait of Matochkin Shar. It is part of the Russian Soviet Federated Socialist Republic. Fishing, sealing, and hunting are the main occupations.

NOVGOROD. Capital of Novgorod region situated 105 miles (168 km) SSE of Leningrad on the Volkov River, in the Russian Soviet Federated Socialist Republic. The city was first recorded in 859. It became an important settlement in the Russian state controlled by Kiev; in 1019 Yaroslav I (*q.v.*) of Kiev gave it a charter of self-government. The medieval prosperity of Novgorod was based on its fur trade and other raw materials from N forests; trade routes covered E Europe from Byzantium to the Baltic territories of the Hanseatic League. The town elected its own prince until 1270; after that the town itself was the sovereign power, as Lord Novgorod the Great. A struggle for supremacy with Moscow from *c.* 1300 ended with the recognition of Moscow's sovereignty in 1478; popular resentment of Moscow continued and was suppressed by massacre and deportation under Ivan IV (the Terrible) (*q.v.*) in 1570. The subsequent decline of Novgorod accelerated under Peter the Great (1682–1725). Industries today include sawmilling, brewing, flour milling, and the manufacture of footwear and clothing.

Buildings of special interest include the Kremlin, begun as a timber stockade in 1044, and, inside it, St. Sofia Cathedral (1045–50). There are many outstanding churches of the 12th and the 14th centuries, including St. Nicholas (1113) and St. Prascovia. Population (1981) 198,000.

Vernadsky, George V. et al. (eds.), *A Source Book for Russian History from Early Times to 1917*, 1972.

NOVGOROD CYCLE. Novgorodian literature included an oral tradition that had a special cycle of *byliny* (*q.v.*).

NOVI, ALEVISIO (*fl.* 1490–1510). Milanese architect. He rebuilt the cathedral of St. Michael the Archangel in Moscow (1505–09), which was to serve as the burial place of the tsars. The interior still conforms to the style used in medieval Vladimir, while the exterior for the first time displayed Renaissance decorative details and was an important source of inspiration for later buildings.

NOVIKOV, IVAN ALEXEYEVICH (1879–1959). Author. He was much influenced by the Turgenev school and gained success with his two novels about Pushkin: *Pushkin v Mikhailovskom* (Pushkin in Mikhailovskoye) (1937) and *Pushkin na yuge* (Pushkin in the South) (1944).

NOVIKOV, NICHOLAS IVANOVICH (1744–1818). Writer and publisher. He edited and published four periodicals and a historical dictionary, *The Library of Old Russian Authors* (1772–75) in 30 volumes. He took over the Moscow University Press in 1778 and published the first Russian magazine for children. His press was closed by Catherine II in 1791 and he was later imprisoned. He was released only on the accession of Paul I.

NOVIKOV-PRIBOY, ALEXEY SILYCH (1877–1944). Author and former sailor. He wrote narratives about the sea and the revolutionary tendency of his *Morskye rasskazy* (Stories of the Sea) (1914) caused its confiscation. He also wrote two documentary novels, *Tsushima* (1932–35, trans. 1936) and *Kapitan pervo ranga* (1943; *Captain of the First Rank*, 1946).

NOVOCHERKASSK. Town situated 20 miles (32 km) ENE of Rostov, in the Russian Soviet Federated Socialist Republic. It was founded in 1805. Manufactures include locomotives, machinery, machine tools, mining equipment, and textiles. It trades in timber, grain, and wine. Population (1981) 186,000.

NOVODVORSKY, ANDREY OSIPOVICH (1853–82). Populist author who also wrote under the pseudonym A. Osipovich. His work is mainly concerned with the failure of intellectuals in the 1870s to come to terms with the people. His heroes are mostly typical "superfluous men."

NOVOKUZNETSK. (formerly Stalinsk) Town situated in the Russian Soviet Federated Socialist Republic 115 miles (184 km) SSE of Kemerovo on the Tom River. Founded in 1617 by the Cossacks, it developed in the 20th century into an important transportation and industrial center with one of the largest iron and steel works in the world. Manufactures include locomotives, machinery, and metal and aluminum products, chemicals and cement. Population (1981) 551,000.

NOVOMOSKOVSK. Town situated 120 miles (192 km) SSE of Moscow. Founded in 1930, it is the center of a lignite-mining district and manufactures chemicals and machinery. Population (1974) 143,000.

NOVOROSSIYSK. Port situated on the NE shore of the Black Sea. It was founded in 1839 on the site of Genoese and Turkish settlements and is an important center of the cement industry, which was started in 1882 and is the largest in the USSR. Other manufactures include agricultural machinery, bicycles, and machine tools. Cement, petroleum, and grain are exported. Population (1981) 165,000.

NOVOSIBIRSK. Capital of the Novosibirsk region of the Russian Soviet Federated Socialist Republic, situated on the Ob River. Founded in 1893 during the construction of the Trans-Siberian railway, it is an important industrial center and the largest town in Siberia. Industries include sawmilling, flour milling, brewing, and the manufacture of trucks, bicycles, agricultural and mining machinery, machine tools, and textiles. It trades in grain, meat, and dairy produce. Population (1981) 1,343,000.

NOVOSIBIRSKYE OSTROVA. *See* **New Siberian Islands.**

NOVOSILTSEV, COUNT NICHOLAS NIKOLAEVICH (1761–1836). Statesman. He was a confidant of Tsar Alexander I *(q.v.)* and was a member of the unofficial committee (1801–03) that was established to investigate reforms. He wrote *Constitutional Charter of the Russian Empire.* In this he saw the empire divided into 12 large administrative areas enjoying limited autonomy. The plan was presented to Alexander I (1820), who accepted it and began to implement it. The scheme was abandoned on the death of the tsar in 1825.

NOVO-TAGIL. *See* **Nizhny Tagil.**

NOVO TROITSK. Town situated 10 miles (16 km) W of Orsk in the Orsk-Khalilovo industrial center on the Ural River, in the Russian Soviet Federated Socialist Republic. The main industry is the manufacture of steel, and nickel, cobalt, and chromium are mined. Population (1973) 88,000.

***NOVY MIR* (NEW WORLD).** Monthly literary magazine, first published in January 1925 in Moscow. Many well-known works, such as A. Tolstoy's *Peter the First* (1929–45) and Michael Sholokhov's *(q.v.)* four-volume *The Quiet Don* (1937–40), and numerous sketches by Leonid Leonov, Alexander Tvardovsky, Konstantin Simonov, Konstantin Fedin, Fedor Gladkov, and Yury Trifonov *(q.q.v.)* have been serialized in *Novy Mir.* Solzhenitsyn's *One Day in the Life of Ivan Denisovich* was serialized in *Novy Mir.*

Glenny, Michael (ed.), *Novy Mir: A Selection, 1925-67,* 1972.

NUKHA. Town situated 150 miles (240 km) WNW of Baku, in the Azerbaijan Soviet Socialist Republic. It is the center of the silk industry. Population (1970) 74,000.

NUKUS. Capital of the Kara-Kalpak Autonomous Soviet Socialist Republic. It is situated 500 miles (800 km) WNW of Tashkent at the head of the Amu Darya River delta. Manufactures include cotton and food products, footwear, and furniture. Population (1970) 74,000.

NUREYEV, RUDOLF (1939-). Ballet dancer. At the age of 16 he was accepted by the Kirov Ballet School, having joined the corps de ballet at Ufa the previous year. He rose to become a leading dancer of the Russian Kirov Ballet but he defected to the West while the company was in Paris (May 1961), and he went to Britain. There he won new fame in the Royal Ballet, especially when he was partnered with Margot Fonteyn in such ballets as *Le Corsair, Marguerite and Armand, Giselle,* and *Swan Lake.* He adapted the choreography of some ballets, such as *Raymonda,* to meet the demands of his technical skill.

Nureyev, Rudolf, *Nureyev,* 1962.

NYSTAD, TREATY OF. Treaty between Russia and Sweden of September 10, 1721 concluding the Great Northern War (1720-21) (*q.v.*) and the period of Sweden's military greatness. Sweden ceded to Russia Ingria, part of Karelia, Livonia (including Estonia), and several islands in the Baltic. Russia retained Vyborg but returned the rest of Finland to Sweden, and paid Sweden an indemnity. Peter the Great formally assumed the title of emperor after the ratification of the treaty, thus officially inaugurating the imperial period of Russian history, and Russia's predominant power in the Baltic.

O

OB RIVER. River formed SW of Bisk, in Altay Territory, by the union of the Biya and Katun rivers. It flows 2,113 miles (3,381 km) through W Siberia, first NW past Kamen and Novosibirsk into swampy forests and on to Narym; then E past Surgut to receive the Irtysh River near Khanty-Mansisk; then N dividing into numerous arms and entering Ob bay at Salekhard 75 miles (120 km) S of the Kara Sea. Frozen for six months of the year, it is otherwise an important trade route. Main tributaries are the Irtysh, Tom, Chulym, Ket, Vakh, Kazam, Vasyugan, Konda, and N Sosva rivers. It is navigable throughout. With the Irtysh it forms a 3,230-mile (5,168-km) waterway.

OBEDIENCE, POPULAR. Passive obedience to the autocracy, which was considered to be part of the Russian character. This abdication of responsibility continued until the beginning of the 19th century. Some commentators say it continues into the Soviet period.

OBER-PROCURATOR OF THE GOVERNING SENATE. In 1711 Peter the Great established the Governing Senate. Its function was to supervise administrative, financial and judicial matters while the tsar was away on his Turkish campaign, but it became a permanent body. Senators numbered nine, later increased to ten. The Ober-Procurator was a liaison official between the tsar and the senate. His signature was needed on all decisions of the senate.

OBLAST. An administrative unit in Russia; a province; a region.

OBLOMOVSHCHINA (Oblomovitis). Disease suffered by Oblomov, the main character of Ivan Goncharov's *(q.v.)* novel of that name, published in 1859. Oblomov is symbolic of the sloth of the Russian gentry, and *oblomovshchina*, Goncharov implies, is a disease suffered by a considerable section of 19th-century society, and to a lesser extent, by most of humanity. Oblomov is the epitome of a person with potential and wealth, but lacking the discipline to do anything at all. Indeed, for the first few hundred pages of the novel, Oblomov fails to succeed in getting out of bed. A love affair fails to come to fruition, as he cannot bring himself to abandon his ingrained indolence. The final part of the novel shows *oblomovshchina* running its full course; Oblomov is sucked deeper and deeper into apathy and inertia and dies in the arms of his landlady, to the delight of her family who wish to exploit his wealth yet further.

OBOLENSKY, PRINCE YEVGENY PETROVICH (1796–1865). Soldier and member of one of the oldest families in Russia. A leader of the Northern Society (*q.v.*), he took part in the Decembrist revolt (*see* **Decembrists**) on the accession of Nicholas I in December 1825. He was condemned to death but his sentence was changed to banishment to Siberia.

Mazour, Anatole Grigorevich, *The First Russian Revolution 1825: The Decembrist Movement, its Origins, Development and Significance*, 1961.

OBROK. *See* **Emancipation, Edict Of.**

OBROK. Quit-rent; payment in kind or money of a serf's obligation or dues to the nobleman.

Blum, Jerome, *Lord and Peasant in Russia from the Ninth to the Nineteenth Century*, 1961.

OBSERVATORY, RUSSIAN. Pulkovo Observatory, situated 10 miles (16 km) S of Leningrad, is the chief astronomical observatory of the Soviet Academy of Sciences. It was built in 1839 and rebuilt in 1946–54, following damage during the Second World War.

OBSHCHESTVO. Society or commune; it can also mean company, as in joint-stock company.

OBSHCHINA. Russian peasant village commune, also known as *mir* (*q.v.*).

Blum, J., *Lord and Peasant in Russia from the Ninth to the Nineteenth Century*, 1961.

OBZHA. Old unit of tax assessment and also old measure of tillable land.

OCHAKOV. Turkey ceded the fortress of Ochakov and the Black Sea shore as far as the Dnestr River to Russia by the Treaty of Jassy (1792) (*q.v.*). This marked the end of the second Turkish war (1787–92).

OCTOBER CHILDREN. Organization founded in 1925 by the communists for children aged 6 to 9.

OCTOBER REVOLUTION (1917). One of the most dramatic landmarks in the history of Russia. On November 7 (October 25, O.S.), the military revolutionary committee of the St. Petersburg Soviet, left Socialist revolutionaries and anarchists, supported by the Red Guards, succeeded in overthrowing Kerensky's provisional government. A provisional workers' and peasants' government (council of people's commissars) was formed. Concerned by the threat of possible Western intervention, its leader, Lenin, saw no solution other than taking over the government.

Dukes, Paul, *October and the World: Perspectives of the Russian Revolution,* 1979.

OCTOBER REVOLUTION ISLAND. Part of the Severnaya Zemlya archipelago, in the Krasnoyarsk Territory, Russian Soviet Federated Socialist Republic, in the Arctic Ocean. It has an area of 5,000 square miles (12,950 sq km). Nearly 50 percent of the area is covered with glaciers.

OCTOBRISTS. The "Union of October 17" was a political party founded in November 1905 with the aim of ensuring the implementation of the promises made in Nicholas II's manifesto of 1905 which granted a constitution. The party was led by Alexander Ivanovich Guchkov and Michael Vladimirovich Rodzyanko (*q.q.v.*), and the party won 12 seats in the first duma, 32 in the second, 150 in the third, and 97 in the fourth. In the third and fourth dumas the Octobrists had an overall majority. They joined the "progressive bloc" in 1915 and took part in the provisional government of 1917.

Hosking, Geoffrey A., *The Russian Constitutional Experiment: Government and Duma 1907–14,* 1973.

Pearson, R., *The Russian Moderates and the Crisis of Tsarism 1914–1917,* 1977.

Radkey, O. H., *The Election of the Russian Constituent Assembly of 1917,* 1950.

ODESSA. Capital of Odessa region of the Ukraine and port situated on the Black Sea. Scene of a mutiny on the cruiser *Potemkin* in the 1905 uprisings. Industries include oil and sugar refining, engineering, and the manufacture of machine tools, agricultural machinery, chemicals, and bricks. Timber, grain, sugar, and wool are exported. Population (1981) 1,072,000.

ODESSA CIVIL WAR. Three months of violent revolutionary disorder in the port of Odessa resulted in a two-day civil war in 1905, with the strikers led by sailors from the cruiser *Potemkin* fighting Cossacks, police, and members of the Black Hundreds. On June 15 Odessa was put under martial law.

Hough, Richard Alexander, *The Potëmkin Mutiny,* 1961.

ODNODVORETS (pl. Odnodvortsy). A "one-homesteader," or state peasant descended from the small servitors who settled on the S frontiers in the 16th and 17th centuries.

ODOYEVSKY, PRINCE ALEXANDER IVANOVICH (1802–39). Poet. He participated in the 1825 Decembrist revolt (*see* **Decembrists**) after which he was exiled to Siberia for 10 years. In 1837 he was sent as a private soldier to the Caucasus where he met Michael Lermontov (*q.v.*). His poetry was heavily influenced by contemporary idealism, and patriotism and freedom provide the main themes.

Raeff, Marc, *The Decembrist Movement,* 1966.

ODOYEVSKY, PRINCE VLADIMIR FEDOROVICH (1803–69). Author and editor. He was a member of a group called Lovers of Wisdom (*q.v.*), formed in 1823. In 1824–25 he edited, with Wilhelm Kuchelbecker, four issues of the influential *Mnemosyne*. He believed in the decline of the West and of the future greatness of Russia. *Russkie nochi* (Russian Nights) (1844) is his best-known work.

OGAREV, NICHOLAS PLATONOVICH (1813–77). Revolutionary poet and writer. He was a friend and collaborator of Alexander Herzen (*q.v.*) with whom he went into voluntary exile in London.

Carr, Edward Hallett, *The Romantic Exiles: A Nineteenth Century Portrait Gallery*, 1933.

OGNEV, N. (MICHAEL GRIGOREVICH ROZANOV) (1888–1938). Writer. His best-known work is *The Diary of a Communist Schoolboy* (trans. 1928), and he also wrote *The Diary of a Communist Undergraduate* (trans. 1929).

OISTRAKH, DAVID FYODOROVICH (1908–74). Violinist and teacher. He made his debut in 1933 and from 1934 taught at the Moscow Conservatory. His repertoire included all the most important classical and modern works. He gained a worldwide reputation for his outstanding technique.

OISTRAKH, IGOR DAVIDOVICH (1931–). Violinist and son of David Oistrakh. He won first prize in the Wieniawski competition in Warsaw in 1949. He performed and recorded with his father and is considered by many to be the latter's technical equal.

OKA RIVERS. (1) River rising W of Maloarkhangelsk in the central Russian upland. It flows 918 miles (1,469 km) N past Orel, Beler, and Chekalin to Kaluga, then E to Ryazan, and NE past Murom to join the Volga River at Gorky. It is navigable for large vessels 550 miles (880 km) below Kolomna but subject to flooding in spring, low water in summer, and ice 220-240 days of the year. It carries grain and timber. (2) River rising in the E Sayan range in the Buryat-Mongol Autonomous Soviet Socialist Republic. It flows 500 miles (800 km) N to enter Angara River at Bratsk.

OKHOTSK, SEA OF. Arm of the NW Pacific Ocean lying W of the Kamchatka peninsula and the Kurile Islands. It has an area of 590,000 square miles (1,528,100 sq km). The sea connects on the SW with the Sea of Japan, by the Tatar and La Perouse straits, on the SE with the Pacific between the Kurile Islands. Average depth 2,750 feet (838 m). It is ice-bound November-June, and subject to thick fog.

OKHRANA. Department for defense of public security and order (security police), which existed from 1881 until it was abolished by the provisional government in 1917. *See* **Secret Police.**

Smith, E. E., *The Okhrana, the Russian Department of Police: A Bibliography*, 1967.

Vasilev, Aleksei T., *The Ochrana,* 1930.

OKOLNICHI. Courtiers, and next to the boyars, the most important rank of the medieval Russian nobility.

OKRUG. Administrative area, subdivided into oblasts and further into *raions.*

OKTEMBERYAN. Town situated 27 miles (43 km) W of Yerevan, in the Aras River valley of the Armenian Soviet Socialist Republic. It is the center of an irrigated agricultural area. Industries include cotton ginning, fruit canning, tanning, oil processing, and metalworking.

OKTYABRSKY. Town situated 100 miles (160 km) WSW of Ufa on the Ik River, in the W Bashkir Autonomous Soviet Socialist Republic of the Russian Soviet Federated Socialist Republic. Founded in 1937 as a petroleum center in the Tyuimazy oil field, it is linked by pipeline to Chernikovsk and Urussu. Population (1970) 77,000.

OKUDZHAVA, BULAT SHALOVICH (1924-). Soviet poet, and member of the CPSU since 1955. Having graduated from Tbilisi University in 1950, Okudzhava had his first work published in 1953. Many of his poems, dealing with incidents at the front or with scenes taken from every day life, are written in a colloquial style. He has also produced lyrical songs, short stories, and a screenplay and composed popular "underground" songs.

OLD BELIEVERS. Patriarch Nikon *(q.v.)* introduced reforms into religious texts and rituals of the Orthodox Church to correct errors that had crept in since the translation from the original Greek. His reforms were opposed by a section of the church led by Archpriest Avvakum, Stephen Vonifatiyev, and Ivan Neronov *(q.q.v.),* who accused him (1653) of heresy. Nikon was vindicated, and his opponents withdrew as a separate sect. They were persecuted severely and some, believing the reforms to be an indication of the end of the world, committed self-immolation.

They rejected the sign of the cross made with three fingers (used in the Greek Church), the return to the pure Greek texts, the new spelling of "Jesus," and other small innovations. They had no theological basis for dissent, but simply refused to recognize any departure from Muscovite custom, regarding their own Muscovite culture as the true Russian tradition, to be copied by others and to be above compromise.

The movement split during the 18th century into two sects. The *popovtsy* (priestly ones) continued to have priests, although they obtained them with difficulty. Some *popovtsy* eventually set up their own episcopate; others were reconciled to the Orthodox Church, keeping their own rites. The *bespopovtsy,* as their name indicates in Russian, had no priesthood, and developed a new religious life with no sacraments except baptism and confession.

They carried their conservatism into political life, denouncing the reforms of Peter the Great, whom they saw as the Antichrist. They suffered periodic persecution until an edict of toleration was passed in 1905. In 1971 the old rites were recognized as valid by the council of the Orthodox Church.

Some surviving groups, in the USSR and abroad, maintain a 17th-century way of life. The group as a whole was always identified with the well-to-do peasant, shopkeeper, or small businessman who had plenty of commercial acumen and little sympathy for the landed gentry of the Orthodox establishment.

Avvakum (trans. Nabokov, V.), *The Life of The Archpriest Avvakum, by Himself,* 1960.

Crumney, R. O., *The Old Believers and the World of Antichrist,* 1970.

Fedotov, Georgii P., *The Russian Religious Mind,* 2 vols., 1946, 1966.

OLD CHURCH SLAVONIC. Slavic language based on Macedonian dialects spoken around Thessalonika. Its once relatively widespread usage is attributed to the fact that this is the language used by Saints Cyril and Methodius (*q.v.*) when translating the Bible and when preaching to the Moravian Slavs. The language as used after the 12th century is referred to as Church Slavonic.

OLDENBURG, SERGEY FEDOROVICH (1863–1934). Orientalist. He was secretary of the Academy of Sciences (1904–29) and minister of education in the provisional government of 1917. A prolific writer on the art and ethnography of the Russian people, he was also an authority on the history of Buddhism.

OLEG, GRAND PRINCE (?–913). Founder and first historical ruler of the Kievan Rus state. According to the *Primary Chronicle,* he was ruler of Novgorod from 879, having succeeded his kinsman Ryurik (*q.v.*). He captured Kiev in 882, and subsequently made it his capital. Further conquests followed in which he defeated the Slavic tribes along the Volkhov-Dnepr waterway. Toward the end of his life he led a successful expedition against Constantinople (907) and as a result obtained an advantageous trading treaty with Byzantium in 911. Prince Igor (*q.v.*) was his successor, ruling from 913 to 945.

Vernadsky, George V., *Kievan Russia,* 1948.

OLEG SVYATOSLAVICH (fl. late 10th century). Brother of Prince Vladimir (St. Vladimir) of Kiev, Oleg was the second son of the warrior-prince Svyatoslav and was appointed by his father as ruler of the Drevlans (*q.v.*). His elder and younger brothers were entrusted with Kiev and Novgorod respectively; civil war between the brothers followed Svyatoslav's death, and Oleg was killed.

Vernadsky, George V., *Kievan Russia,* 1948.

OLEKMA RIVER. River rising in the Yablonovy mountains and flowing 794 miles (1,270 km) N to enter the Lena River below Olekminsk. Gold is mined along its course. Its main tributaries are the Nyukzha, Tungir, and Chara rivers.

OLESHA, YURY KARLOVICH (1899–1960). Writer and dramatist.

He is best known for his short work *Envy* (1927, trans. 1947), a satire on technological society. He found himself in conflict with the demands of Socialist Realism in the early 1930s, and in 1934 he was arrested and imprisoned for openly speaking about his feelings. He was released in 1956.

Brown, Edward J. (ed.), *Major Soviet Writers*, 1973.

OLGA, SAINT (*c.* 890–969). Widow of Grand Duke Igor of Kiev and grandmother of St. Vladimir, Kiev's first Christian prince. She ruled during her son's minority as regent, her husband having been murdered in 945. She was baptized a Christian *c.* 957 after suppressing her husband's enemies with some ferocity. She began the conversion of Kievan Russia, which was completed by St. Vladimir.

Obolensky, Dimitri, *The Byzantine Commonwealth: Eastern Europe 500–1453*, 1971.

OLGIERD. *See* **Algirdas.**

OLMÜTZ, PUNCTATION OF. Agreement of 1850 signed at Olmütz (Olomouc) between Prussia and Austria, reconstituting the German Confederation on terms favorable to Austria.

OMSK. Capital of Omsk region of the Russian Soviet Federated Socialist Republic. It is situated at the confluence of the Irtysh and Om rivers and was founded in 1716. In 1918–19 Admiral Alexander Kolchak (*q.v.*) made Omsk the headquarters of the anti-Bolshevik government. It is a center of industry, transport, and oil refining, as well as a terminus of the oil pipeline from Tyumazy. Manufactures include locomotives, automobiles, agricultural machinery, tires, synthetic rubber, and food products. Population (1981) 1,044,000.

ONEGA BAY. Inlet of the White Sea in NW European USSR, W of the Onega peninsula. The Kem, Vyg, and Onega rivers flow into it. It is 100 miles (160 km) long and 30–50 miles (48–80 km) wide, with the Solovetskye Islands at the entrance. Main ports are Kem, Onega, and Belomorsk.

ONEGA, LAKE. Situated in Karelia, Russian Soviet Federated Socialist Republic, in NW USSR, it is the second largest lake in Europe. It has an area of 3,817 square miles (9,886 sq km). Lake Onega is drained by the Svir River into Lake Ladoga and is connected by canals with the White Sea and the Volga River.

OPRICHNINA. An institution of ruthless men, loyal to Ivan IV, drawn mainly from the lower gentry, was established in 1565. The *oprichnina* was the forerunner of the present political police.

At first 1,000 men were recruited to the *oprichnina*, but later the number increased to 6,000. The members of the *oprichnina*, known as the *oprichniki*, conducted a reign of terror, being above the law and answerable only to the tsar. Boyars were deprived of their land and executed. Archbishops Pimen and Leonid of Novgorod were both murdered, and in 1570 the city was sacked and tens of thousands massacred. This was the most infamous of all the actions of the *oprichnina*.

The *oprichnina* was no longer effective after 1572. Scholars differ on the reasons for Ivan's action in forming the *oprichnina*; it is possible that it was to ensure the tsar's personal safety, but the effect was to contribute to the centralization of the state and to reduce the power of the boyars.

Payne, Robert and Romanoff, N., *Ivan the Terrible*, 1975.

OPTINA PUSTYN. Former monastery situated in the Kaluga oblast of central Russia. Founded in the 15th century, it was a center for the activities of the *startsy* during the 19th century.

ORCHESTRAS. The principal orchestras are the Symphony Orchestra of the USSR (Moscow); Leningrad State Philharmonic Orchestra; the Symphony Orchestra of the State Philharmonic Society (Moscow); and the Moscow Radio Symphony Orchestra.

ORDER NO. 1. An order issued by the Petrograd Soviet of Workers' and Soldiers' Deputies on March 14, 1917. It stated that military affairs should be administered by elected committees. This order, which stripped officers of much of their power, contributed to the eventual collapse of the Russian army.

ORDYN-NASHCHOKIN, AFANASY LAVRENTYEVICH (*c.* 1605–80). Statesman and diplomat. A capable administrator under Tsar Michael (1613–45), Ordyn-Nashchokin was Tsar Alexis's principal adviser on foreign affairs. Having helped defend Russia against Poland-Lithuania in 1654, he was made governor of Kokenhausen on the Dvina, and gradually extended his rule to all the Livonian lands captured by Russia. In 1658 he arranged the terms of an armistice between Russia and Sweden, but he was unsuccessful in his attempts to persuade the tsar to end the war with Poland. In 1665 he was made governor of Pskov, but was recalled the following year in order to conclude the truce of Andrusovo with Poland. As a result of his successful negotiations, he was made a boyar, minister of foreign affairs, and head of several departments. An ardent advocator of developing Russia along Western lines, he strove to protect Russian merchants from foreign competition, developed shipbuilding, and built up trading links with Central Asia and Persia. In 1671, however, Ordyn-Nashchokin was accused of friendship with Poland and dismissed. The following year he became a monk.

ORDZHONIKIDZE, GRIGORY KONSTANTINOVICH (1866–1937). Georgian communist. He joined the Bolsheviks in 1903, and in 1912 he was made a member of the central committee. After spending some years in prison and banishment, Ordzhonikidze was appointed extraordinary commissar of the Soviet government in S Russia. Once Soviet government in Georgia was established, he merged Armenia and Azerbaijan with Georgia, thus establishing the Transcaucasian Federal Republic. Chairman of the central control commission in 1926, in 1930 he was made a Politburo member and chairman of the supreme council of national economy. Having played an important part in organizing and developing Soviet industry during the first Five-Year Plan, in 1932 Ordzhonikidze was made commissar for heavy industry. He disagreed, however, with Stalin's industrial policy and thus fell from favor. He died in mysterious circumstances at the time of the Great Purge.

ORDZHONIKIDZE. Capital of the North Ossetian Autonomous Soviet Socialist Republic of the Russian Soviet Federated Socialist Republic. It is situated on the Terek River in the Caucasus mountains, 142 miles (227 km) W of Makhachkala. Founded as a fortress in 1784, it was known as Vladikavkaz and known as Dzaudzhika, from 1944 to 1954. Industries include metallurgy plants, food processing, woodworking, and glass manufacture. Zinc, lead, and silver are obtained from the Sadon mines. Population (1981) 287,000.

OREKHOVO-ZUYEVO. Town situated 50 miles (80 km) E of Moscow on the Klyazma River in the Russian Soviet Federated Socialist Republic. It was created in 1917 by the amalgamation of a number of industrial communities. Industries include cotton milling, weaving and dyeing, flour milling, sawmilling, metalworking, and the manufacture of plastics. Population (1970) 120,000.

OREL. City situated 200 miles (320 km) SSW of Moscow on the Oka River, in the Russian Soviet Federated Socialist Republic. Founded as a fortress and town in 1564, it became the oblast capital in 1779. It was largely destroyed in 1943 when it was the scene of heavy fighting. It is a communications and industrial center and its manufactures include tractor parts, textile machinery, beer, spirits, footwear, and iron products. Population (1981) 315,000.

ORENBURG. Town (Chkalov: 1938–58) situated on the Ural River NNE of the Caspian Sea, in the Russian Soviet Federated Socialist Republic. Founded as a fortress in 1735 where Orsk now stands, it was moved to present site in 1743. It is an important industrial and transport center trading in livestock, meat, hides, grain, wool, and textiles. Industries include railway engineering, sawmilling, flour milling, and the manufacture of metal goods and clothing. Population (1981) 482,000.

ORGBURO. Agency established in 1919 to direct all Communist Party organization. The orgburo was abolished in 1952.

Schapiro, Leonard B., *The Communist Party of the Soviet Union,* 1970.

ORLOV, PRINCE ALEKSEY FYODOROVICH (1786–1861). Army officer and statesman. He was an adviser to Nicholas I (1825–55) and Alexander II. Having joined the army in 1804, in 1825 Orlov was appointed commander of a cavalry regiment, and as a result of his part in the suppression of the Decembrist (*see* **Decembrists**) revolt, he was made a count. Appointed lieutenant general during the war with Turkey, Orlov played a leading part in the conclusion of the Treaty of Adrianople (1829) (*q.v.*). In

1833 he was made ambassador to Turkey and commander in chief of Russia's Black Sea fleet; he enhanced Russia's defenses by means of the alliance with Turkey at Hünkâ Iskelesi. From 1839 to 1942 he served on the secret committee that examined the possibility of limited improvements of the peasantry. In 1844 he was head of the sinister Third Department, and also of the chancellery. In 1854 he was dispatched on an unsuccessful trip to persuade Austria to refrain from taking sides during the Crimean War. After helping negotiate the Treaty of Paris (1856) (*q.v.*), he was made prince and also president of the state council and the council of ministers. In 1858 he was appointed chairman of a committee established to examine the question of the emancipation of the serfs (*q.v.*). He was unsuccessful in his attempts to prevent the emancipation.

ORLOV, COUNT ALEKSEY GRIGORYEVICH (1737–1808). Russian nobleman and joint leader of the conspiracy to put Catherine II (*q.v.*) on the throne. Having joined the cadet corps in 1749, Orlov later became an officer in the Russian guards. After his brother had become Catherine's lover, Orlov helped him plan the overthrow of Tsar Peter III (*q.v.*). When Catherine had been proclaimed empress Orlov received Peter's abdication and took him into custody. Since the latter was killed shortly afterward while still in Orlov's hands, it is alleged that Orlov murdered him. Appointed as a major general and commander of the Russian fleet, he succeeded in destroying the much larger Turkish fleet at Chesme. After imprisoning a possible rival to the throne, Yelizaveta Alekseyevna Tarakanova, Orlov retired from the army.

ORLOV, COUNT GRIGORY GRIGORYEVICH (1734–83). Military officer and lover of Catherine II (1762–74). Having put her on the throne, he remained her close adviser. Orlov joined the cadet corps in 1749 and fought in the battle of Zorndorf during the Seven Year's War. He became Catherine's lover *c.* 1760; in 1762 he succeeded in overthrowing Tsar Peter III and in putting Peter's wife, Catherine, on the throne. He was then made count, director general of engineers and general in chief. Motivated by the desire to update Russia's agricultural system, Orlov was one of the founders of the Free Economic Society; Catherine, however, disregarded his schemes for the emancipation of the serfs. In 1722 he was chief delegate to the peace conference that was to end the Russo-Turkish War, but peace was not concluded until two years later. He ceased to be Catherine's lover *c.* 1772, left Russia in 1775, and married in 1777. In 1782 he went mad.

ORLOV, VLADIMIR NIKOLAYEVICH (1908–). Soviet literary historian and critic. From 1941 to 1945 Orlov worked as a military correspondent of TASS, and from 1956 to 1970 he was editor of *The Poet's Library*. He has written several works on democratic and revolutionary tendencies in the literature of the late-18th and early-19th centuries.

ORLOV, YURY ALEKSANDROVICH (1893–1966). Soviet paleontologist and member of the Academy of Sciences from 1960. Having graduated from Petrograd University in 1917, Orlov taught at Perm, Leningrad, and Moscow. He was named head of Moscow's department of paleontology in 1943. He edited the *Paleontology Journal* (1959–66) and was chief editor of the 15-volume *Basic Paleontology*. He was awarded the Order of Lenin and various other medals.

ORSHA. Town situated 50 miles (80 km) S of Vitebsk on the Dnepr River in Belorussia. It is an important railway junction, and industries include meat packing, flour milling, brewing, and the manufacture of textiles. Population (1970) 101,000.

ORSK. Town situated on the Ural River and NE of the Caspian Sea in the Russian Soviet Federated Socialist Republic. It was founded in 1735 as Orenburg. Industries include oil refining, nickel smelting, heavy engineering, meat packing, and the manufacture of locomotives and agricultural machinery. Population (1981) 254,000.

ORTHODOX CHURCH. The most important church in Russia and in the Soviet Union. In 1448, the Russian church became autocephalous, in that it was placed under the jurisdiction of an independent metropolitan of Moscow; it was thus no longer under the authority of Rome. In 1458, however, Rome appointed another "metropolitan of Kiev and all Russia." This metropolitanate, controlled by Roman Catholic Poland, accepted union with Rome in 1596 (*see* **Uniates**). In 1686, however, the metropolitanate of Kiev was attached to the patriarchate of Moscow. Muscovite Russians came to regard themselves as the last true Orthodox believers, considering Moscow to be the "Third Rome." Patriarch Nikon's (*q.v.*) liturgical reforms resulted in a major schism in the Russian church. Millions of clergy and laity refused to accept a reformed Russian liturgy closely modeled on the Greek (*see* **Old Believers**). Peter the Great rejected the Byzantine heritage and abolished the patriarchate in 1721, replacing it by a state department. Because of the church's reluctance to involve itself in social issues, the radicals of the 19th century grew increasingly disillusioned with it. On January 20, 1918, the Bolshevik government published a decree depriving the church of all legal rights. Following imprisonment for opposing the regime's religious policy, Patriarch Tikhon decided to conform with the state, and this tendency to conformism is still pursued. Savagely persecuted under Stalin and to a large extent suppressed under Khrushchev, the Orthodox Church continues to survive. *See* **Patriarch**.

Bourdeaux, Michael, *Opium of the People: The Christian Religion of USSR*, 1965.

Bulgakov, Sergei N., *The Orthodox Church*, 1935.

Ware, Timothy, *The Orthodox Church*, 1963.

ORUZHEYNAYA PALATA. The Oruzheynaya Palata (Kremlin Armory, Moscow) was started early in the 15th century as an arsenal but was used for many other purposes including a technical, scientific, educational, and art institute. Icons, bookbinding, leatherwork, and jewelry could also be purchased there, but arms manufacture continued throughout. One of the armory's most famous uses was as the school of the tsar's icon painters in the 17th century.

OSH. Capital of the Osh region of Kirghizia, 198 miles (317 km) ESE of Tashkent. It is situated at the E end of the fertile Fergana valley, and the highway to Pamir begins here. Manufactures include silk and food products. Population (1981) 178,000.

OSORGIN, MICHAEL ANDREYEVICH (M. A. Ilyin) (1878–1942). Author. A Russian émigré who wrote short stories and novels with the 1917 Revolution as his main theme. His works included *A Quiet Street* (trans. 1930) and *My Sister's Story* (trans. 1932).

OSSETIA. Area of the N Caucasus inhabited by the Ossetes, who were descendants of a Scythian tribe (Alani) speaking an Iranian language. The area is mainly in the Severo Ossetian Autonomous Soviet Socialist Republic, of which the chief town is Ordzhonikidze. The area was annexed by Russia 1801–1806.

OSSETIANS (properly **Ossetes**). *See* **Ossetia.**

OSSETIC. Language spoken by people of Ossetia numbering about 400,000 who inhabit the N and S slopes of the central part of the main Caucasus range. The majority are Orthodox Christians, but there are also Sunni Muslims. The majority speak the Iron dialect, which is now written in the Cyrillic alphabet. The other dialect is Digor. The national poet Kosta Khetagurov (1859–1906) established the literary language.

OSTANKINO PALACE. Late-18th century Moscow residence of the Sheremetev family. Since 1918 it has served as a museum of peasant art. The palace has a theater, galleries, and pavilions, and fine furniture, chandeliers, and parquet flooring. Part of the landscaped garden has been preserved as a park.

OSTERMANN, COUNT ANDREY IVANOVICH, (Heinrich Johann Friedrich Ostermann) (1686–1747). Statesman. Born in Westphalia, he went to Russia in 1704 and was appointed interpreter at the foreign office in 1708 and secretary in 1710. His success in negotiations with Sweden and Persia gained him the rank of baron and the vice-presidency of the foreign office. His period of greatest influence began in 1725 with the accession of Catherine I, when he became vice-chancellor, a member of the supreme privy council, and president of the commission on commerce. He was the dominant influence on foreign policy until 1740, cultivating Austria as an ally. This brought him the hostility of France, and he was overthrown by French-inspired intrigue after the death of the Empress Anna in 1740. He was sentenced to death, but was reprieved and banished to Siberia.

OSTROG. Town in the center of the Ostrozhsky region of the Rovenskaya oblast. It is noted for a school that taught Latin and Greek. It was opened by the brotherhood of the Russian Orthodox Church during the 16th and 17th centuries, and sponsored the printing of the first complete Slavonic Bible in 1576–80.

OSTROGOTHS. The Goths, a German people, originally from the Baltic region, invaded Russia during the Gothic period in Russia (200–370). The Ostrogoths settled in the Ukraine and the Visigoths in the W.

OSTROMIR CODEX (Ostromirovo Gospel). A richly illustrated and decorated collection of gospels used in church services and arranged for daily use. It was compiled in Novgorod during 1056–57 and is the oldest surviving Russian manuscript.

OSTROVSKY, ALEXANDER NIKOLAYEVICH (1823–86). Playwright. He is regarded as the greatest dramatist of the period of critical realism. At first he was influenced by Nicholas Gogol (*q.v.*). His plays were concerned with contemporary Russian society, particularly the merchant class of Moscow. They are still popular and include *The Storm* (trans. 1898), *The Forest* (trans. 1926), and *Easy Money and Two Other Plays* (trans. 1944).

Slonim, Marc, *Russian Theatre from the Empire to the Soviets*, 1961.

OSTROVSKY, NICHOLAS ALEXEYEVICH (1904–36). Author. Disabled and blinded as a result of the Civil War, he turned to writing. He wrote *Kak zakalyalas stal* (How the Steel was Tempered) (1932–34), which sold 6 million copies by 1950 and won him the Order of Lenin. His next novel, *Rozhdenye burey* (1937, trans. 1939), was incomplete at his death.

Brown, A., *The Making of a Hero*, 1937.

Tregub, S., *Nikolay Ostrovsky*, 1948.

OTECHESTVENNYE ZAPISKI. *See* **Annals of the Fatherland.**

OTREPIYEV, GREGORY. *See* **Dmitriy, False.**

OWEN, ROBERT (1771–1858). Welsh industrialist and reformer. A utopian socialist who influenced the early unions, he advocated the formation of self-governing workshops. He influenced early Russian social thinkers.

Cole, G.D.H., *Life of Robert Owen*, 1965.

OZEROV, VLADISLAV ALEXANDROVICH (1769–1816). Playwright. He wrote in the pseudoclassic tradition, and his *Polixena* is still considered the best Russian pseudoclassic tragedy.

P

PACHMANN, VLADIMIR VON (1848–1933). Pianist. Born in Odessa, Pachmann studied under Joseph Dachs in Vienna and then toured Germany, Austria, and France, and later the United States. He was particularly noted for his interpretation of Chopin.

PACIFICATION. The policy of suppressing revolutionary terrorist activity and restoring order, carried out by Stolypin's government after 1905. Widespread terrorism was countered by placing different areas of Russia under different centers of control, censoring the press, organizing infiltration of revolutionary movements by police spies, and summary court-martial.

PAHLEN, COUNT PETER ALEKSEYEVICH (1745–1826). Military governor of St. Petersburg and key figure in the conspiracy against Paul I (*q.v.*).

PALCHINSKY, PETER IOAKIMOVICH (?–1929). Engineer and politician. During the First World War Palchinsky was a leading member of the central war industries committee. Following the 1917 February Revolution he was appointed the provisional government's deputy minister of trade and industry and defended the Winter Palace against the Bolsheviks. A technical expert of Gosplan (*q.v.*), he was accused of sabotage and shot at the beginning of the purges. He was said to have founded the underground league of engineering organizations.

PALEKH. Lacquerwork on papier-mâché produced in the village of Palekh. In 1796 Peter Korobov established a factory at Fedoskino in Moscow district, where the technique was introduced by lacquer workers brought from Germany. The art spread to nearby villages (where icon painting was a traditional skill) of which Palekh, Mstera, and Kholui are outstanding. The craft exists today.

Zinoviev, Nikolai M., *Palekh*, 1975.

PALITSYN, AVRAAMY (?–1626). Writer. He was bursar of the Trinity Monastery. He is renowned for his powerful and dramatic work describing events before the accession of the first Romanov tsar, known as the Time of Troubles (*q.v.*).

PAMIR, CENTRAL ASIA. Plateau extending through the Gorno-Badakhshan Autonomous Region into NE Afghanistan and Sinkiang-Uygur, China. It is a series of high mountain valleys at 12,000–14,000 feet (3,657–4,267 m) above sea level with ranges including the Akademiya Nauk, rising to Kommunizma Peak at 24, 590 feet (7,495 m) above sea level. The high valleys have grass on which sheep and goats are reared.

PANEVEZYS. Lithuanian town 60 miles (98 km) NNE of Kaunas on the Nevezys River. It is a railway center with repair shops; industries include flour milling, textiles, meat packing, sugar refining, and tobacco processing; manufactures include metal products, paints, turpentine, cement, and soap. Population (1973) 84,000.

PANFEROV, FEDOR IVANOVICH (1896–1960). Author. His four-volume novel *Bruski* (1931–37) brought him renown. The novel *The Mother River Volga* (1953) was an early critical work in the post-Stalin period. It incurred displeasure, and he was dismissed from the editorship of the literary journal *Oktyabr* and expelled from the Writers' Union but was reinstated in 1958.

PANIN, COUNT NIKITA IVANOVICH (1718–83). Russian statesman and diplomatic adviser to Catherine the Great. As Russian minister to Stockholm he adopted an anti-French policy. In 1760 he was appointed to supervise Grand Duke Paul's education, and supported Catherine during the 1762 Revolution. In 1763 he was head of the foreign college and instigated the Northern Accord, but was taken by surprise by the Confederation of the Bar and the Turkish War. From then on his influence waned, and Panin was dismissed in 1781.

PANIN, COUNT V.N. (1801–74). Reactionary member of Alexander II's secret committee on serfs.

PAN-SLAVISM. A 19th century movement to unite all Slavic peoples for cultural and political ends. It was formed in the early 19th century by intellectuals among W and S Slavs seeking cultural identity for emerging national groups. In 1848 it became a political movement for Slavic emancipation from the Austrian empire. In the 1860s in Russia it developed as an idealistic campaign whereby Holy Russia was to save a spiritually bankrupt Europe; Russian liberation of other Slavs from Austrian or Turkish rule was seen as a prerequisite. In this respect the movement influenced Russian foreign policy in the Russo-Turkish war of 1877–78.

Kohn, Hans, *Panslavism, its History and Ideology*, 1960.

PAPANIN, IVAN DMITRIYEVICH (1894–). Polar explorer. He joined the CPSU in 1919. In 1931 he took part in his first polar expedition, and in 1937, led the North Polar Drift Expedition. In the following year he was appointed head of the Northern Sea Route administration. Papanin's publications include *Life on an Icefloe* (1947) and *Northern Sea Route* (1952).

PARIS, TREATIES OF. The major treaties signed in Paris concerning Russia are the treaties of 1814–15 and the treaty of 1856. At the former Austria, Britain, Portugal, Prussia, Russia, and Sweden met to discuss the fate of France following Napoleon's defeat. At the latter the influence of Russia in the Ottoman Empire following the Crimean War was discussed, and Russia ceded Bessarabia to Moldavia and agreed to the neutralization of the Black Sea area.

PÄRNU. Estonian port 73 miles (117 km) S of Tallinn, situated at the mouth of the Parnu River on the Gulf of Riga. It was a Hanseatic city founded in the mid-13th century. Industries include textiles and sawmilling; manufactures include leather goods. It exports timber and flax and is a tourist resort. Population (1970) 46,000.

PASKEVICH, IVAN FEDOROVICH (1782–1856). Army officer who suppressed the Polish insurrection of 1831. He served in the army in wars with Turkey, France, and Persia. Paskevich took part in the prosecution at the trial of the Decembrists, and in 1829 he was appointed field marshal. He was commander in chief of the Russian forces against Polish insurgents. Paskevich was made prince of Warsaw and viceroy of Poland, which he ruled harshly from 1832 to 1856.

PASTERNAK, BORIS LEONIDOVICH (1890–1960). Poet. After studying philosophy, Pasternak directed his attentions to poetry and was for a time influenced by the Futurists. His most important collections of poetry include *My Sister Life* (1922) and *On Early Trains*. He also translated some of Shakespeare's works. His famous novel *Dr. Zhivago*, which is about the intelligentsia at the time of the Revolution, was offensive to officialdom because it did not conform to Socialist Realism and because it sided with the individual. It was published in Italy in 1957, and in the same year Pasternak received the Nobel Prize in literature but was obliged to renounce it. He died in Peredelkino near Moscow, officially in disgrace, but 2,000 people attended his funeral.

Hingley, Ronald, *Nightingale Fever*, 1982.

Ivinskaya, Olga, *A Captive of Time*, 1978.

Mandelstam, Nadezhda, *Hope Against Hope*, 1971.

PASTERNAK, LEONID O. (1862–1945). Impressionist painter and father of Boris Leonidovich Pasternak. Pasternak was a founding member of the Union of Russian Artists.

PASTERNAK, ROSA KAUFMAN (1867–1939). Concert pianist and mother of Boris Leonidovich Pasternak. In 1921 she left Russia in order to seek medical advice abroad.

PATERIKON. Name of a collection of lives of the saints who lived at the Monastery of the Caves (Pechorskaya Laura) near Kiev.

PATRIARCH. The patriarch of Moscow and All Russia is the head of the Russian Orthodox Church (*q.v.*). Prior to 1589 when the see of Moscow and All Russia was established, the Russian church recognized the patriarch of Constantinople. Since some 17th century patriarchs viewed their office as higher than the tsar's, Peter the Great abolished it, establishing the Most Holy Synod in its place. The patriarchate was reestablished after the fall of the monarchy in 1917, and the patriarch is now assisted in his duties by the Holy Synod.

Cracraft, James, *The Church Reform of Peter the Great*, 1971.

Hackel, Sergei, *The Orthodox Church*, 1971.

PATRIKEYEV, VASSIAN (*fl.* 15th century). Trans-Volga elder and supporter of Nil Sorsky (*q.v.*).

PATRONYMIC. A name received from a paternal ancestor almost always one's father (nowadays). The use of patronymics began early in Russia and survived the general use of hereditary surnames. A Russian has three names: A Christian (or first name), a patronymic, and surname. The first two names are used as a polite form of address. Ivan Sergeyevich Turgenev, the Russian author, has Sergeyevich as his patronymic, as his father's name was Sergey. *See* **Names.**

PAUL I, TSAR (Paul Petrovich) (1754–1801). The son of Catherine II (*q.v.*), Paul was taken from her by Elizabeth Petrovna (*q.v.*) as a child. His shock at Catherine's coup d'état in 1762 against his father, Peter III (*q.v.*), was great, as was Paul's belief later, that Catherine had instigated the murder of his father. In 1783, Catherine gave Paul and his second wife an estate at Gatchina, where he planned various reforms. He reigned from 1796 mostly in a despotic manner, hoping to save Russia from a revolution such as France had seen. In 1798 he joined the second coalition against France, but eventually turned against Great Britain. He was murdered in 1801 by guards officers who had grown tired of Paul's incompetence and his harsh treatment of them.

Ragsdale, H. (ed.), *Paul I: A Reassessment of His Life and Reign*, 1978.

PAUPER'S ALLOTMENT. The so-called pauper's allotment was an additional provision of the emancipation reform law of 1861 by the state council (*see* **Agrarian Reforms**). Under this law serfdom was abolished and those serfs who had worked on the land received a plot for their own use. There were variants on the application of the land settlement in different areas of the country, but the basic plan was that the peasants would receive that part of the land which they had cultivated for themselves, which was roughly half of the total. They had to pay the landlords for the land they acquired, or, alternatively, they could take a quarter of their normal parcel of land, the pauper's allotment, without payment.

Blum, Jerome, *Lord and Peasant in Russia from the Ninth to the Nineteenth Century*, 1961.

PAVLODAR. Capital of Pavlodar region in Kazakhstan, situated 250 miles (400 km) ENE of Tselinograd on the Irtysh River. Industries include meat packing, milk canning, and flour milling. Population (1981) 288,000.

PAVLOV, IVAN PETROVICH (1849–1936). Physiologist. Having studied at the University of St. Petersburg and at the Military Medical Academy, Pavlov directed the department of physiology at the Institute of Experimental Medicine, and in 1897 he was appointed professor of physiology at the Military Medical Academy. After concentrating on circulation, Pavlov directed his attention to digestion and developed a theory of conditional reflexes, which he then applied to human psychology. Although an ardent churchgoer, he was supported by the Soviet government because it viewed his work as promoting materialist ideology. In 1904 Pavlov was awarded the Nobel Prize in medicine.

PAVLOVA, ANNA PAVLOVNA (1881–1931). Prima ballerina. Having trained under Per Christian Johansson (*q.v.*) and Paul Gerdt at the Imperial Theater School, Pavlova danced with the Maryinsky Theater in 1899 and was made prima ballerina in 1906. In 1909 she joined Diaghilev's (*q.v.*). Ballets Russes, but in 1911 she left the company after becoming a traditionalist and rejecting the innovations of Diaghilev. She settled in London, formed her own company, and toured extensively with it. She is considered one of the greatest prima ballerinas of all time.

Bell, J.C., *Anna Pavlova: A Photographic Essay*, 1981.

Franks, A. H., *Pavlova: A Biography*, 1956.

Kerensky, Oleg, *Anna Pavlova*, 1973.

Money, Keith, *Anna Pavlova: Her Life and Art*, 1983.

PAVLOVNA, KAROLINA KARLOVNA (1807–93). Poet. She loved the Polish poet Adam Mickiewicz in her youth but was unhappily married to the novelist Nicholas Pavlov, and much of her poetry expresses suffering. Her literary salon in Moscow, however, was most popular.

PEACEFUL COEXISTENCE. Term referring to peaceful coexistence between socialist and capitalist states. At the Allied Supreme Council at Cannes in 1922 the Allies endorsed Georgy Chicherin's (*q.v.*) coexistence thesis, stating that each nation should choose its own system of government and economy. Khrushchev pursued a foreign policy of so-called peaceful coexistence but this was interpreted as coexistence of different social systems, rather than toleration of different ideologies.

Treadgold, Donald W., *Twentieth Century Russia*, 1958.

Ulam, Adam, *Expansion and Coexistence* , 1968.

PEASANT LAND BANK. Bank established in 1883 by Nicholas Bunge, (*q.v.*), minister of finance. Owned by the state, the bank enabled peasants to purchase land by lending money on favorable terms.

Blum, Jerome, *Lord and Peasant in Russia from the Ninth to the Nineteenth Century*, 1961.

PEASANTS' UNION. Organization established in 1905 as a result of populist activity. The union demanded that land be nationalized, and that it be used only by those who tilled it. Its members disagreed as to whether to use peaceful or violent methods to achieve their aims, and the union disintegrated in 1906.

PECHENEGS. Primitive Turkic nomads. In the second half of the 10th century they began to carry out attacks on the Kievan state. In 1037, however, Yaroslav The Wise (*q.v.*) succeeded in defeating them. The Pechenegs were then pushed back towards the Danube by the Polovtsy (Cumans).

PECHENGA. Town in Murmansk oblast on the Kola peninsula, in the Russian Soviet Federated Socialist Republic, at the head of Pechenga Bay in the Barents Sea. Between 1919 and 1940 it belonged to Finland, as Petsamo. Founded in the 16th century as a trading outpost of the Muscovite Empire. Through its outport, Linakhamari, it acts as a supply base for local copper and the nickel mining industry.

PECHORA RIVER. River rising in the N Ural mountains and flowing 1,100 miles (1,760 km) N and W to enter the Gulf of Pechora on the Barents Sea by a delta. It is used for transporting coal, timber, and firs and is ice-free from June to September.

PEIPUS, LAKE. Lake on the frontier between Estonia and the Russian Soviet Federated Socialist Republic, comprising two lakes joined by a 15-mile (24-km) strait. The larger is Lake Peipus (Lake Chudskoe) to the N, with Lake Pskov to the S. The total area is 1,356 square miles (3,512 sq km). It is drained by the Narova River into the Gulf of Finland and is frozen from December to March.

PEKING, TREATY OF. Treaty signed November 14, 1860 between Russia and China, confirming the agreement of Aigun (1858) whereby China ceded to Russia all the territory N of the Amur River and that strip of Pacific coast S of the Amur, E of the Ussuri River, and N of Korea; Vladivostok was built on this strip.

PENZA. Capital of Penza region of the Russian Soviet Federated Socialist Republic. It is situated on the Sura River 130 miles (208 km) NNW of Saratov. It was founded in 1666. Industries include engineering, sawmilling, and papermaking; manufactures include watches, cement and matches. Population (1981) 500,000.

PEOPLE'S WILL (*Narodnaya Volya*). Populist revolutionary organization, established in 1879 by former members of the populist group, Land and Liberty (*Zemlya i Volya*). It aimed to overthrow the government, by violent means if necessary, and rejected the gradual spread of socialism through the education of the peasants. Many, including approximately 70 army officers, joined the organization following the suppression of the Northern Union of Russian Workers (*q.v.*) in 1879 and the economic crisis and unemployment of 1880. Workers in St. Petersburg, Moscow, Rostov-on-Don, and Kharkov were organized into groups. The executive committee condemned Alexander II, (*q.v.*). to death in 1879 and finally succeeded in blowing up his carriage in March 1881. Nearly all prominent members of the People's Will were arrested by the end of that year, although a few fled abroad.

Venturi, Franco, *Roots of Revolution*, 1960.

PEREDVIZHNIKI. *See* **WANDERERS, THE.**

PEREKOP ISTHMUS. Isthmus joining the Crimean peninsula to the Ukrainian mainland. It is 4 miles (7 km) wide at the narrowest point.

PERELOG. Primitive system of crop rotation in Kievan Russia; the farmer used one part of his land, but left the other fallow, and would alternate the two after a certain number of years. Eventually a two-field system emerged, and the land was rotated annually.

PEREYASLAVL-KHMELNITSKY. Town in the Kiev oblast of the Ukrainian Soviet Socialist Republic on the Trubezh River. One of the oldest Russian towns, it was first mentioned in 907. In the 11th century it was made the seat of a princedom by Yaroslav the Wise (*q.v.*) for his third son. In 1096 it was besieged by the Polovtsy and in 1239 sacked by the Tatars.

PERM. Capital of Perm region of the Russian Soviet Federated Socialist Republic, situated on the Kama River. Founded in 1780, its industries include engineering, tanning, and sawmilling; manufactures include aircraft parts, tractor parts, agricultural and construction equipment, fertilizers, paper, and matches. It is a river port. Population (1981) 1,018,000.

PEROV, VASILY GRIGORYEVICH (1833–82). Critical Realist painter and founding member of the *peredvizhniki* (see **Wanderers, The**). Most of his works illustrate the cruelty of the government, the inefficiency and corruption of the police, and the harsh lot of the serf; at times his paintings border on the sentimental. Toward the end of the 1860s Perov directed his attention to painting portraits, such as *The Stranger* (1870). From 1871 to 1882 he taught in Moscow; Perov's pupils include Michael Nesterov and Andrei Petrovich Ryabushkin, and in 1877 he broke with the *peredvizhniki*. In the West his paintings are now considered more important as social documents than as works of arts.

PEROVSKAYA, SOFYA (1853–81). Member of the Chaykovsky Circle, a Lavrovist group (*see* **Lavrov, Peter**). Together with Andrey Zhelyabov (*q.v.*), Perovskaya directed plans to assassinate the tsar.

PERROT, JULES (1810–90). French choreographer. He was ballet master in St. Petersburg (1848–60) where he produced *Esmeralda, Faust, Giselle,* and *Catarina* for Fanny Elssler and Carlotta Grisi. His work revived the Russian company, which had declined on the removal of Charles Didelot (*q.v.*) in 1829.

PERUN. The chief god of the pagan Slavs.

PERVOURALSK. Town 26 miles (42 km) WNW of Sverdlovsk in the central Urals on the Chusovaya River, in the Russian Soviet Federated Socialist Republic. It is a railway junction. Industries include metalworking, brickmaking, and sawmilling. Population (1974) 122,000.

PESTEL, COLONEL PAUL I (1799–1826). Member of the Union of Salvation (*q.v.*). The former aide-de-camp to General Wittgenstein and a colonel of a regiment, he joined the union, and maintained a secret group (the Southern Society) in Tulchin after the union had been dissolved. After the failure of the Decembrist (*see* **Decembrists**) uprising, Pestel was condemned to death.

Mazour, Anatole Grigorevich, *The First Russian Revolution, 1825,* 1937.

Raeff, Marc, *The Decembrist Movement,* 1966.

PETER I (the Great) (1672–1725). Tsar of Russia (1682–1721) and emperor of Russia (1721–25), who with tireless energy established Russia as an important European power, and who began the Westernization and modernization of Russia by a number of ad hoc reforms. Interested in the army and in shipbuilding from an early age, in the 1690s Peter undertook a tour of W Europe, studied foreign countries, and worked as a shipwright. He returned home with many skilled technicians. he set up schools, arranged for textbooks to be translated, brought the church under state control by abolishing the patriarchate and establishing the Holy Synod, reformed trade, industry, and the army, introduced a poll tax, and established the famous Table of Ranks (*q.v.*), by which state service was made compulsory for the nobility. Disregarding the massive cost in human lives, and the extreme unsuitability of the swampy site given to flooding, Peter built a new capital of Russia, the city of St. Petersburg, on land conquered from Sweden, thereby creating the "window on the West." After initial defeats in the war with Sweden (1700–21), he defeated Charles XII at Poltava and annexed parts of Finland, Estonia, and Livonia, gaining access to the Baltic. His campaign against the Turks (1710–13) met with less success, but in the war with Persia (1722–23), Peter gained extra land in the Caspian region.

Anderson, M. S., *Peter the Great,* 1978.

de Jonge, Alex, *Fire and Water: A Life of Peter the Great,* 1979.

Jay Oliva, L., *Russia in the Era of Peter the Great,* 1962.

Sumner, Benedict H., *Peter the Great and the Emergence of Russia* , 1951.

PETER II (1715–30). Emperor of Russia from 1727. The Grandson of Peter I (*q.v.*), son of Alexis (*q.v.*), he was proclaimed emperor according to the will of the late Empress Catherine I. Taken from St. Petersburg to Moscow by the Dolgoruky (*q.v.*) family, he was crowned in 1728 and led a pleasure-seeking life, but died of smallpox on the day arranged for his wedding to Princess Dolgorukaya (*q.v.*).

PETER III, EMPEROR (1728–62). Emperor and duke of Holstein. Peter succeeded to the throne in 1762. He returned the Prussian provinces conquered during the Seven Years' War and released the nobility from obligatory state service. Somewhat weak-minded and ineffective as a ruler, he was overthrown by a guards' plot. It is alleged that he was killed by Orlov (*q.v.*), his wife's lover. She was later crowned empress and ruled as Catherine II (*q.v.*).

PETER AND PAUL FORTRESS. Built on Hare Island in 1703 by Peter the Great, from 1718 onward the hexagonal fortress served as a prison for political offenders. It was built according to the designs of Lambert, a pupil of Vauban. Within the fortress is the Cathedral of St. Peter and St. Paul, by Domeniko Andrea Trezzini, the golden spire of which is a focal point of Leningrad.

PETERSBURG SOVIET. Because St. Petersburg was the center of the March Revolution, the St. Petersburg Soviet carried out the role of a national Soviet for a few months but relinquished this in June to an All-Russian Congress of Soviets. After this, in theory at least, it became solely a local city Soviet. Its voice and directorate was the executive committee which the delegates elected.

Katkov, George and Shukman, H., *Lenin's Path to Power: Bolshevism and the Destiny of Russia*, 1971.

Katkov, George, *Russia: February 1917*, 1967.

PETIPA, MARIUS (1822–1910). French choreographer and teacher. In 1847 Petipa settled in St. Petersburg and worked under Jules Perrot (*q.v.*). In 1858 he was made ballet master. *La Fille du Pharaon* (1862) brought him his first major success. Using music of the highest standard, he introduced new steps and achieved a fusion of elements from French classical ballet and Italian acrobatics. He choreographed *The Sleeping Beauty*, *Swan Lake*, and *The Nutcracker*, taught Michael Fokine (*q.v.*), Gorslay, and Legat, and in general profoundly influenced the development of Russian ballet.

PETLYURA, SEMYON VASILYEVICH (1879–1926). Ukrainian patriot who worked tirelessly to gain independence for the Ukraine. In 1905 Petlyura helped found the Ukrainian Social Democratic Workers' Party. Having served in the Russian army in World War I, in 1917 he joined the Ukrainian central council, and was minister of defense in the first Ukrainian government. In 1920 he not only fought the Red Army in the N but the anti-Soviet forces of General Anton Ivanovich Denikin (*q.v.*). He spent some months in Warsaw, but after the peace of Riga he moved his government to Paris and was assassinated by a communist agent.

Bulgakov, M., *The White Guard*, 1925.

PETRASHEVSKY, MICHAEL VASILYEVICH (1821–66). Minor official of the foreign ministry and host to gatherings held on Friday evenings that met to discuss literary, social, and political subjects. Petrashevsky was cowriter of a *Pocket Dictionary of Foreign Words* (1845–46).

PETRASHEVTSY. Name given to a group of several hundred people who met in secret every Friday at the house of Michael Butashevich-Petrashevsky (1821–66) in order to discuss economic and sociopolitical thought. Influenced by Blanc, Proudhon, and Leroux, the general philosophy of the group eventually combined elements of Feuerbachian and Fourierist thought; great emphasis was placed on the natural sciences and on the need to build a socialist utopia. Petrashevsky himself favored legal struggle in order to achieve partial reforms; the radicals, on the other hand, under the leadership of Nicholas Speshnev (1821–82), favored armed revolt. In 1845 and 1846 the Petrashevtsy published their ideas in the celebrated *Pocket Dictionary of Foreign Terms.* In 1849, 21 of the Petrashevtsy were charged with plotting to overthrow the state, but the death sentence was commuted at the last minute; one of the condemned was the writer F. M. Dostoyevsky. The Petrashevtsy did, however, make a valuable contribution in pioneering socialist ideas that were to be discussed by radical groups later in the century.

Walicki, A., *A History of Russian Thought*, 1980.

PETRODVORETS (prior to 1944, Peterhof). Town in the Leningrad oblast on the S shore of the Gulf of Finland. It has several 18th- and 19th-century imperial palaces and parks. In 1941–43, when the Germans occupied the town, it was destroyed but has been rebuilt for the most part.

PETROGRAD. Name given to St. Petersburg in August 1914 as an anti-German gesture. *See* **Leningrad.**

PETROKREPOST (Prior to 1611, Oreshek; 1611–1702, Noteborg; 1702–1944, Shlisselburg). Town in the Leningrad oblast on Lake Ladoga at the start of the Neva River. Petrokrepost is renowned for its old fortress, which from the 18th century to 1917 was used as a prison for political offenders. Founded by Novgorodians in 1323, from 1611 to 1702 it was Swedish, and from 1941 to 1943 it was occupied by the Germans.

PETROPAVLOVSK. City on the Trans-Siberian Railway in N Kazakhstan 875 miles (1,400 km) NNW of Alma Ata. Founded in 1752, it became a commercial center trading in grain, furs, and textiles. Industries include engineering, meat packing, flour milling, and tanning. Population (1981) 212,000.

PETROPAVLOVSK-KAMCHATSKI. City in the NE situated on the SE coast of the Kamchatka peninsula on the Bering Sea. Industries include shipbuilding, sawmilling, and fish canning. It is a naval base and seaport that is ice-free for seven months of the year. Population (1981) 223,000.

PETROV, VASILY PETROVICH (1736–99). Poet, most of whose work is written in imitation of Michael Lomonosov (*q.v.*). He also translated some of Alexander Pope's work.

PETROV, YEVGENY PETROVICH (1903–42). Pseudonym of an author named Katayev. Having worked on the newspaper *Gudok*, Petrov together with Ilya Ilf started to write novels such as *The Twelve Chairs* (1928) and *The Golden Calf* (1931), which are satirical accounts of life in the 1920s. Ilf and Petrov also wrote articles on America, following their visit to the United States. These were published widely in *Pravda*, *Krokodil*, and *Literaturnaya Gazeta*. After Ilf's death in 1937, Petrov continued to write, producing sketches, plays, and scenarios for film.

PETROV-VODKIN, KUZMA (1878–1939). Artist. Having studied at Anton Azbe's studio in Munich and under Leonid Pasternak (*q.v.*) in Moscow, Petrov-Vodkin traveled to Africa where he was influenced by primitive art. He deliberately did not adhere to any one school of painting, although he was a close friend of many of the Blue Rose group. He evolved the theory that the best method of depicting space on canvas is by means of a curved horizontal axis, a theory he expounds in two books. Petrov-Vodkin became an influential professor at the Leningrad Art Academy. Among his best-known paintings is *The Playing Boys* (1911).

Gray, Camilla, *The Russian Experiment in Art*, 1962.

PETROZAVODSK. Capital of Karelian Autonomous Soviet Socialist Republic in the Russian Soviet Federated Socialist Republic, 185 miles (296 km) NE of Leningrad. It is situated on W shore of Lake Onega. Founded in 1702 by Peter the Great as a site for an armaments factory, its industries include sawmilling and mica processing; manufactures include cement, furniture, and machinery. Population (1981) 241,000.

PEVSNER, ANTON (1886–1962). Constructivist artist. Having spent a year at the St. Petersburg Academy of Art in 1910, Pevsner went to Paris and then Norway, where he painted in the Cubist style. In the early 1920s Pevsner began working on constructions, and together with his brother, Naum Gabo (*q.v.*), joined the antiproductionist group Inkhuk.

Gray, Camilla, *The Russian Experiment in Art*, 1962.

PHILARET, PATRIARCH (1553?–1633). In secular circles, Philaret was known as Fedor Nikitich Romanov, as a successful soldier and diplomat. Compelled to take monastic vows by Boris Godunov, he was released by the first False Dmitry and made metropolitan of Rostov in 1606. In 1609 the second False Dmitry made him patriarch of All Russia. He was arrested and sent to Poland in 1611. After his son Michael was elected tsar he returned to Moscow and was enthroned as patriarch in 1619. From that time on he ruled Russia jointly with Tsar Michael.

PILNYAK, BORIS (B. A. Vogau) (1894–1937). Writer. Pilnyak's novel

The Naked Year (1922) was the first novel to deal with the Revolution and its effects on Russian life. Pilnyak became disillusioned with the regime, and the publication of *Mahogany* (1929) caused him to be expelled from the author association. His novel about the Five-Year Plan, *The Volga Flows into the Caspian Sea,* was an attempt to reinstate himself in official favor. He survived the purges by publicly denouncing his "antirevolutionary" writings.

Struve, Gleb, *Russian Literature Under Lenin and Stalin,* 1972.

PINEAU, NICHOLAS (1684–1754). French wood-carver. In 1716 he was invited to Russia by Peter the Great and became chief decorative artist to the court. His most important work is the carved tsar's cabinet in the Peterhof Palace.

PINSK. Town 135 miles (216 km) SSW of Minsk, in Belorussia, situated in Pripet Marshes. Part of Kievan Russia in 1097, it was part of Lithuania in 1320 and of Poland in 1569. It was ceded to Russia in 1793 but was returned to Poland in 1921 and became Russian again in 1945. Industries include the manufacture of paper, furniture, soap, matches, and leather. Population (1976) 84,000.

PIONEERS. Young peoples' group for those between the ages of 10 and 14 to 15 years, founded as an auxiliary to the Komsomol in 1922. The aim of the movement is outlined in the Komsomol statute: it should make its members "convinced fighters for the Communist Party cause, inculcate in them a love of labor and knowledge, and assist the formation of the younger generation in the spirit of communist consciousness and morality." Regular meetings are held; visits are arranged to places of revolutionary interest; and Pioneers parade and take part in summer camps. Pioneer activities often provide a useful addition to the school curriculum. Those wishing to join must take the Pioneer oath and undertake to obey the Pioneer laws. Nearly all children in this age range are Pioneers.

PIROGOV, NICHOLAS I. (1810–81). Surgeon in charge of the Sevastopol hospitals during the siege of Sevastopol. In 1856 he was made curator of the educational district of New Russia, although he was later transferred to Kiev.

PIROSMANASHVILI, NIKO (1860–1918). Artist. A Georgian sign painter, Pirosmanashvili attracted the attention of Michael Larionov *(q.v.)* and other Futurists. He exhibited works with the Donkey's Tail group *(q.v.).* Among his most famous paintings is his *Recumbent Woman* (1905).

PISAREV, DMITRY IVANOVICH (1840–68). Radical social thinker and leading Russian nihilist. Having studied at St. Petersburg University, Pisarev was imprisoned for writing an article in which he defended the socialist Alexander Herzen *(q.v.).* He wrote for several radical journals, including *Notes of the Fatherland,* and he edited *Russian Word.*

Lampert, Evgeny, *Sons Against Fathers,* 1965.

PISEMSKY, ALEKSEY FEOFILATOVICH (1820–81). Writer. Having been educated at Moscow University, Pisemsky entered the civil service and joined the young editorial staff of the *Moskvityanin,* where he met Alexander Ostrovsky and Apokon Grigoryev *(q.q.v.).* In 1858 he embarked on a career in journalism. Becoming increasingly hostile toward the radicals and increasingly embittered, Pisemsky watched his talents wane. *A Thousand Souls* (1858) and the tragedy *A Hard Lot* (1859) rank among his greatest writings and are noted for their plots and characterizations.

PLATONOV, SERGEY FEDOROVICH (1860–1933). Historian and professor at St. Petersburg University. A specialist on the Time of Troubles, Platonov protested loudly at the falsification of history by the Soviet authorities. As a result he was dismissed from the Academy of Sciences and banished. His publications include the textbook *A History of Russia* (1925).

PLEHVE, VYACHESLAV KONSTANTINOVICH (1846–1904). Russian statesman and staunch supporter of the autocracy. Having served in the department of justice from 1867, in 1881 Plehve was appointed director of the police department. As a result of his harsh suppression of terrorism, he was made deputy minister of the interior in 1884 and head of the imperial chancellery in 1894. In 1902 he was appointed minister of the interior. He was assassinated in 1904.

PLEKHANOV, GEORGY VALENTINOVICH (1857–1918). Politician. When the organization *Zemlya i Volya* (*see* ***Land and Liberty Organization***), of which Plekhanov was a member, split into violent and nonviolent factions, Plekhanov became leader of the new nonviolent *Cherny Peredel* (Black Repartition). Having become a Marxist in W Europe, in 1883 he founded the Liberation of Labor group *(q.v.).* Collaborating with Lenin, Plekhanov at first supported the Bolsheviks, but in 1903 joined the Mensheviks, and in 1910 he established the faction of "party-minded" Mensheviks. He played a unique part in converting the Russian intelligentsia to Marxism. After the February Revolution of 1917, Plekhanov set up the right-wing Social Democratic organization Unity, but died shortly after the Bolshevik seizure of power.

Baron, Samuel, *Plekhanov: The Father of Russian Marxism,* 1963.

PLETNEV, PETER ALEKSANDROVICH (1792–1865). Minor poet. He was Pushkin's literary agent and friend. Pletnev was editor of *Sovremennik* after Pushkin's death.

PLISETSKAYA, MAYA (1928–). Ballerina. Having studied at the Bolshoi School, Plisetskaya is considered one of the greatest ballerinas of her time. She is noted particularly for her interpretation of the role of Odette-Odile in *Swan Lake.*

POBEDA PEAK. Highest peak of the Tien Shan mountains in the E Kirghiz Soviet Socialist Republic. It is 24,406 feet (7,438 m) above sea level.

POBEDONOSTSEV, KONSTANTIN PETROVICH (1827–1907). Courtier and politician. He was appointed procurator of the Holy Synod of the Russian Orthodox Church in 1880. He was reactionary and was responsible for the illiberal schemes of Alexander III *(q.v.)*.

PODGORNY NICHOLAS VIKTOROVICH (1903–1983). Soviet state official. Podgorny joined the CPSU in 1931 and rose in the ranks of the party in the Ukraine. He was a member of the Presidium and Politburo of the central committee of the CPSU from 1958 to 1960. He was secretary of the central committee of the CPSU (1963–66) and chairman of the Presidium of the USSR Supreme Soviet, from 1965 to 1977.

PODOLIA. Region in the Ukraine between the Dnestr River to W and S Bug River to E. The chief towns are Vinnitsa and Kamenets-Podolski. Polish settlers began the transformation of the steppe to farmland in the 14th century. Before this Podolia had been part of Kievan Russia. Belonging in turn to Poland, Lithuania, and the W area of Austria, it became a Polish possession again in 1919 and was annexed by the USSR in 1939.

PODOLSK. City situated 26 miles (42 km) S of Moscow on the Pakhra River. It was owned by the Danilov Monastery until 1781, when it received its charter as a city. Industries include railway engineering and oil refining; manufactures include cables, sewing machines, lime, and cement. Population (1981) 205,000.

PODSEKA. Slash-and-burn agriculture, sometimes used in forested areas.

PODVOYSKY, NICHOLAS ILICH (1880–1948). Soviet politician. Having joined the Social Democratic Labor Party in 1901, Podvoysky later adhered to its Bolshevik faction. He was the owner of a publishing house specializing in Social Democratic literature before the First World War. Following the February Revolution of 1917, he was a member of the executive branch of the first legal Bolshevik St. Petersburg committee and chairman of the military commission of the central committee and of the military revolutionary committee of the Petrograd Soviet. After the seizure of power, Podvoysky set about the task of organizing the Red Army. In spite of the fact that he served as a commissar in the Civil War, he fell out of favor and from the 1930s was relegated to serving on the staff of the Marx-Engels-Lenin Institute.

PODZOL. Light gray soil of the forest zone.

POGODIN, MICHAEL PETROVICH (1800–75). Journalist. The son of a serf, Pogodin met the Lovers of Wisdom *(q.v.)* at Moscow University. He was appointed a professor of Russian history and later became editor of several magazines, including *Moskivtyanin.*

POGROM (Devastation). An attack on Jews and Jewish property, especially in the Russian Empire. Russian pogroms, which were condoned by the government, were particularly common in the years immediately after the assassination of Alexander II in 1881 and again from 1903 to 1906, although mob persecution of Jews continued until the 1917 Russian Revolution.

POKROVSKY, MICHAEL NIKOLAYEVICH (1868–1932). Historian. In 1918 Pokrovsky was appointed people's commissar for education and director of the Central Archives. He wrote several works on general Russian history, including *Russian History from the Earliest Times* (1924).

POLEVOY, NICHOLAS ALEKSEYEVICH (1796–1846). Journalist. The son of a tradesman, Polevoy's magazine the *Moscow Telegraph* (1825–34) pioneered Romanticism, but in 1834 it was suppressed as a result of an unfavorable review of a play by Nestor Kukolnik. He also wrote a somewhat pretentious satire, *A History of the Russian People.*

POLEZHAYEV, ALEXANDER IVANOVICH (1805–38). Poet. Having led a life of debauchery and drunkenness at Moscow University, Polezhayev was summoned by Nicholas I as a result of having expressed liberal opinions in his poem *Sashka* (1825–26). He was made to serve in the army and was eventually recommended for a commission, but this came after his death. His best-known poems include *Song of the Sailor in the Process of being Wrecked* and *The Song of the Captive Iroquois.*

POLICE. Known as the people's militia, the Soviet police force is organized by the Ministry of Internal Affairs. The militia departments are divided into various branches, including a special transport militia. The militia's work is similar to that of a Western police force, with additions such as the enforcement of the internal passport system and the exposure of social parasites such as people who don't have assigned jobs. Appointment of recruits is approved by the local Soviet, as well as by the militia chief.

POLISH INSURRECTION (also known as the **January Insurrection**) 1863–64). An uprising that attempted to overthrow the Vienna Congress *(q.v.)* Kingdom of Poland. In the early 1860s a variety of conspiratorial groups organized nationalistic demonstrations. The Agricultural Society, headed by Andrew Zamoyski, won the support of many sections of the population, and other groups more interested in open revolt and protest formed in Warsaw, affiliating themselves with the Military Academy. Faced with growing anti-Russian feeling, Marquis Alexander Wielopolski, virtual leader of the government of the Congress Kingdom, decided to draft the radical youths into the army. The conscripts, however, escaped, and on January 22, 1863, with the aid of the revolutionary committee, issued a manifesto calling for a nationwide insurrection. The rebels won widespread support. There were peasant revolts in other areas of Poland, and an underground government was set up in Warsaw. The ill-equipped and untrained rebel army waged guerrilla warfare against the Russian army. The rebels' heroism is the subject of important works of

Polish literature, including Stephan Zeromski's *The Faithful River.* Without strong leadership and military assistance, however, the insurrection was losing momentum by October. In 1864 those leaders who had not escaped the country were executed.

Dyboski, R., *Outlines of Polish History,* 1925.

POLITBURO. The political bureau of the Communist Party central committee is the most powerful institution of the party. It is responsible for the work of the party between plenary sessions of the central committee. The chief policy-making organ of the party, it consists of 14 full members and eight candidate members, although the numbers sometimes vary.

Hough, J. and Fainsod, Merle, *How the Soviet Union is Governed,* 1979.

McAuley, M., *Politics and the Soviet Union,* 1977.

Schapiro, Leonard B., *The Communist Party of the Soviet Union,* 1971.

POLITICAL AGITATION. It is estimated that there are 37 million political agitators in the Soviet Union whose function is to hold short talks and discussions weekly on increasing factory and farm production. In addition political speakers hold lectures on economic, political, or cultural topics, and a smaller number of *dokladchiki* (lecturers) give longer talks on items of foreign or domestic policy on important occasions.

POLOTSK. Town 120 miles (192 km) NNE of Minsk in Belorussia, situated on the W Dvina River. It was the capital of the principality of Polotsk in the 10th to the 13th century; it then became a Lithuanian possession and became part of Russia in 1772. Industries include sawmilling, oil refining, and flour milling. Population (1976) 75,000.

POLOTSKY, SIMEON (1629–1680). Monk, preacher, playwright, and poet. In his rhymed *Psalter* (1680) he used a form of rhymed couplets with an equal number, 11 or 13, of stressed syllables to a line; this meter was taken from the Poles. Polotsky is important for the metrical innovations rather than for the quality of his verse.

POLOVNIK. Sharecropper.

POLOVTSIANS (Cumans). Turkic nomadic tribe that defeated the Pechenegs and occupied the SE steppe; they were the dominant people in the Kipchak tribal confederation. In the mid-11th century they commanded an extensive territory stretching from the N of the Aral Sea westward to the area N of the Black Sea. A threat to Kievan Russia, in 1111 the Polovtsians were defeated at Salnitsa by Prince Vladimir Monomakh *(q.v.)*; his "Testament" records 83 major campaigns. As a result of weakened resources, the tribe fell to the Golden Horde (1237–42).

POLTAVA. Ukrainian town 190 miles (304 km) ESE of Kiev situated on the Vorskiya River. It is the commercial center of an agricultural area. It was the site of a Slavic settlement in the eighth century. Destroyed by the Tatars in the 13th century, it became part of Lithuania in 1430. A Cossack regiment was based in

Poltava in the 17th century and nearby the Battle of Poltava (*q.v.*) took place in which Charles XII of Sweden was defeated by Peter the Great. Industries include textiles, brewing, meat packing, tanning, and flour milling. Population (1981) 284,000.

POLTAVA, BATTLE OF. Battle fought on July 8, 1709 between Russian forces under Peter the Great and Swedish forces under Charles XII (*q.v.*), during the Great Northern War (*q.v.*) for control of the Baltic. The Swedes besieged the town of Poltava. The Russians set up a counter-siege, which successfully drew the Swedes off, and engaged them in conditions favorable to Russia. The Russian commander under Peter the Great was General Prince Alexander Menshikov. The battle was immortalized by Pushkin in his epic poem *Poltava.*

POLTINA. A monetary unit in medieval Russia; one *poltina* equaled half a ruble, or 50 kopecks.

POLYCLINICS. Outpatient clinics. Although the majority of people attend free polyclinics, there are also self-financing polyclinics in large towns.

POLZUNOV, IVAN IVANOVICH (1730–66). Designer and builder of the first steam engine in Russia. Having studied at the Metallurgical School in Yekaterinburg, Polzunov worked as a mechanic in Barnaul before designing his steam engine and a number of other related technical innovations. He died a week before his engine was put into use.

POMERANTSEV, A. N. (1848–98). Architect. He built the GUM department store (1889–93), an extraordinary eclectic classical building, despite the interior use of iron and glass.

POMESHCHIK. Until the early 18th century, the name for a holder of land on service tenure; later, the name used for noble landowners.

POMESTIYE. Until the early 18th century, land held on service tenure; later, the general name for estates owned by nobles.

POMYALOVSKY, NICHOLAS GERASIMOVICH (1835–63). Novelist. Educated at a clerical seminary, Pomyalovsky spent the rest of his life in a gloomy struggle to exist. He died of alcoholism at the age of 28. Pomyalovsky's most famous works include his horrifying *Seminary Sketches* (1862–63) and *Bourgeois Happiness* (1861).

POOD (Pud). Measure of weight equal to 36.113 pounds (16.38 kg.).

POPOV, ALEXANDER STEPANOVICH (1859–1905). Physicist and electrotechnician. He demonstrated a wireless receiver in 1895, and a transmitter in 1896, before Marconi had invented radiotelegraphy. A special commission established Popov's priority in this invention in 1908.

POPOVTSY (Priestly sect). Old Believer movement (*q.v.*) that agreed to accept priests ordained by the official church. The *popovtsy* gradually made their peace with the Orthodox Church (*q.v.*).

POPULATION. The first modern census (*q.v.*) was taken in 1897.

Total Population	
1796	36,000,000
1811	41,000,000
1815	45,000,000
1835	59,000,000
1846	65,900,000
1859	74,000,000
1870	86,000,000
1887	98,000,000
1897	106,000,000
1908	155,000,000
1915	131,000,000
1926	147,000,000
1939	170,000,000
1959	209,000,000
1970	242,000,000
1979	262,000,000

The estimated loss of population in the Second World War was 20 million, of which 7 million were military fatalities.

POPULISM (*Narodnost*). Socialist movement of intellectuals in the 19th century. The populists sought to transform society by basing it on the traditional peasant *mir* (community) (*q.v.*). Inspired by Michael Bakunin (*q.v.*), in 1873–74, the *narodniki* (populists) adopted the tactic of "going to the people" *(khozhdeniye v narod)* with the aim of educating the masses with revolutionary ideas. This having failed, the more secretive Land and Liberty *(Zemlya i Volya)* (*q.v.*) group was formed in 1876. Three years later, those members advocating more violent methods formed the People's Will (*q.v.*) terrorist group (*Narodnaya Volya*). It was this group which was responsible for the assassination of Alexander II in 1881. The moderates, the Black Repartition (*Cherny Peredel*), continued to employ more peaceful means.

PORT ARTHUR. Town, port, and naval base in Manchuria. Port Arthur was a Russian naval base from 1898 but was ceded to Japan as a result of the Russo-Japanese War (*q.v.*). In 1945 it was occupied by Russians and the Soviet government secured the renewal of the concession, but in 1955 it was forced to return the base to the Chinese.

POSADA. A suburb inhabited by taxpayers.

POSADNIK. An elected city official in Novgorod.

POSOSHKOV, IVAN TIKHONOVICH (1652–1726). Tradesman and author of *On Indigence and Wealth.*

POTEMKIN, PRINCE GRIGORY ALEKSANDROVICH (1739–91). Statesman and favorite of Catherine II. The viceroy of New Russia from 1774, from 1784 Potemkin was president of the war department and field marshal. Having persuaded the khan of Crimea to abdicate, Crimea was annexed to Russia. In 1787 Potemkin erected fake villages in New Russia, so that Catherine, visiting the area, would believe it to be more populated than it actually was; hence, the term "Potemkin village."

POTEMKIN MUTINY. Mutiny occurring on June 14, 1905 by the crew of the cruiser *Potemkin* of the Black Sea fleet in Odessa. They put out to sea, but eventually surrendered to Rumanian authorities at Constanta. The mutiny is the subject of a much-acclaimed film by Sergey Eisenstein *(q.v.)*.

Hough, R., *The Potemkin Mutiny*, 1961.

POTI. Georgian town 40 miles (64 km) N of Batumi, on the Black Sea at the mouth of the Rioni River. A Greek colony in the fifth century, it later became a Turkish fort and was taken by Russians in 1828. Industries include fish canning and ship repairing. It also exports manganese from the Chiatura mines. Population (1976) 54,000.

POTRESOV, ALEXANDER NIKOLAYEVICH (1869–1934). Social Democrat. Having worked with Lenin in the *Iskra* movement, he then changed allegiance, becoming leader of the Mensheviks after the 1905 Revolution. In 1917, however, he refused to join the Menshevik Party, maintaining that opposition to the Bolsheviks by legal means only was too limited. In 1927 Potresov emigrated.

POTSDAM AGREEMENT. According to the Potsdam Agreement concerning Germany, a committee of foreign ministers was to be set up in order to work out peace treaties with Germany's allies. The commanders in chief of Great Britain, France, the United States, and the USSR would exercise supreme authority in their respective zones of Germany and would cooperate on the control council on German matters. Germany was to be disarmed, the people reeducated, and no central German government was to be formed for the time being. Part of E Prussia and Königsberg was to be given to the USSR, and the Oder-Neisse line was to be the provisional W frontier of Poland. In addition, war criminals were to be tried.

Feis, Herbert, *Between War and Peace: The Potsdam Conference*, 1960.

POTSDAM CONFERENCE. Conference held between July 16, and August 1, 1945 at Potsdam. Churchill and Attlee, Truman, and Stalin met to discuss the future of Germany after its unconditional surrender on May 7, 1945.

Feis, Herbert, *Between War and Peace: The Potsdam Conference*, 1960.

POZZO DI BORGO, COUNT (1764–1842). Corsican nobleman who later became a Russian diplomat and champion of French interests after the downfall of Napoleon.

PRAGUE SPRING. Name given to the spring of 1968 in Czechoslovakia, which was characterized by a growing freedom of speech, the press, and the arts. The Soviet government became increasingly alarmed at the liberalization of Czechoslovakia and ordered Dubček to take harsh action. Warsaw Pact troops on maneuvers surrounded Czechoslovakia and on August 21, 1968 invaded the country.

PRAVDA (Truth). The daily newspaper of the Communist Party, founded in 1912, which is printed in 44 major cities. Although most of the paper is devoted to party affairs and production achievements, there are also foreign news items, sports, and weather reports. The circulation is about 10 million.

PRAVDA RUSSKAYA. First Russian legal codex. It was compiled by Yaroslav the Wise *(q.v.)*.

PREOBRAZHENSKAYA, OLGA (1870–1962). Famous ballerina and pupil of Christian Johansson *(q.v.)*.

PREOBRAZHENSKOYE. Village in which Peter the Great *(q.v.)* spent some time as a child and from which the Preobrazhensky regiment derived its name. The Preobrazhensky was the senior guards infantry regiment in the Imperial Russian Army.

PRE-PARLIAMENT. A preliminary assembly, sometimes known as the Council of the Republic, set up as a kind of temporary constitutional assembly on Kerensky's *(q.v.)* initiative in October 1917. Because, in Lenin's view, it was rigged, the Bolsheviks walked out of it on the first day. It was closed down in the uprising as part of the seizure of power.

PRESIDIUM. The Presidium is elected by the Supreme Soviet of the USSR, consisting of a chairman and 37 members. It amends statutes, interprets laws, and ratifies treaties. According to the 1977 constitution, the Presidium is more powerful even than the Supreme Soviet; the Presidium can call elections, proclaim martial law, or order mobilization, for example.

McAuley, M., *Politics and the Soviet Union*, 1977.

PRIKAZ. A department of Muscovy's government headed by either a boyar or an *okolnich* and run by a *diyak*. These departments were numerous.

PRIKAZCHIK. An official of the central government in cities or provinces.

PRIMARY CHRONICLE. The *Povest vremennyk let* (Tale of Bygone Years) is a Chronicle written by the monks of the Kievan Monastery of the Caves, including Nestor, who edited the work. The Chronicle includes lives of saints, folk legends, accounts of battles, and a will, as well as the *Instruction of Vladimir Monomakh*, a literary work complete in itself, and containing a portrait of the ideal Kievan prince. *The Primary Chronicle* covers the period up to 1118.

Fennell, John and Stokes, Anthony, *Early Russian Literature*, 1974.

PRIMORE TERRITORY. Territory in SE Siberia situated on the Sea of Japan. It has an area of 65,000 square miles (168,350 sq km). The capital is Vladivostock. Mountainous in the E, with the Sikhote Alin range, and consisting of lowland in the W, it is drained by the Ussuri River. The main products are coal and timber. Population (1970) 1,722,000.

PRIPYAT' MARSHES. Largest area of swamp in Europe, in the basin of the Pripyat' River in the Brest and Gomel oblasts of the Belorussian Soviet Socialist Republic and covering parts of the Ukrainian Soviet Socialist Republic. This area was divided between the USSR and Poland during World War I. Measures have been taken to drain the area.

PRIPYAT' RIVER. River rising in NW Ukraine and flowing 500 miles (800 km) ENE into Belorussia. It then turns E and SE to join the Dnepr River above Kiev. Most of it is navigable and linked by canals to the Bug and Neman rivers.

PRISHVIN, MICHAEL MIKHAILOVICH (1873–1954). Writer, naturalist, and ethnographer. His main works include *In the Land of Unfrightened Birds* (1907), *Roots of Life* (1932), and the novel *The Chain of Kashchy* (1930).

PROCURACY. The office of procurator was an important one in tsarist times. Under the Soviet system, the procurator is appointed by the USSR Supreme Soviet, and it is his task to control his officials throughout the union. He authorizes arrest, prosecutes offenders, supervises prisons and investigations in criminal cases, and can refer judicial decisions to higher courts. He also serves as a channel for citizens' complaints. There is no exact Western equivalent of the procuracy.

PROKOFIEV, SERGEY SERGEYEVICH (1891–1953). Pianist and composer. Having studied under Rimsky-Korsakov, Glazunov, and Glière *(q.q.v.)* at the St. Petersburg Conservatory, in 1918 Prokofiev went on a world tour. He finally returned home in 1934. A diverse and original talent he is regarded as one of the leading Soviet composers. His works include the music for the ballet *Romeo and Juliet* (1936), music for the plays *Boris Godunov* (1936) and *Hamlet* (1938), and the film score for *Ivan the Terrible.* The first performance of his opera *War and Peace* was held in 1944.

Nestyev, I. V., *Prokofiev*, 1961.
Samuel, Claude, *Prokofiev*, 1971.

PROKOPEVSK. Town in S central Siberia 17 miles (27 km) WNW of Novokuznetsk and situated in the Kuznetsk basin. A small village in the 18th century, it expanded in the early 1920s. The main industry is coal mining. Population (1981) 167,000.

PROKOPOVICH, FEOFAN (1681–1736). Ukrainian theologian and archbishop. After studying at Rome, Prokopovich taught at the theological academy in Kiev and later became the rector of the academy. In 1716 Peter the Great *(q.v.)* summoned him to St. Petersburg where Prokopovich assisted Peter with his reforms, both ecclesiastical and secular. In 1705 he produced a tragicomedy in which the hero is a thinly disguised portrait of Peter the Great. He tried to found a secular drama but was not successful.

PROLETARIAT. Class that, according to Marxism, is exploited by capitalist society, and that lives by selling its labor. According to Marxist theory, the bourgeoisie was to be overthrown by the proletariat, and a dictatorship of the proletariat was to be established as a transitional phase to the establishment of communism. According to Lenin, the proletariat need a highly centralized revolutionary party to organize and lead them.

Briefs, G. (trans R. A. Eckhart), *The Proletariat*, 1937.

PROLETKULT. Abbreviation for Proletarian Cultural and Educational

Organizations, established by the Bogdanovists after the February Revolution of 1917. It aimed to produce a proletarian culture that would be indispensable as a foundation for socialist revolution. Subordinated to the commissariat of education in 1919, it was abolished in 1932.

Paul, M. Eden and Cedar, *Proletcult*, 1921.

Thomson, Boris, *The Premature Revolution, 1972.*

PROTOPOPOV, ALEXANDER DMITRYEVICH (1866?–1918). Russian landowner, industrialist, and, in 1916–17, minister of the interior. In 1907 Protopopov joined the left wing of the Octobrist Party (*See* **Octobrists**). In 1916 he led a parliamentary delegation to Great Britain, France, and Italy but was accused of indiscretion. Believing it was his mission to save Russia he devised schemes for organizing the country along totalitarian lines, which were rejected. He failed to relieve the serious food shortages of 1917 and ordered that harsh measures be taken against rioters. He was imprisoned and shot on the orders of the Cheka.

PROVISIONAL GOVERNMENT. Government formed by the duma in February 1917 in Petrograd upon the collapse of the autocracy. The provisional government promised to form a constitutional assembly and to hold free elections. It abolished the secret police and granted religious freedom. Many of its leaders were of a conservative outlook, although Kerensky (*q.v.*) was a moderate socialist. Because of the war effort grave problems, such as redistribution of land and the rights of non-Russian people to self-government, could not be resolved. As a result, discontent continued to grow. At the same time as the provisional government, the Soviet of workers' deputies had been established; this had the support of industrial workers and socialists, and in October 1917 they overthrew the provisional government.

PRUT RIVER. River rising in the Carpathian Mountains in SW Ukraine and flowing 530 miles (848 km) N, then E past Kolomyya and Chernovtsy, and then SSE, forming the Rumania-USSR frontier, to join the Danube River 8 miles (13 km) E of Galati, Rumania.

PRZHEVALSK. Town 190 miles (304 km) E of Frunze near the SE shore of Lake Issyk-kul, in the Kirghiz Soviet Socialist Republic. It was founded in 1869 as a military outpost. It is a food-processing center in a wheat-growing area; manufactures include wines, beverages, machinery, and furniture. Population (1973) 47,000.

PSKOV. Town in the W situated on the Velikaya River, in the Russian Soviet Federated Socialist Republic. It is the capital of Pskov region. It became an outpost of Novgorod in 903 and from 1347 to 1510 was a city-state with commercial links to the Hanseatic League. In 1510 it was annexed by Moscow. Industries include manufacturing linen from local flax, and the manufacture of rope, leather, and agricultural machinery. Pskov railway station was the scene of the abdication of Tsar Nicholas II on March 3, 1917. In the walled city is a kremlin dating from the 12th century. Population (1976) 155,000.

PUBLISHING. The preparation of books for distribution dates from the end of the 10th century with scriptoria in monasteries, princely courts, and some towns. Early in the 16th century the White Russian Frantsisk Skorina was printing books in Vilnius. The first dated Russian printed book (1563–64) was printed by Ivan Fedorov and Peter Mstislavets at the Imperial Printing House. The reforms of Peter the Great encouraged publishing, which was a government monopoly until 1783. Publishing flourished under enlightened scholar-entrepreneurs like Nicholas I. Novikov (*q.v.*) but inspired by reaction to the French Revolution, Catherine the Great curbed the press in 1796. 9,500 titles were published in the 18th century. The 19th century saw the growth of capitalist publishing, mainly by enlightened aristocrats or booksellers. In 1860 2,085 titles were published; in 1880 10,562. Throughout the century there were various decrees on censorship varying in severity, and to escape these some publishers set up abroad, e.g., Alexander Herzen in London. A breakdown of types of literature at the end of the 19th century shows a predominance of religious literature followed by light fiction "for the people" published by various "improvement" societies. In 1913, 30,079 titles were published, 9.1 percent in languages other than Russian.

After the 1917 Revolution, publishing was taken over by the state, although some private publishers survived for a year or two. Decrees of November 10, 1917 and January 11, 1918 laid down administrative and policy foundations. Over 500 cheap editions of literature and textbooks were brought out during the Civil War (1918–21). The state publisher (Gosizdat) was set up on May 21, 1919 to regulate publishing in general as well as issue its own work. Under the New Economic Policy, commercial trading was reintroduced and publishers were made self-accounting units. Publishing regained prewar levels by 1925. During this period the present specialization patterns of publishers began to take shape.

An administrative reorganization of July 1930 established the Union of State Book and Periodical Publishers of the Russian Soviet Federated Socialist Republic (Ogiz). During the 1930s annual title production averaged 44,000. This dropped to 18,353 in 1945 because of war damage and diversion of resources.

In February 1949 Ogiz was replaced by the Chief Board for the Printing Industry, Publishers, and the Book Trade (Glavpoligrafizdat). In 1963 this was replaced by the Committee for the Press, which became the SCP in August 1972.

Dewhirst, Martin and Farrell, Robert (eds.), *The Soviet Censorship*, 1973.

Gorokhoff, Boris I., *Publishing in the USSR*, 1959.

Walker, Geoffrey, P. M., *Book Publishing in the U.S.S.R.: Reports of the Delegations of U.S. Book Publishers Visiting in the U.S.S.R.*, 1972.

Walker, Geoffrey, P. M., *Soviet Book Publishing Policy*, 1978.

PUDOVKIN, VSEVOLOD ILLARIONOVICH (1893–1953). Soviet film director. Wounded and imprisoned in the First World War. Pudovkin entered the State Institute of Cinematography in Moscow, and at first worked with Lev Kuleshev (*q.v.*). Among Pudovkin's best-known films are *The End of St. Petersburg* (1927), *Mother* (1926), and *Deserter* (1933). Pudovkin edited for continuity and not, as Eisenstein (*q.v.*), did for shock effect. He was thus able to develop his characters and their emotional growth smoothly. He has also written books on film production.

Leyda, Jay, *Kino: A History of the Russian and Soviet Film*, 1960.

Taylor, R., *The Politics of the Soviet Cinema, 1917–29*, 1979.

PUGACHEV, YEMELYAN IVANOVICH (1726–75). Cossack leader of a revolt during Catherine II's reign. Declaring himself Emperor Peter III in 1773, he issued a manifesto promising to liberate the serfs. Pugachev won widespread support in the Volga area and in the Urals, but the revolt was eventually crushed and he was executed.

Avrich, Paul, *Russian Rebels, 1600–1800*, 1972.

PUGACHEVSHCHINA. Peasant rising led by Yemelyan Pugachev (*q.v.*) in 1773–74.

Avrich, Paul, *Russian Rebels, 1600–1800*, 1972.

PULKOVO. Village in the Leningrad oblast of the Russian Soviet Federated Socialist Republic and home of the chief astronomical observatory of the Academy of Sciences of the USSR. Prior to the Revolution, Russian maps were based on the Pulkovo meridian.

PUNIN, NICHOLAS. Art critic who advocated that art should no longer be an object of worship, stating that art "is not a holy shrine where things are lazily regarded, but work, a factory which produces new artistic things." Punin edited the weekly paper *Art of the Commune* from 1918 to 1919 and was a close friend of Vladimir Tatlin (*q.v.*)

Gray, Camilla, *The Russian Experiment in Art*, 1962.

PURGES. Campaigns by which the government wished to eliminate "socially alien" elements in trade unions, the party, and the bureaucracy. The old intelligentsia were purged in 1928–31, but the still more sinister Great Purge organized by Nicholas Yezhov (*q.v.*) occurred in 1936–38. It is thought that between 8 and 10 million died in this purge. In 1939–41 there were purges in the Baltic states, Bessarabia, part of Bukovina, and E Poland. There was also a wave of purges in 1944–46 in territory that had been occupied by the enemy.

PURISHKEVICH, VLADIMIR M. (1870–1920). Founding member of the Union of Russian People, created in 1905 and a right-wing member of the duma.

PUSHKIN, ALEXANDER SERGEYEVICH (1799–1837). One of the great figures of world literature, and Russia's greatest poet. He came from a poor but noble family. A maternal great-grandparent was an Ethiopian who became a general under Peter the Great. He was influenced by the Enlightenment and the French Revolution, and was a personal friend of many of the Decembrists. He was twice exiled for his views, once to New Russia in 1820 and once to the family estate in 1824. Nicholas I freed him from the ordinary censorship by undertaking to be censor himself. He was killed in a duel with a French nobleman whom he suspected of being the lover of his wife.

Pushkin's first poem was published when he was 15; and early in his writing career he was influenced by Anacreon, Parny, and Voltaire. Later Byron was his main inspiration and even later he adopted Realism. He was fully conversant with all literary forms of the West, but he assimilated them and used them to create an entirely Russian literature. His masterpiece is the "novel in verse" *Eugene Onegin* (1823–31). Other works include *Ruslan and Lyudmila* (1819), *Caucasian Prisoner* (1821), *Poltava* (1828), *The Bronze Horseman* (1833), and the play *Boris Godunov* (1825).

Larvin, Janko, *Pushkin and Russian Literature,* 1947.

Troyat, Henri, *Pushkin,* 1974.

PUSHKIN (prior to 1917, **Tsarskoye Selo;** 1917–37, **Detskoye Selo).** Town in the Leningrad oblast, 15 miles (24 km) S of Leningrad. Founded in 1718, it is the site of the famous 18th-century baroque palace built by Rastrelli, 18th century parks, the Pushkin Memorial Museum, and the lycée attended by the noble youth of 19th-century Russia.

PUTYATIN, ADMIRAL COUNT YEFIM V. (1803–83). Putyatin led an expedition sent to obtain Russian access to Chinese Treaty Ports. Having had a successful career in the Far East as a negotiator, in 1861 he was appointed minister of education. As a result of his severe policies, a number of prominent professors resigned their positions.

PYANDZH RIVER. River formed by junction of the Pamir and Wakhan rivers near Qala Panja, on the Afghanistan-USSR frontier. It flows approximately 400 miles (640 km) SW, then NW along the frontier, and SW again as far as Nizhni Pyandzh where it joins the Vakhsh River to form the Amu Darya River.

PYATAKOV, GRIGORY L. (1890–1937). Politician and leader of the left wing of the Ukrainian Communist Party. In December 1918 Moscow ordered that a concealed Soviet government be set up in Kursk under Pyatakov. Pyatakov accordingly set up a Soviet regime and invaded the Ukraine with Red troops. In 1937, however, he was tried at the "anti-Soviet Trotskyite Center" trial.

Treadgold, Donald W., *Twentieth Century Russia,* 1958.

PYATIGORSK. Town founded in 1780, and a spa since 1803, situated 216 miles (346 km) ESE of Krasnodar in the N Caucasus. Industries include metalworking and manufactures are clothing and furniture. Some of Lermontov's (*q.v.*) *Hero of Our Times* is set in Pyatigorsk.

PYATOK. Old dry measure equal to 5 *gorsti,* literally, 5 handfuls.

Q

QUADRUPLE ALLIANCE. An alliance, first formed in 1813, among Russia, Great Britain, Austria, and Prussia, to defeat Napoleon. It was officially renewed in 1815 to enforce the peace settlement devised at the Congress of Vienna; Article VI instituted the "Congress System," an attempt to monitor and control the political development of Europe by conferences among the four powers. There were four such meetings: in Aix-la-Chapelle (1818), Troppau *(q.q.v.)*, Laibach (1820–21), and Verona (1822); by then, differences had emerged between Great Britain, which was opposed to direct intervention in the internal affairs of sovereign states, and the others, which were prepared to intervene directly to suppress revolution. Further differences emerged (between Russia and Austria) in 1825 and the system was abandoned.

Lobanov-Rostovsky, A., *Russia and Europe 1789–1825*, 1947.

QUARENGHI, GIACOMO (1744–1817). Italian neoclassical architect invited to Russia by Catherine II, as court architect. Main buildings include the Raphael Loggias of the Hermitage, St. Petersburg (1788); the Academy of Sciences, St. Petersburg (1783–87); the English Palace in Peterhof (1781–89); and the Alexander Palace at Tsarskoye Selo (1796).

QUINTUPLE ALLIANCE. Drawn up in 1818 on the admission of France to the former Quadruple Alliance *(q.v.)* of Russia, Great Britain, Austria, and Prussia, its purpose was to preserve the balance of power in Europe.

R

RABA. Female slave.

RABKRIN. Commissariat of the workers' and peasants' inspectorate, established in 1919. As a supervisory body of the Soviet civil service, the Rabkrin's task was to eradicate bureaucratic mismanagement. Teams of peasants and workers were sent to inspect government departments.

RACHMANINOV, SERGEY VASILYEVICH (1873–1943). Pianist and composer. After studying at St. Petersburg Conservatory and at Moscow Conservatory as a pupil of Ziloti, Zverev, Sergey Taneyev, and Anton Arensky *(q.q.v.)*, Rachmaninov traveled abroad, and left Russia in 1917 to live in the United States. He composed operas, symphonies, choral works, the best-known of which is *The Bells* (1910), piano concertos, symphonic poems, and songs. "Rhapsody on a Theme by Paganini" earned him great popularity.

Leyda, Jay, *Sergie Rachmaninov: A Lifetime of Music,* 1956.

Norris, G., *Rakhmaninov,* 1976.

RADA. Ukrainian council, used in the 17th to the 20th century.

RADEK, KARL BERNARDOVICH (SOBELSOHN) (1885–1940?). Russian author and politician. Born in Poland of Jewish ancestry, he became a journalist and supported the German Social Democratic Party from 1904 on. He was imprisoned several times, fought in the Russian Revolution (1917), and tried to organize a communist revolution in Germany (1918–19). He was a member of the presidium of the Communist International (1919–23) but his influence declined when the Comintern proved ineffective. He became head of the Sun Yat-Sen Communist University for Chinese students in Moscow (1923–27) until he was expelled from the Communist Party (1927) on a charge of having supported Trotsky and was banished to the Urals. He was rehabilitated and wrote for *Izvestiya.* He also helped draft the 1936 constitution. In 1937 he was sentenced to 10 years' imprisonment for treason and is thought to have died in prison.

Lerner, W., *Karl Radek, the Last Internationalist,* 1970.

Radek, Karl, *Portraits and Pamphlets,* 1935.

RADICALS. Term applied to a group of people in the 1860s to the 1880s who wished to change the existing structure of society radically and to overthrow the autocracy. The majority were anarchists and wished to overthrow the economic system, the church, and the state by means of the weapons of positivist philosophy. Leading radicals included Nicholas Chernyshevsky, author of the influential *What Is To Be Done?* (1863), Dimitry Pisarev, Michael Bakunin, and Peter Lavrov *(q.q.v.).* In 1874 several thousand students abandoned their studies in an unsuccessful attempt to "go to the people." The radical movement then split into several groups.

Pipes, Richard, *Russia Under the Old Regime,* 1974.

Venturi, Frances, *Roots of Revolution,* 1960.

RADIMICHI. East Slavic tribe who came from the W and who passed NE up the Desna. According to archaeological finds, they consisted of eight groups. By the middle of the ninth century, the Radimichi were paying taxes to the Khazars, and by the end of the ninth century they had come under the rule of Prince Oleg of Kiev.

RADISHCHEV, ALEXANDER NIKOLAYEVICH (1749–1802). Writer and revolutionary thinker. His *Journey from St. Petersburg to Moscow* (1790) exposes the injustices of serfdom and earned him the death sentence. This was commuted to 10 years' exile in Siberia, where he continued his literary activity. Following the death of Catherine the Great, Radishchev was permitted to return and in 1801 served on the commission for the codification of laws. He committed suicide in 1802, despairing that he had been unable to alleviate the lot of the serf.

Lang, David Marshall, *The First Russian Radicals: Alexander Radishev, 1749–1802,* 1960.

RADOMYSLSKY. *See* **Zinoviev.**

RAGLAN, FITZROY JAMES HENRY SOMERSET (1788–1855). Commander in chief of the British forces during the Crimean War *(q.v.).* He was made a field marshal for his victory at Inkerman but he was largely blamed for the disaster of the Charge of the Light Brigade at Balaclava.

RAILWAYS. The first Russian railway line was opened in 1837, and in 1851 the St. Petersburg-Moscow line was completed. However, it was in the 1860s–1870s that the basic network was constructed, and in 1891, work on the Trans-Siberian Railway was started. Expansion was rapid during the First World War, during which 6,769 miles (10,900 km) of railway were built. Railways are still largely concentrated in European Russian, especially in the Moscow area, the Donets Basin, and the W Ukraine. The USSR is still building a considerable number of new lines such as the Baikal-Amur mainline across E Siberia. Railways are constructed to a gauge of 5 feet (1,524 mm); thus coaches are more spacious than in the W.

The total length of railways in January 1981 was 88,058 miles (141,800 km) (1913: 36,328 miles/58,500 km). By the end of 1979, 87,250 miles (140,500 km) of mainline railways had changed to electric and diesel traction; 27,321 miles (42,461 km) were wholly electrified; and 99.9 percent of railway freight went by these means. In 1979, 60 percent of all goods traffic and 40 percent of passenger transport went by rail (in 1913, 57 percent and 91 percent respectively). The Moscow-Donetz, Leningrad-Leninakan (2,111 miles/3,400 km) and western frontier-Baikal (4,657 miles/7,500 km) lines have been electrified.

RAKOVSKY, KHRISTIAN GEORGYEVICH (1873–1938). Communist leader and diplomat of Bulgarian origin. Because of his involvement with the socialist movement, Rakovsky was not able to enter Sofia University, but studied abroad. In 1900 he was an officer in the Rumanian army, but in 1907 he was expelled from Rumania. After the communists came to power, Rakovsky was made a member of the All-Russian Central Executive Committee, and in 1919 of the central committee of the Communist Party. The chairman of the council of people's commissars of the Ukraine, he occupied several diplomatic posts, including Soviet ambassador to France (1926–27). He was, however, expelled from the Communist Party in 1927 as a result of his support of Trotsky. He was readmitted in 1935 and was a departmental head of the People's Commissariat of Health. In 1937 he was dismissed, and in 1938, arrested. He was sentenced to 20 years' imprisonment, and it is believed that he died in a concentration camp.

RAPALLO, TREATY OF. Treaty signed in 1922 by the two defeated states of World War I, Germany and the Russian Soviet Federated Socialist Republic, although the treaty was later extended to apply to other republics of the USSR. According to the treaty all diplomatic and consular relations between Germany and Russia would be resumed; claims for war reparations and compensation would be dropped; and most-favored-nation treatment would be adopted with regard to trade. As a result of the treaty, Germany was able to develop in Russia weapons forbidden by the Treaty of Versailles.

RASKOL. *See* **Old Believers.**

RASPUTIN, GRIGORY YEFIMOVICH (1872-1916). Siberian peasant who exerted a pernicious influence at court and on political affairs. Although without education, he allegedly possessed hypnotic powers, which he did not hesitate to exploit, claimed to be able to work miracles, preaching that physical contact with himself had a healing effect. As a youth Rasputin had been influenced by the *Khlysty* (Flagellants) sect. In 1903 Rasputin arrived in St. Petersburg as a *starets* (holy man) *(q.v.)* and as such gained access to the highest circles of society. He exercised virtually unlimited influence on Tsaritsa Alexandra (*q.v.*) by using hypnotism to stop the hemophiliac tsarevich's bleeding. She viewed him as a divine missionary, sent to save the dynasty. The church denounced him as an imposter, and in 1912 he was sent back to Siberia. In 1914 he returned, and in 1915, when the tsaritsa was left in charge of domestic affairs, Rasputin's influence was vast, and many of the more capable ministers were dismissed. He continued his dissolute habits until his assassination in 1916.

de Jonge, Alex, *The Life and Times of Griogorii Rasputin,* 1982.

Minney, R. J., *Rasputin,* 1972.

RASTRELLI, COUNT BARTOLOMMEO (1700–71). Architect. Rastrelli served as court architect to Elizabeth and designed the Winter Palace (1754–62), the palaces of Peterhof and Tsarskoye Selo (1783, later altered by Charles Cameron), and the Smolny Convent (1748). He also built St. Andrew's Cathedral in Kiev (1747), which exemplifies the mature baroque style in Russia.

RAYON. Administrative area, for example, a city district.

RAZIN, S. T. *See* **Stenka Razin.**

RAZNOCHINTSY. Semiofficial term (literary men of various ranks) in the 19th century applied to those who belonged neither to the peasantry nor to the nobility; they consisted of merchants' sons without capital, priests' sons who had not taken holy orders, sons of civil servants and "freed" serfs. Many of this intermediate class wrote or taught for a living; the *raznochintsy* were to become one of the main sources of the intelligentsia. The leading *raznochinets* was Vissarion Belinsky *(q.v.).*

Pipes, Richard (ed.), *The Russian Intelligentsia,* 1961.

Schapiro, Leonard B., *Rationalism and Nationalism in Russian Nineteenth-Century Political Thought,* 1967.

RAZUMOVSKY, COUNT ALEKSEY (1709–71). Cossack shepherd and singer. Razumovsky's brilliant talent attracted attention, and he was brought to the court as a singer. Empress Elizabeth fell in love with him, and may have been morganatically married to him. Razumovsky had some slight influence on state affairs.

RAZUMOVSKY, FIELD MARSHAL COUNT CYRIL (1728–1803). The brother of Aleksey Razumovsky, he was well educated and eventually was appointed president of the Academy of Sciences, field marshal, and hetman of the Ukraine.

REALISM. Dominant trend in art in Russia in the second half of the nineteenth century. Paul Feodotov *(q.v.)* and the Realists of the 1860s–1880s concentrated on painting scenes from everyday life, rather than subjects from mythology, and hoped that in so doing, they could focus attention on social injustices; Fedotov's *The Major's Betrothal* (1848) deals with the inequality with which women were treated. Thus, all Realists believed that art should serve serious social functions. Realist painters, however, are not as renowned as the great Realist writers of the day.

Talbot Rice, Tamara, *A Concise History of Russian Art,* 1963.

REBIKOV, VLADIMIR IVANOVICH (1866–1920) Composer. He composed operas, including *In the Storm* (1894), church music, piano works, and orchestral pieces. At first influenced by Tchaikovsky *(q.v.)*, his later music is individualistic and experimental.

RED ARMY. Bolshevik army whose task is to protect the country from its external enemies. The workers' and peasants' Red Army was formed by Lenin on January 28, 1918 from the workers' militia, the Red Guards. At first consisting of proletarian volunteers, conscription was introduced during the Civil War; at this stage the army was under Trotsky. The Red Army was demobilized at the end of the Civil War and the war with Poland, although a core of half a million men was retained. Owing to the party's commitment to war as a means of bringing about revolution, expansion was rapid during the 1920s and 1930s, and in the 1930s ranks were reintroduced and officers' privileges reinstated. At first during the Second World War the Red Army was fighting mainly a defensive war, but from 1943 the army embarked on offensive operations. Following the war the name Red Army was changed to Soviet Army, and it was reorganized along traditional Russian lines. In 1981 there were about 187 divisions, of which some 100 were at combat readiness with a total force of about 1.8 million.

O'Ballance, E., *The Red Army.* 1964.

RED FLAG. *See* **Flag.**

RED GUARDS. Armed factory workers who stormed the Winter Palace *(q.v.)* with Bolshevik-led soldiers and sailors in the October Revolution of 1917.

Daniels, Robert V., *Red October: The Bolshevik Revolution of 1917,* 1968.

RED SQUARE *(Krasnaya Ploshchad).* Square in Moscow that lies along the NE wall and moat of the Kremlin *(q.v.)* in front of the Kitay Gorod *(q.v.)*. It is linked to the Kremlin by three gates. It has existed since the 15th century as a market, and many main roads converged at this point. In 1812 the burning of Moscow destroyed much of Red Square. Osip Bovet replanned the square, and his buildings include the present state department store GUM. It is the site of military parades and displays on public holidays. Lenin's mausoleum lies in front of the E walls.

RED TERROR. An attempt was made on Lenin's life in 1918, and as a result, the Bolsheviks instigated large-scale arrests and executions and suppressed non-Bolshevik newspapers.

Carr, Edward Hallett, *The Russian Revolution: From Lenin to Stalin,* 1979.

REDEMPTION PAYMENTS. Fixed amount of money paid annually to the government by peasants who were former serfs, for the land they received from the landlord at the time of the emancipation of the serfs (*see* **Emancipation, Edict of**) (1861). The government had immediately compensated the landowners and redemption payments were to last for 49 years, but the government reduced the amount of debt and in 1906 they were remitted. *See* **Agrarian Reforms.**

Blum, Jerome, *Lord and Peasant in Russia from the Ninth to the Nineteenth Century,* 1961.

Robinson, Geroid Tangrary, *Rural Russia under the Old Regime,* 1949.

REED, JOHN (1887–1920). American journalist who covered the war in Eastern Europe, becoming a close friend of Lenin. He was an eyewitness of the 1917 October Revolution and wrote his account *Ten Days that Shook the World* (1919). In 1919 he organized the Communist Labor Party in the United States and was founder and first editor of the *Voice of Labor.* For a short period he was the Soviet consul in New York. He left the United States for Russia, where he died of typhus and was buried in the Kremlin wall. Other works include, *The War in Eastern Europe* (1916) and *Red Russia* (1919).

Gelb, B., *John Reed,* 1973.

REFORMISTS. Reformists aimed at altering conditions by working legally through the existing regime. There were many radical changes effected by the reforms of Alexander II (*q.v.*): emancipation of the serfs (*see* **Emancipation, Edict of**), reform of the *mir* (*q.v.*), local government reform, the establishment of the autonomy of the universities, the introduction of universal military service, and judicial reforms. After 1905 the Stolypin (*q.v.*) government carried out moderate reforms, while the Constitutional Democrats and right-wing socialist groups favored radical reforms.

REINSURANCE TREATY. Secret treaty concluded between Germany and Russia in 1887 after the Three Emperors' League (*q.v.*) had expired. Each country was to remain neutral if the other engaged in warfare, with the exception of an aggressive war of Germany against France, or Russia against Austria-Hungary. After Bismarck's resignation in 1890, Germany abrogated the treaty.

REMIZOV, ALEKSEY MIKHAILOVICH (1877–1957). Writer. Expelled from Moscow University, he spent the next few years at Penza, Ust-Sysolsk, and Vologda. In 1904 he was released from police surveillance and settled in St. Petersburg. He organized the satirical Great and Free House of Apes, of which he was "chancellor," and sent most Russian writers and publishers handwritten charters, stating their position in the House. By the First World War, Remizov was head of a new school of fiction. His *Mara* and *The Lament for the Ruin of Russia* (1917) convey conditions in Petrograd (Leningrad) from 1914 to 1921. His work, however, is extremely varied in style and content. His prose consists of contemporary stories, the best-known of which is *The Story of Ivan Semyonovich Stratilatov* (1909), legends, folk stories, dreams, and plays. His verse is less successful. In 1921 Remizov emigrated and settled in Paris.

RENNEKAMPF, GENERAL PAUL KARLOVICH VON (1854–1918). Having taken part in the suppression of various uprisings, Rennekampf was commander of the first Russian army at the time of the First World War. In 1915 he was dismissed and sent into retirement. He was shot by Soviet forces in 1918.

REPIN, ILYA YEFIMOVICH (1844–1930). Painter. Having worked with icon painters, Repin studied at the Society for the Encouragement of Art in 1863, and from 1864 to 1871 at the Academy of Arts. After his second visit to Paris in 1863, Repin's work became gradually more impressionistic in style. He was a leading member of the Wanderers *(q.v.)*, a group of nonacademic painters who sought to bring art to a mass audience through social realism. Repin spent the later years of his life in Finland and turned to religious paintings. His best-known paintings include *The Volga Boatmen, The Religious Procession in Kursk Province,* and *Ivan the Terrible with the Body of his Son.*

Gray, Camilla, *The Great Experiment: Russian Art, 1863–1922,* 1971.

Talbot Rice, Tamara, A *Concise History of Russian Art,* 1963.

REPUBLICS, CONSTITUENT. The Union of Soviet Socialist Republics was formed by the union of the Russian Soviet Federated Socialist Republic, the Ukrainian Soviet Socialist Republic, the Belorussian Soviet Socialist Republic, and the Transcaucasian Soviet Socialist Republic. The Treaty of Union was adopted by the first Soviet congress of the USSR on December 30, 1922. In May 1925 the Uzbek and Turkmen Autonomous Soviet Socialist Republics and in December 1929 the Tadzhik Autonomous Soviet Socialist Republic were declared constituent members of the USSR, becoming union republics.

At the eighth congress of the Soviets, on December 5, 1936, a new constitution of the USSR was adopted. The Transcaucasian Republic was split into the Armenian Soviet Socialist Republic, the Azerbaijan Soviet Socialist Republic, and the Georgian Soviet Socialist Republic, each of which became constituent republics of the union. At the same time the Kazakh Soviet Socialist Republic and the Kirghiz Soviet Socialist Republic, previously autonomous republics within the Russian Soviet Federated Socialist Republic, were proclaimed constituent republics of the USSR.

In September 1939 Soviet troops occupied E Poland as far as the "Curzon line," which in 1919 had been drawn on ethnographic grounds as the E frontier of Poland, and incorporated it into the Ukrainian and Belorussian Soviet Socialist Republics. In February 1951 some districts of the Drogobych Region of the Ukraine and the Lublin Voyevodship of Poland were exchanged.

On March 31, 1940 territory ceded by Finland was joined to that of the autonomous Soviet socialist republic of Karelia to form the Karelo-Finnish Soviet Socialist Republic, which was admitted into the union as the 12th union republic. On July 16, 1956, the Supreme Soviet of the USSR adopted a law altering the status of the Karelo-Finnish Republic from that of a union (constituent) republic of the USSR to that of an autonomous (Karelian) republic within the Russian Soviet Federated Socialist Republic.

On August 2, 1940 the Moldavian Soviet Socialist Republic was constituted as the 13th union republic. It comprised the former Moldavian Autonomous Soviet Socialist Republic and Bessarabia (17,095 square miles/44,290 sq km., ceded by Rumania on June 28, 1940), except for the districts of Khotin, Akerman, and Ismail, which, together with N Bukovina (4,029 square miles/10,440 sq km), were incorporated in the Ukrainian Soviet Republic. The Soviet-Rumanian frontier thus constituted was confirmed by the peace treaty with Rumania, signed on February 10, 1947. On June 29, 1945 Ruthenia (Sub-Carpathian Russia, 4,903 square miles/12,742 sq km) was by treaty with Czechoslovakia absorbed in the Ukrainian Soviet Socialist Republic.

On August 3, 1940 Estonia, Latvia, and Lithuania were incorporated in the Soviet Union as the 14th, 15th, and 16th union republics. The change in the status of the Karelo-Finnish Republic has reduced the number of union republics to 15.

After the defeat of Germany it was agreed by the governments of Great Britain, the United States, and the USSR (by the Potsdam agreement) that part of E Prussia should be ceded to the USSR. The area 4,498 square miles (11,655 sq km), which includes the towns of Königsberg (renamed Kaliningrad). Tilsit (renamed Sovyetsk), and Insterburg (renamed Chernyakhovsk), was joined to the Russian Soviet Federated Socialist Republic by a decree of April 7, 1946.

By the peace treaty with Finland, signed on February 10, 1947, the province of Petsamo (Pechenga), ceded to Finland on October 14, 1920 and March 12, 1946, was returned to the Soviet Union. On September 19, 1955 the Soviet Union renounced its treaty rights to the naval base of Porkkala-Udd and on January 26, 1956 completed the withdrawal of forces from Finnish teritory.

In 1945, after the defeat of Japan, the S half of Sakhalin (13,896 square miles/36,000 sq km) and the Kuril Islands (3,937 square miles/10,200 sq km) were, by agreement with the Allies, incorporated in the USSR. Japan, however, asked for the return of the Etorofu and Kunashiri Islands as not belonging to the Kuril Islands proper. The Soviet government informed Japan on January 27, 1960 that the Habomai Islands and Shikotan would be handed back to Japan on the withdrawal of American troops from Japan.

RESHETNIKOV, FEDOR MIKHAILOVICH (1841–71). Author, much of whose work is about the peasants. His story *The People of Podlipnoye* (1864), about the hardships endured by the Finnish Permians, had a powerful impact and aroused the social conscience and feelings of guilt among nobles of liberal disposition.

REUTERN, COUNT MICHAEL (*c.* 19th century). Minister of finance from 1822 to 1878. Reutern worked toward the stabilization of the paper ruble and the improvement of his country's balance of payments through the strengthening of Russia's export position. He sought to encourage railway construction and private banking but was unsuccessful in preventing the war with Turkey of 1877–78, although he argued that war would harm the country's economic position. He was in favor of the sale of Alaska to the United States.

REVISIONISM. Term used to describe change in the officially accepted interpretation of Marxism. It is considered by Marxists detrimental to the prospects of revolution and to the dictatorship of the proletariat.

REVOLUTION OF 1905. An insurrection in Russia. It was an expression of the widespread discontent that foreshadowed the Russian Revolution of 1917. It began on Bloody Sunday, January 22, 1905 when a group of striking workers, led by Father Gapon, marched peacefully to the Winter Palace in St. Petersburg only to be met by gunfire. The massacre precipitated nationwide strikes, uprisings, and mutinies (including the mutiny on the cruiser *Potemkin*). By October Russia was gripped by a general strike, which with the establishment of the St. Petersburg Soviet (workers' council) dominated by the Mensheviks, including Trotsky, forced Emperor Nicholas II *(q.v.)* to promise a constitutional government (*see* **Duma**). The Revolution was substantially crushed by the end of December.

REZANA. Monetary unit in medieval Russia. One *rezana* equaled one-fiftieth of a *grivna (q.v.)*.

RICHTER, SVYATOSLAV TEOFILOVICH (1914–). Pianist. He first studied the piano with his father, then at the Moscow Conservatory under Genrikh Neuhaus, and made his debut in Odessa in 1949, winning the Stalin Prize. In 1960 he made an international tour, visiting Great Britain in 1961. Since then he has made a great impact at the Aldeburgh and Edinburgh festivals. He returns to France each year to take part in his own music festival, near Tours. He is outstanding in his interpretations of Bach and Beethoven.

RIGA. Latvian capital on the Dvina River 8 miles (13 km) from the mouth. Riga became a Hanseatic town in 1282 and an important trading center in the Baltic. Industries include shipbuilding and textiles; manufactures include cement, footwear, rubber products, paper, and telephone equipment. Riga is a seaport trading in flax, timber, paper, butter, and eggs; the harbor is open approximately 8 months of the year. Population (1981) 850,000.

RIGA, GULF OF. Inlet of the Baltic Sea off the coasts of Latvia and Estonia. It has a length of approximately 100 miles (160 km) and a width of up to 60 miles (96 km). It is ice-free from May to December.

RIGHT OPPOSITION. Opposition to the party on the part of those who stress compromise and cooperation with noncommunists. The Right Opposition of 1928–29 was led by Nicholas Bukharin, Aleksey Rykov, and Michael Tomsky (*q.q.v.*).

RIMSKY-KORSAKOV, NICHOLAS ANDREYEVICH (1844–1908). Composer, conductor, and music teacher, and one-time pupil of Ulich and Feodor Kanille. Professor of composition and instrumentation at St. Petersburg Conservatory, he was also conductor of the Free Music School concerts and the Russian Symphony concerts. Rimsky-Korsakov wrote operas, including *The Snow Maiden* (1880–81) and the *Golden Cockerel* (1906–07), choral and orchestral works such as *Scheherazade* (1888), chamber music, vocal works, works for the piano, and folk songs. He brought the atmosphere of Russian folk music into his works.

Abraham, Gerald E. H., *Rimsky-Korsakov: A Short Biography,* 1948.

RINALDI, ANTONIO (1709–94). Principal architect of Catherine II (*q.v.*). Rinaldi built the Marble Palace in St. Petersburg (1768–85) and a pavilion in Lomonosov.

RIONI RIVER. River rising in the Caucasus mountains of Georgia and flowing 180 miles (288 km) WSW past Kutaisi to enter the Black Sea at Poti. It is used for hydroelectric power.

RIURIK. *See* **Ryurik.**

ROCKETS AND SPACE TRAVEL. *See* **Space Travel.**

RODZYANKO, MICHAEL VLADIMIROVICH (1859–1924). President of the duma. Having supported the autocracy's suppression of the 1905 Revolution, he unsuccessfully opposed the idea that Tsar Nicholas II should take command of the army. With Alexander Guchkov he led the Octobrists, a party of right-wing liberals who constituted the majority party in the 3rd and 4th dumas.

ROERICH, NICHOLAS KONSTANTINOVICH (1874–1947). Artist. In the 1880s Roerich worked for Mamontov's Private Opera theater productions. He was also interested in archaeology, took part in many digs, and from the 1890s contributed work on scientific discoveries to historical journals. In 1893 he enrolled at the St. Petersburg Academy, where he embarked on formal training in painting. He later contributed to the *World of Art* magazine and was a stage designer for Diaghilev. One of his best-known works is his stage set for *Prince Igor* (1909).

Selivanova, N. N., *The World of Roerich,* 1924.

ROKOSSOVSKY, KONSTANTIN KONSTANTINOVICH (1896–). Marshal of the Soviet Union. Of Polish origin, Rokossovsky joined the Red Army in 1919 and became a member of the Bolshevik Party. During the Second World War he was an outstanding Soviet commander. He acted with great heroism at the battles of Moscow (1941–42), Stalingrad (1942–43), Kursk (1943), and in Belorussia and at the battle for Berlin (1944–45). In 1944 he became a marshal and commanded the Soviet forces in Poland. In 1949 he was transferred to the Polish army. He became minister of defense and a member of the Politburo of the Polish Communist Party. In 1956 he was dismissed by Wladyslaw Gomulka and was appointed a deputy minister of defense of the USSR.

ROMAN CATHOLIC CHURCH. Roman Catholics are most numerous in Lithuania, Latvia, and the W Ukraine. There are two Roman Catholic archepiscopates and four episcopates in Lithuania with a seminary at Kaunas providing a five-year course. In 1946 some 3 million Uniates (*q.v.*) in the USSR withdrew their allegiance to Rome and came under the jurisdiction of the Orthodox Patriarchate in Moscow. In Latvia there is an archepiscopate and one episcopate (Riga and Liepaja) of the Roman Catholic Church.

ROMANOV, KONSTANTIN NIKOLAYEVICH (1827–92). General, admiral, prince, and son of Tsar Nicholas I. In 1850 Romanov was made a member of the state council, in 1857 a member of the secret committee, and in 1860 the leader of the committee for peasant affairs. He carried out reforms in the army and navy, and in 1862–63 he was governor-general of Poland.

ROMANOV, MICHAEL FEDOROVICH (1596–1645). Elected to the throne in 1613 at the end of the Time of Troubles (*q.v.*), in order to restore internal order Michael expelled the Swedes and Poles from Moscow and tried to restore the country's ailing economy. Under his rule, Russia continued to expand westward.

Vernadsky, George, *The Tsardom of Moscow, 1547–1682,* 1959.

ROMANOV, PANTELEYMON SERGEYEVICH (1884–1938). Author. While his short sketches give a picture of life during the Civil War (*q.v.*) and the period of the New Economic Policy (*q.v.*), many characters of his novels are recognizable descendants of the 19th-century "superfluous man." His most important novel, *The New Table of Commandments* (1928), however, deals with a Soviet marriage. In 1927 Romanov met with official disapproval, and was forbidden to publish, although the ban was later lifted.

ROMANOVS. The last ruling dynasty of Russia (1613–1917), noted for their absolutism and for transforming Russia into a large empire. The first Romanov tsar was Michael (*q.v.*), whose election ended the Time of Troubles. Peter I (*q.v.*) was succeeded by his second wife, Catherine, the daughter of a Livonian peasant, and she by Peter II (*q.v.*), the grandson of Peter, with whom the male line of the Romanovs terminated in the year 1730. The reign of the next three sovereigns of Russia, Anne, Ivan VI, and Elizabeth, of the female line of Romanov, formed a transition period, which came to an end with the accession of Peter III (*q.v.*), of the house of Holstein-Gottorp. All the subsequent emperors, without exception, connected themselves by marriage with German families. The wife and successor of Peter III, Catherine II, daughter of the prince of Anhalt Zerbst, general in the Prussian army, left the crown to her only son, Paul, who became the father of two emperors, Alexander I and Nicholas I (*q.q.v.*), and the grandfather of a third, Alexander II (*q.v.*). All these sovereigns married German princesses, creating intimate family alliances, among others, with the reigning houses of Wurttemberg, Baden, and Prussia.

The emperor was in possession of the revenue from the crown domains, consisting of more than 1 million square miles (2.6 million km) of cultivated land and forests, besides gold and other mines in Siberia, and producing a vast revenue, the actual amount of which was, however, unknown as no reference to the subject was made in the budgets or finance accounts, the crown domains being considered the private property of the imperial family.

In March 1917, during the Russian Revolution, Romanov rule ended with the abdication of Nicholas II. He and his family were executed.

House of Romanov—Male Line	
Michael	1613
Alexis	1645
Feodor	1676
Ivan and Peter I	1682
Peter I	1689
Catherine I	1725
Peter II	1727
House of Romanov—Female Line	
Anne	1730
Ivan VI	1740
Elizabeth	1741
House of Romanov—Holstein	
Peter III	1762
Catherine II	1762
Paul	1796
Alexander I	1801
Nicholas I	1825
Alexander II	1855
Alexander III	1881
Nicholas II	1894

Bergamini, J., *The Tragic Dynasty,* 1970.

Grey, Ian, *The Romanovs: The Rise and Fall of Russian Dynasty,* 1971.

Kluychevsky, Vasily, *The Rise of the Romanovs,* 1970.

Massie, R. K., *Nicholas and Alexandra,* 1967.

Seton-Watson, Hugh, *The Russian Empire,* 1967.

ROMODANOVSKY, PRINCE FEDOR (1640–1717). Companion of Peter the Great (*q.v.*), and member of the Most Drunken *Sobor* (council) of Fools and Jesters. He was later appointed head of the secret police.

ROSSI, KARL IVANOVICH (1775–1849). Architect of Italian descent. Rossi was the chief architect of Alexander I (*q.v.*) and was in charge of the building of the *ensembles* of the Mikhail Palace, the Alexandra (Pushkin) Theater, Palace Square, and the Admiralty and Senate Squares. The replanning of St. Petersburg was in the style and on the scale of imperial Rome.

Auty, Robert and Obolensky, Dimitri (eds.), "An Introduction to Russian Art and Architecture," *Companion to Russian Studies,* Vol. 3, 1980.

ROSTOPCHIN, COUNT FEDOR VASILYEVICH (1763–1826). Statesman under Paul I (*q.v.*). In May 1812 Rostopchin was appointed military governor and chief commander of Moscow. He was held responsible for the burning of Moscow and in 1814 was dismissed and exiled, although the fire was a major factor in Napoleon's withdrawal from Moscow and his disastrous retreat. Rostopchin defended himself in *The Truth Concerning the Fire of Moscow* (1823).

ROSTOV-ON-DON. Capital of Rostov region situated NE of the Sea of Azov on the Don River and founded in 1749. It is a communications and commercial center. Industries include shipbuilding, railway and agricultural engineering, textiles, and chemicals; manufactures include tobacco and leather products. A port, it handles overseas trade through Taganrog, situated 50 miles (80 km) W on the Sea of Azov. Population (1981) 957,000.

ROSTOVTSEV, GENERAL YAKOB IVANOVICH (1803–60). Having warned the government of the impending Decembrist (*see* **Decembrists**) revolt, Rostovtsev was appointed chief of the military schools. In 1857 he became a member of the secret committee, and in 1859 chairman of the editing commission. Having played a leading part in preparations for the emancipation of the serfs, he died from overexertion.

ROSTROPOVICH, MSTISLAV LEOPOLDOVICH (1927–). Cellist, pianist, and conductor. Rostropovich studied under his father and under Semyon Kozolupov and Vissarion Shebalin, making his debut in 1942. In 1947 he started teaching at the Moscow Conservatory. In 1974 he left the USSR and in 1975 accepted an offer to become director of the National Symphony Orchestra in Washington, D.C. In 1978 he was stripped of his Soviet citizenship.

ROVNO. Capital of region of the same name in the Ukraine situated 110 miles (176 km) ENE of Lvov. It is a railway junction. Industries include textiles; manufactures include machinery and food products. Population (1981) 192,000.

RSFSR. *See* **Russian Soviet Federated Socialist Republic.**

RTISHCHEV, FEDOR MIKHAILOVICH (1625–73). Boyar who built a monastery in 1648–49 in Moscow and invited 30 monks to teach there. He also founded hospitals and compiled a Slavonic-Greek dictionary.

RUBINSTEIN, ANTON GRIGORYEVICH (1829–94). Pianist and composer. Having studied under Alexander Villoing and Siegfried Wilhelm Dehn in 1862, Rubinstein founded the St. Petersburg Conservatory. He wrote operas, the best-known of which is *The Demon* (1875); symphonies, piano, cello, and violin concertos; and chamber music, orchestral works, and the symphonic poem *Rossiya* (1882). *See* **Moguchaya Kuchka.**

RUBINSTEIN, NICHOLAS GRIGOROVICH (1835–81). Pianist. Having studied under Theodor Kullak and Siegfried Wilhelm Dehn in 1859, Rubinstein founded the Russian Musical Society in Moscow, and in 1864 the Moscow Conservatory. Although his compositions are largely disregarded, he is remembered as teacher of Sergey Taneyev *(q.v.)* and Ziloti. *See* **Moguchaya Kuchka.**

RUBLE. Monetary unit of the Soviet Union. There is a recorded use of the term "ruble" as far back as the 13th century. The ruble is divided into 100 kopeks. Originally a silver ingot of fixed weight, it was first issued as a coin by Peter the Great in 1704. The export of the ruble is prohibited and it is not convertible.

RUBLEV, ANDREY (*c.* 1360–1430). Icon painter in Moscow and Vladimir. Rublev was considerably influenced by Paleologos painting brought from Constantinople to Russia by Feofan the Greek (*q.v.*). His *Trinity* (1422–25) in the Troitsa-Sergeyeva Monastery (*q.v.*) is one of his best works and in general one of the finest Russian icons. It is set in enamel work characteristic of the Moscow style.

Stuart, J., *Ikons,* 1975.

Uspensky, L. A. and Lossky, V. N., *The Meaning of Icons,* 1952.

RUBTSOVSK. Town 80 miles (128 km) NNE of Semipalatinsk near the border with Kazakhstan, in the Russian Soviet Federated Socialist Republic. Industries include flour milling and agricultural engineering. Population (1981) 158,000.

RUFFO, MARCO (*fl.* 15th century). Italian architect. Together with Petrio Antonio Solario and other Italians he built the Banqueting Hall and the Redeemer Gate in the Kremlin in the early Italian Renaissance style.

RUMYANTSEV, COUNT PETER ALEKSANDROVICH (1725–96). Statesman and army officer. He achieved fame during the Seven Years War (1756–63) and the Russo-Turkish war of 1768–74. Having enjoyed favor under Peter III (*q.v.*), he was appointed governor-general of the Ukraine by Catherine II (*q.v.*). After the peace of Kuchuk-Kainarji (1774) (*q.v.*), he was made field marshal and given the title Count Zadunaysky. In 1794 Catherine II enlisted his help to pacify the Poles.

RUNICH, DMITRY P. (*fl.* 19th century). First curator of the university at St. Petersburg, known as "a corpse stimulated to life by Magnitsky." Of reactionary tendencies, Runich and Magnitsky (*q.v.*) enforced the application of misguided and supposedly biblical principles and in 1821 managed to dismiss the university's three leading professors.

RUS. Slavic lands, the capital of which was Kiev (*q.v.*).

Vernadsky, George V., *Kievan Russia,* 1948.

RUSSIA. Colloquial name of the pre-1917 Russian empire and of the present Union of Soviet Socialist Republics.

RUSSIAN REVOLUTION (1917). The revolution of March and November (Old Style February and October) 1917 that overthrew the Russian monarchy and established the world's first communist state. It began with the February Revolution, when riots over shortage of bread and coal in Petrograd (formerly St. Petersburg) led to the establishment of the Petrograd Soviet of workers' and soldiers' deputies, dominated by the Mensheviks and Social Revolutionaries, and of a provisional government of duma deputies, which forced Nicholas II (*q.v.*) to abdicate. The failure of the provisional government, under Prince George Lvov (*q.v.*) and then Kerensky (*q.v.*), to end Russia's participation in the First World War and to deal with food shortages led to the demand of the Bolsheviks under Lenin for "all power to the Soviets." The Bolsheviks, who had gained a majority in the Soviet by September, staged the October (or Bolshevik) Revolution, seizing power and establishing the Soviet of people's commissars. The new government made peace with Germany in early 1918 but almost immediately faced opposition at home. In the subsequent Civil War (1918–21) the Red Army was ultimately victorious against the anticommunist Whites but with the loss of some 100,000 lives. In addition, some 2 million Russians emigrated.

Chamberlin, William Henry, *The Russian Revolution, 1917–1921*, 2 vols., 1952.

Daniels, Robert V., *Red October: The Bolshevik Revolution of 1917*, 1968. *The Russian Revolution. Documents*, 1972.

Katkov, George, *Russia: February 1917*, 1967.

Liebman, Marcel, *The Russian Revolution*, 1970.

Reed, John, *Ten Days that Shook the World*, 1961.

Shukman, H., *Lenin and the Russian Revolution*, 1977.

RUSSIAN SOCIAL DEMOCRATIC LABOR PARTY. Founded in 1898 as the Social Democratic Labor Party, the party consisted of orthodox Marxists, revisionists, and trade unionists. Although the party split into Bolsheviks and Mensheviks at the second party congress in 1903, it was formally reunited, but both factions continued to exist. In 1919 the Bolsheviks no longer used the name of Russian Social Democratic Party, but the Mensheviks opted to retain it.

Mendel, Arthur P., *Dilemmas of Progress in Tsarist Russia*, 1961.

RUSSIAN SOVIET FEDERATED SOCIALIST REPUBLIC. Largest of the constituent republics containing over 76 percent of the total area and approximately 55 percent of the total population. The Russian Soviet Federated Socialist Republic consists of: (1) Territories (*kray*): Altay, Khabarovsk, Krasnodar, Krasnoyarsk, Primorye, and Stravropol. (2) Regions (*oblasty*): Amur, Arkhangelsk, Astrakhan, Belgorod, Bryansk, Chelyabinsk, Chita, Gorky, Irkutsk, Ivanovo, Kaluga, Kalinin, Kaliningrad, Kamchatka, Kemerovo, Kirov, Kostroma, Kuibyshev, Kurgan, Kursk, Leningrad, Lipetsk, Magadan, Moscow, Murmansk, Novgorod, Novosibirsk, Omsk, Orel, Orenburg, Penza, Perm, Pskov, Rostov, Ryazan, Sakhalin, Saratov, Smolensk, Sverdlovsk, Tambov, Tomsk, Tula, Tyumen, Ulyanovsk, Vladimir, Volgograd, Vologda, Voronezh, and Yaroslavl. (3) Autonomous Soviet Socialist Republics: Bashkir, Buryat, Chechen-Ingush, Chuvash, Dagestan, Kabardino-Balkar, Kalmyk, Karelian, Komi, Mari, Mordovian, North Ossetian, Tatar, Tuva, Udmurt, and Yakut. (4) Autonomous Regions: Adygey, Karachay-Cherkess, Gorno Altay, Jewish, and Khakass. (5) National Areas (*okrugi*): Agi-Buryat, Chukchi, Evenki, Khanty-Mansi, Komi-Permyak, Koryak, Nenets,

Taymyr (Dolgan-Nenets), Ust'Orda Buryat, and Yamal-Nenetz. The total area is 6,501,500 square miles (16,838,900 sq km). The capital is Moscow. The republic produces approximately 70 percent of the total industrial and agricultural output of the USSR. The republic has a variety of climates, ranging from Arctic to subtropical, and a range of geographical conditions, which include tundra, forest lands, steppes, and rich agricultural soil. It also contains great mineral resources: iron ore in the Urals, the Kerch peninsula and Siberia; coal in the Kuznetz basin, E Siberia, Urals, and the sub-Moscow basin; oil in the Urals, Azov-Black Sea area, and Bashkiria. It also has abundant deposits of gold, platinum, copper, zinc, lead, tin, and rare metals. Population (1981) 139,100,000.

RUSSIFICATION. Various tsars carried out a policy of russification. The Bolsheviks, however, in the face of growing national consciousness among the national minorities, promised to liberate ethnic minorities from russification. In the republics, however, the Russian language and Russian traditions are favored. As a result, discontent, especially among republics annexed during the Second World War, is growing.

RUSSKAYA PRAVDA. Russian Justice (or Truth). The first compilation of Russian laws, it was collected under Yaroslav the Wise (1019–54) (*q.v.*). It consists largely of lists of fines to be paid to injured persons.

RUSSKI, NICHOLAS (1854–1918). Soldier. He studied at the staff college in St. Petersburg and was made a general (1896). In 1914 he was posted to the SW front, and in September he defeated the Austrians at Rawa Ruska near Lvov. Later he was reassigned to the W front, and he prevented Hindenburg from breaking through near Lodz. He is believed to have been killed by the Bolsheviks in 1918.

RUSSO-CHINESE BANK. Bank founded in China in December 1895 by Count Witte (q.v.). Although under the patronage of the Russian imperial government, its capital was predominantly French. The bank was established to finance the Chinese Eastern Railway Company.

RUSSO-FINNISH WAR (OR WINTER WAR) (1939–40). The war between the Soviet Union and Finland at the beginning of the Second World War. It was won by the Soviet Union, the aggressor, which gained part of the Karelian isthmus.

RUSSO-GERMAN NON-AGGRESSION PACT. On August 23, 1939 the Russo-German Non-aggression Pact was signed enabling Germany to attack Poland without fear of Russian reprisals and to fight a war against Great Britain and France. The Baltic states and about half of Poland passed under Russian influence.

RUSSO-JAPANESE WAR (1904–05). War arising from the conflict of Russian and Japanese aspirations in Asia. Russia refused to withdraw from Manchuria, despite having agreed to do so in 1902, and also wished to gain concessions in Korea. Alexander

Bezobrazov's (*q.v.*) timber company began work on the Korean side of the Yalu River, and in 1904 the Russian fleet was attacked by the Japanese at Port Arthur. In May 1905 the Japanese virtually destroyed the Baltic fleet at Tsushima. Britain's proposal of American mediation was accepted. At the peace conference, presided over by Theodore Roosevelt, in Portsmouth, New Hampshire, Russia ceded Port Arthur, the S line of the Chinese Eastern railway, and the S half of Sakhalin Island to Japan.

RUSSO-TURKISH WARS. Name given to wars between Russia and the Ottoman Turkish empire. As a result, Russian territory was extended to include the Prut River and the land beyond the Caucasus. The first Russo-Turkish war was fought from 1676 to 1681. Subsequent wars occurred in 1735–39, 1768–74, 1787–91, 1806–12, 1828–29, 1853–56, and 1877–78.

Anderson, M.S., *The Eastern Question 1774–1923: A Study in International Relations,* 1966.

RUSTAVI. Town 20 miles (32 km) SSE of Tbilisi on Kura River, in the Georgian Soviet Socialist Republic. The main industries are iron and steel milling; manufactures include metal products, fertilizers, and synthetic fibers. Industry is based on coal from Tkibuli and Tkvarcheli and on ore from Dashkesan. Population (1973) 111,000.

RUTHENIA. A region comprising the S slopes of the Carpathian mountains, now part of the Ukrainian Soviet Socialist Republic (Soviet Union). It was part of Hungary until it was attached to Czechoslovakia in 1920. Following Hitler's seizure of Czechoslovakia in 1939, Ruthenia briefly proclaimed its independence, before being reannexed by Hungary. After the Second World War it was ceded to the Soviet Union.

RYAZAN. Town situated 130 miles (208 km) SE of Moscow on S bank of the Oka River. Industries include engineering and petrochemical and oil refining. Population (1981) 470,000.

RYBACHY. Town in the Russian Soviet Federated Socialist Republic 20 miles (32 km) NE of Zelenogradsk, on the lagoon inland of Courland Spit, on the Baltic coast near the Lithuanian Soviet Socialist Republic border. It is a resort and fishing port.

RYBAKOV, BORIS ALEKSANDROVICH (1908–). Historian and archaeologist. Since 1953 he has been a member of the Academy of Sciences, and since 1951 a member of the Communist Party. In 1939–43 Rybakov lectured at Moscow University. He is a specialist in the field of the history of the USSR and in ancient Slavic history. In 1952 he was awarded the Stalin Prize for his work *The History of the Culture of Ancient Russia* (1948–51).

RYBINSK. Town situated 170 miles (274 km) NE of Moscow, at the SE end of Rybinsk reservoir on the Volga River. Industries include shipbuilding, wire, and matches. Rybinsk trades in timber, grain, and petroleum. Population (1981) 243,000.

RYBINSK RESERVOIR. Lake 170 miles (274 km) NE of Moscow in the Russian Soviet Federated Socialist Republic, fed by the Andoga, Mologa, Chagoda, Suda, Sheksna, and Volga rivers.

RYKOV, ALEKSEY IVANOVICH (1881–1938). Member of the militant wing of the Social Democratic Labor Party and of its Bolshevik faction. Rykov worked as an underground agent in Russia but broke with Lenin in 1910 to become leader of the "party-minded Bolsheviks," a subfaction, which was more tolerant toward the Mensheviks. After the October Revolution in 1917 he advocated a coalition government of all socialist parties. Chairman of the supreme council of national economy in 1918–20 and 1923–24, in 1921–24 he was deputy chairman of the council of people's commissars, and later chairman. A member of the Politburo, he became a leading member of the Right Opposition. He was executed following the last show trial of the Great Purge.

Carr, Edward Hallett, *The Russian Revolution: From Lenin to Stalin,* 1979.

RYLEYEV, KONDRATY FEDOROVICH (1795–1826). Decembrist (*see* **Decembrists**) and poet. In 1823, Ryleyev and Alexander Bestuzhev (*q.v.*) began publishing a yearly "almanac," the *Polar Star.* While he frequently wrote narrative verse similar to that of Byron, his best poems are those inspired with revolutionary zeal, such as "The Citizen" (1826). He was arrested and hanged in the Peter and Paul fortress after the suppression of the Decembrist revolt.

Mirsky, D. S., *A History of Russian Literature,* 1948.

Raeff, Marc, *The Decembrist Movement,* 1966.

RYSAKOV, NICHOLAS IVANOVICH (1861–81). Terrorist. In 1881 he threw a bomb at Alexander II's (*q.v.*) carriage in St. Petersburg. The tsar was unharmed. Later on the same day another attempt was made, this time having the desired result. Rysakov was arrested and executed.

RYURIK (?–*c.* 879). The semi-legendary founder of the Ryurik dynasty of Russian princes (862–1598). A Varangian chieftain, Ryurik was allegedly prince of Novgorod from 862. His descendants were grand princes of Kiev, Vladimir, and Muscovy. The Kievan state was founded by Oleg, Ryurik's successor.

RYURIKIDS. Ruling house established by Ryurik, to which the princes and grand princes of Kiev, the grand princes of Vladimir, and the grand princes and tsars of Muscovy, until 1598, belonged.

RZHEV. Town in the Russian Soviet Federated Socialist Republic situated 70 miles (112 km) SW of Kalinin on S Bank of the Volga River. Industries include agricultural engineering, paper, and distilling. Population (1970) 49,000.

S

SAAREMAA. Estonian island at the mouth of the Gulf of Riga. Ruled at first by the Livonian Knights, it became a Danish possession in 1560, a Swedish possession in 1645, a Russian possession in 1710, and was part of independent Estonia in 1917. It has an area of 1,050 square miles (2,720 sq km). The chief town is Kingisepp. It is low-lying and the main occupations are farming, fishing, and tourism.

SABUROV, MAKSIM ZAKHAROVICH (1900-). Communist functionary. He joined the party in 1926 and volunteered for work suppressing armed resistance to the regime. He studied at the Sverdlov Communist University (1923–26) and then studied engineering at Moscow University. From 1941 to 1944 and 1949 to 1955 Saburov was chairman of Gosplan. He was chairman of the state economic commission from 1955 to 1956 and a first deputy prime minister from 1955 to 1957. In 1952 he was a member of the central committee and its presidium. As a result of accusations of membership in the antiparty group, in 1957 he was removed from positions of governmental responsibility. Since then he has worked as deputy chairman of the committee for the economic cooperation of the Soviet bloc countries and as a factory manager.

SADKO. Hero of many *byliny (q.v.)* (heroic ballads), written in Kiev and Novgorod.

SAIN BULAT. *See* **Beksulatovich, Simeon.**

ST. GEORGE'S DAY. Feast day celebrated on November 25. In the 15th century a number of monasteries were given the right to forbid their peasants to move, except for three weeks around St. George's Day. In 1601, the serf owners were granted the right to take peasants from other landowners at a two-week period around St. George's Day.

Clarkson, J. D., *A History of Russia*, 1961.

ST. LÉON, ARTHUR (1821–70). French ballet master at St. Petersburg. He trained the ballerina, Marfa Muravyeva and created the ballet *The Little Hump-backed Horse* (1864), based on a Russian fairy story and containing national dances.

ST. PETERSBURG. *See* **Leningrad.**

ST. PETERSBURG CRYSTAL FACTORY. The St. Petersburg crystal factory, then called the Sparrow Hills glass factory, was established by English masters and glassblowers, who trained Russian craftsmen early in the 18th century. By 1750 it had moved from the Sparrow Hills in Moscow to St. Petersburg.

SAINT SERGIUS OF RADONEZH (1314–92). Founder of the Troitsa-Sergeyeva Lavra (Monastery) *(q.v.)*. He is a patron saint of Russia. His popularity is largely due to the fact that he blessed Dmitriy Donskoy *(q.v.)* before the battle of Kulikovo and believed that he would win.

ST. SERGIUS TRINITY (TROITSA) MONASTERY. Monastery founded in the 14th century near Moscow by St. Sergius of Radonezh (1314–92). The monastery was an important center of religious life and culture, and eventually owned vast amounts of land.

Mirsky, D. S., *Russia: A Social History*, 1931.

SAINT-SIMON, HENRI DE (1760–1825). French social reformer who founded a religion of socialism, which combined the teachings of Jesus with scientific ideas. The Saint-Simonians had considerable influence on Alexander Herzen and Vissarion Belinsky *(q.q.v.)*.

Berlin, Isaiah, *Russian Thinkers*, 1978.

SAINT STEFAN OF PERM (1340–96). A missionary to the Zyrian people, Stefan translated the scriptures and liturgy into their language, creating a Zyrian alphabet in order to do so.

SAINTS. Among the first saints to be canonized were the princes Boris and Gleb *(q.v.)*. Martyred in 1015, their feast was celebrated three times a year. In 1072, Feodosy was canonized, and in 1240, Vladimir. In the Kievan period, the lives of saints were popular material for literature.

SAKHALIN. Island off E Siberia in the Sea of Okhotsk, forming part of Khabarovsk territory. Noted in the late 19th century as a Russian prison colony, its possession was disputed between Russia and Japan until 1945. It has an area of 19,700 square miles (76,923 sq km). The chief town is Aleksandrovsk. The central valley runs N to S and is flanked by parallel mountain ranges. The land is mainly tundra and forest. Chief occupations are fishing and growing rye, oats, potatoes, and other vegetables. There is some extraction of coal, timber, and petroleum. Population (1970) 600,000.

SAKHAROV, ANDREY D. (1921–). Physicist and dissident. In 1970 Sakharov founded the human rights committee. He won the Nobel Peace Prize in 1975 and in 1980 was sentenced to internal exile in Gorky. He wrote *My Country and the World* (1975).

Sakharov, Andrey D., *Sakharov Speaks,* 1974.

SAKULIN, PAUL NIKITICH (1868–1930). Scholar and man of letters. He was a lecturer at Moscow University (1902–11), but left his job in protest against the tsarist regime. He wrote various works on the history of Russian literature.

SALTYKOV-SHCHEDRIN, MICHAEL YEVGRAFOVICH (1826–89). Satirical writer. Coeditor of *The Contemporary,* he was editor of the radical journal *Annals of the Fatherland.* He aimed to expose the injustices of the Russian regime by means of his social and political satire.

Fennell, John L. I. (ed.), *Nineteenth-Century Russian Writers,* 1973.

SALYUT SPACE STATIONS. Series of orbiting space stations. The first Salyut station went into orbit on April 19, 1971 at an altitude of approximately 124 miles (200 km) from the earth's surface. The spaceship *Soyuz 10* joined the Salyut station for a routine checking of equipment and left again after five and a half hours. A similar experiment was repeated with *Soyuz 11.* A number of photographs of the earth's surface and atmosphere of geological and meteorological significance have been taken from the stations. A second Salyut space station was launched in 1973, and a third and fourth in 1974. They have enabled a series of experiments in space to be carried out. Klimuk and Sevastyanov spent 63 days in space in 1975. *See* **Space Travel.**

SAMARIN, YURY FEDOROVICH (1819-76). Slavophile leader and writer. A supporter of Alexander II's *(q.v.)* Great Reforms, he was active in the drafting of plans for the emancipation of the serfs; because of his belief in the great benefits of peasant communes, he influenced the authorities to transfer land to communes rather than to the individual peasant.

Petrovich, Michael B., *The Emergence of Russian Panslavism, 1856–70,* 1956.

SAMARKAND. Capital of the Samarkand region of the Uzbek Soviet Socialist Republic. It is located in the Zeravshan valley, on the Trans-Caspian Railway. The city was recorded as Maracanda in 329 B.C. when, as the capital of Sogdiana, it was taken by Alexander the Great. In the eighth century it was captured by Arabs; in the 9th, 10th, and 11th centuries, it was ruled by a succession of Persian and Turkic peoples. In 1220 it was destroyed by Genghis Khan. In 1369 Timur (Tamerlane) rebuilt it as his capital. It became the most important cultural center of Central Asia, and a rich trading city on the Silk Road to China, the point where a network of other important routes converged. In 1500 it was conquered by the Uzbeks, who subsequently moved their capital from Samarkand to Bukhara *c.* 1550. Samarkand declined until it was virtually deserted in the 18th century. It was annexed by Russia in 1868. Economic revival came when the railway (1896) was restored to its earlier status as a route center. It is now the trading center of a fertile area. Industries are brewing, distilling, flour milling, and tobacco processing; manufactures are textiles, chemicals, clothing, and footwear. Outstanding historical buildings include Registan Square, a complex of 15th-century colleges, 13 mausoleums of the time of Timur, including his own (1405), the Shah-Zindah mosque, and the mosque of Bibi-Khanum (1404). Population (1981) 499,000.

Maclean, Fitzroy, *Eastern Approaches*, 1949.

SAMIZDAT. Term coined by Soviet dissenters for the system of preparing and circulating writings, usually in typescript form, so as to avoid official censorship. Though the large-scale appearance of this phenomenon occurred in the late 1950s during the period of destalinization, the word itself dates from the mid-1960s. It is a parody of the official acronym *Gosizdat* (State Publishing House) and means "self-publishing" or "do-it-yourself publishing." In *samizdat,* materials are circulated on the chain-letter principle. Typescript copies of the original text are passed on to trusted colleagues who in turn make further copies and hand them on to their friends to do likewise.

The authors and distributors of *samizdat* often operate under conditions of great difficulty and risk arrest and imprisonment in the event of discovery. Two articles of Soviet law specifically prescribe terms of imprisonment for citizens who seek to express their opinions in ways disapproved of by the authorities. Article 190–1 of the Russian Soviet Federated Socialist Republic Criminal Code, "dissemination of fabrications known to be false which defame the Soviet state and social system" and Article 70 of the same code, "anti-Soviet agitation and propaganda," carry maximum penalties of 3 and 12 years imprisonment respectively.

Samizdat has become a permanent feature of Soviet life in the post-Stalin period. It has provided an alternative, unofficial, and uncontrolled channel of communication. *Samizdat* provides a forum for opinions, as well as a source of information on political, national, religious, and literary themes that cannot find expression in the official press and publishing. It is not limited to the larger Russian cities but is also well developed in some of the non-Russian republics of the Soviet Union, particularly in Lithuania and the Ukraine. A striking feature of *samizdat* is the wide range and volume of its material. The range of subjects vary from petitions, protests, and statements to complete novels, e.g., Pasternak's *Doctor Zhivago*, and lengthy historical works, e.g., Solzhenitsyn's *The GULag Archipelago.* Perhaps the most outstanding achievement of *samizdat* has been the appearance between 1968 and 1980 of over 50 issues of the journal *A Chronicle of Current Events*, the mouthpiece of the human rights movement in the

USSR. The *Chronicle* reports on human rights violations throughout the Soviet Union and is noted for its objectivity and accuracy.

The practice of circulating uncensored material privately has a long tradition in Russia. It can be traced as far back as the 1820s when the poet Pushkin, the playwright Aleksander Sergeyevich Griboyedov, and others are known to have distributed privately manuscripts of works disapproved of by the censors. The practice flourished in the second half of the 19th century as various revolutionary groups, and later political parties and national movements, emerged. It continued after the Bolshevik seizure of power in October 1917, and their creation of a new system of censorship. By the mid-1930s, however, the practice was effectively stamped out everywhere except in the labor camps, and it did not begin to reappear until after Stalin's death in 1953.

SAMOGITIA. Historical region of W Lithuania situated N of the Neman River. It is inhabited by the Lithuanian tribe of Samogitians. The area was ceded to Lithuania by the Teutonic Knights in 1411.

SAMOYED. Breed of sturdy working dog kept by the Samoyed people and developed in N Siberia.

SAMOYEDS (NENETS). People living on the shores of the Arctic Ocean from the White Sea in the W to the Khatanga River in the E. They speak languages of the Ural-Altaic family, similar to the Finno-Ugrian family, and number about 25,000. They are seminomadic reindeer breeders in the N and sedentary hunters and fishers farther S.

Hajdú, P., *The Samoyed Peoples and Languages,* 1963.

SAMSONOV, ALEXANDER VASILYEVICH (1859–1914). General. Samsonov commanded the army that invaded E Prussia in August 1914 and was defeated at the battle of Tannenberg, where two Russian corps were destroyed and three others were reduced to half their size. Samsonov committed suicide.

Solzhenitsyn, Alexander, *August 1914,* 1972.

SANIN, JOSEPH. *See* **Joseph of Volokolamsk.**

SAN STEFANO, TREATY OF. Treaty signed at the village of San Stefano near Istanbul on March 3, 1878 by Russia and Turkey at the end of the Russo-Turkish war of 1877–78. The main terms were that Turkey should recognize Montenegro, Rumania, and Serbia as independent states; that Bulgaria should be granted the status of an independent principality; and that Batum, Kars, Turkish Armenia (Bayazet), and part of Bessarabia should be ceded to Russia. The treaty was, however, replaced by the Treaty of Berlin (1878) *(q.v.)* following pressure by Austria-Hungary and Great Britain.

SARAFAN. Item of Russian women's national dress. The *sarafan* is a sleeveless jacket worn on the shoulders. Before the days of Peter the Great, *sarafany* were worn by the boyars, but by the 10th century they were worn by peasant women in Russia and Siberia. They are still worn in parts of the Arkhangel, Vologodsk, and Kursk oblasts.

SARANSK. Capital of the Mordovian Autonomous Soviet Socialist Republic situated 155 miles (248 km) SSE of Gorky. It was founded as a fort in 1680. Center of an agricultural area. Industries include the processing of grain, hemp, sugar beets, and dairy products; manufactures are agricultural machinery and electrical equipment. Population (1981) 280,000.

SARAPUL. Town in the Udmurt Autonomous Soviet Socialist Republic, situated 142 miles (227 km) SW of Perm on the Kama River. Founded in the 16th century, it was destroyed in the Pugachev *(q.v.)* rebellion of 1773. It is a trading center for grain and timber. Manufactures are leather, footwear, rope, and machine tools. Population (1970) 97,020.

SARATOV. Capital of Saratov region situated on the Volga River. It was founded at the end of the 16th century. Industries are oil refining, natural gas, flour milling, and sawmilling; manufactures are agricultural machinery, diesel engines, and railway rolling stock. Population (1981) 873,000.

SAREMA. *See* **Saaremaa.**

SARMATIANS. Nomads who inhabited an area E of the Don River in the fourth century B.C. and who continued to move westward for about 700 years. In the third and fourth centuries A.D. they were defeated by the Goths and the Huns. Sarmatian art from Siberia was preserved by Peter the Great for the Siberian collection now in the Hermitage Museum in Leningrad.

Harmatta, A., *Studies in the History of the Sarmatians,* 1950.

Phillips, E. D., *The Royal Hordes: Nomad People of the Steppes,* 1965.

SART. Name referring to the urban and rural sedentary peoples living in the oases of Central Asia, as opposed to the nomadic Uzbeks. Iranian in origin, from the sixth century these peoples endured Turkicization following conquests by Turkic tribes. While a minority still speak Tadzhik, the majority now speak the Turkic Chagay. From 1924 Tadzhik-speaking *sarts* have been officially registered as Tadzhiks, while Chagay-speaking *sarts* have been considered to be Uzbeks.

SATELLITES. The world's first artificial satellite was launched on October 4, 1957 from a secret base in Central Asia. *Sputnik I,* as it was named, was designed by S. P. Korolev (1906–66) and V. P. Glushko (1908–). The second Sputnik carried a dog, and *Sputnik III* housed a geophysical observatory and sent back by television the first pictures of the far side of the moon.

Riabchikov, Evgeny, *Russians in Space,* 1972.

SATIRE. Owing to the restrictions of censorship both in tsarist times and during the present regime, satire has been of considerable significance in Russia as a means of expressing discontent with the regime. For example, Ivan Goncharov's *Oblomov (q.v.)* satirizes the inefficiency of serfdom, while Gogol's witty comedy *The Government Inspector* satirizes bureaucratic inefficiency. Vladimir Voinovich's *(q.v.)* novel *The Life and Extraordinary Adventures of Private Ivan Chonkin* satirizes the bureaucratic shortcomings of the Soviet regime.

SAYAN MOUNTAINS. Two mountain ranges in the extreme S of the USSR. The E Sayan mountains extend SE from Yenisey River to the Mongolian border, rising to Munku Sardyk, 11,457 feet (3,492 m) above sea level. The W Sayan mountains extend ENE from the Altay mountains, rising to 9,000 feet (2,743 m) above sea level and join the E range. Gold, silver, lead, and coal are found as well as timber.

SAZONOV, SERGEY DMITRIYEVICH (1861–1927). Diplomat and statesman. Sazonov started working for the foreign ministry in 1883 and in 1910 was appointed foreign minister. He attempted to ease relations with Germany, but relations with Great Britain deteriorated. He eventually forced the Germans to relinquish command of Turkish troops in Constantinople. After the assassination of Archduke Francis Ferdinand, Sazonov pressured the tsar to agree to complete mobilization. He was dismissed in 1916 as a result of his view that an autonomous Poland should be created. In 1917 he was appointed ambassador to London and then acted as foreign minister for Admiral A. V. Kolchak *(q.v.)*.

SCHISM OF 1054. Schism whereby the Eastern Orthodox Church broke away from the Latin Church. The Byzantine Empire had disagreed with Rome over a variety of doctrinal matters, such as methods of tonsuring monks, and the West's inclusion of the *Filioque* clause in the Creed. Although attempts have been made to bridge the schism, it still exists.

Obolensky, Dimitri, *The Byzantine Commonwealth: Eastern Europe 500–1453*, 1971.

SCISSORS CRISIS. Name given to the economic crisis of 1923–24. Prices of farm produce were falling, while those of industrial goods were rising. As a result, the standard of living of the peasants was falling; to offset this, the government took measures to keep prices of industrial products artificially low.

SCRIABIN, ALEXANDER NIKOLAYEVICH (1872–1915). Composer of piano and orchestral music. In 1888 he entered the Moscow Conservatory and from 1898 to 1903 he taught there. He married pianist Vera Isakovich in 1897. From 1900 on he was interested in mystical philosophy, and the end of his First Symphony was designed to be a glorification of art as religion. Theosophical ideas inspired his *Le Divin Poème* (1905) and *Poème de l'estase* (1908). He eventually viewed himself as a messiah who would reunite Russia with the Spirit. He devised a "liturgical act," which made use of poetry, dancing, colors, and scents, as well as music, in an attempt to induce a "supreme final ecstasy." His music became progressively more idiosyncratic.

Brook, Donald, *Six Great Russian Composers*, 1946.

SCRUB. *See* ***Klet.***

SEBASTOPOL. Ukrainian town on the SW point of the Crimean peninsula. Although Greek and Roman settlements had existed there, it was Catherine the Great who founded the city and port. Its history is one of great sieges including one in 1854–55 during the Crimean War when the city held out for 349 days against British, French, Turkish, and Sardinian forces, and again in 1941–42 when it held out for eight months against German and Rumanian forces. Sailors at Sebastopol mutinied in the 1905 Revolution. Industries include shipbuilding, fish processing, tanning, flour milling, and tourism. The town is a naval base and seaport. Population (1981) 315,000.

SECHENOV, IVAN MIKHAILOVICH (1829–1905). Professor at St. Petersburg and Moscow universities, regarded as the father of Russian physiology. Strongly influenced by Nicholas Chernyshevsky and Charles Darwin, he proposed a materialist explanation for spiritual and psychic occurrences. Sechenov wrote *Object, Thought, and Reality* (1892), *Physiology of the Nervous System* (1866), and *Impressions and Reality*.

SECOND ECONOMY. General term referring to unofficial trading and manufacturing, the black market, and speculation.

SECOND NORTHERN WAR. *See* **Great/Second Northern War.**

SECOND WORLD WAR. *See* **World War II.**

SECRET COMMITTEE. Committee established in 1802 by Alexander I. It consisted of four of the tsar's friends and met to discuss ways in which the Enlightenment could be brought to Russia.

SECRET POLICE. From 1917 to 1922 the Soviet security service was known as the Cheka (All-Russian Extraordinary Commission for Combating Counter-Revolution and Sabotage). This was reorganized as the GPU (State Political Administration) in 1922 and as the OGPU (United State Political Administration) in 1923. In 1934 the OGPU was succeeded by the NKVD (People's Commissariat for Internal Affairs), by the NKGB (People's Commissariat for State Security) in 1943, by the MGB (Ministry for State Security) in 1946, and by the MVD (Ministry of Internal Affairs) in 1953. Since 1954 the Secret Police has been known as the KGB (Committee for State Security).

The Secret Police has directed its energies against the church, private traders, *kulaks*, the intelligentsia, and any who disagree with the regime. It became a particularly sinister and powerful tool under Yezhov during the Great Purge in which 8 to 10 million people perished. The KGB is also responsible for foreign espionage. It is now part of the USSR council of ministers and it is estimated that it has half a million employees.

SECRETARIAT OF THE CENTRAL COMMITTEE. The secretaries of the central committee are in charge of the party apparatus and oversee work in the departments of the central committee. The secretariat has at present 10 members, of whom half are also members of the

Politburo, but all members of the secretariat usually attend meetings of the Politburo.

SELENGA RIVER. River rising in the Khangay mountains of NW Mongolia and flowing 750 miles (1,200 km) ENE to the Russian border near Altan Bulak, then N through Buryat Autonomous Soviet Socialist Republic, past Ulan Ude into Lake Baikal. It is navigable in summer along the Russian section.

SELF-DETERMINATION. The right of the people of a state to choose their own government. The Soviet role in Eastern bloc countries has caused concern among Western members of the United Nations where the concept has been developed and defined; the right to self-determination was reaffirmed in the Declaration of the Inadmissability of Intervention in the Domestic Affairs of States and the Protection of their Independence and Sovereignty.

SEMEVSKY, VASILY IVANOVICH (1848–1916). Historian and professor at St. Petersburg University. One of the founders of populism *(q.v.)*, Semevsky wrote many works on the history of serfdom in Russia.

SEMIPALATINSK. Town in Kazakhstan situated on the Irtysh River. Founded in 1718, it is the capital of Semipalatinsk region. Industries include meat packing, flour milling, and tanning. Population (1981) 291,000.

SEMYONNOVSKY GUARDS. Regiment founded by Peter the Great in 1687.

SERAFIM, METROPOLITAN (1763–1843). Senior metropolitan of St. Petersburg, opposed to modern commentaries on the Bible.

SERAFIM OF SAROV, SAINT (1759–1833). The first known *starets* (holy man). A monk of the Sarov Monastery, Serafim spent most of his life as a hermit and recluse. He was canonized in 1903.

SERAFIMOVICH, ALEXANDER (POPOV) (1863–1949). Writer. Born in the Don region, and son of a Cossack officer, Serafimovich entered the mathematical faculty at the University of St. Petersburg in 1883, and there met the elder brother of Lenin. In 1887, he wrote a revolutionary proclamation for which he was exiled to Archangel until 1919. In 1889 he wrote his first work, *On the Ice*, and he joined the literary art group *Sreda*. His fame rests mainly on *The Iron Flood* (1924), a somewhat journalistic and epic account of the Civil War.

SERAPION BROTHERS. A group of 12 young writers who were fellow-travelers and who had met in Petrograd in 1921. They took their name from E.T.A. Hoffmann's "Storyteller and Hermit." They rejected the idea that their literature should be in any way associated with propaganda, thus incurring the suspicion of party critics. Frequently original in style and form, as a group the Serapion brothers are characterized by their irreverence and wit. Perhaps the most promising of them, Lev Lunts, died at the age of 23; others, such as Konstantin Fedin, Nicholas Tikhonov, and Venyamin

Kaverin, later adopted the party line on literature.

SERFS. Peasants who could be bought, sold, and generally treated as chattels, by the landowner. Although the 1649 code forbade the owner to kill, wound, or mistreat his serfs, this code was frequently infringed. Tax had to be paid on a serf and he spent half his working day on the landowner's estate. At times, peasant rebellions occurred, such as the uprising led by Stenka Razin *(q.v.)* in 1670. Serfdom was abolished in 1861. *See* **Agrarian Reforms.**

Blum, Jerome, *Lord and Peasant in Russia from the Ninth to the Nineteenth Century,* 1961.

Kochan, Lionel, *The Making of Modern Russia,* 1962.

Smith, Robert E. F., *The Enserfment of the Russian Peasantry,* 1968.

SERGIUS ALEXANDROVICH, GRAND DUKE (1864–1905). Governor-general of Moscow who was assassinated in 1905 in the Kremlin by a bomb thrown by Ivan Rakonovich Kalyayev, the Socialist Revolutionary. The grand duke had succeeded in alienating virtually every sector of society.

SEROV, ALEXANDER NIKOLAYEVICH (1820–71). Composer and critic. After visiting Wagner in 1858, he became a firm supporter of his music. His works comprise three operas, *Judith* (1863), *Rogneda* (1865), and *The Power of Evil* (1867–71), which was completed by Nicholas Solovev. He also composed orchestral works, some piano pieces, and sacred music.

SEROV, VALENTIN ALEKSANDROVICH (1865–1911). Painter. Having studied under Ilya Repin *(q.v.)* and at the Academy of Arts (1880–84), Serov was particularly fond of painting portraits of the Russian aristocracy. Serov's best-known paintings are his intimate portraits, very often of children. His *Girl with Peaches* is a landmark in Russian art.

SEROV. Town situated 190 miles (304 km) N of Sverdlovsk in the Sverdlovsk region of the Russian Soviet Federated Socialist Republic. It was founded during the construction of the Trans-Siberian Railway in 1894. It is an important metallurgical center, manufacturing metal goods and special steels. Population (1974) 100,000.

SERPUKHOV. Town situated 60 miles (96 km) S of Moscow at the confluence of the Oka and Nara rivers. It was founded in the 14th century, and a stone kremlin built in the 16th century still stands. It is a commercial center of an agricultural area, trading in grain and timber. Industries include textiles, sawmilling, and metalworking. Population (1974) 130,000.

SEVASTOPOL. *See* **Sebastopol.**

SEVEN YEARS WAR (1756–63). Properly named the Austro-Prussian War of 1756–63. Russia fought Prussia until the beginning of 1762, when the two countries made a separate peace. Britain allied with Prussia against Austria, France, Russia, Sweden, and Saxony. The Treaty of Itubertusburg (Hubertsburg), between Austria, Prussia, and Saxony, was signed in 1763.

Russia succeeded in eliminating French influence from Poland.

SHAKHTY. Town situated 40 miles (64 km) NE of Rostov in Donets Basin, Rostov region. It was founded in 1829 as a coal-mining center. Manufactures include clothing, furniture, and machinery. Population (1981) 214,000. It is the site of Shakhty Trials (1928), a forerunner of the Great Purge *(Yezhovshchina)*, of engineers accused of trumped-up sabotage charges.

SHALYAPIN, FEDOR IVANOVICH (1873–1938). Russian bass singer who strongly influenced the style of performance in opera. Born in Kazan of humble origin, Shalyapin began to study singing with Dmitry Ussatov in 1892. As a member of Sarva Ivanovich Mamontov's private opera company he learned the roles that were to bring him fame later on. Although a supporter of the Bolshevik Revolution, he left Soviet Russia in 1921 and visited the United States and London. He wrote *Pages from My Life: An Autobiography* (1927).

SHAMANISM. Religion adopted for a time by some primitive Mongol tribes, such as the Buryats and the Kalmyks.

SHAMIL, IMAM (1797–1871). Religious and political leader of the Muslim population in N Caucasia. Shamil led their resistance to Russian conquest but surrendered at Gunib in 1859. He died in Mecca. Under Stalin's regime Shamil was viewed as a British and Turkish agent.

Baddeley, John F., *The Russian Conquest of the Caucasus*, 1908.

SHAPORIN, YURY ALEKSANDROVICH (1887–). Composer. He studied at the St. Petersburg Conservatory under Sokolov and Nicholas Cherepnin *(q.v.)* and in 1939 was appointed professor at the Moscow Conservatory. His best-known works include the opera *The Decembrists* (1947–53), the oratorio *The Lay of the Battle for the Russian Land* (1943–44), and the music for the film *Kutuzov*.

SHEKSNA RIVER. River rising in Lake Beloye in W Russian Soviet Federated Socialist Republic, and flowing 100 miles (160 km) S to the Rybinsk reservoir, forming part of the Mariynsk canal system.

SHELEKLOV, GRIGORY. *See* **Alaska.**

SHELEPNIN, ALEXANDER NIKOLAYEVICH (1918–). Communist official. Having studied in Moscow, Shelepnin joined the party in 1940, and worked in the Komsomol apparatus; in 1958 he was appointed first secretary of its central committee, and became a member of the party central committee. He was chairman of the committee of state security (KGB) (1958–61). He was removed from the leadership, and thus eliminated as a potential opponent to Brezhnev, in 1975.

SHELEST, PETER YEFIMOVICH (1908–). First secretary of the Ukraine. From 1963 he has been a member of the Politburo of the CPSU, and from 1966 a member of the central committee. After graduating from the Mariupol Evening

Metallurgical Institute, Shelest worked on farms, on the railway, and as a factory worker before holding a number of executive party posts in Chelyabinsk, Moscow, Saratov, Leningrad, and Kiev. He eventually rose to become a Presidium member of the USSR Supreme Soviet in 1966, and the head of the USSR Supreme Soviet delegation to Hungary in 1965.

SHELGUNOV, NICHOLAS VASILYEVICH (1824-91). Coauthor of the revolutionary leaflet *To the Young Generation*, circulated in the summer of 1861. Shelgunov demanded a social radicalism combined with what he saw as Russia's special mission.

SHEPILOV, DMITRY TROFIMOVICH (1905-). Politician. Head of the propaganda department of the central committee in 1948, in 1952 Shepilov was chief editor of *Pravda*, secretary of the central committee (1955–56 and 1957), and foreign minister in 1956. After eventually joining the antiparty group in 1957, he was expelled from the central committee, and it is thought that he then taught political economy at Frunze.

SHESTOV, LEV (LEV ISAKOVICH SCHWARTZMANN) (1866–1938). Writer. Of Jewish origin, he studied for the bar, and turned to literature late in life. His first book, *Shakespeare and His Critic Brandes* (1898), contains an attack on positivism and rationalism, and later works, such as *Dostoyevsky and Nietzsche* and *The Philosophy of Tragedy* (1901), illustrate his profound lack of belief in Idealism. He spent many years abroad studying the history of philosophy and mysticism. Opposed to the Bolsheviks, in 1917 Shestov settled in Paris.

SHEVCHENKO, TARAS HRYHOROVYCH (1814–61). Ukrainian poet. Bought out of serfdom by a group of intellectuals, Shevchenko took part in the clandestine Pan-Slavic society, the Brotherhood of Saints Cyril and Methodius, as a result of which he was banished to Orenburg for 10 years. He then moved to St. Petersburg. Shevchenko made a considerable impact on the Ukrainian national movement. His best-known poems were published in the collection, *Kobzar* (1840).

SHIPKA PASS. Bulgarian pass through the Balkan mountains on the main road from Ruse to Adrianople (Edirne) in Turkey. Fierce fighting occurred there in the Russo-Turkish war of 1877–78, in which 5,500 Russians and 13,000 Turks fell, and eventually the Turkish General Vessil Pasha surrendered.

SHIPOV, DMITRY NIKOLAYEVICH (1851–1920). Liberal politician. Chairman of the Moscow *Zemstvo*, Shipov organized unofficial congresses of *zemstvo* representatives in the 1890s and 1900s. In 1905 he was one of the founders and 10 leaders of the Octobrist *(q.v.)* party, and in the following year, a leader of the party of peaceful renovation.

Fischer, George, *Russian Liberalism, from Gentry to Intelligentsia*, 1958.

SHIRINSKY-SHIKHMATOV, PRINCE P. A. (1790–1853). Minister of education under Nicholas I (*q.v.*), and of a somewhat reactionary outlook.

SHKLOVSKY, VIKTOR BORISOVICH (1893–). Formalist (*q.v.*) critic and leader of the formalist critical group *Opoyaz* (Society for the Study of Poetic Language). He was a member of LEF. He also wrote *Sentimental Journey*, describing life in literary circles in Petrograd in 1918–20.

SHLYAPNIKOV, ALEXANDER GAVRILOVICH (1883–1943). Bolshevik. He joined the party in 1903 and participated in the labor movement in France, before being appointed by Lenin to establish the Russian bureau of the central committee. In 1917 Shlyapnikov assisted with plans for the October seizure of power, and worked with the trade unions. Commissar for labor in the first Soviet government, and leader of the workers' opposition in 1920–21, he was expelled from the party in 1933. He disappeared in the Great Purge.

SHOCKWORKERS' MOVEMENT (1927–35). Workers were encouraged by trade unions to become "shockworkers" (*udarniki*), a particularly dedicated kind of worker who, according to the party, actively directed participation in economic construction.

SHOLOKHOV, MICHAEL ALEKSANDROVICH (1905–84). Author. Born in a small Cossack village in the Don region, Sholokhov was educated in Moscow and worked as a teacher, clerk, and journalist. In 1920 he started to publish sketches and joined several literary circles. The start of his literary career was boosted by Alexander Serafimovich's (*q.v.*) help. In 1926 Sholokhov is thought to have begun his famous novel *Tales of the Don*, although it has been alleged that he did not in fact write it. *The Quiet Don* was published in 1926–40, *And Quiet Flows the Don* in 1934, and *The Don Flows to the Sea* in 1940. A member of the Communist Party from 1931, he was elected to the Soviet Academy of Sciences, and later to the central committee of the Soviet Union. From 1946 he has served as a deputy to the Supreme Soviet. He was awarded the Nobel Prize for literature in 1965. He later launched an attack on Andrey Sinyavsky.

Ermolaev, Herman, *Mikhail Sholokhov and His Art*, 1982.

Struve, Gleb, *Russian Literature under Lenin and Stalin*, 1972.

SHOSTAKOVICH, DMITRY DMITRIYEVICH (1906–75). Composer, pianist, and teacher. He studied under Leonid Vladimirovich Nikolayev and Lev Petrovich Shteynberg at the Leningrad Conservatory, was named a professor there, and later taught at the Moscow Conservatory. Although accused of "formalism" by party officials, particularly over his tragic opera *Lady Macbeth of Mtsensk* (1934), in 1960 Shostakovich was secretary of the Russian Soviet Federated Socialist Republic Union of Composers. Highly individual, his music is frequently dignified and austere, although at times it seems garish. His best-known works include the opera *The Nose* (1927–28), the ballet *The Golden Age* (1929–30), the choral work *The Poem of Our Coun-*

try (1947), symphonies, piano concertos, quartets, music for plays and films, and the song-cycle *From Jewish Folk Poetry* (1948).

Kay, Norman, *Shostakovich*, 1971.

SHOW TRIALS. Trials of alleged "wreckers," mostly held between 1928 and 1931. The trials were to serve as a reminder that vigilance was necessary, since "bourgeois specialists" were trying to sabotage the country's industrial growth.

SHUISKY, PRINCE ANDREY (?–1544). Eminent boyar. In 1544, Ivan the Terrible *(q.v.)*, then age 13, ordered his arrest and savage murder.

SHUISKY FAMILY. An old princely family, directly descended from Ryurik *(q.v.)*. Three members of the family were regents during Ivan the Terrible's *(q.v.)* minority, and most of them survived Ivan the Terrible's reign by submitting to his every whim. Banished from Moscow by Boris Godunov *(q.v.)*, Vasily Shuisky was permitted to return to Moscow later. At first the Shuiskys served against the uprising led by the pretender to the throne, the False Dmitry *(q.v.)*. In private, however, Vasily Shuisky is said to have claimed that Dmitry was the tsarevich. Under Dmitry's rule, however, the Shuiskys were once more banished, although they were allowed later to return to Moscow, where they clandestinely made plans with King Sigismund of Poland to put his son Wladyslaw on the throne of Moscow.

SHUISKY, PRINCE VASILY (*fl.* early 17th century). After the False Dmitry's *(q.v.)* accession to the throne in 1605, it was announced that Vasily Shuisky had denounced him as an impostor. The general assembly of land *(Zemsky Sobor)* found Vasily guilty and sentenced him to death. The pretender, however, reprieved him. Vasily continued to conspire against Dmitry and in 1606 he charged into the Kremlin, and the pretender was killed. In 1606 he was made tsar. Though Vasily was popular with the upper classes, the majority of people supported the new pretender. Eventually, representatives of every class called on him to descend from the throne on July 17. He was seized and forced to become a monk.

SHUKSHIN, VASILY (1929–74). "Village" writer, many of whose stories deal with the life and problems faced by uprooted peasants. A popular screenwriter and director, one of his most famous movies, *Kalina Krasnaya (The Red Snow-ball Tree)* was shown in the United States.

SHURATOV, MALYUTA (*fl.* late 16th century). Notorious henchman of Ivan the Terrible. In 1570 he murdered Metropolitan Philip. He died at the hands of the *oprichniki.*

SHUVALOV, COUNT IVAN (1727–97). In 1755 Shuvalov suggested that Peter the Great *(q.v.)* found the first university in Russia, at Moscow, and the first state-controlled secondary schools, and proposed that *gimnazii* (high schools) be set up in all large cities, although this did not come to pass. In 1757 he was responsible for the creation of the Academy of Arts.

SHUVALOV, COUNT PETER ANDREYEVICH (1827–89). Russian government official and ambassador. A member of an old noble family, Shuvalov began his military career in 1845, and his diplomatic career in 1856 at the Paris Peace Conference. After being in charge of the St. Petersburg police, he was made director of the political police (1861–64), and in 1866 he was chief of staff of the gendarmerie corps and head of the Third Section. He then became an influential adviser of Alexander II *(q.v.)* and was opposed to liberal reform. In 1876 he was sent to London as ambassador. He died in St. Petersburg.

SHVERNIK, NICHOLAS MIKHAILOVICH (1888–). Communist. Having joined the party in 1905, Shvernik took part in underground work. After the Bolshevik coup, he was chairman of the Samara Soviet, and a commissar in the Red Army during the Civil War. In the early 1920s he was a member of the presidium of the central control commission, and in 1930 he was secretary of the trade union central council. In 1944 he was appointed first deputy chairman of the presidium of the USSR Supreme Soviet and the following year was chairman. In 1956 he was chairman of the committee of party control.

SIBERIA. Region in the Russian Soviet Federated Socialist Republic extending W and E from the Ural mountains to the Pacific Ocean and N and S from the Arctic Ocean to the Central Asian mountain ranges. It has an approximate area of 5,200,000 square miles (about 13,500,000 sq km). The plains in the W are drained by the Yenisey and Ob rivers and bounded on the S by the Altay and Sanay mountain ranges. The central area is a plateau, bounded on the E by the Lena River. The E is mountainous. All rivers except the Amur flow into the Arctic Ocean and are frozen for most of the year. The climate is continental. Verkhoyansk in E Siberia has a mean January temperature of – 59°F (– 50°C). Chief occupations of the N are lumbering, fur trapping, and fishing. In the S and the SW, where agriculture is concentrated, cereal is grown and cattle and sheep are raised. Coal, oil, gold, and iron ore exist in large quantities. Important industries are concentrated in the Kuznetsk coal basin and the adjoining industrial region centered on Sverdlovsk and Chelyabinsk in the Ural mountains. Other chief towns are Novosibirsk, Omsk, and Vladivostok on the Trans-Siberian Railway.

SIBERIAN KHANATE. Tatar state established in W Siberia in the 15th century. Conquered by Yermak *(q.v.)* and his Cossacks, it was annexed to Muscovy in 1582. *See also* **Stroganov.**

SICH (SECH). Originally *sich* referred to a fortified camp on the Dnepr River, which in the 16th, 17th, and 18th centuries was the center of the Ukrainian Cossacks. The word was extended in meaning to include the entire region and the Cossack military organization there.

SIDE-BURNITES. In 1837 Nicholas I issued a decree forbidding the wearing of beards and whiskers by civil servants and this was later extended to include students.

SIEGE OF LENINGRAD. *See* **Leningrad, Siege of.**

SIEGE OF STALINGRAD. *See* **Stalingrad, Siege of.**

SIKHOTE ALIN RANGE. Mountain range in the Primore and Khabarovsk territories, extending 750 miles (1,200 km) along the Pacific coast from Vladivostok to Nikolaevsk. It rises to 6,000 feet (1,829 m) above sea level. It is forested, and has mineral resources especially coal, iron, lead, and zinc.

SIKORSKI, WLADYSLAW (1881–1943). Polish prime minister of the government-in-exile during the Second World War. In 1941 he concluded an agreement on cooperation with the USSR. Stalin severed Polish-Soviet diplomatic relations when Sikorski demanded an inquiry into the murder of Polish prisoners at Katyn. Sikorski died in an air crash in 1943.

SIKORSKY, IGOR IVANOVICH (1889–1972). Aircraft designer. In 1913 he constructed and flew the first successful four-engine airplane and during the First World War designed bombers for the Russian air force. He emigrated to the United States in 1919, and from 1930 on Sikorsky was one of the foremost designers of helicopters.

SILVER AGE. Period of approximately 30 years between the last decade of the 19th century and the October Revolution. It was a most fruitful time of exploration in literature and the arts. Writers of this era include Alexander Blok, Osip Mandelstam, and Anna Akhmatova (*q.q.v.*); artists include Kasimir Malevich (*q.v.*), El Lissitsky, and Alexander Rodchenko.

Poggioli, R., *Poets of Russia, 1880–1930,* 1960.

SIMEON OF POTOLSK (1629–1680). Belorussian monk and educator of Sofia Alekseyevna (*q.v.*), regent of Russia.

SIMFEROPOL. Ukrainian city situated 35 miles (50 km) NE of Sevastopol on the Salgir River. It is the capital of Crimea and the center of a farming and horticultural area. Industries are fruit and vegetable canning, flour milling, and tanning. Population (1981) 314,000.

SIMONOV, KONSTANTIN MIKHAILOVICH (1915–79). Novelist, dramatist, and poet. His novel *Days and Nights* (1944) is an epic account of the Battle of Stalingrad. His haunting war poem "Wait for Me" deeply touched millions of people, although his play of the same title was less successful. In 1956 he argued the case that the writings of Isaac Babel, Yury Olesha, and Anna Akhmatova (*q.q.v.*) should be made available again.

Struve, Gleb, *Russian Literature Under Lenin and Stalin,* 1972.

SINOP, BATTLE OF (1853). Naval battle fought between Russia and Turkey. Russian vice-admiral P. S. Nakhimov destroyed a division of the Turkish fleet, and a portion of Sinop was burned. This partly influenced Great Britain's participation in the Crimean War.

SITKA. Settlement in Alaska. It was founded in 1799 by Alexander Baranov, first Russian governor of Alaska, although the present town was founded in 1804. Sitka was the headquarters of the Russian-American Company until 1867 and the center of trading in Alaska. Alaska was formally transferred from Russia to the United States at Sitka on October 18, 1867.

SIXTUS IV, POPE (FRANCESCO DELLA ROVERE) (1414–84). Pope from 1471–84. He continued Sixtus III's attempts to reunite the Russian church with the Roman see, and negotiated with Ivan III with this aim in view. He was unsuccessful.

SKOBELEV, MICHAEL DIMITRIYEVICH (1843–82). Russian army officer. In 1875–76 he held a command in the expedition against Kokand, as a result of which he was promoted to major general and made first Russian governor of Fergana. He distinguished himself during the war between Russia and Turkey, commanding the Caucasian brigade of Cossacks in the attack on the Green Hills at the second battle of Plevna. In January 1878, Skobelev crossed the Balkans and defeated the Turks near Shipka Pass. He then captured Göktepe in 1881 and forced the people of Akhal-Tekke to submit. He was then put in charge of the Minsk army corps.

SKOMOROKHI. Itinerant mummers. They performed comic songs, dances, and tumbling at court and for the peasants in the 16th and 17th centuries. They thus played an important role in the history of Russian folklore, as they spread songs and dances, both secular and sacred. The church succeeded in suppressing them in the mid-17th century.

SKOPKIN-SHUISKY, PRINCE MICHAEL (?–1610). Nephew of Tsar Vasily. Skopkin-Shuisky assisted in recovering Yaroslavl from the Poles and in relieving Moscow. He died suddenly in 1610, and it is suspected that the Shuiskys murdered him on account of his popularity.

SKOROPADSKY, HETMAN PAUL P. (1873–1945). A former tsarist general, Skoropadsky was installed as hetman by the Germans in the Ukraine. He was overthrown by the peasant leader Semyon Petlyura (*q.v.*).

SLAVIC LANGUAGES. A western branch of the Satem division of Indo-European, closely connected with the Baltic languages. There are 13 living Slavic languages, classified in three groups: (1) the E Slavic group, consisting of Great Russian, Ukrainian, and Belorussian; (2) the W Slavic group, consisting of Polish, Slovak, Czech, High and Low Serbian; (3) the S Slavic group, consisting of Slovene, Serbo-Croatian, Macedonian, Bulgarian, and Church Slavonic. The now extinct Polabian and Pomeranian languages also belong to this group.

SLAVOPHILE. An adherent of a mid-19th-century Russian philosophy that opposed the Westernization of Russia. The Slavophiles believed Russia to be culturally, morally, and politically superior to the West. They idealized Russian rural society and, though favoring autocratic government, desired such reforms as the emancipation of the serfs and the granting of civil rights. The leading Slavophiles were Aleksey Khomyakov (*q.v.*) (1804–60) and the brothers Konstantin (1817–60) and Ivan (1823–86) Aksakov (*q.q.v.*).

Masaryk, Tomás G., *The Spirit of Russia: Studies in History, Literature and Philosophy*, 2 vols., 1919; rev. ed. 1955.

Riasanovsky, Nicholas V., *Russia and the West in the Teaching of the Slavophiles: A Study of a Romantic Ideology*, 1952.

SLAVS. Ethnic group, living mostly in Europe, but also in N Asia. The main area they inhabit includes most of E Europe; to the W this area stretches as far as the Oder and Lusatian Neisse rivers and to Erzgebirge; to the E, to Siberia and the Pacific Ocean. Slavs also live in Yugoslavia and Bulgaria. Slavs can be divided into the E Slavs (Russians, Ukrainians, and Belorussians), the W Slavs (Poles, Czechs, Slovaks, and Lusatians) and the S Slavs (Serbs, Croats, Slovenes, Macedonians, Montenegrins, and Bulgars).

SLAVYANSK. Ukrainian town situated 60 miles (96 km) NNW of Donetsk. Founded in 1676, its industries include chemicals. Manufactures include glass, porcelain, and salt. Population (1970) 124,000.

SLEPTSOV, VASILY ALEKSEYEVICH (1836–78). Writer of noble birth and follower of Nicholas Chernyshevsky (*q.v.*). He was a brilliant master of the technique of realistic dialogue, at the same time not sacrificing artistic merit. His best-known work is *Hard Times* (1865), a satire for liberal society in the 1860s.

SLITTE, HANS (*fl.* mid-16th century). German. In 1547 Slitte went to Moscow, where he became a close friend of the tsar. Ivan entrusted him with the responsibility of recruiting engineers, artisans, doctors, architects, chemists, printers, and other specialists from Germany, but the Hanseatic League at Lübeck refused to let many of them pass.

SLUCHEVSKY, KONSTANTIN KONSTANTINOVICH (1837–1904). Poet. His poetry met with a frosty reception from both nihilists and radicals. His poems inspired by the landscapes of N Russia and the Murmansk coast are considered his best, but generally his poetry is of a low standard.

SLYUDYANKA. Town 50 miles (80 km) SSW of Irkutsk at SW end of Lake Baikal, in the Russian Soviet Federated Socialist Republic, on the Trans-Siberian railway. It is a mining center for mica, marble, and quartz, and has some metalworking.

SMERD. The category of free peasant. A peasant was "free" in that if murdered, his murderer had to provide the deceased *smerd*'s family with compensation and had to compensate the prince. A *smerd*, unlike a slave, could be fined by the prince, and he was technically free to move about at will. It was the prince's duty to protect the *smerd*.

SMERSH. Acronym for *Smert' Shpionam* (Death to Spies). A division of the Soviet security organ, which eliminated real, suspected, or potential opponents to the Soviet government. Most of those had lived for a while outside the control of the Soviet regime during the Second World War, as civilian deportees, refugees, or prisoners of war. Smersh favored large-scale arrests, executions, or deportation.

SMOLENSK. Oblast in the Russian Soviet Federated Socialist Republic. It was formed in 1937. Most of the oblast lies in the basin of the Upper Dnepr River. An area long settled by Russians, its forests have mostly been cleared.

SMOLENSK. Town and center of the Smolensk on the banks of the Dnepr River. One of the oldest Russian towns, it dates back to the ninth century. Most of the historic buildings were destroyed in the Second World War, although the 12th-century churches of Saints Peter and Paul, the Sviskaya, and the church of St. John the Divine have been restored. The main center of the Baltic-to-Byzantium "Water Road," under Kiev, Smolensk was given to one of the sons of Yaroslav the Wise. In the 12th and the 13th centuries, there was extensive trading with Germany. Following the Tatar invasion (1238–40) the town was given to the grand duchy of Lithuania. A bitter source of conflict between Muscovy and the West, the town was burned during Napoleon's advance on Moscow (1812). A severe battle was fought there in 1941 and also in 1943. Population (1981) 311,000.

SMOLNY INSTITUTE. Building in Leningrad, at present the seat of the town and oblast committee of the CPSU. At the beginning of the 18th century, tar for ships was prepared on the site of the future institute; the institute takes its name from the Russian word for tar, *smola*. In the middle of the 18th century a convent was built here by V. Pastrelli. In 1764 the Smolny Institute became the first school for well-bred young ladies to be supported by the state. The Smolny Monastery was closed in 1797. In 1917, however, the institute took on a new role as the center of the defense of Petrograd, and the military-revolutionary committee of the Petrograd Soviet of workers' and soldiers' deputies was housed here, and after the October Revolution, the second congress of the All-Russian executive committee was held here.

SNITKINA, ANNA G. (1846–1918). Stenographer and then wife of F. M. Dostoyevsky *(q.v.)*. Her calming influence was such that he was able to give up gambling and keep out of debt.

SOBOLEV, LEONID SERGEYEVICH (1898–). Novelist. He rose to fame in 1957 when he accused dissident writers of obeying the Russian émigrés' demands for silence. As a result, Khrushchev appointed him chairman of the Union of Writers.

SOBORNOST **(Conciliarism).** Concept of free unity while working for higher values held in common. While Aleksey Khomyakov *(q.v.)* developed *sobornost* as fundamental to the Orthodox Church consciousness, it was applied to social philosophy as well. For the Slavophiles *sobornost* was embodied in the life of the Russian peasant *mir,* or commune. *Sobornost* forms the basis of modern Russian solidarism.

Masaryk, Tomás G., *The Spirit of Russia: Studies in History, Literature and Philosophy,* 2 vols., 1919; rev. ed. 1955.

SOCHI. Town in the Russian Soviet Federated Socialist Republic situated 110 miles (176 km) SSE of Krasnodar on the Black Sea coast, in the foothills of the Caucasus. Manufactures include food and tobacco products. It is a leading seaside resort and became a spa in 1910. Population (1981) 295,000.

SOCIAL DEMOCRATIC LABOR PARTY. Political party founded in 1898. Most of the founders were subsequently arrested, so it was not until 1903 that the party could function. Many opted for middle-class liberalism, which Lenin opposed.

Mendel, Arthur, *Dilemmas of Progress in Tsarist Russia,* 1961.

Plamenatz, J., *German Marxism and Russian Communism,* 1954.

Ulam, Adam B., *Lenin and the Bolsheviks: The Intellectual and Political History of the Triumph of Communism in Russia,* 1969.

SOCIAL SECURITY. The origins of the Soviet social security system date back to the tsarist workmen's compensation scheme. This has been extended considerably under the present regime, and benefit levels have increased in order to keep in line with the increase in earnings; in 1974 approximately 12 percent of the national income was spent on social security. Social security benefits are usually related to employment, but they also include child allowances, family income supplement, student stipends, and burial grants.

SOCIALISM. Term designating differing systems of public ownership and management of production and distribution of goods, which, unlike capitalism, do not involve private ownership or management.

Kolakowsk, L. and Hampshire, S. (eds.), *The Socialist Idea,* 1974.

Lichtheim, G., *The Origins of Socialism,* 1969. *A Short History of Socialism,* 1970.

SOCIALISM IN ONE COUNTRY. Policy inaugurated in the 1920s by Stalin when he announced that the Soviet Union could build socialism without help from other countries.

SOCIALIST PARTIES. By the time of the 1917 Revolution, four main socialist parties were in existence in Russia: the Socialist Revolutionaries, the Left Socialist Revolutionaries, the Bolsheviks, and the Mensheviks *(q.v.).*

Mendel, Arthur A., *Dilemmas of Progress in Tsarist Russia*, 1961.

SOCIALIST REALISM. The "basic method" of art and literature. Although works of Socialist Realism existed prior to 1930, in 1934 the doctrine was officially adopted at the first all-union congress of Soviet writers. Accordingly, art should be the truthful, historically concrete presentation of reality in its revolutionary development and must also assist with the ideological remaking and education of writers in the spirit of socialism. Thus all art was constrained by the duty to base it on Marxist-Leninist philosophy.

Ermolaev, Herman, *Soviet Literary Theories, 1917–1934: The Genesis of Socialist Realism*, 1963.

Tertz, A., *On Socialist Realism*, 1960.

Vaughan, James C., *Soviet Socialist Realism*, 1973.

SOCIALIST REVOLUTIONARIES. Political party, founded in 1902 by the leaders of revolutionary populism. It was led by Viktor Chernov and Nicholas Avksentev *(q.q.v.)*. It demanded socialization of the land, a federal state structure, and self-determination for non-Russian peoples. One section of the party, the Left Socialist Revolutionaries, having supported the Bolsheviks in 1917, played a part in the Bolshevik government until the Treaty of Brest-Litovsk of 1918. In 1922 the Bolsheviks suppressed the party.

Footman, David, *Red Prelude*, 1968.

Venturi, Franco, *Roots of Revolution*, 1960.

SOFIA ALEKSEYEVNA (1657–1704). Regent of Russia from 1682 to 1689. The sixth child of Tsar Alexis, she was very well educated by Simeon of Potolsk. On the death of her brother, Tsar Fedor III, Sofia strove to prevent her half brother, Peter I *(q.v.)*, from ruling, and persuaded the *streltsy* that her brother Ivan V should rule with Peter, with herself as regent; the *Zemsky Sobor* agreed. She was greatly assisted in her regency by her lover, V. V. Golitsyn *(q.v.)*. A treaty of peace and alliance was concluded with Poland in 1686, but her handling of matters in the Crimea was widely criticized. Hoping to have her enemies, the Naryshkins, silenced, Sofia instigated a plan that backfired. Her name was removed from the tsar's joint title, and she was forced to retire to a convent.

SOFIA PALEOLOGUE (*fl.* late 15th century). Wife of Ivan III and niece of the last Roman emperor of Byzantium, Constantine Paleologue. Sofia was brought up as a refugee in Rome but adopted the Orthodox faith on her marriage to Ivan III in 1472. Her son Vasily III ruled from 1505.

Fennell, John L. I., *Ivan the Great of Moscow*, 1963.

SOKOLNIKOV, GRIGORY YAKOVLEVICH (BRILLIANT) (1888–1939). Politician. In 1905 Sokolnikov was a member of the Bolshevik faction of the Social Democratic Labor Party *(q.v.)*. In 1910 he disagreed with Lenin's treatment of the Mensheviks. A member of the central committee following the February 1917 Revolution, he was later in charge of nationalizing the banks. Chairman of the third Soviet delegation, he was a commissar in the Red Army during the Civil War, people's commissar of finance (1921–26), and ambassador to Great Britain (1929–32). He was imprisoned in 1937 and died two years later.

SOLIKAMSK. Town in the Russian Soviet Federated Socialist Republic situated 115 miles (184 km) N of Perm. It is the center of a mining area and manufactures chemicals. Population (1970) 85,000.

SOLOGUB, COUNT VLADIMIR ALEKSANDROVICH (1814–82). Author. He came from an aristocratic family and his work is mostly superficial, being directed against the Slavophiles and romantic idealists. *Tarantas* (1844), an account of a journey from Moscow to Kazan, is his best-known work.

SOLOUKHIN, VLADIMIR ALEKSEYEVICH (1924–). Writer. He studied at the Gorky Institute of Literature. Among Soloukhin's works are the verse collection *Rain in the Steppes* (1953), *Postcards from Viet-Nam* (1962), the novel *Mother-Stepmother* (1971), and the poetry collection *A Winter's Day* (1969). In 1952 he was made a member of the Communist Party.

SOLOVETSKY MONASTERY. Monastery founded on the White Sea in 1429 by St. Sergius. In 1668–76 the monastery revolted against the revised versions of the Church services. *See* **Nikon.**

SOLOVEV, SERGEY MIKHAILOVICH (1820–79). Scholar. He was a professor of Russian history at Moscow University (1847–49), and his *History of Russia from Ancient Times* is regarded as a landmark in the writing of Russian history. He viewed Russia as having evolved from the clan to the patriarchal state, and then to enlightened absolutism. He also stressed that Russia was an integral part of Europe. A liberal, he supported Alexander II's *(q.v.)* reforms.

SOLOVEV, VLADIMIR SERGEYEVICH (1853–1900). Philosopher and theologian. He studied science, philosophy, and theology at Moscow University, writing his thesis, *The Crisis of Western Philosophy*, against the positivists. This met with disfavor from the reactionary members of the staff, as a result of which he went abroad for a time. He rejected atheistic materialism, accepted certain aspects of Christianity, and claimed that the ideal essence of the world existed in the mind of God; this essence he named Sophia. Having revived aspects of the Christian humanism of Erasmus and Thomas More, and influenced by Dostoyevsky and the *startsy* (see **Starets**), Solovev profoundly influenced the Symbolist poets and Russian religious philosophers in the early 20th century. He also strove to reunite the Orthodox and Roman Catholic churches.

West, James D., *Russian Symbolism*, 1970.

SOLZHENITSYN, ALEXANDER ISAYEVICH (1918–). Writer and dissident. He studied mathematics and physics at Rostov University, as well as obtaining a degree in literature. Solzhenitsyn served in the army at the front as a gunner and artillery officer, for which he was decorated. In February 1945 he was arrested in Königsberg by *Smersh (q.v.)* on the grounds that he had criticized Stalin; he spent eight years in labor camps. Released in 1953, Solzhenitsyn spent three years in exile, during which time he suffered from stomach cancer. Back in the Soviet Union, Solzhenitsyn taught in a secondary school in Ryazan. In 1962, he was permitted to publish *One Day in the Life of Ivan Denisovich*, which was an overnight success. In 1968 he was attacked in the *Literaturnaya Gazeta (q.v.)*. He won the Nobel Prize in Literature in 1970, but was expelled from the writers' union in 1970 and arrested and deported in 1974, following the publication in Europe of *The GULag Archipelago*. Other works include *Cancer Ward, The First Circle, August 1914*, and *The Oak and the Calf*.

SOPHRONIA OF RYAZAN. Priest and poet of the early 15th century. He wrote *Zadonshchina*, a long poem describing the Russian defeat of the Tatars at Kulikovo. It is one of the best-known works of early Russian literature.

SOROKI. Town in the Moldavian Soviet Socialist Republic 85 miles (136 km) NNW of Kishinev on Dnestr River. Industries include flour and oilseed milling, brewing, and soap manufacture.

SORSKY, NILS. *See* **Joseph of Volokolamsk.**

SORTAVALA. Town in the Karelo-Finnish Soviet Socialist Republic 120 miles (192 km) W of Petrozavodsk on the N shore of Lake Ladoga. It is a resort and commercial center. Industries include sawmilling, manufacturing woolens, furniture, felt, leather, and beer; the town is also a center for dairy produce. Population (1975) 23,000.

SOTNYA. From the Russian *sto*, meaning a hundred; a military unit, originally consisting of a hundred men.

SOUL TAX (POLL TAX). Tax introduced by Peter the Great *(q.v.)*. Although this placed a considerable burden on the peasants, it resulted in the extension of the area of land cultivated, since it was in the peasant's interests to cultivate as much as possible in order to pay the tax. When it was abolished by Nicholas Bunge *(q.v.)* the state lost 40 million rubles (1883–86).

SOUTH-EASTERN LEAGUE. Organization of Cossacks, Caucasian mountain peoples and the nomadic wanderers of N Caucasus, formed in 1917. The South-eastern League declared itself an independent republic, but this was short-lived.

SOUTH OSSETIAN AUTONOMOUS REGION. Autonomous region on the S slopes of the Great Caucasus mountains in Georgia. It has an area of 1,505 square miles (3,898 sq km). The capital is Tskhinvali. The main occupations are stock rearing and lumbering. Population (1970) 100,000.

SOUTHERN SOCIETY. Society led by Col. Paul Pestel (*q.v.*), which had as its goal the forcible establishment of a republic. In 1825 it merged with the Northern Society led by Nikita Muravev (*q.v.*), and staged the abortive Decembrist uprising of December 14, 1825.

Mazour, Anatole Grigorevich, *The First Russian Revolution, 1825,* 1937.

Raeff, Marc, *The Decembrist Movement,* 1966.

SOVETSK (formerly **Tilsit**). Town situated 60 miles (96 km) ENE of Kaliningrad on the Neman River in the Kaliningrad region. Founded in the 13th century, it became an E Prussian town where the treaties of Tilsit were negotiated in 1807. It was ceded to the USSR at the Potsdam Conference in 1945. It is a trading center for dairy produce and manufactures cheese, wood pulp, leather, and soap. Population (1970) 65,000.

SOVIET. Term derived from the Russian word meaning council. Any organ of state power in the USSR, which, in the words of the 1936 constitution, is the USSR's "political basis." There are Soviets at every level of the party apparatus, ranging from the Supreme Soviet, to the republican, provincial and local Soviets. Membership is by election. The function of Soviets is summed up in Stalin's description of Soviets as "transmission belts from the party to the masses."

Fainsod, M. and Hough, J., *How the Soviet Union is Governed,* 1979.

McAuley, M., *Politics and the Soviet Union,* 1977.

SOVIET-GERMAN NON-AGGRESSION PACT. *See* **Russo-German Non-aggression Pact.**

SOVIET MAN. In the eyes of the party, the ideal Soviet man is devoted to communism and has a communist attitude toward work and to the social economy, thus putting the collective before his individual desires. He has no bourgeois morals or opinions and is an atheist. It is the role of agitprop and various study groups to form Soviet man.

SOVIET OF NATIONALITIES. One of the two chambers of the USSR Supreme Soviet. It is elected on the basis of 25 deputies from each union republic, 11 from each autonomous republic, 5 from each autonomous region, and 1 from each autonomous area; but the deputies are not required to be, and very often are not, of the nationality they are supposed to represent. In 1979 there were 750 members. It is the successor of the Soviet of Nationalities within the central executive committee, which existed from 1918 to 1936.

SOVIET OF THE UNION. One of the two chambers of the USSR Supreme Soviet. It is elected on the basis of 1 deputy for 300,000 people. In 1979 there were 750 members. It is the successor of the Soviet of the Union, which existed before 1936 within the central executive committee.

SOVKHOZ. State farm. Although *sovkhozy* were important in cultivating virgin land and as places of agricultural experimentation, they werc often inefficient, and many of them were changed to *kolkhozy*, or collective farms.

Davies, R. W., *The Socialist Offensive: the Collectivization of Soviet Agriculture, 1929–1930*, 1980.

SOVNARKHOZ. Name given to councils that were set up and operated in the USSR from 1917 to 1932 and from 1957 to 1967. They were subordinate to the councils of ministers of the union republic. Their function was to supervise industry and building, and it was hoped that these councils would help to compensate for the disadvantages of centralization.

SPACE TRAVEL. The first manned space flight, in which Yury A. Gagarin orbited the earth, occurred on April 12, 1961, and on March 18, 1965, A. A. Leonov was the first man to walk in space from the *Voskhod* 2. The Soyuz program was deferred following cosmonaut V. V. Komarov's death, and following the *Soyuz II* mishap of 1971, when three men died in a depressurization accident as they were returning to the earth. In 1978, however, V. V. Kovlenko and A. S. Ivanchenkov spent a record 139 days and 14 hours in space, and in 1979 V. A. Lyakhov and V. V. Ryumin spent a record 175 days orbiting the earth.

Riabchikov, Evgeny, *Russians in Space*, 1972.

SPASSKY, BORIS (1937–). Journalist and chess player. he studied at the Leningrad State University faculty of journalism and worked as a trainer at the Leningrad section of the voluntary sport society. Spassky has played in numerous international chess tournaments; in 1956 he was the USSR Grand Master, the international Grand Master, and world chess student champion. He was world champion from 1969 to 1972.

SPERANSKY, COUNT MICHAEL MIKHAILOVICH (1772–1839). Russian minister of state. As Alexander I's *(q.v.)* adviser he devised a liberal constitutional system for Russia, but the intrigues of his opponents drove him from office and nullified his work. Under Nicholas I *(q.v.)* he took a prominent part in the proceedings against the Decembrist conspiracy and also codified Russian law.

Raeff, Marc, *Michael Speransky, A Statesman of Imperial Russia*, 1969.

SPESIVTSEVA, OLGA (1895–). Dancer. Trained at the Imperial School attached to the Maryinsky Theater, she joined the Russian Ballet in 1916. In 1918 she was appointed ballerina. She danced for Diaghilev *(q.v.)* in 1921, then returned to Russia. She worked with the Paris Opera from 1924 to 1932. Spesivtseva was considered the leading ballerina of her time in the Romantic style. Her most famous roles were *Esmeralda, Giselle,* and *The Sleeping Beauty.*

SPORTS. Private sporting clubs were first set up in Russia in the 19th century by liberal noblemen and industrialists. They grew steadily in number as interest in sports increased, and in 1912 the government established a physical fitness committee. After the Revolution, it was at first debated whether competitive sports should occur in a worker's state; the Hygienists and Proletkultists regarded competitive sports as potentially dangerous in that it fostered nonsocialist tendencies. On the other hand, the Hygienists claimed that sports should be integrated into all activities, and Proletkultists strove to devise exercises that were not inherited from bourgeois society; factory workers, for instance, were made to swing hammers and sickles in time to music. Realizing the need for greater fitness, the government began to promote competitive sports throughout the Soviet Union, and in 1928, 4,000 participated in the sports contest known as the first worker's *spartakiad.* In 1925, the party announced that physical culture was to be an integral part of political and cultural education, and sports came to be regarded as an extremely effective instrument for carrying out the party's social policies. Sports now is directed centrally by the committee on physical culture and sport. There are many sports organizations, with opportunity for all sectors of the population to participate, and special sports schools for children showing exceptional prowess, all of which account for the Soviet Union's role in world sports.

Riordan, James W., *Sport in Soviet Society: Development of Sport and Physical Education in Russia and the USSR,* 1977.

SPUTNIK (SATELLITE). Russia launched the first earth satellite on October 4, 1957, with two more successful launchings following on November 3, 1957 and May 15, 1958.

STAKHANOV, ALEKSEY GRIGORYEVICH (1906–77). Coal miner who was much extolled by the party in that his output was 12 tons of coal per shift. The normal output was 7. Stalin praised his achievement and established the Stakhanovite movement to raise Soviet industrial output.

STAKHANOVITE. Member of a Soviet labor movement that strove to increase industrial production. Named after Aleksey Grigorevich Stakhanov *(q.v.)*, a coal miner who in 1935 reorganized his work gang to increase its daily production seven-fold, the movement failed because quality could not be maintained.

STALIN, JOSEPH VISSARIONOVICH (DZHUGASHVILI) (1879–1953). Dictator of the USSR and leader of the World Communist movement. The son of a Georgian shoemaker, he was expelled from the Tbilisi Theological Seminary in 1898, as a result of his interest in the revolutionary movement. He then joined the Russian Social Democratic Party *(q.v.)*, and, in 1903, its Bolshevik faction. Having worked in the underground movement in Transcaucasia, he was made part of the Bolshevik central committee by Lenin and Zinoviev *(q.v.)*. Banished to Petrograd after the February Revolution of 1917, Stalin edited the party's newspaper, *Pravda.* Stalin served as commissar for nationalities and commissar for worker-peasant inspection (1919–23) and became a very close collaborator of Lenin. During the Civil War he served as a commissar for nationalities. In 1922 he was appointed secretary-general of the central committee, although Lenin, nurturing misgivings about Stalin's suitability for this position, was planning to remove him from it. Lenin's death, however, prevented this, and Stalin's political career continued unchecked. Together with Zinoviev and Kamenev he defeated Trotsky, and then with Bukharin and Rykov's help he defeated Zinoviev and Kamenev in the struggle for power. Molotov, Voroshilov, Kaganovich, Ordzhonikidze, and Kirov *(q.v.)* then helped him to defeat Bukharin's and Rykov's Right Opposition. From 1929 to 1934 he ruled with them, assuming the position of leader until they opposed him. This provided the catalyst for abandoning collective leadership and for instigating the Great Purge. With Stalin as official head of government in 1940 and chairman of the state defense committee, a reign of terror ensued. Generalissimo during the Second World War, he outwitted Churchhill and Roosevelt. He became increasingly more obsessed with problems of security. He was jealous, anti-Semitic, chauvinistic, and xenophobic, while demanding to be treated as a virtual demigod by all. He died in 1953.

Alliluyeva, Svetlana, *Twenty Letters to a Friend,* 1967.

Deutscher, Isaac, *Stalin: A Political Biography,* 1949.

Djilas, Milovan, *Conversations with Stalin,* 1962.

Hingley, Ronald, *Joseph Stalin: Man and Legend,* 1974.

McNeal, Robert H., *Stalin's Works: An Annotated Bibliography,* 1967.

Souvarine, Boris, *Stalin: A Critical Survey of Bolshevism,* 1939.

Trotsky, Lev, *Stalin: An Appraisal of the Man and His Influence,* 1941.

Tucker, Robert C., *Stalin as Revolutionary 1879–1929,* 1974.

Ulam, Adam B., *Stalin, The Man and His Era,* 1973.

STALINABAD. Name used for Dushanbe *(q.v.)* from 1929 to 1961.

STALINGRAD. *See* **Volgograd.**

STALINGRAD, SIEGE OF (1942–43). In May and June of 1942 German tanks, dive-bombers, and other forces were approaching the lower Volga River and the Caucasus. Having crossed the Don River, they reached the outskirts of Stalingrad and besieged the city. By mid-November 1942, the British victory at El Alamein and the pursuit of the defeated Germans resulted in no more reinforcements for the German army near Stalingrad. Fresh Russian reinforcements were brought in, and on November 20 Yeremenko broke the enemy line. The Russians launched a great thrust from the N, and Mannstein was forced to retreat. The Germans under Paulus surrendered on February 2, 1943, having sustained a loss of 200,000 men.

Werth, Alexander, *The Year of Stalingrad,* 1947.

STALINISM. Name given to Stalin's political theorizing and rule of the USSR, the Eastern Europe Bloc countries, and the World Communist movement. Based on Marxism, Leninism, and national Bolshevism, Stalin with the help of Molotov, Zhdanov, and Vyshinsky *(q.q.v.)* added such doctrines and ideas as the existence of the state under full communism, Socialist Realism in the arts, the concept of building socialism in one country, the people's great love for the Communist Party, their unanimous support of Stalin, and the security organs to eliminate "misguided" dissenters. Concentration camps were much in use, especially during Stalin's Great Purge. Some aspects of Stalinism became obsolete, particularly after Khrushchev's *(q.v.)* secret report to the 20th party congress, others; such as the role of the Communist Party, remain.

Khrushchev, Nikita S., *Khrushchev Remembers,* 1977.

Mandelstam, Nadezhda, *Hope Against Hope,* 1971.

Payne, Robert, *The Rise and Fall of Stalin,* 1966.

Randall, Francis B., *Stalin's Russia: An Historical Reconsideration,* 1965.

Tucker, Robert C., *The Soviet Political Mind: Stalinism and Post-Stalin Change,* 1972.

______ (ed.), *Stalinism: Essays in Historical Interpretation,* 1977.

STALINO. *See* **Donetsk.**

STALINSK. *See* **Novokuznetsk.**

STANISLAVSKY, KONSTANTIN SERGEYEVICH ALEKSEYEV (1863–1938). Actor and producer. Stanislavsky began acting at the age of 15 in the Alekseyev Circle, a group of family and friends. In 1888, he founded the Society of Art and Literature, which became one of the most popular amateur theater companies in Moscow. In 1897, Vladimir Nemirovich-Danchenko *(q.v.),* director of the Moscow Philharmonic Society's drama school, invited him to establish a new theater; this was the Moscow Art Theater *(q.v.),* a joint enterprise, and it was itself, in part, influenced by the German Meiningen Players. Stanislavsky's new method of training actors involved a psychological study of the character to be played, and his first success was his production of Chekhov's *The Sea Gull* (1898), which brought Stanislavsky world fame. Chekhov wrote *The Three Sisters* (1901) and *The Cherry Orchard* (1903), specifically for the Moscow Arts Theater. His writings on stagecraft include *My Life in Art, Building a Character,* and *An Actor Prepares.*

Magarshack, David, *Stanislavsky: A Life,* 1951.

Mikailovich, N., *Stanislavsky Directs,* 1976.

STANKEVICH, NICHOLAS VLADIMIROVICH (1813–40). Key figure and inspirer of the most important philosophical circle in Moscow in the 1830s. Future members of the Westernizers, such as Michael Bakunin and Vissarion Belinsky, and of the Slavophiles, such as Konstantin S. Aksakov and Michael Katkov *(q.q.v.),* belonged to Stankevich's group.

Berlin, Isaiah, *Russian Thinkers,* 1978.

STANOVOY RANGE. Mountain range in SE USSR extending 500 miles (800 km) E from the Olekma River and rising to Skalisty Mountain, 8,143 feet (2,682 m) above sea level. It forms part of the watershed between rivers flowing to the Arctic and those flowing to the Pacific.

STARETS. Term for an elder of the Orthodox church, a greatly respected monk, and spiritual overseer of younger monks. The *startsy* of the *Optina Pustyn (q.v.)* considerably influenced members of the intelligentsia, such as Dostoyevsky and Vladimir Solovev *(q.q.v.)*. Perhaps the best-known *starets* is *Zossima* in Dostoyevsky's novel *The Brothers Karamazov*.

STAROV, IVAN YEGOROVICH (1744–1808). Architect. He is mainly remembered for the Tauride Palace, built in St. Petersburg in 1782–88. He simplified the classical style, and initiated the use of columns in Russian interiors.

STATE, CONCEPT OF. As Marx and Engels had before him, Lenin considered the state to be a bourgeois instrument of class oppression. In his *State and Revolution* Lenin outlined his theory that a dictatorship of the proletariat was to be established. Eventually the state with its repressive armies, bureaucracies, law courts, and police would wither away. In the 1960s it was considered that the dictatorship of the proletariat could be replaced by an all-peoples' state; this state was to maintain law and order and defend the USSR, world peace, and international socialism; in practice the state plays an important role in administration, education, and management. It shows little sign of withering away.

STATE CONFERENCE IN MOSCOW. Conference convened by Alexander Kerensky in order to unite the state power with all organized forces in the country. Over 2,000 people were invited from different sectors of the population. It opened on August 25, 1917 at the Bolshoi Theater. The conference met with Bolshevik disapproval, and the main result of the conference was to sharply split the revolutionaries into left and right.

STATE FARMS. *See Sovkhoz.*

STAVROPOL. *See* **Togliatti.**

STENKA RAZIN (?–1671). Cossack leader of the great peasant rebellion of 1670–71 in the SE area of the Volga. Many members of the upper classes were massacred; the peasants and soldiers welcomed him. By the time Stenka Razin's army reached Simbirsk it was 200,000 strong. It was nevertheless defeated by the Muscovite troops. He escaped but in 1671 was handed over to Muscovite officials and executed.

Avrich, Paul, *Russian Rebels, 1600–1800,* 1972.

STEPANAKERT. Town in the Azerbaijan Soviet Socialist Republic 60 miles (96 km) SSW of Yevlakh. Industries include food processing, silk milling, and wine making. Population (1974) 33,000.

STEPNYAK, SERGEY MIKHAILOVICH. See **Kravchinsky, Sergey Mikhailovich.**

STEPPES. Belt of forest steppe and prairie grassland. It is a cool temperate region. The prairie grassland area originally was covered with grasses, legumes, and sedges; the forest steppe consisted of oak woodland and areas of grassland. Much of both areas has been cleared for farmland; the famous *chernozem* soil is especially fertile. It has been necessary to plant shelterbelts of trees to combat wind and water erosion. The belt of a steppe land runs approximately S of Kiev, Kursk, Tula, and Ulyanovsk, although there is also an area of steppe in Siberia to the E of the Urals.

STERLITAMAK. River port in the Russian Soviet Federated Socialist Republic situated 85 miles (136 km) S of Ufa on the Belaya River in Bashkir Autonomous Soviet Socialist Republic. Industry includes heavy engineering; manufactures include synthetic rubber, chemicals, cement, clothing, and food products. Population (1981) 228,000.

STOLBOVO PEACE TREATY (1617). Treaty concluded between Muscovy and Sweden in 1617; the Swedes evacuated Novgorod but retained the coastal stretch lost by Ivan the Terrible.

STOLNIK. Russian courtier. A *stolnik* was lower in rank than a boyar *(q.v.)*.

STOLYPIN, PETER ARKADYEVICH (1862–1911). Statesman. As a liberal conservative, he failed to win the approval of either the extreme right or the radicals. From 1906 Stolypin was minister of the interior and chairman of the council of ministers. While firmly suppressing the 1905 Revolution, he wished to carry out liberal reforms. Under his agrarian reforms of 1906–11, peasants were permitted to leave village communities, settle in separate farms, buy land, and were encouraged to settle in less populated areas. In 1907 Stolypin altered the electoral system by imperial decree. He was assassinated by a Socialist Revolutionary terrorist in 1911.

Hare, Richard, *Portraits of Russian Personalities between Reform and Revolution,* 1959.

Levin, Alfred, "Peter Arkad'evich Stolypin: A Political Appraisal," *Journal of Modern History,* 1965.

STRAKHOV, NICHOLAS NIKOLAYEVICH (1828–96). Philosopher and literary critic. Strakhov adopted A. Grigorev's theory of "soil-boundness." A Slavophile *(q.v.)* and anti-Darwinist, he was a friend of Dostoyevsky *(q.v.)*, who was influenced by his philosophical views, and of Count Lev Tolstoy *(q.v.)*.

STRATEGIC ARMS LIMITATION TALKS. Talks at which the United States and the USSR meet to agree to limit nuclear weapons production in their respective countries. SALT I took place in 1972. Owing to the Soviet invasion of Afghanistan in 1979, the United States was reluctant to agree to the terms set by the Soviet Union in SALT II.

Gray, Colin S., *The Soviet-American Arms Race,* 1976.

STRAVINSKY, IGOR FEDOROVICH (1882–1971). Composer and pianist. After studying law at St. Petersburg University, Stravinsky took music lessons from Nicholas Rimsky-Korsakov *(q.v.)*, who with Claude Debussy influenced his early music.

In 1908 he met Serge Diaghilev (*q.v.*) and composed the music for a number of famous ballets, such as *The Firebird* (1910), *Petrushka* (1911), *Les Noces* (1923), and *Orpheus* (1947). His operas include *The Nightingale* (1914) and *The Rake's Progress* (1951). In 1934 Stravinsky visited the United States, and then settled in France, becoming a French citizen in 1934, before returning to the United States to live. He is one of the most influential and versatile composers of the century.

Stravinsky, Vera, *Stravinsky in Pictures and Documents,* 1979.

STRELETS. A member of the military corps (from the verb *strelyat'*, to shoot). This corps was established by Ivan the Terrible (*q.v.*) (c. 1568), but after becoming seditious it was suppressed by Peter the Great (*q.v.*). *Streltsy* enjoyed special privileges.

STRIGOLNIKI. Religious sect in 14th century Novgorod. The *strigolniki* believed that priests were unnecessary, that laymen could preach, and that prayers for the dead served no purpose.

Pares, Bernard, *A History of Russia,* 1926.

STROGANOV. Russian merchant family who in 1515 were granted the right to establish saltworks at Solvychegodsk in the Urals. Free from all tax for 20 years, they built their own towns, using Cossack mercenaries as guards; one of these, Yermak (*q.v.*), acquired the Siberian Khanate for Muscovy by conquest in 1582.

STROGANOV SCHOOL. Style of icon-painting created by craftsmen working for the Stroganov family at the end of the 16th and the beginning of the 17th century.

STRUVE, FRIEDRICH GEORG WILHELM VON (1793–1864). German astronomer. Summoned by Tsar Nicholas I in 1835 to superintend the building of Pulkovo Observatory (*q.v.*) near St. Petersburg, he was appointed its director in 1839.

STRUVE, PETER BERNARDOVICH (1870–1944). Economist and sociologist. Of German origin, Struve was one of the main theorists of Marxism in Russia in the 1890s. In 1898, he drafted the Social Democratic Labor Party's (*q.v.*) manifesto, but then changed allegiance and became leader of the Liberal constitutional movement. In 1905 he joined the Constitutional Democratic Party and was an important member of the *Vekhi* movement (*q.v.*).

Pipes, Richard, *Struve: Liberal on the Left, 1870–1905,* 1971. *Struve: Liberal on the Right, 1905–44,* 1980.

STUNDISTS. Religious sect, not unlike the German Baptists, living in S Ukraine. They broke away from the Russian Orthodox Church (*q.v.*) in 1870. Stundist meetings were forbidden in 1894 but they were again granted freedom to worship in 1905.

STÜRMER, BORIS VLADIMIROVICH (1848–1917). Prime minister. A previous master of ceremonies at court, Stürmer was appointed prime minister in 1916. He was also in charge of the ministry of foreign affairs. A puppet of Rasputin (*q.v.*), he was not liked and was dismissed from the duma on November 23, 1916.

SUB-CARPATHIAN RUSSIA. Name of Transcarpathia at the time of its incorporation into Czechoslovakia, which lasted from 1919 to 1939.

SUBBOTNIK. *Subbotnik* refers to unpaid voluntary work, originally performed on Saturdays (from the word *Subbota,* meaning Saturday). A day is declared a *subbotnik* day, and everyone is expected to put in a day's work for no pay.

SUBWAYS. The construction of a subway for Moscow was discussed before the Revolution but no action was taken. The first section (7 miles/11.5 km) of double track was opened to the public in May 1935. The heaviest surface traffic had always been in the NE of the city, in the vicinity of the railway stations, and the first section or the subway was the line from Komsomol Square via the city center to Gorky Park, with a branch line from Okhotny Ryad to Smolensk Square. Every station has a distinctive design following a definite theme associated with some date, place, person or event.

Subway systems have also been built in Leningrad, Kiev, Tbilisi, Kharkov, Tashkent, Baku, and Yerevan. Others are under construction at Minsk, Gorky, Novosibirsk, Omsk, and Sverdlovsk, and lines are planned for Riga and Dnepropetrovsk.

SUDEBNIK. Word used to refer to the code of laws. The most famous are the *sudebniki* of 1497 and 1550.

SUKHOVO-KOBYLIN, ALEXANDER VASILYEVICH (1817–1903). Playwright. Although fascinated by the philosophical thought of Hegel, and by German Idealism, Sukhovo-Kobylin is remembered for his comedies. He wrote three, the most famous of which is *The Wedding of Krechensky* (1855), a work of pure comedy. *The Affair* and *The Death of Tarelkin,* however, are bitterly satirical. He was under investigation for seven years for the suspected murder of his mistress but was acquitted in 1857.

Mirsky, D. S., *A History of Russian Literature,* 1949.

SUKONNAYA SOTNYA. An association of Moscow's lower-ranking textile merchants in the 16th and 17th centuries.

SUMAROKOV, ALEXANDER PETROVICH (1718–77). Playwright, journalist, literary critic, and man of letters. In 1756 he was director of the first permanent theater in Russia. Arguably his best-known work is his tragedy *Khorev,* first performed in 1749, which is written in the French neoclassical style. In 1757 his company, which by then included women, was given a court subsidy, becoming the first professional Russian theater company.

Slonim, Marc, *Russian Theatre from the Empire to the Soviets,* 1961.

SUMGAIT. Town in Azerbaijan situated 15 miles (24 km) NW of Baku on the Caspian Sea. Industries are dependent on the Baku oil fields and include manufacturing chemicals and synthetic rubber. Population (1981) 201,000.

SUMY. Capital of Sumy region of the Ukraine situated 195 miles (312 km) ENE of Kiev. Founded in 1658, it is the center of an agricultural area, specializing in wheat and sugar beet production. Industries are sugar refining, tanning, sawmilling, agricultural engineering, and textiles; manufactures include food products and fertilizers. Population (1981) 240,000.

SUPREMATISTS. Name of group of painters, the chief of whom was Kazimir Malevich *(q.v.)*; other Suprematists include Puni, Menkov, and Ivan Klyun *(q.v.)*. Malevich issued a Suprematist manifesto in 1915 at the time of the Last Futurist Painting Exhibition, in which he stated that "to reproduce the hallowed objects and parts of nature is to revivify a shackled thief." Malevich's *Eight Red Rectangles* (1915) accordingly shows rectangles of color on a white background, rather than objects taken from nature.

SUPREME PRIVY (SECRET) COUNCIL. Established in 1726, the privy council reduced the power of the senate, subjecting the senate to the council. On the death of Catherine I in 1727, the supreme privy council ruled in the name of the young Peter II. Following his death, they appointed Anna Ivanovna as ruler, provided she remain subject to the council. This was widely unpopular, and the supreme privy council was abolished in 1730.

SUPREME SOVIET. The highest legislative organ is the Supreme Soviet of the USSR. It consists of two chambers with equal legislative rights, elected for a term of five years: the Soviet of the Union and the Soviet of Nationalities *(q.v.)*.

SURIKOV, VASILY Y. (1848–1916). Painter. Surikov won fame with his historical scenes such as *The Execution of the Streltsy* (1881) and *The Boyarnya Morozova* (1887).

SURKHAN DARYA RIVER. River rising in two branches in the Gissar mountains, in the Uzbek Soviet Socialist Republic, and flowing approximately 150 miles (240 km) SSW through a cotton-growing area, past Dzhar-Kurgan to enter the Amu Darya River near Termez. It is linked by canal to Kafirnigan River.

SURKOV, ALEKSEY ALEKSANDROVICH (1899–1983). Poet and party member from 1925. His patriotic poems were warmly received in the Second World War. In 1954 Surkov was made secretary of the writers' union. At the third writers' congress in 1959 he was removed from his post.

SUSANIN, IVAN (*fl.* 17th century). Peasant. Polish partisans, wishing to capture Michael Romanov, seized Susanin and demanded to know where Michael was hiding. Susanin refused to divulge his whereabouts and died under torture. Glinka *(q.v.)* wrote an opera, *Ivan Susanin*, based on the story.

SUSLOV, MICHAEL ANDREYEVICH (1902–82). Party official and member of the CPSU since 1921. He attended the Institute of Red Professors, lectured at Moscow University, and held executive posts with the central control committee. From 1937 to 1939 he was secretary of the Rostov oblast committee of the All-Union Communist Party. From 1937 on he was deputy to the USSR Supreme Soviet. He had held a number of other important official posts, including that of head of Stavropol Kray headquarters for partisan forces (1941–45). From 1950 to 1954 he was a member of the Presidium and of the Politburo central committee.

SUSLOVA, APPOLLINARIA (?–1918). Mistress of F. M. Dostoyevsky *(q.v.)* from (1862 to 1863). Proud, cruel, and evil, as an "infernal" woman, she played an important part in revealing the unpleasant side of life that was so profoundly to affect Dostoyevsky's writing. She later married Vasily Rozanov.

SUVORIN, ALEKSEY SERGEYEVICH (1844–1912). Journalist and publisher. He published the right-wing newspaper *New Time,* and cheap editions of classics from world literature. His *Diary* was published posthumously in 1923.

SUVOROV, COUNT ALEXANDER VASILYEVICH (1730–1800). Russian military commander. Suvorov enlisted at the age of 12 and first saw action in the Seven Years War of 1756–63. He was promoted to lieutenant colonel. He took part in the battle of Kunersdorf (1759) and the Russo-Turkish war of 1768–74. Suvorov brilliantly commanded the Russian armies in the Russo-Turkish war of 1787–91 and was created Count Rymnitsky by Catherine II *(q.v.)* and a count of the Reich by the Holy Roman Emperor. In 1794 he successfully but harshly suppressed an insurrection in Poland. Out of favor during Paul I's *(q.v.)* reign, he went into exile in Novgorod, but was recalled when Russia joined the coalition against France. He expelled most of the French from Italy, and in 1799, was appointed generalissimo of the Russian forces. His most brilliant exploit was the 1799 Swiss expedition. He died, however, in disgrace. Suvorov's *The Science of Conquering* strongly influenced Russian military thought.

Osipov, K., *Alexander Suvorov,* 1944.

SUZDAL. Popular tourist town in the Russian Soviet Federated Socialist Republic situated 120 miles (192 km) NE of Moscow in Vladimir region. Founded in the 11th century, it is important as a religious and monastic center.

SVERDLOV, YAKOV MIKHAILOVICH (1885–1919). Politician. He joined the Social Democratic Labor Party *(q.v.)* in 1901 and from 1902 to 1917 acted as a professional revolutionary for the Bolsheviks. In 1913 he was made part of the central committee. Following the February 1917 Revolution Sverdlov was the chief organizer of the party and became chairman of the All-Russian Central Executive Committee of the Soviets. He was a close collaborator of Lenin.

SVERDLOVSK. Capital of Sverdlovsk region in the E foothills of the central Ural mountains in the Russian Soviet Federated Socialist Republic. Founded in 1721, the first ironworks were constructed in 1726. Industries are mainly metallurgical, especially the manufacture of steel, mining and heavy engineering equipment, railway rolling stock, ball bearings, and aircraft; copper smelting and gem cutting and polishing are also important. It is an important junction on the Trans-Siberian Railway. Formerly called Yekaterinburg (after Catherine I), it was the place of execution of Tsar Nicholas II and his family in 1918. Population (1981) 1,239,000.

SVIR RIVER. River rising in Lake Onega and flowing 140 miles (224 km) WSW past the Svirstroy hydroelectric plant to Lake Ladoga, forming part of the Maryinsk canal system.

SVOD ZAKONOV. Code of laws promulgated in 1833. It continued in use until 1917. The *Svod Zakonov* presented Russian laws in a modern form derived from the Napoleonic codes.

SVYATOPOLK I, GRAND PRINCE (*c.* 11th century). After seizing Kiev, Svyatopolk murdered his brothers Boris and Gleb *(q.v.)*. He was later defeated by another brother, Yaroslav the Wise *(q.v.)*.

Vernadsky, George V., *Kievan Russia,* 1948.

SVYATOSLAV I (980–1019). Grand prince of Kiev from 945. A heroic warrior, Svyatoslav defeated the Khazars on the lower Don, the Ossetians and Circassians in N Caucasus, stormed the Volga Bulgars' capital, and defeated the Bulgars in 967. Ambushed by the Pechenegs, he was killed in 972.

Vernadsky, George V., *Kievan Russia,* 1948.

SVYATOSLAV II, GRAND PRINCE (?–1076). He was prince of Chernigov following the partition of Kiev after the death of Yaroslav in 1054.

SYKTYVKAR. Capital of Komi Autonomous Soviet Socialist Republic of the Russian Soviet Federated Socialist Republic. It is situated on the Vychegda River. An important trading center for timber, its industries include sawmilling, boatbuilding, fur processing, wood pulp production and papermaking. Population (1981) 180,000.

SYMBOLISM. The leading literary school in Russia at the beginning of the 20th century. The period of Symbolism is usually taken to refer to the years of 1900 to 1910. Not only did Symbolism develop a new literary technique, but it also developed a new spiritual and aesthetic outlook, coinciding as it did with the growth of religious idealism. The leading Symbolist, Andrey Bely *(q.v.)*, aspired to create of Symbolism a religion. Symbolism was superseded by Acmeism (*See* **Acmeists**) and Futurism *(q.v.)*.

Struve, Gleb, *25 Years of Soviet Russian Literature,* 1944.

SYR DARYA RIVER. River rising as Naryn River in the E Kirghiz Soviet Socialist Republic and flowing 1,400 miles (2,240 km) generally W and SW to irrigate the Fergana valley in the

Uzbek Soviet Socialist Republic. It turns NW, bounding Kyzyl Kum desert to the W, and enters the Aral Sea by a delta. It was known to the ancients as the Jaxartes.

SYZRAN. Capital of Kuibyshev region of the Russian Soviet Federated Socialist Republic, situated 500 miles (800 km) SE of Moscow on the Volga River. Industries include oil refining, and manufactures include machinery, building materials, and clothing. It is important as a river port and railway center, handling grain and oil. Population (1981) 169,000.

T

TABLE OF RANKS. A system devised by Peter the Great *(q.v.)* in 1722 that assigned military, court, and civilian service to 14 parallel grades. Each rank in one section had a corresponding rank in the other two. All those entering service began on the bottom rung, and promotion was to be dependent on ability and length of service, rather than on birth. Membership of the *dvoryanstvo (q.v.)* or nobility was automatically granted to those who had succeeded in climbing the first eight ranks of the civil or court ladder and the first 14 of the military ladder. Theoretically, therefore, even those not of noble birth could become hereditary noblemen with the right to possess serfs. The Table of Ranks simultaneously consolidated the rights and the obligations and duties of the nobility.

Massie, R. N., *Peter the Great,* 1980.

Raeff, Marc (ed.), *Peter the Great Changes Russia,* 1972.

TADZHIKISTAN. The Tadzhik Soviet Socialist Republic was formed from those regions of Bukhara and Turkestan where the population consisted mainly of Tadzhiks. It was admitted as a constituent republic of the Soviet Union in 1929. It has an area of 55,240 square miles (143,100 sq km). The capital is Dushanbe *(q.v.)*. Horticulture and cattle breeding are important as is other farming. There are rich deposits of brown coal, lead, and zinc. Oil is found in the N of the republic. Other minerals found are asbestos, mica, corundum, and emery, lapis lazuli, potassium salts, and sulphur. Population (1981) 3,400,000.

TAGANROG. Port situated on the Gulf of Taganrog in the Sea of Azov. A settlement was destroyed by the Mongols in the 13th century. Refounded in 1698 as a naval base by Peter the Great, it is now an important industrial center manufacturing iron and steel goods, including agricultural machinery, aircraft, boilers, machine tools, and hydraulic presses. There are three harbors exporting coal and grain. It is the birthplace of Anton Chekhov. Population (1981) 281,000.

TAGLIONI, MARIE (1804–84). Ballet dancer born in Stockholm. Taglioni developed a style of dancing that was graceful, light, and full of illusion. In 1837 she made her debut at St. Petersburg, thus introducing Romantic ballet to Russia. She died in Marseilles.

Roslavleva, Natalia, *Era of the Russian Ballet, 1770–1865,* 1966.

TAIROV, ALEXANDER YAKOVLEVICH (KORNBLIT) (1885–1950). Actor and director. He studied law at St. Petersburg University, and had wide experience in the theaters of St. Petersburg, Moscow, and Riga. In 1914 he founded the Kamerny Theater in Moscow. In 1946 he was dismissed as the artistic director, and in 1949 he ceased to produce plays there. He particularly stressed the need for form and technique on the part of the cast.

TALLINN. Capital of Estonia and port situated on the S coast of the Gulf of Finland. First recorded in 1154, although there is evidence of iron-age and later settlements. Formerly known as Reval, the city joined the Hanseatic League of Baltic trade in 1285, passed into Swedish control in 1561, and was captured by Russia in 1710. The Toom Church (13th century), Oleviste and Niguliste churches, the Guildhall (1410), Rathaus, and castle date from its medieval mercantile prosperity. Icebreakers keep the port open during most of the winter, and timber, textiles, and paper are exported. Industries include woodworking, engineering, and the manufacture of textiles and food products. Population (1981) 442,000.

TAMARA, QUEEN OF GEORGIA (?–1213). Queen of Georgia (1184–1213) and daughter of Gregory III. Her reign was characterized by the continual strengthening of Georgia's power. Her first marriage to Yury, the son of the Vladimir prince, Andrey Bogolyubsky *(q.v.)*, helped develop political links between Georgia and Russia. A successful war with Persia in 1211 resulted in the submission of Iranian Azerbaijan to Georgia.

TAMBOV. Capital of Tambov region of the Russian Soviet Federated Socialist Republic, situated 260 miles (416 km) SE of Moscow on the Tsna River. Founded in 1636 as a fortress, it is now the industrial center of an agricultural district producing grain, potatoes, sugar beets, and sunflowers. Industries include sugar refining, distilling, flour milling, and the manufacture of machinery, textiles, chemicals, and synthetic rubber. Population (1981) 277,000.

TANEYEV, SERGEY IVANOVICH (1856–1915). Pianist, composer, and music teacher. Having studied under Langer Hubert, Nicholas Rubinstein, and Peter Tchaikovsky *(q.q.v.)* at the Moscow Conservatory, Taneyev was appointed professor of harmony and instrumentation in 1880, and in 1885 he was made director of the conservatory.

Taneyev is considered one of the great Russian contrapuntalists, and as such, it is felt that his work lacks emotion. His celebrated *Invertible Counterpoint* appeared in 1909. His other works include the trilogy *Orestes* (1895), symphonies, orchestral works, chamber music, and organ and piano music.

TANNENBERG, BATTLE OF (1410). Battle in which the Pan-Slavic army led by the Polish-Lithuanian Prince Vitovit (*q.v.*) defeated the Teutonic Knights. This marked the E limit of German expansion for centuries.

TARKOVSKY, A. (1932–). Film director. He is particularly noted for the historical epic *Andrey Rublev* (1966).

TARLE, YEVGENY VIKTOROVICH (1875–1955). Historian and member of the Academy of Sciences. He graduated in 1896 from Kiev University and held a number of professional appointments in prerevolutionary Russia. He wrote works on the history of France, including several on the history of the working class in France, and on Napoleon, international relations and the foreign policy of Russia. In 1942 he published *Napoleon's Invasion of Russia, 1812.*

TARTU. Estonian town situated W of Lake Chudskoye and on the Ema River. A Hanseatic port founded in 1030, it was captured by Peter the Great in 1704 and was ceded to Russia by the Treaty of Nystad (*q.v.*) in 1721. Tartu State University was founded here in 1802. It was the scene of much fighting during the Russian Civil War (1918–1919). Manufactures include agricultural machinery, metal and food products, textiles, and cigars and cigarettes. Population (1973) 95,000.

TASHKENT. Capital of the Uzbek Soviet Socialist Republic (Uzebekistan) on the Kazakhstan border, in an oasis on Chirchik River. It was under Arabic rule until the 12th century when it was taken by the Turks. Ghengis Khan captured it in the 13th century and Tamerlane in the 14th. It was taken by Russian forces in 1865. It is a trading center on important routes and the center of an irrigated area producing fruit, cotton, rice, and tobacco. Industries include the manufacture of textiles, flour, oils, and agricultural and textile machinery, fertilizers. Population (1981) 1,858,000.

TASS (TELEGRAPHIC AGENCY OF THE SOVIET UNION). The official Soviet news agency, founded in 1925. The agency deals with news both at home and abroad. It is attached to the council of ministers, and its work is carefully controlled by the propaganda department.

TATAR AUTONOMOUS SOVIET SOCIALIST REPUBLIC. It has an area of 26,250 square miles (67,987 sq km). Region constituted as an autonomous republic of the Russian Soviet Federated Socialist Republic in 1920. The capital is Kazan, 450 miles (720 km) E of Moscow. The chief industries are engineering, and oil and chemicals, and timber, building materials, textiles, and the manufacture of clothing and food are also becoming important. There are 9.5

million acres (3.7 million hectares) under crops. Population (1981) 3,453,000.

TATARS. The Turkic-speaking descendants of the Mongols of the Golden Horde. In the 15th century the Horde split into several groups. The Kazan Khanate fought with Muscovy, until in 1552 Ivan the Terrible captured Kazan. Tatars have settled along the central section of the Volga and along the Kama towards the Urals, in S Siberia, and in the E and SE of the European part of the USSR. The name "Tatar," however, sometimes is used to refer to all nomads and tribes of the Asian deserts and steppes. From the fifth to the ninth century, the Tatars were predominantly farmers, but from the 18th century onward, they became renowned as traders. The majority of Tatars adopted the Islamic faith in the 14th century.

Katz, Zev (ed.), *Handbook of Major Soviet Nationalities,* 1975.

TATISHCHEV, VASILY NIKITICH (1686–1750). Historian, administrator, and geographer. Tatishchev aided Peter the Great *(q.v.)* by discussing Peter's reforms, and carrying them out, particularly in the Urals where he was chief of the mining administration. His five-volume *History of Russia from the Earliest Times* is considered by many the foundation of modern Russian historiography.

TATLIN, VLADIMIR (1885–1953). Artist and founder of Constructivism *(q.v.)*. After an unhappy childhood, at the age of 18 Tatlin ran away to become a sailor and traveled to Egypt. This had a profound influence on his art. After studying at the Penza School of Art and at the Moscow College of Painting, Sculpture, and Architecture, Tatlin worked as a free-lance painter, and sent works to the Union of Russian Artists and the Union of Youth exhibitions. He later contributed works to the Knave of Diamonds *(q.v.)* of 1913. In the same year, he journeyed to Berlin with some Ukrainian singers and played the accordion with them at the Russian Exhibition of Folk Art. With the proceeds, he went to Paris and visited Picasso. From 1913 to 1914, Tatlin began to explore the possibility of "painting relief" and became known as the founder of Constructivism.

Gray, Camilla, *The Russian Experiment in Art,* 1962.

TAURIA. Name by which the Crimea was known in the Middle Ages. The name "Tauria" is still used to refer to the mainland bordering the Crimea to the S of the lower Dnepr River. A rich agricultural area, Tauria belongs to the Kherson and Zaporozhe oblasts.

TBILISI (TIFLIS). The capital of the Georgian Soviet Socialist Republic, it is situated on the Kura River. A commercial and transportation center with engineering and woodworking industries, it also manufactures textile machinery, machine tools, electrical equipment, textiles, and food products. Many ancient buildings still exist and the hot sulphur springs in the vicinity make it a spa. Population (1981) 1,095,000.

TCHAIKOVSKY, PETER ILYICH (1840–93). Composer. After studying at the St. Petersburg school of jurisprudence, in 1862 Tchaikovsky entered the St. Petersburg Conservatory and in 1865 was appointed professor of the Moscow Conservatory. He resigned his professorship in 1878. In 1888 he made an international tour as conductor and met many of the leading musicians of the day. In 1891 he again traveled, to America and England. His works include the operas *Eugene Onegin* (1877–78) and *The Queen of Spades* (1890); the ballets *Swan Lake* (1875–76), *The Sleeping Beauty* (1888–89), and *The Nutcracker* (1891–92); and choral works, church music, symphonies, piano and violin concertos, chamber music, and the overture-fantasy *Romeo and Juliet* (1880). He was the most important Russian composer of the 19th century and was the towering figure of Russian romanticism. He was also instrumental in introducing nationalism into Russian music.

Evans, Edwin, *Tchaikovsky*, 1935.
Warrack, J., *Tchaikovsky*, 1973.

TECHNICUM. Professional secondary school devoted to technical studies, including agricultural and commercial subjects.

TEREK RIVER. River rising in the glaciers near Mount Kazbek, Georgia, and flowing 382 miles (611 km) N through the Daryal Pass to Malchik, then E to enter the Caspian Sea by a delta 70 miles (112 km) wide 50 miles (85 km) N of city of Makhachkala, in Dagestan Autonomous Republic. It is used for irrigation, especially for rice on its lower course.

TERESHKOVA, VALENTINA VLADIMOROVNA (1937–). The first spacewoman, famed for her trip (1963) in which she circled the earth 48 times in *Vostok 6*, in 70 hours and 50 minutes.

Sharpe, M., *"It is I, Sea Gull": Valentina Tereshkova, First Woman in Space*, 1974.

TERNOPOL. Capital of the Ternopol region of the Ukraine 76 miles (120 km) ESE of Lvov, on the Seret River. Manufactures include agricultural machinery, cement and food products, especially refined sugar. Population (1974) 104,000.

TEUTONIC KNIGHTS. A religious body of knights that played an important part in E Europe in the late Middle Ages. In 1240 armies of Teutonic Knights together with the Swedish army attacked Novgorod, and two years later attacked Pskov. In 1558, Russia received part of Livonia when the master of the Teutonic Knights surrendered his territory.

THEATER, PREREVOLUTIONARY. The first Romanov tsar, Michael III, ordered the construction of the first known theater in Russia in 1613. The actors were probably German. Apart from court performances by foreign actors and fairground shows, there was little interest in drama in Russia until Empress Elizabeth *(q.v.)* established the first public theater in 1756, at St. Petersburg, directed by Alexander Sumarokov *(q.v.)*. Theater became more popular under Catherine the Great; she founded the Imperial Theater School in 1779 and authorized the construction of the Petrovsky (Bolshoi) Theater. Until the appearance of the first Russian playwright, Denis Fonvizin *(q.v.)*, plays consisted of translations and imitations of French neoclassical plays. In 1824 the Maly (small) theater was opened with a company originally formed in 1806; it is the oldest Moscow theater. In 1832 the Alexandrinsky theater was built in St. Petersburg on the orders of Nicholas I. The tsar used the theater for political ends and is considered to have virtually invented the patriotic play, a form of drama through which playwrights flattered him. The number of theaters increased under Alexander I and Nicholas I, but many of the best plays were banned by censorship; Alexander Griboyedov's *(q.v.)* *Woe from Wit* (1823) was not staged in its full version until 1869. Similarly, Pushkin's *Boris Godunov* (1825) was not performed until 1870. Under Alexander II, censorship was relaxed, and the plays of Alexander Ostrovsky *(q.v.)* were popular. In 1883 all Yiddish plays were forbidden as a part of the anti-Semitic measures taken after the tsar was assassinated. Many dramatists left Russia to settle in the United States, making New York the new center of Yiddish drama. In 1898 Konstantin Stanislavsky and Vladimir Nemirovich-Danchenko *(q.q.v.)* founded the Moscow Art Theater *(q.v.)*, which was to influence profoundly the theater worldwide. They produced Chekhov's plays and some of Gorky's. The Symbolists *(q.v.)* experimented with nonrealistic productions.

Slonim, Marc, *Russian Theater from the Empire to the Soviets*, 1961.

Varneke, Boris V., *History of the Russian Theatre, 17th through 19th Century*, 1951.

THEATER, SERF. Theaters built by wealthy landowners who trained actors from among their serfs. Many serfs achieved such success that their owners emancipated them. The most famous of the serf theaters were at Penza, Kazan, St. Petersburg, and Moscow.

THEATER, SOVIET. After the Revolution the theater was nationalized and expanded, and today nearly 600 professional theaters produce work in 45 languages. In the 1920s the Soviet theater ranked as one of the most innovative in the world. Yevgeny Vakhtangov *(q.v.)* evolved a style of "fantastic realism," and Alexander Tairov *(q.v.)* brought Constructivism to the theater and in his "total theater" incorporated acrobatics and mime. The theater of Vsevolod Meyerhold *(q.v.)* was more abstract still, as he searched for a means of nonrealistic expression. Playwrights of this period include Nicholas Erdman, Michael Bulgakov, Yevgeny Shvarts, and Viktor Rozov; directors include Georgy Tovstonogov, Yu. P. Lyubimov, and Yefremov.

Glenny, Michael, "The Soviet Theatre" in R. Auty and D. Obolensky (eds.) "An Introduction to Russian Language and Literature," *Companion to Russian Studies*, Vol. 2, 1977.

Gorchakov, Nicholas Mikhailovich, *The Theater in Soviet Russia*, 1957.

Slonim, Marc, *Russian Theater from the Empire to the Soviets*, 1961.

THEOPHANES THE GREEK. *See* **Feofan the Greek.**

THIRD ELEMENT. Name given to the medical, agronomic, and general helpers of the *zemstva* toward the end of the 19th century; the first two elements of rural society were the peasants and nobles. The Third Element comprised young, idealistic professional men and women who worked for little money in conditions of severe hardship in order to better the lives of the peasants. In their aspirations they were the heirs of the *narodniki* (*see* **Populism**) of the 1860s and 1870s.

THIRD METALLURGICAL BASE. Name given to a proposed series of widely scattered iron and steel plants in Kazakhstan, Siberia, and the Soviet Far East. Plans for the Third Metallurgical Base have been discussed since the Second World War.

THIRD ROME, DOCTRINE OF THE. In the 14th century the authors of the Bulgarian Chronicles wrote of Trnovo, capital of Bulgaria, that it would become the Third Rome, fulfilling the role that Rome and Constantinople had had. In the 16th century, however, some monks saw Moscow as the Third Rome. This was preceded by Russian adoption of the two-headed eagle, symbol of the Eastern Roman Empire, and by the marriage of Ivan III to the niece of the last Byzantine emperor. Philotheus of the Eleazer Monastery in Pskov wrote that the First Rome had fallen because of Apollinarian heresy; the second, Constantinople, had fallen because of the Hagarenes; but that the Third Rome radiated Orthodox Christianity to the ends of the earth. He added that there would not be a Fourth Rome. This doctrine was later amended by the monk Arsenius Sukhanov, who claimed that Orthodox Christianity had been corrupted by Latin elements, and that all Christendom was awaiting the liberation of Constantinople by Russia. Moscow was regarded not only as the Third Rome, but as the New Jerusalem. Fundamentalists, on the other hand, tended to view the Muscovy theocracy and the New Jerusalem as the Kingdom of the Antichrist.

Billington, James H., *The Icon and the Axe,* 1966.

Fedotov, Georgii P., *The Russian Religious Mind,* 2 vols., 1946–66.

Obolensky, Dimitri, *The Byzantine Commonwealth: Eastern Europe 500–1453,* 1971.

THIRD SECTION OR DEPARTMENT. Formed by Tsar Nicholas I *(q.v.)* in 1826 as one of the six departments of His Majesty's Own Chancery. It was a secret police force responsible for political security and was the tsar's chief weapon against subversion; it symbolized his reign. Designed by Count Alexander Bencuendorff *(q.v.)*, head of the department (1826–44), its chief functions were surveillance, the gathering of information on undesirables such as political dissidents and foreigners, the running of state prisons, prosecution of forgers, banishment of political criminals, and censorship. The department had a vast network of spies and informers and the cooperation of the military corps of gendarmes, established in 1836.

The department, although supposed to protect the proletariat, became increasingly repressive, causing the arrest of many populists (*narodniki*) (*see* **Populism**). This led to the assassination of the then head of the Third Section, General N. V. Mezentsov (*q.v.*), in 1878.

The failure of the department to achieve much, largely due to the proliferation of false reports brought in by informers, resulted in its closure in 1880 by General Michael Loris-Melikov (*q.v.*). Its functions were transferred to the Ministry of the Interior.

Monas, Sidney L., *The Third Section: Politics and Society in Russia under Nicholas I*, 1961.

THOMAS, ALBERT (1878–1932). French statesman, historian, and (from 1919) director of the International Labor Office. Following the fall of the imperial government in Russia in 1917, Thomas was sent to Russia where he worked with the Kerensky government and supervised the production of munitions.

THREE EMPERORS' LEAGUE. League formed in 1873, with Russia, Germany, and Austria-Hungary as members. The league was valuable during a war scare with Britain over Afghanistan in 1885, but less helpful during the period of tension caused by the union of E Rumelia and Bulgaria (1885–86). In 1887 the Reinsurance Treaty (*q.v.*) between Russia and Germany replaced the league.

TIFLIS. *See* **Tbilisi.**

TIKHOMIROV, MICHAEL NIKOLAYEVICH (1893–). Marxist historian. He graduated from Moscow University in 1917. In 1934 he returned to embark on a lecturing career there and has been a member of the Academy of Sciences since 1946. He has written extensively on the history of the peasants in feudal Russia, and on ancient Russian culture and Russian law (*Russkaya Pravda*). His *The Towns of Ancient Rus* was published in 1959.

TIKHOMIROV, VASILY (1876–1956). Dancing teacher. He was a pupil of Paul Gerdt and became a teacher at the Bolshoi school of ballet in 1896. He taught many leading dancers and was considered one of the best teachers of his time.

TIKHONOV, NICHOLAS SEMYONOVICH (1896–). Poet. He was influenced at various stages in his career by Nicholas Gumilev, Vladimir Mayakovsky, and Boris Pasternak (*q.q.v.*). He became chairman of the Writers' Union in 1944, but he was removed by Andrey Zhdanov in 1946 and replaced by Alexander Fadeyev (*q.q.v.*). He received the Order of Lenin and the Stalin Prize for his work and in the 1950s was one of those who instigated a critical campaign against Pasternak. His first publications, two collections of poems, were *The Horde* (1922) and *Meade* (1923).

TILSIT. *See* **Sovetsk.**

TILSIT, TREATIES OF (1807). The treaties that France signed at Tilsit with Russia and Prussia, respectively, after Napoleon's defeat of the Prussians at Jena and Auerstadt, and the Russians at Friedland. Russia became an ally of France, and Prussia, its territory considerably reduced, was occupied by French troops. Both Russia and Prussia joined the continental system of blockade against British trade.

TIME OF TROUBLES (1598–1613). Period that began with the death of Boris Godunov *(q.v.)* and that lasted until the establishment of the House of Romanov. During the Time of Troubles there was widespread discontent, invasions by Poland and Sweden, and five tsars in Moscow at one time or another, most of whose claims to the throne were of doubtful validity. The Time of Troubles ended when the Poles were expelled from Moscow and Michael Romanov was elected tsar.

Platonov, Sergei F., *The Time of Troubles,* 1970.

TIMIRYAZEV, KLIMENT ARKADYEVICH (1843–1920). Botanist. His main work is devoted to a study of photosynthesis, but he is also remembered for his work on Darwin, *Charles Darwin and His Teaching* (1865). His teaching is used as support for Trofim Lysenko's *(q.v.)* views.

TIMOFEYEV, IVAN (*fl.* early 17th century). Historian and writer. From the end of the 16th century until 1607 Timofeyev was deacon in the Moscow department and was then transferred to Novgorod, Astrakhan, Yaroslav, and Nizhny-Novgorod, before returning to Moscow in 1628. He is the author of the well-known *Vremennik* (1630), which gives, in a rhetorical style, a reliable account of events in the reign of Ivan IV *(q.v.)* until 1619.

TIMOSHENKO, SEMYON KONSTANTINOVICH (1895–). Marshal of the Soviet Union. Of Ukrainian origin, Timoshenko commanded a division in Semyon Budyonny's *(q.v.)* first cavalry army during the Civil War and commanded Red Army units during the 1939–40 war with Finland. In 1940 he was appointed commissar for defense and was responsible for the introduction of stricter army regulations. His work as commander on the Western front following the German invasion of the Soviet Union was not particularly successful. He later commanded a number of military districts and retired in 1960.

TIMUR (TAMERLANE) (1336–1405). Turkish-Mongol ruler of Central Asia. After 1388 he ruled under the title of sultan. After cruel fighting Timur reclaimed Iran and the Caucasus. Timur died while preparing for a journey to China. Despite the cultural significance of Timur's kingdom, the kingdom fell apart soon after his death.

Vernadsky, George, *A History of Russia, The Mongols and Russia,* vol. 3, 1953.

TISZA RIVER. River rising below the Pass of the Tatars in the E Carpathians, in the Ukrainian Soviet Socialist Republic, and flowing 840 miles (1,344 km) W into Hungary, turning SW across the Hungarian plain to Szeged and on into Yugoslavia where it joins the Danube River above Belgrade. It is used for power and irrigation, especially in NE Hungary.

TKACHEV, PETER NIKITICH (1844–85). Publicist and leader of the revolutionary "Jacobins." A contributor to radical journals, Tkachev was a member of various underground revolutionary groups in the 1860s and early 1870s. As a result of the Sergei Nechayev (*q.v.*) affair, Tkachev emigrated and published the journal *Alarm Bell* in Geneva, in which he developed his ideas of a seizure of power in order that socialist reforms could be carried out by the state. This influenced the populist *Narodnaya Volya* (*see* **People's Will**) organization, the Fokin organization, and Lenin.

Hardy, D., "Tkachev and the Marxists"; *Slavic Review,* Vol. 29, No. 1, 1970.

Karpovich, Michael, "A Forerunner of Lenin: P. N. Tkachev," *Review of Politics,* 6, 1944.

TOBOL RIVER. River rising in the S Ural mountains in N Kazakh Soviet Socialist Republic and flowing 800 miles (1,280 km) NE past Kustanai and Kurgan to enter the Irtysh River at Tobolsk. It is navigable up to Kurgan.

TOBOLSK. Town in W Siberia, Russian Soviet Federated Socialist Republic, situated at the confluence of the Irtysh and Tobol rivers. Founded in 1587 it is the center of a lumbering region and trades in fish and furs. The ancient craft of bone carving is still carried on. Population (1970) 49,000.

TOGLIATTI. River port 600 miles (960 km) E of Moscow situated near S end of the Kuibyshev reservoir, in the Russian Soviet Federated Socialist Republic. Formerly known as Stavropol, it was renamed in 1964 in honor of the Italian communist leader Palmiro Togliatti (1893–1964). It is an industrial center with ship repairing, engineering, and food processing. Manufactures include vehicles (in 1970 the Volga car works began operating and in cooperation with Fiat of Italy is producing the popular *Zhiguli* car), synthetic rubber, chemicals, and furniture. Population (1981) 533,000.

TOKTAMYSH, KHAN (*fl.* 14th century). Leader of the Mongol attack on Moscow in 1382. He besieged Moscow but was unable to capture it. He therefore swore that fighting would cease and requested permission to enter and look around Moscow. Once inside the walls, however, he sacked and burned it, and then retreated. Dmitriy Donskoy (*q.v.*) was forced to accept the overlordship of Toktamysh, who confirmed his position as crown prince of Russia.

TOLSTOY, COUNT ALEKSEY NIKOLAYEVICH (1883–1945). Novelist, playwright, and National Bolshevist. He rose to fame as a neo-Realist before the 1917 Revolution, and supported the Whites during the Civil War. He emigrated, but as a member of the Change of Landmarks organization, Tolstoy returned to Russia. At first, as a fellow-traveler, he was regarded with suspicion, but by the mid-1930s, he was regarded as a loyal Stalinist and did much to create the Stalin cult. He is also remembered for his trilogy on the intelligentsia between 1914 and 1921, *The Road to Calvary* (1920–41).

Struve, Gleb, *Russian Literature Under Lenin and Stalin,* 1972.

TOLSTOY, COUNT DMITRY (1823–89). *Oberprokuror* of the Holy Synod in 1864, Tolstoy continued his career as a reactionary minister of education. He assumed office in 1866, and much greater importance was accorded to classical languages in order to distract students' attentions from the issues of the day. In 1882, Tolstoy was appointed head of the Ministry of the Interior.

TOLSTOY, COUNT LEV NIKOLAYEVICH (1828–1910). Novelist and philosopher. Born at the family estate of Yasnaya Polyana into a family of the Russian nobility, by the age of nine Tolstoy was an orphan. He studied oriental languages and law at Kazan University. He joined an artillery unit in the Caucasus and took part in the siege of Silistria and in the defense of the Fourth Bastion during the Crimean War. Some of his experiences are recorded in his *Sevastopol Stories* (1855). During the years 1856–61, spent in St. Petersburg, Moscow, and Yasnaya Polyana, Tolstoy grew increasingly disgusted with European civilization, egotism, and materialism in general and began to turn to the Russian peasants as the repository of all virtues. In 1862 he married Sofia Andreyevna Behrs and for a time was absorbed in the pleasures of family life. It was at this period in his life that he wrote *War and Peace* (1862–69), considered by some to be the greatest novel in the world, which gives a panoramic view of Russian society during the Napoleonic wars. While writing *Anna Karenina* (1873–77) Tolstoy underwent a spiritual crisis, described with powerful sincerity in *A Confession*. He became estranged from his wife, renounced art and literature, and lived a life of asceticism while evolving an ethical theory of nonresistance to evil, largely based on a rational interpretation of the Sermon on the Mount. He was tormented by the question of how one should conduct one's life; this obsession prompted the writing of the masterpiece *The Death of Ivan Ilyich* (1886). Having denied the deity and resurrection of Christ, and the deity of the Holy Spirit, he was excommunicated in 1901. He died in 1910 at Astapovo railway junction.

Christian, R. F., *Tolstoy: A Critical Introduction*, 1969.
Greenwood, Edward B., *Tolstoy: The Comprehensive Vision*, 1975.
Maude, Aylmer, *Leo Tolstoy*, 1918.
Troyat, Henri, *Tolstoy*, 1970.

TOLSTOY, COUNT PETER ALEKSANDROVICH (1761–1844). Russian ambassador to Paris and army general. Tolstoy started his military career serving with the Preobrazhensky regiment (*see* **Preobrazhenskoye**), and took part in the Italian campaign of 1799, after which he was promoted to general-adjutant. He was governor-general of St. Petersburg 1803–05 and then commanded a corps during the war with Napoleon. From 1807 to 1808 he was a special envoy in France, and from 1828 he served as commander in chief of St. Petersburg and Kronstadt. Tolstoy was a member of the state Soviet and the committee of ministers.

TOLSTOY, COUNTESS SOFIA ANDREYEVNA. Wife of Lev Nikolayevich Tolstoy. Having married Tolstoy in 1862, she settled down to domestic pursuits at the Tolstoy estates at Yasnaya Polyana and was invaluable in aiding him with his manuscripts. *The Diary of Sophie Andreyevna Tolstoy* was published in 1928.

Edwards, Anne, *Sonya: The Life of Countess Tolstoy,* 1981.

TOMASHEVSKY, BORIS VIKTOROVICH (1890–1957). Formalist writer. A member of *Opayaz* (The Society for the Study of Poetic Language), Tomashevsky wrote on the subject of the theory of literature. *See* **Formalists.**

TOMSK. Capital of Tomsk region in W central Siberia, in the Russian Soviet Federated Socialist Republic. It is situated on the Tom River. Founded in 1604, it is an important transportation and industrial center. Manufactures include machinery, chemicals, electrical equipment, ball bearings, wood products, and matches. It is also a major cultural center of Siberia. Population (1981) 439,000.

TOMSKY, MICHAEL PAVLOVICH (?–1936). Trade union official. Tomsky wished to obtain a degree of autonomy for the unions but was purged in 1929. *See* **Right Opposition.**

TON, KONSTANTIN (1794–1881). Architect. He built the Kremlin Palace, Moscow (1838–40), which is a hybrid of Russian and Renaissance styles, foreshadowing later 19th-century eclecticism in Russian architecture. He also built the Cathedral of the Redeemer in Moscow (1839–83) as the first neo-Byzantine building in Russia.

TOURISM. Prerevolutionary Russia was never a country for any but the most hardy and better-off tourists, as the introductory pages of Baedeker's guide made clear. For its subjects, too, touring was no more inviting. The acute shortage of hotels and boarding-houses, poor roads, and lack of ordinary services for visitors were among the least of their difficulties. These have not by any means been fully overcome, but great efforts have been made. In 1975 there were 3,690,751 foreign visitors, of whom 1,582,741 were from nonsocialist countries. Soviet citizens traveling abroad totaled 2,450,087 of whom 932,119 went to nonsocialist countries. Intourist (the USSR company for foreign travel) has its headquarters in Leningrad, with 11 branches in major cities. The 1980 Olympics caused a slight improvement in tourist facilities for foreigners in the USSR.

Within the USSR, tourism by Soviet citizens has been much encouraged by the trade unions, which are developing an extensive network of facilities, particularly for hikers, campers, and climbers. These facilities number more than 10,000 tourist camps, 650 tourist "bases" (supply depots for hiring equipment), and over 4,000 huts for anglers, hunters, and mountaineers. The Central Council of Trade Unions also owns or controls 137 river or seagoing ships, 120 trains, and 8,000 buses exclusively for tourist use.

Soviet tourists numbered about 19 million in 1978.

TOZ. Acronym for Partnership for the Cultivation of Land. It was a simple form of collective farming in the 1920s. Tenure of land remained individual, but peasants pooled animals and equipment. This was not enforced, although its practice was encouraged. The *toz* was abolished and replaced by the *kolkhoz (q.v.)* during the collectivization of agriculture.

TRADE UNIONS. Trade unions are organized on an industrial basis. All workers, whether manual or white-collar, in every branch of a given industry are eligible for membership of the same union. Collective farmers may also join trade unions.

Since 1933 the trade unions have carried out the functions of the former labor commissariat; they control and supervise the application of labor laws, introduce new labor laws for approval by the government, and administer social insurance and factory inspection. Social insurance is noncontributory. The All-Union Congress has met at irregular intervals; the 14th congress met in 1968, the 15th in 1972, and the 16th in 1977. Membership (1982) 130,000,000.

Blair, A. Ruble, *Soviet Trade Unions: Their Development in the 1970s*, 1981.

Brown, Emily C., *Soviet Trade Unions and Labor Relations*, 1966.

TRANSCAUCASIA. Territory S of the Caucasus, separated from the rest of European Russia. It comprises the republics of Georgia, Azerbaijan, and Armenia.

TRANSCAUCASIAN FEDERATION. State established in 1912 and dissolved in May 1918. It was an independent democratic republic, led by Georgian Mensheviks, the Azerbaijani party *Mussavat*, and the Armenian party *Dashnaktsutyun*. In May 1918 the republics of Armenia, Azerbaijan, and Georgia were created from the federation. These republics, conquered by the Red Army, became the Transcaucasian Soviet Socialist Republic in 1922 and a union republic of the USSR. It was abolished in 1936.

TRANSLITERATION. *See* **Alphabet and Transliteration.**

TRANS-SIBERIAN RAILWAY. Railway, running from Chelyabinsk in the Urals to Vladivostok on the Pacific, constructed between 1891 and 1915. It is 4,388 miles (7,021 km) long and is the world's longest railway. The construction of it greatly aided Russian colonization of Siberia and the Far East.

Dmitriyev-Mannonon, A. I. and Zdziarski, A. F., *Guide to the Great Siberian Railway*, (1900), reprinted 1971.

TREATY OF 1686. Treaty with Poland that confirmed the permanent Russian possession of all it had gained, including Kiev. This treaty of "eternal peace" was largely the work of Vasily Golitsyn *(q.v.)*.

TREDIAKOVSKY, VASILY KIRILLOVICH (1703–69). Astrakhan poet. The son of an impoverished priest, Trediakovsky was educated in Paris and was appointed acting secretary to the academy on his return to Russia. While his translations are deemed clumsy and his verse inferior, his *View of the Origin of*

Poetry and of Verse (1752) is the first Russian statement of the classical theory of imitation.

TRENGOV, KONSTANTIN ANDREYEVICH (1884–1945). Playwright and author of the melodrama *Lyubov Yarovaya* (Springtime Love).

TREPOV, GENERAL DMITRY FEDOROVICH (1855–1906). Military official. From 1896 to 1905 Trepov was the much disliked chief of police in Moscow, and from 1905 he served as governor-general of St. Petersburg. He was the instigator of the pogroms carried out by the Black Hundred antirevolutionary group, and in 1905, he was made commandant of the Winter Palace.

TREPOV, GENERAL FEDOR FEDOROVICH (*fl.* late 19th century). Military governor of St. Petersburg. On his orders Alexis Bogolyubov, a member of Land and Liberty (*q.v.*), was flogged for a minor breach of discipline. A riot ensued, and preparations were made for Trepov's murder. He was fatally shot by Vera Zasulich (*q.v.*).

TRESSINI, DOMENICO (1670–1734). Architect who built the Cathedral of Saints Peter and Paul (1714) as part of the Peter and Paul Fortress, and Peter I's palace in the Summer Gardens in St. Petersburg.

TRETYAKOV, SERGEY MIKHAILOVICH (1892–1939). Author and journalist. Tretyakov's poetry includes the collection *Iron Pause*, but it was as a playwright that he achieved fame. His grotesque anticolonial *Roar China* (1926) was widely successful. He proclaimed the death of fiction and a new empirical writing that would be the true expression of Marxist-Leninist materialism and suggested the creation of literary workshops. He was arrested and executed during the Purges as an alleged Chinese spy.

TRETYAKOV ART GALLERY. Moscow art gallery, founded by P. M. Tretyakov, a textile manufacturer (1832–98), in 1892. He had bought the best paintings at the Association of Traveling Art Exhibitions, and these formed the core of the gallery.

Rostovkseva, I., *The Tretyakov Gallery, Moscow,* 1975.

TREZZINI, DOMENICO. *See* **Tressini, Domenico.**

TRIFONOV, YURY (1925–81). Writer. Many of his stories explore urban morality. Having established his reputation under Stalin with his politically cautious novel *Students* (1956), Trifonov wrote many short stories and novels. Skilled at creating convincing characters, he portrays in detail Soviet life in the large cities. Among Trifonov's best-known works are the novels *The House on the Embankment* (1976) and *A Long Goodbye.*

Brown, D. B., *Soviet Russian Literature Since Stalin,* 1978.

TROITSA-SERGEYEVA LAVRA. Monastery of the Holy Trinity, 44 miles (70 km) N of Moscow. Founded by St. Sergius of Radonezh in 1337, Troitsa-Sergeyeva Lavra is the largest Russian Orthodox monastery. The cathedral is built in the early Muscovite style, and the bell tower (1741–70) in the baroque style. From the 14th to the 17th century the monastery was an important religious and political center. In 1920 it was seized and turned into a museum. Since 1948 it has been the patriarch's residence.

TROPPAU, CONGRESS OF. Congress held in 1820 as one in a series following the defeat of Napoleon. Alexander I of Russia, Francis I of Austria, and Frederick William III of Prussia met to discuss what action should be taken concerning the democratic revolution that had taken place in Naples.

TROTSKY, LEV DAVIDOVICH (BRONSHTEYN) (1879–1940). Politician. Trotsky joined the Social Democrats *(q.v.)* in 1896. He was banished to Siberia but escaped and became a member of *Iskra (q.v.)*. In 1903 when the party split, he became a Menshevik, prophesizing that Leninist theory would result in a one-man dictatorship. He was again banished as a result of his role in the 1905 Revolution, when he held the position of chairman of the St. Petersburg Soviet. While trying to reunite the factions of the Russian Social Democrats, he led the internationalist wing of the Mensheviks during the First World War. Expelled from France as a result of his pacifist propaganda, Trotsky settled in the United States. Back in Russia, following the February 1917 Revolution, Trotsky became a Bolshevik and the chief supporter of Lenin, and played a leading role in organizing and carrying out the October Revolution. Trotsky was head of the St. Petersburg Soviet and its military revolutionary committee, commissar for foreign affairs (1917–18), commissar for war (1918–25), leader of the Red Army during the Civil War, and from 1919 to 1927 was a member of the Politburo. A frequent opponent of Lenin, Trotsky was expelled from the party in 1927. The "combined opposition" of Trotsky, Grigory Zinoviev, and Lev Kamenev *(q.q.v.)* was unsuccessful, and in 1929, he was expelled from the Soviet Union. He was accused of espionage during the Great Purge and was murdered in Mexico City by Soviet agents. In 1930 he wrote *My Life: An Attempt at an Autobiography*.

Carmichael, Joel, *Trotsky: An Appreciation of His Life*, 1975.

Deutscher, Isaac, *The Prophet Armed: Trotsky, 1879–1921; The Prophet Unarmed: Trotsky, 1921–29; The Prophet Outcast: Trotsky, 1929–40*, 3 vols., 1954–63.

TRUBETSKOY, PRINCE DMITRY TIMOFEYEVICH (?–1625). Leader of the Tushino Cossacks and, together with Lyapunov and Zarutsky *(q.v.)*, a leader of the provisional government established as a result of the *Prigovor*, or Decision of June 30, 1611 during the Time of Troubles.

TRUBETSKOY, PRINCE SERGEY NIKOLAYEVICH (1790–1860). Decembrist (*see* **Decembrists**). In 1823 he was appointed leader of the Northern Society *(q.v.)*. He wished to abolish serfdom while retaining the administrative apparatus of the government. In 1826 he was banished to Siberia.

Mazour, Anatole G., *The First Russian Revolution, 1825*, 1937.

TRUBETSKOY, PRINCE YEVGENY NIKOLAYEVICH (1863–1920). Legal philosopher and liberal politican and professor at Kiev and Moscow universities. He edited the *Moscow Weekly.* His main works include *Religious and Social Ideal of Western Christianity in the Fifth Century. St. Augustine* (1892), *The Philosophy of* V. I. *Solovev* (1913), and *The Metaphysical Assumption of Knowledge* (1917).

TRUDOVIKI. Party in the state duma, 1906–17. Its deputies consisted of intellectuals of humble origins, peasants, and village priests. The party had no existence outside the duma.

Hosking, Geoffrey, *The Constitutional Experiment,* 1973.

TRUVOR (*fl.* 9th century). One of three Varangian brothers. According to the *Primary Chronicle* (*q.v.*), Ryurik (*q.v.*), Sineus and Truvor were invited by the E Slav tribes to come and rule the land of Rus.

TSAR (CZAR). Title from the Latin *Caesar* used by the rulers of Muscovy from the 15th century to Peter the Great, who adopted the title Emperor of All Russia. The title "Tsar," however, remained in popular usage during the imperial period.

TSARSIS, VALERY YAKOVLEVICH (1902–). Author. A former communist, Tsarsis revised his opinions of the regime and produced highly satirical accounts of Stalinism and bureaucratic mismanagement, while the hero of his *What a Gay Life* can be seen as a caricature of Khrushchev. After his work had been published in England, Tsarsis was arrested and sentenced to a year in a mental institution. This is the basis of his *Ward 7 1965,* an outspoken attack on communism. In 1965 he was deprived of his citizenship and settled in W Europe.

TSARSKOYE SELO. *See* **Pushkin.**

TSELINOGRAD. Capital of Tselinograd region in the central N of Kazakhstan, situated on the Ishim River. It is an important industrial and railway center with asphalt and reinforced concrete works, meat packing plants, and engineering works. Population (1981) 241,000.

TSELOVALNIK. A sworn man; a person who has kissed the cross; officials of local or central government in Muscovy.

TSIOLKOVSKY, KONSTANTIN EDUARDOVICH (1857–1935). Pioneer in space travel whose work laid the foundation of later research into the subject. He worked as a schoolteacher, and his theories on cosmic travel met with cynicism in his day.

TSUSHIMA, BATTLE OF (1905). Sea battle during the Russo-Japanese War of 1904–05. The Russian fleet, under Admiral Z. P. Rozhdestvensky, was completely defeated.

TSVETAYEVA, MARINA IVANOVNA (1892–1941). Poet. Born into a highly cultured family. Tsvetayeva was educated in Switzerland. Her first collection of poetry was published in 1911, and in 1922 the Moscow State Editions published two of her books *The Tsar Maiden* and *Versty*, which were highly praised by Boris Pasternak. Her husband was Sergey Efron, an anticommunist, and they eventually settled in Germany, Prague, and France, where the family lived in great poverty. Efron became a Soviet sympathizer and worked for the secret police, and Tsvetayeva decided to return to Russia where she worked in the Soviet Union as a translator of poetry. She hanged herself in 1941. Two decades later, she was hailed as a great poet. Collections of poetry, particularly *Craftsmanship* and *The Pied Piper*, are highly esteemed.

Hingley, Ronald, *Nightingale Fever*, 1982.

Karlinsky, Simon, *Marina Cvetaeva (Tsvetaeva): Her Life and Art*, 1966.

Mandelstam, Nadezhda, *Hope Against Hope*, 1971.

TSYGANOV, NICHOLAS G. (1797–1831). Songwriter and itinerant actor. Tsyganov wrote folk songs, imagery and symbolism of which is considered very beautiful, and the content unsentimental. Tsyganov's songs were published posthumously in 1834.

TUGAN-BARANOVSKY, MICHAEL IVANOVICH (1865–1919). Economist. He held the position of professor at the universities of St. Petersburg and Kiev. In 1917 he was appointed minister of finance of the Ukrainian national government. His most important works include *The Theoretical Assumptions of Marxism* (1905) and *Modern Socialism and its Historical Development* (1913).

TUKHACHEVSKY, MICHAEL NIKOLAYEVICH (1893–1937). Marshal of the Soviet Union. Of a noble family, Tukhachevsky served as an officer in the First World War, but in 1918 he joined the Bolsheviks and the Red Army. He was commander in 1918–19 and was commander of all the Red forces in the Caucasus in 1920. In 1921 he was commander of the government forces against the Kronstadt uprising. He was head of the military academy, commander of the western and Leningrad military districts, and the Red Army's chief of staff (1925–28). Deputy commissar for military and naval affairs in 1931, in 1935 Tukhachevsky was appointed one of the first five marshals. He was accused of leading a military conspiracy and was tried and shot during the Great Purge. His reputation was rehabilitated in 1958.

TULA. Capital of Tula region in central European Russia, first mentioned in the 12th century. Peter the Great built an arms factory there in 1712, and it is the chief center of the Moscow coal basin with metallurgical and engineering industries. It is famous for fine metalwork; the best samovars come from Tula. Population (1981) 521,000.

TULUP. A type of headgear.

TUPOLEV, ANDREY NIKOLAYEVICH (1888–). Aircraft designer and lieutenant-general of the air force. Having studied under N. Y. Zhukovsky at the Moscow Higher Technical School, in 1916 Tupolev established the Aerodynamic Aircraft Design Bureau. He has designed and directed work on both civil and military aircraft, including the ANT25 and the TU104 and TU114. Arrested during the Great Purge in 1938, he was released and rehabilitated in 1943.

TURGENEV, IVAN SERGEYEVICH (1818–83). Writer. The son of an impoverished squire, Turgenev was educated at the Universities of Moscow and St. Petersburg and then studied at Berlin where he was influenced by Hegel and where he met the Westernizers Timofei Granovsky and Nicholas Stankevich *(q.q.v.)*. After an abortive attempt at a career in the civil service, in 1845 Turgenev devoted himself to literature. In 1847 some of the stories from the famous *A Sportsman's Sketches* were published. The sketches, illustrating the plight of the serf, are said to have persuaded the future emperor, Alexander II *(q.v.)*, to emancipate the serfs. Turgenev was arrested and banished to his estates from 1852 to 1853 as the result of composing an overenthusiastic obituary of Gogol. He eventually settled in Paris, where he met Flaubert and Mérimée and where he became the first Russian author whose works were highly esteemed abroad. Turgenev's novels include *Rudin* (1856), *On the Eve* (1860), and the much-loved *Fathers and Children* (1862). He also wrote the play *A Month in the Country*, the first Russian psychological drama, and a number of short stories.

Freeborn, Richard, *Turgenev: A Study*, 1960.

Pritchett, Victor Sawdon, *The Gentle Barbarian*, 1977.

Schapiro, Leonard B., *Turgenev: His Life and Times*, 1978.

TURGENEV, NICHOLAS IVANOVICH (1789–1871). Decembrist (*see* **Decembrists**) and economist. Having studied at the universities of Moscow and Gottingen, Turgenev became a Decembrist. After the failure of the Decembrist uprising, he was condemned to a life sentence of penal servitude, but he wrote to the tsar, renouncing his revolutionary stance. He produced many books on the emancipation of the serfs and on economics.

TURKESTAN. Former name for the historical area in Asia that now consists of the Soviet Central Asian republics of the USSR, together with part of the Sinkiang Province of China and the N part of Afghanistan.

TURKIC LANGUAGES. Turkic languages may be divided into Old Turkish, Middle Turkish, and Modern Turkish. The latter consists of the Turkmen, Uzbek Kipchak, and Uighur groups. In 1928, Mustafa Kemal Ataturk tried to modernize Turkish by adopting the Latin script and by eradicating Arabic and Persian words. In 1939, however, the Soviet government adopted the Cyrillic script, in order to alienate Soviet Turkic peoples from other Turks, and introduced words of Russian origin into the language. Both the Soviets and the Turkish government have simplified syntax and phonetics. Turkish is the primary language of 19 million people in the USSR.

TURKMANCHAY, TREATY OF (1828). Treaty at which Persia surrendered Yerevan and the Nakhichevan Khanates.

TURKMEN SOVIET SOCIALIST REPUBLIC. Constituent republic of central Asian USSR bounded on the W by the Caspian Sea, on the N by Kazakhstan and Uzbekistan, and on the S by Iran. It has an area of 186,400 square miles (482,776 sq km). The capital is Ashkhabad. The region is about 80 percent desert, rising to the Kopet Dagh foothills in the S and settled in a chain of oases. Irrigation is highly developed, and agriculture depends on it. The main crops are cotton, maize, fruit and vegetables, grapes, and olives. Livestock raised includes karakul sheep, horses, and cattle. Mineral deposits are extensive, including oil, coal, ozocerite, sulphur, salt, and magnesium. Industries include mining, oil refining, engineering, textiles, and chemicals. Population (1981) 2,900,000.

TURKSIB. Acronym for Turkestan-Siberian railway built in 1913–30, which connects the Trans-Siberian and the Orenburg-Tashkent lines.

TUVA AUTONOMOUS SOVIET SOCIALIST REPUBLIC. Part of the Russian Soviet Federated Socialist Republic situated to the NW of Mongolia and bounded on the E, W, and N by Siberia and to S by the Republic of Mongolia. Incorporated in the USSR as an autonomous region in 1944, it became an autonomous republic in 1961. It has an area of 65,810 square miles (170,448 sq km). The capital is Kizyl. The chief occupation is pastoral farming. Gold, cobalt, and asbestos are mined in the region. Population (1981) 269,000.

TVARDOVSKY, ALEXANDER TRIFONOVICH (1910–71). Writer. In 1936 Tvardovsky published *The Land of Muravia* and in 1942, the famous portrait of the Soviet soldier, *Vasily Terkin*. He edited the literary journal *Novy mir*, was dismissed from this post in 1954, but was reinstated in the 1960s. Tvardovsky was responsible for publishing Solzhenitsyn's *A Day in the Life of Ivan Denisovich* in the Soviet Union, where it appeared in *Novy mir*.

TVER. *See* **Kalinin.**

TVER, PRINCES OF. Under the rule of Prince Yaroslav Yaroslavich, Tver became a principality, and its power grew under Michael I (*q.v.*). Michael's son Dmitry was executed in 1326. Dmitry's brother, Alexander I, fled to Pskov after the Mongol massacre of 1327. During the reign of Basil II (1346–47), the principality had to contend with an internal dynastic conflict between Basil and his uncle and cousins. Alexander's son, Michael II, challenged Moscow's position until he was defeated by Dmitriy Donskoy in 1375. Under Boris Aleksandrovich (1425–61), Tver enjoyed a period of economic prosperity.

TYAGLO. A tax or an obligation in kind or money, or both, paid by city inhabitants and peasants.

TYNYANOV, YURY NIKOLAYEVICH (1896–1943). Writer. Having graduated from Petrograd University, Tynyanov was appointed professor at the age of 29. He is regarded as an initiator of the historical biographical novel, having written *Kukhyla* (1925), which deals with Wilhelm Kuchelbecker, *The Death of Vazir Mukhtar* (1929), which recounts the life of Alexander Griboyedov (*q.v.*), and *Pushkin*. He was a Formalist (*q.v.*) critic of the group *Opoyaz* (Society for the Study of Poetic Language).

Slonim, Marc, *Soviet Russian Literature, 1917–77,* 1977.

TYSHLER, ALEXANDER (1898–1980). Artist and one of the leaders of the Society of Easel Artists. Owing to the stifling demands of Socialist Realism, Tyshler in later life turned to theater design.

TYSYATSKY. Elected by the Novgorod *veche (q.v.)*, the *tysyatsky* assisted the prince in his duties. He resolved commercial disputes and commanded the town regiment or thousand; his name is probably derived from the Russian *tysyacha*, meaning thousand. The office *tysyatsky* was abolished in Moscow in 1374 and in Novgorod in the late 1470s by Ivan III.

TYUMEN. Capital of Tyumen region of the Russian Soviet Federated Socialist Republic located in W Siberia on the Tura River. Founded in 1586, it is the oldest city in Siberia. Industries include boatbuilding, sawmilling, tanning, and the manufacture of chemicals and carpets. Population (1981) 378,000.

TYUTCHEV, FEDOR IVANOVICH (1803–73). Slavophile and poet. After studying at Moscow University, Tyutchev entered the diplomatic service in 1822. In Munich he met the philosopher Friedrich Schelling and the poet Heinrich Heine and wrote about 40 lyrical poems. Although he was expelled from the diplomatic service, he returned to Russia and worked as a censor and became known as a reactionary and Pan-Slavist. Despondent and guilt-ridden after a love affair, he continued to write political verse and died after suffering a stroke. Much of his poetry is metaphysical, such as his *Silentium* (1835), and expresses his pantheistic views. His tragic love poetry is considered very moving, but the style is archaic. He was a forerunner of the Symbolists *(q.v.)* and Dostoyevsky described him as Russia's first philosopher poet.

Gregg, R. A., *Fyodor Tyutchev,* 1965.

Mirsky, D. S., *A History of Russian Literature,* 1948.

U

UDALTSOVA, NADEZHDA (1886–1961). Painter and one of the chief representatives of the Cubist school in Russia. Udaltsova studied with Lyubov Popova at Arseneva's gymnasium (1907–10) and they then took a studio together in Moscow. They went to Paris in 1912, but Udaltsova returned to Russia in 1914. One of her best-known paintings is *At the Piano* (c. 1914).

Gray, Camilla, *The Russian Experiment in Art*, 1962.

UDEL. Independent and semi-independent domains of princes in the era of the Mongol domination; in the 19th century the term referred to the land belonging to the imperial family.

UDMURT AUTONOMOUS SOVIET SOCIALIST REPUBLIC. It is part of the Russian Soviet Federated Socialist Republic that was constituted an autonomous region in 1920 (then named Votyak) and then an autonomous republic in 1934. It has an area of 16,250 square miles (42,087 sq km). The capital is Izhevsk, situated 600 miles (960 km) ENE of Moscow. Chief industries include the manufacture of locomotives, machine tools, and other engineering products; there are also varied light industries. Population (1972) 1,424,000.

UDMURTS (Votyaks). Finnish-speaking people numbering about 70,000 who live near the Kama River in the Udmurt Autonomous Soviet Socialist Republic and in neighboring areas. They are Orthodox Christians and are chiefly peasants.

UEZD. Administrative district or county comparable to the *okrug* (*q.v.*) and comprising several *volosts* (*q.v.*).

UFA. Capital of the Bashkir Autonomous Soviet Socialist Republic situated at the confluence of the Ufa and Belaya rivers 715 miles (1,144 km) E of Moscow. One of the largest industrial centers of the Urals, it has important heavy and light engineering industries, including oil refining, with pipelines to the Volga-Ural oil field, and has the largest petrochemical plant in the USSR. Sawmilling and food processing are also important. Population (1970) 773,000.

UFA DIRECTORY. An anti-Bolshevik government established on September 23, 1918 in Ufa by some committee members of the Constituent Assembly. It was disbanded in December 1918 by Admiral Kolchak (*q.v.*).

UFA RIVER. River rising in the S Urals and flowing NW and SSW for 450 miles (720 km) to join the Belaya River at Ufa.

UGLICH. Town in the center of the Uglich region of the Yaroslavskaya oblast, on the right bank of the Volga. Slavic tribes settled there in the eighth and ninth centuries. Uglich was later to become an appanage of the Moscow princes. The Uglich Kremlin contains several churches and other buildings of architectural interest. The castle, built in 1481–83, was where Dmitry, son of Ivan the Terrible, was allegedly murdered in 1591.

UGRA RIVER, BATTLE OF (1480). Bloodless confrontation between Muscovite and Mongol forces at the Ugra River, 150 miles (241 km) SW of Moscow, following Ivan III's (*q.v.*) renunciation of allegiance to the Golden Horde. Khan Ahmad formed an alliance with Lithuania and Poland, but his allies failed to send forces. The khan, hearing that his base camp at Saray was being raided, withdrew.

UKAZ (or **Ukase**). An edict (statute or administrative decree) first used in medieval times and continued by the tsars until 1917. Under the 1936 constitution the expression was revived in the USSR.

UKRAINE. The Ukrainian Soviet Socialist Republic was proclaimed in 1917 and was finally established two years later. In 1920 it concluded a military and economic alliance with the Russian Soviet Federated Socialist Republic, and in 1923 it joined together with the other Soviet socialist republics to form the USSR. It has an area of 231,990 square miles (603,700 sq km). The capital is Kiev. The Ukraine contains rich land and is therefore important agriculturally. Coal and iron ore are mined extensively; other important minerals are manganese, oil, gypsum, and alabaster. Population (1981) 50,100,000.

UKRAINIAN DIRECTORY. A Ukrainian *rada* (council), led first by the author Vladimir Vinnychenko and then by Simon Petlyura, assumed power in Kiev on November 7, 1917. A Ukrainian People's Republic was proclaimed, but in January 1918 the Bolsheviks overran the Ukraine and the *rada* was overthrown.

ULANOVA, GALINA SERGEYEVNA (1910–). Prima ballerina. She made her debut in 1928 at the Kirov Theater, Leningrad, in *Les Sylphides*. Her dancing represented a survival of the best of the prerevolutionary Russian school. She was taught by Agrippina Vaganova, who was in turn taught by Nicholas Legat; her parents were dancers at the Imperial Theater in St. Petersburg, the Maryinsky. Although comparatively unknown outside the Soviet Union until her visit to London in 1956, she established herself as one of the world's greatest dancers. In addition to her stage performances, she appeared in the films *Giselle* and *Romeo and Juliet.* On retiring in 1963, she joined the Bolshoi Theater as ballet mistress.

Bogdanov-Berezovsky, V. M., *Ulanova and the Development of the Soviet Ballet,* 1952.

Kahn, Albert Eugene, *Days with Ulanova,* 1962.

ULAN-UDE. Capital of the Buryat Autonomous Soviet Socialist Republic in Siberia, situated at the confluence of the Selenga and Uda rivers. It was founded in 1649 as a Cossack winter encampment. An important railway center, its industries are railway engineering, ship repairing, and sawmilling. Manufactures include glass and food products. Population (1970) 254,000.

ULOZHENIYE. A legal code, approved by the *Zemsky Sobor* in 1648 and enacted in 1649, which provided the first comprehensive set of laws since 1550. The aim was to give certainty to economic, social, and political affairs after the Time of Troubles (*q.v.*). One of its important provisions was the final establishment of serfdom. It remained in force until 1835.

Vernadsky, George V., et al. (eds.), *A Source Book for Russian History from Early Times to 1917,* 1972.

Vernadsky, George V., *Russia at the Dawn of the Modern Age,* 1959.

ULYANOV, ALEXANDER ILYICH (1866–87). Elder brother of Vladimir Ilyich Ulyanov (Lenin), a member of the People's Will (*q.v.*), and the manufacturer of the bombs intended for the assassination of Alexander III. Ulyanov was executed on May 8, 1887. His involvement in the revolutionary movement and his execution made a great impact on Lenin's subsequent development.

ULYANOV, VLADIMIR ILYICH. *See* **Lenin.**

ULYANOVSK. Capital of the region of the same name situated 110 miles (176 km) NW of Kuibyshev between the Volga and Sviyaga rivers, in the Russian Soviet Federated Socialist Republic. It is an important transportation center. Industries are engineering, sawmilling, tanning, and food production. Lenin's birthplace. Population (1981) 485,000.

UNDERGROUND MAN. Main character in Dostoyevsky's *Notes from the Underground* (1864), a work of considerable psychological and philosophical insight. The Underground Man asserts man's right to freedom and the need for the irrational. Central to Dostoyevsky's work and thought, the Underground Man was a profound influence on many subsequent writers.

Villadsen, P., *The Underground Man and Raskolnikov,* 1981.

UNDERGROUND RAILWAYS. See **Subways.**

UNIATES. Uniates is the term used to describe those Christians who are doctrinally united with the Church of Rome, but whose practices are similar to those of the Orthodox Church. Use of the term occurred when the Orthodox bishops in Poland recognized the pope's authority at the Union of Brest-Litovsk in 1596. They retained most of the external features of the Orthodox Church, such as the rites and the use of Church Slavonic as the ritual language. After the partitions of Poland in the 18th century, the union with Rome was abrogated in the territories annexed to Russia, but the denomination remained intact in the Austrian-held provinces.

UNION OF LIBERATION. Revolutionary organization founded in 1903 that was responsible for the organization of the Constitutional Democratic Party (Kadets) (*q.v.*). Its organ, *The Liberation*, was published abroad under the editorship of the economist, Peter Struve.

UNION OF PEREYASLAV. In 1654 a *rada* (assembly) of the Ukrainian people agreed to declare allegiance to Moscow because of their exposure to attack. Hetman Bogdan Khmelnitsky (*q.v.*) explained that the alternatives were subjection to Poland or allegiance to Turkey. The decisions were accepted by Tsar Alexis (*q.v.*).

UNION OF THE RUSSIAN PEOPLE. A reactionary organization founded in 1905, by the secret police, which directed most action against the revolutionaries. For the most part, the Union of Russian People blamed the Jews for the granting of civil liberties, and hence the Union encouraged the street mobs' anger against the Jews.

UNION OF SALVATION. A secret society established in 1816. It was led by Paul Pestel (*q.v.*) and in 1817 was reorganized as the Union of Welfare. The society was dissolved in 1821.

Mazour, Anatole Grigorevich, *The First Russian Revolution, 1825*, 1937.

UNION OF SOVIET SOCIALIST REPUBLICS. Until 1917 the territory now forming the USSR, together with that of Finland, Poland, and certain tracts ceded in 1918 to Turkey, except for the territories then forming part of the German, Austro-Hungarian, and Japanese empires—E Prussia, E Galicia, Transcarpathia, Bukovina, E Sakhalin, and the Kurile Islands—which were acquired during and after the Second World War, was constituted as the Russian Empire.

In 1917 a revolution broke out, a provisional government was appointed, and in a few months a republic was proclaimed. Late in 1917 power was transferred to the second All-Russian Congress of Soviets. This elected a new government, the Council of People's Commissars, headed by Lenin. Early in 1918 the third All-Russian Congress of Soviets issued a Declaration of Rights of the Toiling and Exploited Masses, which proclaimed Russia a republic of Soviets workers', soldiers' and peasants' deputies; and in the middle of 1918 the fifth congress adopted a constitution for the Russian Soviet Federated Socialist Republic. In the course of the Civil War other Soviet republics were set up in the Ukraine, Belorussia, and Transcaucasia. These first entered into treaty relations with the Russian Soviet Federated Socialist Republic and then, in 1922, joined with it in a closely integrated union. The total area is 8.65 million square miles (22.4 million sq km). The capital is Moscow. Population (1977) 260 million.

The USSR, until 1928 predominantly agricultural in character, has become an industrial-agricultural country. Of the gross product, industry and transport accounted for 42.1 percent in 1913 and 78.1 percent in 1971; agriculture accounted for 57.9 percent in 1913 and 15.7 percent in 1971. Of the total state land fund of 2,227,500,000 hectares, agricultural land in use in 1971 amounted to 607.3 million hectares, state forests and state reserves to 1,124,000,000 hectares. The total area under cultivation is 207.3 million hectares. There are 747 million hectares of forest land in the USSR; the largest forested areas are 515 million hectares in the Asiatic part of the USSR, 51.4 million hectares along the N seaboard, 25.4 million hectares in the Urals, and 17.95 million hectares in the NW.

The USSR is rich in minerals and claims that it contains 58 percent of the world's coal deposits, 58.7 percent of its oil, 41 percent of its iron ore, 76.7 percent of its apatite, 25 percent of all timber land, 88 percent of its manganese, 54 percent of its potassium salts, and nearly 33 percent of its phosphates.

Under eight successive Five-Year Plans over 31,940 large-scale modern industrial works have been constructed.

Berg, L. S., *The Natural Regions of the USSR*, 1950.

Dewdney, John C., "The USSR," *Studies in Industrial Geography*, 1978.

Hooson, David J. M., *The Soviet Union: People and Regions*, 1966.

Maxwell, R. (ed.), "Information USSR," trans. *Great Soviet Encyclopedia*, 1962.

UNION OF SOVIET WRITERS. Under a decree of April 23, 1932, all existing literary organizations were abolished, and the Union of Soviet Writers was founded, holding its first congress in 1934. Membership is essential for the pursuit of a professional career in literature. In 1976 there were 7,833 members, of whom 1,097 were women, writing in 76 languages. There are branches in all the union republics.

Hingley, Ronald, *Russian Writers and Soviet Society, 1917–1978*, 1979.

Walker, Gregory P. M., *Soviet Book Publishing Policy*, 1978.

UNION OF SPIRITUAL COMMUNITIES OF CHRIST. *See* ***Dukhobory.***

UNION OF WELFARE. *See* **Union of Salvation.**

UNITED NATIONS. The USSR was a founding member of the United Nations in 1945. It is one of five permanent members of the Security Council.

UNIVERSITIES. In 1978–79 there were 4,332 technical colleges with 4.7 million students, and 866 universities, institutes, and other places of higher education, with 5.1 million students (including 2.25 million taking correspondence or evening courses); 68,000 students, enrolled after work in factories, collective farms, or the armed forces, were attending preparatory courses at 524 places of higher education (similar to the "workers' faculties" of early Soviet years).

Among the 65 university towns are Moscow, Leningrad, Kharkov, Odessa, Tartu, Kazan, Saratov, Tomsk, Kiev, Sverdlovsk, Tbilisi, Alma-Ata, Tashkent, Minsk, Gorky, and Vladivostok. On January 1, 1979 there were 1.3 million scientific workers in places of higher education, research institutes, and academies of sciences. There were 33,000 foreign students from 130 countries.

The Academy of Sciences of the USSR had 693 members and corresponding members. Total learned institutions under the USSR Academy of Sciences numbered 244, with a scientific staff of 45,721. Fourteen of the union republics have their own academies of sciences, with a scientific staff numbering 47,177. On January 1, 1978 there were 96,668 postgraduate students.

The Academy of Pedagogical Sciences had 14 research institutes with a staff of 1,693.

Grant, Nigel, *Soviet Education*, 4th ed., 1979.

UNIVERSITY STATUTE OF 1835. Statute issued in 1835 by Count Sergey Uvarov (*q.v.*), minister of education. Despite Uvarov's conservatism, his statute provided for considerable autonomy for the universities.

UNKIAR SKELESSI, TREATY OF. Treaty signed on July 8, 1833, between Russia and Turkey, aiming at peace and friendship for eight years, and allowing for consultation and aid in the event of attack by third parties. By this treaty the Ottoman Empire became a virtual protectorate of Russia.

UNKOVSKY, ALEXIS (1828–93). Marshal of the nobility of Tver. In 1858 he proposed immediate emancipation of the peasants with land, with compensation for the owner. These measures were rejected by the government. Unkovsky continued his interest in the peasant question and in legal concerns throughout his life.

UNOFFICIAL SECRET COMMITTEE. Alexander I (*q.v.*) formed the so-called unofficial committee on July 6, 1801 by inviting four friends, Nicholas Novosiltsev (*q.v.*), Paul Stroganov, Viktor Kochubey, and Adam Czartoryski, to meet as a council of advisers to discuss reforms and questions of the day.

URAL-ALTAIC LANGUAGES. A language family composed of Finno-Ugric, Samoyedic, and Altaic groups. The latter includes Mongolian, Tungus, and Turkic languages.

URAL COSSACKS. A number of Don Cossacks settled by the Ural River in the 16th century, and formed autonomous communities. The Ural Cossacks supported Stenka Razin's (*q.v.*) uprising in 1670. In 1773 there occurred another uprising of the Ural Cossacks, led by Yemilyan Pugachev (*q.v.*), who claimed to be Peter III.

URAL MOUNTAINS. Mountain range running N to S from the Arctic Ocean and forming part of the boundary between Europe and Asia. It extends for over 1,400 miles (2,240 km), mainly of low elevation, the highest peak being Narodnaya, 6,214 feet (1,894 m) above sea level. There are rich mineral resources, including iron, copper, nickel, manganese, gold, and platinum. Apart from the N ranges, the Urals are densely forested.

URAL RIVER. River rising in the S of the Ural mountains and flowing for 1,400 miles (2,240 km) S to enter the Caspian Sea through a delta at Chapayev, 10 miles (16 km) SW of Gurev.

URALSK. Capital of the Uralsk region of Kazakhstan on the Ural River. It was founded in 1622 and is the center of an agricultural area. The chief occupations are meat packing and wool processing. Population (1970) 134,000.

URITSKY, MOYSEY SOLOMONOVICH (1873–1918). Revolutionary. Friend of Trotsky and one of the organizers of the October Revolution. He was appointed head of the Cheka in Petrograd but was assassinated.

URQUHART, DAVID (1805–77). Scottish diplomat and Russophobe who, as a journalist, helped to spread the near hysterical anti-Russian feelings of the 1830s. Following the publication of his *Turkey and its Resources* in 1833, he was sent on a secret mission to Turkey to investigate the potential for trade between Great Britain and Turkey and gained the complete confidence of the Turkish government. He was recalled from Constantinople because of his outspokenness. In 1835 he returned to Constantinople only to be recalled again in 1837 because his actions threatened to lead to an international crisis over Russian influence in Circassia. Just before his return his pamphlet *England, France, Russia, and Turkey* was published, and this enhanced his reputation and influence. He founded *Portfolio* in 1835, in which he published a series of Russian state papers. Sitting in Parliament (1847–52), he attacked Lord Palmerston's foreign policy, and during the Crimean War (*q.v.*) he contended that Turkey could fight its own battles without European intervention. He founded *Free Press* (later renamed *Diplomatic Review*), to which Karl Marx was a contributor.

USHAKOV, ADMIRAL FEDOR FEDOROVICH (1744–1817). An outstanding naval commander and one of the founders of the Russian navy. When Russia became a member of the second coalition against France, Ushakov won a victory against the French in the Mediterranean and the Adriatic by seizing the Ionian Islands in 1798.

USHINSKY, KONSTANTIN DMITRYEVICH (1824–70). Educational theorist. He advocated the establishment of training colleges for teachers and the introduction of departments of education at universities. This led to the foundation of modern methods of primary education in Russia.

USPENSKY, GLEB IVANOVICH (1840–1902). Novelist. His important writings were mainly about peasant life. *Power of the Soil* (1882) was noted for its realism which contrasted with the then prevailing romantic approach to peasant life.

Glinka, A. S., *Uspensky*, 1935.

USSURI RIVER. River rising 50 miles (80 km) from Ussuri Bay, an inlet of the Sea of Japan, and flowing 560 miles (896 km) N to the Amur River SW of Khabarovsk.

UST-KAMENOGORSK. Town situated 110 miles (176 km) ESE of Semipalatinsk on the Irtysh River in Kazakhstan. It was founded in 1720 as a military outpost. The industrial center of a district mining zinc, copper, and lead, it has the largest nonferrous metallurgical plant in the USSR. At Ablaketka, 10 miles (16 km) to the S, there is a large hydroelectric power station. Population (1981) 286,000.

UST URK. Desert plateau between the Caspian and Aral seas in the Uzbek Soviet Socialist Republic. It has an altitude of approximately 490–980 feet (180–300 m). It is inhabited by seminomadic tribes raising goats, sheep, and camels.

USTINOV, DMITRY FEDOROVICH (1908–). Soviet party official. Ustinov joined the Communist Party of the Soviet Union in 1927. In 1934 he graduated from the Institute of Military Mechanical Engineering and worked as a fitter and machine operator. From 1934 until 1941, Ustinov was USSR people's commissar. He climbed up the ranks of party posts, being made a member of the central committee in 1952. He was the USSR minister of the defense industry (1953–57), chairman of the USSR supreme economic council (1963–65), and a member of the Presidium and Politburo central committee. From 1976 Ustinov has been minister of defense, general of the army, and marshal of the Soviet army.

U–2. Single seated, high-altitude jet reconnaissance and research aircraft used by the United States. In 1960 a U-2 flown by Gary Powers was brought down while on a spying exercise over the USSR. This caused the collapse of a summit conference in Paris among the United States, the USSR, Great Britain, and France.

UVAROV, COUNT SERGEY SEMYONOVICH (1786–1855). Minister of education (1833–49). In 1848 the aim of education was declared to be the preparation of "loyal sons for the orthodox church, loyal subjects for the tsar, and good and useful citizens for the fatherland." Uvarov needed trained bureaucrats but while expanding the educational facilities, he wished to avoid subversive infiltration. He encouraged the establishment of specialist courses where original thought was less likely to be encouraged. He expanded existing universities and created one new one. He also kept watch over textbooks used and the activities of schoolmasters, professors, and students with the aid of full-time inspectors after 1834.

Riasanovsky, Nicholas V., *Nicholas I and Official Nationality in Russia*, 1959.

UYGURS. People of the Uygur state in E Turkestan in the eighth and ninth centuries. They are Muslims and a Turkic-speaking people, living chiefly in the Sinkiang Province of China, but also forming a national minority in Soviet Central Asia.

UZBEKISTAN. In 1917 the Tashkent Soviet assumed authority, and in the following years established its power, throughout what had been Turkestan. The semiindependent khanates of Khiva and Bokhara were first (1920) transformed into "People's Republics," then (1923–24) into Soviet socialist republics, and finally merged in the Uzbek Soviet Socialist Republic and other republics. The Uzbek Soviet Socialist Republic was formed in 1924 from lands formerly included in Turkestan. The area of the region is 172,819 square miles (447,600 sq km). The capital is Tashkent. There is intensive farming and high cotton production. Population (1981) 16,200,000.

UZBEKS. Turkic-speaking people of Central Asia, numbering about 11 million in 1970. They take their name from Uzbek, a descendant of Genghis Khan, and live in Uzbekistan. Many Uzbeks also live in parts of Kazakhstan, Kirgizia, Tadzhikistan, and Turkmenia.

Wheeler, Geoffrey E., *The Peoples of Soviet Central Asia*, 1966.

V

VACETIS, IOAKIM IOAKIMOVICH (1873–1938). Red Army colonel. He suppressed a revolt in Moscow on July 6 and 7, 1918. On July 10 he was appointed commander of the Eastern Front and commander of the Fifth Army. He was commander in chief of the Red Army from September 4, 1918 to July 8, 1919.

VAGANOVA, AGRIPPINA (1879–1951). Ballerina and teacher. She published *Fundamentals of the Classic Dance* (1934) and was an influential teacher who stressed that technique is grounded in developing bodily strength, balance, and coordination. Her pupils included Natalya Dudinskaya and Galina Ulanova.

VAKHTANGOV, YEVGENY BAGRATIONOVICH (1833–1927). Actor and director. He was a pupil of Konstantin Stanislavsky (*q.v.*). Vakhtangov joined the Moscow Art Theater (*q.v.*) in 1911 as an actor and producer in its First Studio, and in his own Third Studio from 1920. In 1926 the Third Studio was renamed the Vakhtangov Theater. He experimented with the concept of the modern mystery play.

Glenny, Michael, "The Soviet Theatre" in Auty, Robert and Obolensky, Dimitri (eds.), "An Introduction to Russian Language and Literature," *Companion to Russian Studies*, 1977.

Slonim, Marc, *Russian Theatre from the Empire to the Soviets*, 1961.

VALUYEV, COUNT PETER ALEKSANDROVICH (1814–90). Minister of the interior (1861–68) and president of the committee of ministers (1877–81). He helped to establish the *zemstva* (*q.v.*) and was active in planning the Great Reforms (*q.v.*). He produced a constitutional plan in 1863 that would have established a consultative assembly combining elected and appointed ministers. The scheme was not implemented, but was, however, reexamined in 1880.

Starr, S. Fredrick, *Decentralisation and Self-government in Russia, 1830–1870,* 1972.

Yaney, G., *The Systematization of Russian Government,* 1973.

VARANGIANS. An old Russian name given to the Scandinavians, who raided the eastern shores of the Baltic in the ninth century and penetrated into Eastern Europe toward Byzantium along the Dnepr River. The Varangian leader Ryurik (*q.v.*) made Novgorod (*q.v.*) his headquarters in 862, and a number of tribes invited him to rule their territories.

VASILY I, II, AND III, GRAND PRINCES OF MOSCOW. *See* **Basil I, II, and III.**

VASILYEV, FEDOR (1850–73). Painter. Vasilyev adhered to the Realist (*q.v.*) school of artists and was a prominent member of the group of painters known as the Wanderers (*q.v.*).

VASNETSOV, VIKTOR MIKHAILOVICH (1848–1926). Painter. He was a Slavophile (*q.v.*) artist who turned to folklore for most of his painting, using the epics telling of the valor of warriors of the past as inspiration.

VAVILOV, NICHOLAS IVANOVICH (1887–1943). Botanist and chemist. He held many important posts, including that of director of the All-Union Institute of Plant Breeding (1924–40), and enjoyed an international reputation as one of the greatest contributors to the study of botanical populations. Although he had supported some of the experiments of Trofim D. Lysenko (*q.v.*), he opposed many of the latter's more outrageous scientific claims. As a result he was arrested (1940) and died in a concentration camp. After the death of Stalin his reputation was rehabilitated.

VECHE. A village or city assembly sharing decision making with the local prince in medieval Russia. In Novgorod, Pskov, and Vyatka the *veche* acquired total power and determined the domestic and foreign policy of the town, elected the officials, and discharged certain judicial functions.

***VEDOMOSTI* (NEWS).** The first Russian newspaper, published irregularly from 1703. The first edition was edited by Peter the Great (*q.v.*).

VEDRO. Liquid measure equal to 3.25 gallons (12.30 liters). *See* ***Botchka.***

VEDROSHA RIVER, BATTLE OF. Battle in 1500 won by Russia against Lithuanian forces.

***VEKHI* (LANDMARKS).** Political movement exemplified by articles published in 1909 by seven authors, including Peter Struve, Nicholas Berdyaev, Sergey Bulgakov, Semyon Frank, and Michael Gershenzon, which attacked the radical intelligentsia and their mystique of revolution.

VELIKY KNYAZ. A grand prince.

VELIKYE LUKI. City situated in the Pskov oblast of the Russian Soviet

Federated Socialist Republic on the Lovat River. It was founded in 1166 and was governed first by Novgorod, then by Lithuania, and, after 1448, by Moscow. It is an important railway junction and manufactures bricks, electronic equipment, and furniture. Population (1971) 95,000.

VENEDI. Term used by Roman writers when referring to Slavs.

VENETSIANOV, ALEKSEY GAVRILOVICH (1779–1847). Painter. He spent a large part of his life painting scenes of peasant life at his country estate at Safonkovo.

VENEVITINOV, DMITRY VLADIMIROVICH (1805–27). Poet. A friend of Pushkin, he helped to organize the first Russian philosophical society, Lovers of Wisdom (*q.v.*). His poetry belonged to the "golden age" of Russian poetry.

VENGEROV, SEMYON AFANASYEVICH (1855–1920). Literary historian and bibliographer. An Idealist, Vengerov at first supported the populist *Narodnaya Volya* (*q.v.*) movement, but later retracted from this viewpoint. In 1899 he was made minister for education. Dismissed from Petersburg University, Vengerov was not able to return there until after the 1905 Revolution. In his articles on literature he expressed the view that Russian literature has never been divorced from social issues. Vengerov also wrote critical commentaries on Pushkin, Shakespeare, Schiller, Byron, and Molière.

VENIAMINOV, INNOKENTY (1794–1892). Metropolitan in the Russian Orthodox Church who worked in Kamchatka, Alaska, and the Aleutian Islands.

VERESAYEV, VIKENTY VIKENTEVICH (SMIDOVICH) (1867–1946). Writer. A physician by profession, he explored the minds of perplexed intellectuals in many of his novels. His early works included *Without Road* (1895) and *At the Turning Point* (1902). In 1901 he published *A Doctor's Sketches*; other nonfiction includes essays on Dostoeyvsky, Tolstoy, and Pushkin. His two best-known books since the Revolution are *In a Blind Alley* (1922) and *The Sisters* (1933).

VERESHCHAGIN, VASILY VASILYEVICH (1842–1904). Painter. He was totally opposed to war and used his art to paint large canvases of the horrors of conflict. His *Apotheosis of War* was dedicated to all great conquerors, present, past, and future, and depicted a pile of skulls. He died in Petropavlovsk during the Russo-Japanese War.

VERKHOYANSK. Town in Siberia situated 385 miles (616 km) NNE of Yakutsk on the Yana River. Founded in 1638, it was used as a place of exile until 1917. It is one of the coldest places on earth, with a recorded temperature of nearly −100°F. The main occupations are tin mining and fur trapping. Population (1975) 1,400.

VERNADSKY, GEORGE (1887–1973). Scholar who was particularly interested in the early history of Russia. His publications include *Ancient Russia* (1943), *Kievan Russia* (1943), *The Origins of Russia* (1959), and *Russia at the Dawn of the Modern Age* (1959).

VERNADSKY, VLADIMIR IVANOVICH (1863–1945). Geochemist and mineralogist. He was considered a founder of geochemistry. Although he was active in the *zemstvo* (*q.v.*) movement and opposed the Bolsheviks, he returned to his work after the Civil War and was founder of the biogeochemical laboratory of the Academy of Sciences in Leningrad, becoming its director in 1928.

VERST. A linear measure; unit of distance equal to 0.6629 miles, or about 3,500 feet (1.067 km).

VERTOV, DZIGA (KAUFMANN, DENIS ARKADYEVICH) (1896–1954). Film director and pioneer in film documentary, editing, and montage techniques. At first an extreme realist, Vertov strove to portray the raw details of daily life. He founded an extremist school of filmmakers, which in 1922 denounced "artificial art." In the early 1930s Vertov was denounced by the authorities as a "formalist" (*q.v.*). He disappeared during the Great Purge, but was permitted to pursue his career later. His main films include *Anniversary of the Revolution* (1918), *History of the Civil War* (1921), *Kino-Pravda* (1922–25), and *Three Songs of Lenin* (1934).

Leyda, Jay, *Kino: A History of the Russian and Soviet Film*, 1960.

Taylor, R., *The Politics of the Soviet Cinema, 1917–1929*, 1979.

VESELOVSKY, ALEXANDER NIKOLAYEVICH (1838–1906). Literary historian. Having studied at Moscow University, Veselovsky worked abroad before being appointed professor at Moscow University in 1872. He was an expert in Slavic, Byzantine, and West European literature and folklore and theorized on the history of mythology. He is remembered for his erudite work on Pushkin, Zhukov, Dante, and Boccacio and for his works on aesthetics.

VESELY, ARTEM (NICHOLAS IVANOVICH KOCHKUROV) (1899–1939). Novelist. He wrote several novels about the Revolution, including *The Fiery Rivers* (1942). *Land of My Birth* (1926), and *Russia Washed with Blood* (1929–31). His historical novel about Yermak (*q.v.*) a 17th-century adventurer and conqueror of Siberia, *The Sporting Volga,* was published in 1933. He was detained in 1939 in the Great Purge, and nothing has been heard of him since.

VESTNIK EVROPY **(CHRONICLE OF EUROPE).** Russian magazine expressing conservative ideas, founded in Moscow in 1802, and until 1804 edited by Nicholas Karamzin (*q.v.*). Publication ceased in 1830. A different journal of the same name was started up in 1866 under the editorship of Professor M. M. Stacjulevic. It expressed more liberal views. The leading liberals of the day contributed to the second *Vestnik Evropy*, including Ivan Turgenev and Ivan Goncharov (*q.v.*). Publication ceased in 1918.

VIENNA, CONGRESS OF. The assembly (1814–15) that reorganized Europe after the defeat of Napoleon. It was attended by the four countries mainly responsible for the overthrow of Napoleon: Austria, Great Britain, Prussia, and Russia. Although Castlereagh was anxious to oppose Russian expansionism, Russia gained the Duchy of Warsaw, thereafter called the Kingdom of Poland.

VILNIUS. Capital of the Lithuanian Soviet Socialist Republic, founded in 1323. It is an educational center and also a railway center trading in grain. Industries include chemicals, sawmilling, food processing, papermaking and the manufacture of leather and matches. Population (1981) 503,000.

VINIUS, ANDREW (*fl.* early 17th century). Dutchman and director of the first Russian ironworks, which made use of waterpower, established at Tula in 1632.

VINNITSA. Capital of the Vinnitsa region of the Ukraine, situated 125 miles (200 km) SW of Kiev on the S Bug River. Industries include meat packing, flour milling, engineering, and the manufacture of machinery, electrical equipment, and fertilizers. Population (1981) 332,000.

VINOGRADOFF, SIR PAUL GAVRILOVICH (1854–1925). Historian. He was professor of history at Moscow University but resigned in 1902 because of difficulties with the authorities. After 1903 he was professor of jurisprudence at Oxford.

VINOGRADOV, ANATOLY KORNEILEVICH (1888–). Author. In 1930 he wrote *Three Colors at a Time* (trans. 1946), about Stendhal. *The Black Consul* (1931, trans. 1934) took as its theme Toussaint L'Ouverture's rising in Haiti.

VIRGIN LAND CAMPAIGN. In 1953 Khrushchev ordered the reclamation of virgin and waste land in Central Asia. Within three years nearly 90 million acres (36.4 million hectares) had been cultivated in Kazakhstan, Siberia, and the S Urals. The aim was self-sufficiency in cereals. After the initial stage of the campaign, intensive rather than extensive cultivation was practiced. The campaign was interpreted by some as an attempt to russify minor nationalities.

Hahn, W., *The Politics of Soviet Agriculture*, 1972.

VIRTÁ, NICHOLAS (1906–). Novelist and playwright. His first novel, *Solitude* (1935), was dramatized as *The Land* (1937). Other works include *Our Daily Bread* (1947) and *The Conspiracy of the Condemned* (1948).

VISHNEVSKY, VSEVOLOD (1900–51). Novelist and playwright. He was basically a propagandist, and in the screen play *The Unforgettable Year 1919* (1949) he flatters Stalin by the sheer exaggeration of his involvement in the Civil War. His plays included *Trial of the Kronstadt Mutineers* (1921) and *The Optimistic Tragedy* (1932).

VITEBSK. Capital of the Vitebsk region of Belorussia, situated in the W on the W Dvina River. Founded in the 11th century, it passed to Russia in 1772. Manufactures include agricultural machinery, machine tools, textiles, glass, footwear, and furniture. Population (1981) 310,000.

VITEN (VYTENIS) (?–1316). Grand prince of Lithuania (1293–1316). Following a period of internal strife, he managed to unite his people. He was succeeded by his son Gedymin (Gedimines), who reigned from 1316 to 1341 and who finally established the Lithuanian state.

VITIM RIVER. River 1,100 miles long (1,760 km) rising in a small lake E of Lake Baikal in the Buryat Autonomous Soviet Socialist Republic and flowing S, then NE, and then N to enter the Lena River at Vitim. The plateau between the Vitim and Olekma rivers is an important source of gold.

VITOVIT (*fl.* late 14th–early 15th centuries). Grand Prince of Lithuania. During his reign (1392–1430) the Lithuanian territory was greatly extended. In 1410 he successfully led his forces with Polish support against the Teutonic Knights at the Battle of Tannenberg (Grünwald) (*q.v.*). His defeat in 1399 in a battle against the Mongols is disputed by some historians.

VIZE, VLADIMIR YULYEVICH (1888–1954). Geographer and explorer. He was part of the team led by G. Ya. Sedov that attempted to reach the North Pole in 1912–14. He helped organize the North Polar Drift Expedition in 1937, and between 1910 and 1937 he participated in 14 Arctic expeditions.

VKHUTEMAS. Name given in the 1920s to the higher state art technical studios, which provided a meeting place for the exchange of ideas between artists and architects, as well as a place for research.

VLADIMIR. Capital of the Vladimir region of the Russian Soviet Federated Socialist Republic, situated 110 miles (176 km) ENE of Moscow on the Klyazma River. It was founded in the 12th century by Vladimir II of Kiev. The town has many fine works of Russian art of the 12th–19th centuries, including the cathedrals of the Assumption (built 1158–61) and of St. Demetrius (1193–97), both of which house frescoes by Ruslev. The Church of the Intercession at Bogolyubovo is particularly beautiful. Manufactures include tractors, chemicals, textiles, machine tools, and precision instruments. Population (1981) 307,000.

VLADIMIR, SAINT (VLADIMIR I) (*c.* 956–1015). Grand prince of Kiev (980–1015). He was baptized before his marriage to the sister of the Byzantine emperor, Basil II, in Kherson in the Crimea. In *c.* 987 he introduced the Byzantine rite to Kiev and Novgorod. This action marks the end of the Varangian (*q.v.*) period of Russian history. Vladimir ordered that all pagan works of art be destroyed, and pagan motifs only survived when they were incorporated in Christian art.

Obolensky, Dimitri, *The Byzantine*

Commonwealth: Eastern Europe 500–1453, 1971.

VLADIMIR MONOMAKH (1053–1125). Grand prince of Kiev (1113–25). For most of his life he was involved in wars. He is credited with 83 campaigns and the death of 200 Polovtsy princes. His *Testament*, which is a vivid personal and political autobiography, records these battles. It was written for his sons and is the earliest known literature written by a layman. He had great administrative ability and founded the city of Vladimir, which replaced Kiev as the capital towards the end of the 12th century.

VLADIVOSTOK. Capital of the Primorye territory and port in the extreme SE situated on the Pacific coast between Amur Bay and Golden Horn, at the end of the Trans-Siberian Railway. Founded in 1860, it became a naval base after the loss of Port Arthur to Japan in 1905. It is an important transport center and naval base. Industries include shipbuilding, sawmilling, food processing, fish canning, fishing, and whaling. Exports include coal, timber, fish, oil cake, and soybean oil. Population (1981) 565,000.

VLADYKA. Title of an archbishop, bishop, or other high cleric in the Russian Orthodox Church.

VLASOV, ANDREY ANDREYEVICH (1900–46). General and leader of the anticommunist movement among Soviet prisoners of war during the Second World War in Germany. He enlisted in the Red Army in 1919 and played a prominent part in the defense of Kiev and Moscow (1941–42). After capturing him in 1942, German officers persuaded him to assist with the Russian anticommunist movement. He was chairman of the Committee for the Liberation of the Peoples of Russia in 1944. He surrendered to the Americans in 1945 and was returned to the Soviets, who executed him.

VNESHTORGBANK. The Soviet foreign trade bank.

VODKA. Popular drink in Russia. Its name in Russian is a diminutive term meaning "little water." First produced in Russia in the 14th century, vodka was obtained from wheat, maize, sugar beets, rye, or potatoes. Today, potato spirit vodkas are preferred in Russia. Vodka is traditionally filtered through beds of vegetable charcoal and reduced to potable strength with distilled water. Russian vodka is generally 40 percent alcohol by volume (80 proof) and consumed neat in glasses of one ounce capacity.

VODKA MONOPOLY. Monopoly on vodka created by Peter the Great's government.

VOINOVICH, VLADIMIR (1932–). Exiled writer who lives in Paris. After serving in the Soviet army in Poland, Voinovich worked as a carpenter and started to write. In 1963 he published *I Want to be Honest* in *Novy Mir*. In 1966 he signed a letter defending Yu Daniel (*q.v.*) and Andrey Sinyavsky and in 1968 signed one protesting the arrest of Alexander Ginzberg and Yuri Galakovsk. In 1973 Voinovich refused to attack Andrey Sakharov (*q.v.*), although pressure was put on him to do so. In 1974 he was expelled from the Writer's Union and in 1980 went into exile. His satirical novel *The Life and Extraordinary Adventures of Private Ivan Chonkin* has won him much support abroad, as well as in Russia among those who have managed to read it in *samizdat* (*q.v.*).

VOLGA-CASPIAN SEA TRADE ROUTE. A principal waterway in Europe. The Volga rises in the Valday upland NW of Europe and flows S into the Caspian Sea.

VOLGA RIVER. River rising in the Valday hills approximately 200 miles (320 km) NW of Moscow and flowing 2,325 miles (3,720 km) first SE to Rzhev, then NE to Kalinin, through the Rybinsk reservoir, whence it turns SE past Yaroslavl, Kostroma, Kineshma, Gorky, and Cheboksary to Kazan. Below Kazan it receives the Vyatka and Kama rivers and flows S past Ulyanovsk to Kuibyshev, SSW past Saratov and Volgograd, and finally SE to enter the Caspian Sea by a delta below Astrakhan. It is linked by canal with the Don River at Volgograd, and with the Neva River at Moscow. It is the most important Russian river, used for transport, water storage, and power. The Greater Volga development scheme provided channeling, hydroelectric plants, reservoirs, and dams. It is ice-bound for 3–5 months of the year, and prone to spring flooding and shoals in summer. Its middle course is important for irrigation and wheat-growing areas.

VOLGOGRAD (formerly **Tsaritsyin** and **Stalingrad**). Capital of the Volgograd region of the Russian Soviet Federated Socialist Republic and port situated on the Volga River near its junction with the Volga-Don canal. It was founded in 1589 as a base to defend possessions along the Volga. It was twice captured by the Cossacks; first by Stenka Razin (*q.v.*) (1670) and then by Yemelyan Pugachev (*q.v.*) (1774). Industries include oil refining, sawmilling, iron and steelworks, and the manufacture of tractors, oil-field machinery, railway equipment, machine tools, footwear, clothing, and cement. Population (1981) 948,000.

VOLIN, V.M. (1886–1957). After working in the interests of Bolshevik underground literary activities before the 1917 Revolution, Volin was appointed chief censor of the Soviet Union. He subsequently headed the people's commissariat of enlightenment.

VOLKHOV RIVER. River rising in Lake Ilmen in the Russian Soviet Federated Socialist Republic flowing 140 miles (224 km) NE to enter Lake Ladoga. There is an important power station at Volkhov.

VOLKONSKAYA, PRINCESS MARIA NIKOLAYEVNA (1805–63). Wife of the Decembrist Sergey Grigorevich Volkonsky. She accompanied him during his long years of penal servitude in the Nerchinsky mines. Volkonskaya provided the inspiration for Nekrasov's (*q.v.*) poem *Russian Women*.

VOLKONSKY, PRINCE SERGEY GRIGORYEVICH (1788–1865). Decembrist and major-general. Volkonsky fought in the Napoleonic Wars (1806–12) and in the Patriotic War (1812). After the failure of the Decembrists' uprising, Volkonsky was sentenced to death but served 20 years in the Nerchinsky mines. After the amnesty of 1856 he returned home.

VOLKOV, FEDOR GRIGORYEVICH (1729–63). Merchant and actor. In 1751 he founded the first Russian provincial public theater in Yaroslavl on the Volga, and later he was asked to establish a similar theater in St. Petersburg.

Slonim, Marc, *Russian Theatre from the Empire to the Soviets,* 1961.

Varneke, Boris V., *History of the Russian Theatre,* 1951.

VOLOGDA. Capital of the Vologda region of the Russian Soviet Federated Socialist Republic, situated NE of the Rybinsk reservoir on the Vologda River. The merchants of Novgorod founded the city in 1147. It is an industrial and railway center. Industries include railway engineering and the manufacture of agricultural machinery, textiles, glass, and cement. It also trades in dairy produce. Population (1981) 247,000.

VOLOKOLAMSK. Town in the center of the Volokolamsk region of the Moscow oblast, 75 miles (120 km) W of Moscow. Volokolamsk is one of the oldest Russian towns. There are records of settlement there dating from the first half of the 12th century, and it was on an important trading route. Chief industries are now textiles, weaving, and brickmaking.

VOLOSHIN, MAKSIMILIAN ALEKSANDROVICH (1877–1931). Symbolist poet. Born in S Russia, he traveled extensively in Central Asia and around the Mediterranean. He also lived in Paris, studying painting there. Voloshin's poetry reflects the influence that Catholic mysticism, the occult, the Aegean, and ancient Greek culture had on him. He wrote a series of historical poems on the subject of the destiny of Russia, as a result of the Revolution, in which he developed the concept of a "Holy Russia." He felt that a country of Christian mysticism was being oppressed by the state.

West, James, *Russian Symbolism,* 1970.

VOLOST. The smallest administrative division in rural Russia, comprising several villages.

VOLPE, GIOVANNI BATTISTA. *See* **Fryazin, Ivan.**

VOLTAIRE, FRANCOIS MARIE AROUET (1694–1778) French philosopher and writer whose influence extended to Russia. During Elizabeth's reign he was elected an honorary member of the Academy of Sciences, and was commissioned by the government to serve as a historian of Peter the Great. Catherine, desirous of strengthening ties with France, corresponded with Voltaire (1768–78). French ideas, particularly educational theory, came to inform part of Russian life among the upper echelons of society.

VOLYNIA. Area in NW Ukraine consisting of the Rovno Zhitomir and Volynia oblasts. Thus Volynia refers both to the area as a whole, and more specifically to the Volynia oblast. The region belonged to the Kievan state from the ninth century, and later became independent before becoming Lithuanian in the 14th century, then Polish in 1569, and Russian in 1793. It was occupied by the Germans in both world wars.

VONIFATIEV, STEPHEN (*c.* 17th century). Father confessor to the tsar in the 17th century. He campaigned for the setting up of schools and the translation and dissemination of educational works. He summoned together various popular preachers in an attempt to improve public morality. *See* **Old Believers.**

VORONEZH. Capital of the Voronezh region of the Russian Soviet Federated Socialist Republic, situated on the Voronezh River near its confluence with the Don, 300 mi S of Moscow. It was built in 1586 as a fortress on the site of the 11th-century town of Khazar. In 1695 Peter the Great (*q.v.*) established shipbuilding here during the Azov campaign. It is the principal industrial center of the Black Earth (*q.v.*) area. Manufactures include machinery, chemicals, excavators, electrical equipment, machine tools, tires, synthetic rubber, and food products. The poet Osip Mandelstam, in exile here, wrote the *Voronezh Notebooks* (1935–39). Population (1981) 809,000.

VORONIKHIN, ANDREY (1760–1814). Architect and painter. After studying architecture, mechanics, natural sciences, mathematics, and physics in Sweden and Paris, Voronikhin returned to Russia. He designed the Institute of Mines and Kazan Cathedral and generally laid the foundations of the Russian classical style.

Hamilton, George H., *Art and Architecture of Russia*, 1975.

VORONSKY, ALEXANDER KONSTANTINOVICH (1884–1935). Critic and editor of *Krasnaya Nov*, the main journal for fellow-travelers. Voronsky and The Pass group were the targets for official attack in 1927, and Voronskyism became synonymous with nonconformity, since Voronsky was accused of being a Bergsonian, a Freudian, and a Trotskyist. His theory of "shedding the veils" (*snyatiye pokrovov*) involved a rejection of political propaganda in literature. This met with the party's disapproval, although Voronsky was a Marxist. He produced essays, memoirs, and short stories.

VORONTSOV-DASHKOV, ILLARION IVANOVICH (1837–1916). Following the assassination of Alexander II, he was appointed head of the tsar's guards. He was opposed to the growing revolutionary movement. From 1905 to 1915, Vorontsov-Dashkov was governor-general in the Caucasus. Although he planned several moderate reforms, particularly in the sphere of economics, the majority were not implemented.

VORONTSOV, MICHAEL (1714–67). A page at Elizabeth Petrovna's court, he assisted her in the coup d'état which made her empress. In

1744 Vorontsov was appointed vice-chancellor of the empire. After the Seven Years War, he was made imperial chancellor, replacing Aleksey Bestuzhev-Ryumin (*q.v.*). At first refusing to serve under Catherine, he was put under house arrest but swore allegiance to her after learning of Peter's death. He was then reinstated as chancellor, until he resigned in 1763.

VOROSHILOV, KLIMENT EFREMOVICH (1881–1969). Military and political leader, and a close friend of Stalin. He joined the Bolsheviks in 1903, organized the workers of Lugansk in the 1905 Revolution, and was subsequently deported. After returning to Russia in 1917, Voroshilov was a member of the central committee of the Communist Party and entered the Politburo in 1926. Following Stalin's death in 1953, he was appointed chairman of the Presidium of the Supreme Soviet. In 1960, however, he was dropped from the Presidium and in 1961 was expelled from the central committee; he was later restored to full membership.

VOROSHILOVGRAD. Capital of the Voroshilovgrad oblast of the Ukraine, situated on the Lugan River 70 miles (112 km) N of Rostov in the Donets Basin. Founded around a cannon factory in 1796, it has twice been called Lugansk and twice Voroshilovgrad. An important industrial center, it manufactures diesel locomotives, coal-mining equipment, automobile parts, machine tools, steel pipes, and ball bearings. Population (1981) 474,000.

VOROTYNSKY, MICHAEL (*c.* 1510–77). Outstanding general in the Russian army who fought in Ivan IV's (*q.v.*) campaigns. He is particularly noted for his position as chief of the border guards and for strengthening the SE border. Vorotynsky later fell from favor, was arrested in 1577, and committed suicide on his way to exile.

VOSTOKOV, ALEXANDER KHRISTOFOROVICH (OSTENECK) (1781–1864). Philologist and chief librarian of the Rumiantsev Museum in Moscow and a member of the Academy of Sciences. Vostokov's *Discourse on the Slavonic Language* (1820), *Russian Grammar* (1831), and *Description of Russian and Slavonic Manuscripts of the Rumiantsev Museum* (1842) are considered indispensable to the study of Slavonic philology.

VOTCHINA. Hereditary landed property of a noble and also the landed patrimony of princes in medieval Russia.

VOTCHINNIK. The owner of a *votchina.*

VOTKINSK. Town situated 115 miles (184 km) SW of Perm in the Russian Soviet Federated Socialist Republic. Industries include railway engineering, and the manufacture of boilers and agricultural machinery. Tchaikovsky was born here. Population (1970) 74,000.

VOTYAKS. *See* **Udmurts.**

VOVCHOK, MARKO (MARIA ALEKSANDROVNA VILINSKAYA MARKOVICH) (1834–1904). Prominent Ukrainian writer. Her stories *Folk Tales* (1859) and *Stories from Russian Folk Life* (1859) were much acclaimed at the time and depict the tragic life style of the serfs. She also wrote stories for children.

VOYEVODA. A military and administrative leader of medieval Russia. He was usually a member of the nobility. It was also the name of the tsar's appointed official in a city or a district.

VOYEVODSTVO. An administrative unit in medieval Russia, presided over by a *voyevoda.*

VOZNESENSKY, ANDREY A. (1933–). Poet. After studying architecture Voznesensky embarked on a full-time career as poet. His first work was published in 1958, and he has traveled abroad on reading tours, which have included several visits to the United States. He has enjoyed the approval of the regime apart from a short time in 1963. His first book, *Mosaica* (1960), consists mostly of lyrical poems; later collections of his work, such as *The Triangular Pear* (1962) show greater subtlety and irony.

VOZNESENSKY, NICHOLAS ALEKSEYEVICH (1903–50). Communist. Having joined the party in 1919, Voznesensky studied at Sverdlov Communist University and at the Economic Institute of Red Professorship, and in 1934 he was appointed a member of the committee of party control. From 1935 he worked with Andrey Zhdanov (*q.v.*) in Leningrad and rose to the posts of chairman of Gosplan (1938), deputy prime minister (1939), and a member of the state defense committee during the Second World War. In 1947, Voznesensky was made a full member of the Politburo. As a result of Georgy Malenkov's (*q.v.*) persecution of Zhdanovites, he was arrested and shot.

VPERYOD (FORWARD). A radical Bolshevik faction founded in 1909 by Bogdanov, Anatoly Lunacharsky and Maxim Gorky (*q.q.v.*).

VRUBEL, MICHAEL ALEKSANDROVICH (1856–1910). Painter. He was a fine draftsman whose work prepared the way for Cubism in Russia.

Kaplanova Sofia G., *Vrubel,* 1975.

VYATICHI. A Slavic tribe who were defeated by Svyatoslav *c.* 964 and who became subjects of Kiev; before this they had paid tribute to the Khazars.

VYATKA. *See* **Kirov.**

VYAZEMSKY, PRINCE PETER ANDREYEVICH (1792–1878). Poet. He belonged to the Pushkin circle and his poetry was classical in form and romantic in content. He wrote much criticism and some essays on Nicholas Gogol, Ivan Krylov and Vladislav Ozerov (*q.q.v.*), and his correspondence has great literary value.

Auty, Robert and Obolensky, Dimitri (eds.), "An Introduction to Russian Language and Literature," *Companion to Russian Studies,* Vol. 2,

1977.

Fennell, John L. I. (ed.), *Nineteenth-Century Russian Literature*, 1973.

VYBORG. Port situated on Vyborg Bay 70 miles (112 km) NW of Leningrad in the Russian Soviet Federated Socialist Republic. Vyborg developed round a Swedish castle built in 1293 and later became a Hanseatic port. It was seized by Russia in 1710, passed to Finland in 1812, and became part of the USSR under the Finnish-Soviet peace treaty of 1947. Manufactures include agricultural machinery and electrical equipment. Timber and wood products are exported. Population (1973) 68,000.

VYBORG MANIFESTO. About 180 deputies met in Vyborg to protest the dissolution of the first duma by Nicholas II (*q.v.*) in July 1906. The largest majority were Kadets (*see* **Constitutional Democratic Party [Kadets]**) and the manifesto urged the people not to pay taxes or undertake military service when conscripted. The plan failed and the deputies were arrested, given three months' imprisonment and, probably more important for Russia, deprived of their right to stand for election to the second duma.

Hosking, Geoffrey A., *The Constitutional Experiment*, 1973.

VYSHINSKY, ANDREY YANUARYEVICH (1883–1954). Lawyer and politician. He became public prosecutor (1931) and was soon notorious for the rancor and vindictiveness with which he conducted state trials, notably in the Metropolitan-Vickers trial (1933) and the purges of 1936–37. After 1940 he became active in foreign affairs and was Molotov's successor as foreign minister (1949–53), having been deputy minister (1940–49). As a delegate to the United Nations Organization he often attacked Western policies with the same venom that he had shown in the Soviet courts.

VYSOTSKY, VLADIMIR (1938–80). Popular actor in the Taganka Theater and writer of humorous songs, many of which are circulated clandestinely, although others have been released as records in the Soviet Union.

VYT. Medieval unit of tax assessment and also an old measure of tillable land.

VYVOZ. "Exportation" of peasants by landlords.

W

WAGNER, NICHOLAS PETROVICH (1829–1907). Writer of fairy tales and professor of zoology at St. Petersburg University. His writings are unusual in that he is the only author of his day who did not adhere strictly to the rules of the "natural" school of writing. His most delightful children's book is *Tales of the Purring Cat* (1872).

WALACHIA. A vassal state of the Ottoman Empire. In 1859 Walachia, together with Moldavia, became part of Rumania. Separated from Moldavia by the Seret River, Walachia was divided into Greater Walachia and Lesser Walachia.

WANDERERS, THE (*PEREDVIZHNIKI*). The Wanderers, Peripatetics or Itinerants were 13 artists who opposed the accepted academic standards in the 19th century. They wished to bring art to the people by showing realistic paintings in traveling exhibitions, and believed that art should have the purpose of encouraging social reforms. They also opposed those who wished Russia to develop along W European lines. They were encouraged by the Moscow patron and collector, P.M. Tretyakov (1832–98). The Wanderers' leader was Ivan Kramskoy (1837–87) (*q.v.*).

WAR COMMUNISM. Name given to the Bolshevik government's social and economic policies of 1918–21. In order to support the Bolsheviks in the Civil War fully, and to build communism in general, War Communism was characterized by the nationalization of industry and trade, wages in kind for workers and enforced labor service. These measures were unpopular, and in 1921 there occurred several uprisings. War Communism was replaced by the New Economic Policy (*q.v.*) in 1921.

Carr, Edward Hallett, *The Russian Revolution: From Lenin to Stalin*, 1979.

WARSAW PACT, THE. The Warsaw Treaty of Friendship, Co-operation, and Mutual Assistance was established in May 1955. Its members are Bulgaria, Czechoslovakia, East Germany, Hungary, Poland, Rumania, and the USSR; Albania withdrew its membership in 1968. It was prompted by the inclusion of West Germany in the Western Alliance. In theory, the Warsaw Pact was to provide resources of men and money to be used for defense purposes; in practice, the available forces are controlled by the USSR, which benefits from it, since it provides a buffer zone between E and W and reduces Soviet military expenditure. Its close work with Comecon has encouraged the rapid growth of arms factories in E Europe. The organization prevents any one non-Soviet army from becoming too powerful. No E European officer can command national forces without Soviet approval. Many E European officers are trained at the Frunze Military Academy in the Soviet Union.

Fetjö, F., *A History of the Peoples' Democracies*, 1974.

Hanak, H., *Soviet Foreign Policy since the Death of Stalin*, 1972.

WESTERN INFLUENCES. The Renaissance, Reformation, and Counter-Reformation made very little impression on Muscovy, and during that period the Orthodox Church was well able to dominate intellectual life. Peter the Great (*q.v.*), hailed as the first Westernizer, strove to open up his country to Western influences, and profit from foreign technological skills. He established St. Petersburg, the "Window on the West." Under Catherine II (*q.v.*), Voltaire and Blackstone were widely read by the educated, especially by those who traveled abroad. Hegel and Schiller were also popular in the early 19th century. The Westernizers (*q.v.*) strove to expose Russia to Western influences, in order to develop along Western lines. In the 20th century, the West is, in official eyes, synonymous with the United States, decadence, poverty, and exploitation. Symbols of Western culture, however, such as pop records and blue jeans remain highly sought after, as is Western technology.

Billington, James H., *The Icon and the Axe*, 1966.

Kochan, L., *The Making of Modern Russia*, 1962.

WESTERNIZERS. Name given to those intellectuals who felt that the future of Russia lay with the West and that Russian society should be organized along Western lines. Westernizers believed that the absence of Catholicism, and hence the Renaissance, was the root of Russia's backwardness. Westernizers tended to believe in the universality of human culture, the highest expression of which was to be found in Germany, and tended to be liberals and atheists, influenced by Hegel. Leading Westernizers include the liberal, Timofei Granovsky (*q.v.*), although he later became a Slavophile, and Vissarion Belinsky and Alexander Herzen. A fierce debate raged between the Westernizers and the Slavophiles, which intensified in the 1840s. The Westernizers admired Peter the Great (*q.v.*) as the first Westernizer and Belinksy in particular praised him highly, but the Slavophiles believed that Russia should be left to develop along its own unique lines.

Berlin, Isaiah, *Russian Thinkers*, 1978.

Carr, Edward Hallett, *The Romantic Exiles: A 19th Century Portrait Gallery*, 1949.

Herzen, Alexander, *My Past and Thoughts*, 5 vols., 1924–26.

WESTERN PROVINCES. The provinces of the Ukraine, Belorussia, Moldavia, Lithuania, Latvia, and Estonia.

WHISTLER, MAJOR (GEORGE WASHINGTON) (1800–49). American engineer invited to Russia as a consultant. He assisted in the completion of the important St. Petersburg-Moscow railway. As Whistler advocated the use of a five-foot gauge, the Russian railway gauge was made three and one-half inches wider than European gauges.

Westwood, John N., *Endurance and Endeavour: Russian History 1812–1971*, 1973.

WHITE ARMY. During the Civil War (1917–22) the anti-Bolshevik forces were known as the White Army. *See* **Whites.**

WHITE RUSSIA. *See* **Belorussia.**

WHITE RUSSIANS. *See* **Belorussians.**

WHITES. Name given to the anti-Bolshevik forces at the time of the Civil War. The majority of Whites were Social Revolutionaries, right-wing Social Democrats who disagreed with the official Menshevik party, and other right elements. The White Army was first formed in an area of Don Cossacks and was led by General Lavr Kornilov and the former tsarist chief of staff, Anton Denikin (*q.q.v.*). In 1919 General Nicholas Yudenich (*q.v.*), advised by the British, marched from Estonia to take Petrograd. This was unsuccessful, and once back in Estonia, his forces disintegrated. As a result, Denikin withdrew and handed over his position to General Peter Wrangel (*q.v.*). Wrangel was defeated, and his forces evacuated from the S of Russia in 1920. By 1922 the Reds had taken Vladivostok, the last stronghold of the Whites. The Whites were unsuccessful because they lacked leadership of the caliber mustered by the Reds, a common sense of purpose, and an inability to generate peasant support.

Footman, David, *Civil War in Russia*, 1961.

Luckett, Richard, *The White Generals: An Account of the White Movement and the Russian Civil War*, 1971.

Stewart, George, *The White Armies of Russia*, 1933.

WHITE SEA. A gulf of the Barents Sea, the entrance to which lies between the peninsulas of Kola and Kanin. It has an area of 36,680 square miles (95,110 sq km). The principal port is Arkhangelsk. The Onega, N Dvina, and Mezen rivers discharge into it. Herring and cod fishing and sealing occur in the N.

WIELOPOLSKI, MARQUIS ALEXANDER (1803–77). Polish aristocrat who was put in charge of the civilian administration of Poland by Alexander II, when Poland was under Russian rule. Although he obtained the emancipation of Polish Jews and established the Main School, he pleased neither the Red nor the White Polish factions, who wished above all to restore the frontiers of 1772. In 1863 he introduced conscription, and this prompted a slaughtering of Russian soldiers which was the beginning of the Polish Insurrection (*q.v.*).

WINDOW ON THE WEST. Name given to the city of St. Petersburg, founded in 1703 by Peter the Great, on territory captured from Sweden. Owing to its geographical location, the city, fortress, and shipyard served as the much longed-for window on the West. As a result, Russia was opened up to some Western influences, and technological progress was facilitated. Later the Slavophiles were to claim that Peter had directed Russia away from its natural course and had tried to force it into an alien mold.

Sumner, Benedict H., *Peter the Great and the Emergence of Russia*, 1951.

WINTER PALACE. Palace built in St. Petersburg by Bartolommeo Rastrelli (*q.v.*) in the mid-18th century on the left bank of the Great Neva. It is built in the Russian baroque style. Partially destroyed by fire, it was rebuilt by Kleinmikhel in the first half of the 19th century. It and several adjoining buildings now house the Hermitage Museum of Art.

Kennett, Victor and Andrey, *The Palaces of Leningrad*, 1973.

WIPPER, ROBERT YURYEVICH (1859–?). Historian. He came to public attention with the publication of *The Church and State in 16th Century Geneva at the Time of Calvinism* (1894). His work *The Origin of Christianity* (1918) met with harsh criticism from Lenin. In 1924 Wipper left the Soviet Union and settled in Latvia but he returned to Moscow when Soviet power was established in Latvia.

WITTE, COUNT SERGEY YULYEVICH (1849–1915). Statesman. In 1892 Witte was appointed minister of transport and from 1892 to 1903 was minister of finance. He encouraged industrial growth in Russia by protectionist tariffs, large foreign loans, and the large-scale building of railways. From 1903 to 1906 Witte was prime minister. He was in charge of negotiating the peace treaty with Japan at Portsmouth, New Hampshire. As a moderate convervative, Witte was attacked by both liberals and the extreme right. After his dismissal by the tsar, he continued as an independent member of the council of state.

von Laue, Theodore H., *Sergei Witte and the Industrialization of Russia*, 1963.

WITTRAM, REINHARD (1902–). German historian and professor at Riga University (1941–45) and Göttingen University (1946–54). A specialist in the Baltic Germans, Wittram has also written on Russian subjects such as *Three Generations, Germany, Livonia, and Russia 1830–1914* (1949) and *Peter the Great* (1954).

WLADYSLAW, PRINCE OF POLAND (1595–1648). Son of King Sigismund III of Poland. During the winter of 1610–11, when Moscow was occupied by the Poles, Wladyslaw was proposed as the new tsar of Russia, and accordingly, at 14 years of age, was brought to Russia and adopted the Orthodox faith. Sigismund secretly hoped to be able to take Muscovy, and made preparations to take the throne. Wladyslaw refused to renounce his claims to the throne even when Michael Romanov was elected tsar by the boyars in 1613.

WORKERS' OPPOSITION. Opposition, mainly from trade unionists within the Bolshevik party, which in 1920 criticized the bureaucratic control of industry by the government and the central party organs and advocated the establishment of an All-Russian Congress of Producers to run the country's economy. At the 10th party congress (1921) the opposition was condemned and a resolution was carried forbidding "factionalism." The Workers' Opposition was alleged to have continued during the following year. Most of the Workers' Opposition leaders were expelled from the party, and all the known leaders, except Alexandra Kollontay (*q.v.*), disappeared during the Great Purge.

WORLD OF ART, THE. In 1870 Savva Marmantov, a businessman, established an artists' colony at Abramtsevo near Moscow. The setup was similar to that of William Morris. The World of Art group was devoted to art for art's sake, in contrast with the social aims of the Wanderers (*q.v.*). In 1904 Diaghilev founded a magazine called *The World of Art,* which became the organ of the group. Leon Bakst was probably the colony's best known member.

Spencer, Charles, *The World of Serge Diaghilev,* 1974.

WORLD WAR I (1914–18). War broke out in July 1914 between Austria and Serbia. The Russians stepped in since they were bound by treaty to fight if Germany were to attack France. The Russian government hoped that a war would unite the Russian people in a common purpose. Patriotism and enthusiasm, as well as support for the tsar, Nicholas II (*q.v.*), waned when Russia sustained great losses in fighting with Germany, and when the western provinces were lost. Communications broke down, and there were widespread shortages of food and ammunition. To make matters worse, the tsar dismissed the assembly and took personal charge of the war, leaving internal government in the incapable hands of Tsaritsa Alexandra and Rasputin the monk (*q.v.*). The February Revolution (1917) was the outcome of widespread misery and bitterness, and Nicholas II abdicated. In the spring of 1918 the Bolsheviks made peace with the Germans at Brest-Litovsk, at which Russia accepted Germany's harsh demands. Great Britain and France, alarmed at losing their ally and fearing that the Germans might discover large consignments of arms sent to Russia, themselves marched into Russia, together with the Americans and Japanese.

Florinsky, Michael, T., *Russia: A History and an Interpretation,* 2 vols., 1953.

Katkov, George (ed). *Russia Enters the Twentieth Century, 1894–1917,* 1971.

Riasanovsky, Nicholas V., *A History of Russia,* 3rd ed., 1977.

WORLD WAR II. In order to concentrate Hitler's attentions on the West, in 1939 Stalin secretly arranged with Hitler to allow German armies to enter Poland. Following the invasion Great Britain and France declared war but Russia remained neutral and secured E Poland and the Baltic states. Russia then attacked Finland. In 1941 Hitler ordered the invasion of Russia, which began on June 22. The Nazis advanced eastward, overpowering Russian resistance with great barbarity and violence. By the summer of 1941 Leningrad was besieged and defeat seemed imminent, but the Russians put up determined resistance and stymied the Germans. The bitter winter of 1941–42 killed thousands of German soldiers, while in the East the Red Army prepared to counterattack. In the spring the German advance began for a second time, and in September they reached Stalingrad, the scene of an extremely fierce battle. In November the Red Army launched a counterattack, surrounded the Germans, and forced them to surrender in February 1943. The Russians then began driving westward. The following year, the British and Americans landed in France, and the Germans, attacked from E and W, were defeated. In 1945, Stalin, Churchill, and Roosevelt met at Yalta (*q.v.*) to discuss the surrender and occupation of Germany, the war against Japan, and the future establishment of the United Nations.

Shulman, M. D., *Stalin's Foreign Policy Reappraised,* 1963.

WRANGEL, BARON PETER NIKOLAYEVICH (1878–1928). General. Following service in the Russo-Japanese War and the First World War, he joined the anti-Bolshevik forces of General Anton Denikin (*q.v.*). After Denikin's defeat in November 1919 he was left in command of the disorganized White army. He advanced against the Bolsheviks but was forced to retreat and the remnants of his troops were evacuated to Turkey from Sevastopol in 1920. He spent the rest of his life in Belgium.

Footman, David, *Civil War in Russia,* 1961.

WRANGEL ISLAND. Island situated about 80 miles (128 km) from the coast of NE Siberia. It has an area of 1,800 square miles (4,662 sq km). The terrain is mainly tundra.

WRITERS, UNION OF SOVIET. *See* **Union of Soviet Writers.**

Y

YABLONOVY MOUNTAINS. Range in E Siberia running NE and SW for about 700 miles (1,120 km) at an average height of 5,000 feet (1,524 m), E of Lake Baikal, dividing the basins of the Lena and Amur rivers and forming part of the watershed of rivers flowing to the Arctic and Pacific oceans. The highest peak is Sokhondo at 8,200 feet (2,499 m). The watershed is continued in the NE by the Stanovoy Mountains.

YADRINTSEV, NICHOLAS MIKHAILOVICH (1842–94). Ethnographer and historian. His *Siberia as a Colony* (1882) was the first study of Siberian regionalism. He also founded and edited an influential newspaper, the *Eastern Review.* In 1889 he discovered the location of Genghis Khan's capital, Karakorum, and the Orkhon River Inscriptions, where are Turkic and Chinese writings dating from the 8th century.

YAGODA, GENRIKH GRIGOREVICH (1891–1938). Soviet political official. He became deputy chairman of the GPU in 1924 and chief of the security police (*q.v.*) in 1934. He was responsible for the first purge. In 1936 he was dismissed, having been accused of slackness by Stalin. He was a defendant at the show trial of the "Anti-Soviet bloc of Rightists and Trotskiyites" and in 1937 was executed.

Conquest, Robert, *The Great Terror,* 1971.

Mandelstam, Nadezhda, *Hope Against Hope,* 1971.

YAGUZHINSKY, PAUL. One of the assistants to Peter the Great (*q.v.*). Said to have been a swineherd in Lithuania originally, he was one of the able men taken by the tsar from the lower classes when he found the nobility hostile to reform. Yaguzhinsky became the first procurator-general of the senate.

YAKUBOVICH, PETER FILIPPOVICH (1860–1911). Radical poet, member of the revolutionary terrorist group People's Will (*q.v.*). He served an eight-year term of hard labor in Siberia from 1887 to 1895; his stories *Mir otverzhennykh (The World of the Outcasts)*, written under the pen name of L. Melshin, describe this experience.

YAKUT AUTONOMOUS SOVIET SOCIALIST REPUBLIC (YAKUTIA). Part of Russian Soviet Federated Socialist Republic that was constituted an autonomous republic in 1922. It has an area of 1,197,760 square miles (3,102,198 sq km). The capital is Yakutsk. Chief industries are mining, including gold, tin, mica, and coal, and livestock breeding; there is also trapping and breeding of fur-bearing animals. Population (1981) 883,000.

YAKUTS. The most numerous of the N peoples of Russia, inhabiting the Lena basin and the neighboring area of E Siberia. They number over 250,000 and are Turkic speaking. They are mainly breeders of livestock. The Yakuts have been known since the 14th century and have been subject to Russia since the 17th century.

YAKUTSK. Capital of the Yakut Republic situated near the Lena River. The mean temperature in January is −46°F. (−43°C). Founded in 1632, it is a commercial center trading in furs, ivory, and hides. Industries are sawmilling, tanning, brick making, and food production. Population (1979) 149,000.

YALTA. Ukrainian town situated 32 miles (51 km) ESE of Sevastopol on the coast. Built on the site of an ancient Greek colony, it is the center of the Crimean health resort area. Industries are fish canning and wine making. The historic conference between Churchill, Roosevelt, and Stalin took place at Yalta in February 1945. There is an important Chekhov museum. Population (1970) 62,000.

YALTA CONFERENCE. Conference between President Roosevelt, Prime Minister Winston Churchill, and Premier Joseph Stalin held at Yalta on February 4-11, 1945 to plan the final defeat and subsequent occupation of Nazi Germany. The Allied agreement that only unconditional surrender was acceptable was reaffirmed, and a four-power occupation of Germany was planned. A promise that the USSR would declare war against Japan was obtained. The USSR also agreed to join in the establishment of the United Nations.

Feis, Herbert, *Churchill, Roosevelt, Stalin*, 1957.

YAMAL-NENETS NATIONAL AREA. Situated in Tyumen region, in Siberia, between the Gulf of Ob and the Kara Sea, and including the Yamal peninsula. It has an area of 259,000 square miles (670,810 sq km). The capital is Salekhard. The chief occupations are fishing, fur trapping, and reindeer breeding.

YAN, V. (1874–1954). Pseudonym of the popular novelist Vasily Yanchevetsky, who wrote a trilogy (completed 1945) on the Mongol invasions:

Genghis Khan, Batu Khan, and *Alexander Nevsky.*

YANA RIVER. River rising in the Yerkhoyansk range in Yakut and flowing 750 miles (1,200 km) N to the Laptev Sea.

YANKOVICH DE MIRIEVO, THEODORE (*c.* 1740–1814). Serbian educator brought to Russia by Catherine the Great (*q.v.*) in 1782. Catherine admired the educational system that the Austrian empire had instituted in 1774. She formed a commission for the establishment of popular schools to carry out plans recommended by Yankovich de Mirievo; he devised a three-tier school system, laid down an educational program, and supervised the training of teachers. He also translated a number of Austrian textbooks into Russian.

YARLYK. Word for a privilege-granting edict of the khans of the Golden Horde. In modern times it is a term meaning trademark or customs stamp.

YAROPOLK, GRAND PRINCE (?–1139). Ruler of the Kievan state. Son of Vladimir Monomakh, Yaropolk succeeded his elder brother Mstislav (ruled 1125–32) and reigned until his death in 1139.

Vernadsky, G. V., *Kievan Russia,* 1948.

YAROPOLK SVYATOSLAVICH (*fl.* late 10th century). Brother of Vladimir, who was ruler of the Kievan state from about 980. His sympathetic interest in Christianity led to its considerable spread in Russia.

Vernadsky, George V., *Kievan Russia,* 1948.

YAROSLAV I VLADIMIROVICH, THE WISE (1019–54). Grand prince of Kiev. He was considered the consolidator of the Kievan state. He promoted Christianity and was the builder of many churches, including the Cathedral of St. Sophia in Kiev. He gained the throne by defeating his brother Svyatopolk in the Civil War, regained Galicia which Svyatopolk had ceded to the Poles, and suppressed the aggressive Pecheneg (*q.v.*) nomads (1037) to the S. He developed trading, diplomatic, and dynastic links with W Europe.

Vernadsky, George V., *Kievan Russia,* 1948.

YAROSLAV OSMOMYSL (?–1187). One of the most able and famous of the princes of Galicia, a principality which became more important as Kiev declined. Osmomysl is said to mean eight-minded, i.e., exceptionally wise.

YAROSLAV OF TVER (*c.* 13th century). Grand prince, brother of Alexander Nevsky and Basil of Kostroma.

YAROSLAVL. Capital of the region of same name in the Russian Soviet Federated Socialist Republic, at the confluence of the Volga and Kotorosl rivers. It is an important railway junction for four lines and was Moscow's Volga port until the opening of the Moscow canal in 1937. Known since 1071, it began to develop its industry with the establishment of shipyards in 1564. It is an industrial center with large engineering, textile, chemical, and rubber plants. Population (1981) 608,000.

YAROSLAVL, GRAND PRINCE OF. Title of the ruler of the city of Yaroslavl and its surrounding area, which together made up an independent principality from 1218 to 1463.

YAROSLAVSKY, YEMELYAN MIKHAILOVICH (MINEY IZRAILEVICH GUBELMAN) (1878–1943). Jewish politician active in the Social Democratic Labor Party (*q.v.*) from 1898, for which he was imprisoned and exiled. As a supporter of Lenin he was involved in the Bolshevik Revolution 1917, but in 1918 he became critical of Lenin's policies and joined the Left Communists. He became a supporter of Stalin and the official historian of the Communist Party in Russia and was instrumental in falsifying the history of the party. He was also a militant atheist. He wrote *Twenty-five Years of Soviet Power,* which was published in 1943.

YASNAYA POLYANA. Village situated 7 miles (11 km) S of Tula, in the Russian Soviet Federated Socialist Republic. It is the birthplace and home of Lev Tolstoy (*q.v.*), who is buried there. His house is now a museum.

YASSAK. Tax in furs paid by non-Orthodox subjects of the tsar.

YAVORSKY, STEFAN (1658–1722). Orthodox Russian churchman and writer. He was acting patriarch from 1700 and later president of the Holy Synod. He wrote a number of important theological works, including *The Rock of Faith* (*c.* 1713), an account of fundamental Orthodox doctrine.

YAYLA MOUNTAINS. Range in the S Crimea, rising to 4,986 feet (1,520 m) and well forested. Otherwise called the Crimean Mountains, the range runs parallel with the S Crimean coast, sheltering its resorts from N winds.

YAZYKOV, NICHOLAS MIKHAILOVICH (1803–46). Writer of lyric verse in the style of Pushkin, whom he knew and admired. He was a member of the group called the Pushkin Pleiad. Many of his verses have become popular songs.

YEFIMOV, MICHAEL NIKIFOROVICH (1881–1920). Pilot. In 1910 he won first prize in aviation competitions at Nice and at St. Petersburg and was appointed the first Russian pilot instructor of military aviation. In 1920 he was shot by White Guards in Sevastopol.

YEFREMOV, OLEG (1927–). Director of the *Sovremennik* (Contemporary) Theater in Moscow. One of his best-known productions is the 1965 production of Aksyonov's avant-garde play *Your Murder.*

YEKATERINBURG. *See* **Sverdlovsk.**

YELENA IVANOVNA (*fl.* late 15th century). Eldest daughter of Ivan III. In 1495, with great ceremony, she married the grand prince of Lithuania, Alexander. It was hoped that the union would improve relations between the two countries, but instead relations deteriorated.

YELENA VASILYEVNA GLINSKAYA (?–1538). The second wife of Basil III and mother of Ivan the Terrible. After Basil's death Yelena ruled Russia with the help of her uncle, Michael Glinsky, and her lover Prince Obolensky. She grew steadily less popular after she had Glinsky imprisoned and had a number of rivals to the throne killed or imprisoned. She died of poisoning in 1538.

YELISEYEV, ALEXANDER VASILYEVICH (1858–95). Explorer and anthropologist. He traveled extensively around Sweden, Norway, Finland, Egypt, Arabia, Tunisia, Algiers, the Sudan, and Ethiopia. His writings were a valuable source of information on geographical, anthropological, and ethnographical subjects.

YENAKIEVO. Ukrainian town situated immediately SE of Gorlovka in the Donbas industrial area, on the oil pipeline from the Caucasus to Gorlovka. It was founded in 1883 with the discovery of coal. Population (1970) 92,000.

YENIKALE. Tatar name for the Kerch strait, which connects the Sea of Azov with the Black Sea, separating the Taman peninsula, in the Russian Soviet Federated Socialist Republic, from the Kerch peninsula, in the Crimea.

YENISEY RIVER. River rising in the Sayan mountains of Siberia, in two headstreams that unite at Kyzyl. It flows for 2,364 miles (3,782 km) N to enter the Kara Sea at Yenisey Bay. The main tributaries are the Angara, Stony Tunguska, and Lower Tunguska rivers. Navigable throughout most of its length, despite being frozen for a considerable part of the year, it is one of the longest rivers in the world.

YEREVAN. Formerly Erivan, capital of Armenia, it is situated on the Zonga River 110 miles (177 km) S of Tbilisi. One of the world's most ancient cities, it was established in the eighth century B.C. It was taken by Russia in 1827 but was the capital of independent Armenia from 1918 to 1920. It is an important industrial center producing chemicals, synthetic rubber, electrical equipment, machinery, textiles, and plastics. It is famous for its brandy. There are many old Turkish and Persian buildings in the city. Population (1981) 1,050,000.

YERMAK TIMOFEYEVICH (?–1584). Cossack headman. The merchant family of the Stroganovs (*q.v.*) enlisted Yermak to defend their possessions and, in 1581, commanding 840 Cossacks and soldiers, he invaded the Siberian Khanate and conquered its capital, Kashlyk. This led the way to the annexation of W Siberia by Muscovy.

YERMOLOV, GENERAL ALEXEY PETROVICH (1772–1861). Commander of the Russian forces in the Napoleonic wars and commander of the Caucasian corps from 1816 to 1827.

YEROPKIN, PETER MIKHAILOVICH (1690–1740). Architect and town planner. He was sent to Italy by Peter the Great (*q.v.*) to study architecture. Appointed a member of the committee for the building of St. Petersburg in 1737, Yeropkin played a leading role in the planning of the city and in particular designed the Admiraltyeska part of St. Petersburg. Under his leadership, the first Russian treatise on architecture was produced. A loyal patriot, he was a member of A. P. Volynsky's group, for which he was arrested and executed in 1740.

YERSHOV, PETER PAVLOVICH (1815–69). Poet. Born in Siberia, Yershov was educated at St. Petersburg University, after which he worked as head of the Tobolsky Gymnasium (school). His narrative verse *Konek Gorbunek* was published in 1834, and was warmly received. He also wrote short stories, among them *Autumn Evenings*. Satirical, humorous, and sometimes coarse, Yershov's work is similar in style to folktales.

YEVREYNOV, NICHOLAS NIKOLAYEVICH (1879–1953). Playwright, director, and producer who specialized in spectacle. He rejected the Stanislavsky (*q.v.*) method and adopted a nonrealistic formal theater, which he said satisfied a fundamental human instinct. He left Russia in 1920.

YEVTUSHENKO, YEVGENY ALEKSANDROVICH (1933–). Poet. A descendant of Ukrainian exiles in Siberia, he attracted attention with the publication of his first important long poem, *Zima Junction* (trans. 1962). He became a spokesman for the post-Stalin generation of poets. He fell into disfavor but in 1965, after the publication of *Bratsk Station*, his privileges were restored. In 1979 he published *Ivan the Terrible and Ivan the Fool*, an allegory of Russian history.

Yevtushenko, Yevgeny, *A Precocious Autobiography*, 1963.

YEZHOV, NICHOLAS IVANOVICH (1895–1939?). Party official. He joined the Communist Party after the Revolution but was not well known until 1934, when he became a member of the central committee. He was appointed chairman of the commission of party control and from 1936 to 1938 was chief of security police (NKVD), directing the Great Purge (*Yezhovshchina*). He was succeeded by Lavrenty Beria in 1938 and disappeared in 1939.

Conquest, Robert, *The Great Terror*, 1971.

Mandelstam, Nadezhda, *Hope Against Hope*, 1971.

YIDDISH. Language widespread among Jews of the USSR and E Europe. Originally a mixture of German dialects, it developed as an individual language *c.* 1100 and spread with Jewish migration. It is written in the Hebrew alphabet.

Herzog, I. M., et al. (eds.), *The Field of Yiddish*, 1969.

YOSHKAR-OLA. Town situated 80 miles (128 km) NW of Kazan, in the Mari Autonomous Soviet Socialist Republic. Founded in 1578, it is the capital of the republic. The main industries are wood and food processing. Population (1981) 213,000.

YOUNG GUARD (*MOLODAYA GVARDIYA*). Organization of about 100 Komsomol members that existed from September to December 1942 in Krasnodon, Ukraine. The group showed much heroism against the occupying Germans but was betrayed by an informer; most of its members were arrested, tortured, and murdered. The novelist Alexander A. Fadeyev (*q.v.*) describes the group in *The Young Guard* (1946, rev. 1951).

YUDENICH, NICHOLAS NIKOLAYEVICH (1862–1933). General commanding a Russian force in the war against Japan (1905) and during the First World War. In 1919 he led a White Russian army (based on the Baltic) against Petrograd but was defeated and driven back. He died in exile. *See* **Whites.**

Footman, David, *Civil War in Russia*, 1961.

YUON, KONSTANTIN (1875–1958). Painter. A pupil of Mstislav Dobrzhinsky, he was later a member of the World of Art Society (*q.v.*). One of his best-known paintings is *A Sunny Spring Day*, executed in a neoclassical style. Yuon was first chairman of the Union of Soviet Artists.

Gray, Camilla, *The Russian Experiment in Art*, 1962.

Talbot Rice, Tamara, *Russian Art*, 1949.

YUREVSKAYA, PRINCESS. *See* **Dolgorukaya, Princess Catherine.**

YUROVSKY, YANKEL (*fl.* early 20th century). Grand commander and regional commissar for justice, who, on behalf of the local Soviet, it is claimed, shot Nicholas II (*q.v.*) and his family in Yekaterinburg.

Summers, A. and Mangold, T., *The File on the Tsar*, 1976.

YURY, PRINCE (?–1434). Claimant to the principality of Moscow after the death of his brother Basil I in 1425. Basil's son was just 10 years old, Yury claimed seniority and had the support of a section of the feudal nobility. After his death his claim was unsuccessfully upheld by his sons, Basil the Squint-Eyed and Dmitry Shemyaka. The war of succession ended in 1450.

Vernadsky, George V., *The Tsardom of Muscovy*, 1969.

YURY, PRINCE OF DIMITROV (*fl.* late 15th century). Brother of the Muscovite Tsar Ivan III (*q.v.*); he died childless in 1472 and his brother inherited his principality.

YURY DANILOVICH (?–1325). Grand Prince of Moscow. He was a grandson of Alexander Nevsky, son of Daniel of Moscow, whom he succeeded in 1303 as ruler of Moscow but not yet as grand prince. He annexed the territory of the prince of Mozhaysk, thus gaining control over the Moscow River, and then began a struggle with Michael of Tver (*q.v.*) for the leadership of Russia. To this end he made a marriage alliance with the khan of the Golden Horde, who gave him the title of grand prince already held by Michael. Michael defeated

Yury in battle and captured his wife, who died in prison. This in turn led to Michael's execution for her murder, and Yury was confirmed as grand prince in 1319. In 1322 the khan changed his mind and gave the title to Michael's son Dmitry. In 1325 Yury was killed by Dmitry. He was the first ruler of Moscow to hold the position of grand prince.

Fennell, John L. I., *The Emergence of Moscow, 1304–1359*, 1968.

YURY DOLGORUKY (*c.* 1090–1151). Prince of Rostov-Suzdal, son of Vladimir Monomakh. He won the grand princedom of Kiev (*q.v.*) and is also traditionally credited with the foundation of Moscow. The first reference to the city (1147) records his inviting his ally Svyatoslav of Novgorod-Seversk to visit him there.

Vernadsky, G. V. et al. (eds.), *A Source Book for Russian History from Early Times to 1917*, 1972.

YUSHKEVICH, SEMYON SOLOMONOVICH (1868–1927). Novelist, playwright, and short-story writer who based his work on Jewish life in Odessa, his birthplace, and other Russian cities. He emigrated after the Revolution of 1917.

YUSUPOV, PRINCE FELIX FELIXOVICH (*fl.* early 20th century). He conspired with Tsar Nicholas I's cousin, Grand Duke Dmitry (*q.v.*), to assassinate the tsaritsa's adviser, Rasputin (*q.v.*), whose influence they considered personally and nationally disastrous. Yusupov and another murdered Rasputin in 1916.

YUZOVKA. Former name (until 1924) of the city of Donetsk in the Ukraine. The name is a Russian version of "Hughes-ouka," the original town (1869), which was founded as a metallurgical center by the New Russia Metallurgical Company and its Welsh head, John Hughes (*q.v.*).

Z

ZABOLOTSKY, NICHOLAS ALEKSEYEVICH (1903–). Poet. A member of the short-lived Leningrad literary group *Oberyu,* Zabolotsky was exiled and sent to prison camps between 1938 and 1946. Prior to this, it is considered that his poetry displayed genuine talent and potential. After Zabolotsky's political rehabilitation, publication of his work resumed in 1948. Something of a puppet in the hands of the government, he has won much critical esteem in the Soviet Union.

Hingley, Ronald, *Russian Writers and Soviet Society,* 1979.

Poggioli, R., *Poets of Russia,* 1960.

ZADONSHCHINA. Late 15th-century epic poem telling the story of the Battle of Kulikovo (the defeat of the Mongols by Dmitriy Donskoy [*q.v.*], prince of Moscow in 1380).

ZAGORSK. Town situated 44 miles (70 km) NE of Moscow. It is noted as a center of the wood-carving industry, which has flourished there since the 15th century. Other occupations include engineering and textile manufacture. The town originated as a settlement serving the Monastery of the Trinity (Troitsa-Sergeyeva Lavra; *q.v.*), founded by St. Sergius (*q.v.*) in 1337 and now a museum. Boris Godunov is buried in the Uspensky Cathedral. Population (1973) 93,000.

ZAGOSKIN, MICHAEL NIKOLAYEVICH (1789–1852). Patriotic, popular historical novelist. His best-known work is *Yury Miloslavksy* (1829).

ZAITSEV, BORIS KONSTANTINOVICH (1881–). Novelist of pre-1917 Russia, which he described with a melancholy lyricism. He emigrated to Italy in 1922, began to write of émigré society and continued in an increasingly nostalgic vein for many years. His works include *The Golden Pattern* (1926), *Gleb's*

Journey (1935), *Moscow* (1939), and *The Tree of Life* (1953).

ZAKHAROV, ANDREYAN DMITRIYEVICH (1761–1811). Outstanding architect of the classical school. He was born in St. Petersburg, where he designed the Admiralty building (1803).

Auty, Robert and Obolensky, Dimitri (eds.), "An Introduction to Russian Art and Architecture," *Companion to Russian Studies,* Vol. 3, 1980.

Hamilton, George H., *The Art and Architecture of Russia,* 2nd ed., 1975.

ZAKON. Legislative measure or a fundamental law.

ZAKUP. Indentured peasants of the Kievan era.

ZAMYATIN, YEVGENY IVANOVICH (1884–1937). Neo-realist writer. A Bolshevik in his early life, he became critical of the regime after the Revolution. His 20th-century novel *My* (*We,* trans. 1925), anticipated Huxley's *Brave New World* and Orwell's *1984,* and also prophesied the reign of Stalin, which estranged him from the authorities. He lived in France from 1931.

Richards, David J., *Zamyatin,* 1962.

Struve, Gleb, *Russian Literature under Lenin and Stalin,* 1972.

ZAPOROZHYE. Capital of region of the same name in the Ukraine, situated on the Dnepr River. Founded in 1770 on the site of the Zaporozhye Cossack camp, it is an important industrial and transport center with a large hydroelectric power station. It is known mainly for engineering and metallurgical industries with allied products. Population (1981) 812,000.

ZARUDNY, SERGEY IVANOVICH (1821–87). Lawyer. Head of the law department of the state council from 1861 on, he became a senator in 1869. He played an important part in the judicial reforms of 1864, advocating trial by jury and the independence of judges and magistrates.

Yaney, G., *The Systematization of Russian Government,* 1973.

ZARUTSKY, IVAN MARYONOVICH (?–1614). Cossack leader. He supported False Dmitry II (*q.v.*) and his infant son in the Time of Troubles. Tsar Michael defeated Zarutsky in 1614 at Astrakhan, where he was captured and executed.

ZASULICH, VERA IVANOVNA (1849–1919). Revolutionary who shot and wounded General Fedor Trepov (*q.v.*), the military governor of St. Petersburg. She stood trial by jury and was acquitted. As a result of this, political cases ceased to be taken through normal judicial procedures. She was a founding member of Liberation of Labor in 1883.

Haimson, Leopold H., *The Russian Marxists and the Origins of Bolshevism,* 1955.

Mendel, Arthur P., *Dilemmas of Progress in Tsarist Russia,* 1961.

Venturi, Franco, *Roots of Revolution* 1961.

ZAYONCHKOVSKY, PETER ANDREYEVICH (1904–). Historian and member of the Communist

Party from 1931. He studied at the Moscow Institute of History, Philosophy, and Literature and took part in the war of 1941–45. His areas of special interest include the history of the Russian peasantry, and the domestic and foreign policies of the 19th century; he has edited and published the diaries of Dmitry Milyutin and Valuev.

ZAYSAN, LAKE. Lake situated in the E Kazakhstan district of the Kazakh Soviet Socialist Republic, between the Tarbagatay and Altay ranges. Fed by the Black Irtysh River, it drains into the Irtysh River, where it helps to power the Bukhtarma hydroelectric power station. It is frozen from November to April but is navigable in summer.

ZEMLYA I VOLYA. *See* **Land and Liberty Organization.**

ZEMSKY SOBOR. Occasional gatherings of the estates of the realm, including boyars, clergy, gentry, and sometimes burghers and peasants, called by Muscovite tsars to consider matters of special importance. First called by Ivan IV (*q.v.*) in 1549, they met five or six times before 1613, when an assembly convened to elect a new tsar, Michael Romanov (*q.v.*). It met continually as an influential advisory body until 1622. It continued to be important until *c.* 1660. It was abandoned by Peter the Great (*q.v.*). Historians are divided as to the extent of its power; the most important was that of 1613 which represented the highest authority in the state.

Vernadsky, George V., *Russia at the Dawn of the Modern Age*, 1959.

ZEMSTVA. Name for institutions of local self-government for European Russia and the Ukraine, established in 1864 during the period of the Great Reforms (*q.v.*). The aim of the *zemstva* was to provide social and economic services. Although they were limited from time to time in their authority and revenues and were dominated by the nobility, their existence and liberal influence achieved much in the field of education, communications, agriculture, and health. The authority of the *zemstva* was increased after the February Revolution of 1917, but they were replaced by Soviets after the Bolshevik seizure of power.

Starr, S. Frederick, *Decentralization and Self-Government in Russia, 1830–1870*, 1972.

ZEMSTVO UNION. The union or association of *zemstva* and their professional employees, which acted as a body campaigning for social reform and supported revolutionary activity in 1904–05 and 1917. The *zemstva* were introduced in 1864 as elected local government assemblies at the provincial and county level. They were elected by all classes from the peasants upward; they had power to levy taxes and to spend on schools, roads, and public health. Much of their effort at social amelioration was obstructed by the central government. They were abolished in 1918.

Fischer, George, *Russian Liberalism*, 1958.

Galai, S., *The Liberation Movement in Russia 1900–1905*, 1973.

ZERAVSHAN RIVER. River rising in the Zeravshan mountains and flowing 450 miles (720 km) W through Tadzhikistan and Uzbekistan before disappearing in the desert near the Amu-Darya River.

ZHALOVANNAYA GRAMOTA. Charter.

ZHDANOV, ANDREY ALEXANDROVICH (1896–1948). Politician. From 1934 to 1944, he was first secretary of the Leningrad Party, holding also the secretaryship of the central committee. As secretary he was in charge of ideological affairs. He introduced strict political control and extreme nationalism into the arts and opposed Western cultural influences. *Decisions of the Central Committee . . . on Literature and Art,* published by the Communist Party of the Soviet Union in 1951, is an English text of the decrees initiated by Zhdanov. He wrote *Essays on Literature, Philosophy, and Music* (1950). He participated in the defense of Leningrad during the Second World War, and organized the establishment of the Cominform in 1947. He died in 1948, and in 1953 a group of Jewish doctors was accused of his murder, but the charges were dropped after Stalin's death.

Conquest, Robert, *The Politics of Ideas in the USSR*, 1967.

Mandelstam, Nadezhda, *Hope Against Hope,* 1971.

Swayze, Harold, *Political Control of Literature in the USSR, 1946–1959,* 1962.

ZHDANOV. Port situated on the Sea of Azov. It is an important industrial center manufacturing iron and steel, machinery, and chemicals. Fishing and fish processing are carried on, and coal, grain, and salt are the chief exports. Population (1981) 511,000.

ZHELEZNOVODSK. Town situated 7 miles (11 km) NNW of Pyatigorsk in the Russian Soviet Federated Socialist Republic at the S foot of Zheleznaya Mountain, in the N Caucasus. It is a health resort with mineral springs and sanatoriums.

ZHELYABOV, ANDREY IVANOVICH (1850–81). The son of an ex-serf from Odessa, he was one of those on the executive committee of the revolutionary People's Will (*q.v.*) organization, which was founded in 1879. He was a leader in the plan to assassinate Tsar Alexander II, and although he and Michael Mikhailov were arrested before the assassination took place, the final arrangements were made by his accomplice and lover, Sofya Perovskaya (*q.v.*).

Venturi, Franco, *Roots of Revolution,* 1961.

ZHIDOVIN. Legendary figure of Jewish origin who appears in the oral epics or Russian *byliny.*

ZHITOMIR. Capital of the region of the same name in the Ukraine situated 80 miles (128 km) WSW of Kiev. It was part of the Kievan state and was subsequently ceded to Lithuania in 1320 and to Poland in 1569. It became Russian again in the second partition of Poland in 1793. It is an industrial and transportation center; manufactures include metal goods, furniture, and clothing. Population (1981) 254,000.

ZHORDNIA, NOAH NIKOLAYEVICH (1870–1953). Georgian revolutionary and Menshevik leader. He served as head of the government of the Georgian independent republic (1918–21) and stated, "We prefer the imperialists of the west to the fanatics of the east." He emigrated to Paris when the Bolsheviks took over Georgia in 1921.

ZHUKOV, GEORGY KONSTANTINOVICH (1896–). Marshal of the Soviet Union. He joined the Red Army in 1918 and the Communist Party in 1919. During the Second World War he was at first chief of the general staff and subsequently deputy commissar of defense and deputy supreme commander in chief of the Soviet armed forces. He was prominent in the planning of Soviet operations and is particularly remembered in the defense of Moscow (1941), the Battle of Stalingrad (1942), the relief of Leningrad (1943), and the advance toward Germany (1943–44). On May 8, 1945 he received the surrender of the German High Command in Berlin, but in 1946 he was removed from the post by Stalin, and after a brief period as commander in chief land forces and deputy minister of the armed forces he was sent into semi-retirement. He again became a first deputy minister of defense upon Stalin's death in 1953 and in 1955 was appointed minister of defense. He took Khrushchev's side against Malenkov, Kaganovich, and Molotov (*q.v.*), and he became a full member of the Presidium upon their expulsion in 1957. However, he was himself expelled from the Presidium and the central committee and was dismissed as minister of defense later that year. In 1964 he was partially rehabilitated after the fall of Khrushchev and was awarded the Order of Lenin (1966).

Salisbury, Harrison E. (ed.), *Marshal Zhukov's Greatest Battles*, 1969.

Zhukov, Georgy Konstantinovich, *Memoirs and Reflections*, 1969 (trans. 1971).

ZHUKOVSKY, VASILY ANDREYEVICH (1783–1852). Poet and translator of Byron, Firdausi, Goethe, Gray, Homer, and Schiller. He translated Gray's *Elegy in a Country Churchyard* (1802). He was also tutor to Tsar Alexander II (*q.v.*) and was part of the Pushkin circle, having paved the way for the Russian Romantic school. His contribution to Russian literature was to introduce, through his translations, the works of great English and German writers. He also wrote musical lyrics of unrequited love, as well as ballads and folk narratives.

Fennell, John L. I. (ed.), *Nineteenth-Century Russian Literature*, 1973.

Mirsky, D. S., *A History of Russian Literature*, 1949.

ZILUPE. Latvian town situated 32 miles (51 km) ESE of Rezekne on the border with the Russian Soviet Federated Socialist Republic.

ZINOVIEV, GRIGORY YEVSEYEVICH (RADOMYSLSKY) (1883–1936). Politician. He joined the Social Democratic Labor Party (*q.v.*) in 1901 and its Bolshevik faction in 1903. He emigrated after the 1905 Revolution and accompanied Lenin on his return to Russia after the February 1917 Revolution, but he was not in agreement with the April Theses (*q.v.*), the October Revolution, or the Treaty of Brest-Litovsk. He was chairman of the Petrograd Soviet after the October Revolution, became a candidate member of the Politburo in 1919, was a full member from 1921 to 1926, and was chairman of the executive committee of the Communist International from 1919 to 1926. After Lenin's death he first opposed Trotsky and then joined him against Stalin. He was falsely accused of complicity in the murder of Sergey Kirov (*q.v.*) and in 1935 was sentenced to 10 years' imprisonment. He was retried in the great treason trial (1936) and executed. He became notorious in British politics with the publication (1924) of a letter, allegedly by him, urging supporters in Great Britain to prepare for violent insurrection. This contributed materially to Ramsay MacDonald's electoral defeat and the deterioration of British-Soviet relations.

Carr, Edward Hallett, *The Russian Revolution: From Lenin to Stalin*, 1979.

ZLATOUST. Industrial town of Chelyabinsk region, situated in the S Urals. Founded in 1754, it is a notable metallurgical center producing special steels and manufacturing tools, precision instruments, and cutlery. Population (1981) 201,000.

ZLATOVRATSKY, NICHOLAS NIKOLAYEVICH (1845–1911). Author with populist (*q.v.*) tendencies. His best work was the novel *Ustoy* (1878–82), in which he described the contrast between the old village and the new. A strong believer in agrarian socialism, he idealized the Russian *muzhik* and the peasant commune.

ZOË PALAEOLOGA (?–1503). Second wife of Ivan III (*q.v.*) and niece of the last Byzantine emperor, Constantine XI. In November 1472 she arrived in Moscow from Rome and was received into the Orthodox Church as Sofia.

Fennell, John L. I., *Ivan the Great of Moscow*, 1963.

ZOLKIEWSKI, STANISLAW (*fl. c.* 1610). Polish commander responsible for defeating Dmitry Shuisky (*q.v.*) when the latter attempted to relieve Smolensk in 1610. Sigismund III of Poland had invaded Russia in 1609 and Zolkiewski, having defeated Shuisky, marched on Moscow. The population of the territories occupied by Polish troops swore allegiance to Wladyslaw (*q.v.*), Sigismund's son, following the mob's deposition of Tsar Vasily Shuisky. In August the Muscovites came to an arrangement with Zolkiewski that the 14-year-old Wladyslaw should be invited to rule Russia. Polish troops then entered Moscow in September and held it for two years. Sigismund, however, would not accept the conditions of the agreement and claimed the throne in his own right. In 1612 the war was resumed.

ZORNDORF, BATTLE OF (1758). Also called the Battle of Sarbinowo, it was fought against Prussia as part of Russia's involvement in the Seven Years' War. This Prussian victory halted the Russian advance into Brandenburg.

ZOSHCHENKO, MICHAEL MIKHAILOVICH (1895–1958). Ukrainian satirical writer. From 1921 he began to gain popularity with his short stories depicting the bewilderment and disbelief of the ordinary citizen in Soviet Russia. In 1946 he was the main target of Andrey Zhdanov's (*q.v.*) attacks when the latter began his campaign to impose absolute party control over cultural life. He was expelled from the Union of Soviet Writers (*q.v.*) and his works were banned. His books include *Youth Restored* (1933), *Russia Laughs* (trans. 1935), *The Woman Who Could Not Read* (trans. 1940), and *The Wonderful Dog* (trans. 1942).

Slonim, Marc, *Soviet Russian Literature*, 1967.

Struve, Gleb, *Russian Literature under Lenin and Stalin*, 1972.

ZUBATOV, SERGEY VASILYEVICH (1864–1917). Chief of the Moscow *Okhrana* (1890–1903) (*see* **Secret Police**). In 1901 he founded, with others, the society of mutual help for workers in mechanical production. Under police protection this society flourished and such legal trade unions were established in Minsk, Odessa, and St. Petersburg. He was able to maintain control of the movement in Moscow but elsewhere the unions got out of control and were used for revolutionary purposes. In 1903 the government withdrew its protection and Zubatov was dismissed.

ZUBOV, PLATON ALEXANDROVICH (1771–1804). Lover and favorite of Catherine II (*q.v.*). The last in a long line of Catherine's lovers, he was the only one of Potemkin's successors who had any political importance, and there is some evidence to suggest that he and Catherine were secretly married. He had plans for the revival and extension of Potemkin's "Greek Project," an advance toward India as well as toward Constantinople, but they were abandoned at Catherine's death in 1796. He was involved in the plot to murder Catherine's son, Paul I (*q.v.*).

ZUCCHI, VIRGINIA (1847–1930). Italian ballerina and pupil of Carlo Blasis. She was responsible, with Isadora Duncan, for interesting Diaghilev (*q.v.*) in ballet.

ZYRIANE. *See* **Komi.**

CHRONOLOGY

It should be noted that many early dates are dubious or mythical, as are some "facts" which are currently under discussion.

6th–8th centuries	Slavs migrate from central Europe into the forest zone of Russia.
7th century	Turkic Khazars conquer Black Sea steppe and establish their kaganate; at the end of the eighth century they are converted to Judaism; in the eighth and ninth centuries, Slavs in south pay tribute to Khazars.
c. 800	Old Ladoga, Norse settlement in Russia; in ninth century, Norsemen spread out along Volga and Dnepr basins and raid Constantinople.
860	First Slav attack launched against Constantinople. First Varangian expedition against Constantinople.
862	Traditional date of the establishment of Ryurik dynasty in Novgorod. Varangian princes invited to rule over the Slavs.
862–879	Reign of Prince Ryurik in Novgorod.
882	Transfer of the capital to Kiev. Prince Oleg unites Novgorod with Kiev to form one state.
907	First agreement between Oleg and the Greeks. Oleg's campaign against Byzantium.
911	Second agreement between Oleg and the Greeks. Trade treaty between Kiev and Byzantium.
913	Oleg's death.
941–944	Igor's expedition against Constantinople.
943	Kievan campaign in Persia.
945	Igor's death.

945–957	Olga's reign.
955	Olga, the Kievan grand duchess, christened at Byzantium.
957	Olga visits Constantinople.
964–966	Svyatoslav's defeat of the Khazars on the Volga.
966–967	Prince Svyatoslav attacks and destroys Khazar state.
967–992	Svyatoslav's expedition in the Balkans.
968	Kiev attacked by the Pechenegs.
970–971	Svyatoslav conquers Bulgaria.
971	Peace treaty with Byzantium; Russia loses the Balkans and the Crimea.
973	Svyatoslav's death.
973–978	Yaropolk's rule.
978–1015	Vladimir's rule.
988–989	Vladimir adopts Christianity (the Greek Orthodox rite) as the official religion.
1015	Death of the Grand Duke Vladimir.
1015–1019	Struggle for power among Vladimir's sons.
1019–1054	Yaroslav's reign.
1025	Traditional date of the founding of Yaroslavl.
1030	Yaroslav founds Dorpat.
1034	Yaroslav's victory over the Pechenegs.
1037	St. Sophia, Kiev, begun.
1045–1052	Building of St. Sophia, Novgorod.
1054	Polovtsians arrive at Kievan frontiers.
1054–1073	*Russkaya Pravda* (Russian Justice) prepared.
1068	Invasion of the Kievan state by the Polovtsians; uprising in Kiev against Prince Izyaslav.
1095	First election of a prince in Novgorod.
1097	Partition of Kievan Rus into patrimonial estates at Lyubekh conference.
1108	Traditional date of the founding of Vladimir.
1113	"Monk Nestor," possibly several authors in reality, completes the writing of the Primary Chronicle.
1113–1125	Reign of Vladimir Monomakh in Kiev.
1126	First election of a *posadnik* (mayor) by the Novgorod *veche* (assembly).
1147	First reference to Moscow in a chronicle.
1151	Death of Yury Dolgoruky.
1156	First election of a bishop in Novgorod.
1167	Destruction of Kiev by Andrey Bogolyubsky, prince of Vladimir-Suzdal.
1169	Transfer of the seat of government from Kiev to Suzdal.
1174	Death of Andrey Bogolyubsky.

1185	Unsuccessful expedition of Prince Igor of Novrogod-Seversk against the Polovtsians (May).
1195	Novgorod concludes the first treaty with German cities and Gottland.
c. 1200	Polovtsians cut the Kiev-Constantinople trading route.
1204	Crusaders capture and sack Constantinople.
1206	Genghis Khan assumes command of the Mongols.
1209	First recorded reference to Tver.
1212	Death of Grand Duke Vsevolod III of Vladimir-Suzdal.
1215–1280	Mongols conquer China.
1218–1221	Mongols conquer Central Asia.
1221	Founding of Nizhny-Novgorod (now Gorky).
1223	First invasion of Rus by the Mongols and the battle on the Kalka River.
1227	Death of Genghis Khan.
1236	Batu, Genghis Khan's grandson, begins conquest of western territories.
1237–1238	Mongols invade Russia under Batu.
1237–1241	Invasion and conquest of Rus by Batu Khan.
1240	Alexander Nevsky's victory over the Swedes on the Neva River.
1240–1242	Mongols attack southern Russia, Poland, and Hungary and then withdraw to Mongolia.
1242	Alexander Nevsky's victory over the Teutonic Order at Lake Peipus.
c. 1243	Formation of the Golden Horde, of which northeastern Russia and Novgorod become tributaries.
1245–1247	Journey of Giovanni da Pian del Carpini to Mongolia.
1246	First census of the population by the Mongols in the Kiev and Chernigov territories.
1252	Emergence of Moscow as an independent hereditary principality.
1252–1263	Reign of Alexander Nevsky, Great Prince of Vladimir.
1253–1255	Journey of William of Rubrock (or Ruysbroeck) to Mongolia.
1256–1259	Mongols conquer the Caucasus and Iran.
1257	Mongols conduct the first census of Russia.
1257–1259	Anti-Mongol uprisings.
1263	Death of Prince Alexander Nevsky.
1270	Novgorod negotiates a treaty with the Hanseatic League.
c. 1276	Appanage principality of Moscow carved out for Nevsky's son, Daniil, who ruled *c.* 1276–1303.
1300	Transfer of Metropolitan office from Kiev to Vladimir.
1302	Moscow annexes Pereyaslavl, Kolomna, and Mozhaisk.
1303–1325	Yury Danilovich, prince of Moscow.
1318	Prince Yury of Moscow acquires the Charter *(Yarlik)* of the Grand Prince from the Mongols.

1322	Charter *(Yarlik)* of the Grand Prince passes to Dmitry of Tver.
1325–1340	Ivan I (*Kalita,* or "Moneybags"), prince of Moscow (Grand Prince of Vladimir, 1328–40).
1327	Anti-Mongol uprising in Tver, suppressed by Ivan I with Mongol help.
1328	Ivan *Kalita* gains the *Yarlik* of Grand Prince. Metropolitan moves his see from Vladimir to Moscow.
1340	St. Sergius founds the Trinity Monastery.
1341	Ivan I dies; succeeded by his son, Simeon the Proud.
1348	By mutual agreement, Pskov separates itself and forms an independent city-state.
1352	Black Death in Novgorod and Moscow.
1353	Death of Simeon the Proud.
1353–1359	Reign of Ivan II (of Moscow) the Meek.
1359–1389	Rule of Dmitry Donskoy, prince of Moscow (Grand Prince after 1362).
1360–1362	Struggle between Moscow and Suzdal for the title of Grand Princedom.
1367–1368	First stone fortifications of the Moscow Kremlin laid.
1368	Olgerd of Lithuania attacks the Muscovy state.
mid-1300s	Mongol power collapses in Iran.
1360s–1370s	Dynastic crises in Golden Horde.
1368	Collapse of Mongol power in China.
1370s	Moscow begins to interfere with boyar departure rights.
1371–1375	Heresy of *Strigolniki* (shearers) in Novgorod.
1375	Tver acknowledges Moscow as a Grand Principality.
1378	Dmitry Donskoy defeats Mongols on the banks of the Vozha River.
1380	Dmitry Donskoy defeats Khan Mamay at Kulikovo.
1382	Moscow taken by Khan Tokhtamysh; first mention of firearms in Moscow; first coining of money in Moscow.
	Moscow sacked by Mongols.
1386	Dynastic union of Lithuania with Poland and conversion of Lithuanian dynasty to Catholicism.
1389–1395	Timur (Tamerlane) attacks Golden Horde and sacks Saray, its capital.
1389–1425	Basil (Vasily) I.
	Rule of Basil I in Moscow.
1392	Moscow absorbs Suzdal and Nizhny-Novgorod.
1395	Defeat of the Golden Horde by Tamerlane.
1408	Principality of Moscow devastated by the Golden Horde.
1425–1462	Rule of Basil (Vasily) II, the Blind.
1427	Formation of the Crimean Khanate.
1430–66	Disintegration of the Golden Horde.

1436	Foundation of Solovetsky Monastery.
1437	Formation of the Kazan Khanate.
1439	Council of Florence attempts to reunite eastern and western churches. Russian hierarchy rejects attempt.
1441	Metropolitan Isidore deposed in Moscow for acceptance of Council of Florence.
1448	Church of Moscow declared autocephalous.
c. 1450	Golden Horde disintegrates; formation of Kazan, Astrakhan, and Crimean principalities (khanates).
1452	For the first time a Mongol prince accepts Russian suzerainty when the princedom of Kasimov is established.
1453	Ottoman Turks capture Constantinople.
1458	Kievan metropolitan assumes independence from Moscow.
1459	Formation of the Astrakhan Khanate.
1462–1505	Rule of Ivan III, the Great.
1463	Moscow annexes the principality of Yaroslavl; Moscow conquers the Mari Lands.
1463–1468	First limitations upon freedom of peasant movement.
1470	The Judaizer Heresy spreads throughout Novgorod.
1471	Moscow attacks Novgorod and defeats its armies.
1472	Moscow annexes the principality of Perm; Ivan III marries Sophia Paleologue, niece of last Byzantine emperor.
1474	Moscow annexes Rostov.
1475–1479	Building of the *Uspensky Sobor* (Cathedral of Assumption) in the Moscow Kremlin.
1476	Ambrosio Contarini, the first westerner, visits and writes about Moscow.
1477	Moscow again attacks Novgorod and annexes it. (After 1477 massive land expropriations carried out by Moscow in Novgorod; introduction of conditional land tenure *[pomeste]*.)
1480	Ivan III terminates the "Tatar of Mongol Yoke." Overthrow of Mongol rule.
1484,1489	Massacres in Novgorod and deportation of its leading citizens to inland Russia.
1485	Moscow annexes Tver.
1485–1516	Building of the new Kremlin in Moscow.
1489	Moscow annexes Vyatka.
1494	Hansa depot in Novgorod shut down.
1497	Ivan III issues *Sudebnik* (Code of Laws).
1503	Church Council condemns the heresy of Judaizers and rejects Nil Sorsky's appeal for voluntary renunciation of ecclesiastical properties (beginning of battle between pro- and anti-property parties in the Russian church).
1505-33	Rule of Basil (Vasily) III.
1510	Moscow annexes Pskov, followed by mass deportations.

1514	Moscow annexes territories of Smolensk.
1517,1526	Baron Herberstein's missions to Moscow.
1521	Basil III deposes Metropolitan Varlaam.
1525	Metropolitan Daniil authorizes Basil's divorce.
1533–1538	Regency of Ivan's mother, Elena.
1533–1584	Rule of Ivan IV, the Terrible.
1535	Edicts against further monastic acquisitions of land.
1547	Ivan IV assumes the title "Tsar." Marriage and coronation of Ivan IV. Fire of Moscow.
1549	First meeting of the *Zemsky Sobor* (Landed Assembly).
1550	Organizations of the *streltsy; Sudebnik* (Code of Laws) of Ivan IV. *Tsarsky Sudebnik* (Second of Laws Code): 1,064 "boyars' sons" given *pomestya* in the environs of Moscow.
1550–1551	Council of *Stoglav* (Hundred Chapters). *Stoglavy* (Hundred-headed) Synod.
1550s	First *prikazy* formed and reforms of local administration.
1552	Capture and annexation of Khanate of Kazan.
1553	Discovery of northern maritime route to Russia by Richard Chancellor.
1550s	Moscow constructs chain of stockades along the southern border and Russian colonization of the steppe begins.
1555	Formation of the Muscovy Company in London and extension of privileges to it for trade throughout the Moscow state.
1556	Conquest of Astrakhan.
1558–1583	The Livonian War of Ivan IV. A sustained but unsuccessful effort by Ivan IV (the Terrible) to secure a Russian coastline on the Baltic at the expense of Poland and Sweden.
1561	The Livonian Order disbanded.
1564	First book printed in Moscow by Ivan Fedorov.
1564–1572	*Oprichnina* terror.
1565–1584	Ivan IV's reign of terror.
1566	Land Assembly convened to discuss Livonian War.
1569	Union of Lublin resulting in the merger of Poland and Lithuania.
1570	Novgorod razed on orders of Ivan IV; massacres of inhabitants.
1571–1572	Crimean Tatars raid and burn Moscow.
1572	*Oprichnina* abolished by Ivan IV.
1577	Establishment of commercial ties with Holland.
1581–1592	New cadaster books drawn up that serve as basis for serfdom.
1582	Yermak conquers the Khanate of Sibir. Conquest of Siberia.
1584	Founding of Archangel.
1584–1598	Rule of Tsar Fedor Ivanovich.
1587–1598	Boris Godunov acts as regent.

1588	Giles Fletcher visits Moscow.
1589	Formation of the office of patriarch in Moscow. Metropolitan is raised to rank of patriarch.
1591	Murder of Prince Dmitry at Uglich.
1596	Creation of Uniate Church in Poland-Lithuania.
1597	*Ukaz* grants nobles five years to claim their fugitive peasants.
1598	End of the Ryurik dynasty. End of the dynasty of Ivan Kalita. Coronation of Boris Godunov.
1598–1605	Rule of Tsar Boris Godunov.
1601–1602	Edicts further restricting peasant mobility.
1601–1604	Years of famine.
1605	Death of Boris Godunov and beginning of period of unrest.
1605–1606	Rule of the First False Dmitriy.
1605–1613	"Time of Troubles": Russia threatened with Polish and Swedish conquest. Ends with the accession of the Romanov dynasty.
1606–1607	Bolotnikov's revolt.
1606–1610	Rule of Tsar Vasily Shuisky.
1607–1610	Rule of Second False Dmitriy.
1610–1612	Poles occupy Moscow.
1610–1613	Interregnum.
1610	Russians offer throne to Polish Prince Wladyslaw.
1611–1612	National uprising against Poles.
1611–1617	Swedes occupy Novgorod.
1613	*Zemsky Sobor* elects Michael Romanov as tsar.
1613–1917	Romanov dynasty.
1613–1645	Rule of Tsar Michael Romanov: between 1619 and 1633, his father, Patriarch Philaret, co-ruler.
1617	Peace of Stolbovo. Swedes evacuate Novgorod.
1631	Peter Mogila, Metropolitan of Kiev, founds Kiev Academy.
1632–1634	Russian attempt to capture Smolensk from the Poles.
1632	Winius and Marselis found Tula and Kashira iron foundries.
1637	Don Cossacks conquer Azov.
1643–1646	Peyarkov reaches the Sea of Okhotsk.
1645–1676	Rule of Tsar Alexis.
1648	Ukrainian Cossack uprising against Poland. Urban rebellions.
1648–1649	*Zemsky Sobor* issues *Sobornoye Ulozheniye* (Code of Laws). Important assembly in session.
1649	Trading privileges of the Muscovy Company abolished. *Ulozheniye* (New Code). British commercial privileges withdrawn.
1652	Foundation of the German settlement in Moscow; founding of Irkutsk.
1652–1658	Nikon as patriarch institutes his reforms.
1652–1666	Nikon, Patriarch of Moscow.
1653	Last full meeting of *Zemsky Sobor.*

1654	Ukrainian Cossacks swear allegiance to the tsar of Moscow; Church Council adopts Nikon's reforms thereby causing a schism.
1654–1667	Russo-Polish war over the Ukraine.
1662	"Copper riots" in Moscow.
1664	Russian official, Grigory Kitoshikhin, flees to Sweden.
1666	Establishment of postal service in Russia; Church Council deposes Patriarch Nikon. Synod condemns Nikon, retains his reforms; beginning of schism *(raskol)*.
1667	Poland cedes Kiev and Smolensk to Russia in the Peace of Andrusovo; *Novotorgovy ustav* (New Commercial Code) promulgated; Church Council condemns Old Believers. Russia makes large territorial gains from Poland (confirmed and made permanent by a treaty of 1686).
1667–1676	Revolt of Solovetsky Monastery against church reforms.
1670–1671	Revolt of Stenka Razin.
1672	Birth of Peter the Great. Russians establish embassies to all major European states.
1676	Death of Tsar Alexis and accession of Fedor III.
1676–1681	War with the Ottoman Empire and in the Crimea.
1676–1682	Rule of Tsar Fedor Alekseyevich (Peter's half-brother).
1682	Death of Fedor III. After *streltsy* attack on the Kremlin Ivan V and Peter are established as co-tsars. Beginning of the regency of Sophia. Execution of Archpriest Avvakum. *Mestnichestvo* abolished.
1682–1689	Sophia regent, with Peter first as co-ruler and then as tsar. Regency of Sophia; Vasily V. Golitsyn is the actual ruler.
1684	Institution of formal persecution of Old Believers.
1686	Russia enters the Holy League with the Holy Roman Emperor, Venice, and Poland.
1687	Slavo-Greek-Latin Academy in Moscow begins to function. Unsuccessful campaign against the Crimean Tatars.
1688	Peter begins experiments in shipbuilding on Lake Pleshcheyev.
1689	Peter marries Yevdokiya Lopukhina. Treaty of Nerchinsk with China signed. Unsuccessful campaign against the Crimean Tatars. Sophia's regency overthrown, Peter takes over (until 1696 co-ruler with his brother, Ivan).
1693	Peter visits Archangel and has his first sight of the sea.
1696	Death of Ivan V. Capture of Azov, after an unsuccessful attack in the previous year. Building of a naval squadron begins there.
1697–1698	"Great Embassy" to western Europe. Peter visits the Netherlands, England, and Austria, but fails to secure help against the Ottoman Empire.
1697	*Preobrazhensky Prikaz* given exclusive authority over political crimes.

1698	*Streltsy* revolt breaks out and is savagely suppressed.
1699	Rapid growth of metal production in the Ural Sea begins.
1700	Peace is made with the Ottoman Empire. Outbreak of war with Sweden and great Russian defeat at Narva. Patriarch Adrian dies but no successor is appointed; replaced by acting head of church. Abolition of the patriarchate.
1701	Monasteries required to turn over revenues to state.
1703	Peter founds St. Petersburg, foundations of new city laid. *Vedomosti,* Russia's first newspaper, published.
1705	Systematic conscription for the armed forces established; outbreak of uprising in Astrakhan, which lasts into the following year. Recruitment obligation instituted.
1707	Great advance of Charles XII against Russia begins. Outbreak of Cossack rising in the Don area, which lasts into the following year. St. Petersburg replaces Moscow as capital of Russia.
1708	Effort at reform of local administration by the creation of the *gubernii* and their subdivisions (followed by further changes, notably in 1715). The Swedes are defeated at the battle of Lesnaya but are joined by Mazepa.
1709	Decisive Russian victory over Sweden at Poltava, followed by rapid rise in Russia's prestige and international standing. Construction of St. Petersburg begins.
1710	Russians take Livonia and Estonia.
1711	Outbreak of war with the Ottoman Empire and Russian defeat on the Prut. Creation of the senate. Peter abolishes most trading monopolies. Tsar's Council ("Boyar Duma") replaced by the senate.
1713	Peace treaty with the Ottoman Empire.
1714	Decree forbids subdivision of estates among the heirs when the holder dies. Edict requiring landowners to bequeath estates intact to a single heir. *Kormleniya* abolished and civil servants placed on a salary.
1716	Flight of the Tsarevich Alexis to Vienna and Naples. Russian occupation of Mecklenburg provokes the hostility of Britain and Emperor Charles VI. *Ustav voinsky* (Military Code) issued.
1717	Peter's second journey to western Europe. He visits the Netherlands and Paris. Alexis returns to Russia.
1718	Death of Alexis. Creation of the administrative colleges starts. Unsuccessful peace negotiations with Sweden in the Aland islands begin. Beginning of first "soul" census. Colleges replace *prikazy*.
1720	*Morskoy ustav* (Naval Code) and *Generalny reglament* (General Regulation) issued; increasing efforts being made to systematize the machinery of government.
1721	War with Sweden is ended by the treaty of Nystad. Peter assumes

	the title of emperor. *Dukhovny reglament* (Spiritual Regulation) issued and synod established. Merchants allowed to purchase villages in order to attach laboring force to industrial and mining enterprises. Senate proclaims Peter "Emperor." Ecclesiastical Regulations: Patriarchate abolished and replaced with Holy Synod.
1722	Table of Ranks promulgated. War with Persia begins. Peter assumes the right to nominate his own successor. Succession law abolished: emperors free to choose successors.
1724	Catherine, Peter's second wife (married privately in 1707), is crowned as empress. "Soul" tax introduced. First comprehensive protective tariff.
1725	Death of Peter and accession of Catherine. Establishment of the Academy of Sciences in St. Petersburg.
1725–1727	Rule of Catherine I.
1727	Death of Catherine and accession of Peter II, son of the Tsarevich Alexis.
1727–1730	Rule of Peter II.
1730–1740	Rule of Empress Anna.
1730	Constitutional crisis; unsuccessful attempt by Supreme Privy Council to impose "Conditions" on Anna. Inheritance law of 1714 repealed.
1731	Establishment of Noble Cadet Corps.
1736	Compulsory state service limited to 25 years and may begin at age 20; one son of landlord may remain home. "Possessional" serfs attached in perpetuity to factories and mines.
c. 1740	Imperial Ballet School established at the Winter Palace.
1740–1741	Rule of Emperor Ivan VI.
1741–1762	Rule of Empress Elizabeth.
1753	Internal tariffs and tolls in Russian Empire abolished.
1755	University of Moscow founded.
1761–1762	Peter III.
1762	"Manifesto of *Dvoryanstvo* Liberty" exempting *dvoryanye* from compulsory state service. Church and monastic properties sequestered; law goes into effect in 1764. Most commercial and manufacturing monopolies *(regalia)* abolished. Law of 1721 allowing merchants to buy villages revoked.
1762–1796	Catherine II, the Great, gains throne by *coup d'etat*; her husband, Peter III, is murdered.
1764	Automatic promotion for certain categories of civil servants.
1767	Automatic promotion rules for civil servants extended.
1767–1768	Legislative Commission convoked to draft new code of laws.
1769	Russia's first satirical journals (*Vsyakaya vsyachina* and *Truten*) published.
1772	First Partition of Poland.

1773–1775	Peasant and Cossack uprising under Yemelian Pugachev.
1775	Provincial reform. All manufacturing activity open to all estates.
1783	*Dvoryanye* allowed to operate private printing presses.
1785	Charter of *Dvoryanstvo* and Charter of Cities (April).
1787–1791	War with the Ottoman Empire.
1790	Publication of Radishchev's *Journey,* followed by his arrest.
1792	Novikov arrested.
1793	Second Partition of Poland.
1795	Third Partition of Poland.
1796–1801	Rule of Paul I.
1801–1825	Rule of Alexander I.
1802	Reorganization of senate. Establishment of Ministries.
1804	Kharkov and Kazan universities founded. Statute on Jews.
1807	Treaty of Tilsit with Napoleon.
1809	Abortive attempt to introduce civil service examinations. Conquest of Finland.
1811	Ministry of the Police created; abolished in 1819.
1812	French invade Russia and take Moscow.
1814	Paris taken and Alexander enters in triumph.
1815	Holy Alliance and Quadruple Alliance.
1816	Establishment of League of Salvation, first secret organization of the future Decembrists.
1825–1855	Rule of Nicholas I.
1825	Decembrist Revolt. Pushkin's *Boris Godunov.*
1826	Execution of conspirators; organization of political police (Third Section of Imperial Chancery). Supreme Criminal Commission set up to try Decembrists. Third Department established. Censorship Code.
1826–1828	War with Persia. Treaty of Turkmanchai.
1828–1829	War with Turkey. Treaty of Adrianople.
1830	Full Collection of Laws published. "Cholera Riots."
1830–1831	Suppression of Polish revolt. Polish constitution abrogated.
1831	Pushkin completes *Yevgeny Onegin.*
1832	Code of Laws issued.
1832–1833	First Mohammed Ali crisis. Treaty of Unkiar-Skelessi.
1833	Münchengrätz agreement.
1834	Alexander Herzen banished to Vyatka. New radical intelligentsia from now on in conflict with censors and police.
1835	Reform of University Statutes.
1836	Publication of Chaadayev's First Philosophical Letter. Paul A. Chaadayev declared insane by Nicholas for critique of Russian backwardness. First performance of Gogol's *Government Inspector* and Glinka's *A Life for the Tsar.*
1837	Pushkin killed in a duel. Ministry of state domains established.
1839–1840	Second Mohammed Ali crisis.

1840	Bakunin leaves Russia for Germany.
1841	Lermontov killed in a duel.
1845	Hereditary *dvoryanstvo* restricted to top five ranks. Revised version of Criminal Code.
1846	Dostoyevsky publishes *Poor Folk.*
1847	Turgenev publishes *A Sportsman's Sketches.*
1848	Revolution in France, Austria, Italy, and Germany. Chartist Petition in England. Publication of Marx's *Communist Manifesto.* Death of Vissarion G. Belinsky.
1849	Nicholas intervenes to help Austria put down Hungarian revolt. Dostoyevsky and others sentenced to death but reprieved on scaffold.
1851	Opening of St. Petersburg-Moscow Railway.
1852	Louis Napoleon proclaimed emperor of France. Leo Tolstoy publishes *Childhood.* Death of Gogol.
1853–1856	Crimean War.
1855	Death of Nicholas I.
1855–1881	Rule of Alexander II.
1856	Treaty of Paris ends Crimean War. Hereditary *dvoryanstvo* restricted to top four ranks.
1857	Herzen founds *The Bell* in London.
1858–1860	Russian penetration in NE Asia. Acquisition of Amur and Maritime provinces from China.
1859	Shamil surrenders: conquest of Caucasus complete except for Circassia (1864).
1860	Foundation of Vladivostok. Rural courts introduced. State bank established.
1861	Emanicipation of serfs. Formation of first revolutionary groups. Turgenev publishes *Fathers and Sons.*
1862	Bismarck becomes chancellor of Prussia. Start of Russian railway boom.
1863	Poland rebels. Leo Tolstoy begins *War and Peace.*
1863–1864	Reforms of law, education, and local government *(zemstva).*
1864	Nicholas G. Chernyshevsky banished to Siberia. Court reform. Introduction of *zemstva* and city self-government.
1864–1868	Conquest of Central Asia.
1864–1880	Russia conquers Turkestan.
1866	Prussia defeats Austria at Königgrätz. First attempt on Alexander's life. Moscow Conservatory founded. Dostoyevsky's *Crime and Punishment* published.
1867	Sale of Alaska to United States.
1868	Tolstoy's *War and Peace* finished.
1869	Tchaikovsky's first opera *The Voyevodye* performed.
1870	Compulsory military service introduced. Municipal dumas reorganized.

1870–1871	Prussia defeats France. Bismarck unites Germany under William.
1871	London Convention on the Straits. Bakunin's *Dieu et l'etat.*
1873	Three Emperors' League.
1873–1874	First "Going to the People" movement.
1877–1878	Russo-Turkish war. Treaty of San Stefano. Mass trials of radicals and revolutionaries ("Fifty" and "193").
1878	Bismarck presides over the Congress of Berlin. Vera Zasulich shoots St. Petersburg police chief. Terrorist assassinates Chief of Gendarmes (Aug.). Temporary laws introducing courts-martial for terrorists (Aug.). Secret circular authorizing arrest and exile of persons suspected of seditious intent (Sept.).
1878–1881	Development of terrorist activity. Dynamiting of Winter Palace; wrecking of imperial trains.
1879	"Temporary Governors General" created (April). Tchaikovsky's *Eugene Onegin.*
1880	Terrorists succeed in planting bomb in Winter Palace. Third Department abolished; establishment of new Department of State Police.
1881	Alexander II assassinated.
1881–1894	Rule of Alexander III.
1881	Reaction. Institution of Emergency Powers. Ascendancy of Pobedonostsev. Major edict concerning "Temporary Laws."
1882	Rules for overt surveillance.
1883	Law requiring peasants to buy out their land allotment.
1885	Anglo-Russian crisis over Afghanistan. New edition of Criminal Code.
1885–1887	Bulgarian crisis.
1886	Special rules governing forced labor.
1887	"Reinsurance Treaty" between Russia and Germany. Execution of Lenin's brother for participating in attempt on Alexander III. Soul tax abolished.
1889	Land Commandants created.
1890	Famine.
1891	Start of Trans-Siberian Railway.
1891–1893	Maturing of Franco-Russian alliance.
1892–1903	Witte revolutionizes industry, commerce, and transport.
1893	Clauses in Emancipation Edict permitting the leaving of communes are abrogated.
1894	Death of Alexander III.
1894–1917	Rule of Nicholas II.
1896	Expansion into Manchuria: Chinese Eastern railway.
1897	Foundation of Moscow Art Theater.
1898	Foundation of Marxist Russian Social-Democratic Labor Party.
1899	Diaghilev founds *Mir Isskustva (The World of Art).*
1900	Boxer rebellion in China.

1901–1903	Zubatov active.
1902	Foundation of Socialist Revolutionary Party. Assassination of D. S. Sipyagin (minister of interior).
1903	Lenin splits Social-Democratic party into Bolshevik and Menshevik wings. Kishinev pogrom.
1904–1905	Russo-Japanese war.
1904	Assassination of V. I. Plehve (minister of interior). Zemstvo "banquet" campaign demanding constitution (Nov.).
1905	Bloody Sunday (Jan. 9). Battle of Mukden (Feb.–Mar.). Destruction of Russian fleet at Tsushima by Japanese (May). Treaty of Portsmouth, New Hampshire ends Russo-Japanese conflict (Aug.). Assassination of Grand Duke Sergey. Abortive revolution (general strike; establishment of Soviets of Workers' Deputies; violent repression. Concession of representative assembly, or state duma, Oct. 17). Manifesto promising civil liberties and representative institutions.
1906	Fundamental Laws (constitution) and First Duma. New legislation enabling peasants to consolidate holdings and leave communes (Nov.).
1906–1911	The Stolypin era. Successive dumas convened and prorogued. Revolutionary agricultural reforms. Industrial progress. Rasputin gains ascendancy over Tsaritsa and Tsar.
1907	Anglo-Russian entente. Redemption payments and arrears canceled.
1908	Annexation of Bosnia-Herzegovina by Austria.
1909	*Vekhi.* Symposium published by a group of politicians and philosophers.
1910	Death of Leo Tolstoy.
1911	Agadir crisis. Assassination of Stolypin.
1912	Massacre in Lena goldfields. Strike wave. First issue of *Pravda,* Vyacheslav M. Molotov heads editorial board.
1914–1917	War with Germany and Austria.
1916	Rasputin murdered (Dec.).
1917	Nicholas abdicates (Feb.). Outbreak of the Revolution. Bolshevik seizure of power (Oct.). Provisional government formed but duma takes over.
1918–1921	Civil War and War Communism.
1918	Murder of former tsar and his family (July). Proclamation of the "Red Terror" (Sept.).
1921	New Economic Policy (NEP) inaugurated.
1923	Union of Soviet Socialist Republics formed.
1925	Constitution ratified by Soviet Congress. USSR-German commercial treaty and defensive alliance and Turkey. Trotsky dismissed.

1927	Soviet Criminal Code enacted.
1928–1932	"Collectivization": creation of *kolkhozy.*
1929	Sholokhov publishes *Quiet Flows the Don.*
1934	Clauses added to Criminal Code sections dealing with anti-state ("counter-revolutionary") crimes. USSR joins League of Nations. Doctrine of Soviet Socialist Realism officially tabulated at Writers' Congress. Sergey Mironovich Kirov assassinated.
1936–1938	Great Purges.
1936	"Stalin Constitution" instigated.
1939	Molotov-Ribbentrop (Soviet-German nonaggression) Pact.
1940	Bulgakov completes *The Master and Margarita.*
1941	Germany invades USSR (June). Siege of Moscow.
1941–1944	Siege of Leningrad (lasting almost 900 days).
1942	USSR victorious at Stalingrad.
1943	USSR victorious in Kursk tank battle.
1945	Victory over Germany (May 9).
1947–1954	Cold War.
1949	Industry and agriculture restored to level of pre-Second World War output.
1953	Death of Stalin.
1957–1965	Regional economic councils established.
1957	Sputnik I. Boris Pasternak's *Dr. Zhivago* published.
1959	Russian spacecraft Lunik III photographs moon. Ulanova appointed ballet mistress of the Bolshoi Ballet.
1960	USSR cancels economic and technical aid to China. Death of Pasternak.
1961	Gagarin becomes first man to travel in space.
1962	Cuban Missile Crisis (Oct.). *One Day in the Life of Ivan Denisovich* by Alexander Solzhenitsyn published.
1963	Nuclear test ban treaty between U.S., USSR and Britain. *A Precocious Autobiography* by Yevgeny Yevtushenko published.
1964	Mikoyan named president of USSR. Khrushchev falls and is replaced by Brezhnev and Kosygin.
1965	Soviet cosmonaut Alexei Leonev becomes first man to walk in space.
1966	*The Master and Margarita* by Mikhail Bulgakov published. Treaty of Friendship between USSR and Mongolia.
1968	Censorship again tightened. Film *Andrei Rublev* not released because of its "negative" view of history. "Prague Spring" Liberalism and Soviet invasion.
1970	Treaty of Friendship between USSR and Czechoslovakia. Extension, for 20 years, of Finnish Treaty of Friendship and Mutual Assistance. Treaty of Renunciation of Force between USSR and Federal Republic of Germany.

1971	Khrushchev dies. Mars 3 makes soft landing on moon.
1974	Alexander Solzhenitsyn expelled from USSR after publication of *Gulag Archipelago.*
1975	Apollo-Soyuz link up in space (July). Completion of first section of the Baikal–Amur Magistral railway.
1977	Brezhnev elected president of USSR Supreme Soviet. Fourth Constitution since 1917 published.
1979	Salt II signed by U.S. President Jimmy Carter and Brezhnev. Invasion of Afghanistan.
1980	Olympic Games in Moscow. Kosygin dies.
1982	Brezhnev dies. Yury Andropov elected General Secretary of the Communist Party of the Soviet Union Central Committee and member of the Presidium.
1983	Andropov elected President of the Presidium.
1984	Andropov dies. Konstantin Chernenko elected General Secretary of the Communist Party of the Soviet Union Central Committee and President of the Presidium.

SELECT BIBLIOGRAPHY

General

Great Soviet Encyclopaedia. Trans. of the 3rd ed. of *Bol'shaya Sovetskaya Entsiklopediya, 1970,* 17 vols. in progress. 1973–.

Brown, Archie; Fennell, John; Kaser, Michael; and Willetts, H. T. (eds.). *The Cambridge Encyclopedia of Russia and the Soviet Union*. 1982.

Davies, R. W. and Shaw, Denis J. B. (eds.). *The Soviet Union*. 1978.

Florinsky, Michael T. *McGraw-Hill Encyclopedia of Russia and the Soviet Union*. 1961.

Kaiser, Robert G. *Russia: the People and the Power*. 1976.

Murarka, Dev. *The Soviet Union*. 1971.

Smith, Hedrick. *The Russians*. 1976.

Thompson, Anthony. *Russia/U.S.S.R.: a Selective Annotated Bibliography of Books in English*. 1979.

Utechin, S. V. *Everyman's Concise Encyclopaedia of Russia*. 1961.

Wieczynski, Joseph L. *Modern Encyclopedia of Russian and Soviet History*. 1976–.

History (General)

Blum, Jerome. *Lord and Peasant in Russia from the Ninth to the Nineteenth Centuries*. 1961.

Carr, Edward Hallett. *History of Soviet Russia,* 14 vols. 1952–78.

Clarkson, J. *A History of Russia*. 1961.

Crankshaw, Edward. *In the Shadow of the Winter Palace*. 1976.

Pares, Bernard. *A History of Russia*. 1926.

Pipes, Richard E. *Russia Under the Old Regime*. 1974.

Rauch, Georg von. *A History of Soviet Russia*. 1957.

Riasanovsky, Nicholas V. *A History of Russia,* 3rd ed. 1977.

Treadgold, Donald W. *Twentieth-Century Russia*. 1964.

Vernadsky, George. A *History of Russia,* 5th rev. ed. 1961.
______. *Kievan Russia.* 1948.
Vernadsky, George and Karpovich, Michael. A *History of Russia,* 5 vols. 1943–69.

History (Medieval)

Dmytryshyn, Basil. *Medieval Russia.* 1972.
Fennell, John L. I. *Ivan the Great of Moscow.* 1961.
______. *The Emergence of Moscow, 1304–1359.* 1968.
Grey, Ian. *Ivan III and the Unification of Russia.* 1964.
______. *Ivan the Terrible.* 1964.
______. *Boris Godunov, the Tragic Tsar.* 1973.

History (Early Romanovs)

Anderson, M. S. *Peter the Great.* 1978.
Avrich, Paul. *Russian Rebels, 1600–1800.* 1972.
Dukes, Paul. *Catherine the Great and the Russian Nobility: a Study Based on the Materials of the Legislative Commission of 1767.* 1967.
Lentin, A. *Russia in the Eighteenth Century: from Peter the Great to Catherine the Great, 1696–1796.* 1973.
Sumner, Benedict H. *Peter the Great and the Emergence of Russia.* 1951.
Talbot Rice, Tamara. *Elizabeth, Empress of Russia.* 1970.

History (Imperial Russia)

Almedingen, Edith Martha. *So Dark a Stream: a Study of the Emperor Paul I of Russia, 1754–1801.* 1959.
______. *The Emperor Alexander II: a Study.* 1962.
______. *The Emperor Alexander I.* 1964.
Charques, Richard D. *The Twilight of Imperial Russia: the Reign of Tsar Nicholas II.* 1958.
Crankshaw, Edward. *The Shadow of the Winter Palace: the Drift to Revolution, 1825–1917.* 1976.
Florinsky, Michael T. *The End of the Russian Empire.* 1931.
Frankland, Noble. *Crown of Tragedy: Nicholas II.* 1960.
Graham, Stephen. A *Life of Alexander II, Tsar of Russia.* 1935.
de Grunwald, Constantin. *Tsar Nicholas I.* 1954.
Herzen, Alexander Ivanovich. *My Past and Thoughts.* rev. ed., 4 vols., 1968.
Hough, Richard Alexander. *The Potemkin Mutiny.* 1961.
Kelly, Aileen. *Mikhail Bakunin: A Study in the Psychology and Politics of Utopianism.* 1982.
Kochan, Miriam. *The Last Days of Imperial Russia.* 1976.
Lowe, Charles. *Alexander III of Russia.* 1895.
Mazour, Anatole Grigorevich. *The First Russian Revolution 1825: the Decembrist Movement, Its Origins, Development and Significance.* 1961.
Mendel, Arthur P. *Michael Bakunin: Roots of Apocalypse.* 1982.

Monas, Sidney L. *The Third Section: Police and Society in Russia under Nicholas I.* 1961.
Palmer, Alan W. *Alexander I, Tsar of War and Peace.* 1974.
Pares, Bernard. *The Fall of the Russian Monarchy: a Study of the Evidence.* 1939.
Seton-Watson, Hugh. *The Decline of Imperial Russia, 1855-1914.* 1952.
Solzhenitsyn, Alexander. *August 1914.* 1972.
Strakhovsky, Leonid Ivan. *Alexander I of Russia: the Man Who Defeated Napoleon.* 1947.
Youssoupoff, Princc. *Rasputin: His Evil Influence and His Murder, by One of the Men Who Killed Him.* 1974.

History (Provisional Government, 1917 to Stalin)

Alexandrov, Victor. *The End of the Romanovs.* 1966.
Browder, Robert P. and Kerensky, Alexander Fedorovich (eds.). *The Russian Provisional Government, 1917,* 3 vols. 1961.
Deutscher, Isaac. *The Unfinished Revolution: Russia 1917-1967.* 1967.
Fitzpatrick, Sheila. *The Russian Revolution.* 1983.
Kerensky, Alexander Fedorovich. *The Kerensky Memoirs: Russia and History's Turning Point.* 1965.
Kochan, Lionel. *The Russian Revolution.* 1971.
Reed, John. *Ten Days that Shook the World.* 1961.
Treadgold, Donald W. *Twentieth-century Russia,* 3rd ed. 1971.
Ulam, Adam B. *Bolsheviks.* 1968.

History (Stalin era to the end of the war, 1945)

Dallin, David J. *From Purge to Coexistence: Essays on Stalin's and Kruschchev's Russia,* 1964.
Deutscher, Isaac. *Stalin: A Political Biography.* n.d.
Fadeyev, Alexander Aleksandrovich. *Leningrad in the Days of the Blockade, 1941-43.* 1945.
Gibson, Michael. *Russia under Stalin.* 1972.
Medvedev, Roy Alexandrovich. *Let History Judge: the Origins and Consequences of Stalinism.* 1972.
Tolstoi, Nikolai. *Victims of Yalta.* 1978.
Werth, Alexander. *Russia at War, 1941-1945.* 1964.

History (From 1945)

Crankshaw, Edward. *Khrushchev's Russia.* 1959.
______. *Khrushchev: a Biography.* 1966.
Kennan, George Frost. *Memoirs, 1950-1963.* 1973.
Medvedev, Roy Alexandrovich. *Let History Judge: the Origins and Consequences in Power.* 1976.
Strobe, Talbot. *Khrushchev Remembers.* 1971.

Nationalities

Allworth, Edward. *The Nationality Question in Soviet Central Asia.* 1973.
Bazhan, M. P. (ed.). *Soviet Ukraine.* 1969.
Bilmanis, Alfred. *A History of Latvia.* 1951.
Demko, George J. *The Russian Colonization of Kazakhstan, 1898–1916.* 1969.
Greenberg, Louis. *The Jews in Russia: the Struggle for Emancipation.* 1976.
Jukes, Geoffrey. *The Soviet Union in Asia.* 1973.
Jurgela, Constantine R. *History of the Lithuanian Nation.* 1948.
Katz, Z., Rogers, R. and Harned, F. (eds.). *Handbook of Major Soviet Nationalities.* 1975.
Kendrick, D. and Puxon, G. *The Destiny of Europe's Gypsies.* 1972.
Kochan, Lionel (ed.) *The Jews in Soviet Russia since 1917,* 3rd ed. 1978.
Kolarz, W. *Russia and Her Colonies.* 1953.
Lang, David M. *Armenia: Cradle of Civilization.* 1978.
______ *The Georgians.* 1966.
______ and Walker, C. *Armenians.* 1977.
Lewis, R. A., Rowland, R. H. and Clem, R. S. *Nationality and Population Change in Russia and the USSR: An Evaluation of Census Data, 1897–1970.* 1976.
Maclean, Fitzroy. *To Caucasus, End of all the Earth.* 1976.
Manning, Clarence A. *Twentieth-century Ukraine.* 1951.
Nove, Alec and Newth, J. A. *The Soviet Middle East.* 1967.
Parming, Tönu and Järvesoo, Elmar (eds.). *A Case Study of a Soviet Republic: The Estonian SSR.* 1978.
Rauch, Georg von. *The Baltic States: the Years of Independence; Estonia, Latvia, Lithuania, 1917–1940.* 1974.
Semyonov, Yuri. *Siberia: Its Conquest and Development.* 1963.
Tuzmuhamedov, R. *How the National Question was Solved in Soviet Central Asia.* 1973.
Vakar, Nicholas P. *Belorussia, the Making of a Nation.* 1956.

Literature (General)

Alexandrova, Vera. *A History of Soviet Literature.* 1963.
Brown, Edward J. *Russian Literature since the Revolution.* 1963.
Chizhevsky, Dmitri. *History of Russian Literature from the Eleventh Century to the End of the Baroque.* 1972.
Davies, Ruth. *The Great Books of Russia.* 1968.
Freeborn, Richard. *The Rise of the Russian Novel.* 1973.
Glenny, Michael (ed.). *Novy Mir: a Selection, 1925–67.* 1972.
Gudzy, N. K. *History of Early Russian Literature.* 1970.
Hayward, Max and Labedz, Leopold (eds.). *Literature and Revolution in Soviet Russia, 1917–62.* 1963.
Hingley, Ronald. *Russian Writers and Society in the 19th Century,* 2nd rev. ed. 1977.
Markov, Vladimir. *Russian Futurism: a History.* 1969.

Mirsky, Dmitri, P. A *History of Russian Literature, Comprising a History of Russian Literature and Contemporary Russian Literature.* 1949.
Simmons, Ernest J. *An Outline of Modern Russia Literature, 1880–1940.* 1943.
Slonim, Marc. *Soviet Russian Literature: Writers and Problems, 1917–1977,* 2nd rev. ed. 1977.
Struve, Gleb. *Soviet Russian Literature, 1917–50.* 1951.
Unbegaun, Boris Ottokar. *Russian Versification,* 2nd rev. ed. 1963.

Literature (Biography)

Bearne, C. G. *Sholokhov.* 1969.
Berlin, Isaiah. *The Hedgehog and the Fox: an Essay on Tolstoy's View of History.* 1953.
Brown, Clarence. *Mandelstam (1892–1938).* 1973.
Brown, Edward J. *Mayakovsky: a Poet in the Revolution.* 1973.
Carden, Patricia. *The Art of Isaac Babel.* 1972.
Dalton, Margaret. *Andrei Siniavski and Julii Daniel: Two Soviet "Heretical" Writers.* 1973.
Gifford, Henry. *Pasternak: a Critical Study.* 1977.
Gilles, Daniel. *Chekhov, Observer Without Illusion.* 1969.
Grossman, Leonid. *Dostoevsky: a Biography.* 1974.
Haight, Amanda Chase. *Anna Akhmatova: a Poetic Pilgrimage.* 1976.
Hingley, Ronald. *Chekhov: a Biographical and Critical Study.* 1966.
Jordan, M. *Andrei Platonov.* 1973.
Kodjak, Andrej. *Alexander Solzhenitsyn.* 1978.
Lavrin, Janko. *Dostoevsky: a Study, With a Portrait Frontispiece.* 1943.
______. *Goncharov (1812–91).* 1954.
______. *Lermontov.* 1959.
Levin, Dan. *Stormy Petrel: the Life and Work of Maxim Gorky.* 1967.
Magarshack, David. *Chekhov: a Life.* 1952.
______. *Gogol: a Life.* 1957.
______. *Turgenev: a Life.* 1954.
McVay, Gordon. *Esenin: a Life.* 1976.
Pyman, Avril. *Aleksandr Blok: a Biography. Volume 1: Distant Thunder, 1880–1908.* 1978.
Schapiro, Leonard B. *Turgenev: His Life and Times.* 1979.
Troyat, Henri. *Gogol: the Biography of a Divided Soul,* 1974.
______. *Pushkin (a Biography).* 1974.
______. *Tolstoy.* 1970.
Yarmolinsky, Avrahm. *Dostoevskii: His Life and Art.* 1957.

Art and Culture

Alpatov, M. *Art Treasures of Russia,* 2nd ed., 1975.
Barna, Yon. *Eisenstein.* 1973.
Benois, Alexandre. *The Russian School of Painting.* 1916.

Berton, Kathleen. *Moscow: An Architectural History.* 1977.
Brown, David. *Mikhail Glinka: a Biographical and Critical Study.* 1974.
Buxton, David R. *Russian Mediaeval Architecture.* 1975.
Calvocoressi, Michel D. *Mussorgsky.* 1946.
______. *A Survey of Russian Music.* 1944.
Carmichael, Joel. *A Cultural History of Russia.* 1968.
Fabritsky, B. and Shmeliov, I. *Treasures of Mediaeval Rus.* 1974.
Faensen, Hubert and Ivanov, Vladimir. *Early Russian Architecture.* 1975.
Fitzpatrick, Sheila (ed.). *Cultural Revolution in Russia, 1928–1931.* 1978.
Golubova, E. *Art of the Autonomous Republics of the Russian Federation.* 1973.
Gostelow, Mary. *Embroidery of All Russia.* 1977.
Gray, Camilla. *The Russian Experiment in Art, 1863–1922.* 1971.
Hamilton, George H. *The Art and Architecture of Russia.* 1954.
Ivanova, E. (ed.). *Russian Applied Art: 18th to Early 20th Century.* 1976.
Kahn, Albert Eugene. *Days with Ulanova.* 1962.
Kennett, Audrey and Kennett, Victor. *The Palaces of Leningrad.* 1973.
Kerensky, Oleg. *Anna Pavlova.* 1973.
Kopp, Anatole. *Town and Revolution: Soviet Architecture and City Planning, 1917–1935.* 1970.
Korshunova, T. (ed.). *Russian Tapestry.* 1975.
Kostochkin, V. (ed.). *Old Russian Towns.* 1972.
Krebs, Stanley, D. *Soviet Composers and the Development of Soviet Music.* 1970.
Lazarev, Victor. *Russian Icons, from the 12th to the 15th Century.* 1969.
Lebedev, A. *Soviet Painting in the Tretyakov Gallery.* 1976.
Loukomski, George K. *Charles Cameron, 1740–1812; an Illustrated Monograph on His Life and Work in Russia, Particularly at Tsarskoye Selo and Pavlovsk.* 1943.
Martynov, Ivan I. *Dmitri Shostakovich (1906–): the Man and His Work.* 1976.
Miliukov, Paul Nikolayevich. *Outlines of Russian Culture.* 1942.
Onasch, Konrad. *Russian Icons.* 1977.
Popov, Oleg. *Russian Clown.* 1970.
Pronin, Alexander and Pronin, Barbara. *Russian Folk Arts.* 1975.
Rimberg, J. D. *The Motion Picture in the Soviet Union, 1918–1952: a Sociological Analysis.* 1973.
Roslavleva, Natalia. *Era of the Russian Ballet.* 1966.
Samuel, Claude. *Prokofiev.* 1971.
Sarabianov, D. and Bowlt, John. *Russian and Soviet Painting.* 1977.
Schwarz, Boris. *Music and Musical Life in Soviet Russia, 1917–1970.* 1972.
Shneerson, Grigory. *Aram Khachaturyan.* 1959.
Sobolevsky, Nikolai Dmitrievich (ed.). *The Art of Soviet Palekh.* 1958.
Spencer, Charles. *The World of Serge Diaghilev.* 1974.
Stravinsky, Vera and Craft, Robert. *Stravinsky in Pictures and Documents.* 1979.
Talbot Rice, David. *Russian Icons.* 1947.
Talbot Rice, Tamara. *A Concise History of Russian Art.* 1963.
Tcherepnin, A. *Anthology of Russian Music.* 1966.

Valkenier, Elizabeth. *Russian Realist Art.* 1977.
Voronov, N. and Rachuk, E. (eds.). *Soviet Glass.* 1973.

Religion

Beeson, T. *Discretion and Valour.* 1974.
Bennigsen, G. and Lemercier-Quelquejay, C. *Islam in the Soviet Union.* 1967.
Bourdeaux, Michael. *Religious Ferment in Russia.* 1968.
Cracraft, James. *The Church Reform of Peter the Great.* 1971.
Curtiss, John S. *The Russian Church and the Soviet State 1917–1950.* 1953.
Fedotov, Georgii P. *The Russian Religious Mind,* 2 vols., 1946–66.
Hackel, Sergei A. *The Orthodox Church.* 1971.
Hayward, Max and Fletcher, William C. (eds.). *Religion and the Soviet State: A Dilemma of Power.* 1969.
Lane, C. *Christian Religion in the Soviet Union: A Sociological Study.* 1978.
Simon, G. *Church, State and Opposition in the USSR.* 1974.
Stroyen, W. *Communist Russia and the Russian Orthodox Church, 1943–1962.* 1967.
Struve, N. *Christians in Contemporary Russia,* trans. 1967.
Timasheff, N. *Religion in Soviet Russia.* 1942.

Republics and Autonomous Regions of the Soviet Union, 1983

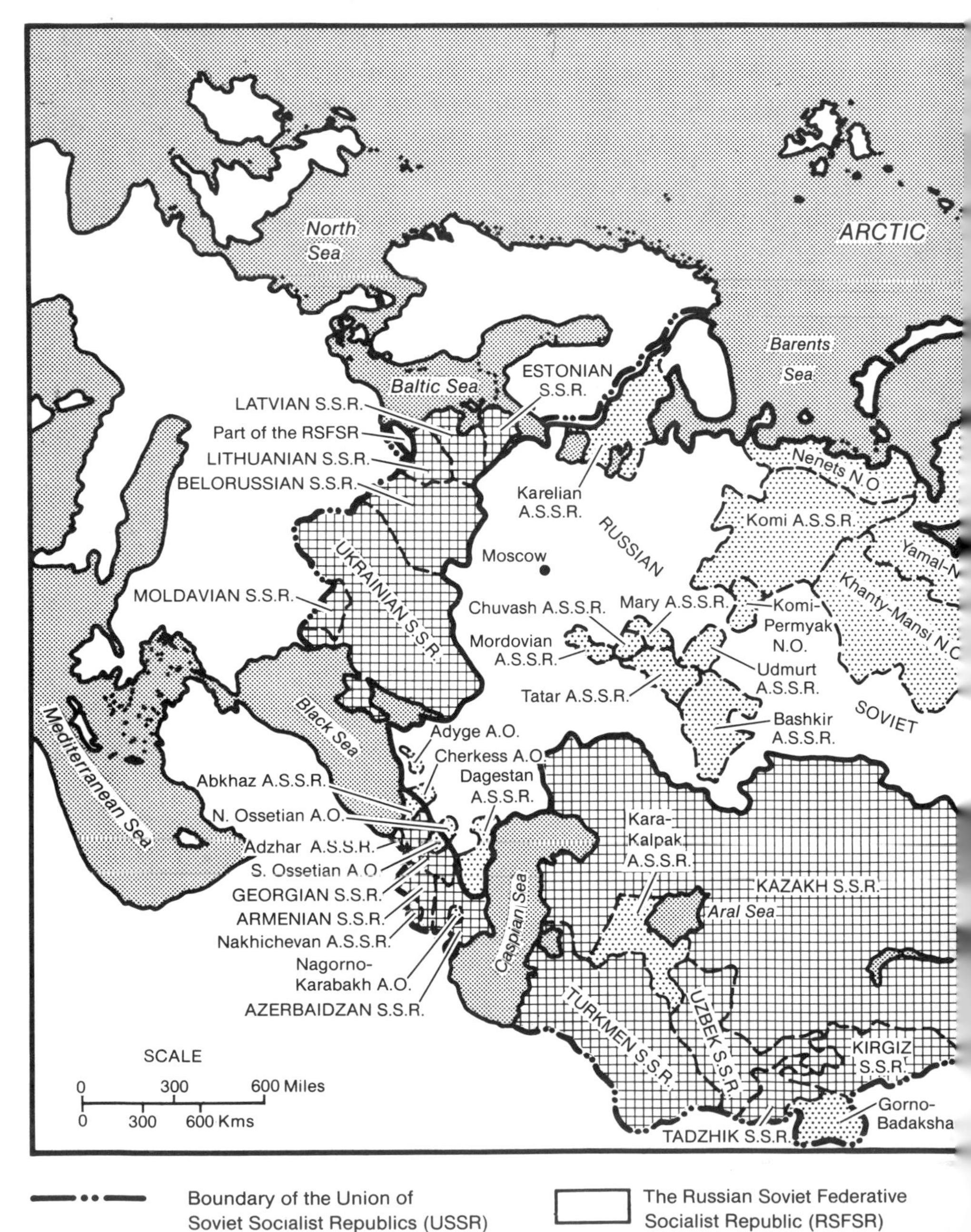

Boundary of the Union of Soviet Socialist Republics (USSR)

The Russian Soviet Federative Socialist Republic (RSFSR)

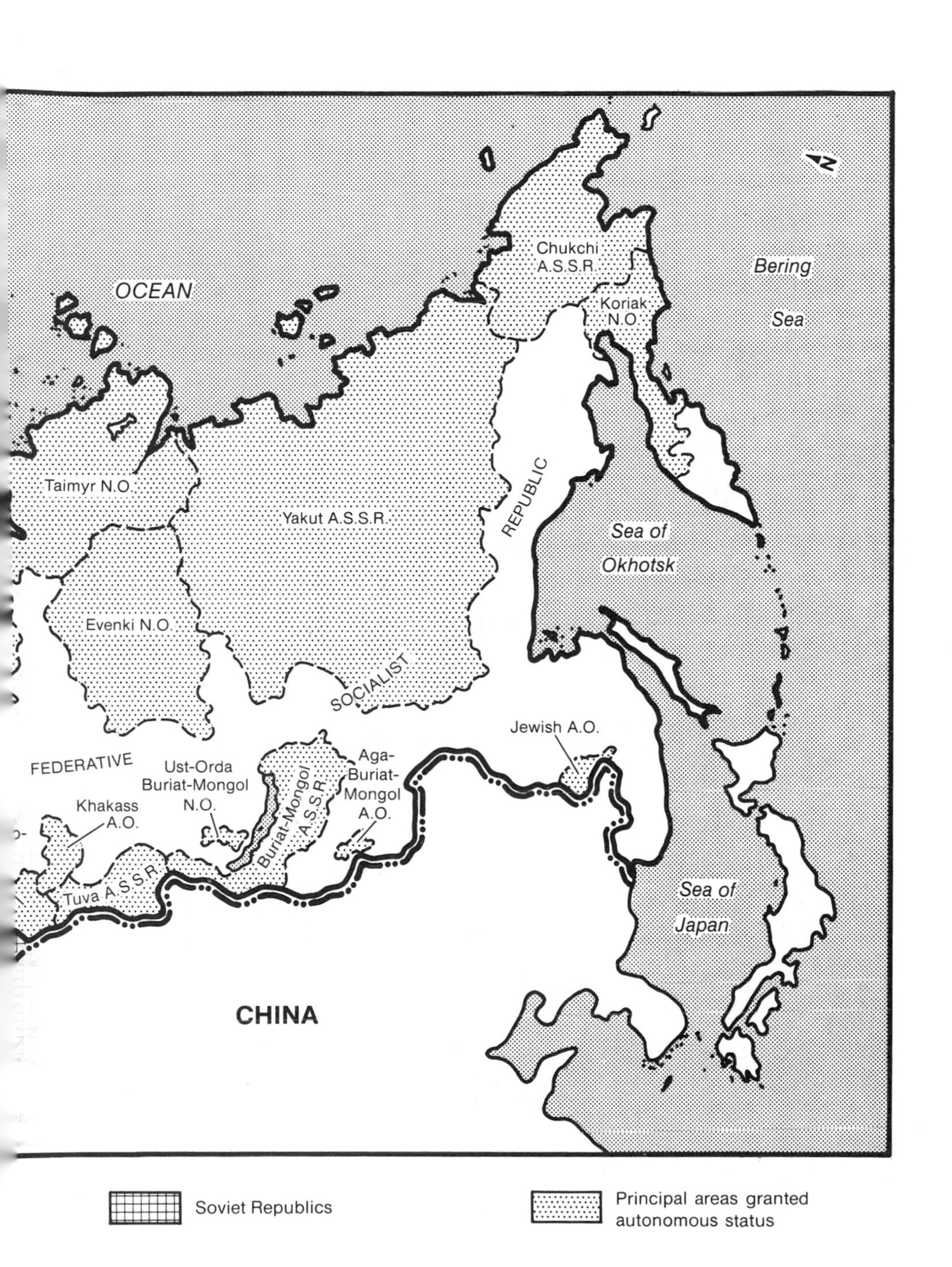
OCEAN
Chukchi A.S.S.R.
Koriak N.O.
Bering Sea
Taimyr N.O.
Yakut A.S.S.R.
REPUBLIC
Sea of Okhotsk
Evenki N.O.
SOCIALIST
Jewish A.O.
FEDERATIVE
Ust-Orda Buriat-Mongol N.O.
Aga-Buriat-Mongol A.O.
Buriat-Mongol A.S.S.R.
Khakass A.O.
Tuva A.S.S.R.
Sea of Japan
CHINA
Soviet Republics
Principal areas granted autonomous status

Soviet Union: Ethnic Composition

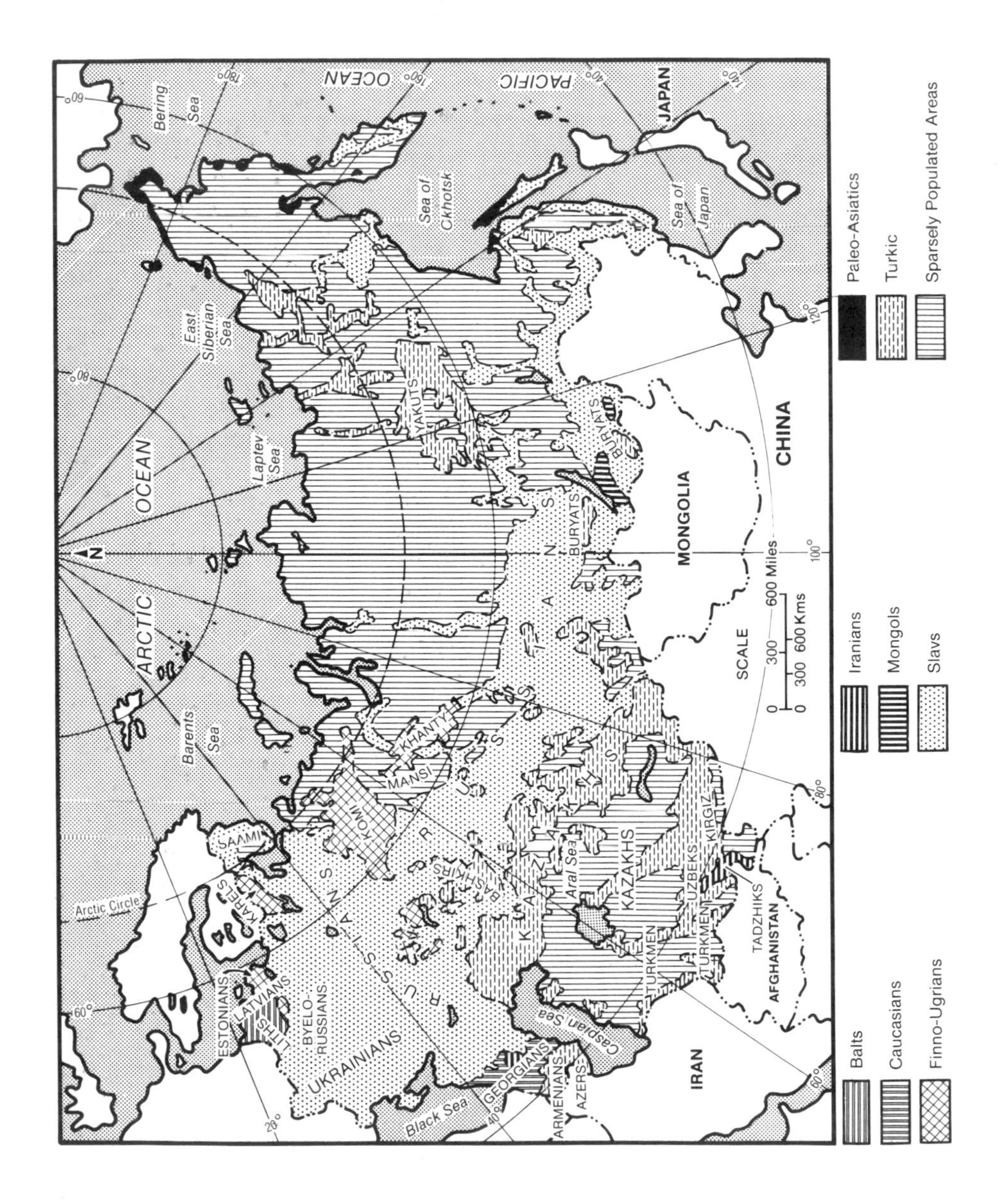

Soviet Union: Climates

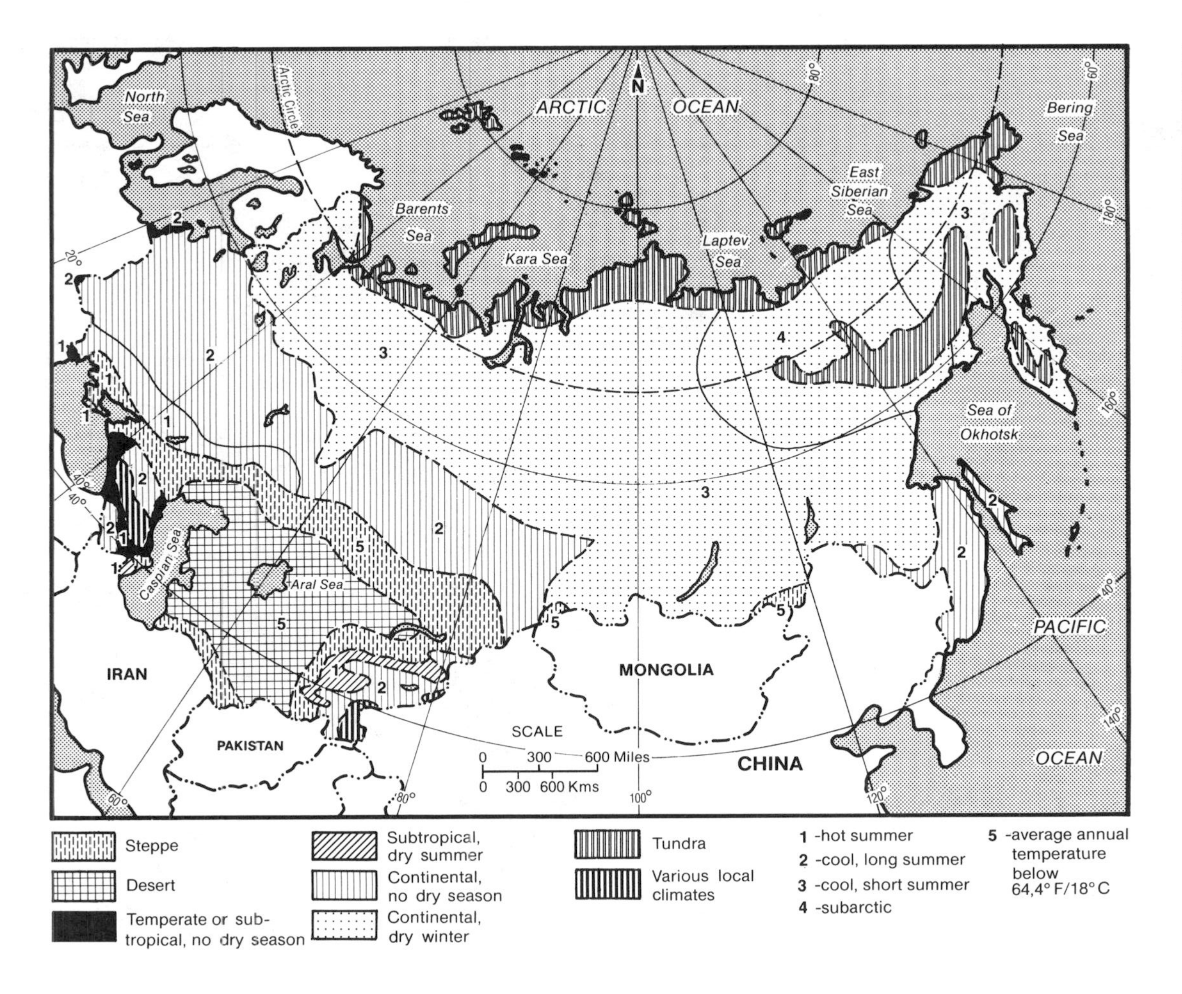

Soviet Union: Physical Regions

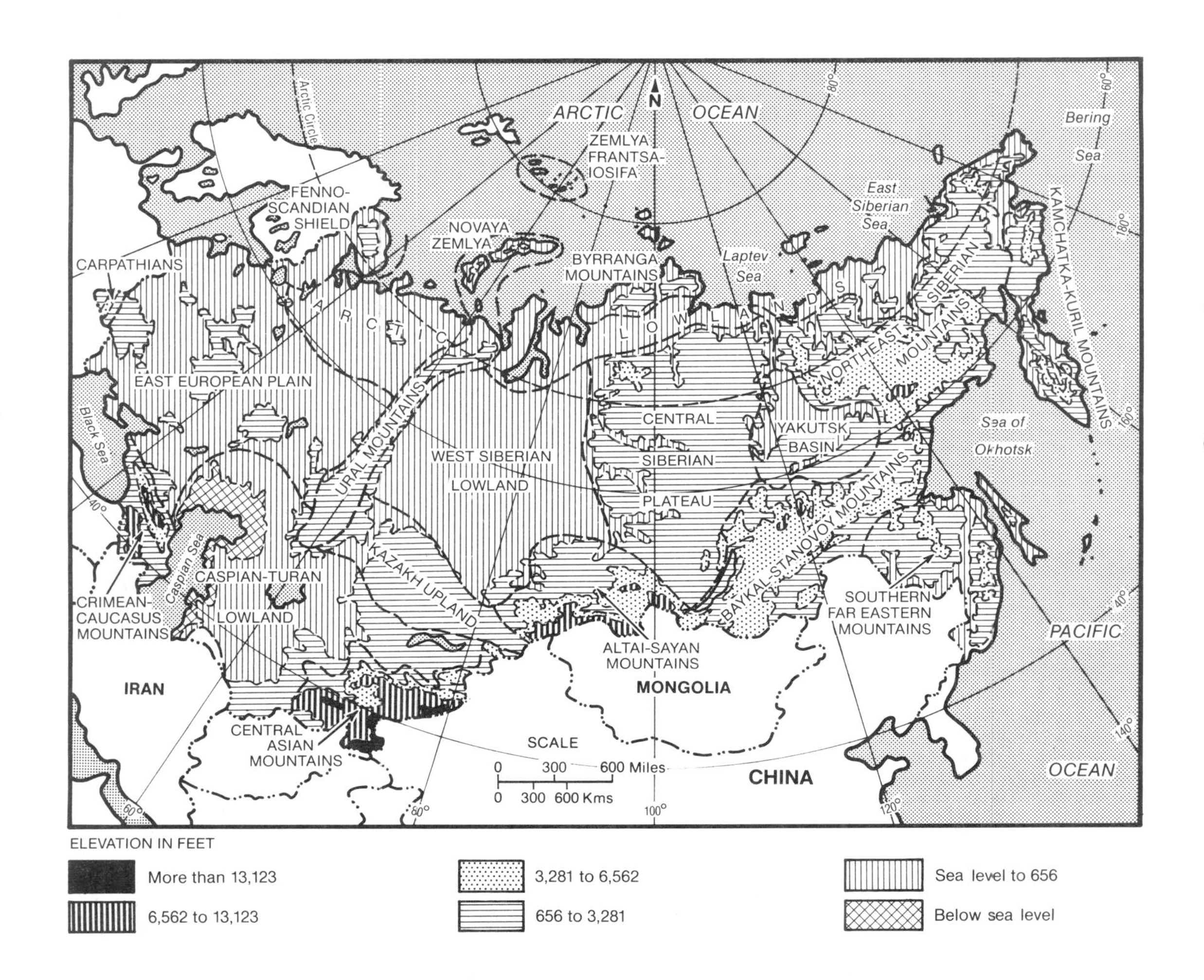

Soviet Union: Vegetation

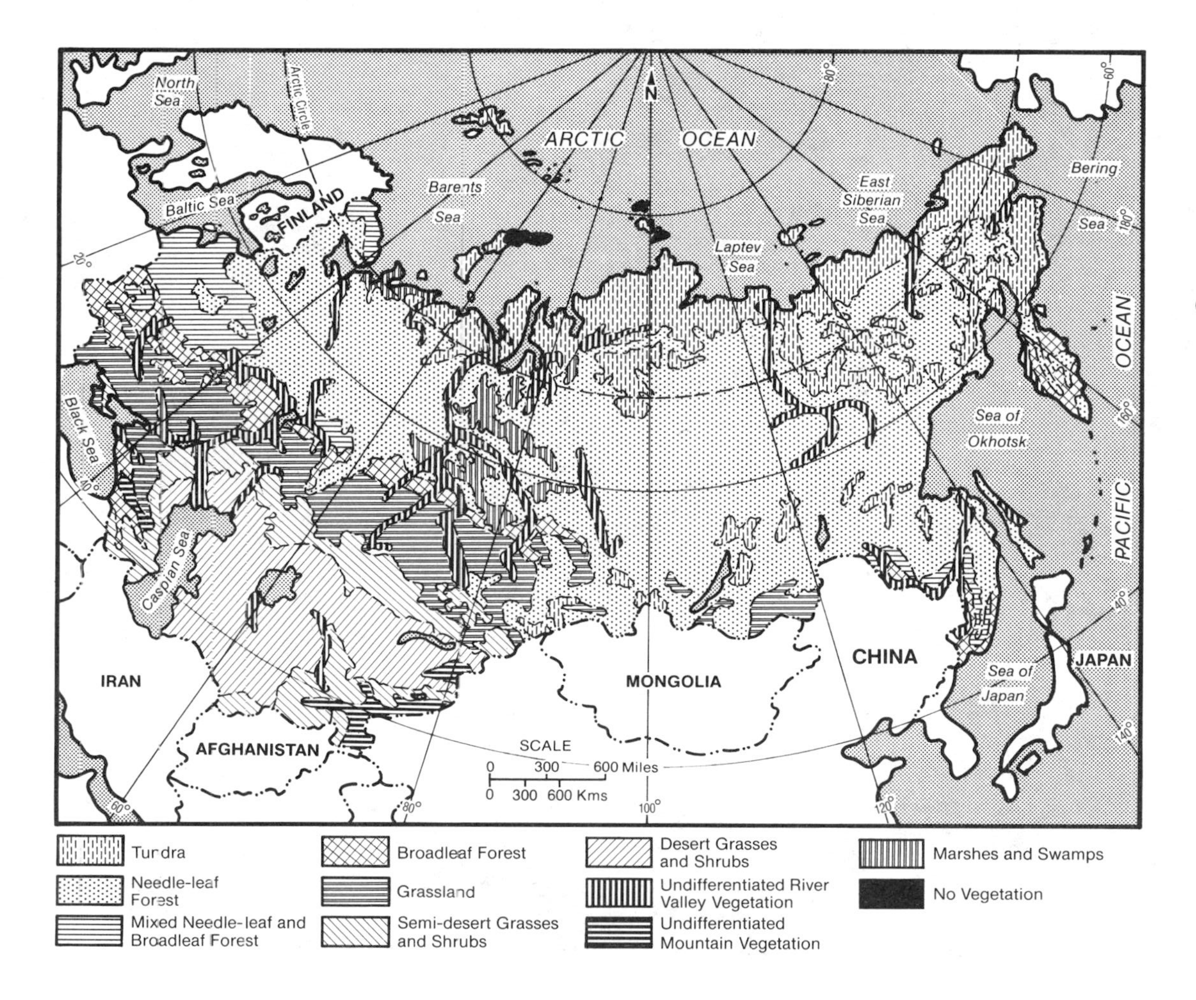

The Growth of Russia, 1462–1533

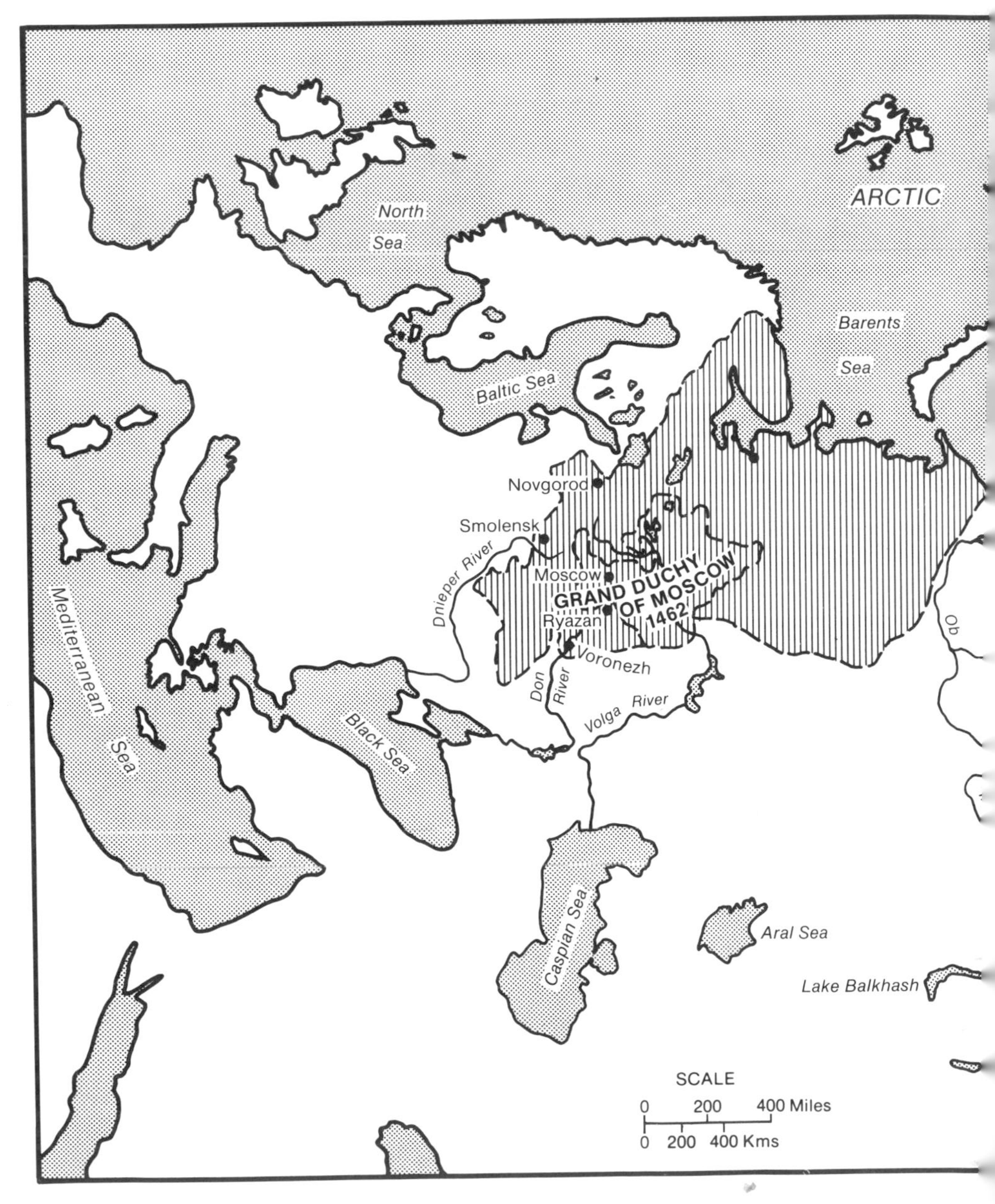

Grand Duchy of Moscow 1462 & Russia in 1533

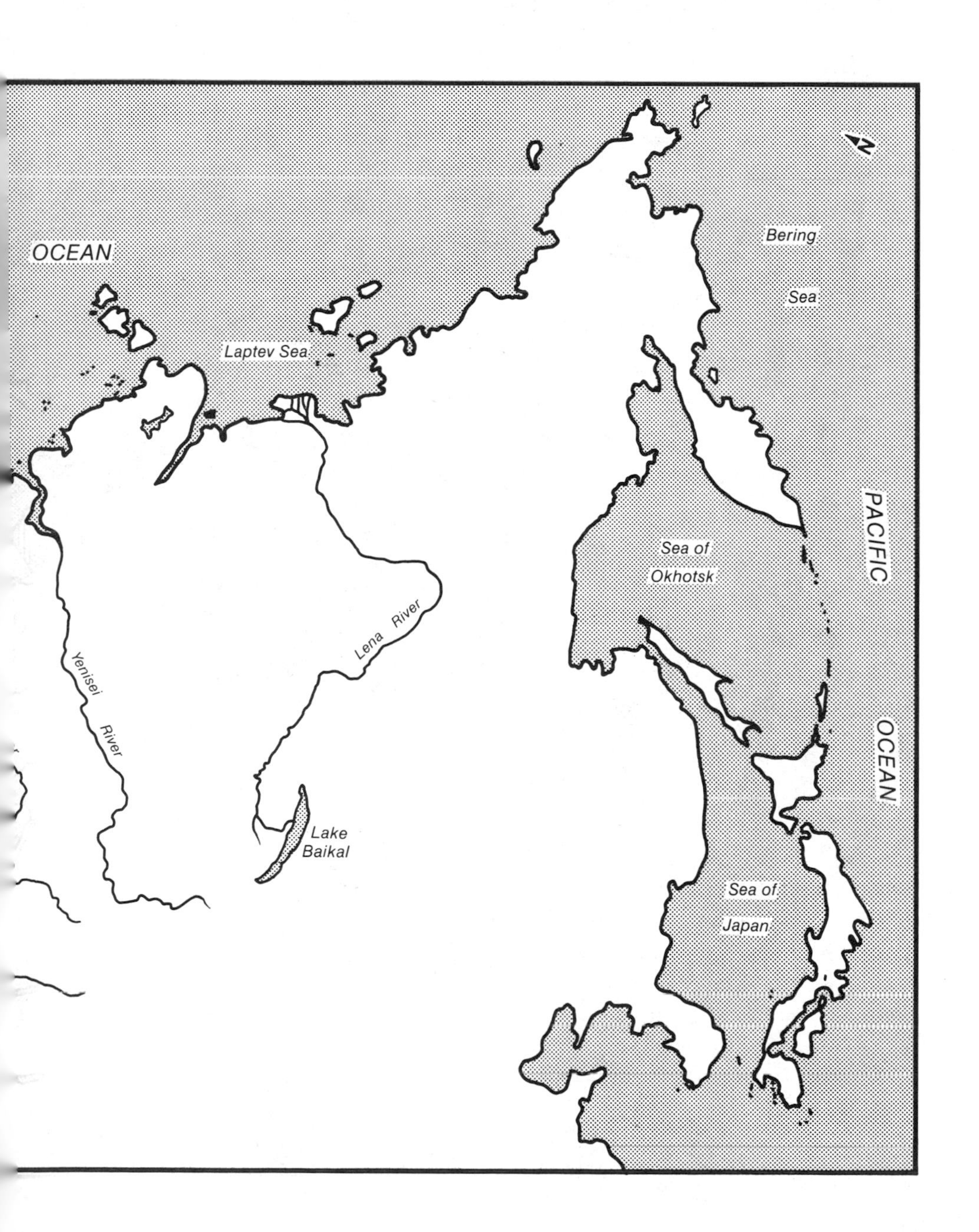
OCEAN
Laptev Sea
Bering
Sea
PACIFIC
OCEAN
Sea of
Okhotsk
Lena River
Yenisei
River
Lake
Baikal
Sea of
Japan

The Growth of Russia, 1533–1598

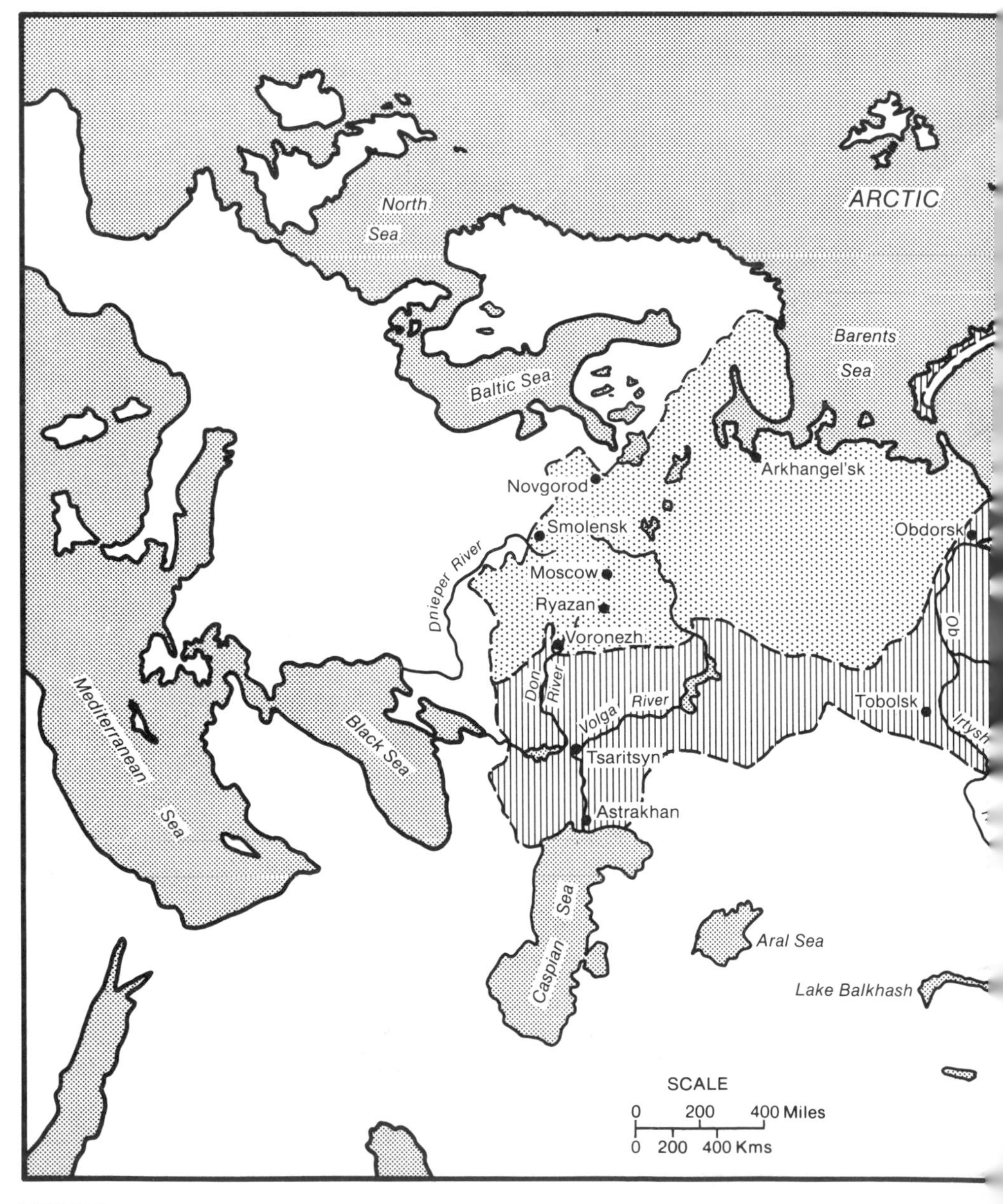

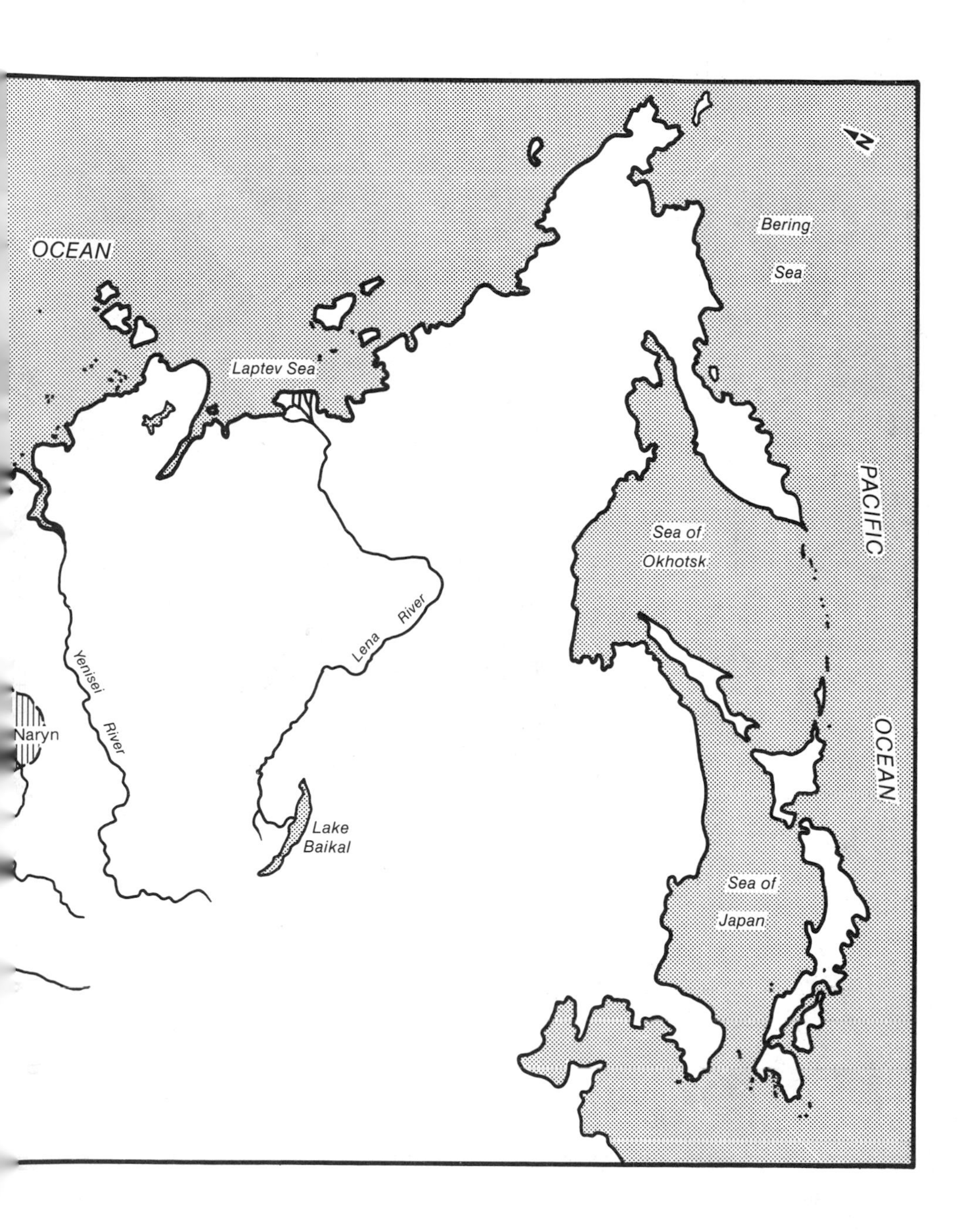
OCEAN
Laptev Sea
Bering
Sea
PACIFIC
OCEAN
Sea of
Okhotsk
Lena River
Yenisei River
Naryn
Lake
Baikal
Sea of
Japan
N

The Growth of Russia, 1598–1689

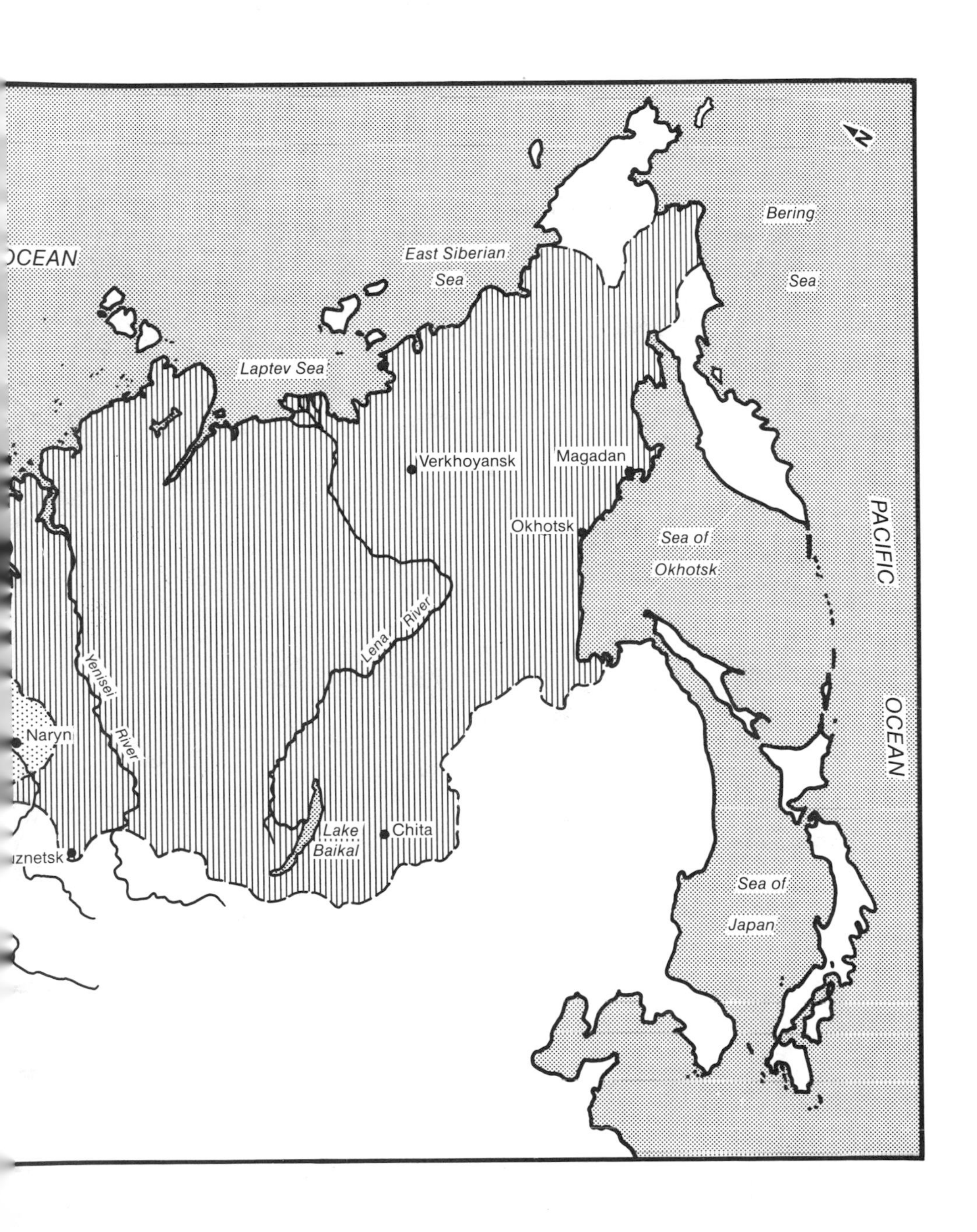

OCEAN
East Siberian
Sea
Bering
Sea
Laptev Sea
Verkhoyansk
Magadan
Okhotsk
Sea of
Okhotsk
PACIFIC
OCEAN
Lena River
Yenisei
River
Naryn
Lake
Baikal
Chita
znetsk
Sea of
Japan

The Growth of Russia, 1689–1725

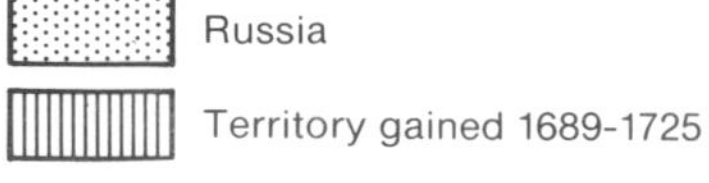

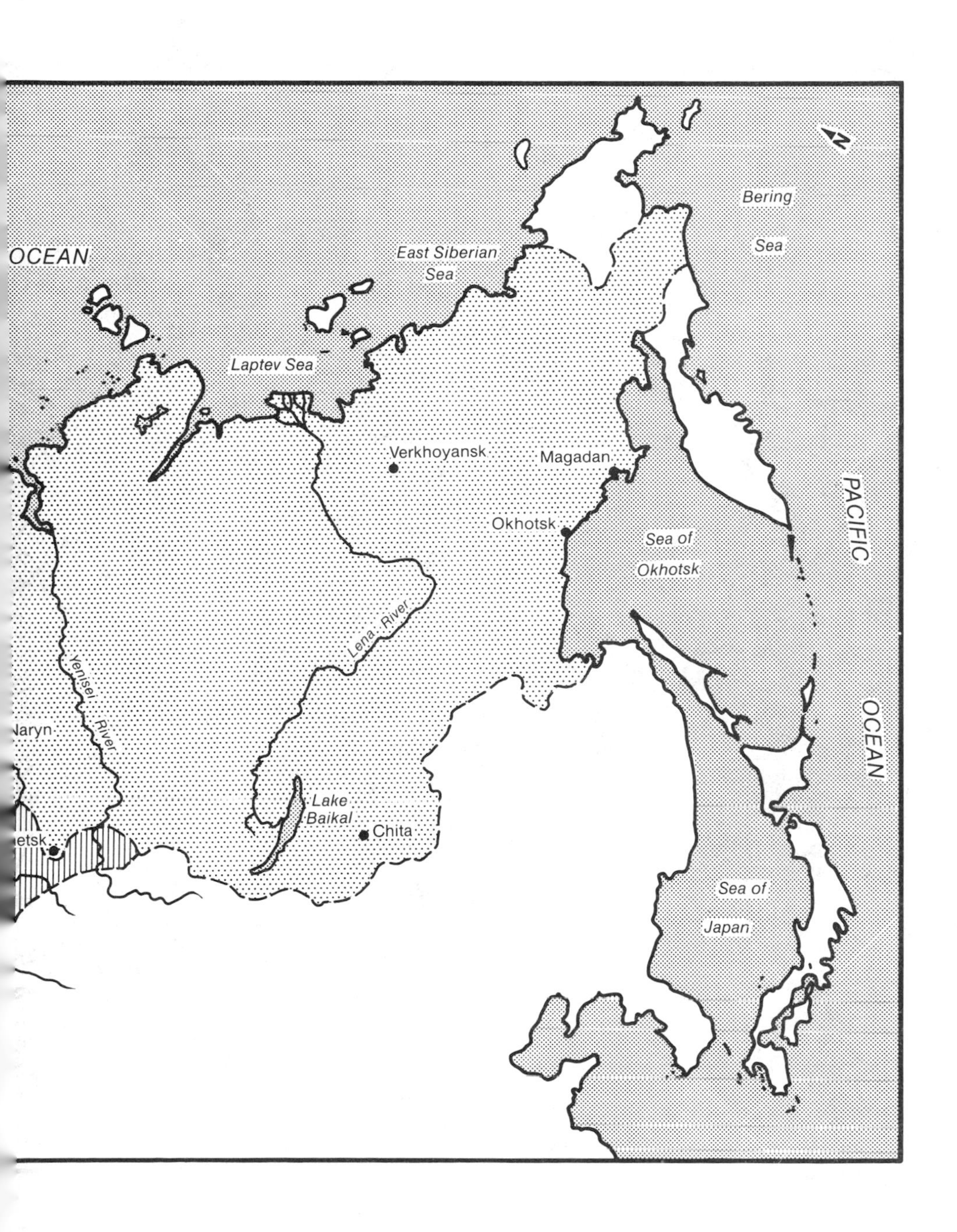
OCEAN
East Siberian Sea
Bering Sea
Laptev Sea
Verkhoyansk
Magadan
Okhotsk
Sea of Okhotsk
PACIFIC OCEAN
Lena River
Yenisei River
Naryn
Lake Baikal
Chita
etsk
Sea of Japan

The Growth of Russia, 1725–1763

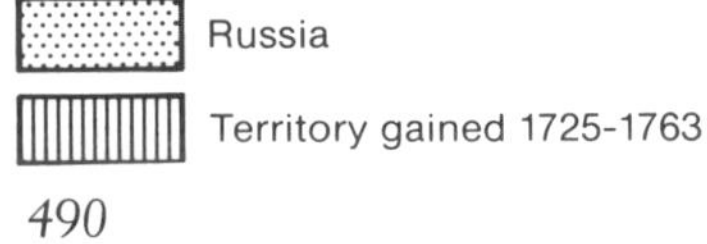

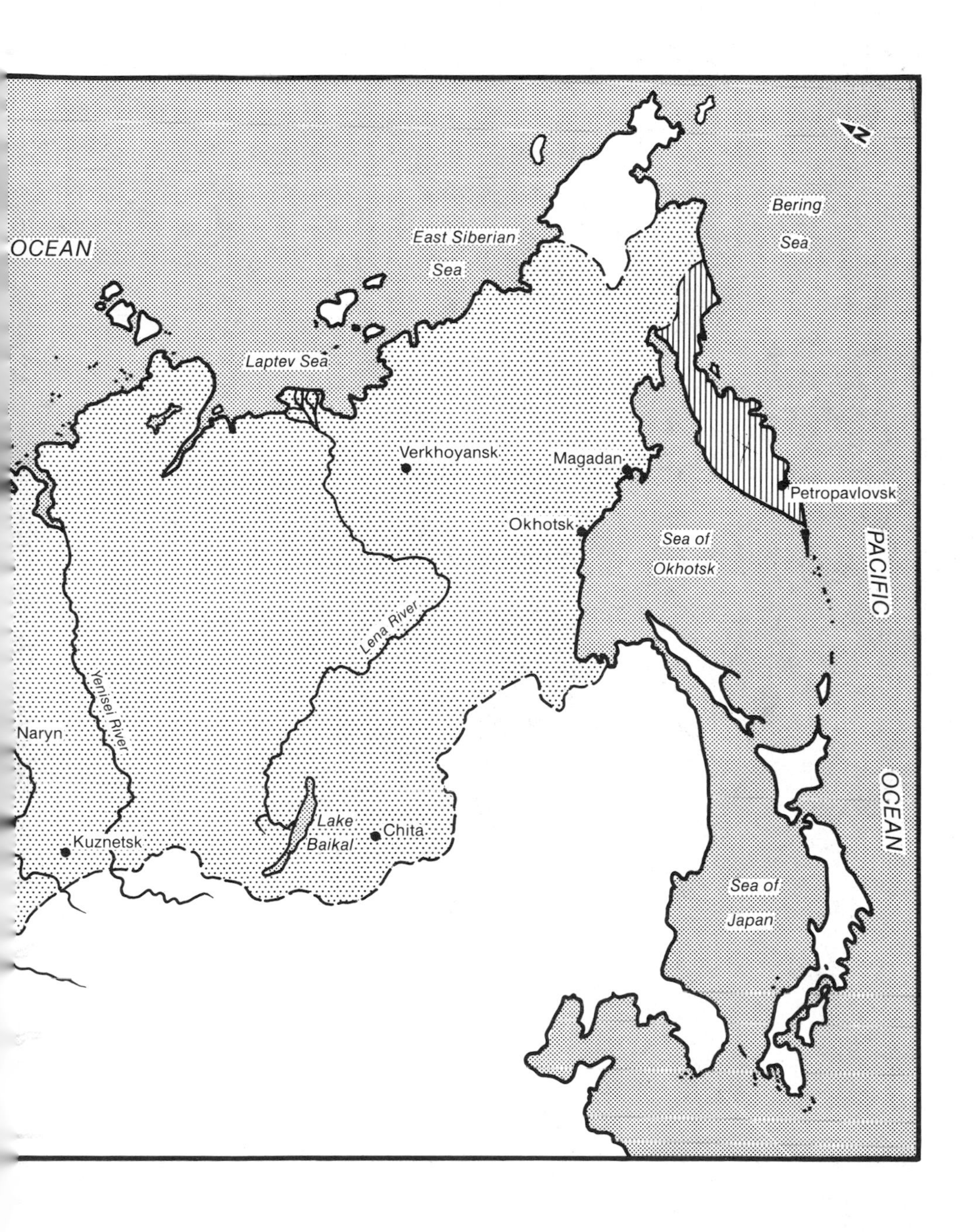
OCEAN
East Siberian Sea
Bering Sea
N
Laptev Sea
Verkhoyansk
Magadan
Petropavlovsk
Okhotsk
Sea of Okhotsk
PACIFIC OCEAN
Lena River
Yenisei River
Naryn
Lake Baikal
Chita
Kuznetsk
Sea of Japan

The Growth of Russia, 1763–1801

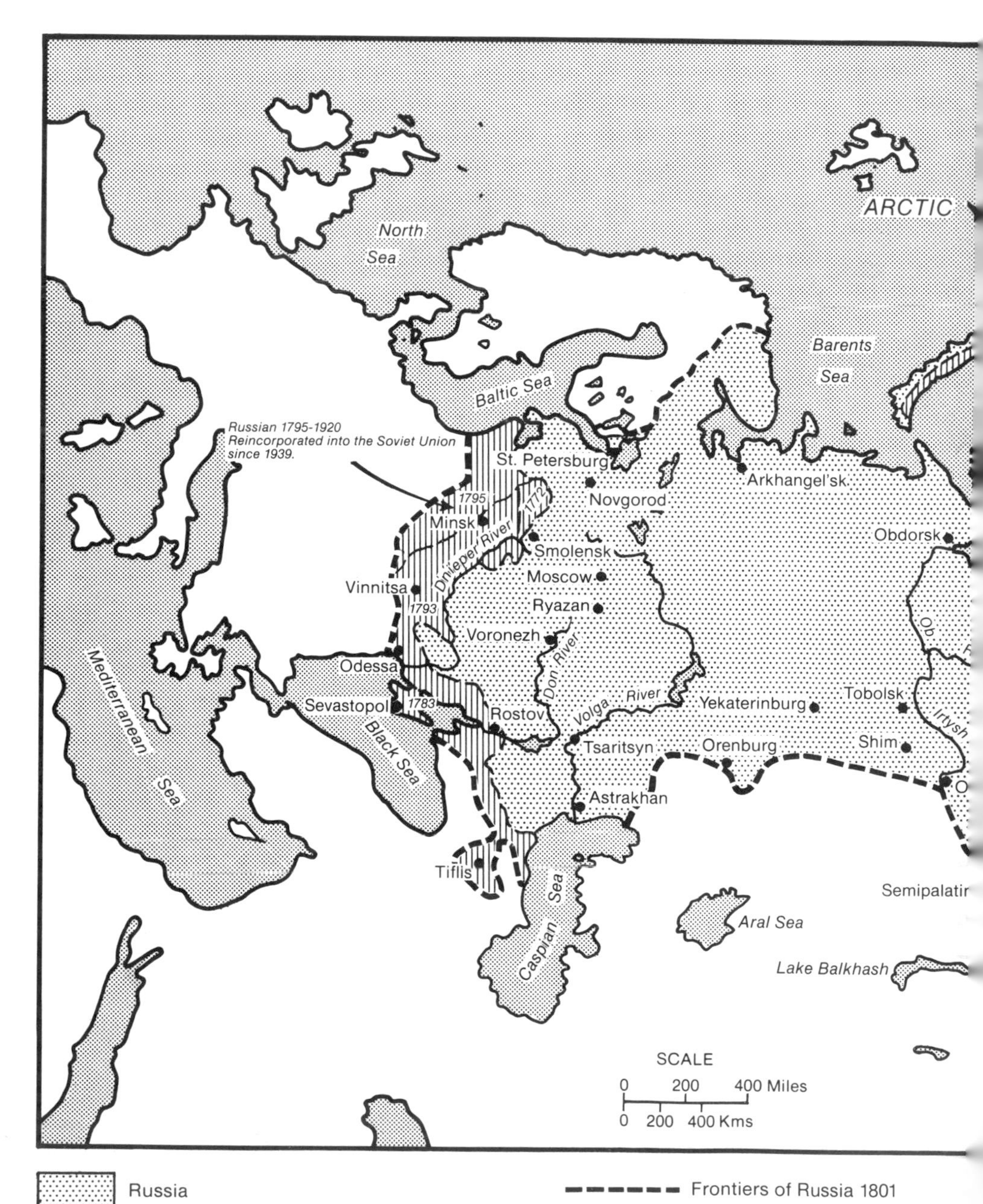

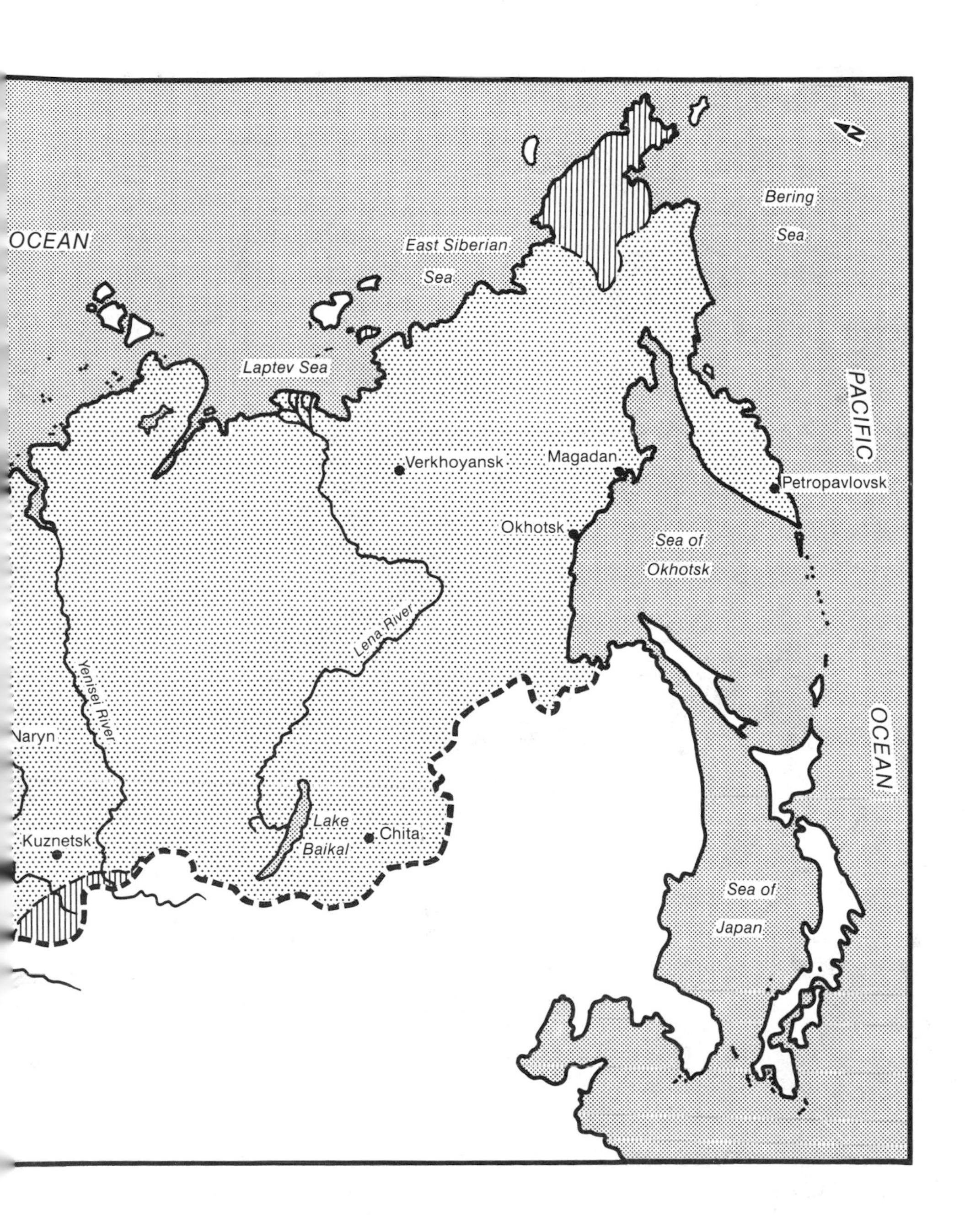
OCEAN
East Siberian Sea
Bering Sea
Laptev Sea
PACIFIC OCEAN
Verkhoyansk
Magadan
Petropavlovsk
Okhotsk
Sea of Okhotsk
Lena River
Yenisei River
Naryn
Lake Baikal
Chita
Kuznetsk
Sea of Japan

The Growth of Russia, 1801–1855

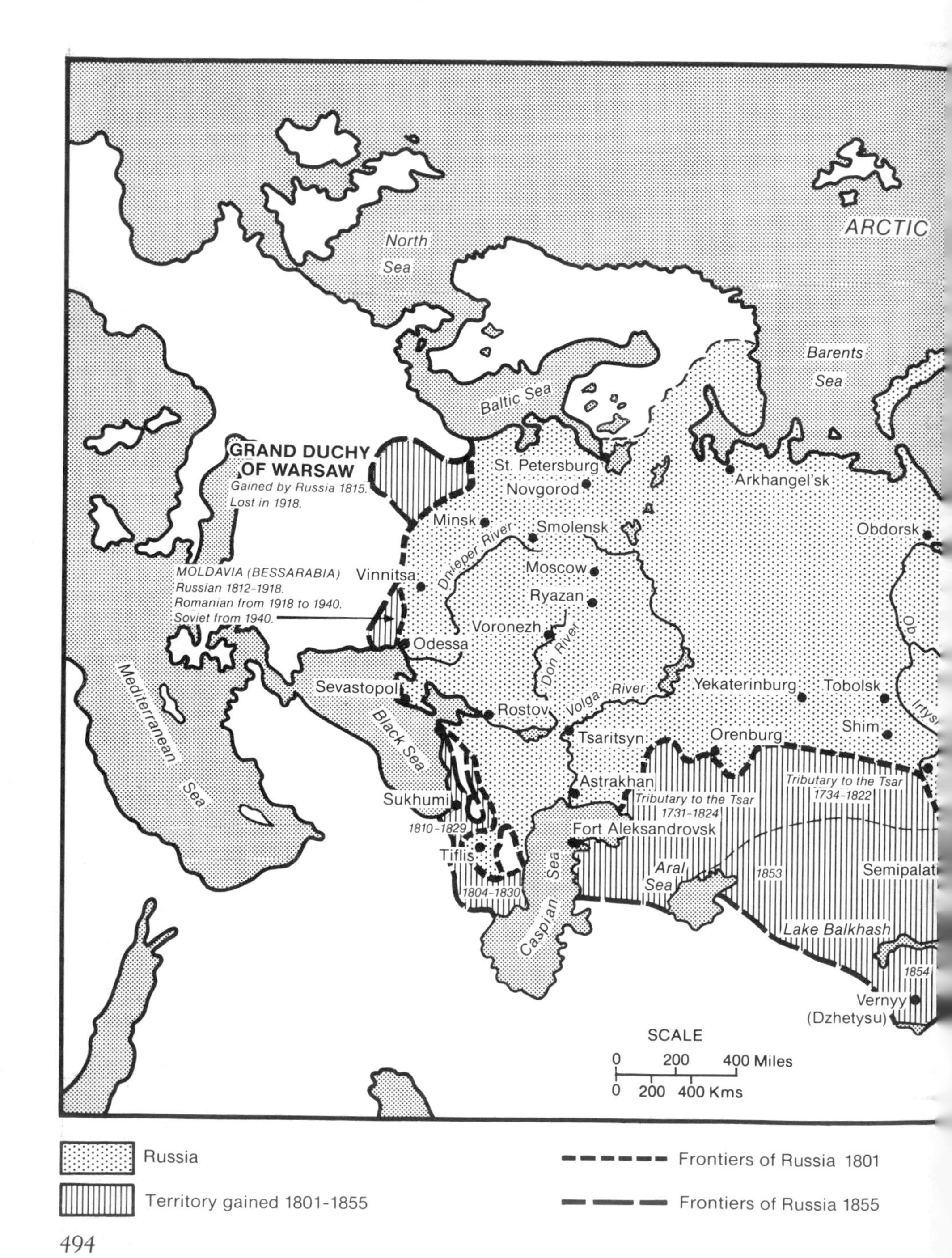

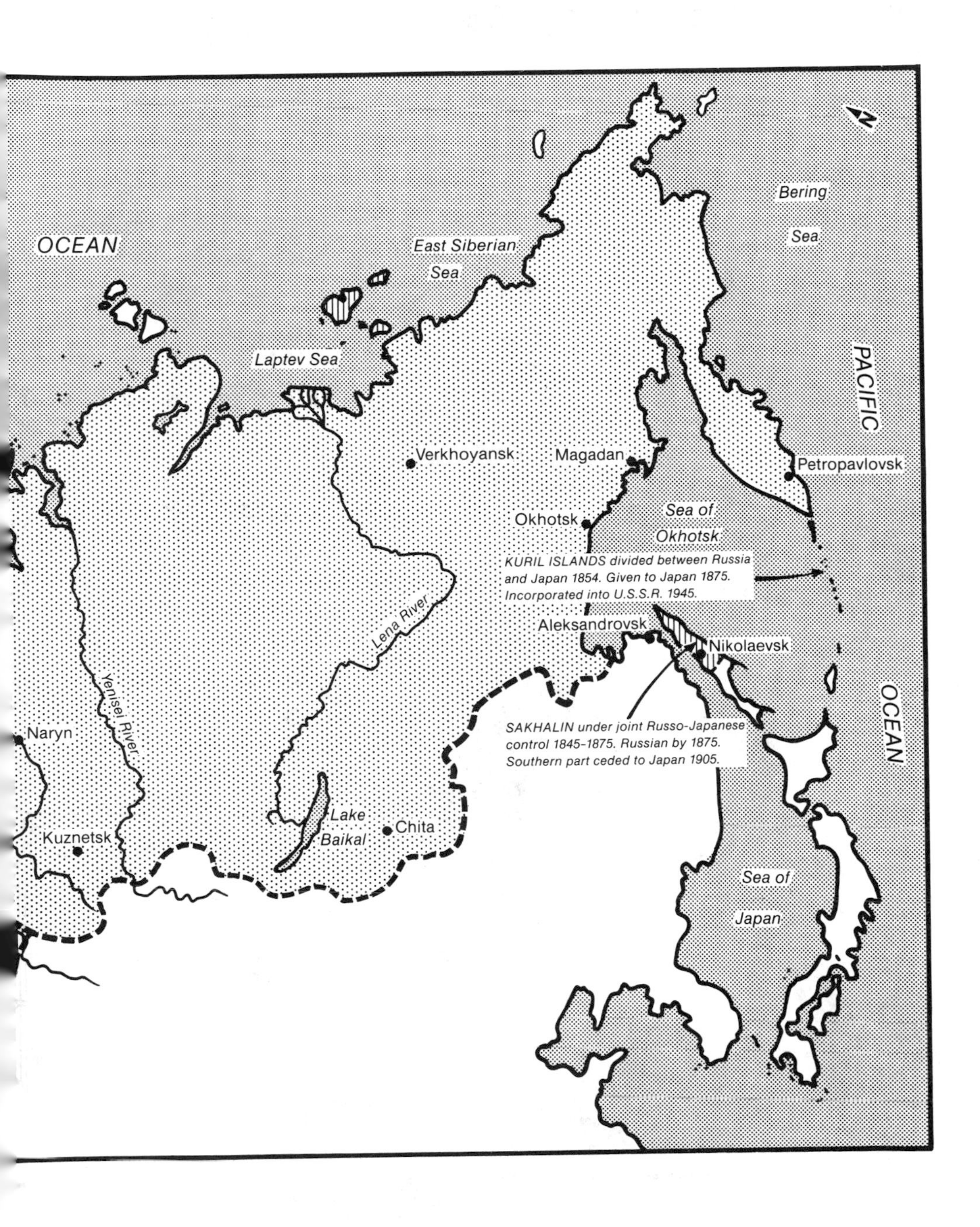
OCEAN
East Siberian Sea
Bering Sea
Laptev Sea
PACIFIC OCEAN
Verkhoyansk
Magadan
Petropavlovsk
Okhotsk
Sea of Okhotsk
KURIL ISLANDS divided between Russia and Japan 1854. Given to Japan 1875. Incorporated into U.S.S.R. 1945.
Lena River
Aleksandrovsk
Nikolaevsk
Yenisei River
Naryn
SAKHALIN under joint Russo-Japanese control 1845-1875. Russian by 1875. Southern part ceded to Japan 1905.
Lake Baikal
Chita
Kuznetsk
Sea of Japan

The Growth of Russia, 1855–1904

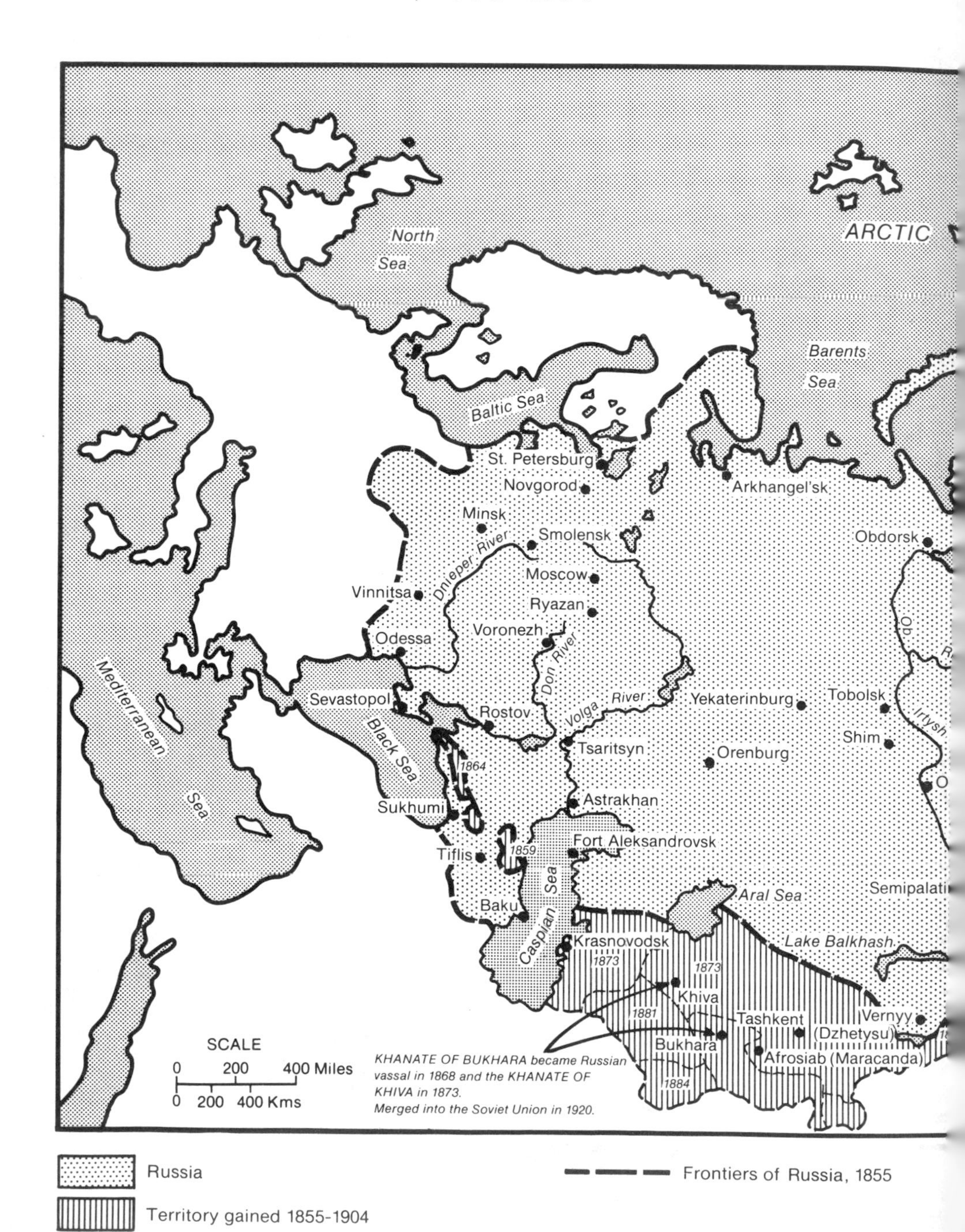

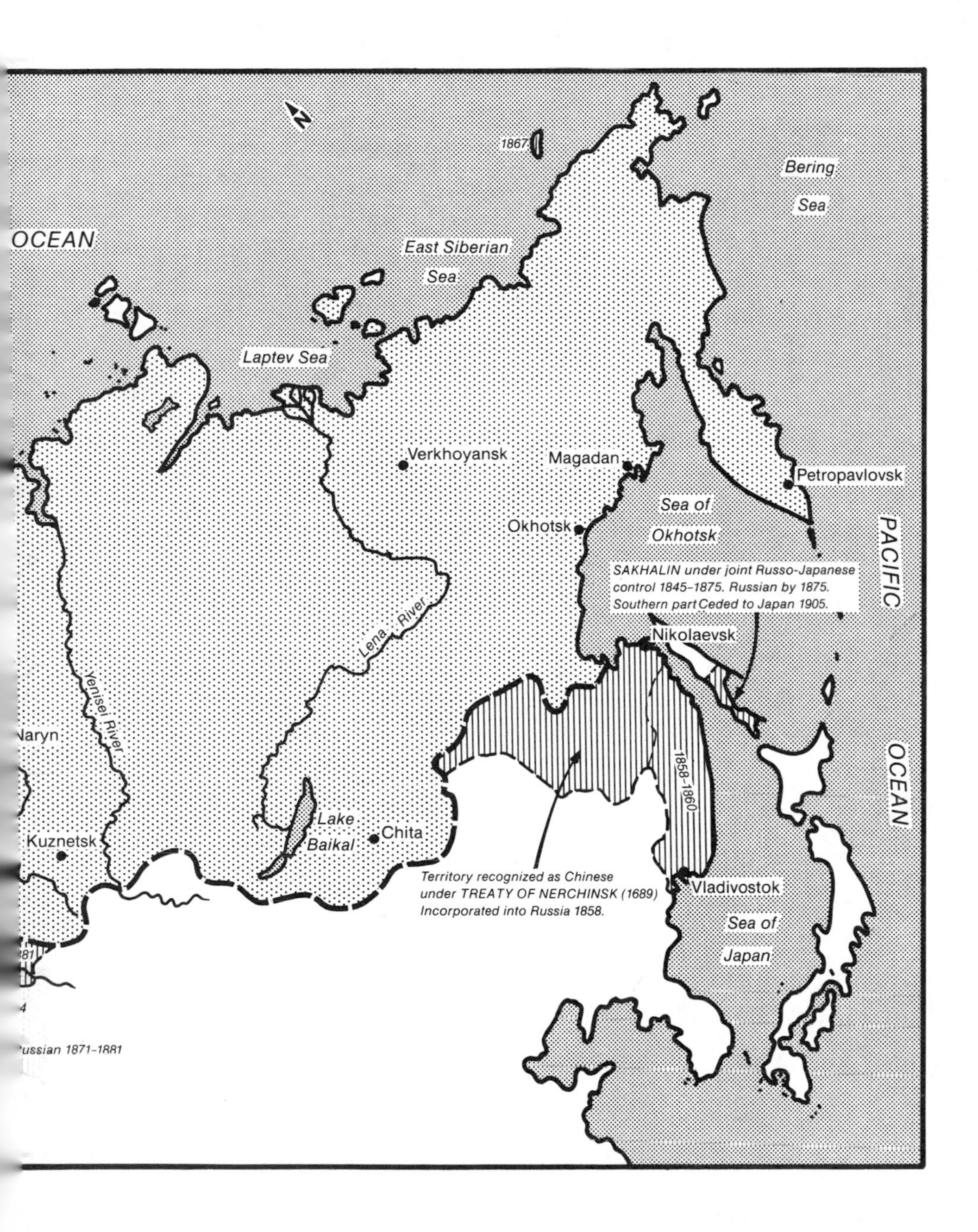
1867
Bering
Sea
OCEAN
East Siberian
Sea
Laptev Sea
Verkhoyansk
Magadan
Petropavlovsk
Sea of
Okhotsk
Okhotsk
PACIFIC
SAKHALIN under joint Russo-Japanese
control 1845–1875. Russian by 1875.
Southern part Ceded to Japan 1905.
Nikolaevsk
Lena River
Yenisei River
Naryn
1858–1860
OCEAN
Lake
Baikal
Chita
Kuznetsk
Territory recognized as Chinese
under TREATY OF NERCHINSK (1689)
Incorporated into Russia 1858.
Vladivostok
Sea of
Japan
ussian 1871–1881

The Growth of Russia, 1904–1955

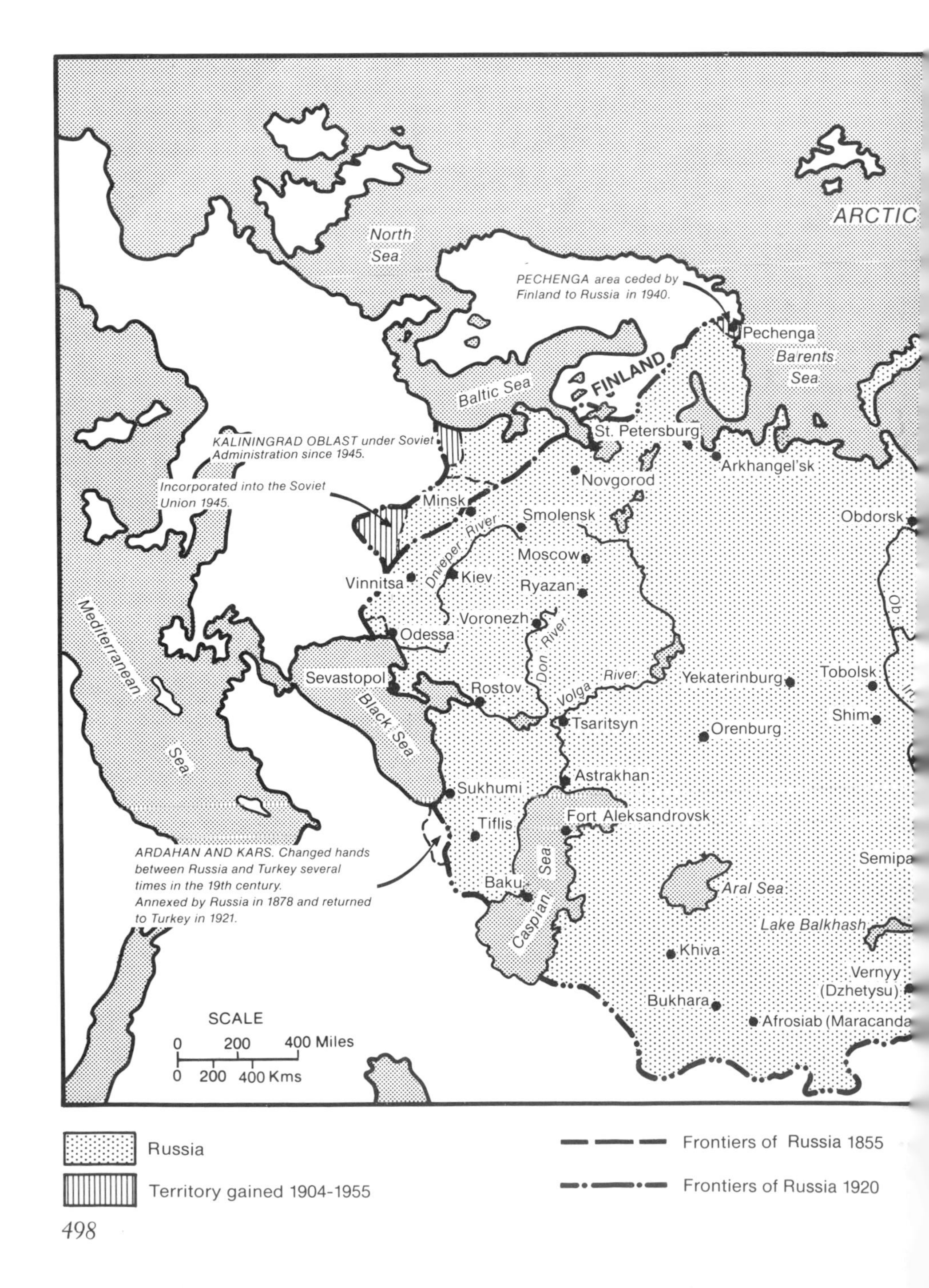

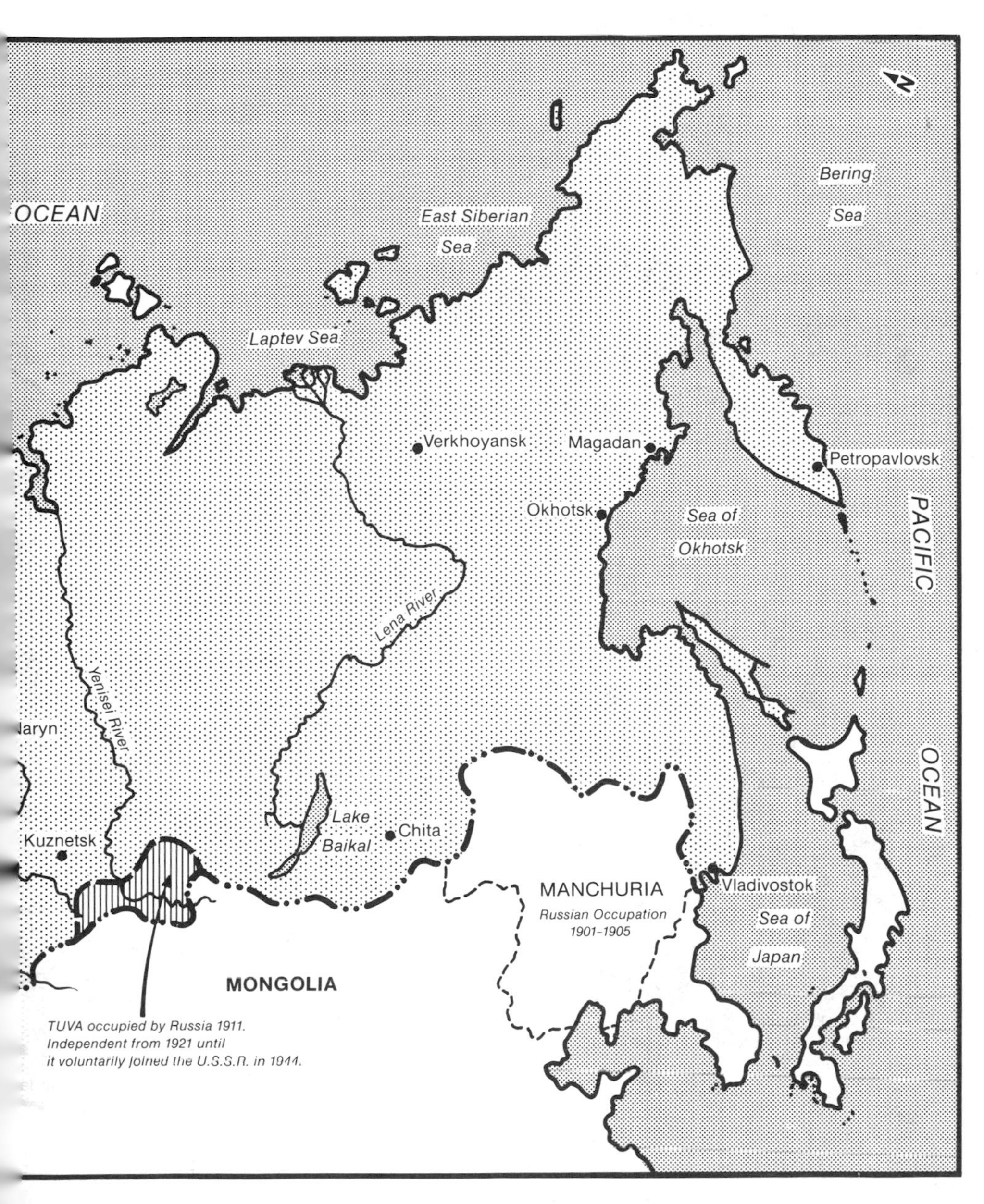

Frontiers of Russia 1955

Invaders of Russia, 1240–1945

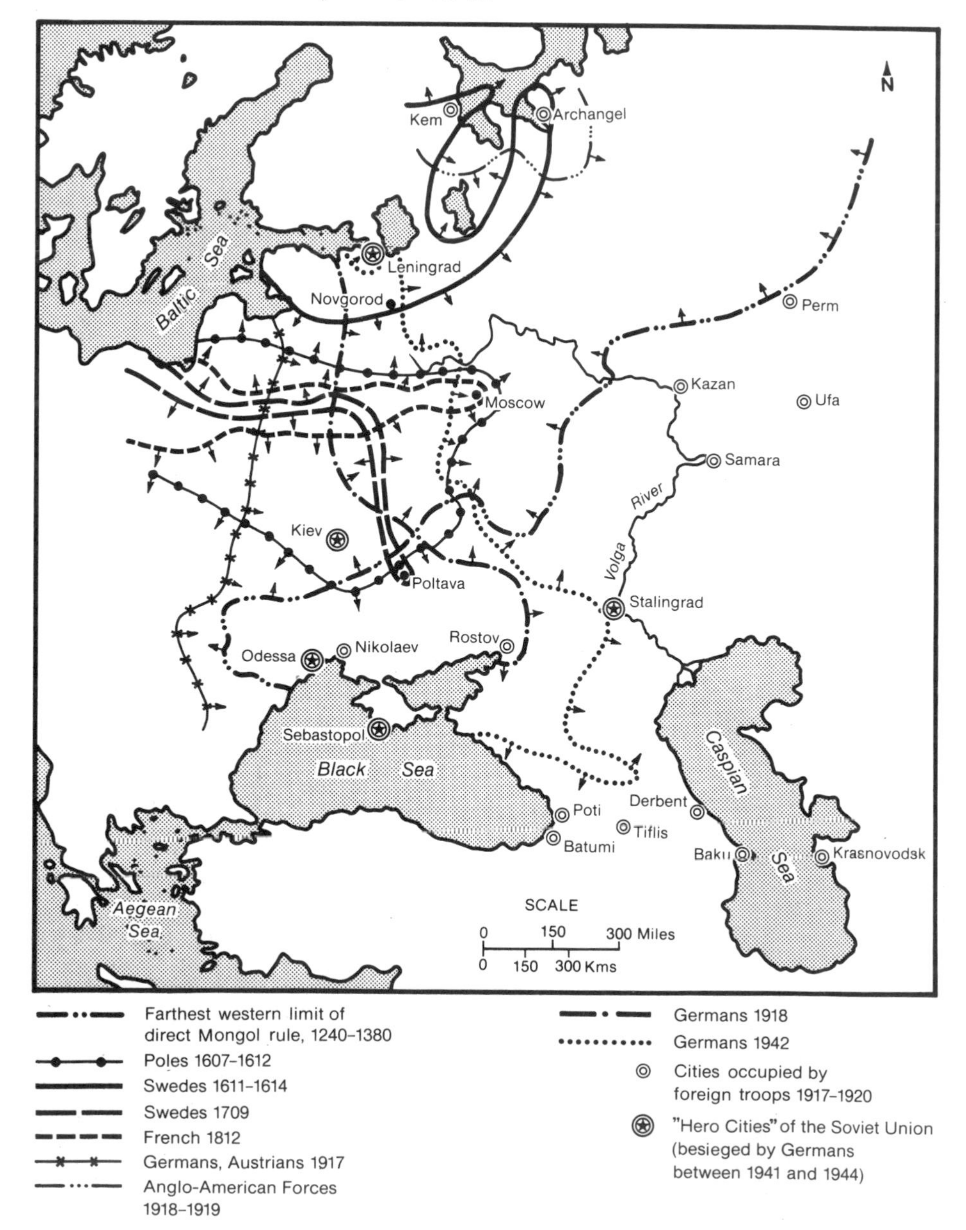

Sino-Soviet Border Disputes, 1858–the Present

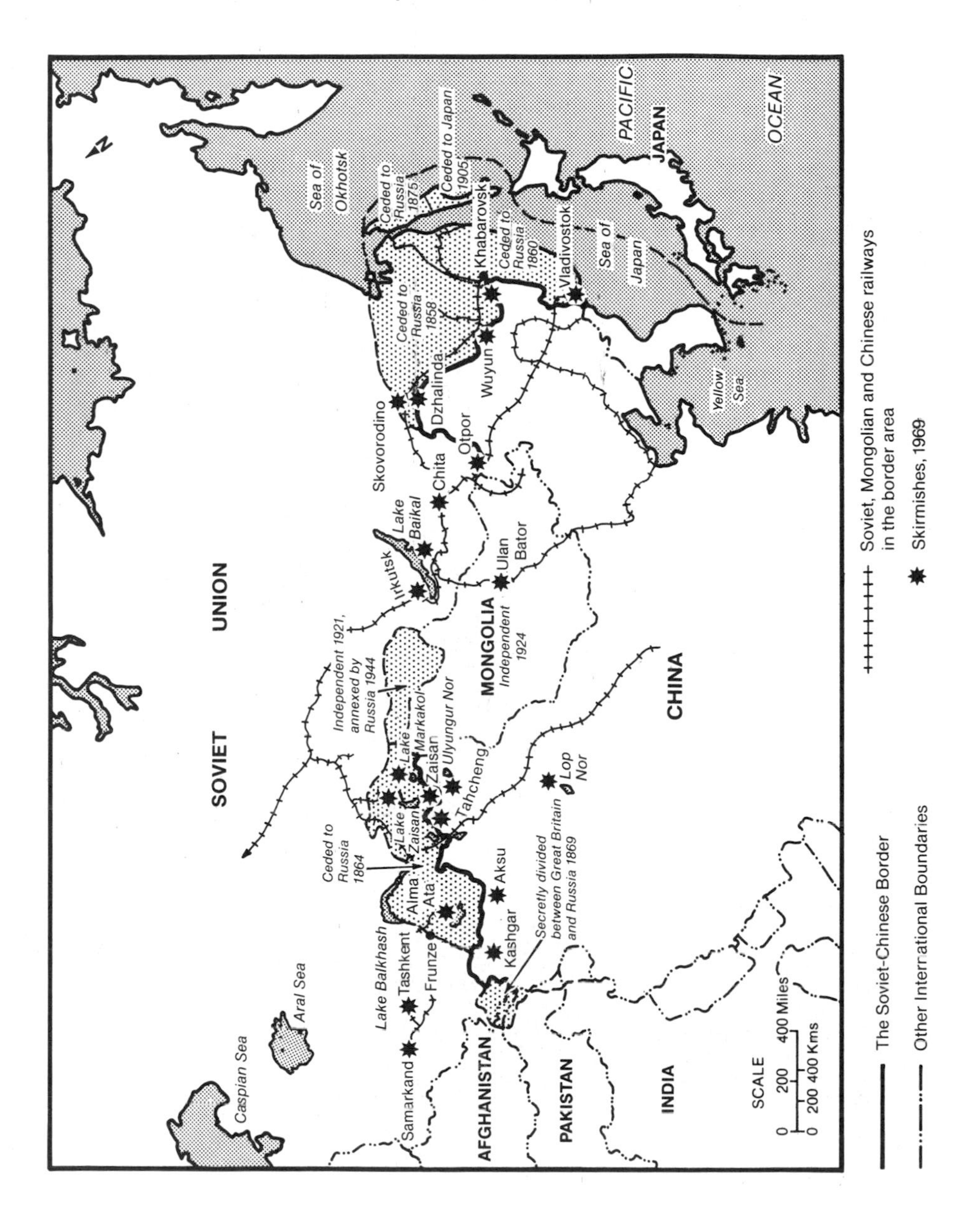

Russia in America, 1784–1867

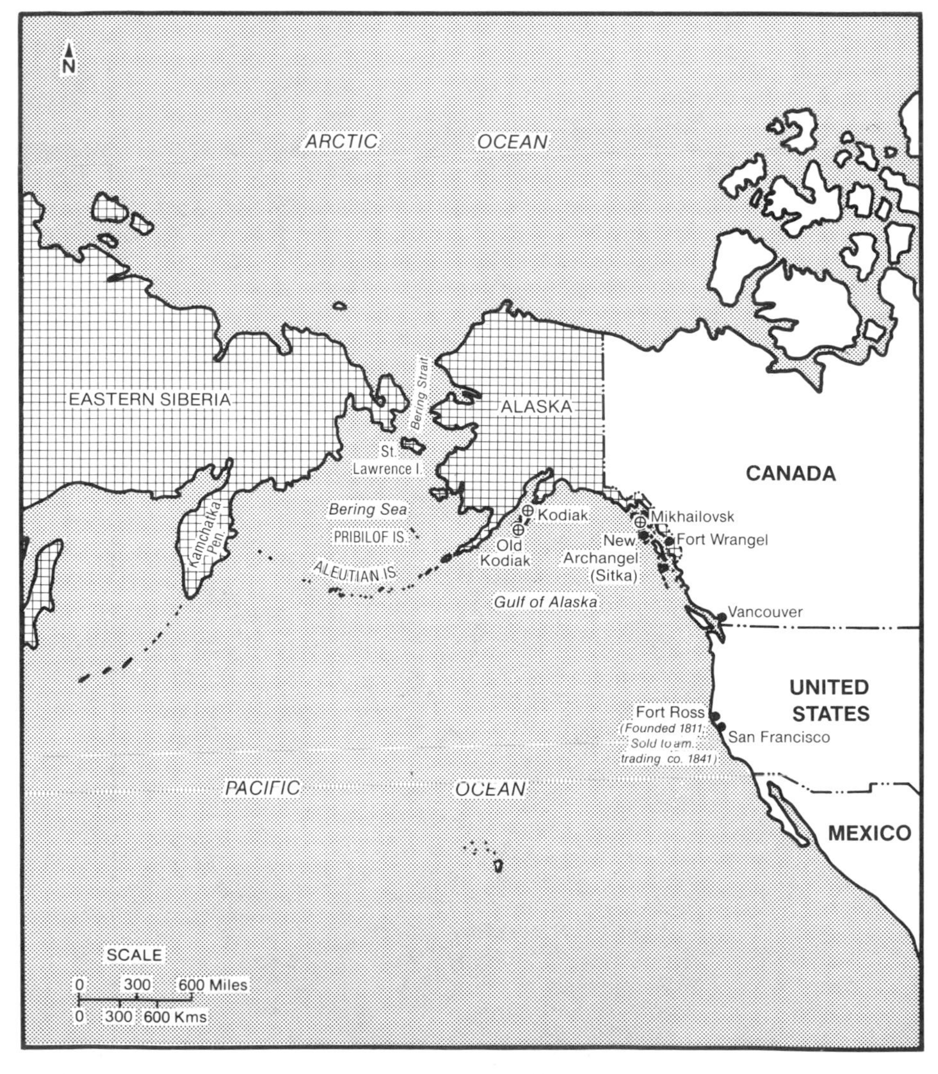

⊕ Cities founded in the 18th century • Cities founded in the 19th century

THE NORTHEAST PASSAGE AND THE TRANS-SIBERIAN RAILROAD

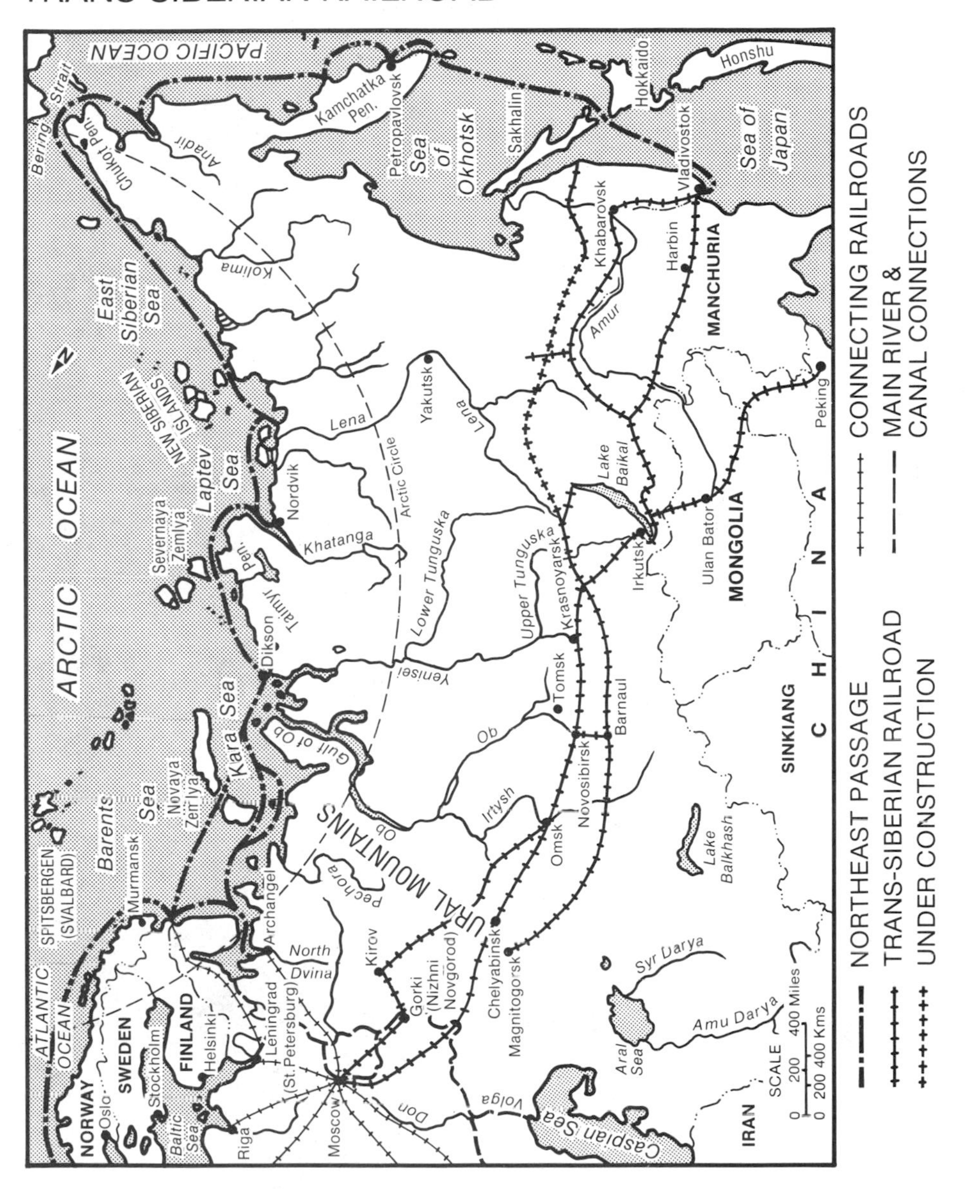